90 0757326 6

WITHDRAWN
FROM
UNIVERSITY OF PLYMOUTH
LIBRARY SERVICES

Dialect Change

Dialects are constantly changing, and due to increased mobility in recent years, European dialects have 'levelled', making it difficult to distinguish a native of Reading from a native of London, or a native of Bonn from a native of Cologne. This comprehensive study brings together a team of leading scholars to explore all aspects of recent dialect change, in particular dialect convergence and divergence. Drawing on examples from a wide range of European countries – as well as areas where European languages have been transplanted – they examine a range of issues relating to dialect contact and isolation, and show how sociolinguistic conditions differ hugely between and within European countries. Each specially commissioned chapter is based on original research, giving an overview of current work on that particular area and presenting case studies to illustrate the issues discussed. The first ever book devoted to the position of dialects in Europe, *Dialect Change* will be welcomed by all those interested in sociolinguistics, dialectology, and European languages.

Dialect Change

Convergence and Divergence in European Languages

Edited by

Peter Auer, Frans Hinskens, and Paul Kerswill

CAMBRIDGE
UNIVERSITY PRESS

CAMBRIDGE UNIVERSITY PRESS
Cambridge, New York, Melbourne, Madrid, Cape Town, Singapore, São Paulo

Cambridge University Press
The Edinburgh Building, Cambridge CB2 2RU, UK

Published in the United States of America by Cambridge University Press, New York

www.cambridge.org
Information on this title: www.cambridge.org/9780521806879

© Cambridge University Press 2005

This book is in copyright. Subject to statutory exception
and to the provisions of relevant collective licensing agreements,
no reproduction of any part may take place without
the written permission of Cambridge University Press.

First published 2005

Printed in the United Kingdom at the University Press, Cambridge

A catalogue record for this book is available from the British Library

Library of Congress Cataloguing in Publication data
Dialect change : convergence and divergence in European languages / edited by
Peter Auer, Frans Hinskens, and Paul Kerswill.
   p.   cm.
Includes bibliographical references and index.
ISBN 0-521-80687-9
1. Europe – Languages – Dialects.   2. Sociolinguistics – Europe.   3. Linguistic
change – Europe.   I. Auer, Peter, 1954–   II. Hinskens, Frans.   III. Kerswill, Paul.
P380.D52   2004
471′.2′094 – dc22   2004051858

ISBN-13 978-0-521-80687-9 hardback
ISBN-10 0-521-80687-9 hardback

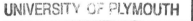
UNIVERSITY OF PLYMOUTH

9007573266

Cambridge University Press has no responsibility for the persistence or accuracy of
URLs for external or third-party internet websites referred to in this book, and does not
guarantee that any content on such websites is, or will remain, accurate or appropriate.

Contents

Maps

Figures

Contributors

PETER J. C. AUER, Professor of German Linguistics, University of Freiburg

GAETANO BERRUTO, Professor of General Linguistics and Sociolinguistics, University of Turin

LEONIE CORNIPS, Senior Research Fellow, Meertens Instituut, Amsterdam

KAREN CORRIGAN, Reader in Linguistics, University of Newcastle-upon-Tyne

JENNY CHESHIRE, Professor of Linguistics, Queen Mary, University of London

FRANS L. M. P. HINSKENS, Head of the Department of Linguistics, Meertens Instituut, Amsterdam, and Professor of Language Variation and Change, Vrije Universiteit, Amsterdam

JENS NORMANN JØRGENSEN, Professor, Department of Nordic Studies, University of Copenhagen

JEFFREY L. KALLEN, Senior Lecturer in Linguistics and Phonetics, University of Dublin, Trinity College

PAUL E. KERSWILL, Professor of Linguistics, Department of Linguistics and English Language, University of Lancaster

TORE KRISTIANSEN, Lecturer, Institute for Danish Dialect Research, University of Copenhagen

INGE LISE PEDERSEN, Director of the Institute for Danish Dialect Research, University of Copenhagen

PETER ROSENBERG, Lecturer, European University, Viadrina

JOHAN TAELDEMAN, Chair of Dutch Linguistics, University of Ghent

PETER TRUDGILL FBA, Professor of English Linguistics, University of Fribourg

JUAN ANDRES VILLENA-PONSODA, Chair of General Linguistics, Universidad de Málaga

ANN WILLIAMS, Department of Linguistics, University of Wales, Bangor

CURT F. WOOLHISER, Preceptor in Slavic Languages and Literatures, Harvard University

Preface

Between 1995 and 1998, the European Science Foundation funded an international research Network on social dialectology with the title 'The Convergence and Divergence of Dialects in a Changing Europe'. The Network was founded and chaired by Peter Auer (Universities of Hamburg and later Freiburg, Germany, and Frans Hinskens (University of Nijmegen, at the time). Eleven European countries were officially represented by a scientific committee, which had as its members (in addition to the chairpersons):

> *Wolfgang Dressler (Vienna)*
> *Walter Haas (Fribourg, Switzerland)*
> *Toon Hagen (Nijmegen)*
> *Jeffrey Kallen (Dublin)*
> *Paul Kerswill (Reading)*
> *Klaus Mattheier (Heidelberg)*
> *Inge Lise Pedersen (Copenhagen)*
> *Alberto Sobrero (Lecce)*
> *Johan Taeldeman (Ghent)*
> *Mats Thelander (Uppsala)*
> *Juan Villena Ponsoda (Málaga).*

As part of the activities of the Network, three workshops (in Nijmegen, Ghent, and Heidelberg) and an open conference (in Reading) were held. The Network also organised a summer school for Ph.D. students (in Málaga). A series of publications relating to the theme of the Network has already appeared: a special issue of *Sociolinguistica* (10, 1996) edited by Auer, Hinskens, and Mattheier; a special issue of *Folia Linguistica* (22/1–2) edited by Auer in 1998; the volume *Dialect and Migration in a Changing Europe* edited by Mattheier (Frankfurt, etc.: Lang, 2000) and a special issue of the *International Journal of the Sociology of Language* edited by Kallen, Hinskens, and Taeldeman (145, 2000).

Following an extensive introduction by the editors, the present volume is divided into three parts which together contain thirteen chapters, the embryonic versions of several of which are based on presentations at the Reading conference; the remaining chapters were specially commissioned. Although this volume is thus the youngest of the offspring of the ESF Network, it definitely stands on its own feet as the outcome of much fruitful cross-fertilisation of ideas both during and after the formal period of the Network. It distils the essence of this new research area with a coherence that would not have been possible without the Network and the many cross-national links it fostered.

As the editors, we would like to thank Dr Antonio Lamarra of the European Science Foundation, which, apart from funding the activities of the research Network, also financially supported part of the production and publication of the present volume. We would also like to thank Dr Aniek IJbema for her assistance in compiling the index.

Freiburg, Amsterdam, and Reading   PA, FH, AND PK
March 2004

European countries discussed in this book.

1 The study of dialect convergence and divergence: conceptual and methodological considerations

Frans Hinskens, Peter Auer, and Paul Kerswill

1 Introduction

Dialect change can have several different manifestations. Among these, dialect convergence (dc) and dialect divergence (dd) noticeably affect the relationships between related dialects. Dc and dd have probably been present for as long as dialects have existed. Various historical developments, including the 'modernisation' of society, have left their mark on the very nature of dialects and have partly changed the dynamics of dc and dd; moreover, they have broadened them to dialect – standard language convergence.

This chapter sets the stage for the various aspects of the study of dc and dd presented in this book, in that it both provides a general introduction and constitutes a springboard for the discussion of the themes and approaches which play a role in the individual chapters. As an introduction, the chapter presents the central terminology (section 2), provides the background information necessary for the interested non-specialist (section 3), sketches what we see as the main research methods (section 4), and binds together the issues featured in the various chapters (section 5).

2 Definitions of the Key Concepts

We will use the notion of 'dialect' to refer to a language variety which is used in a geographically limited part of a language area in which it is 'roofed' by a structurally related standard variety; a dialect typically displays structural peculiarities in several language components (cf. Chambers and Trudgill 1998: 5), though some of the authors in this book deal mainly with phonetic (or 'accent') features. Usually dialects have relatively little overt prestige and are mainly used orally. Lacking in this definition is the fact that the dialects of a certain language area (including the standard variety) maintain very specific historical relationships (cf. Agard 1971: 21–24).

The notions of dc and dd can be defined, respectively, as the increase and decrease in similarity between dialects. Whereas dc involves the linguistic unification, focusing (*sensu* Le Page and Tabouret-Keller 1985), and homogenisation of the linguistic repertoire, including the traditional dialects,[1] dd amounts to linguistic diversification, growing diffuseness and heterogenisation – although divergence may lead to focusing in a repertoire, making the varieties which survive the process more distinct from each other. Weinreich (1954: 395) defines convergence as 'partial similarities increasing at the expense of differences' (though, in his view, divergence is the main subject matter of diachronic dialectology). As should be clear from these definitions, convergence and divergence are relational notions, referring to either processes or the results of processes.

Dialect convergence may lead to simplification (Trudgill 1986) and to the reduction of intrasystemic, especially 'quantitative', variation. However, in most studies of dialect convergence or divergence, attention is only paid to the question of how processes of linguistic change affect intersystemic variation, i.e. differences between dialects. These differences can pertain to either categorical or quantitatively variable features.

Sometimes dc and dd are two sides of the same coin. Gilles (1998b), for instance, shows that the dc of Letzebuergesch towards the central Luxemburg variety implies its giving up of east Luxemburg features and, hence, a divergence from Mosel Franconian dialects of German. Ó Curnáin (1998) demonstrated how, in the same West Galway vernacular of Irish, in the segmental phonology dc and dd can coexist. Pedersen (1998) showed how, in the course of the nineteenth century in Copenhagen and Stockholm, the convergence of the *stylistically* marked differences between urban dialect and the spoken standard and divergence of the *socially* marked differences between both systems occurred simultaneously.

Dc and dd can change the relationships between the dialects involved and may, hence, necessitate the reclassification of the dialects involved (cf. Samuels 1972: 92).

3   Background and Conceptual Frameworks

To bring the concepts of dc and dd more clearly into focus, we will now present a rough overview of the historiography of the study of dc and dd (section 3.1) as well as a short discussion of related concepts in contemporary approaches to dialectology, in two branches of sociolinguistics, and in the study of language contact (section 3.2).

---

[1] Mattheier (1996) separates convergence from advergence, the latter referring to unilateral manifestations of the process. For convergence in bilingual societies, Hock (1991: 492) proposes a similar distinction; 'the convergence between different languages may be mutual (between adstratal languages) or unidirectional (in an unequal prestige relationship)'.

3.1   Historiographical sketch

Here, we briefly discuss some of the main models, theories, proposals, findings, and individual observations which are relevant to, and can sometimes retrospectively be seen as precursors of, much of the present-day study of dc and dd. We will largely concentrate on the areas of historical linguistics and traditional dialectology.

The manifestations of dialect divergence are most visible in language history. The long-lasting process of the diversification of Proto-Indo-European into (what are retrospectively referred to as) language families, and of language families into languages, etc., largely took place in linguistic prehistory. The results of divergence are represented visually in the branching lines in the family tree diagrams of historical linguistics.

Undoubtedly, the most influential school of historical linguistics is that of the Neogrammarians, one of the main spokesmen being Hermann Paul. Applying a partial analogy from nature, Paul recognises only the language of the individual, the idiolect, which is the product of ontogenesis and phylogenesis. 'Dialect split means, simply, the increase of individual differences beyond a certain measure' (Paul 1920: section 22; our translation). He asks the question of why it is that 'a greater or lesser amount of agreement is maintained in this group of individuals which is constituted in this or that way'. The reason is that language habits ('*Sprachusus*') are determined by human interaction ('*Verkehr*'), which has either a levelling or a differentiating effect (Paul 1920: section 23). 'Each change in language use is the product of the spontaneous behaviour of single individuals on the one hand, and the nature of interaction on the other. If instances of spontaneous behaviour are very differently distributed in the various districts, then the levelling (to the extent that it is necessary) taking place in districts which are remote from each other and have no mutual interaction must necessarily lead to different results' (Paul 1920: sections 22–25, our translation).

The Neogrammarians distinguished between language change in the strict sense and borrowing. Language change has language-internal origins. Formal (rather than semantic) change can take the form of either sound change, which is achieved spontaneously, or analogical change. When a change is not achieved autonomously, that is, when it does not have an internal origin, it can either stem from another language or 'from within the same speech area', as stated by Bloomfield (1933: 444), who referred to the latter type as 'dialect borrowing'. Sound change was claimed by the Neogrammarians to be lexically exceptionless, hence the designation 'sound laws'.

Only a few historically attested instances of sound change appear to be completely exceptionless, however. The fact that, in the grammar and lexicon of individual dialects, regular and exceptional ('residual') forms can often be found to exist side by side has led many scholars to subscribe to the idea that 'sound laws', especially, tend to operate sporadically, which leads some, including Schuchardt, to conclude that sound laws do not exist.

A process of language change that has not come to completion in some respect leaves behind language variation, either intrasystemically (as in, for example, lexically diffuse sound change) or between closely related language varieties (e.g. dialects or style levels). In traditional dialectology much attention is paid to intersystemic variation. Natural and man-made borders were typically looked upon as explanations of the location of dialect boundaries as the outcomes of dialect divergence (or, rather, non-convergence).

Apart from divergence, lexical dialect mixing (*Mischung*) and the levelling of variation (differences) between dialects (*Ausgleich*)[2] were thought to be the key mechanisms that destroy regularity and the alleged exceptionlessness of the 'sound laws' and thus made it impossible to reconstruct historical developments from the geographical distribution of particular forms, the original aim of nineteenth-century historical linguistics and dialectology (Dauzat 1922: 22). The insight developed that the forces constituting individual dialects and dialect landscapes are not only the human linguistic 'hardware' (to use a modern expression), such as the articulatory organs (the possibilities and limitations of which were held responsible for 'sound laws') and the 'software' located in the brain (cognition being held responsible for analogy), but also social interaction, social networks, contact between places, etc., leading to all types of what the Neogrammarians labelled dialect borrowing. 'The maps showed . . . that local dialects do not exist in a state of isolation from one another' (Bynon 1983: 185).

As early as 1870 Schuchardt, who, after the publication in 1885 of his *Über die Lautgesetze, gegen die Junggrammatiker*, was the first leader of the opposition against the Neogrammarian views, distinguished between two opposite forces working on language. What he labelled 'centrifugal force' (*Zentrifugalkraft*) leads to the differentiation of language, whereas 'centripetal force' (*Zentripetalkraft*) aims at unity. Centripetal force exerts its influence through such institutions as the school, the church, and the state. In Schuchardt's later writings, these notions occur under the headings of *Spaltung* (split) or *Divergenz* (divergence) and *Ausgleich* (levelling) or *Konvergenz* (convergence), respectively.[3] Reflecting on the mutual influence between the standard variety and a dialect (*'langue littéraire et idiome local'*), one of the founding fathers of modern linguistics, de Saussure, writes that language history is a continuous struggle between *'la force d'intercourse et l'esprit de clocher'*, i.e. between the tendencies towards unification and those towards particularism and cultural

---

[2] Terminology as used by Wrede (1919) as well as other German dialectologists such as Haag (1929–1930).

[3] Cf. Hagen 1982: 242–243.

fragmentation.[4] German dialectologists coined the notion of *Abbau* to refer to levelling in the dialect-standard language dimension.

Applying these insights to historical dialectology, Frings (1936) accounted for the emergence of a German *Gemeinsprache* (common language) as a consequence of the convergence of the Middle German settlers' dialects in what was to become the Upper-Saxonian area. Migration as a force for levelling will be a recurring theme in this volume. Historical dialectology provides evidence for divergence, too. Goossens (1970) points to the following trends, which led to the divergence of the dialects of Dutch and German:

1. specific linguistic elements or structures in the German 'dialect cluster' underwent changes that did not occur in the Dutch cluster;
2. the Dutch cluster underwent changes that the German one did not undergo;
3. both clusters underwent different changes.

Little by little the dialect-geographical investigation of dialect boundaries was given up in favour of the study of the history of individual words, leading to extreme positions such as the one expressed in the famous dictum '*chaque mot a son histoire*'. In the eyes of many linguists, traditional dialect geography is characterised by atomism and, in the worst cases, complete abstinence from theoretical reflection. That this extreme position was perhaps rare is indicated by the fact that most dialect atlases contain maps based on phonological parameters, implying that there is a general rule behind the change in the phonological shape of the words.

3.2   *Fencing off dialect convergence and divergence from related concepts*

In this section, dc and dd will be compared to closely related notions from sociolinguistics, especially the social psychology of language; from both traditional and more modern approaches to dialectology, including levelling and koineisation; from pidgin and creole studies; and, finally, from the study of 'mixed languages'.

3.2.1 Accommodation and variation   Convergence and divergence both have short-term and long-term manifestations. Their short-term manifestations are often discussed under the heading of *accommodation*, and, in Giles' *et al.*'s (1987) model, are the opposite of non-accommodation, though more usually (e.g. Trudgill 1986) accommodation is associated just with convergence. Short-term convergence is exemplified by the observation that in babies' utterances F_0 often has lower values when the infant is interacting with the father than during interactions with the mother (Giles and Powesland after Daan *et al.* 1985: 72; see Kerswill 2002a for further examples and discussion). In

---

[4] In part IV ch. 2 and part III, ch. 4 of his *Cours de linguistique générale*.

adults, short-term convergence can be either 'upwards', i.e. from a geographical or a social dialect towards the standard language (although there is usually an upper boundary that cannot be transgressed without sanctions) or 'downwards' (as when members of the local elite speak dialect (Daan *et al.* 1985: 76; Voortman 1994), a phenomenon for which there are such telling labels as '*magistratenplat*' ('magistrate's dialect').[5] Of course, Giles' description presupposes a neatly hierarchically structured society in which dialect and standard can be related in a straightforward way to social position, but this may not be the general pattern. A demonstration of short-term accommodation is Coupland's (1984) account of a Cardiff travel agent's response to her clients. Coupland argues that the accommodation on various phonetics variables is not a mechanistic matching of frequencies, but rather an attempt at 'identity projection'. (See Kerswill 2002a; and AUER AND HINSKENS.)

Motivations for short-term divergence may range between strictly situational (the desire to distance oneself from one's conversational partner) or more general (the need to develop, maintain, or stress social or personal identity, or to demarcate the ingroup from the relevant outgroup). In the longer term, language can thus become the symbol of an entire minority group (as in the case of Welsh, Basque, Catalan, Frisian, and maybe also in the case of Letzebuergesch).[6] The divergence of African American Vernacular English (Labov and Harris 1986) from white dialects, which resulted from the fact that the AAVE speakers have not participated in any of the sound shifts characteristic of the white vernaculars, may originally also have had this motivation.

Both short-term convergence and short-term divergence can take place psychologically and/or linguistically. Psychological accommodation (convergence or divergence) has to do with the communicative intentions and attitudes of a speaker towards his interlocutor or audience, and may not result in actual linguistic accommodation. While linguistic convergence can be described as the linguistic manifestation of speakers adapting 'to the speech of others to reduce differences' (Siegel 1985: 367), divergence is the exploitation of differences, for example by using different features more often and thus making them more salient. In sum, 'according to this theory, people may adjust their speech with

---

[5] Short-term convergence can even be exploited as a sociolinguistic research strategy. Peterson (1996) discusses the several types of short-term convergence of an interviewer towards his black interlocutors, responsively as well as initiatively. He did this with 'the specific goal of promoting natural conversation in each of the interviews. The most appropriate strategy [he adopted] for accomplishing this task was to establish himself as a member of an AAVE vernacular speaking community' (168). Something similar holds for Trudgill (1974), who established empirically that as an interviewer he himself glottalised his ts in concert with his various informants from Norwich. In this case, the interviewer actually *was* a member of the speech community.

[6] According to Giles (1977: 35) 'non-convergent language can be used by ethnic groups as a symbolic tactic for maintaining their identity and cultural distinctiveness'.

others either to reduce or to accentuate linguistic (and hence social) differences between them' (Siegel 1987: 240).

While Labovian sociolinguistics associates language use primarily with social structures and social behaviour, research on linguistic accommodation is grounded in theories of 'social action' (how social meaning is produced from interaction), more specifically 'rational action' (Turner 1996). Linguistic accommodation is analysed as the outcome of more or less conscious choices on the part of rational social actors, the choices being tailored to expectations about their extralinguistic consequences. If the boundaries between linguistically distinct groups are permeable (Mummendey 1999), the speaker may benefit by moving closer to the other group by converging linguistically, either by the avoidance of salient features of the speaker's own dialect or by the adoption of features of the interlocutor's dialect. This can affect the interlocutor's attitudes and behaviour in positive ways. As in Giles' theory, accommodation by Trudgill's (1986) more restricted definition of linguistic convergence may take the form of the reduction of differences or the adoption of features from the dialect spoken by the interlocutor.

Some of Gilles' (1998a: 73) findings show that psychological convergence (or divergence, for that matter) is not necessarily expressed in linguistic convergence (or divergence, respectively). Gilles' findings do not provide any evidence for short-term, interactional convergence between speakers of different dialects of Lëtzebuergesch: 'We are dealing with a process of convergence which can be located solely in the speakers' mind, but has no effect on their actual verbal behaviour' (73).[7] Blom and Gumperz's (1972) finding that students from Hemnesberget (a village in Norway) who had been living in the city claimed to speak the local dialect yet had adapted their speech to one of the standard varieties, shows how psychological non-accommodation can go hand in hand with long-term objective linguistic divergence.

In the case of Serbian/Croatian, psychological divergence between several ethnic and religious groups seems to be leading to growing structural divergence between the respective dialect groups (cf. Janich and Greule 2002; Grčević 2002; Gvozdanović in press). Psychological convergence may be the reason why some linguists (Angelov 2000) have come to regard Macedonian as a dialect of Bulgarian. However, national ideologies probably also play an important part in this judgement.

    3.2.2 Dialectology   Whereas in connection with the analysis of dialect borrowing the focus is on the overall effects on the 'recipient' dialect, in connection with geographical diffusion (or expansion or areal diffusion),

---

[7] AUER AND HINSKENS provide more details of this study.

the focus is on specific dialect features. The German dialectologist Theodor Frings (e.g. Aubin *et al.* 1926) can be called the main protagonist of the 'expansionist' approach in dialect geography, which was essentially an elaboration of Johannes Schmidt's 1872) '*Wellentheorie*' (wave theory). As Bynon (1983: 192–193) points out, Schmidt's wave model can also account for dc through 'the elimination of specific isoglosses which previously served to differentiate . . . two dialects through the spread of features from one dialect area over the territory of the other . . . The degree of such convergence will clearly depend both upon the length of time during which they previously underwent separate developments as well as the length of time during which they were subsequently subjected to the influence of a common centre' such as the growing influence of the standard language. (See Britain 2002a.)

A textbook example of the wave-like areal diffusion of an innovation is Kloeke's (1927) account of the spread of the diphthongisation of West Germanic /uː/ to /œy/ (via an intermediate /yː/) from the cities in the northwestern Netherlands to the more peripheral parts of the language area in the sixteenth and seventeenth centuries. With respect to this phoneme, three rather than two 'clusters' of dialects resulted from the incomplete spread of the change, leading to dd.

Trudgill (1983) developed his 'gravity' formula (which we will sketch in section 5.4 below) in order to model the areal diffusion of innovations. Innovations are supposed to jump from large, influential cities to smaller, less influential ones, in order of decreasing size (the 'urban hierarchy'). To judge from Trautmann's (1880) and Trudgill's (1983) account of the spread of the uvular 'r' in northwestern Europe, this can occasionally even have Sprachbund-type effects. Trudgill (1992) compares the (1) dialectological, (2) macrosociolinguistic/geolinguistic, and (3) microlinguistic approaches to diffusion. In connection with (1), he discusses isogloss bundles and transition zones; in connection with (2) corridors of variability; and with respect to (3) linguistic accommodation. He points out that accommodation is usually not perfect. 'At the micro level, the best-known form of imperfect accommodation is hyperadaptation, and the best-known form of this is hypercorrection' (78). He illustrates this with data for the so-called Bristol 'l', which refers to the addition of /l/ word-finally in words such as *idea* and *Norma*, giving forms homophonous with *ideal* and *normal*. (See also Britain 2002b, 622–627; 2003.)

Bailey *et al.* (1993) introduce quantitative techniques to analyse the areal diffusion of grammatical, phonological, and lexical innovative dialect features of English in Oklahoma. Their findings led them to conclude that 'different patterns of diffusion are tied to the different social meanings that linguistic features carry' (386), and that 'innovations that diffuse hierarchically represent the encroachment of external norms into an area, whereas features that diffuse in contrahierarchical fashion represent the revitalisation of traditional norms'.

We will return to this issue in section 5.4 below. Kerswill (2003) discusses differences in the rate and extent of diffusion of vowels and consonants, finding that, in Britain, consonantal features spread rapidly across the whole country, while innovations in vowels seem restricted to smaller regions.

In his work on the structural consequences of language contact, Van Coetsem (1988) draws a general distinction between source versus recipient linguistic systems, assuming that either can take the 'agentivity' role. Which linguistic system is proactive as the 'agent' depends on dominance, that is, on the bilingual's relative proficiency in the two languages. In this model, *borrowing* is a matter of recipient-language agentivity, while *imposition*[8] stems from source language agentivity (2000: 5, 32). Strictly speaking, the notion of dialect borrowing refers to the process of one dialect copying an element or structure from another dialect; a long-term result can be the convergence of the recipient dialect with the source dialect. Kruijsen (1995) discusses examples of phonological (stress patterns) and morphological traits which were imported with French loan words in the Limburg dialects of Dutch spoken in the Belgian region of Haspengouw/Hesbaye near the Dutch–French language border.

A mechanism countering dialect borrowing is sociolinguistic *polarisation*. 'This force can act defensively, by retarding structural borrowing, but also offensively, by engendering developments diametrically opposed to what is found in other dialects or by bringing about something like hypercorrections in reverse' (Hock 1991: 428). The first type of effect comes down to resistence to convergence; the second one results in divergence towards the other dialects through hyperdialectisms. It would seem that a precondition for sociolinguistic polarisation, be it defensive or offensive in nature, is a certain level of awareness of the spreading feature in the consciousness of the speakers of the 'threatened' dialect. This may have played a role in the history of Hiberno-English (cf. Hinskens, Kallen, and Taeldeman 2000: 4). The defensive or offensive reaction may well have sociopsychological motivations, particularly non-integrative attitudes towards the speakers of the 'threatening' dialect. Some effects of polarisation in the creation of hyperdialectisms in the Flemish context are discussed in Taeldeman 2000.

Initially, because of extensive borrowing, dialect contact often leads to abundant variation as a result of *dialect mixing*, the partial merging of the lexicons and grammars of different but related dialects. Logically, the effects are visible only in areas where the original dialects used to be different. An example from historical dialectology is the enormous pool of variation resulting from interdialectal contact in sixteenth-century Judeo-Spanish, after the expulsions of Jewry from the Iberian Peninsula and their migration to the Balkans, Asia Minor, and North Africa (Minervini 1998).

---

[8] Often called 'transfer' in the study of second language acquisition.

Whenever dialect mixing leads to the stabilisation of the variants that are typical of the respective 'pure' lects along with additional 'compromise' variants, one usually speaks of *fudging* (cf. Chambers and Trudgill 1998: 110–118; Britain 2002, 2004). A well-known lexically intermediate or compromise form from the Cologne area in the German Rhineland and the dialects in the neighbouring transition area between Ripuarian and East Limburg dialects of Dutch is '*öllich*', /ʌlɪç/, or '*öllik*', /ʌlɪk/, 'onion', which has been analysed as a fusion (a 'mixed compound', as Singh 1981 has baptised this type of formation) of the lexical variants '*ön*' /ʌn/ (< Lat. *unio*), used in the dialects west and southwest of Cologne, and the more northern '*look*' /lok/, related to standard German *Lauch* (Aubin *et al.* 1926: 32–33). As is evident from the latter example, convergence (and divergence for that matter) has consequences for the dialect landscape. Dialectal transition zones can result from partial cross-dialectal convergence (cf. Mazur 1996). In his discussion of what he labels *interdialect*, Trudgill (1992: 77–78) presents examples of intermediate forms in the phonological component (vowel quality in certain lexical sets of dialects of East Anglia) and the lexicon. Trudgill goes on to discuss the variation between German dialects in the word for 'potato', viz. *Grundbirne*, lit. 'ground pear', which is used in an area in between the areas with *Erdbirne*, 'earth pear', and *Erdapfel*, 'earth apple', respectively;[9] a similar, more recent, example from British English, discussed by Trudgill, concerns central and southern *take away*, the northern variant *carry out*, and the intermediate *take out*, which is used in the southern part of northern England.

Phonologically intermediate forms are exemplified by the spread of '/oi/ instead of standard German /ai/, replacing the base dialectal form /a/ in the Rheno-Franconian area' (Ziegler, after Auer 1998a: 5). A similar example comes from the dialects of Dutch spoken in the extreme southeast of Limburg. The easternmost dialects have undergone dorsal fricative deletion with compensatory lengthening, yielding forms such as /naːt/, 'night', and /liːət/, 'light', which do not occur in the dialects spoken west of this area, which have preserved /naxt/ and /lɪçt/ (which are identical with the standard variants). In a subset of the relevant items, the dialects in an intermediate area show vowel lengthening but no dorsal fricative deletion, hence /naːxt/ and /leːçt/ (cf. Hinskens 1992: section 12.2.1; 1998a: 47–48).

Independently of whether fudging occurs, in situations marked by heavy dialect mixing, after a certain period of time a process of selection usually takes place. After all, 'many mundane events suggest that people have a deeply ingrained attraction to linguistic conformity. The stigmatization of certain dialect features appears to be an overt attempt by communities to stamp out

---

[9] Cf. *Erdbirne* which is used in an area between the areas with *Erdapfel* and *Grundbirne* (König 2001: 206).

certain variants' (Chambers 1995: 209). This sifting through dialect levelling sometimes, though not necessarily, leads to koineisation, i.e. structural convergence between closely related linguistic systems, eventually leading to the stabilisation of some compromise variety (Hinskens 2001: 200; cf. Kerswill 2002a).

3.2.3 Levelling and koineisation   Dialect levelling, the process which reduces variation both within and between dialects,[10] is structural *dialect loss*. Functional dialect loss, the gradual giving up of the dialect in favour of another language variety, is often referred to as *dialect shift*. Dialect levelling makes (a) individual dialects more homogeneous; and (b) different dialects more similar and, consequently, diasystems more homogeneous. Thus, our definition does not entirely coincide with Berruto's (1995: 226) usage of the notions *convergenza* and *livellamento dialettale*. Whereas for Berruto convergence is the (vertical) reduction of variation between a dialect and the overarching standard language (German *Abbau*), he defines dialect levelling as the (horizontal) reduction of variation between different dialects (German *Ausgleich* – cf. section 3.1 above).

Complete dialect loss, i.e. the disappearance of a dialect without leaving any traces behind, resembles language death (Craig 1997), though dialect death can be gradual and (to the speakers at least) virtually imperceptible. As it turns out, however, it does not usually come to this, because some of the features of the old dialects will be recycled into new nonstandard varieties such as regiolects and sociolects. Moreover, 'old dialects are being continually wiped out only to make room for new ones' (Sapir 1921: 152).

Unlike dialect levelling, *koineisation* 'involves the mixing of features of . . . different dialects, and leads to a new, compromise dialect'. It results 'from integration or unification of the speakers of the varieties in contact' (Siegel 1985: 365, 369). Koineisation has been defined as the development through dialect mixing, simplification, and reduction of a regional lingua franca which incorporates features of various varieties. Berruto (1995: 226–227) describes a koine as a compromise between different dialects which results from the elimination of their most peculiar and marked features.

Apart from the original Koine of Hellenistic Greek, the ancestral Arabic koine is a famous example. The development, in the nineteenth century, of *Nynorsk*, one of the two official standard languages of Norway, may also largely be a matter of (deliberate) koineisation by its creator, Ivar Aasen, since it incorporates features from a number of dialects, as well as being grammatically simpler than most of the 'input' dialects in avoiding the use both of the dative case and separate plural forms of verbs.

---

[10] Bloomfield 1933: 476ff.; Weinreich 1954: 396.

Siegel (2001) draws a distinction between *immigrant* and *regional* koines. Referring to the former, that is, the results of the koineisation of different dialects after colonisation, Bynon (1983: 193) argues that 'the outcomes of such convergence is by no means complete uniformity'. As Sobrero (1996) shows for the modern Italian situation, the development of regional koines can be a complicated matter. Sobrero distinguishes three types of koineisation: an active one, concerning the spread of a koine of 'a strong urban centre into the neighbouring territory' (e.g. Milanese and Neapolitan); a passive one, which levels out dialectal differences under the pressure of the standard language; and a third type, which concerns 'the reinforcement and expansion' of transition zone dialects. This last type 'can be compared to the "passive" one' (108). While the social basis of active urban koineisation can, according to Sobrero, be characterised as 'bourgeois', the third type is 'proletarian' in nature. Regional koines may replace the input varieties, and are thus akin to *regional dialect levelling* or *dialect supralocalisation*, which refer to the loss of distinctiveness at the local level in favour of distinctiveness at the regional level (Torgersen and Kerswill 2004; Kerswill 2002a; Milroy, Milroy, and Hartley 1994; Britain 2002b).

Kerswill and Williams (2000) studied the emergence of a new dialect in the new town of Milton Keynes (which was founded in 1967) from the point of view of koineisation and first language acquisition; for that reason they paid particular attention to the youngest generations. Davies (1992) is an interesting, partly historical, dialectological study of dialect mixing, koineisation, and focusing in the development of modern standard Chinese. The same holds for Trudgill, Gordon, Lewis, and Maclagan's work on New Zealand English (2000).

Koines are the results *par excellence* of dc. It can be argued that dc and dd do not constitute autonomous, separate types of linguistic change in themselves; rather, they are epiphenomena, resulting from common processes of linguistic change. Processes of linguistic change resulting in dc or dd are sometimes internally motivated (and typically structurally directional, such as simplification, regularisation, and paradigmatic levelling). However, external motivations, particularly those pertinent to contact with other varieties of the same language (such as mixing, cross-dialectal levelling, and koineisation), seem to predominate.[11]

In his work on migrant Turkish, Boeschoten (1997: 5, 7) interprets dc and dd as spin-offs of processes such as acquisition, borrowing or calquing, interference, dialect levelling, restructuring, and attrition. Riehl's (2001) work on '*extra muros*' German (that is, outside the German-speaking heartland and including territories such as Eastern Belgium, Romania, Russia, Australia, and

---

[11] See Farrar and Jones (2002) for a succinct exposé of the interplay of internal, contact-induced, and extra-linguistic factors in language change.

Texas) facilitates an interesting comparison. She ascribes the partly convergent developments in the varieties of German in her corpus to the catalysis of
internal tendencies (e.g. the loss of morphological case marking), tendencies
towards typological redefinition (e.g. embedded $SV_{fin}O$ word order), cognitive
principles,[12] and the exploitation of latent categories because of language contact (as the *am V-en* continuous construction, as in e.g. *am arbeiten*, 'working',
which has a limited geographical distribution *intra muros*), among other things.
More about the place of Riehl's study is given in section 5.8 below.

It seems that there are no processes of linguistic change which are unique
to dc and dd. The main question for our present purposes is whether
the common processes or the outcomes of common processes of linguistic
change can be plausibly interpreted as dc or dd. This is not least a methodological issue; we will return to this issue in section 4 below.

3.2.4 Pidginisation and creolisation   The sociocultural settings of
Old- or New-World dialects, on the one hand, and pidgins and creole languages,
on the other, barely overlap. Yet, sociolinguistically, processes resulting in dc
or dd and *pidginisation, creolisation*,[13] and *decreolisation* can be compared in
several dimensions.

As Hock and Joseph (1996: 387, 423) point out, koineisation, the convergence
between different languages, and pidginisation usually involve structural simplification as well as the development of an interlanguage. Siegel (2001) argues
that (a) pidginisation and koineisation both involve second language learning,
transfer, mixing and levelling; and (b) the differences between pidginisation
and creole genesis, on the one hand, and koineisation, on the other, are due
to differences in the values of a small number of language-related, social, and
demographic variables.[14] Koineisation is usually a gradual, continuous process
which takes place over a long period of sustained contact; whereas pidginisation and creolisation are traditionally thought of as relatively rapid and sudden
processes. This corresponds with Samuels' (1972: 92) distinction between 'two
main types of contact: Type A: stable and continuous contact between neighbouring systems that are adjacent on either the horizontal (regional) or the vertical (social) axis; Type B: sudden contact, resulting from invasion, migration
or other population-shift, of systems not normally in contact hitherto'. Nowadays, however, both pidginisation and creolisation are generally seen as rather

---

[12] E.g. the breaking up of the brace construction, i.e. the surfacing of the non-finite verbs (in the
main clause) and the entire verb cluster (in the embedded clause) in final position.
[13] 'Pidginisation is that complex process of sociolinguistic change comprising reduction in inner
form, with convergence, in the context of restriction in use. . . . Creolisation is that complex
process of sociolinguistic change comprising expansion in inner form, with convergence, in the
context of extension in use.' (Hymes 1971: 84). In the past thirty years of research, the insight
has grown that the two processes are not always that distinct.
[14] Cf. Hinskens (2001) for a summary of, and comments on, Siegel (2001).

gradual processes – like koineisation. Moreover, Kerswill (2002a) argues that koineisation can, in fact, be relatively abrupt, since the 'normal' transmission (Thomason and Kaufman 1988: 9–10) of language/dialect across generations is interrupted in cases where children are demonstrably the 'koineisers'.

Afrikaans developed out of processes of koineisation of several different seventeenth-century Dutch dialects, but it also has 'creoloid' characteristics.[15] To the extent to which the diachronic study of Afrikaans is feasible, this language seems to provide unique possibilities for testing Siegel's claims regarding the essential differences between koineisation and creolisation.

Drawing parallels between decreolisation (Bickerton 1975) and dc is made difficult by the fact that the historical relationship between a basilect (the 'deep' variety of a creole language) and its acrolect (the language – usually European – which supplied most of the lexical material) differs from that between a dialect and the related standard language and even more so from that between related dialects. Whereas in most cases the acrolect is one of the ancestors of the basilect, a dialect, and the related standard language, or a related dialect, are usually 'siblings' in the sense that many modern standard languages developed from a dialect or a group of dialects. Second, whereas decreolisation is by definition a movement in the direction of the acrolect, dc need not necessarily proceed in the direction of the standard language (cf. Hinskens 1992: section 1.2.4).

3.2.5 Mixed languages   The convergence between languages can ultimately result in the development of *mixed languages* through *language intertwining*. Bakker and Mous (1994: 4–5) define mixed languages as languages 'showing a combination of the grammatical system (phonology, morphology, syntax) of one language with the lexicon of another language', the main difference (according to these authors) between a mixed language and a language with extreme lexical borrowing being the fact that mixed languages can have over 90 per cent 'foreign' elements even in the core lexicon, while languages which have undergone heavy borrowing do not typically have more than 45 per cent 'foreign' words. A famous mixed language is Spanish-Quechua Media Lengua (Muysken 1981). Some of the descendants of Romani also qualify as mixed languages (Bakker and Cortiade 1991).

The line distinguishing language intertwining from dc is not always easy to draw. According to Sarhimaa (2000), Karelian, a Balto-Finnic language spoken in northwest and central Russia and, until the Second World War, in the easternmost part of present-day Finland, has some features of a mixed language. Because of the close historical relationship between Dutch and Frisian, Town

---

[15] According to, for example, Muysken and Smith (1995: 5); Den Besten, Muysken, and Smith (1995: 93); Mühlhäusler (1997: 7).

Frisian (Stadsfries) is even more problematic for a proper distinction between language intertwining and dc. Town Frisian is a centuries-old, originally urban, 'variety of Dutch that preserves substratal Frisian peculiarities' such as the fact that it is 'spoken with a Frisian accent' (Van Coetsem 2000: 100; cf. Van Bree 1994).

It is not yet clear whether the differences between the convergence between different languages, such as may result in mixed languages, on the one hand, and dc, on the other, are of a gradual, hence quantitative, nature or if they are essentially qualitative in nature.

4   Methodologies

In this section, we will present a compact, yet critical, discussion of some of the methods applied in the study of dc and dd. We will give short comparative overviews of the standard (as well as some not-so-standard) techniques used to collect, analyse, and interpret data in historical linguistics, dialectology, and sociolinguistics. Then we will point out a number of requirements for the proper study of either the processes or the results of dc and dd.

It is obvious that the study of dc and dd is relevant to historical linguistics, dialectology, and sociolinguistics. Apart from differences in orientation between these three subdisciplines, there are also basic differences in methodology that are relevant to the study of dc and dd. These differences concern the techniques used to collect, analyse, and interpret data, and they pertain to aspects such as

- the nature of the data (written or oral, elicited, or spontaneous)
- the ways in which the material is collected ('armchair-method' or 'tape recorder-method', recording one, a few, or a larger number of speakers)
- the types of analysis (e.g. are quantitative, statistical approaches relevant and feasible?)

Moreover, the fact that historical linguists often try to follow large numbers of changes in outline over a long period of time, whereas sociolinguists usually investigate a comparatively small number of changes in great detail (cf. Aitchison 1991: 18), affects not only the research questions but also the type of conclusions and inferences that are possible.

In its approach to, and interpretation of, linguistic change, traditional dialectology pays a great deal of attention to the relationships between the dialects affected – in other words, the nature of the *diasystem* constituted by the dialects. It is also concerned with geographical directionality, as we have seen. In having these concerns, dialectology showed little interest in the linguistic and sociolinguistic processes involved. Variationist sociolinguistics, on the other hand, concentrates on the actuation, embedding, and evaluation of the processes, sometimes at the expense of directionality and intersystemic relationships.

Thus, the two subdisciplines complement each other. The study of dialect convergence and divergence therefore needs to be informed by both subdisciplines.

Processes resulting in dc or dd often have consequences not only for the variation between related varieties (intersystemic variation) but also for 'inherent', quantitative, intrasystemic variation. Prototypically, dc and dd result from dialect contact, though language contact may (exceptionally) be involved if this results in dialects diverging from neighbouring ones as a result of borrowing of material from another language, or the effect of convergence across unrelated languages which are in contact – the *Sprachbund* phenomenon. For instance, on both sides of the Dutch–French border in Belgium, a rising diphthong develops out of /ɛ/ as in e.g. /pjɛrt/ (<Flemish, Brabant, and Limburg dialect /pɛrt/, standard Dutch <paard>, 'horse') and /pjɛrt/ ∼ /pjɛt/ (< Fr. <perdre>, 'to lose'). Another example is the fact that, in a part of the same area, both French and Dutch systematically lack /h/, as in French 'h aspiré' and 'h muet' (cf. Van Bree 1990: 321–322).[16] Research into dc and dd lies at the crossroads between contact linguistics and variationist linguistics, i.e. between the study of language change as a result of language contact and the study of language variation as a synchronic manifestation of language change, but without contact being implicated.

As we pointed out in section 2, processes leading to dc or dd may involve variable, rather than categorical, dialect features. Moreover, independently of whether the dialect features involved are categorical or variable in nature, the convergence and divergence processes will probably proceed gradually – which makes it necessary to apply quantitative techniques in their analysis.

In order to be able to interpret the outcomes of processes of linguistic change as dc or dd, at least two different dialects need to be studied and compared either diachronically, at minimally two different points in time, or in apparent time. However, in many cases the probes are limited to one single dialect, contemporary data for which are then typically compared to older ones. Descriptions of data for an older stage or stages usually constitute the calibration point; often the data representing the older stage(s) are distilled from either monographs or comparative studies, which are often based on questionnaires or maps.

In practice, in most studies only one dialect is studied in detail – which *may* make the method somewhat unreliable, since the dialect with which the dynamics in the analysed dialect is being compared may itself in the meantime have changed. This may have resulted from 'drift', by which dialects undergo parallel changes even after they have split and are not in contact with each other, that is, without any 'interdialectic influencing' (Sapir 1921: 171–172). In Sapir's view, this is brought about by 'fundamental' features which the dialects, despite

---

[16] Cf. Hinskens, Kallen, and Taeldeman (2000: 18) for an additional example.

their split, still have in common and which are 'fundamental to the genius of the language'.

The fact that until recently only few representatives of formal linguistic theory were concerned with language variation (let alone with dc or dd) has to do with their outspoken preference for (1) their own intuitions regarding their standard language, and, in so far as the object of their investigations is not their own standard language; for (2) the 'armchair method', i.e. the fact that they hardly ever study 'undocumented' language systems (cf. Kiparsky 1972: 193) – which is equally at the expense of nonstandard varieties. The number of theoretically oriented linguists who do fieldwork is still very limited. Besides, many linguists still regard formal theory as merely synchronically relevant. Nevertheless, there is a growing number of representatives of formal theory working on language variation and change, including dc and dd. In several of his articles, beginning with 'Linguistic universals and linguistic change' (1968), Kiparsky explicitly takes the position that a theory which, apart from the relevant synchronic data, can also explain diachronic data is superior to a theory which can only handle synchronic data. In this volume formal theory is most clearly represented in the chapters by CORNIPS AND CORRIGAN (syntax) and KALLEN (phonology).

5   Research Questions and Hypotheses

In this section, we attempt to summarise the main current insights that have been achieved by relating them to ten sets of questions. In doing so, we will make ample reference to what we view as the most important relevant literature as well as to the relevant chapters of the present book.

5.1   Internal factors

What is the relationship between structural forces and contact in dc and dd? What is the use of formal linguistic theory for the understanding of dc and dd?

 5.1.1 Intrasystemic forces versus contact   We need to ask which types of internal factors play a role in processes leading to dc and dd. Among the internal, structural factors which can bring about dc are 'drift' and the 'genius of language' (Sapir – briefly discussed in section 3, above), along with natural-ness.[17] An example of drift is the historical diphthongisation of Germanic /iː/ and /uː/ in English, German and Dutch (e.g. *ice, Eis, ijs* and *house, Haus, huis*, respectively). Another example may be phrase-internal covariation in noun phrase number agreement in Puerto Rican Spanish and Brazilian Portuguese

---

[17] Cf. the output constraints of Optimality Theory as teleological motivations. Closely related to Sapir's 'drift' is Keller's (1994) concept of the 'invisible hand'.

which, according to Scherre (2001: 103), in this respect display more similarities than differences. In Mattheier's (1996: 36–37) conception, dc is mainly
contact (i.e. externally) induced, while dd in the first place results from 'indigenous innovations' (our translation) in one of the dialects. The latter result, in
turn, from what Mattheier refers to as articulatory-perceptual or intrasystemic
variation.

In section 3.2 we discussed mixing and fudging as lexical or structural manifestations of cross-dialectal convergence. In line with these considerations the
question may arise whether, in cases of contact-induced phonemic merger, dc
prevails, while dd prevails in cases of split. Labov (1994: 313–321) discusses
the expansion of mergers at the expense of distinctions in dialect geography, a
tendency which he refers to as 'Herzog's Principle'.

5.1.2 Formal linguistics   The question arises as to whether research
into dc and dd can profit from the types of theories that have been developed in
formal linguistics. If so, we must also ask whether formal theories, apart from
post hoc explanations, also provide *predictions* which can serve to structure the
empirical study of dc and dd as well as interpret its outcomes.

Formal theory has proved to be useful to the study of language variation and
change, including dc and dd, in four respects:
1. in the selection of dialect features to be studied, although the selection will
   typically not only be based on considerations of a linguistic nature;
2. a formal explanation of the *raison d'être* of specific dialect features may be
   the basis for predictions about possible future changes, provided the formal
   account is grounded in a general theory;
3. linguistic analysis is indispensable when it comes to answering the question
   if and to what extent similarities and differences in changes between related
   dialects are motivated either by shared or even universal structural tendencies
   or, rather, by common external factors;
4. linguistic analysis can counteract the 'atomistic' approach to dialect features
   which is typical of traditional dialectology in its tendency 'to treat linguistic
   forms in isolation rather than as parts of systems or structures' (Chambers
   and Trudgill 1998: 33).

The latter three points can be illustrated on the basis of insights from the theory
of lexical phonology. In this theory, three types of sound change can generally be distinguished, two of which (postlexical and lexically diffuse sound
change) are productive. The third type concerns lexicalised, hence unproduc-
tive, sound change. While postlexical rules, which can introduce new allophones, have no lexical exceptions and are blind to morphological structure
(i.e. they are instances of Neogrammarian regular change, or '*Lautwandel*')
yet operate variably, lexically diffuse sound change ('*Lautersatz*', i.e. sound
substitution through the redistribution of lexical sets over the available sound

segments) is the analogical, item-by-item extension of a nearly lexicalised sound change.

Typically, phonological innovations start as postlexical, i.e. combinatorial, strictly phonetically motivated, changes. They gradually change into morphologically motivated (lexical) processes of alternation, or else they get lexically frozen and maintain a low level of productivity, spreading on an item-by-item basis. Whatever direction they develop, ultimately they lose their productivity altogether and end up as lexicalised rules, that is, as the lexical remnants of former rules; intrasystemically (i.e. quantitatively) they do not vary. Because of their synchronically unpredictable nature, they make it impossible to establish transparent cross-dialectal correspondence rules (Hinskens 1998b).

Since sound changes have their own dynamic, what in dialect A is a postlexical rule can be a lexically diffuse rule in dialect B, and a lexicalised, hence 'dead', rule in dialect C. Word-final [t] deletion is a postlexical process in most of the relevant dialects of Dutch (such as the dialect of Nijmegen), a postlexical rule with lexical traits (because of its morphological structure sensitivity) in some dialects of Dutch (this holds for Limburg dialects of Dutch), and a lexicalised (morpheme structure type) rule in Afrikaans, a daughter language of Dutch.[18] The tensing and raising of /æ/, as in *man*, similarly has a different status in the grammars of dialects of American English. The process is spreading in a lexically diffuse fashion in several Midatlantic dialects of American English. As Labov has shown (1994: 429–437), in Philadelphia the rule, which can result in vowels that are identical to AE /ɛ/ (as in *dress*), /e/ (as in *face*), and even /ɪə/ (as in *idea*) (as manifested in the fact that *Ann* and *Ian* can be homophonous), has affected /æ/ preceding tautosyllabic /m/, /n/, /f/, /t/, /s/, /r/, and, in some items, /d/. It is also subject to prosodic and grammatical conditioning. Currently, it is spreading to items with following hetero- or ambisyllabic /n/ and /l/, such as *planet* and *personality*. Whereas this sound change is lexically diffuse in Philadelphia and New York City (Labov 1994), it operates postlexically in the Northern Cities as well as in the Midwest (for Columbus, Ohio, cf. Hartman Keiser *et al.* 1997). Differences in the dynamics in the status of a particular sound change, as it progresses, can hence lead to dd.[19]

In so far as dc consists of a decrease in the usage of dialect-specific features in the sound component, lexically diffuse and lexicalised sound changes can be expected to be given up earlier, as (1) they tend to be more salient; and (2) they are not automatic rules, that is to say, they are not rules that speakers are usually unaware of. The patterns of accommodation across different dialects of German revealed by Auer (1997) provide evidence for this idea.

---

[18] Cf. Hinskens (1992, 2002); Hinskens and van Hout (1994).
[19] See Hinskens (1998b) for an overview of phonological, historical linguistic, dialectological, and sociolinguistic aspects of these three types of sound change.

Borrowed sound changes will usually be embedded in borrowed lexical items. Initially a sound change thus adopted will entrench itself in the borrowing dialect in the loan words, before starting to spread in a lexically diffuse fashion.

As was pointed out in section 4 above, among the representatives of formal linguistic theory there is a growing focus on quantitative (intrasystemic) and geographical (intersystemic) variation. In phonology, both non-linear theory (especially lexical phonology and prosodic theory – cf. Nespor and Vogel 1986; and Selkirk 1984) and non-derivational, declarative models such as Optimality Theory (OT) have inspired a surprisingly large number of studies of language variation.[20] After so many years of neglect, there are few reasons to complain.[21] But there are hardly any studies in which there is any recognition of the fact that one is dealing with a nonstandard variety. In other words, the subordinate position of the language variety under scrutiny does not usually seem to matter. At best, one finds statements such as: dialect nature, standard language culture (as it is put in the title of Van Marle 1997). Somewhat more appealing is But-skhrikidze and van de Weijer's (2001: 49) 'speculation' that standard varieties are more restricted phonologically in that they tend to rank 'faithfulness' con-straints, i.e. constraints that require the phonetic output form to be maximally identical with the underlying form, higher than 'markedness' constraints, that is, constraints that make the phonetic output conform to prosodic and articulatory requirements. To the extent that standard varieties reflect the speech norms of the higher social classes, this speculation comes close to Kroch's (1978) claim that prestigious varieties tend to suppress natural phonetic tendencies such as contraction, deletion, monophthongisation and diphthongisation, etc. (cf. Van Oostendorp 1997).

KALLEN deals with phonological convergence (the type of diachronic devel-opment which made Dauzat and Gilliéron reject the idea of blind sound laws) in Hiberno-English, and considers the question of how phonological convergence can be accounted for from both linguistic and extra-linguistic angles.

As far as syntax is concerned, Principles and Parameters (P&P) theory is generally relatively well represented. This theory, which formed part of the pre-minimalist generative model of grammar, looks at Universal Grammar as an invariant system of highly abstract principles, some of which permit at most a specified degree of variation within a given language. Originally, this notion of variation referred to differences between languages (macroparametric variation), but the approach came to be applied to language-internal, typically

---

[20] Hinskens *et al.* (1997) contains a collection of contributions on language variation, change and phonological theory, most of which feature OT, showing how language variation can be accounted for either as mutually unranked constraints or the competition between two or more ordered constraint sets and how language change can be represented as change in constraint order.

[21] Among the exceptions from the very beginning are Lightfoot and Kiparsky.

cross-dialectal, variation (microparametric variation). From this line of research, deeper insights are expected into the universal set of parameters, their form as well as the substantial variation they allow. Within the P&P framework, language acquisition is seen as the process of parameter setting. Along these lines, Snyder 2001 presents an analysis of grammatical variation in verb particle constructions and root compounding in first language acquisition. CORNIPS AND CORRIGAN do the same for what is often referred to as syntactic microvariation (variation between related dialects or style levels), elaborating the P&P model with quantitative methods to handle data showing dc and dd from Hiberno-English as well as Limburg and the German Rhineland dialect continuum.

From a considerably wider, but not formal, angle, and on the basis of evidence from English dialects, CHESHIRE, KERSWILL, AND WILLIAMS consider if dc and dd in phonology, grammar, and discourse features (such as the focus marker 'like') show parallel patterns. They explore how variables in different components pattern geographically and socially, taking into account the particular links between, particularly, syntactic variation and discourse context.

5.2   Isolation and contact

A range of seemingly disparate insights exists about the effect of *isolation* on linguistic diversity. While Sapir (1921: 150) claimed that 'dialects arise not because of the mere fact of individual variation but because two or more groups of individuals have become sufficiently disconnected to drift apart, or independently, instead of together',[22] Labov (1972a: 324) stated that 'the fact that diversity is not automatically connected with isolation suggests that it may also be connected with the normal processes of face-to-face communication'. As Samuels (1972: 90) sees it, it is

the mere fact of isolation or separation of groups that accounts for all simpler kinds of diversity. Complete separation, whether through migration or geographical or other barriers, may result in dialects being no longer mutually intelligible; and thus, if there is no standard language to act as a link between them, new languages come into being. Lesser degrees of isolation result in what is known as a dialect continuum – a series of systems in which those nearest and most in contact show only slight differences, whereas the whole continuum, when considered from end to end, may show a large degree of total variation. Dialect continua are normally 'horizontal' in dimension . . . but in large towns they may also be 'vertical'.

A moderate degree of 'horizontal' isolation holds in the case of Balearic islands. Montoya (1995) studied five variable phonological processes in the Catalan dialects spoken in the islands, four of which appear to 'han estat totes

---

[22] Cf. Chambers' (1995: 65–66) 'Dialect laws of mobility and isolation'.

contraries a l'evolució de la resta del català' (198), i.e. 'have all undergone evo-
lutions which were contrary to what happened to them in the rest of [mainland]
Catalonia' (our translation). A relatively high degree of isolation holds in the
case of language enclaves (*Sprachinseln*). The *non plus ultra* of such enclaves
in Europe is Sorbian, a small (west) Slavonic island in a German sea in what
was once the GDR. This language is not spoken elsewhere. For this reason,
there cannot be divergence from a homeland here.

Some of the methodological problems in the study of language enclaves are
discussed in Mattheier (1997). Among the methodological problems which,
in our view, are specific to emigrant dialects (which most of these enclave
languages are) are questions such as: what is the point of reference to establish
dc or dd? Should they be compared to the 'home' dialects or to one another? If
the goal is to look for indications of divergence from the original dialect in the
'home country', is the point of reference the state of the dialect at the time of
the emigration or the dialect in its present state?[23]

Daan (1987: 118–120) studied the Dutch of American descendants of speakers of very precisely localised Dutch dialects. In their speech, Daan found
differences compared to the present-day Dutch dialects. On the basis of the
operational assumption that the American Dutch dialects she studied had not
changed in the course of the generations, Daan tentatively concludes that the
corresponding 'home country' dialects had probably changed. We add that such
claims are only warranted on the basis of dialect use of speakers (a) who after
their emigration no longer had sysematic contacts with speakers of the same
or related varieties who did not migrate; and (b) whose competence did not
deteriorate.

Minervini (1998) seems to try to compare the emigrant dialects both to the
'home' dialects and to one another. Equally relevant is Katsoyannou and Karyolemou's (1998) study of Greco in Calabria (south Italy) in 1985; since this
date, the dialect has become almost extinct.

Do old dialects imported by settlers converge in their new environment?
This question has mainly been studied for language enclaves. A famous example is Schirmunski's (1930) study of a range of geographically and structurally
fairly divergent dialects of German in Russia. ROSENBERG deals with German
dialects in the former Soviet Union and in Brazil. Smits' (1996) study of Iowa
Dutch, which, according to the author, 'is certainly not identical to Standard
Dutch' (15), brings to light some of the results of intensive processes of interdialectal levelling.

In connection with the overseas varieties of Dutch, English, Portuguese, and
Spanish (the languages of the former colonising nations), isolation with respect

---

[23] This problem, including the question how to reconstruct the then (spoken) dialect on the basis
of older (written) sources, is discussed in Nesse (1998).

to 'mother tongue and mother country' and at the same time contact with originally non-contiguous dialects went hand in hand. Did this lead to similar patterns of dc and dd? And what role does the new linguistic environment have?

Russo and Roberts (1999) show that the gradual replacement of the auxiliary *être* by *avoir* in Vermont French (which is also taking place in Canadian French) is being conditioned by internal factors (grammatical properties of the main verb) and the relative frequency of usage of the main verb, but not by social factors. According to the authors, this latter fact corroborates findings of others regarding language death, language loss, and shift to the majority language. The result is divergence from the French of France and older forms of North American French.

That divergence does not need to result from isolation is demonstrated by the developments in standard Dutch as it is spoken in Belgium. There are recent developments in both phonology (Van de Velde 1996) and the lexicon (Geeraerts *et al.* 1999) which lead to divergence from standard Dutch as it is spoken in the Netherlands. Although language systems can hardly be compared to biological species, there seems to be an interesting parallelism with recent insights from evolution theory here. Evolutionary biologists and paleontologists like Stephen Gould have discovered that geographical isolation is not an absolute condition for the development of a new species; at the rim of (rather than separate from) the area of distribution of specific species of insects, fish, and birds, intermediate varieties and new species have been found to develop (Goldschmidt 2000).

Conversely, isolation does not necessarily result in linguistic non-convergence or divergence. Bolognesi (2001: section 7) argues that

the prolonged isolation of Sardinia does not bring about the archaicism of its language at all. In fact, the traits that in the [historical linguistic and dialectological] literature are considered archaic have been found to be extremely limited in number [3 out of the 15 traits discussed by the author] and they occur only in part of the structure in some of the varieties of Sardo. (our translation)

In a sense, *contact* is the opposite of isolation. Historically, contact beyond the borders of one's own village grew with the demise of the economic role of agriculture. While in 1849 no less than 44 per cent of the Dutch population earned a living in agriculture, in 1950 this proportion had sunk to 20 per cent. In 1995 it had shrunk to less than 2 per cent. World-wide, in 1960 about 2/3 of the population lived in the country; according to recent projections by the United Nations, in 2025 only 1/3 of the world population will depend on farming for their living (Mak 1998: 44–45).

The transition from an agrarian to an industrial and, eventually, post-industrial society triggers cultural changes which indirectly and gradually have tremendous effects on the position of the dialects. Among the cultural changes are increased literacy and improved means of transportation, leading to commuting and increased general mobility. This brings about a gradual widening of the horizon from *Gemeinschaft* (community) to *Gesellschaft* (society), as the nineteenth-century German sociologist Tönnies (1887) baptised it. World-wide, the erosion of the relatively closed rural village community, the habitat of the traditional dialects, is manifested geographically in urbanisation and the 'usurpation' of village communities by neighbouring cities. Regular and intensive contact of a dialect with other varieties often leads to short-term accommodation and, as some authors assume, in the long run to convergence (cf. section 5.7 below).

In general dc also plays a role in the stabilisation of standard varieties. PEDERSEN discusses the emergence of standard varieties and considers the question of how decisive the role of sustained and intensive dialect contact, dc and koineisation is in that connection.

In our motorised society, dialect contact has manifestations which are probably surprising to many a traditional dialectologist. Labov (1974) showed that the average daily traffic flow on the highways of the eastern USA allows predictions of the location of the major traditional dialect boundaries, with the exception of New York City – which is probably due to the fact that sociolinguistically the city still constitutes a 'sink of low prestige' (Labov 1966).

5.3   *The role of the standard variety*

To what extent are the processes of convergence and divergence between non-standard varieties dependent on those between nonstandard and standard? In order for this question to be empirically considered at all, there has to be a range of dialects plus a standard language with sufficient geographical and social spread as well as prestige; moreover, structurally they have to be part of the same diasystem (cf. AUER AND HINSKENS 1996: 5–6, 13).

Whereas the convergence and divergence of dialects affect the degree of stuctural distance between them (Kloss' 1967 *Abstand*), the convergence and divergence of a dialect vis-à-vis its roofing standard language may affect not only their structural distance but also the dialect's *Ausbau*, i.e. its stage of functional development, which is maximal in the standard language (Kloss 1967). In the latter dimension, Berruto (1990: 105) distinguishes between 'regionalizzazione dell' italiano' and 'italianizzazione dei dialetti', or, more generally, between the development of regional varieties of the standard language and of relatively standardised varieties of the dialects, respectively. For the Italian situation, both processes are characterised by gradualness and continuity (Berruto 1990). Both in that publication and in his contribution to the present volume, BERRUTO wants to take the discussion further and develop a model to account for the conceptual relationship between these tendencies, on the one hand, and the utterance-internal juxtaposition of both dialect and standard through code-switching and code-mixing, on the other. In his view, mixing and switching are characterised by relative abruptness. Similarly, yet on the double basis of data for the developing dialect of the new town of Milton Keynes (UK) and rural newcomers in the city of Bergen (Norway), Kerswill (1996a) considers the question of what may be revealed about processes of convergence by patterns of variation, co-occurrence, and code-switching.

BERRUTO deals with situations in which, alongside the original dialects A and B, new compromise varieties A^B and B^A emerge, and code-switching between all the varieties occurs. He shows how Myers-Scotton's notion of the matrix language fails in the typical dialect and standard-language case. Still on the theme of standard–nonstandard relations, we note that Van Coetsem's (1988) distinctions between (a) source and recipient language systems; and (b) *agens* or *patiens* roles in language contact are highly useful in setting up a typology of varieties lying between a national standard and a traditional dialect. Levelled nonstandard regional varieties (which may be also be referred to as regiolects or, rather confusingly, regional dialects) typically develop in situations in which traditional dialects absorb features (usually lexical items) of the standard variety, i.e. situations in which the dialect is the recipient and plays the *agens* role.[24] Situations in which the dialect is the recipient but has a passive role will arise where the standard or near-standard variety forces its (grammatical or phonological) structures upon the dialect (Van Coetsem's 'imposition'). This is not uncommon in regional or national capitals or economic centres.

Regional varieties of the *standard* language can result from deliberate, but only partly successful, attempts by dialect speakers at learning the standard variety. For the (typically unstable) learners' varieties which develop in this type of situation and for which nicknames such as *Hollendsj mit knoebele* ('Dutch with bumps') or *Missingsch* exist, the dialect is the source and the dialect speakers attain the *agens* role. Berruto's (1990) 'italianizzazione dei dialetti' is a further example. Probably more common in present-day Europe, where most adults more or less master a variety of the standard, is the situation in which the standard picks out (regional) dialect features, often of a phonetic nature, as may have occurred in the case of the young 'Poldernederlands' (Stroop 1998), a supra-regional, yet northwestern, informal, spoken variety of standard Dutch which stands out, among other things, because of its lowering of the first element in the front unrounded diphthong /ɛi/ into /[ai], which used to be specific to a limited set of northwestern Hollandic dialects. This is an example of the type of situation where the dialect as the source is in the passive role.[25] Another

---

[24] This metaphorically refers to a situation in which the borrowing of standard features occurs as a result of the active involvement of the dialect speakers.

[25] Cf. AUER AND HINSKENS (1996: 7–8) for a more elaborate discussion and additional examples. The regional standard variety that Cornips (1994) refers to as Heerlens Algemeen Nederlands has the dialect as its source and the dialect speakers in the *agens* role type.

potential example is the rise to prominence of regionally accented varieties of standard British English, such as 'Estuary English', which contains much London regional phonology combined with standard morphology and syntax (Rosewarne 1984). However, in this case it seems to be more a matter of the wider acceptance of such speech in contexts where a Received Pronunciation (RP) accent would have been expected (Trudgill 2002a). It is difficult to fit this development into Van Coetsem's model, since it is not a matter of language change but of a change in the sociolinguistic distribution of an existing variety. Equally relevant is PEDERSEN's discussion of the influence standard varieties can exert on the dialects in their diasystem.

Insights into the phenomenon of the regional standard variety, i.e. the types of situation in which a dialect is the source and its speakers attain either the agens or the patiens role, are still limited, which is partly due to its linguistically highly variable and hence elusive nature. Among the many issues are those regarding the relative stability of regional standards and what determines which dialect features may, and which may not, occur in this diffuse type of variety.

From a situation in which traditional dialects, on the one hand, and the national standard language, on the other, were kept neatly apart both on the level of the individual speaker and on the level of the speech community at large, in many parts of Europe a situation is developing in which variants or even varieties actually fill up most parts of the structural space between dialect and standard. Bellmann 1998 has described this development as a change from diglossia, with linguistically and contextually distinct varieties, to 'diaglossia', a more fluid repertoire. In this development, varieties emerge which Coseriu (1980, 1981) would refer to as secondary and tertiary dialects, specifically if destandardisation sets in. On the resulting continua shifting occurs – not switching, as abrupt transitions between the constituent systems no longer exist (cf. Auer in print).

For Flemish and Limburg dialects of Dutch, Taeldeman (1998) and Hinskens (1992, 1993b: 54–56, 1998a), respectively, and for Middle German and Swiss German dialects Bellmann (1998) and Christen (1998), respectively, present findings which show that there can be a dimension in dc which is independent of the standard. In most of these cases, there is even evidence of developments which constitute cross-dialectal convergence and dialect / standard language divergence at the same time.

Largely on the basis of findings from the Málaga Urban Vernacular project, Villena (1996) models the south Andalusian verbal repertoire as a tripolar continuum, the three corners of which are formed by the traditional dialects, the national standard (Castilian), and the regional variety of the standard language ('*andaluz culto*'). Villena's model shows that, significantly, the regional variety of the standard language (which developed out of the various, partly diffuse, processes of dialect / standard convergence and divergence) is for linguistic and ethnographic reasons not located on the dialect / standard continuum.

In some cases the independent cross-dialectal convergence comes about through dialect borrowing; Ramge (1982) found that certain Saarland dialects of German adopt variants of neighbouring dialects, and Dewulf *et al.* (1981: 58) come to the same conclusion for certain Flemish dialects of Dutch.

Additionally, there is evidence that younger regional varieties can develop features of their own which do not result from cross-dialectal or dialect / standard convergence. An example is the spread of the coronalisation of the palatal allophone of the voiceless velar fricative ([ç] > [ɕ]– cf. Herrgen 1986) in the dialects and regional standard varieties in the Middle German area – which constitutes divergence from the standard language.

The standard-language concept is relatively young and mass literacy is a twentieth-century attainment. Therefore, cross-dialectal levelling must be the older and, historically, the main and probably only type of convergence. As 'late' as 1914, Terracher's investigations on the dialects of the Angoulême area brought to light that 'l'agent destructeur de la morphologie des patois n'est pas le français, mais les parlers limitrophes' (Pop 1950: 106).

Of course, the question arises as to whether the present-day levelling of cross-dialectal variation occurs completely independently of the standard language. What may seem to be purely cross-dialectal levelling may be motivated by the fact that the dialect converged towards is perceived as being (and may in fact be) closer to the standard variety by the speakers of the converging dialect. For instance, Lake Constance Alemannic German seems to converge towards the northern adjoining area of Swabian; however, since the Swabian forms adopted are closer to the standard variety, and given the attitudinal predispositions of the converging speakers, the factual convergence towards Swabian may be an 'accidental' result of an intending approximation of the standard variety; cf. Auer (1988, 1997). Most of the situations in which there appears to be an independent cross-dialectal dimension in dc concern speech communities where, alongside a range of dialects, a prestigious standard language is in common use. Is cross-dialectal convergence sociolinguistically independent of the standard language in these communities? Would this type of dynamics also have occurred if there had been either no standard language or another standard language?

Norway, where the two standard varieties are not in common oral use, seems to constitute an instance of the first scenario, i.e. cross-dialectal convergence occurring independently of the standard language. Sandøy (1998b) reports that, rather than adopting morphological features from larger towns (let alone either of the two standards), the various dialects studied undergo independent simplification processes.

In certain cases, the patterns of change are subtle. Some of the developments reported in Hinskens 1998a and Christen 1998b simultaneously result in

structural convergence towards, and a divergence in, the very linguistic substance from the standard language (cf. Auer 1998a: 5 for a brief comparison).

Sometimes, dc or dd have ancient roots. According to Smith (1979), the non-
convergence of a group of Dutch dialects towards the standard language with
respect to part of the system of diminutive formation should be accounted for
by the substrate effect of Frisian. Comparable, yet much older, are the so-called
'ingveonisms' in Old Dutch.[26] These seem to be other situations where there is
a need to distinguish non-convergence from divergence. Another example was
discussed in the preceding section 5.2; cf. section 3.1 above.

5.4   The Role of Social and Physical Geography

What role do geographical distance and borders play? What is the relevance of
nearness, community type, and family structure?

5.4.1 Distance, isolation, and the gravity model

The study of pro-
cesses of dc and dd necessarily has a comparative aspect and, since traditional dialects are primarily geographically defined, the geographical aspect
will inevitably play a role. However, geography as such does not influence
language varieties, but does so through its social effects.

In the first decades of the twentieth century, a group of Italian dialectologists
known as the 'Neolinguistici' (in particular Bartoli and Terracini) proposed
a set of general 'laws' of dialect geography. An example is the insight that
a dialect variant whose geographical distribution is limited to an isolated or a
peripheral area is the older one. These laws (or 'norms' – actually they are to be
understood as tendencies) connect aspects of the spatial diffusion of linguistic
forms to their relative age.[27]

Both social and physical geography feature in Trudgill's (1983: 73–78) application of the *gravity model* to dialect geography. His formula contains both
geographical distance and demographic data. The formula, which is essentially
a refinement of that used in social geography to describe inter-city migration
processes (Zipf 1946; cf. Jones and Eyles 1977: 194ff.) is, in turn, based on those
of Newton. The parameters in Trudgill's formula, which measures 'linguistic
influence', are the populations of, and the distance between, the centres, as well
as their 'prior-existing linguistic similarity'. Hinskens (1992: section 12.2.2,
1993b: 56–57) successfully applied Trudgill's gravity model to account for the
fact that the rural Dutch dialect of Rimburg drops more Ripuarian features than

---

[26] An old theory, recently revitalised by Van Bree (1997), who gives a very extensive overview of
the older literature on the issue. Cf. (12–15) for a brief description of 18 'ingveonisms'.

[27] See Chambers and Trudgill (1998: 167–168) for examples, and a discussion, of these laws and
Benincà (1988: 81–89) for an overview of the intellectual background and some of the main
achievements of this school.

Ripuarian-East Limburg ones – by showing that in the course of the twentieth century the linguistic influence of the nearby city of Kerkrade (where a Ripuarian dialect is spoken) has shrunk dramatically compared to that of the slightly further away city of Heerlen (which lies in the Ripuarian-East Limburg transition zone). Sociogeographical and linguistic shifts appear to coincide nicely. But what exactly is the nature of this relationship?

Directly linked to the gravity model is the idea of the spatial diffusion of a linguistic change down the urban hierarchy, jumping from city to city according to their size (Britain 2002b). TAELDEMAN critically examines this model for West Flemish dialects of Dutch. An interesting new (quantitative) approach to the study of the geographical dispersion of sound change is presented in Horvath and Horvath's 2001 'multilocality' study of l-vocalisation in New Zealand and Australian English. The findings showed 'the failure of the gravity model as an explanatory device' (51).

5.4.2 Borders Borders often have an effect on change, leading mainly to dd between dialects on either side of the border, and simultaneously dc between dialects on the same side. Borders are natural (e.g. rivers, swamp areas, mountain chains) or made by humans (tribal, political, and eclesiastical boundaries).

In Western societies, political borders, particularly state borders, may be the most influential. Linguistically, however, state borders are of different types. With respect to dialects and political borders, in present-day Europe at least three different types of constellation can be distinguished. In the first, almost the same standard language is spoken on both sides of the border; the state borders are often younger than the dialect continua they cut across. Examples are the German-Austrian border and the border between Germany and the German-speaking part of Switzerland, as well as the much more recent, and temporary, border between the Federal Republic of Germany and the former GDR. Further examples are constituted by the border area between the Netherlands and the northern, Dutch-speaking part of Belgium, as well as that between France and the southern, francophone part of Belgium.

The different status of the vernaculars on both sides of the English–Scottish political border, along with earlier phonological changes in the border area, leads Glauser (2000) to hypothesise that eventually it will coincide with the political border. A diverging linguistic effect is also exerted by the national border between Canada and the USA, as the so-called Canadian Raising of the diphthongs /ai/ and /au/ before voiceless obstruents halts at the border. Kallen (2000) deals with the political border between Northern Ireland and the Irish Republic (which coincides with the old cultural border between Ulster and the other provinces of Ireland) on the basis of data collected in the 1950s for the traditional dialects of Irish and Hiberno-English. The hypothesis that

Hiberno-English reflects the dialect divisions of Irish is rejected. The traditional dialects of both languages do show a north–south division. Given the huge difference in the societal position of Irish on both sides of the border, the future may well bring divergence among its dialects along this relatively new political border.

In the second type of constellation, different but related standard languages are spoken on both sides of the border. It is exemplified by the Dutch–German transition areas along a stretch of the Dutch–German border which are part of the larger Continental West Germanic continuum, spanning what was originally one diasystem. Another example of this type of constellation is Spain and Portugal; a more restricted but even more striking example might be Galician and Portuguese. The members of each of the three sub-branches of the Slavonic language family and Scandinavia form still further examples.

The entire Romance dialect continuum, of which Spain and Portugal form a part, is itself an example of the second constellation. Applying methods from dialectometry, Goebl (2000) describes how a single geographical continuum of Romance dialects is cut across by national boundaries, each of which is associated with its own standard. Each of these standard languages, in turn, is based on dialects which are distant from the ones in the continuum at issue.

In the third type of constellation, a dialect area is again divided by a national border, but the corresponding standard language is used only on one side of the border. Since the dialect on the other side of the border does not belong to the same diasystem as the national standard language, we speak of a 'roofless' dialect. Examples are several dialects of Dutch origin spoken in Germany and the northwest of France; the Hungarian dialects spoken in Austria (Gal 1979); the Albanian dialects spoken in Greece; and Spanish in the southwest of the USA.[28] Cf. section 4 for examples of dc and dd across borders of the third type.

A subtype is formed by those cases where there is no immediate geographical contiguity of the roofless dialects with related but roofed dialects. Examples are the Albanian dialects spoken in several parts of southern Italy, the dialects of the German language enclaves in Russia,[29] investigated by Schirmunski (e.g. 1930), and, generally, migrant dialect communities. A further subtype is provided by Welsh and Irish, which have diffuse and non-institutional borders with English-speaking communities. Both these languages have 'roofs' of considerable antiquity, and these function in education and, to some extent, in administration. However, practically all speakers are bilingual and biliterate, and, for most people, English fulfils most 'H' functions. The former Yiddish-speaking communities in Poland and Russia belong to yet another subtype.

---

[28] Cf. AUER AND HINSKENS (1996: 15–18); and Hinskens, Kallen, and Taeldeman (2000: 18–23) for additional discussion and further examples for the three border types.

[29] The situation in the Russian enclaves is slightly more complicated since the German standard language has been around for a long time.

In a language community in which the dialects have no overarching standard roof the standard variety of the dominant linguistic group is part of the repertoire and fulfils many of the functions of a standard variety for the speakers of a non-related dialect as well. However, the speakers of the 'roofless' dialects do not necessarily linguistically orient themselves towards this standard variety in the way they would to a 'real' standard variety.

The French political borders are old and have been quite stable over the centuries. In the northwest the state border was not a language border, as West Flemish was spoken on both sides.[30] Nevertheless, traditionally the West Flemish dialects of French Flanders have three types of features which set them apart from their siblings in what used to be the Netherlands until 1830, and what has been Belgium since 1830. Ryckeboer (2000) discusses the age-old gradual ousting of West Flemish, a cluster of dialects of Dutch, from northwest France, partly as a long-drawn social process, partly as the ultimate form of cross-border dialect divergence. For a long stretch, the River Rhine coincides with the French–German border. According to Klausmann (2000), on the right bank of the river, an intermediate variety, between standard German and the traditional dialects, has emerged. It has no counterpart on the left bank, where French serves as the standard language. Instead, French has found its way into the Alsatian repertoire, in the sense that, in certain situations, left-bank speakers of Alsatian switch to standard French.

The Danish–German border is also relatively old, but has shifted southward. As a result, there are speakers of (Low) German dialects on the Danish side of the border as well as speakers of Danish (Jutland) dialects on the German side (Pedersen 2000). Sarhimaa (2000) discusses the question whether divergence in the dialects of Karelian, as well as both convergence and divergence between Karelian and other parts of the Eastern Balto-Finnic dialect continuum, is his-torically related to the political border between Finland and Russia/the former Soviet Union.

According to Sapir (1921: 213fn.), nationally, state borders tend to have uni-fying effects, although the linguistic unification is never absolute. The comple-ment to this internal convergence is divergence at the borders, which destroys old dialect continua. Despite the fact that the seven contributions to Kallen *et al.* (2000)[31] deal with a range of different European situations, all show that convergence on the dialect standard language and cross-dialectal dimensions (i.e. state-internal linguistic unification) necessarily leads to divergence at the borders. This is one of the ways in which national standard languages 'minimize internal differences and maximize external ones', as Einar Haugen (1968/1972: 244) put it.

---

[30] In most other areas, Walloon dialects of French were spoken on both sides.
[31] Namely, Glauser, Kallen, Goebl, Ryckeboer, Klausmann, Pedersen, and Sarhimaa.

WOOLHISER discusses some results of his recent research on the phonology and morphology of Belarusian dialects of the contemporary Polish–Belarusian border region; as Polish belongs to the Western and Russian, and Belarusian to the Eastern, branch of the family of Slavonic languages, this represents the second type of constellation. What makes the study particularly interesting is the fact that in Woolhiser's research area, the border dates back only to the mid-1940s, which makes it, in principle, possible to observe related processes of dc and dd in progress.

5.4.3 Family structure and community type

5.4.3 *Family structure and community type*   On an entirely different level, on the smallest scale of social geography, we find the organisation of such small communities as the household or the family. In this respect, many Western societies have in the past century or so gone through the decline of the multi-generational family and the rise of the 'nuclear family'. This is one of the microsocial consequences of the historical transition from predominantly agrarian to industrial economies. Growing up in a nuclear family differs in many respects from growing up in a household shared by one's grandparents and other kin. As far as language acquisition is concerned, the effects on the variability in linguistic input are evident. As the dialect is transferred to the new generations, in the nuclear family it will be the variety spoken by the younger or the middle age groups. This variety may well be structurally reduced compared to the one spoken by the older age groups; in any case, such a situation may accelerate linguistic change. KERSWILL AND TRUDGILL consider cases of migration where the third, oldest generation is absent: the development of koineised forms of English in New Zealand and the new town of Milton Keynes is, they argue, accelerated by the lack of a stable local vernacular to act as a model.

Even within small-scale communities, differences lead to different dc and dd outcomes. Sandøy (2003) differentiates between two sorts of isolated, small community: the Faroese type, where it is known that, historically, most people lived in villages of about 150 individuals; and the Icelandic type, where the population lived in isolated family units of about 10 people. In the Faroe Islands, a small degree of social marking of language could take place within villages, while communities remained very close-knit. This led to linguistic differentiation between, rather than within, villages, perhaps as a marker of local allegiance. In Iceland, there was neither social stratification nor, for the children, any peer groups, a situation which inhibited linguistic differentiation both within a family unit and across the country itself.

What the sociological make-up of households and communities, as well as the nature of borders (discussed in section 5.4.2), seem to have in common is a direct effect on the interaction between individuals and groups (age groups, social networks, ethnic groups, groups which are constituted by language background) as well as potentially on sociopsychological aspects of language use (attitudes, the linguistic projection of identity) and thus, indirectly, on language.

5.5   The role of demographic and sociopolitical processes

How do sociopolitical and demographic processes such as centralisation, decentralisation, and regionalisation affect or even trigger processes of linguistic change resulting in dc or dd? What is the role of urbanisation? Are cities hotbeds of processes of linguistic change resulting in dc and dd? What role do mobility and migration play in dc and dd? Is internationalisation relevant to dc and dd?

5.5.1 Centralisation in European nation states   In Europe, cities developed in a postfeudal, civil society not governed by aristocrats, but characterised by trade and the emergence of the nation state; centuries later, these developments were followed by growing mobility and the emergence of the fourth estate of the media. Compared to rural communities, urban ones tend to be relatively dynamic and open to outside influences of all kinds. In cities, cultural and specifically linguistic influence can also be exerted by rural newcomers. In her study of Swedish in four Finnish towns, Ivars (1998) found that immigration from the rural hinterland has brought about levelling between the rural and the urban dialects and increases the social differentiation of the urban dialects. According to Samuels (1972: 93), 'large cities usually show a higher rate of innovation than surrounding areas (to which innovations then radiate), and hence the classic situation in linguistic geography of an "innovating central area" flanked by "conservative peripheral areas"'. TAELDEMAN is a thorough study of both historical and contemporaneous processes of dc and dd in the area of the city of Ghent in Flanders, the southwestern (Belgian) part of the Dutch language area.

   In the course of *national unification*, the process which gradually transforms a state into a nation, the contacts between inhabitants of different regions become more frequent and more intensive, while the inhabitants become socially and culturally more similar and more dependent on one another. In other words, developments generally occur as regards:

- infrastructure: transport and communication, book printing, mass media;
- economy: the increase in scale in production and trade;
- politics: growing importance of the central government, the participation of increasingly large groups in national politics;
- culture: gradual elimination of local and regional cultures.

Behind these developments complex relationships exist. Their intricacies were already appreciated by Bloomfield, who pointed out the importance for this 'process of centralization' of the growth of economic and political units, and the improvement of the means of communication (1933: 481, 485).

Two closely related cultural aspects of the unification process are linguistic homogenisation and standardisation. In general, the processes of national unification and linguistic homogenisation do not appear to run exactly parallel: the former does not stop after a nation state has taken shape; while the latter may require even more time. In a country such as Italy, which in its present shape by European standards is still a relatively young state, the geographical and social spread of the (originally Tuscan) standard variety is far from complete. The fact that Spain, as a much older state, continues to have regional dialects and languages suggests that the age of a state is not the decisive factor, but rather the processes of unification and centralisation which follows statehood. In Spain, political centralisation is much weaker than in France, which has a much reduced dialect diversity, at least in the central and northern areas. PEDERSEN discusses the sociopolitical and ideological aspects of the emergence of standard varieties in Denmark and Sweden, relating this to the development of urban societies in the respective capital cities in the seventeenth and eighteenth centuries. She argues that the greater centralisation of Denmark has all but led to the eradication of dialects there.

The type of diversification of the standard language which is sometimes referred to as *regionalisation* leads to the emergence of regional varieties of the standard language. This issue has been dealt with in section 5.3 above.

5.5.2 Mobility and migration   Do social and geographical *mobility* lead to dc and dd? Because of geographical mobility, dialects do not usually exist in isolation. Hoppenbrouwers (1990) discusses the revolutionary long-term effects of the invention of the bicycle on dialect geography. Similar studies of the impact of motorised means of transportation seem to be lacking.

A special type of mobility is *migration* – a part of the human condition. Kerswill (2005) contains a discussion of the subtypes of migration and summarises their linguistic outcomes; here, we summarise some of the main points. A group of Hollandic dialects of Dutch shows that mobility can indeed lead to processes of linguistic change resulting in dc and dd. After the Fall of Antwerp in 1585, i.e. the occupation of this then very wealthy seaport by the Spanish (whose mission it was to roll back the effects of the Reformation and to reintroduce Catholicism), thousands of inhabitants of this Brabantine city and other parts of Brabant and Flanders fled to the cities in the north, especially to the cities in the The Hague–Amsterdam area. Most of the refugees were well to do and many of them immediately joined the top layers of society in the Hollandic cities. Numerically they were also very significant (cf. Van der Horst and Marschall 1992: 53–55). Ever since this immigration wave, the dialects in and around Amsterdam stand out because of the vowel in such items as *daar*, *maken* ('there', 'make'), etc., which is [o.ɑ], whereas the surrounding dialects have [ɛː]. The deviant Amsterdam variant has been interpreted as a Brabantism, borrowed from the highly respected Brabant refugees (Paardekooper 2001).

Migration started to grow very considerably in the Europe of the mid-nineteenth century, i.e. with the advent of industrialisation. The economic centres attracted many newcomers from the surrounding area as well as from more distant parts of the country concerned. These developments tend to have an impact on the status and, in the longer term, on the structure of the dialects involved. Cross-border labour migration also led to demographic movements hitherto unknown, including both emigration and immigration.

Emigration, and especially the founding and settling of colonies overseas, is one of the possible routes leading to new-dialect formation, the other being the development of new towns. Trudgill (1986) devoted a chapter to the emergence of new overseas dialect varieties. KERSWILL AND TRUDGILL deal with new-dialect formation in New Zealand and Milton Keynes.

Immigration has led to both short-lived and relatively stable bilingualism; the latter seems to be the case of the Turkish communities in the Netherlands and Germany, and of the Indian communities in the UK. In some of the cities in northwestern Europe, ethnic minorities are gradually developing into the new lower class or even 'underclass' of society. Among young people in cities with high concentrations of migrant workers, psychological divergence sometimes results in linguistic divergence. Kotsinas (1988) reports that younger members of ethnic minority groups in Stockholm have developed their own nonstandard varieties of Swedish for in-group use on the basis of both their mother tongues and the local urban nonstandard variety of Swedish. Similar systems are presently being studied in Hamburg (Auer 1999), Amsterdam (Appel 1999), and Utrecht (Cornips 2000). One of the most remarkable things about these new, partly mixed, language varieties is that they are not only spoken by the young members of the ethnic minority groups involved but also by younger members of the majority communities (Nortier 2001). An interesting question is what effect these new, originally ethnic, nonstandards may eventually have on the maintenance and development of the indigenous urban nonstandard varieties.

Apart from labour migration, politically motivated migration has played a role in twentieth-century Europe. Stark examples are the mass movement of people in Central Europe in the period during and after Hitler's Third Reich, as well as the 'ethnic cleansing' in the former Yugoslavia in the 1990s. A less emotionally charged new form of migration is mass tourism. A well-known example is the divergent development of the English diphthongs on Martha's Vineyard off the coast of Massachusetts (Labov 1963). Lanthaler (1997) attributes the increasing use of Federal Republic German (FRG) rather than Austrian German in South Tyrol (the German-speaking part of northern Italy) to the huge numbers of German tourists in this region – an instance of convergence towards FRG German and divergence from Austrian German. De Vink (2004) claims that very similar mechanisms kept the traditional Dutch dialect of the small, orthodox Protestant fishing village of Katwijk aan Zee from converging towards the standard language.[32]

5.5.3 *Internationalism versus 'glocalisation'* It is too early yet to tell if the internationalisation of economic and administrative structures and the increase in international communication in present-day Europe will strengthen or weaken the traditional dialects. Nelde (2001) sees a growing orientation towards local and regional identity in reaction to the internationalisation of the economy and the consequences of this for daily life. Nelde is one of the scholars who refers to this tendency as *Glokalisierung* ('glocalisation'), a blend of the adjective 'lokal' and the noun *Globalisierung* (globalisation). The notion first appeared in the late 1980s in newspaper publications by economists. According to the sociologist Roland Robertson (1993), who has popularised the notion, glocalisation describes the tempering effects of local conditions on global pressures. According to Robertson, glocalisation 'means the simultaneity – the co-presence – of both universalizing and particularizing tendencies'.

The alleged 'dialect renaissance' (German: *Dialektwelle*, Norwegian: *dialektbølge*, 'dialect wave') starting in the 1970s may well be an early manifestation of this growing orientation towards local and regional identity. It is as yet unclear if this dialect renaissance is not largely a matter of attitudes, in particular evaluation, and if it does not mainly concern those social groups who would not speak a dialect anyway. So, even for these latter groups, it seems doubtful whether the 'dialect renaissance' will have significant functional effects: metaphorically, we may be dealing with ripples on the surface rather than a wave. Yet there are national differences: the 'wave' in Norway is clearly at grassroots level and has been maintained (cf. Vikør 2001: 56); in the Dutch language area its effects have tapered off somewhat although they are still clearly observable; whereas in the German language area it seems to have led to a destandardisation and regionalisation of the standard language rather than to a reappraisal of the traditional dialects and their prestige. There have been few, if any, empirical investigations of the effects of the 'dialect renaissance', as well as of the intermediate forms, pseudo-dialectalisms, and hyperdialectalisms to which it seems to lead. Hence its effect on dc and dd are a matter of speculation.

---

[32] Cf. AUER AND HINSKENS (1996: 18–20) for additional discussion and examples for the relevance of migration to dc and dd.

5.6   The role of social networks and other types of mesosocial structures

We now look at the importance of 'mesosocial' structures, that is, structures on a level between the 'micro' level of the interactional situation and the 'macro' level of large-scale social constructs such as socioeconomic class.

One of the best-known mesosocial structure types in sociolinguistics is the social network. Social networks were introduced into sociolinguistics by Blom and Gumperz's study of (presumed) code-switching between the local dialect and standard *bokmål* Norwegian in the village of Hemnesberget (1972).[33] Code-choice and code-switching were analysed as a means of symbolically expressing group membership, rather than against the background of the speakers' socio-economic position. Also in 1972, Labov published his monograph on the Black English Vernacular in New York's inner city (Labov 1972b). He showed how the language behaviour of members of youth gangs called Cobras and Jets depended on their position in the group (where two of the main network membership types are referred to with notions such as 'core' and 'lame'). Lesley Milroy's (1980) Belfast study placed social networks (which she sees as 'norm enforcement mechanism' (175)) at the centre of the sociolinguistic agenda.

These and other studies demonstrate that an individual's socioeconomic position (usually operationalised on the basis of such parameters as educa-tional background and occupational level) is not necessarily the prevalent social factor determining social identification, nor does it account for the survival or loss of traditional dialects. Moreover, people do not typically have a sense of 'belonging' to, let alone derive a sense of security from identifying with, a social class. Unlike social classes, networks, which are often determined by friendship ties, are not anonymous. Accordingly, they are, in principle, open to ethnographic study.

VILLENA-PONSODA implements the social network concept in his quan-titative analyses of phonological variation in the urban/'rurban' Andalucian vernacular in several neighbourhoods in Málaga. In order to answer questions such as whether open vs. closed social networks have differential effects on dc and dd, Villena implements measures of social-network membership both as independent and as spurious (correlated but not causal) variables, along with educational background, sex, and age. His findings lead him to criticise a one-sidedly correlative approach to social networks and to plead for an interpretative understanding of sociolinguistic behaviour.

As is apparent from most sociolinguistic studies of social networks, a closely related mesosocial factor is neighbourhood. As Labov (2001: 259) observes,

---

[33] Norwegian dialectologists have called into question Blom and Gumperz's claim that code-switching was present in Hemnesberget, preferring to refer to style-shifting on a continuous scale (Mæhlum 1996).

'unlike gender or social class, neighborhoods are *particular* products of *particular* historical events' (our emphasis) – arguing that it therefore appears unlikely that the study of neighbourhoods allows for the induction of *general* principles of linguistic change. Careful analysis has led Labov to conclude that change in progress in Philadelphia 'is still led by the oldest and poorest [white] neighborhood' and that 'the neighborhood effects found . . . point toward diffusion of the [new] features from a local centre' – but he adds that all this is 'not enough to allow us to predict that this will hold true in any large city' (260).

Other closely related concepts are integration in the local community (Lippi-Green 1989; Sundgren 2000), and 'Ortsloyalität', i.e. loyalty to the local community, introduced into German dialectology by Mattheier (1980).[34] The results of an investigation by Hofmann (1963) indicate that a decrease of 'Ortsloyalität' has a negative effect on the functional autonomy of the local dialect.

5.7   The role of social psychological factors: identity and attitudes

Several Belgian sociolinguists (Deprez 1981; Jaspaert 1986; Van de Velde 1996) have ascribed the divergent developments in the phonology and lexicon of the Belgian variety of standard Dutch from the variety of standard Dutch spoken in most of the Netherlands (cf. section 5.2 above) to shifting *identification* and slightly distancing attitudes towards the Netherlands. Interestingly, for Northern Ireland McCafferty (1998) treats religious denomination (namely Protestant versus Catholic) as ethnic identity, showing how three sound changes which originated in the largely Protestant east of the country 'tend to be adopted primarily by Protestants, whereas Catholics tend to be more conservative' (97).

In their study of linguistic convergence in adolescents, Kerswill and Williams (2000) are concerned with the nature and extent of peer-group pressure. This is in line with the general insight that 'the prevalence of diversity' is due to 'the natural tendency for people to cling to the linguistic markers that imbue their most personal encounters' (Chambers 1995: 229–230).

Most research on language *attitudes* is experimental in nature, as the methodology centres on the systematic manipulation and control of variables. Another way of obtaining data on language attitudes is to distil them from interviews. Both experimental research and interviewing are difficult tools for eliciting reliable data, especially when used to investigate the covert prestige of a variant or variety. In so far as the methodological problems can be solved, this type of research can provide valuable insights into how certain linguistic forms are stereotypically associated with speaker attributes such as intelligence, profession, likeability, trustworthiness, etc.

---

[34] Cf. Wollersheim (1998: 52) for references to some recent relevant studies of social psychology.

In the case of language attitudes (as with accommodation – cf. section 3.2 above), psychology and language behaviour do not necessarily mirror each other. Particularly intriguing is Hofer's (2000: 106–108) finding that there are large evaluative differences connected with relatively small linguistic differences between varieties of the Basle dialect of Swiss German and, *vice versa*, that relatively big linguistic differences between varieties are connected with small evaluative differences. Very similar findings were made by Kerswill and Williams (2002a); they associated this finding with the level of salience of particular features (see below, section 5.9).

Faced with the contradiction between the rapid diffusion of the Copenhagen variety of Danish[35] and the negative attitudes towards 'low' (nonstandard) Copenhagen features, in what looks like a case of covert prestige, Kristiansen (1996) applied techniques to tap data regarding more 'unconscious' attitudes. These revealed that the traditional dialects are downgraded, rather than the overtly stigmatised low Copenhagen features. KRISTIANSEN AND JØRGENSEN discuss the effects of ideology, affiliation, and language attitudes on dc and dd. The covert subjective correlates were studied in situations where language was not focused on, and in which subjects were unaware of displaying attitudes towards language (speaker evaluations in both experimental and natural settings). In Næstved, adolescents gave a low rating to speakers with even a minimum of local dialect phonetics, while giving a high rating to speakers who used traditional working-class Copenhagen features.

A range of studies has shown that language attitudes have only limited prognostic power for code-choice and for language variation; it is even more difficult to use attitudinal data as predictors of language change;[36] the same holds for dc and dd. In so far as attitudes do affect dialects, one might hypothesise that they do so indirectly, and that attitudes have a certain prognostic value for the choice of the language of socialisation and hence
(1) for the transfer of a nonstandard variety to a new generation;
(2) for the function of this nonstandard variety for the new generation; and
(3) in the longer run, for the structure of the nonstandard variety.

Is levelling foreshadowed by face-to-face *accommodation*? What is the relative impact of accommodation on the part of children, adolescents, and adults? The latter question is empirically considered by Kerswill (1996b), and by KERSWILL AND TRUDGILL, the former by AUER AND HINSKENS. On the basis of various empirical studies, carried out on speakers of dialects of Dutch,

---

[35] The use of low Copenhagen features among young Jutlanders had already been observed by Pedersen (1996).
[36] See e.g. Münstermann and van Hout (1986); Jaspaert and Kroon (1988); Hinskens (1993a: 235–241). See Omdal (1994); Labov (2001: ch. 6) for critical assessments of the relevance of subjective dimensions. AUER AND HINSKENS (1996: 22) speculate about possible explanations for the mismatch between language attitudes and dialect use.

Lëtzebuergesch, and German, AUER AND HINSKENS evaluate the main idea underlying Trudgill's (1986) model of dialects in contact, the idea that prolonged and frequent short-term convergence leads to dialect levelling. Although Trudgill's hypothesis is not rejected, in all the amount of empirical support is far from impressive and seems to urge a revision of the hypothesis.

In connection with convergence and divergence, not everybody thinks along sociopsychological lines. In his study of Romani and 'a possible linguistic area' in the Near East, Matras (2001: 1, 4) claims that convergence is cognitively motivated; according to him, convergence is rooted in simplification by bilingual speakers. He interprets convergence as 'the efficient management of the pragmatics of multilingual interaction: reduce the organizational effort on the one hand, maintain the structural autonomy of the systems on the other'. In this conception, there is no place for social psychology. As Trudgill points out (2002b), simplification of this sort also takes place in dialect contact in high-contact communities where adults, with their cognitive limitations in relation to language acquisition, are faced with learning second dialects.

Does this contradict the interpretations of the relevant findings for dc and dd? We would like to advance the hypothesis that in the case of the convergence and divergence between dialects in contact (where mutual comprehensibility is usually not at stake), volition and, more generally, sociopsychological factors play the *main* role; while in the case of the convergence and divergence between different languages in contact the main (but, of course, not only) role is played by proficiency and, more generally, cognitive factors, the degree to which it plays a role being proportional to the structural distance between the languages.

The proportion of 'bilectal' speakers in a speech community may be inversely related to the degree to which cognitive factors play a role in convergence and divergence between dialects in contact. The model can be even further refined by distinguishing between compound and co-ordinate 'bilectality' (by analogy with 'bilingualism'). Whereas in compound bilectality both lects were acquired simultaneously and are supposed to be cognitively represented as one system, co-ordinate bilectality is the result of the successive acquisition of the dialects at issue, which are supposed to be cognitively represented as two systems.[37]

The obvious relatedness between accommodation, language attitudes, identification, social networks, and loyalty to the local community (the latter two of which were briefly discussed in section 5.6 above) is illustrated by Wolfram and Hazen's (1996) description of the speech of a black woman in a small community on the Ocracoke island in the outer banks of North Carolina. The authors show how the woman's English is distinguished by convergence to, and

---

[37] On compound versus co-ordinate bilingualism see Weinreich (1953); Ervin and Osgood (1954). Cf. van Coetsem (2000: 83) and the references mentioned therein.

divergence from, both the island's dialect (Ocracoke Vernacular English) and African American Vernacular English.

5.8   The interaction of internal, external, and extra-linguistic factors

In their seminal paper from 1968, Weinreich, Labov, and Herzog defined the three main problems in the study of language change as its actuation, its social and linguistic embedding, and its evaluation in the speech community. In our view, either *internal* (language structure, UG) or *external* (contact and borrowing) factors cause the actuation of a language change,[38] including changes that result in dc or dd. Clearly, internal factors determine the linguistic embedding. To the external, contact-related factors we would add *extra-linguistic* factors, which Farrar and Jones (2002: 1) define as 'sociopolitical and economic', that is, factors which are not directly related to the interaction of linguistic systems through contact. Under 'extra-linguistic' we would also include social–psychological factors, especially identities and attitudes. Both external and extra-linguistic factors determine the social and geographical diffusion of a change and its social embedding.

An indication of the interaction of internal, i.e. linguistic and extra-linguistic, motivations is found in Bailey's (1973) model, which builds on Schmidt's (1872) '*Wellentheorie*' (see section 3.2.2 above). According to Bailey, change diffuses (a) simultaneously in linguistic structure and along extra-linguistic dimensions; and (b) in wave-like patterns. Haas (1978) provides an implementation of Bailey's model in the study of a number of sound changes in dialects of Swiss German.

Andersen (1988, 1989) distinguishes adaptive, evolutive, and spontaneous innovations. While adaptive innovations are 'not explainable without reference to factors outside the linguistic system in question', evolutive innovations are 'entirely explainable in terms of the linguistic system that gave rise to it' (Andersen 1973: 778). Adaptive innovations are externally motivated and involve finality, whereas both evolutive and spontaneous innovations are internally motivated and do not involve finality. Andersen specifies a number of subtypes, only some of which seem to be relevant for the present discussion. Contact-induced innovation is a special type of adaptive innovation, usually affecting differences between language systems, and abductive innovation is a special type of evolutive innovation, which typically affects differences within a single system. Abductive innovations, which are a special type of evolutive innovation, result from an 'incorrect' analysis of the primary language data by the language learner, motivated by the 'laws of language' (Andersen 1973); in

---

[38] But even in the case of an externally motivated change, usually language internal factors will ultimately 'decide' to accept or reject it.

abductive innovations, UG motivated reanalysis, which is claimed to have its roots in first language acquisition, plays an essential role (cf. Røyneland 2000: 189–191).

On the basis of Andersen's (1988, 1989) work, we deduce the following probabilistic model:

Internal/external origin	Type of innovation	One or both systems innovating?	Probable outcome
external	adaptive – contact	one	dc
		both	dc
internal	evolutive – abductive	one	dc/dd
		both	dc/dd
internal	spontaneous	one	dd
		both	dc/dd

Two further specifications of the hypotheses are in order, both with respect to the concept of evolutive innovations. In cases where only one of the language systems involved is innovating, *and if* the other system has already carried through the particular innovation, then the chances that the outcome will be convergence seem relatively good (cf. Stroop's view on the lowering of the first element of the diphthong /ɛi/ as a pan-Germanic tendency, paraphrased in section 5.3 above). Where both of the language systems involved are innovating *and if* the relevant areas of the linguistic structure are sufficiently different to begin with, then the evolutive innovations will probably result in divergence – unless there is drift taking place.

Structural factors can apparently also be of overriding importance in dialect / standard convergence, particularly in deciding which dialect features will be levelled out and which ones will survive. Landa and Franco (1998) studied Basque Spanish to test the following two claims: (i) the pre-existence of a certain degree of structural parallelism between the standard variety and the dialect is required for a feature to remain; and (ii) a syntactic phenomenon does not survive in isolation but its future is linked to that of a cluster of syntactic properties (cf. our discussion of parameter theory in section 5.1.2 above).

Some researchers maintain that contact can strengthen language-specific structural forces or more general natural tendencies (e.g. of a prosodic nature). In their study of Greco in Calabria, Katsoyannou and Karyolemou (1998, cf. section 5.2 above) report on the Greco dialects borrowing from the surrounding Calabrese dialects of Italian, but also displaying structures that can be considered as reinforcements of trends which existed already in Greek, where they have minor or peripheral status. Cf. our remarks with respect to Riehl (2001) in section 3.2.3 above. In recent work on the verb–object agreement system in western, Biscayan, and eastern dialects of Basque (which is an ergative language), Elordui (1998) found that what looked like dd appeared on closer consideration to be dc, since the dialects show basically the same dynamic – which they share not only among themselves but also with French and Spanish. ROSENBERG discusses comparable questions on the basis of findings from his investigations of the situation in some of the former German language enclaves in Russia and elsewhere.

In situations of sustained isolation, internal tendencies possibly have free play; Biberauer (to appear) shows that, as far as the syntax of the finite verb is concerned, in its modern spoken versions Afrikaans, a partly creolised daughter language of Dutch, is in the process of diverging further away from Dutch.

VILLENA-PONSODA questions the fine-grained quantitative approach to social networks as it does not allow him to account for the entire amount of variability in the changes in the use of the linguistic variables in his Málaga project. However, as processes of language change are usually determined by a cocktail of factors and are, hence, to be seen as 'multi-causality phenomena' (Dressler 1986: 520; cf. Hinskens 1992: section 2.5.1), in relation to dc and dd each single external, extra-linguistic, and internal factor needs to be understood as a probabilistic explanation – leaving the investigator with the task of developing a model which is at the same time maximally explanatory and maximally simple and parsimonious.[39]

Andersen uses the adjective 'external' in the sense of 'from another linguistic system' (hence[40] it stands for borrowing in the widest sense of the word – and this is the sense in which we use it), but sometimes (as in the chapter by KALLEN) 'external' refers also to language-external, hence extra-linguistic factors. Kallen discusses the relationship between internal and external (extra-linguistic as well as contact-related) factors in dc and dd in the phonology of Irish English.

5.9   Salience

In Kiparsky's conception (1992: 59), the likelihood of an innovation being adopted is 'inversely proportional to its salience, as measured by its distance from the old form'.[41] Salience itself is not defined by Kiparsky, who merely states that, like frequency, salience has 'no structural correlate'.

---

[39] The latter requirement is sometimes referred to as 'Occam's Razor'.

[40] Also in Thomason and Kaufman (1988), who knock the bottom out of a number of common methodological principles on the basis of which historical linguistics keeps potential external explanations (*in casu* borrowing) for particular instances of structural change out of the picture (57–64). This seems to be a matter of conceptual orientation in the first place.

[41] As well as 'to the old form's entrenchment, measured primarily by frequency'. At the same time, the success of an innovation is 'locally proportional to its functional value, and to the productivity . . . of the process that derives it'.

According to some dialectologists, the relative 'salience' of individual dialect features plays a role in short- and long-term accommodation. In Trudgill's (1986) model of the sociolinguistic consequences of dialect contact (to be sketched in section 5.10 below), this factor has both linguistic and extra-linguistic correlates, as shown below (adapted from Trudgill 1986: 11):

- the variable has at least one variant which is overtly stigmatised;
- the variable has a high-status prestige variant reflected in the orthography;
- the variable is undergoing linguistic change;
- variants are phonetically radically different;
- variants are involved in the maintenance of phonological contrasts.

Though plausible, this part of the model is weakened by the fact that salience is sometimes used as an explanation for accommodation (and diffusion or reduction – e.g. 1986: 45) and sometimes to explain why accommodation does *not* take place. In other cases it is simply not possible to decide whether a dialect feature is salient or not. The problem is that it is probably impossible to give an intersubjective operationalisation of this notion.

A predecessor of Trudgill's ideas regarding the factor salience is Schirmunski's (1930) distinction between primary versus secondary dialect features. Here primary dialect features are the 'am stärksten auffallenden' (most strongly salient), as against the secondary ones, which are the 'weniger auffallenden' (less salient). In Schirmunski's conception, primary dialect features are very susceptible to change or loss, while secondary ones are relatively resistant. Though he mentioned derived criteria,[42] Schirmunski has not done much to prevent his critics from accusing him of having introduced an impracticable and basically non-empirical proposal. Despite this pessimistic view, dialectologists have been able to apply Schirmunski's classification of dialect features in a meaningful way. Thus, TAELDEMAN (section 4.2) applies the label 'primary dialect feature' to variants which stand out through their 'conservative insularity' (cf. relic forms). In Taeldeman's view such primary features may even be the result of the polarisation of an existing feature of a regionally or locally limited nature.

Schirmunski's and Trudgill's models are obviously related to Labov's (1972a) tripartite distinction between *indicators* (which signal, passively, membership of a particular speech community), *markers* (which have geographical and sociostylistic differentiation), and *stereotypes* (geographical relevance and sociostylistic differentiation plus conscious awareness). In the case of stereotypes, conscious awareness on the part of speakers can lead to positive or negative evaluations, including stigmatisation. However, Labov does not

---

[42] A typology of the many criteria that have been proposed in relation with the primary versus secondary distinction as well as three possible operationalisations are presented in Hinskens (1986). Cf. Auer (1993); Taeldeman (1993); Auer *et al.* (1998); Kerswill and Williams (2002a).

differentiate between the evaluation by the speakers themselves (which may lead to autostereotypes) and by others (which may result in heterostereotypes).

The same question can be raised in connection with 'salience': salient to whom? To the speakers themselves or to speakers of other dialects? From the point of view of dc and dd, we need to ask the question of whether speakers have to be aware of dialect features at all either to converge with, or diverge from, them. Kerswill and Williams (2002a) considered this question by investigating speakers' awareness of particular features of dialect grammar in three British cities. Awareness varied widely, both between the different features and between different socioeconomic groups. This result led them to conclude that 'salience' has a complex set of determinants including linguistic factors such as phonetic distance. More importantly, and usually decisively, salience is also derived from extra-linguistic cognitive, pragmatic, interactional, social-psychological, and sociodemographic factors. In the end, it may not be possible, even in principle, to predict levels of salience. It may also be impossible to determine whether a given level of salience, once established, leads to the adoption or the non-adoption of a feature in dc or dd.

5.10   Comprehensive models for the outcomes of dialect convergence and divergence?

What are the possible 'results' of dc and dd? Can we construct a comprehensive model which can at the same time accommodate such constructs and processes as koines, 'new dialects' (the subject of the chapter by KERSWILL AND TRUDGILL), new 'regiolectal' varieties, regional standards, dd across borders, language enclaves, dialect loss, and dialect death?

In Trudgill's (1986) model of the sociolinguistic consequences of dialect contact, accommodation between individual speakers of different dialects takes place with respect to features that are salient. As in Giles' theory, the accommodation may take the form of the reduction of differences or even the adoption of features from the dialect of the interlocutor. Trudgill states: 'If a speaker accommodates frequently enough to a particular accent or dialect . . . then the accommodation may in time become permanent, particularly if attitudinal factors are favourable' (39). 'When a speaker employs a new feature in the absence of speakers of the variety originally containing this feature' (40), the accommodation becomes stabilised. This is a necessary condition for the diffusion of features in the contact situation. In this process, geography (distance) and demography (population size) play a role. The accommodation constituting such interdialect convergence need not be complete. The result may be (a) quantitative variation between the 'old' and the 'new' variants; or (b) the occurrence of the 'new' variant, in some words, but not in others, giving rise to a lexically diffuse incidence; this process is termed *transfer* and its product a

mixed dialect; or (c) intermediate, phonetically approximate, forms, the resulting variety being a *fudged dialect*; phonetically intermediate forms are a type
of *interdialect forms*; another type is *hyperdialectalism*. This, however, is the
result of divergence rather than convergence (62–78).

Contact between dialects may lead to 'an enormous amount of linguistic
variability in the early stages' (Trudgill 1986: 107). In this situation, we are
likely to observe *koineisation*, which consists of *levelling* (the reduction in the
number of competing variants through the loss of rare or otherwise linguistically
marked forms) combined with *simplification*. However, not all variation of
the phase preceding koineisation is reduced. The remaining variation, i.e. the
'forms that are not removed during koineisation . . . will tend to be re-assigned
according to certain patterns' (110). This *reallocation* can cause variants to take
on a specialised linguistic (allophonic) or extra-linguistic (social, stylistic, or
geographical) function (110–126).

Siegel (2001) presents an overall model for the comparison of contact
between speakers of closely related language systems (koineisation) and
between speakers of typologically very different, unrelated systems, who do
not speak each other's language (sometimes leading to pidginisation and creole
genesis). We will here mainly summarise the contours of the first part of the
model.[43] Koines result from prolonged contact between related linguistic systems, usually more or less contiguous dialects of the same language, sometimes
closely related languages (cf. Siegel 1993), in other words, between linguistic
systems which are sufficiently similar to be mutually intelligible (Siegel 2001).
However, continuous contact between related systems as such does not necessarily lead to the formation of a koine. What is needed is sufficient 'integration
or unification of the speakers of the varieties in contact' (Siegel 1985: 369).
This may result from 'some large-scale political, economic or demographic
change in society which causes increased interaction among speakers of different dialects and decreased inclination to maintain linguistic boundaries' (Siegel
1992: 110; 1985: 456; 1993: 116–117). In short, social and sociopsychological
conditions have to be favourable.

The process of koine formation itself can be roughly defined as structural
convergence between closely related linguistic systems, eventually leading to
the *stabilisation* of some compromise variety. On the basis of a typology of
standard/dialect repertoires Auer (in print) proposes a general model for the historical development of dialects, koines, standard languages, new 'regiolectal'
varieties, regional standards, dialect loss, and dialect death. The model postulates a sequential arrangement of various repertoire types – from a repertoire
with an exoglossic standard overarching the vernacular varieties via a diglossic
repertoire with a written standard and a diglossic repertoire with a spoken

---

[43] The second part and the comparability have already been sketched in section 3.2 above.

standard variety to a diaglossic repertoire (a more fluid repertoire – cf. section 5.3). Both the diaglossic and the diglossic repertoire may lead to dialect loss, although they do so through different mechanisms of erosion vs. shift. This type of a model enables one to compare seemingly non-comparable situations, ranging from the type of a situation where dialects thrive and the standard language hardly plays a role in the verbal repertoire, to situations where there is almost nothing left of the traditional dialects and where merely some style-shifting occurs between the standard variety and a regional standard.

In the model developed by BERRUTO (part of which has already been sketched in section 5.3 above), a distinction is drawn between language system and language use. On the level of the language system, convergence (which grows in the course of time) or advergence (see note 1) takes the form of interference. On the level of language use convergence or advergence manifest themselves as code-switching and code-mixing. Both interference and code–mixing lead to *hybridisation*, which can, in turn, either lead to complete advergence of one of the dialects involved, to the convergence of all dialects involved (which Berruto equates with the development of a mixed system), or to language shift.

One of the questions that arises, is whether, and to what degree, these models are mutually compatible. Another question is how general these models are. A third question is if and how these models can account for such phenomena as dialect levelling independent of a standard language, tripolar continua (Villena-Ponsoda 1996), the three types of koineisation sketched by Sobrero (1996; section 3.2.3, above), and the like. A fourth, equally important, question is how the basic notions underlying these models are defined and how they can be operationalised in empirical research.

6   Design and Goal of this Volume

In this concluding section, we will outline the rationale underlying the general design of this volume.

There is a general conviction that processes of linguistic change are 'multi-causality' phenomena (cf. section 5.8 above). It is unlikely that processes which result in dc or dd are exceptions to this general rule. Typically, innovations will have either internal (structural and language-specific, more general, or universal) or external (contact-induced) sources. Additionally, extra-linguistic factors play a part, including large-scale (sociological) as well as smaller scale (social-psychological, psychological, and interactional) factors. Moreover the proportions in which the several types of factors exert their influence vary from case to case – though usually not as causes in the strict sense, but as guiding, promoting, or restraining factors.

We have grouped the chapters in this volume according to these general insights. While the chapters in Part 1 deal with a range of issues in connection with internal factors, the chapters in Parts 2 and 3 focus on social issues. Macrosocial dimensions are central in Part 2, while microsocial dimensions are dealt with in Part 3. The chapters all have a similar structure: after a survey of the main literature and a brief discussion of the principal insights, the authors present an example of their own research.

The aim of the each chapter is to discuss critically and test some of the specific insights of our field, and thus reach a more general level of description and explanation in dc and dd. The book achieves this by focusing, on the one hand, on sociolinguistic and dialect geographical issues and, on the other, on linguistic description and theory. In so doing, it shows the fullest range of external and extra-linguistic factors that can lead to dialect change, and illustrates the wide range of approaches to dc and dd taken by scholars in the field. The book also shows that an understanding of linguistic structure, informed by theory, gives us insights into what is frequently, and what is less frequently, subject to contact- or isolation-induced change. Especially with respect to the linguistic aspects, the overall aim is to proceed from the *idiographic* level, i.e. the level of the description of unique, particular, situation-specific findings regarding single dialect features, to the *nomothetic* level, the level of general, preferably universal, principles underlying processes resulting in dc and dd.

Part 1

Convergence, Divergence and
Linguistic Structure

2 Internal and external factors in phonological convergence: the case of English /t/ lenition

Jeffrey L. Kallen

1 Introduction: Phonological Variation and Linguistic Theory

In trying to understand the dynamics of dialect convergence and divergence, we are faced with two sets of problems that are rarely reconciled. One set pertains to the social factors that operate in the initiation, actuation, and diffusion of linguistic variation and change. Viewed as social processes, dialect convergence and divergence can easily be understood as the outcome of speakers' activity, either in the short term as the result of variations which arise in direct, face-to-face communication, or in the long term as the outcome of a process in which patterns of social interaction lead to changes in the linguistic norms of the entire speech community (but cf. Auer and Hinskens, this volume). Viewed in this way, changes in the linguistic system arise from changes in the speech patterns of speakers (see Milroy and Milroy 1985 for further discussion). A second set of factors, however, can also be compelling. If we assume that knowledge of a language is knowledge of an abstract system of rules which operates irrespective of the context of performance, it should equally be possible to bracket out the social dimension and understand dialect convergence and divergence as internally motivated processes that stem from deep-seated general principles such as universal constraints on markedness. Following this logic, classical generative treatments of dialect differentiation (e.g. Saporta 1965; Thomas 1967; King 1969; Brown 1972; Newton 1972) thus focused on the development of dialects as the outcome of rule addition, deletion, reordering, and simplification without regard to social factors. As King's (1969: 87–88) treatment of the development of German shows, the evolution from derivations in which word-final devoicing precedes vowel lengthening (yielding *vek ~ veːgə* nominative ~ genitive 'path' from underlying *veg*) to the modern derivation

I am grateful for help with fieldwork to Seán Devitt and to the teachers and former students of the Westland Row Christian Brothers School in Dublin. Special thanks go to Frans Hinskens and Marc van Oostendorp for discussions on phonology, and to comments which I have received on various oral and written versions of this chapter, notably from William Labov, Lesley Milroy, Ailbhe Ní Chasaide, and Máire Ní Chiosáin. Of course, I alone am responsible for the content of the chapter, including any remaining faults or omissions.

yielding *ve:k* ~ *ve:gə* can be accounted for by a rule re-ordering in which vowel lengthening applies before consonant devoicing. Following Kiparsky's (1968: 200) principle by which 'rules tend to shift into the order which allows their fullest utilization in the grammar', King's analysis thus accounts for the data as the outcome of a language-internal reduction of markedness: an appeal to social factors is not necessary.

Despite the potential of early generative analyses for relating language variation directly to phonological theory, close scrutiny shows that they work best with invariant data and categorical rules. In Saporta's (1965) analysis of Spanish, for example, a phonemic contrast between /θ/ and /s/ is posited for all dialects, including those of Latin America which exhibit no phonetic [θ]; exceptionless rules then apply to neutralise this opposition in the relevant Latin American dialects. The attempt to unite all dialects of a language under a single, fully specified underlying phonological representation gave rise to the polylectal approach exemplified by Bailey (1973) but little used beyond this point. Examination of speech communities, and even the quantitative examination of individual speech, also showed that the categorical operation of phonological rules does not necessarily coincide with linguistic behaviour. Variable rule systems as developed by Labov (1972: 216ff.); Cedergren and Sankoff (1974); Sankoff (1974); Fasold (1978), and others represent a compromise between these two positions. In the variable rule developed, for example, by Cedergren and Sankoff (1974: 344–346) to account for the frication of syllable-final [r] in Panamanian Spanish, a fully specified underlying [r] is fricated to [řˇ] not according to any categorical rule but by a weighted series of probabilities depending on factors such as word position, grammatical function, the phonetics of the following segment, and social-class features of speakers.

Newer approaches in phonological theory have raised other possibilities for the study of language variation. Within the theory of Lexical Phonology (Kaisse and Shaw 1985; Kiparsky 1985), for example, Kaisse (1993) demonstrates that the difference in the operation of rules for obstruentisation and dissimilation between Cypriot Greek and non-Cypriot dialects can be accounted for as a function of their operation in different parts of the grammar. Underspecification in the lexicon plays a crucial role in Kaisse's analysis. Thus, while modern Greek dialects in general show dissimilations for obstruents other than voiced fricatives (as in *ek-timo* → *extimo* 'esteem', *γraf-θike* → *γraftike* 'it was written', and *plek-θike* → *plextike* 'it was knitted'), Cypriot Greek additionally obstruentises the glide /j/, such that (using Kaisse's notation) *aðelfi-a* 'brothers' and *teri-azo* 'to match' are realised as *aðelfkʲa* and *terkazo* rather than *aðelfya* and *teryazo* as otherwise expected. Kaisse accounts for these and related variations by reference to a shift in Cypriot Greek from the lexical rule of dissimilation that applies in certain derived environments in pan-Greek dialects (such that application between stem and suffix is favoured over application between prefix and stem, though both are possible) to the use of a postlexical dissimilation rule. This rule follows a Cypriot lexical rule which obstruentises /j/ following a consonant. The surface effect of Cypriot Greek restructuring is that dissimilation applies in cases (e.g. *avgon* 'egg', *erkete* 'he comes') where it does not apply in other dialects (*avɣo* 'egg', *erxete* 'he comes'), not because the rule has become simplified, but because it now applies in a different derivational stratum. Under Kaisse's view of underspecification, it thus follows that a generalised rule of the form

(1) $[\alpha\text{cont } \beta\text{cont}] \rightarrow [+\text{cont } -\text{cont}]$

will apply more widely in Cypriot Greek because it can be, as Kaisse (1993: 354) puts it, 'triggered by the nondistinctively continuant segments' that 'only become available late in derivations, most likely post-lexically' (Kaisse 1993: 355).

Also adopting a lexicalist perspective, Guy (1994) demonstrates that statistical differences in the frequency of English /t/ deletion according to various phonological and morphological environments are best accounted for within what he terms (139) an 'exponential model', by which coronal stop deletion can apply at different stages of lexical and postlexical phonology. Supporting the exponential model, it emerges that those environments in which the most deletion is found are precisely those in which the deletion rule can apply at both lexical and postlexical levels; conversely, environments least liable to favour deletion are those where the rule can apply only once, postlexically. Though Lexical Phonology has not played a major role in the study of language variation, analyses of this type demonstrate the potential for accounting for cross-dialectal variation through models that are designed to answer other theoretical questions in phonology.

More recently, Optimality Theory (OT) (see Archangeli and Langendoen 1997) has been invoked as another means of accounting for language variation, using a radically different approach to derivation and the interaction between phonological rules. Crucially, it is held in OT that rules do not apply in an extrinsic ordering, but that any rule could apply to an underlying form at any time: what makes the difference in outcome across languages or dialects hinges largely on the differential ranking of output constraints within different systems. Thus the difference between Russian and English treatments of the voice/voiceless contrast in word-final position can be seen in figure 2.1, based on Pulleyblank (1997: 82). In the two tableaux which follow, the same three rules are invoked by both languages: FAITH[VOICE], which dictates that the value for voice of a lexical entry remains unchanged; OBS/VOI, which states that an obstruent must be voiceless; and CONTRASTIVECODA, which stipulates (81) that 'a coda does not bear contrastive features'. In the tableau for English, FAITH[VOICE] ranks above the other two rules, with the result that a voice contrast is

/sɑd/ 'sod'	FAITH[VOICE]	CONTRASTIVECODA	OBS/VOI
☞ sɑd		*	*
sɑt	*!		

English: faithfulness to input voicing

/sɑd/ 'sod'	CONTRASTIVECODA	FAITH[VOICE]	OBS/VOI
sɑd	*!		*
☞ sɑt		*	

Russian: neutralisation of voicing in coda

Fig. 2.1 Optimality Theory and voicing contrasts in English and Russian (following Pulleyblank 1997).

maintained in the preferred derivation (indicated by ☞, where * indicates a violation of rules, *! a so-called fatal violation among dispreferred outputs, and shading shows dispreferred outcomes). In Russian, however, CONTRASTIVE CODA outranks FAITH[VOICE] so that the voicing contrast is lost and the violations of FAITH[VOICE] and OBS/VOI are acceptable (cf. also a contrast between English and German devoicing in Hinskens, van Hout, and Wetzels 1997: 7). The facility with which OT can derive different outcomes from essentially the same materials (underlying forms, universal rules) by the differential ranking of constraints has made this theory particularly attractive in the study of variation.

In this chapter, I assume that both social and systemic factors must be taken into account in order to understand the process of dialect convergence and divergence (see Hinskens, van Hout, and Wetzels 1997 for a review of related arguments). What is in question is the nature of the relationship between these two sets of factors. In order to investigate this question in detail, I examine here some aspects of the realisation of the voiceless alveolar stop /t/ in English, using the system of Irish English as a starting-point. Working from a set of questions centred on what is often referred to as the 'Neogrammarian controversy' (Labov 1981), and invoking some theoretical arguments that are specific to the problem of lenition, I consider several sets of empirical data in complement with relevant arguments from phonological theory. Comparing social and linguistic factors, I argue that a system of internally motivated lenition – which, if motivated by a given universal principle, should lead to a high degree of convergence among related dialects – is more illusory than real. I suggest, instead, that even speech communities which share a process that is favoured by general principles can show significant divergence in linguistic behaviour. This relationship of convergence and divergence suggests, at least in the case considered here, that general principles of phonology can, at best, only define points in the system which are open to change, and establish probabilities that change – if it happens – will operate in a particular direction. The nature of variation and culmination of change will depend in a fundamental way on the social embedding of linguistic norms for speakers and speech communities.

2   Convergence, Divergence, and Principles of Sound Change

In order to develop a testable hypothesis concerning the roles of social and theoretically motivated constraints on convergence and divergence using /t/ lenition as a case study, let us focus first on the Neogrammarian controversy. Space limitations do not allow for a detailed consideration of this issue here: for discussion which is particularly relevant to the concerns of this chapter, see especially Weinreich, Labov, and Herzog (1968); Labov (1981, 1994); Kiparsky (1995); and Hinskens (1998b). Recurring elements in the charac-terisation of Neogrammarian sound change have been expressed by Labov (1981: 277) as follows: (1) 'every word in a given historical class is affected'; (2) 'these changes appear to be gradual'; and (3) 'changes in progress show the most detailed kinds of phonetic conditioning, with no indication of grammatical constraints'. As Kiparsky (1995: 643) also points out, this kind of sound change typically operates rapidly, and results in new phonemic inventories and phono-logical rules rather than the redistribution of words between existing phonemes. Typically as well, according to Labov (1981: 296), the rules which characterise Neogrammarian sound change are readily learnable and carry with them social significance.

Particularly since work by Wang (see Wang 1977), however, alternative views of phonological change have been developed which take account of elements that may present a challenge for the so-called Neogrammarian hypothesis. These challenges include the existence of lexical exceptions to otherwise regular phonological changes, morphological and other non-phonological conditioning factors, and unpredictability in rule application. Lexical exception and gram-matical conditioning are thus seen as hallmarks of lexically diffuse phonological change. Kiparsky (1995) further notes that phonetic abruptness, extension of change by analogy from word class to word class, and structure preservation are also elements of lexically diffuse change. Structure preservation (i.e. change in which no phonemic contrasts are introduced that are not available in the lex-icon) is particularly relevant to our consideration of /t/ lenition and can be understood in considering Kiparsky's analysis of the spread of English short /ū/ (Kiparsky 1995: 643–648). Kiparsky points out that the short vowel whose core environment is preceded by [-anterior] segments and followed by those which are [-anterior, -coronal] (*cook, hook, rook, brook*, etc.) has seen a relax-ation of the conditions both preceding and following the segment, such that *took, nook, book*, etc. and *good, hood, should* now also regularly take /ū/, although environments which are maximally distinct from the original environment for vowel shortening (as in *boom, loom, spoof, snooze*) still predominantly use long /ū/. In Kiparsky's view (1995: 643), such a structure-preserving shift is 'a redistribution of phonemes among lexical items' and therefore 'cannot produce any new sounds or alter the system of phonological contrasts'. As for the temporal and social aspect of lexical diffusion, Labov (1981: 296) remarks that this kind of change tends to be slower in its progress, not easily learnable, and lacking in social affect.

Hinskens (1998b: 164) makes explicit a third type of sound change, which he designates as that consisting of 'lexicalized rules', i.e. rules of change which have operated in the lexicon diachronically, but which only function synchronically in an unpredictable way as the 'lexical remnants ("relicts") of a former rule'. These lexicalised rules are typically dialect-specific, making it impossible to set up transparent cross-dialectal correspondence relationships. Hinskens (1998: 165–166) points out that hypercorrection and hyperdialectism, both of which subject individual lexical items to rules that would not have applied historically to these items, are more common in this kind of 'lexicalised' sound change.

Consideration of the Neogrammarian controversy gives us a set of questions to ask in looking at /t/ lenition: is the spread of lenited forms (a) gradual or abrupt; (b) uniform within word classes or subject to lexical exception; (c) phonologically conditioned or conditioned additionally by grammatical factors; (d) structure-building or structure-preserving; and (e) socially marked or socially below the level of salience? Characterisation of the type of variation and change represented by /t/ lenition might also help to evaluate the balance between internal and external motivations for change across related dialects. This problem could be put as follows: if we can observe the same change occurring in many different dialects, and we can account for this change by an abstract phonological principle, then we can argue that convergence arises not from socially motivated changes activated by speakers but from a principle which would have gone into operation in any event. The discussion which follows thus examines first the problem of lenition in linguistic theory, and proceeds to consider English /t/ lenition in the light of the Neogrammarian controversy.

3   Lenition as a Problem in Phonology

Bauer (1988: 381) has observed that 'most phonological textbooks and treatises do not define lenition or weakening. . . . Instead they provide a list of examples of processes which they wish to term "lenitions" or "weakenings". It is then hoped that the reader will deduce a correct definition'. As an example of this approach, we can cite Crowley (1992: 39–40), who comments that 'the concept

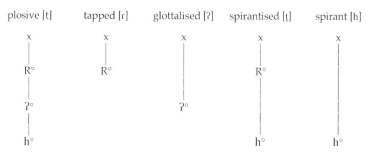

Fig. 2.2 Lenition as the loss of elements (following Harris 1990).

of lenition is not very well defined', but that changes such as *bulan to *fulan* 'moon' and *topu to *tuf* 'sugarcane' in the Kara language of Papua New Guinea constitute 'one good example of lenition'. Lack of definition, or conflicting definitions, have led Sihler (2000: 39–40) to describe the terms 'lenition' and 'fortition' as 'pre-scientific' or 'pseudo-PHONETIC', and to argue against the use of these concepts at all.

Those definitions which have been put forward for lenition can be crudely divided into phonetic and phonological approaches, in both cases relying on a hierarchy of strength for sounds of different types. Phonetic definitions usually refer to sound production, notably the degree of supraglottal obstruction in the airflow. Lass and Anderson (1975: 151) state that 'strength is equated with resistance to airflow through the vocal tract, and weakness with lack of such resistance'; Hock and Joseph (1996: 130) see [t] lenition as a matter of 'relaxation in the gestures required to make a voiceless [t]'. Works by Harris (1990, 1994) and Harris and Kaye (1990) show both a descriptive approach whereby 'lenition processes typically manifest themselves in articulatory terms as a decrease in the degree of supraglottal stricture and in aerodynamic terms as a decrease in resistance to airflow through the vocal tract' (Harris 1990: 257, citing work by Ailbhe Ní Chasaide), and a more abstract, feature-based, view that 'every weakening process can be characterized as the suppression of some aspect of the elementary content of a segment'. In this definition, consideration is also given to 'trajectories' of lenition (e.g. from stop to fricative to deletion, or from non-continuant to resonant to deletion) which show 'a progressive decrease in the melodic complexity of a segment, where complexity is straightforwardly gauged by the number of elements of which a segment is composed' (Harris 1994: 122). The notion of 'number of elements' can be understood as in figure 2.2, adapted from Harris (1990: 285), in which five different realizations of /t/ are defined within the framework of Government Phonology according to the presence or absence of the phonological elements 'coronal' (R°), 'occluded' (?°), and 'noise' (h°).

What I have termed phonological definitions, on the other hand, refer less to the production of sounds than to their role in the development of sound systems, especially their position in a development from plosion to deletion. We note, for example, Hyman's definition based on Theo Venneman's suggestion that 'a segment X is said to be weaker than a segment Y if Y goes through an X stage on its way to zero' (Hyman 1975: 165). Foley's phonological approach explicitly rejects phonetic definitions and uses observed patterns of historical change to argue that 'relative phonological strength refers not to the absolute phonetic strength of elements, but to the relation of the elements to one another in a phonological system' (Foley 1977: 29). Foley's analysis leads to conclusions which differ significantly from those based in articulatory phonetics. By the reckoning of Lass and Anderson (1975) and Harris (1994), for example, a change from stop to fricative is a type of lenition. For Foley (1977), the same change represents fortition or strengthening when considering the strength relationship between segments on his 'resonance' parameter. Citing a diachronic change in which Latin final [t] is deleted in Spanish (Latin *amat* > Spanish *ama*) while Latin final [s] is retained (Latin *amas* > Spanish *amas*), Foley (1977: 37) argues that 'since elision occurs preferentially to weak elements, the elision of Latin final *t* . . . but not of final *s*' provides what he terms 'evidence that occlusives are phonologically weaker than continuants'.

Whatever the definition, the concept of 'lenition' can be applied both synchronically and diachronically. For historical linguistics, the best-known demonstration of lenition is the First Germanic Consonant Shift ('Grimm's Law'), which includes shifts such as that from Latin *piscis* to Gothic *fisks* and Latin *canis* to Gothic *hunds*, Old English *hund*. Observations on this process were ultimately central to the development of the Neogrammarian view of the uniformity of sound change (see Trask 1996: 224–228 for a relevant overview). The term 'lenition' is also used to denote synchronic variation, however, as in the continuum of careful to fast/careless speech described by Giannelli and Savoia for Florentine Italian (cited by Kirchner 2000: 513). In this process, for example, underlying /la tavola/ 'the table' is realised in careful speech as [la θavola], in natural speech as [la θ̬avola], in careless speech as [la (ð̞)aoḷa], and in extremely fast or careless speech as [la aoḷa]. By this account, /t/ progresses synchronically through frication to voicing and frication and to deletion, depending on speech style alone. (On the phonetic gradation and transcription of stops (e.g. [t]), 'close fricatives' such as [θ], and 'open approximants' as with [θ̞], see Kirchner 2001: 197, 257fn.)

Yet another type of lenition – comparable to the lexicalised rules described by Hinskens (1998b) – occurs in the grammatically conditioned reflexes of historical consonantal alternations found in contemporary Celtic languages. In Modern Irish, for example, initial stops are generally realised as fricatives in certain grammatically defined environments: Irish *cóta* 'coat' with initial [k] goes to fricative [x] in *a chóta* 'his coat' but not in *a cóta* 'her coat', while *titeann sé* 'he falls' with initial [tʲ] contrasts with *thit sé* 'he fell' using initial [h]. Fricatives either palatalise (*Seán* with initial [ʃ] vs. *a Sheán* [vocative] with [ç]) or delete, as with the initial [fʲ] of *fiacail* 'tooth', deleted in *mo fhiacail* 'my tooth' ([məˈiəkˠəlʲ] but not in *a fiacail* 'her tooth' ([əˈfʲiəkˠəlʲ]). Though this process has its roots in a basic phonological conditioning which focused on single consonants in intervocalic positions, the rules for initial consonant lenition have become thoroughly grammaticalised (on the Celtic mutations generally, see Russell 1995: 231–257; on Old Irish, see Thurneysen 1946: 74ff.). Thus the Celtic lenitions represent a set of phonologically irregular *synchronic* alternations which reflect the *diachronic* shift from phonological to grammatical conditioning of lenition.

The following discussion uses the notion of lenition without presupposing that a single underlying process can account for all the data to be considered. Taking 'lenition' as a cover term which has been applied to the behaviour of broadly similar segments in broadly similar environments, it remains in this chapter to examine some of the articulatory, auditory, and systemic qualities which contribute to the concept of lenition and which may illuminate its relationship to the social and grammatical influences on language variation and change.

4   Lenition of /t/ in English

Rather than trying to organise the examination of /t/ lenition around a priori rule systems or the notion that lenition progresses from plosion to frication to deletion, I begin this section with a brief discussion of three main trends in the family of alternations we may refer to as lenition: voicing, glottalisation, and spirantisation. The role of syllable structure and syllable boundaries in lenition will be considered as well. It should also be noted that sonority (see Blevins 1995 for review) is a further potential candidate in accounting for lenition. Just as segments may be arranged hierarchically from least to most sonorous in a sonority scale (e.g. stop<fricative<vowel), consonants could be arranged hierarchically in a strength scale (e.g. geminate stop<stop<affricate<fricative), and an account of lenition could be phrased by deriving demotions in strength from promotions in sonority. As Kirchner (2001: 14–17) points out, however, the similarity between these two types of scales rarely stands up to detailed analysis. Even at a simple level, the non-correspondence between maximally sonorous segments (low vowels) and the maximally weak end of a strength scale (deletion) is striking. Though the question of gradation in English /t/ lenition will be discussed further in this chapter, sonority *per se* does not appear as a major factor in trying to understand the data at hand.

4.1   Voicing

Voiced realisations of /t/ have been variously described as flaps, taps, or simply voiced variants of [t]: transcriptions include [ɾ] (used in this chapter), [d], [t̬], and [D] (see Wells 1982: 249). MacMahon (1998: 486) describes tapping in American English as a twentieth-century innovation; it has been widely noted in Australia (Horvath 1985; Tollfree 2001), New Zealand (Bayard 1990; Holmes 1994), and varieties of British English including Glasgow (Stuart-Smith 1999), Newcastle (Watt and Milroy 1999), Liverpool (Knowles 1973), Cardiff (Mees 1987), and London (Tollfree 1999). In Ireland, flapping was noted in Cork by Leahy (1915), in Dublin (Bertz 1975), and extensively in Coleraine in Northern Ireland (Kingsmore 1995). It does not, however, appear to feature in Henry's (1958) survey of traditional rural dialect.

Under voicing, we may also include what Wells (1982: 370) calls the 'T-to-R rule' (e.g. [ʃʊɹ ˈʊp] *shut up*). Noting this rule in the north of England, Wells derives it from the tapped form [ɾ] and the subsequent 'phonological reinterpretation of [ɾ] as /r/, followed then by use of the prevailing /r/ variant, [ɹ]'. This rule has been cited for Tyneside (Wells 1982: 374; Docherty *et al.* 1997), Liverpool (Knowles 1973), and Derby (Docherty and Foulkes 1999). In Irish English, Henry (1958) and Bertz (1975, 1987) do not note it, but Hickey (1999a) does, and I have heard it sporadically in Dublin (e.g. [wəɹ ɪz ɪh pɛh] *what is it, pet?*).

4.2   Glottalisation

Like tapping, glottalisation is well known in world Englishes and appears to be of relatively recent vintage. Wells (1982: 261) notes [ʔ] in 'local accents of London, Glasgow, Edinburgh, in many rural accents of the South of England and East Anglia, and increasingly in urban accents everywhere in England', suggesting that it has spread rapidly in the twentieth century. Collins and Mees (1996: 177–179) point out that glottal realisations of /t/ had been described in Scottish and American English in the nineteenth century, and use sound recordings to suggest the presence of glottalisation in RP in the mid-nineteenth century. Trudgill (1999: 136) suggests that, rather than being a London innovation as commonly proposed, the use of glottals may have diffused from dialects in East Anglia. Thus, while there may be some controversy regarding the age and origins of [ʔ] as a realisation of /t/, there is no evidence to suggest that it is of long standing or that it has now reached all varieties of English. Though it was not noted by Leahy (1915) or Henry (1958), Bertz (1975) records it in Dublin, and it features, particularly among younger speakers, in Coleraine (Kingsmore 1995: 162ff.). It plays a significant role in the Dublin data discussed below.

The term 'glottalisation' has a number of different interpretations. At its simplest, it refers to the use of a glottal stop instead of a voiceless alveolar stop in particular environments – what could be called 'glottal replacement'. Very often, however, glottal closure is co-articulated with supraglottal movements associated with [t], and this co-articulation allows for different phasings of glottal and supraglottal movement. Mees (1987: 29) treats 'all glottalized variants' of /t/ (specifically [ʔ, tˀ, ʔtʰ, tʔ, t']) as members of a single category. Tollfree (2001) similarly notes that the distinction between [tˀ] with no auditory plosion and [tʔ] where glottalisation follows the closure phase is often difficult to perceive. Docherty et al. (1997) and Docherty and Foulkes (1999), however, demonstrate that even where ordinary auditory perception makes it difficult to distinguish [ʔ] from pre-glottalised stops and post-glottalisation, significant social patterning may correlate with differences that are revealed in instrumental analysis, suggesting a need to differentiate among these realisations.

The argument nevertheless to conflate, say, [ʔ, tˀ, ʔt, tʔ] under the heading of lenition rests on the salience of the glottal gesture: glottalisation may affect preceding vowels and may mask any release phase of [t], so that these sounds are perceived as similar and may be left open to similar social evaluation. The instrumental and sociolinguistic results shown by Docherty et al. (1997) and Docherty and Foulkes (1999) argue against this conflation, as does consideration of the mechanism of phonetic production – while glottal replacement may be taken as a weakening process, glottalised articulation of [t] could be taken to represent strengthening in so far as it adds a point of glottal closure to the closure at the alveolar ridge (though it does not create the audible plosion usually associated with consonantal strength in English). In reconciling these arguments, I suggest that any degree of glottalisation is perceptually salient and may incline listeners to group all glottalised realisations together, but that articulatory factors may equally incline listeners to keep glottal replacement and glottalisation distinct. Clearly much more research needs to be done on the extent to which the conflicting trends of auditory similarity and articulatory difference correlate with social evaluation and patterns of articulation. Given our present state of knowledge, it is certainly not self-evident where glottalised variants of [t] fit into the notion of lenition, and the discussion that follows will make specific reference both to glottal replacement and to glottalised articulations of [t].

4.3   Frication

When considering lenition as described in languages generally, it is not surprising to find fricative variants of /t/ in English. What is surprising is that they are not more common, and that they do not often extend to [θ] or [s]. We may note an indication of /t/ frication and affrication in Australian English (Tollfree 2001), strong aspiration tending towards affrication in Sydney (Horvath 1985), and some use of frication in Liverpool (Knowles 1973), Tyneside (Docherty *et al.* 1997), and Edinburgh (Chirrey 1999). The use of an alveolar fricative realisation in Irish English is one of the most salient features of this variety: its phonetic character has been described in detail by Pandeli *et al.* (1997), and approximately twenty different transcriptions have been proposed for it (see reviews in Kallen 1994 and Pandeli *et al.* 1997). The sound, transcribed here as [ṯ] following the recommendations of Ó Baoill (1990, 1997), was noted as a Dublin feature by Hume (1877–1878) and in Cork city by Leahy (1915). Prominent usage in Irish-settled areas of Newfoundland suggests the possibility of robust usage of [ṯ] during the early nineteenth century (see Clarke 1986, 1997), and Tollfree (2001) raises – without confirming – the possibility that it may have come to Australia from Ireland at a similar time. The sound features prominently in Henry's (1958) survey of traditional dialect, except in Ulster and some parts of the south and southwest: for mapping of the data from Henry (1958), see Kallen (1997a, 2000).

Other fricative realisations for /t/ which are commonly noted in Ireland include [θ] and [h], alongside the partial frication of the affricate [tˢ]. Though Henry (1958) suggests limited geographical distribution for [θ], [tˢ] is more widespread and also occurs syllable-initially. Newbrook (1999: 97) and Tollfree (1999: 170) report [tˢ] for intervocalic and word-initial position in Liverpool and southeast London, respectively.

The use of [h] as a lenited realisation of /t/ presents special problems, since the occurrence of /h/ in syllable-final position violates a well-known constraint of English (see Giegerich 1992: 162–163) and of West Germanic languages generally. Nevertheless, syllable-final [h] is a widespread feature of traditional dialects of English in Ireland, especially in the midlands and east (see Henry 1958; Ó Baoill 1990). It is also a common feature in contemporary Dublin, where it has been noted by Hickey (1999a,b), although it is not cited by Bertz (1975). Knowles (1973) does not list [h] as a realisation of /t/ in Liverpool; Harris (1990: 266), however, cites final [h] in function words of Liverpool vernacular English, e.g. *that* [ðæh] and *but* [bʊh]. It has not been cited for Newfoundland. In assessing the factors of convergence which affect the development of Irish English dialects, we should note that any typological constraint against syllable-final [h] in English may be counterbalanced by the lack of such a constraint in Irish. Mhac an Fhailigh (1968: 36) cites syllable-final [h] for words with preceding short /e, a, o/ in Co. Mayo (e.g. *breith* 'judgement' [brʲeh], *leath* 'half' [lʲah], *a sgothadh* 'passing, jumping, etc.' [ə sgoh]), while syllable-final [h] is attested by Ó Cuív (1944: 44) in further examples from Co. Cork (e.g. *cath*, *caith* 'throw' [kɑh], *luath* [luəh]).

4.4   Syllable Structure

Selkirk (1982) puts forward a detailed argument on the role of syllable position in tapping and glottalisation, arguing that certain syllable-final positions –
including both underlying syllable-final segments and those which become
syllable-final by resyllabification rules – present an environment for tapping or
glottalisation, and that the difference between [ɾ] and [ʔ] can be accounted for
by the additional feature of [± release]. Selkirk's argument is a refutation of
the analysis made by Kahn (1976), who accounts for lenition in this instance
as an outcome of *ambisyllabicity*. For Selkirk, the concept of ambisyllabicity
is ruled out on theoretical grounds; a similar position, based on problems such
as English tapping and palatalisation, is also adopted by Blevins (1995: 232).

Harris (1994: 198–203) reviews arguments that lenition is based on ambisyllabicity or syllable-final position, but ultimately takes a distinctive view within
the framework of Government Phonology (cf. Harris 1990; Harris and Kaye
1990). In what Harris terms a 'licensing analysis', consonants in word-final
position are taken to be *onsets* for syllables with empty nuclei; such syllables
are licensed (i.e. permissible) not on the basis of a following nucleus, but by a
'Final-empty nucleus parameter' ('FEN Parameter' in (2) below) which is set
to ON for languages like English but to OFF for languages such as Zulu that do
not allow word-final consonants. Initial consonants in syllables that are licensed
parametrically, like those that occur within a prosodic foot but not preceding
stress, are taken to be intrinsically weaker than foot-initial consonants in their
ability to support a complex set of articulatory gestures. In (2), adapted from
Harris (1994: 209, 211), direct, indirect, and parametric licensing are seen in
the foot-initial, foot-internal, and word-final positions for /t/ in *tunny*, *pity*, and
pit, respectively.

(2)

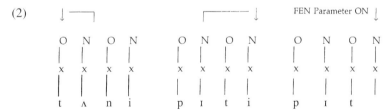

Whether /t/ lenition is understood to arise from ambisyllabicity, coda position, or licensing, there is no doubt that, for many theorists at least, accounts of
lenition must give an important role to syllable structure. The discussion which
follows relies to a large extent on the syllabic analysis of Selkirk (1982) in preference to the ambisyllabicity or licensing arguments: though space limitations
preclude detailed comparisons, I suggest that this approach offers the best fit
with the data at hand.

5   Testing a Hypothesis

The clearest test of the Neogrammarian hypothesis and /t/ lenition would be to treat lenition as a single process which is *phonetically gradual, structure building, exceptionless* within word classes, and *conditioned phonologically* without lexical exceptions or morphological conditioning. To be consistent with Labov's characterisation of Neogrammarian sound change, lenition would also be expected to bear sociolinguistic significance. If this understanding of lenition is correct, and if lenition is motivated by a universal process, then we should also expect to find all dialects of English moving in the same direction in their lenition processes. Conversely, where we find evidence of phonological abruptness, lexical exceptions, or non-phonological conditioning, we must conclude that other factors are at work, including, perhaps, the lexical diffusion of sound change.

To test hypotheses on /t/ lenition, we ought first to distinguish between synchronic and diachronic aspects of lenition. Synchronically, the notion of gradualness suggests a scale from a fully articulated voiceless stop through the sub-processes associated with lenition and, ultimately, it could be argued, to deletion. Elements of this viewpoint have already been put forward by Hickey (1991a,b), who ranks different realisations of /t/ in a lenition 'sequence' as in (3) below (Hickey 1999a: 221):

(3)   /t/   →   [t̪]   →   [ɹ]   →   [h]   →   ø
         motorway   [mot̪ɚwe]   [moɹəwe]   [mohəwe]   [moːwe]

Diachronically, sound change might be predicted to follow the steps of the lenition hierarchy observable in synchronic variation: the argument could be made that dialects pass through a set of intermediate stages on the way to the most lenited segment or to deletion (though note the suggestion above that deletion and lenition are not necessarily part of a common dynamic).

In the sections that follow, data from Dublin, other parts of Ireland, and other English dialects are examined in the light of the so-called Neogrammarian hypothesis and specific theoretical arguments which have been made in regard to lenition. Our empirical evidence will not give any strong support to the notion of a cline of lenition within speech communities (nor does it support the phonetic detail of (3) above). Not coincidentally, the development of dialects in the English-speaking world is not seen to converge towards a given point in this respect.

6   Lenition of /t/: Dublin Data and Style Shift

The data reported on here come mainly from three unpublished sources. All involve the quantitative study of variation, based on phonetic transcriptions

Table 2.1 *Realisation of /t/ in non-initial position (Byrne 1996)*

	t	ṭ	ʔt	t̚	ʔ	ɾ	tʃ	ø	Total
Reading Male	37	35	3	7	6	19	5	20	132
% of each	*28*	*27*	*2*	*5*	*5*	*14*	*4*	*15*	*100*
Reading Female	34	75	0	5	2	1	1	20	138
% of each	*25*	*54*	*0*	*4*	*1*	*1*	*1*	*14*	*100*
Wordlist Male	55	45	12	4	0	7	0	3	126
% of each	*44*	*36*	*10*	*3*	*0*	*5*	*0*	*2*	*100*
Wordlist Female	98	27	0	2	0	0	0	5	132
% of each	*74*	*20*	*0*	*2*	*0*	*0*	*0*	*4*	*100*

from audiotapes. Instrumental analysis was not used. The first (Byrne 1996) is drawn from a group of six speakers (three male and three female) in the social network of the investigator. Speakers were aged between 17 and 24: four were college students, one a qualified nurse, and one in the final year of secondary school. Byrne (1996) did not make use of casual speech data, but observed style shift in the difference between the reading of an informal, humorous text and reading of a wordlist.

Data from this middle-class group are contrasted with two studies from working-class speakers in Dublin's inner city. Pardy (1987) investigates /t/ lenition among a group of ten pre-adolescent inner-city Dublin speakers: the five girls in the sample had a mean age of 11 years, 6 months; while the boys had a mean age of 11 years, 8 months. This study was based on the fieldworker's involvement in a community youth group, and relied on casual speech observation as well as a series of tasks involving increasing degrees of formality. The third Dublin study is based on fieldwork which Seán Devitt from Trinity College Dublin and I did in 1993 in an inner-city Dublin secondary school (henceforth referred to as the 'Westland Row' study). The Westland Row work involved twelve speakers who were approximately 12–13 years old. These students were observed in two contexts: a classroom discussion which was high in narrative content, and a small group session involving seven speakers (five male, two female) which was designed to elicit informal conversation focused on narratives of everyday life and fictive narration.

Table 2.1 shows aggregate realisations of /t/ in word-final, syllable-final, and intervocalic positions, based on data in Byrne (1996). Realisations noted by Byrne include pre-glottalisation [ʔt], unreleased plosion [t̚] (which may contain an element of glottalisation), tapping, deletion, and palatal assimilatory affrication to [tʃ] before [j] (as in dialectal *ye oul' ejit ye*, literally 'you old idiot, you'). Note that [h] never occurs as a realisation of /t/ for the speakers in Byrne's sample. Though table 2.1 shows /t/ deletion, the environments for lenition and

Table 2.2 *Word-final realisations of /t/ in Pardy (1987)*

	t	ţ	?	h	Total
Casual Male	14	9	42	28	93
% of total	*15*	*10*	*45*	*30*	*100*
Casual Female	11	2	55	20	88
% of total	*12*	*2*	*63*	*23*	*100*
Careful Male	32	12	64	34	142
% of total	*23*	*8*	*45*	*24*	*100*
Careful Female	27	2	81	31	141
% of total	*20*	*1*	*57*	*22*	*100*
Reading Male	94	29	95	31	249
% of total	*38*	*12*	*38*	*12*	*100*
Reading Female	101	33	75	40	249
% of total	*41*	*13*	*30*	*16*	*100*
Wordlist Male	63	32	19	6	120
% of total	*52*	*27*	*16*	*5*	*100*
Wordlist Female	97	6	12	5	120
% of total	*81*	*5*	*10*	*4*	*100*

deletion are almost (though not quite) in complementary distribution. Lenition is common in intervocalic position, and deletion usually takes place in complex syllable codas: deletion never occurs intervocalically. Words with complex syllable codas such as *must, harvest, servant, perfect,* and *perfectly*, account for 37 of the 48 deletions. In words of this type, accounting for 128 tokens in all, /t/ is almost always fully realised or deleted: there is only one token each of [tˀ], [?t], and [ţ] (see also table 2.4 below).

Table 2.1 also shows the importance of style shift and gender distribution. For both sexes, the [t] realisation is associated with the shift from informal reading to wordlist style. Males increase the percentage of [t] realisations in wordlists, but also increase the percentage of [ţ] and pre-glottalised [?t] at the expense of [?] and [ɾ]; females dramatically increase the percentage of [t], decreasing their use of [ţ] and virtually abandoning all other realisations. Synchronically, at least, we can say that the two gender groups *diverge* in their treatment of realisations other than [t] in more informal tasks, although they *converge* with increasing formality towards the use of [t]. This kind of gender and stylistic variation may well become an element of language change with the passage of time.

Table 2.2 illustrates the results which Pardy (1987) obtained in investigations of word-final /t/ across a continuum from casual speech through careful speech to reading passages and wordlist reading style.

Table 2.3 *Lenition of non-initial /t/ (Westland Row study)*

	t	tˀ	ʔt	ṭ	ʔ	ɾ	ṭ	h	ø	Total
Male group	26	10	0	2	14	3	2	22	4	83
% of total	31	12	0	2	17	4	2	27	5	100
Female group	13	1	1	1	11	1	0	5	1	34
% of total	38	3	3	3	32	3	0	15	3	100
Male class	18	1	0	1	13	4	0	9	5	51
% of total	35	2	0	2	25	8	0	18	10	100
Female class	4	1	0	0	3	0	0	2	2	12
% of total	33	8	0	0	25	0	0	17	17	100

Table 2.2 contrasts strongly with Table 2.1: [h], absent from table 2.1, is a major realisation type in table 2.2, while [ɾ], which figured especially in male casual speech in table 2.1, is absent from table 2.2. Glottal stop is far more common among Pardy's subjects. Though the variation observable in tables 2.1 and 2.2 does show shared movement in the direction of [t] for wordlist style, important differences remain. Notably, the working-class females of table 2.2 retain use of [ʔ] and [h] in wordlist style, using [ṭ] only marginally more than [h]. Use of [ṭ] among females in table 2.2 is never particularly widespread, reaching only 13 per cent at its maximum in the reading passage. Among the males of table 2.2, [ṭ] is an important rival to [t] in wordlist style, as it is in table 2.1, though unlike table 2.1, table 2.2 also shows use of [ʔ] and [h] in this category. The level of male use of [ṭ] in table 2.2 must be interpreted with some caution, though, as Pardy (1987: 33) notes that many examples of [ṭ] in male speech in her study come from one speaker with a 'wider social network' than the main inner-city networks of his locality. In any case, a comparison of tables 2.1 and 2.2 shows that speakers from different social-class backgrounds in Dublin are convergent in their use of unlenited [t] in the formality of wordlist style; when it comes to lenition, however, there are major differences both in realisation types and in the frequency of use of different types in different situations.

Though relying on naturally occurring data rather than on wordlists or reading passages, the aggregate figures in the Westland Row data seen in table 2.3 afford further comparisons with tables 2.1 and 2.2. Social class emerges as important, since the working-class speakers of table 2.3 pattern more closely with those of table 2.2 than with the middle-class speakers of table 2.1: lenition with [ʔ] or [h] is widespread as in table 2.2, while [ṭ], which features so prominently in table 2.1, is almost entirely absent from table 2.3. Male speakers in table 2.3 may show some tendency to move away from [tˀ] towards [t] in the relative formality of classroom speech, but the percentage of [ʔ] and [h] usage actually increases in the classroom, so it is difficult to see clear evidence of style shift. Though numbers are small for female classroom speech, the percentage of [t] realisations is essentially the same across settings, while [ʔ] increases in the classroom at the expense of [h]. A further gender differentiation is suggested in comparing tables 2.2 and 2.3 that is not applicable for the speakers of table 2.1: in both working-class studies, broadly speaking, [ʔ] is more favoured by females across speech styles, while [h] is more favoured by males. This gender difference is not, however, categorical, and is affected, at least in table 2.2, by the pressure of [t] realisations in more formal styles. Clearly, more quantitative evidence is needed on this point.

6.1   Lenition of /t/: Dublin Data and Phonological Environment

The preceding discussion of data from Dublin looks at differences in the frequencies of realisation of /t/ across speech styles, using social class and gender as relevant non-linguistic conditioning factors. A full assessment of dialect convergence and divergence in the light of possible phonetic gradualness and structure preservation also requires an examination of the role of linguistic environments in conditioning lenition. Crucial in this discussion is the role of syllable structure, though, as anticipated in Lexical Phonology (e.g. Kiparsky 1985), derivation as reflected in word or morpheme boundaries may also be relevant for some types of sound change.

It is uncontroversial that lenition (and, for that matter, deletion) is favoured in syllable coda position (including, in Harris' model, the onsets of syllables with empty nuclei). Non-initial syllable positions pose something of a problem, given the controversy, cited earlier, over ambisyllabicity in phonological theory. In connected speech, phonological phrases can cross word boundaries, so that, for example, the American tapping rule readily applies to unstressed particles within the phonological phrase, as with *to* in *go to* or *me to*. In the Westland Row data, however, no lenition applies for any word-initial /t/ preceded by a vowel (e.g. *go to*, *me to*, *me two*, *we told*). From my experience of Dublin English and General American English, I suggest that this difference is not trivial, but rather represents a deep-seated divergence between the two rule systems.

In the analysis below, I follow the arguments of Selkirk (1982) and Blevins (1995) in rejecting ambisyllabicity. I assume instead that syllable division follows the well-known Maximal Onset Principle in so far as no impermissible onsets are created, but that *resyllabification* as defined by Selkirk (1982) also attaches consonants to the coda of stressed syllables which precede unstressed syllables, thus creating systematic violations of the Maximal Onset Principle. In broad outline, Selkirk's resyllabification analysis is based on a rule of the

Table 2.4 */t/ lenition according to syllable position (Dublin)*

	t	tˀ	ʔt	tʃ	ʔ	ɾ	ṭ	t̪	h	ø	Total
					Complex coda						
Byrne (1996) (e.g. *mart, went out, servant, must, breakfast, perfect, bereft*)											
N =	87	2	1	0	0	0	1	0	0	37	128
%	*68*	*1*	*1*	*0*	*0*	*0*	*1*	*0*	*0*	*29*	*100*
Westland Row (e.g. *start, short, went, sent, just, least, asked, fixed, kept*)											
N =	44	3	0	0	2	0	1	1	0	11	62
%	*71*	*5*	*0*	*0*	*3*	*0*	*2*	*2*	*0*	*17*	*100*
					Simple coda						
Byrne (1996) (e.g. *right, sweet, ticket, merit, hermit, gett.ing, catt.le, lett.er*)											
N =	137	16	14	6	8	27	181	0	0	11	400
%	*34*	*4*	*4*	*1*	*2*	*7*	*45*	*0*	*0*	*3*	*100*
Westland Row (e.g. *right, street, all right, about, lat.er, putt.ing, litt.le, lett.er*)											
N =	17	10	1	0	39	8	1	3	38	1	118
%	*14*	*8*	*1*	*0*	*33*	*7*	*1*	*3*	*32*	*1*	*100*

type in (4), which creates derivations such as (5) (Selkirk 1982: 366–367) in words such as *happ.y, att.itude, heft.y, aft.er, Ast.or, Hask.ins,* etc.

(4)
$$X \left\{ \begin{matrix} [-\text{cons}] \\ [+\text{cons}] \end{matrix} \right\} [-\text{syll}] \begin{bmatrix} +\text{syll} \\ -\text{stress} \end{bmatrix} Y$$
$$1 \quad 2 \quad\quad 3 \quad\quad 4 \quad 5 \quad\quad \rightarrow 1\,2 + 3\,\emptyset\,4\,5$$

(5)

Adopting Selkirk's resyllabification analysis, table 2.4 divides the different realisations of syllable-final /t/ given by Byrne (1996) and in the Westland Row data, according to their occurrence in simple codas (consisting only of /t/) and complex codas that contain at least one other consonant. (In order to facilitate this comparison, Byrne's distinction between [tˀ] and [tˀ] is merged into the category [tˀ] used with the Westland Row data; cf. the preceding discussion on the auditory similarity of these realisations. Data from Pardy (1987) are not reported in sufficient detail as to make their inclusion in table 2.4 possible.)

Table 2.4 shows that both Byrne's middle-class speakers and the working-class speakers of Westland Row share essentially the same constraints on [t] realisation in complex coda environments, albeit with the middle-class group showing a higher percentage of deletion and a more limited range of intermediate realisations. In simple codas, however, the realisations of /t/ are strikingly different. Byrne's speakers favour lenited [ṭ] over [t], with some use of unreleased [t˥], pre-glottalised [ʔt], and [ɾ] accounting for nearly all the remaining realisations: as noted earlier, [h] is not used and [ʔ] is very rare. It is precisely these latter realisations, however, which feature prominently in the Westland Row data. Both [ʔ] and [h] are used more than twice as frequently as [t], each being used in nearly identical proportion. Tapping, though not a major feature, is nearly identical across the two groups. As noted earlier, however, [ṭ] is virtually non-existent in Westland Row. Thus, we may propose that these two groups of Dublin speakers are similar in their treatment of /t/ in complex codas and in their marginal incorporation of the tapping rule for simple codas that has proved to be robust elsewhere (see also below). They differ, however, in their use of [ṭ], [ʔ], and [h] realisations in simple codas, and this difference yields corresponding differences in frequencies of [t] realisation.

Variations of this kind provide a ready basis for dialect convergence and divergence over time. I suggest that the interpretation most compatible with the data presented so far is that cross-dialectal convergence in the realisation of syllable-final /t/ emerges only where general constraints in English effectively block lenition (though not deletion). Divergent effects arise when lenition is possible, with little evidence of convergence towards a favoured lenited realisation.

7   Beyond Dublin: Traditional Dialect

It is difficult to make comparisons beyond the Dublin data scrutinised here, partly because of the lack of comparable study done elsewhere, and partly due to differences in phonetic description or other methodological issues. One set of data, though, which further supports the view that apparently similar phonetic manifestations of lenition do not always stem from the same rule systems is found in Henry's (1958) survey of traditional dialect in Ireland. Though Henry did not use any quantitative or social-stratificational approaches, and does not provide full sets of data for any of his 31 geographical survey points, the results are nevertheless illuminating. If we assume that Henry, in trying to portray variation in the realisation of /t/, included all relevant types, we note two striking points: (1) the non-occurrence of [ɾ] or [ʔ] in traditional dialect; and (2) the extensive use of [h] in word-final and medial position. Following resyllabification as defined above, a tabulation of the 70 tokens of /t/ in simple coda position provided by Henry (1958) from 21 data points is given in table 2.5. Henry's [T] notation is adapted here towards IPA usage as [t̪]; [t̪] denotes the fricative variant of /t/. The low frequency of [t]

Table 2.5 */t/ lenition in simple coda position (based on Henry 1958)*

	t	tˢ	t̪	ʔ	θ	ɾ	ṭ	h	ø	Total
Henry (1958) (e.g. *night, goat, carrot, bleat.ing, cas.'trat.ed, wat.er, butt.er, litt.le*)										
N =	8	2	2	0	1	0	25	32	0	70
%	*11*	*3*	*3*	*0*	*1*	*0*	*36*	*46*	*0*	*100*

realisation in table 2.5 should be interpreted with caution, since Henry's method of data presentation focuses on changes away from [t] rather than reflecting the percentage of [t] usage. Nevertheless, a clear picture emerges in which [t̪] and [h] assume major roles as lenited realisations of /t/, while [θ], [tˢ], and [ṭ] show marginal occurrence, and there are no citations of [ɾ], [ʔ], or deletion.

Turning to the analysis of phonological environments for /t/ lenition, we see that quantitative data obscure a significant difference between [h] usage in Dublin and in traditional dialect. Words cited by Henry (1958) such as *bottom, little, litter, water, butter, buttermilk, eighteen, footed, latted, letters*, and *cas'trat.ed* are all analysed here as having /t/ in the coda of a syllable which has undergone resyllabification in keeping with the arguments of Selkirk (1982). Henry (1958) shows frequent use of lenition for these words, and in at least one token for each of these items, the specific lenited realisation used is [h]. We can contrast this use of [h] with that of Westland Row. Though the Westland Row speakers also use [h] in simple coda environments, those words which show /t/ in the coda following resyllabification do not use [h]: *little* shows [ʔ] 3 times, *letter* [t̪], *later* [ʔ], *better* [t̪], and *ath.'let.ics* [t] once and [tˀ] once. Although more data would be needed to confirm this hypothesis, I suggest that the Westland Row speakers use [h] as a realisation of /t/ only when /t/ occurs in simple coda position in the underlying form, not when /t/ moves into coda position by resyllabification. For the dialect speakers noted by Henry (1958), this latter constraint does not hold. Here again, it would appear that deep-seated differences in phonological systems underlie surface-level similarities between dialects.

8   Lenition of /t/: The Global Picture

The preceding discussion of /t/ lenition in Ireland is not exhaustive. We note, especially, that Kingsmore (1995: 138ff.) details seven major types of realisation for /t/ in the town of Coleraine in Northern Ireland: (1) [t] 'with or without aspiration'; (2) [t̪] 'only when immediately followed by /ɾ/ or /ər/' (where the precise phonetic realization of /r/ is not specified); (3) [d] denoting a voiced 'stop or flap', (4) [?], (5) [t?]; (6) voiced [d?]; and (7) /t/ deletion. Coleraine speakers, however, do not show evidence of [h] or [t̪] realizations (cf. also Barry 1981; Harris 1984). As noted above, Hickey (1999a,b) has also made observations on /t/ lenition, referring (Hickey 1999a: 221) to the 'sequence' as in (3), in which 'fricativised /t/ is further reduced to [h], [r] or zero' in what he terms 'popular Dublin English'. In order to pursue the question of dialectal convergence and divergence further, however, it will be necessary to view the Irish evidence in the light of studies of lenition in other English-speaking areas.

Studies of /t/ lenition constitute a growing field, as an increasing number of communities are subject to detailed study from dialectologists, sociolinguists, phoneticians, and others. From within this field, we can identify some recurring themes which will help us to understand the issues of dialect convergence and divergence. From a phonetic point of view, the global trend of historical development appears to be towards the spread of tapping and glottalisation (including both glottal substitution and glottalisation). Other lenited forms found in Ireland do not fare so well internationally. Clarke (1991, 1997) shows that [t̪] in Newfoundland most strongly correlates with Irish-influenced speech and is declining among younger speakers generally. Tollfree's mention (2001) of a fricated version of /t/ in Australia (combining both affricated [tˢ] and a true fricative for which a transcription is not provided) indicates that it is recessive and associated more with older speakers (younger speakers using more taps and glottal stops). The use of [h] as a realisation of /t/ is hardly noted anywhere outside of Ireland. We should note here, too, the Irish English dentalisation rule which operates in words like *butter* and *water* (cf. tables 2.3 and 2.5 above). Though not strictly speaking a form of lenition (except in so far as it reduces the degree of audible plosion for /t/), dentalisation operates in one subset of the environments for lenition and thus competes with it. Note, for example, that Henry (1958) cites two pronunciations of *butter* from Co. Meath: one using [t̪], the other with [h]; [t̪] is also used in the Westland Row study with *letter* and *better*. Though the dentalisation rule lies outside the scope of this chapter, it appears significant as an Irish divergence from other dialects which in effect bleeds lenition rules proper.

The more attention we pay to the social and phonological conditioning of /t/ realisations, the more we see different rule systems applying in different communities. For example, Docherty *et al.* (1997) report that in Tyneside, both [?] and [?t] are rare pre-pausally or at the end of a speaking turn in wordlist style. Their proposed 'Final Release Rule' (FRR) requires full stop release in such environments and is adhered to by 31 out of 32 speakers in their sample. Though the FRR can be violated in conversational style, observed violations are accounted for by a small number of speakers in the sample and concentrated in a small number of lexical items. On the other hand, Docherty and Foulkes

(1999: 50–51) report that in Derby, [ʔ] is 'almost categorical for word-final /t/' before consonants, and is common before pause. The Westland Row study also shows no evidence of a FRR: [ʔ] shows up in utterance-final *stupid* ['stjupɪʔ] and in many pre-pausal words (e.g. *ten to eight* [tɛn tə eɪʔ], *all that* [ɔl aʔ], *York Street* [jɔk striʔ]). Unlike Derby, however, the situation is complicated in Westland Row by competition in this same linguistic environment from [h], as in *that's it* [dðats ɪh], *couldn't go out* [kʊŋ goʊ aʊh], *what?* [wɑh], and *conked her out* [kaŋkt ər æʊh].

Diversity across communities also holds for the social factors associated with lenition. In Milton Keynes, Reading, and Hull, for example, Williams and Kerswill (1999: 147) report that 'glottal replacement of non-initial /t/ is the norm among young working class people', though working-class males use glottal replacement 'a little more' than females. Among middle-class speakers, however, these three communities differ in that glottal replacement is more associated with females in Reading and Hull, and with males in Milton Keynes. In Glasgow, according to Stuart-Smith (1999: 208), the use of glottals is 'strongly stigmatized yet extremely common', with higher levels of usage in the working class. This picture contrasts with that reported by Mees (1987: 29) for Cardiff, in which upper middle-class speakers use pre-consonantal glottalised realisations significantly more frequently than lower middle-class or working-class speakers. Percentages of glottalisation increase for all groups in the Mees study when moving from interview to wordlist style. Though Mees shows a complex social distribution for glottalisation in Cardiff, in which the categories of gender and social class interact in differing ways with different phonological and stylistic environments for /t/, her evidence is sufficient to show that Cardiff speakers assign different social values for glottalisation from those described by Williams and Kerswill or by Stuart-Smith.

We may also compare the Irish data presented here with Clarke's observations (1986: 73–74) on the use of [t̪] in Newfoundland. Contemporary Newfoundland English (for which nineteenth-century Irish English is a major historical source) and contemporary Irish English are convergent in their adoption of [t̪] as a phonetic element, but the rules which govern their social distribution of [t̪] are different. Clarke's observation that in Newfoundland [t̪] 'displays absolutely no significant socio-economic stratification' would not be true for Dublin. Clarke's Newfoundland data also show females unambiguously leading males in [t̪] realisations across free conversation, reading, and wordlist styles, with the percentage of [t̪] realisation increasing towards wordlist style for both sexes. The Newfoundland pattern can be contrasted with the data of table 2.1 above, in which [t̪] is strongly favoured by females over males for the reading passage (54 per cent vs. 27 per cent), although wordlist style increases male use of [t̪] to 36 per cent yet decreases female usage of [t̪] to 20 per cent in the face of increased use of [t] at 74 per cent.

In short, our global comparisons strengthen and elaborate the conclusion expressed by Docherty *et al.* (1997: 289) with regard to glottalisation as a type of lenition:

glottal reinforcement and glottal replacement cannot easily be ranged on a lenition scale with the glottal stop as the most lenited. They appear to be independent phenomena in that their sociolinguistic distributions systematically covary with the social characteristics of speakers. This forces us to consider the sense in which speakers might be said to be implementing a process of 'lenition'.

Considering the variation which exists in phonetic detail, phonological conditioning factors, interaction with other aspects of phonology, and social significance for all the realisations of /t/ that could be or have been described as 'lenition', I suggest that our review of lenition in Irish and other types of English shows 'lenition' to be at best a very loose cover term for a variety of rule systems. Though further data could, of course, lead to another conclusion, there is little support in either our synchronic or our diachronic evidence for a view that these rule systems are bound by a universal linguistic principle to converge towards a given point.

9   Discussion

In reference to the question of Neogrammarian sound change, it is difficult from the data we have considered here to see any compelling reason to treat English /t/ lenition as a process which is either exceptionless or phonetically gradual. Though it is possible to arrange attested realisations of /t/ on a putative scale of decreasing strength through to deletion, even the assessment of strength is not self-evident: different principles, as discussed above, lead to different conclusions. More to the point, though, the evidence we have seen here suggests that any continuum analysis constructs synchronic phonetic gradualness only by mixing among different systems. Our speakers, from whatever speech community, do not pass through a sequence of points on the way to deletion, but rather make phonetically abrupt choices to lenite or not to lenite within a narrow range of possibilities. Neither is it the case that any supposed stages in lenition lead to deletion as an end-point. Close examination of the evidence shows that lenition is favoured in simple codas as we have defined them, while deletion is conversely favoured in complex codas (cf. table 2.4). The disjunction between these two sets of conditioning environments, while not strictly being a case of complementary distribution, is so great that it is difficult to see how lenition (occurring in one environment) could lead to deletion in a very different environment.

Taking the question of dialect convergence and divergence as a diachronic issue, we also search in vain for evidence that there is any single, purely phonological, principle which is moving different dialects of English closer together or further apart. Lack of historical data puts us at something of a disadvantage, but, as pointed out earlier, at least some of the lenited realisations appear to have originated in the nineteenth century: [ʔ] has spread quite rapidly in British English and exists in a complicated relationship with pre- and post-glottalised variants; [ɾ] is widespread in General American but also in Ulster; [t̞] is widespread in non-Ulster dialects of Ireland and in Irish-based Newfoundland English; and [h] exists in at least two very different patterns within Ireland, but is not common elsewhere. It might still be argued that all these dialects show convergence along a principle that in certain syllable positions (broadly defined), /t/ may become 'weaker' in the sense that it involves voicing, a reduction in audible plosion, reduction in obstruction of the supraglottal airflow, or a combination of these factors. In that sense, convergence towards an abstract notion of lenition could be seen as a diachronic process which is occurring in the English language generally. Yet the evidence we have seen here suggests that the specific /t/ realisations in different English dialects show resistance to any strong form of convergence: both the phonetic realisations and the phonological rules which condition variation vary from community to community. Thus I suggest that the convergence or divergence which does take place for this variable occurs only within a broadly stated phonological tendency, and is crucially conditioned by social factors.

In fact, the greatest divergences that we find when we compare different English dialects may be caused by convergences at other levels. Specifically, divergence within the pool of attested systems of lenition may be triggered by convergences which individual dialects have engaged in with other language varieties or languages. We could suggest, for example, that the [h] realisation in traditional dialects of Irish English may have arisen from convergence with the Irish language, given the morphophonologically conditioned use of [h] as an allophone of /tʲ/ ∼ /tˠ/ and the lack of constraint against syllable-final [h] in Irish, as mentioned earlier. The [t̞] realisation in Irish English could have developed from a convergence between alveolar stops, on the one hand (including [t] in English and [tʲ] ∼ [tˠ] in Irish), and [h], on the other. Though discussions of lenition usually focus on articulatory evidence (for exceptions, see Beckman *et al.* 1992 and Labov 1997), auditory considerations could support the idea of a [t̞] as the outcome of a cross-linguistic convergence process, similar to the dialectal 'fudge' discussed by Chambers and Trudgill (1998). In terms of auditory perception, [t̞] is closer to both [h] and [t] than to the [ʔ] realisation that is more widespread in British English, since [t̞] incorporates the salient frication of [h], the anterior placement of [t], and the voicelessness of both. It could be, in other words, that the historical development of [t̞] is supported by the availability of [h] in Irish as an allophone for /t/.

The entry of [ʔ] into the Irish system would represent yet another kind of convergence, more akin to borrowing. The limited historical and dialectal use in Irish English of [ʔ] (a sound which does not exist in Irish) is certainly compatible with a view that it has come to Ireland from non-Irish varieties of an as-yet unspecified nature, given the wide extent of contact between Ireland and its neighbours both in Britain and in North America. Similarly, the addition of [ɾ] to the Irish system represents an independent convergence with external varieties of English. Given the differential distribution of [ʔ] and [ɾ] across England and Scotland (where English and Scots are both to be considered), it would not be surprising that convergence in Ireland which introduces [ʔ] and [ɾ] into any given system would occur differently for different groups. Speakers in Coleraine will interact with different speakers from those in Dublin – and while both groups may end up using [ʔ] and [ɾ], we can only expect that the sounds will occupy different parts of their respective phonological and sociolinguistic systems.

10   Conclusion

Before reaching conclusions on the question of Neogrammarian sound change and the interaction between internal and external factors in dialect convergence and divergence, it is helpful to summarise the cross-dialectal variation that has been discussed here in terms of the conflicting demands of constraints as understood in Optimality Theory. It turns out that OT offers a ready picture of the differences among lenited realisations of /t/. In this approach, different outcomes in lenition show a conflict between Faithfulness constraints – which dictate that /t/ should be realised as [t] or otherwise maintain an optimum number of place, manner, and voice features – and Agreement constraints which dictate that /t/ agree with adjacent segments on these key features. A Glottal Termination constraint further interacts with Faithfulness and Agreement conditions to produce varied outcomes.

Figure 2.3 thus shows OT tableaux that illustrate the major categories of lenition: (a) tapping; (b) frication; (c) glottal replacement; and (d) glottal fricative realisation. The empirical evidence put forward here shows that deletion should not be considered as part of the same phenomenon with lenition. Patterns for the deletion of /t/ seen in the data are too different from the lenition patterns in (a)–(d) to allow for a unified treatment, and any analysis of /t/ deletion would need to be considered in the context of other rules for English consonant deletion. The four types of lenition seen in figure 2.3 thus show the relationship between /t/ realisations and the constraints of Faithfulness (FAITH$_{manner}$, FAITH$_{place}$, and FAITH$_{voice}$), Agreement relative to the preceding segment (AGREE$_{voice}$, AGREE$_{continuant}$), and Glottal Termination. Additionally, tableau (e) shows the ranking of constraints when lenition does not apply,

/kæt/ 'cat'	F_{place}	AGR_{voice}	F_{manner}	F_{voice}	GLOTERM	AGR_{cont}
☞ kæɾ			*	*	*	*
kæt̪		*!	*			
kæʔ	*!	*		*		*
kæh	*!	*	*			
kæt		*!			*	*

(a) F_{place} and AGR_{voice} outrank all others

/kæt/ 'cat'	F_{place}	F_{voice}	AGR_{cont}	F_{manner}	AGR_{voice}	GLOTERM
kæɾ		*!	*	*		*
☞ kæt̪				*	*	*
kæʔ	*!	*	*		*	
kæh	*!			*	*	
kæt			*!		*	*

(b) F_{place}, F_{voice}, and AGR_{cont} outrank all others

/kæt/ 'cat'	GLOTERM	F_{manner}	F_{place}	F_{voice}	AGR_{cont}	AGR_{voice}
kæɾ	*!	*		*	*	
kæt̪	*!	*				*
☞ kæʔ			*	*	*	*
kæh		*!	*			*
kæt	*!				*	*

(c) GLOTERM and F_{manner} outrank all others

/kæt/ 'cat'	GLOTERM	F_{voice}	AGR_{cont}	F_{manner}	F_{place}	AGR_{voice}
kæɾ	*!	*	*	*		
kæt̪	*!			*		*
kæʔ		*!	*		*	*
☞ kæh				*	*	*
kæt	*!		*			*

(d) GLOTERM, F_{voice}, and AGR_{cont} outrank all others

/kæt/ 'cat'	F_{manner}	F_{place}	F_{voice}	GLOTERM	AGR_{voice}	AGR_{cont}
kæɾ	*!		*	*		*
kæt̪	*!			*	*	
kæʔ		*!	*		*	*
kæh	*!	*			*	
☞ kæt				*	*	*

(e) FAITH constraints outrank all others: lenition does not occur

Fig. 2.3 */t/ lenition and deletion as the outcome of constraint violations.*

that is, when FAITH constraints outrank all others. Following from our position on syllable structure, all constraints apply in essentially the same environment: syllable-final /t/ in simple coda position, including those segments in coda position following resyllabification in violation of the Maximum Onset Principle. If, as suggested above, it is true that [h] realisations in Dublin do not occur following resyllabification, while they do occur in traditional dialect, then a more complete account of lenition would need to account for the interaction between syllabification (which lies outside the scope of this chapter) and the Faithfulness, Agreement, and Glottal Termination constraints.

Figure 2.3 shows that each major realisation of /t/ can be understood by reference to a small set of constraints. Different realisations are considered optimal according to different constraint hierarchies. The fricative realisation at (b), for example, follows F_{place} and F_{voice} but allows for a violation of F_{manner} since it obeys the AGR_{cont} constraint. In other words, for the (b) outcome, AGR_{cont} outranks F_{manner} though faithfulness to place and voice features is maintained. Outcomes (c) and (d) can be compared on the basis that they share high ranking for Glottal Termination, though they differ on the ranking of F_{manner} and F_{voice} as well as AGR_{cont}. The precise details of these constraints could be a matter for further study. Treating the lesser degree of airflow obstruction shared by vowels and fricatives as a matter of agreement on the feature [continuant] (cf. Hyman 1975: 37–39; and Kenstowicz 1994: 35–36), for example, would not accord with all theories of phonological representation, since it is possible to argue that [continuant] is redundant for vowels and should not be applied to them, or even to argue, as does Harris (1994: 41), for a very different approach to problems to which this feature has historically been addressed. While such arguments may require a different formal expression of the relevant constraint, the overall position which I take here – that articulatory similarity between vowels and fricatives relative to plosives can be expressed in terms of an AGR constraint – should not be problematical.

To summarise our results, then, we can see that the development of /t/ lenition in English gives reason to question a strict dichotomy between Neogrammarian sound change and the lexical diffusion of change. The evidence cited here does not suggest that any single system of English has developed lenition by phonetically gradual steps, nor that lenition is a gradual process synchronically. Neither do we see evidence of a phonetically gradual spread of lenition across the English dialects considered here. The patterns in the use of lenited and non-lenited realisations of /t/ in any given system of English also show that the process is by no means exceptionless. The exceptions which do exist, i.e. environments in which lenition does not take place, nevertheless show little evidence of lexical conditioning. There is no word class in which lenition appears to have originated, nor is there any which appears especially resistant to lenition. Morpheme boundaries may play a role in inhibiting lenition where the past tense marker follows verb stems ending in consonants (e.g. *jumped, liked, fixed*), but the grammatical feature in these environments is overshadowed by the complexity of the syllable coda, since lenition rarely takes place in complex coda environments. The role of morpheme boundaries with the past tense marker cannot, of course, be tested in simple codas, since the past tense marker in such cases (*owed, agreed, displayed*, etc.) is realised as /d/ rather than any form of /t/.

Considering phonemic structure-building, which Kiparsky (1995) correlates with Neogrammarian sound change, we see that /t/ lenition is resolutely *structure-preserving* in that it shows little evidence of phonological merger or split. Though [ţ] is admittedly a phonetic innovation in Irish English, its allophonic status poses no threat of merger with /s/. Likewise, [ʔ] is only an allophonic realisation in English and shows no sign of becoming phonemic. The complementary distribution between syllable-final [h] arising from the lenition of /t/ and underlying syllable-initial /h/ affords no realistic chance for the merger of /t/ and /h/ via allophonic [h]. Though the auditory similarity between [d] and [ɾ] can give rise to homophones for some speakers (as between *rider* and *writer*), occasional homophony does not lead towards phonemic merger.

In looking at the development of /t/ lenition in the light of the Neogrammarian controversy, then, we see a mixed picture: lenition resembles Neogrammarian sound change in that it does not appear to be lexically conditioned, and it does exhibit a high degree of social salience. On the other hand, it deviates from the ideal Neogrammarian type in so far as it is not a structure-building process, nor does it proceed by phonetically gradual steps, either within dialectal systems or across systems towards a common English-language pattern.

In this analysis, the role of phonological principles in accounting for the convergence and divergence of English dialects in their use of /t/ lenition may be little more than suggestive. The variation and evidence of change which we have considered here is loosely united by the general principle that changes in the realisation of /t/ pertain to the use of occlusion, voicing, and glottal articulation. Lenited realisations retain a degree of faithfulness to their underlying representations, although changes of voicing and frication, which involve increase in resonance and lessening of stricture, partially assimilate /t/ in simple coda position to the features of preceding vowels. Structure preservation limits the nature of change so that /t/ has not merged with /s/, /θ/, /h/, or /d/, though some dialects show neutralisation of contrasts in certain environments. Yet, beyond these rather elementary principles, purely phonological considerations do not anticipate or explain the precise nature of the different systems we group under the heading of English /t/ lenition. Phonology alone, it would appear, brings us to an understanding of what may happen and how variation and change may be constrained, but – contrary to the universalist approach suggested by Singh (1995), for example – it does not appear able to fill in the details of what happens in any particular system or when systems come into contact.

The precise development of dialectal systems will, I suggest, depend ultimately on the social embedding of variation and the ways in which variation gives rise to change. Though social factors alone cannot account for /t/ lenition (since there are no inherent sociological constraints on realising /t/ as [ɬ] or [f] or anything else), it is equally true that social factors best account for the process of speaker innovation and the diffusion of change within each speech community (cf. Milroy and Milroy 1985b). Since speech communities, in turn, do not exist in isolation, we can expect to find – as we have with /t/ lenition – convergence and divergence of community norms in a state of flux, tempered by principles of phonology that may constrain in at least general terms the direction of language variation and change.

3   Dialect/standard convergence, mixing, and models of language contact: the case of Italy

Gaetano Berruto

Introduction

The main aim of this chapter is to examine some features of the relationship between convergence in a linguistic system and convergence, confluence, or interpenetration of forms from two varieties in use. On the basis of the most salient features of contact between the national language and the Italoromance dialects in Italy the applicability of a theoretical model designed to embrace the apparently very heterogeneous phenomena of language contact within a single concept will be discussed, namely Myers-Scotton's Matrix Language Frame model. This discussion should allow us not only to gain a better sociolinguistic understanding of the Italian situation but also, and above all, to focus on certain features of theoretical significance in the general treatment of convergence and contact.

1   Language Convergence and the Relationship Between Standard Language and Dialects

Let us begin with a few observations of a terminological and conceptual nature with regard to the two main terms involved, namely 'convergence' and 'dialect'. I shall leave aside problems raised by the use of the term 'convergence' with reference to the language behaviour of individual persons in verbal interaction, such as situational accommodation between interlocutors. My employment of the term will be confined to the relationship between language varieties.

The term 'language convergence' is well known as one of the hobby-horses of historical linguistics. This label has been applied to a whole series of phenomena that occur in language contact, and 'convergence' itself has been taken to embrace anything and everything that leads to a reduction of the differences and, hence, an augmentation of the similarities between social and geographical language varieties. As Sasse (1985: 38) put it, 'alle sprachlichen Veränderungen, die zur Vergrößerung der Ähnlichkeit zwischen den beiden Sprachen beitragen, werden als Konvergenzerscheinungen behandelt' ('all language modifications that serve to increase the resemblances between two languages are to be treated as convergence phenomena').

As I outlined some ten years or more ago (Berruto 1989), and as Mattheier (1996: 34) recently and much more elegantly stated, due attention has not always been paid to the fact that 'convergence' strictly speaking implies a certain degree of reciprocity, i.e. the mutual approximation of two language varieties, both of which undergo modifications that reduce the structural distance between them. It is worth pointing out that in what may be called the classic studies, such as Gumperz and Wilson (1971) on convergence between Urdu, Kannada, and Marathi at Kupwar in India, or studies on the Balkan *Sprachbund* (see, for example, McMahon 1994: 213–220), the concept was used in the strict sense.

Language convergence in this restricted sense is a rather specific process and one that occurs relatively rarely among the various manifestations of the influence of one language variety on another. In a broader sense, the term refers to all instances of the reduction of structural distance between linguistic systems through contact. The qualitative difference between the two concepts is by no means negligible and relates both to the structural phenomena involved and to the social and linguistic background in terms of the community's repertoire. Bilateral convergence, for example, presupposes a substantial equality of the sociolinguistic status and the prestige value of the varieties concerned, whereas unilateral convergence presupposes a non-symmetrical social status and a difference in prestige. In principle, the former touches on all the levels of a language system, especially its morphology and syntax, whereas the latter primarily makes its appearance in lexical and phonetic changes. There is thus good reason for drawing a distinction between them. Mattheier (1996: 34) has proposed *Advergenz* ('advergence') as a term for unilateral convergence, a neologism which undoubtedly has advantages.

Of the terms currently employed in linguistics and sociolinguistics, 'dialect' is perhaps the one which enjoys the widest range of meanings and embraces the most dissimilar contents in any given concrete language situation. 'Dialect' may mean something different and even very different according to the specific repertoire within which it is situated. Italy's *dialetti* are not the same thing as the *Dialekte* of Germany or the British dialects. As an illustration of these situations, the structural distance between the standard and the dialects in Italy is much greater; Italoromance dialects have their own history, many of them have a (notable) literary tradition. Coseriu (1980) has, to my mind, provided us with a very useful preliminary distinction between primary, secondary, and tertiary dialects based on the historical, genetic, and derivation/fragmentation relationships that exist between a common, national standard language and the varieties referred to as dialects. Italian dialects are of the primary kind. Partly autonomous, they all came into being at the same time through the transformation of Latin. One of them, the Florentine dialect, later became the national language. Yet this does not mean that Italy has no secondary and tertiary dialects. The regional forms of Italian, i.e. the varieties of the national language found in different parts of the country and which are at least partly the outcome of convergence and more generally of contact between the primary dialects and standard Italian, are typical tertiary dialects.

The distinction between primary, secondary, and tertiary dialects is not devoid of importance with regard to the subject of this chapter. Contact between a standard language and the primary dialects seems destined to give rise to convergence, whereas the very formation of tertiary dialects is principally a process of divergence, of differentiation within the community repertoire. Generally speaking, unilateral convergence or advergence between a standard language and the dialects results in an increasing variability and complexity of the repertoire. One outcome is the formation of intermediate varieties or variants, such as 'interlanguages' (Kristensen and Thelander 1984), 'interdialects' (Trudgill 1988) and others (see Auer and Hinskens 1996: 6–10).

2   Contact Between the National Language and the Dialects in Italy

We can now turn to the contact between Italian and the dialects spoken in Italy through an illustration of some points of general interest that arise from it. In an earlier paper (Berruto 1989) I drew a distinction between four classes of phenomena: (1) dialectisation of Italian; (2) Italianisation of dialect; (3) koineisation; and (4) hybridisation. The first of these is the dialectisation of varieties of the national language, i.e. Italian, in other words situations in which the influence of the dialects on the national language among essentially dialect-speaking people leads to the formation of varieties or variants marked by dialect interference. The result is called *italiano popolare* 'popular Italian', or, better still, 'popular regional Italian', a low diastratic variety which differs from the standard language on several levels of analysis.

The following examples taken from the Piedmontese situation will give an idea of this variety. The first one is on the textual-pragmatic level and shows topicalisation of the infinitive (Grassi and Pautasso 1989: 154):

(1)   *il mangiare si mangiava più bene che in Italia*
       lit: 'the eating, one ate better than in Italy'
       = 'as to eating, one ate better than in Italy'
       std. Ital. *quanto a(l) mangiare si mangiava meglio che in Italia*
       Piedmontese *mangé a-s mangiava pi bin ch'an Italia*

Next, an example at the morphosyntactic level comprising: (a) over-extension (generalisation) of the originally PRO CLIT 1 PL/LOC/INSTRUM *ci* to a PRO CLIT DAT 3 SG; (b) a hanging topic (*nominativus pendens*), *il libro per me*;

(c) generalisation of the PRO 1 SG OBL *me* to a PRO 1 SG NOM (Grassi and Pautasso 1989: 155):

(2)   *ma io ci ho detto che il libro per me ci pensavo me*
        'but I told him that, as to the book for me, I was going to see about it myself'
        std. Ital. *ma io gli ho detto che al libro per me ci pensavo io*
        Piedmont. *ma mi i l'aj dije che ël liber për mi aj pensava mi*

An example at the semantic-lexical level (Grassi and Pautasso 1989: 169):

(3)   *comprare (un bambino)*
        lit. 'to buy (a baby)'
        = 'to give birth to'
        std. Ital. *avere (un bambino)*
        Piedmont. *caté (ën cit/ën mat)* (where *caté = comprare* 'buy')

Finally a phonetic example in which a voiceless alveolar affricate (lacking in the dialect's phonemic inventory) is replaced by the corresponding fricative (Grassi and Pautasso 1989: 202):

(4)   *frisione* [fri'sjone]
        'clutch (of a vehicle)'
        std. Ital. *frizione* [fri'ttsjone]
        Piedmont. *frisiun* [fri'sjuɳ].

The corresponding phenomenon on the dialectal side is the Italianisation of the dialects (Berruto 1997a), with the formation of dialect varieties or variants marked by Italian interference. This is known as an 'Italianised dialect'. As a third class of phenomena, there is koineisation of the dialects (see Sobrero 1996), i.e. the formation of regional or subregional dialect varieties. They are (a) usually founded on the dialect of the region's or the subregion's main town; (b) the result of dialect levelling (see Auer 1998a), with the elimination of features that are linguistically most marked and/or sociolinguistically most stigmatised; and (c) partially Italianised, which means that a distinction cannot readily be drawn between the effects of koineisation and those of Italianisation.

The influence exerted by the standard language on the Italoromance dialects varies considerably. As a simplified, general, statement, we can say that the lexicon is most affected and that phonetics/phonology is also greatly influenced, whereas the imprint of the Italianising hand is less evident in morphology and syntax.

Here, we can refer to a study by Moretti (1988) on Cevio, a village in the Ticino, i.e. in Italian-speaking Switzerland. The sociolinguistic background and the relationship between standard language and dialect (Lombard) in Italian

Switzerland are very similar to those in Italy. Cevio has a dialect continuum with two clearly distinct varieties at its ends: a conservative variety (A), which is archaic and still spoken by some elderly persons; and an Italianised variety (B) spoken by the young. There is a range of partially overlapping intermediate dialect varieties between A and B. For example, three forms for 'milk' (std. Italian *latte* < Latin LACTE(M)) are found: [lɛtʃ], typical of A; [latʃ] and [lat], respectively typical of an intermediate variety near to B and of B. The first form illustrates the application of two productive rules: (a) fronting of stressed *a*; and (b) palatalisation of the consonantal cluster -CT- (voiceless velar stop plus voiceless alveolar stop); the second form results from the application of (b) but not (a); the third form from the application of neither rule, with retention of the central low vowel and simplification of the consonantal cluster. It should be noted that the continuum does not include the theoretically possible form *[lɛt], i.e. application of rule (a), but not (b).

The forms for 'black' (Italian *nero* < Latin NIGRU(M)) appear as ['nejru] in A, and as ['negar] and ['negro] in B and in a variety close to B. The first of these forms is generated from two rules: (a) gliding of the voiced velar stop, followed by a vibrant; and (b) addition of a final vowel to make pronunciation easier; the second from the application of (b) but not (a); the third from the application of neither rule, coupled with the epenthesis of the vowel /a/. The third form is similar to the only form found in the Milanese dialect, ['neger]. Once again, the repertoire does not include the form *['nejar], i.e. the result of the application of rule (a), but not (b). The current Cevio dialect also includes the much more Italianised form [ner] derived from *nero* with a dropping of the final vowel which occurs as a general rule in the dialect unless the vowel is central low. This very productive rule allows insertion of any Italian word into the dialect and is therefore applied to all borrowed items.

The following implicational scales (Moretti 1988: 208–209) illustrate the relationships between these variants:

(5) (a) [a] → [ɛ]/___
           [+stress]

    (b) [−kt] → [tʃ]

	(a)	(b)	
	+	+	[lɛtʃ]
	−	+	[latʃ]
	−	−	[lat]

(6) (a) [g] → [j]/___ [+vibr]

    (b) Ø/[+cons][r] ___ → [+voc]
                              [+back]

	(a)	(b)	
	+	+	['nejru]
	−	+	['negro]
	−	−	['negar]

What conclusions can be drawn from these examples? The first is commonplace: as we have already stated, Italianisation readily produces many alternative forms, and greatly augments variability in the repertoire. Second, Italianisation can lead to forms that are more distant from standard Italian than the original, dialectal forms. This is certainly true of ['negro] and ['negar] as compared to ['nejru]. In this context, interdialectal contact must be taken into account, and hence the influence of the prestige dialect, the koine or the dialect of the towns, on the rural and peripheral dialects. For instance, in the Andorno Valley, Piedmont, innovative and archaic forms coexist: [fø] 'fire' (Ital. *fuoco*) alongside the older [fe]; [bø] 'ox' (Ital. *bue*) alongside older [be]; [œtʃ] 'eye' (Ital. *occhio*) alongside older ['eddǧo], etc. (Berruto 1970: 29–30). The influence of Turin Piedmontese, which serves as the prestige model for the rural dialects of Piedmont, is evident: Turinese has [fø], [bø], and [œj]. Modelling of these phenomena requires two dimensions, one horizontal and one vertical. The third conclusion that can be drawn from our implicational scales is that they represent co-occurrence constraints imposed on the rules that engender variants which allow them to be ranked, whether chronologically or in terms of nearness/distance of the systems: rule (a) is more archaic or typical of the dialect and distant from the standard language than rule (b), etc. This corroborates the conclusions drawn by Auer (1997) in his very convincing and detailed discussion of the importance of such constraints in the treatment of variation and convergence between a standard language and dialects.

Another interesting question can be asked at this point: what is the structural position of the Italianised dialect in the repertoire? Let us go back to the Ticino for a moment. Moretti (1988: 263–264) maintains that, in terms of structural resemblance, B, the more advanced, Italianised dialect variety which comprises [lat] and [ner], is closer to Italian than to the archaic dialect A, which has [lɛtʃ] and ['nejru]. B, therefore, should no longer be regarded as a variety of the dialect, but as a variety of Italian (C), and, hence, it represents an example of what can be called 'dialect assimilation', as in diagram 1:

Diagram 1

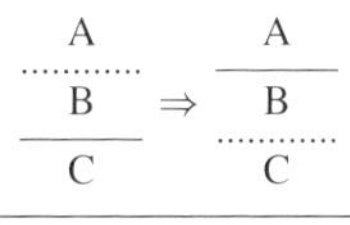

$$
\begin{array}{ccc}
\text{A} & & \text{A} \\
\cdots\cdots & & \overline{} \\
\text{B} & \Rightarrow & \text{B} \\
\overline{} & & \cdots\cdots \\
\text{C} & & \text{C}
\end{array}
$$

This assertion may seem risky. Since they satisfy certain basic dialectal rules, the morphology and the phonetic form of the Italianised dialect are essentially those of the dialect. Even so, it cannot be denied that convergence, or advergence, has led to considerable changes in the structure of the repertoire.

In the polymorphous dynamics of standard/dialect contact, particular attention must be paid to a fourth class of phenomena, namely hybridisation. Hybrid lexical forms are constructed from surface materials and the morphological rules of the two systems (see Kachru 1983: 147–155; Berruto 1989: 114), e.g. a lexical and/or derivational morpheme of the dialect with the inflectional and/or derivational morpheme of std. Italian, or vice versa. *Ner* 'black' in Cevio may represent such a case of hybridisation of the Italian lexical morpheme *nero* (*ner-o*) and the dialectal inflectional morpheme (MASC SG = Ø). Another example is *frisiun* 'clutch' with Italian *fris-,* phonetically adapted to the dialect, and the dialectal derivational nominaliser *-iun-* plus the dialectal inflectional morpheme Ø. An example operating in the opposite direction is regional Italian *rangiare* 'to adjust' (st. Italian *aggiustare*), which is composed of the Piedmontese lexical morpheme [randǧ-] and the std. Italian infinitive ending *-are.*

In the recent literature on language contact, especially in the work of Myers-Scotton, these hybrids are regarded as instances of code-switching or code-mixing, in which a transition from one system to another takes place within a word. My personal feelings run counter to this interpretation. In my opinion, one can no longer speak of code-switching within the limits of the word. The constraints imposed by word formation and morphology are not the same as those imposed by syntax. The difference between code-mixing and hybrids becomes very clear when the mixing of formatives from the two systems is more complicated. For instance, in *ndove* 'where' from Italian *dove* (< Latin DE UBI) and Piedmontese *ndua* (< Latin IN DE UBI) we find Italianisation of the second formative (*-dove*) and retention of the first, dialectal formative *n-* (Grassi and Pautasso 1989: 171, 173). The difference is equally evident in verb forms such as *favo* '(I) was doing' (Grassi and Pautasso 1989: 172), Ital. *facevo,* Biella Piedmontese *fava,* where the dialect stem of the imperfect is combined with the first person singular ending of Italian, and *scrivivo* '(I) was writing' (Grassi and Pautasso 1989: 177), Ital. *scrivevo,* Biella Piedmont. *scrivìa,* where the stem vowel of the dialect morpheme of the imperfect is maintained and combined with the Italian personal ending (hybridisation thus occurs within an inflection morpheme in this case). Another example is provided by *quaiduno* 'someone' (Grassi and Pautasso 1989: 176), Ital. *qualcuno* (or *qualcheduno*), Piedmont. *quaidün,* where the first formative comes from the dialect and the second (including the inflectional ending *-o* = MASC) from Italian.

An utterance such as:

(7)   *lo scrivivo un poco il francese*
       '(I) used to write it a little, the French'

would probably be analysed *à la* Myers-Scotton as code-switching with Italian as the matrix language and a mixed constituent *lo scrivivo* containing an element (a grammatical morpheme? see below) from the dialect (*-ivo*). I, on the other hand, would treat examples of this kind simply as a sentence in Italian (since the morphology is entirely Italian) containing a hybrid lexical form.

The formation of hybrids deserves particular attention for three reasons.

(a) It may be thought to represent a critical moment in the dynamics of the relationship between standard Italian and the dialects, since it implies a certain degree of fusion of the two grammars and may thus promote the birth of a mixed or fused lect. At the present time, however, the forms it gives rise to are, apart from a few exceptions, still attributable either to Italian or to the dialect (and here it is the inflectional morphology which decides). Moreover, hybrids are sporadic manifestations that do not form paradigms.

(b) Hybridisation has to do with Trudgill's 'interdialect' (Trudgill 1988). By this I mean that hybrids would seem to be a particular case in the broad category of forms that arise through the interaction of varieties in contact, and would in no way occur in the original varieties.

(c) There is a link between interaction (discourse) and convergence in the system. This is so because in contexts of structural interference and mixing, there is also convergence in use, i.e. standard language and dialect are simultaneously present in discourse, via code-switching and code-mixing. Their joint presence in the utterance of one and the same speaker is undoubtedly favoured by the existence of a core of lexical forms common to the standard language and the dialects. Whether it is because they are genetically closely related, or because of convergence, the two systems have in their lexicon numerous homonyms: many functional parts of speech, such as prepositions, conjunctions and adverbs, and certain verb forms (cf.: *da* 'from', *fra* 'between/among', *ma* 'but', *prima* 'before', *va* '(he/she/it) goes', *sta* '(he/she/it) stands', etc.) but also some nouns, such as *età* 'age', are the same in standard Italian, Sicilian, Piedmontese, Ticinese, etc.

Clyne (1967) has underscored the importance of such homophonous forms as triggers of code-switching. Alfonzetti (1992: 240) found that standard Italian/Sicilian homophones were involved in one-third (162) of the code-switched utterances in her corpus. Much the same proportion was also observed by Bozzini (1994) in a Ticino corpus.[1] It seems quite natural for the transition from one system to another to take place with the help of a homophone, since this has the effect of 'neutralising' the difference between the two languages.

The effect of this joint presence seems exactly parallel to that of the convergence in the system. There is: (a) a relative absence of conflict between the two

---

[1] In the Italian/Ticinese example given by Bozzini (1994: 111):

(8)   tanto in discesa *va giü anga i sass*
           'when descending in any case, *even the stones go down*'

it is interesting to note that the form *va* is certainly homophonous in Italian and the dialect; its semantics and its morphosyntactics, however, are dialectal (*andà giü* 'to descend', with the third person singular made to agree with a subject in the third person plural).

language systems, and hence they are regarded by the language community as broadly interchangeable in ordinary conversation; (b) a certain functional overlap of standard Italian and dialect; (c) a certain situational underdetermination of the code choice; and (d) an ideological innocence, if one may use such an expression, in the employment of Italian and dialect (see Alfonzetti 1996).

3   Code-switching, Code-mixing, and Language Contact

It is now time to examine the question of code-switching more specifically from the linguistic standpoint. Since the Italian speakers are to some extent bilingual in Italian and dialect, instances of code-switching and/or code-mixing[2] can be studied which provide significant insights for a theory of code-switching in general. Unfortunately, up to date little has been written about code-switching between a standard language and a primary dialect (see, however, Giacalone Ramat 1995; Vandekerckhove 1998). The model which has acquired growing importance in the analysis of code-switching during the last few years is Carol Myers-Scotton's Matrix Language Frame model (cf. Myers-Scotton 1993). Its basic assumption is well known, namely that in all cases where two language systems are intermingled there is always a matrix language that determines and governs the morphosyntactical framework of the sentence produced. We shall come back to the crucial notion of a matrix language later. What is of interest at this point is that in mixed constituents, i.e. syntagmata composed of elements from the two languages – matrix language (ML) and embedded language (EL) – the system morphemes must come from/are supplied by the ML.[3]

In the case of code-switching and code-mixing between Italian and the Italoromance dialects (and it may be said *en passant* that Myers-Scotton draws no distinction between code-switching and code-mixing, i.e. between intersentential and intrasentential code-switching, nor does she make any significant distinction between code-switching and borrowing), this principle is often contradicted. To begin with, one frequently finds utterances that contain a mixed noun phrase in which the article does not belong to what is presumably the ML of the discourse, whereas all the other constituents of the phrase do. The article is typically a system morpheme as identified by Myers-Scotton: it is [+Quantifier], [−θ role-assigner], [−θ role receiver]. Here are some examples (see also Franceschini, 1998: 58):[4]

---

[2] For a concise account, see Berruto 1997b.
[3] It should be added that Myers-Scotton identifies system morphemes from their features as '[+Quantifier]' or '[θ role-assigner]', or '[−θ role receiver]' (in the sense in which these terms are used in generative grammar).
[4] The Italian parts are in Roman script, the dialect parts either in italics or in IPA. The relevant items are underlined.

(9)   al lunedì vado a vedere _el_ mercato
        'on Monday, I go and have a look at *the* market'
        (Marcato, Ursini, and Politi 1974: 110; Ital./*Venetian*)

(10)   _u_ portiere non sta più lì da tanto tempo
        '*the* concierge hasn't been living there for quite some time'
        (Alfonzetti 1992: 175; Ital./*Sicilian*)

(11)   avvocato, _i_ bollette _dô_ o _dâ_ luce è stato provveduto che arrivano al
        suo ufficio?
        'counsellor, have steps been taken to see that *the* bills *for the* gas or
        for the electricity reach your office?'
        (Alfonzetti 1992: 205)

(12)   nel [kan'tun ru ʃku'sa, ar in'vɛrts, el vul'taven sy] _nei_ [bork], e
        bevevano
        'in the *canton, on the other hand, the* (= their) *apron, they chucked it*
        into the *ditches,* and they drank'
        (Tibiletti Bruno 1974: 212; Ital./*Lombard*)

In examples (11) and (12), the definite articles are partly combined with prepositions to form independent morphemes (*d(i)* + *o, d(i)* + *a*), which must here
be regarded as system morphemes taken from the EL, i.e. the dialect in (11)
and Italian in (12). The preposition *di* is also a system morpheme, since it is
$[-\theta$ role-assigner] and $[-\theta$ role-receiver].

There are also numerous examples of noun phrases with a demonstrative
pronoun, another typical system morpheme, taken from the EL:

(13)   d'altra parte _chiddi_ se stanno a casa non producono
        'besides, if *those* stay at home, they do not produce'
        (Alfonzetti 1992: 195; Ital./*Sicilian*)[5]

(14)   se poteva portare, perché c'è _ddu_ poveretto _ca_ mi telefona, avanza
        soldi ancora, devo chiudere quel conticino

        'if he could bring [that], because there is *that* poor chap *who*
        telephones me, he needs more money, I must settle that little
        account' (Alfonzetti 1992: 235)

One can also find noun phrases in which other classes of EL system morphemes are inserted, such as quantifiers:

---

[5] In this example, and there are many like it, it is also difficult to determine the constituent of which
the demonstrative is a part, since it may, in effect, be a noun phrase on its own account. In this
case, we would not be dealing with a mixed constituent, but an EL island, as is clearly envisaged
by the model. A better solution, however, is to regard the entire clause *chiddi . . . non producono*
as a mixed constituent.

(15)   insomma, [tyt] le intemperie che possono capitare
        'in short, *all* the bad weather that can happen'
        (Tibiletti Bruno 1974: 220; Ital./*Lombard*)

possessives:

(16)   allora noi andavamo sempre alla *nosa* messa
        'then we always went to *our* Mass'
        (Grassi and Pautasso 1989: 80; Ital./*Piedmontese*)

relative pronouns/complementizers (see also example 14):

(17)   *acchiappassi a tutti chissi che* possono pagare. *Ci facissi tirari u
        coddu*
        '*I would catch all those* who can pay. *I'd get their necks wrung*'
        (Alfonzetti 1992: 188; Ital./*Sicilian*)

(here I regard *tutti chissi che possono pagare*, a noun phrase with an embedded relative clause, as a mixed constituent); adverbs of time:[6]

(18)   *oh . . . ma adès ül-* ultimamente *quan ch'i sun andà via mi eru lì*
        Albertville
        'oh. . but now la- lastly *when they went away, I was there at*
        Albertville'
        (Pautasso 1990: 146; Ital./*Piedmontese*)

There are also cases in which EL inflectional endings are inserted:

(19)   fac*iavi* quattrocento, cinquecento di profitto
        'you *were* making a profit of four or five hundred'
        (Grassi and Pautasso 1989: 172; Ital./*Piedmontese*)

Here, however, I must repeat that I do not agree with Myers-Scotton's treatment of code-switching on a par with the use of materials from two language systems within the bounds of a single word (see the previous discussion of hybrids): from my point of view, *faciavi* for Italian *facevi* is a typical hybridism.

In short, the general principle that the ML alone supplies the system morphemes within mixed constituents cannot be sustained. Myers-Scotton herself acknowledges the difficulty of applying it in situations 'where the switching is between dialects of the same language' (Myers-Scotton 1993: 17). The fact is, however, as I set out to show at the start of this chapter, that it is highly debatable to regard Italian and the Italoromance dialects as varieties of the same language. It seems to me reasonable to consider the Italian situation as one of

---

[6] On their nature as system morphemes, see Myers-Scotton 1997: 155.

contact and switching between two kindred linguistic systems drawn from a common stock, such as Italian and Spanish, or German and Dutch. Pellegrini (1972) has shown, on the basis of forty-four phonetic/phonologic and morphosyntactic features, that the linguistic distance between Standard Italian and, for example, the dialect of Lucania or the Cadorino (a rural variety of Venetian) is greater than that between Italian and Spanish and is approximately the same as between Italian, Portuguese, and Romanian.

At this point, one may rightly question the validity of the ML concept itself. This is of more than merely secondary importance. 'Matrix language recognition' is a decisive factor in the application of the model to language contact in general. According to Myers-Scotton, an ML is established on both socio-linguistic and psycholinguistic grounds: it is the dominant language within a group, the unmarked choice for interaction, and the language in which the speaker is most fluent and which s/he prefers. One could already object at this point that the two criteria, social dominance and individual preference, do not necessarily coincide. Myers-Scotton (1997: 153–154), however, proposes four working criteria for defining and identifying a matrix language: (i) 'the ML . . . is the language of more morphemes for the entire discourse'; (ii) 'also in the specific CS passage under study, the ML . . . is the language of relatively greater morpheme frequency . . . , if a "discourse-relevant" sample of at least two sentences is studied'; (iii) 'the ML is defined by participant judgements. It is the language which the subjects engaged in CS will perceive as "the language we are speaking"'; (iv) 'the ML is the language from which the lexical-conceptual and predicate-arguments structures, as well as the morphological realization patterns, of mixed constituents are projected'.

Now, criterion (iii) is highly problematical. It cannot be convincingly applied to cases where the speakers continually switch to and fro between two linguistic systems. Situations of this kind can be readily found not only in the case of Italian and the Italoromance dialects but also in the numerous instances of bilingualism due to immigration in Europe (e.g. young Italians in German-speaking Switzerland, Arabic speakers in France, etc.: see Bentahila and Davies 1998). In addition, this criterion cannot be reconciled with the fact that several communities use special terms for the code-switched ways of speaking, such as *mikjimap,* alternating use of the mother tongue and Kriol, an English-based form of Creole, by the Gurindjis of Northern Australia (McConvell 1988); *apneap,* alternating use of pidgin English and Kalawlagawya, by other Australian Aboriginals (Romaine 1989b: 113); *wolof urbain,* a mixture of Wolof and French in Dakar (Swigart 1992). One can also quote conflicting 'participant judgements', such as the well-known remark of one of the English–Spanish code-switchers studied by Poplack (1980): 'Sometimes I'll start a sentence in English *y termino en español*', or that of a young Italian in German Switzerland reported by Pizzolotto (1991: 63): 'Quando parli italiano ti viene un momento, che dopo parli, *wäisch, tuesch mische Tüütsch und Italienisch*' ('when you are speaking Italian, there comes a moment, after that you are speaking, *you know you are mixing Swiss German and Italian*').

Criterion (iv) cannot be taken into consideration by any means, since it is an example of circular reasoning. That the morphosyntactical structural framework and, hence, the selection of the system morphemes are determined by the ML is the *demonstrandum* in this vicious circle: identification of the ML should enable one to both foresee where the system morphemes will come from and determine the restrictions that will decide which structures are admissible and inadmissible in a given code-switching situation. The opposite approach, namely identification of the ML from the system morphemes of which the mixed constituents are composed, could well be an important criterion in itself. However, it is incongruent with the model and poses a substantial threat to its general predictive quality.

We are thus left with the quantitative, objective, and apparently sound criteria (i) and (ii). But here, the very notion of a system morpheme is an initial stumbling-block. Forms that in English and other languages are individual morphemes or monomorphemic words, such as articles, demonstratives, etc., are polymorphemic words in other languages with inflectional endings that could/should be further broken down and analysed. Italian is very much a case in point in this respect: e.g. *la* 'the' (FEM SG), ART DET FEM SG, is decomposable into *l-* ART DET and *-a* FEM SG, *quello* 'that' (MASC), DEM DIST MASC SG, is decomposable into *quell-* DEM DIST and *-o* MASC SG, and so on.

Yet even if we leave aside the well-known difficulties posed by the identification of morphemes in certain, especially inflectional, languages, there is still the question of why it is better to count morphemes rather than words. Let us take a portion of a discourse composed, say, of three sentences containing twenty words, namely fifteen in language A, which is isolating and, hence, each word in it is monomorphemic, and five in language B, which is agglutinating, and each word has an average of four morphemes. Literal application of Myers-Scotton's criteria shows that language B has the highest morpheme score (20 versus 15) and must therefore be the matrix language. The least that can be said about such a conclusion is that it is counter-intuitive.

Both the evidence against one important assumption of the model, namely that the system morphemes in mixed constituents must come from ML, and my theoretical discussion of the concept of a matrix language suggest that there are many instances of language contact and code-switching where there is no matrix language at all and thus, where the concept *à la* Myers-Scotton is inoperative. In a more recent study, Myers-Scotton (1999: 220) suggests that in certain cases a 'compromise strategy' results in the creation of a 'composite matrix language', in other words 'more than one language may participate in providing the components of the lexical structure of the de facto ML'. This solution, however, is not convincing. In the first place, it would take most of the stuffing out of the ML concept itself. In addition, Myers-Scotton (1999) presupposes that this strategy comes into play 'in contact situations such that speakers are NOT fully proficient in the preferred ML'. This is totally inappropriate for the situations described in this chapter. Dialect speakers in Italy, young Italians in German-speaking Switzerland, and Arabic speakers in France are often fully proficient in both language systems.

4   Conclusions

As a way of drawing together the threads I have spun, I would propose an analysis of language-contact phenomena based on the criterion of relative approximation/ progressive interpenetration of the two systems. Instances of such contact can be marshalled along a continuum that starts with an absence of contact and ends with the disappearance or 'annihilation' of the distance between two language systems, resulting in either total blending of the two languages and, hence, the formation of a veritable mixed language (or fused lect), or the disappearance of one of them in ordinary use, i.e. language shift. A third possibility is the assimilation of one linguistic system to the other: the varieties of one system would, in this way, become the varieties of the other through progressive advergence (diagram 1).

As sketched out in diagram 2, one can identify phenomena running along the two lines of this continuum: those concerning the structures or features of a language system, and those concerning the situational usage of a language. The first stage of the system line involves semantic and lexical borrowing; the second in interference, especially in morphosyntax. The usage line has three stages. The first is simple code alternation, in other words, employment of one language or the other to suit the person spoken to, the field of reference, or the situation. The second is (intersentential) code-switching, in other words the alternating use of sentences in two languages during the same discourse and with the same interlocutor. The third is code-mixing, i.e. employment of surface materials of both languages in the construction of individual sentences. Both lines join in a further stage in which hybrids are formed. Each successive stage should correspond to a more intimate degree of approximation in use and of the structural interpenetration of the two systems. Contact does not necessarily lead to one of the scenarios I have described: two systems can remain for centuries in continuous contact, and display the range of phenomena linked to such contact to a more or less marked degree and in a virtually stable manner.

Diagram 2

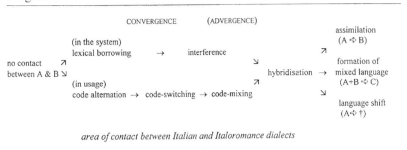

CONVERGENCE   (ADVERGENCE)

assimilation
(A ⇨ B)

(in the system)

lexical borrowing   →   interference

no contact

between A & B

formation of
hybridisation → mixed language
(A+B ⇨ C)

(in usage)

code alternation → code-switching → code-mixing

language shift
(A⇨ †)

area of contact between Italian and Italoromance dialects

There is no space to explain this diagram in detail. I can only point out that the classification of phenomena and the preferential hierarchy indicated in it fit in very well with the typology, albeit founded on a slightly different base, presented and very carefully argued for by Auer (1999b) with a wealth of empirical data.

In contact between Italian and the Italoromance dialects, all the milestones of my continuum are readily visible, in the absence of any substantial indications that any of the 'catastrophic' ends of the road are being reached. It is this multiplicity of contact that makes the Italian situation a very fertile field for the application and testing of theories and methods of analysing variation due to language contact.

4   Convergence and divergence in grammar

Leonie Cornips and Karen Corrigan

1   Introduction

This chapter offers an overview of the most salient current frameworks for analysing processes of convergence and divergence cross-dialectally (including those which occur between standard languages and related dialects) at the grammatical level. It also develops the view expressed in Wilson and Henry (1998) and Kallen (this volume) that combining insights from various models can enhance our understanding of the mechanisms of linguistic variation and change. The paradigms in question are the so-called 'generative' programme of Chomsky (1995) and the 'variationist' approach of Labov (1994). The emphasis in the former on 'top-down' theories of language has led to its being described as an 'Internalist' framework that conceives of 'Grammar' as having no external existence. This perspective is, however, contested by variationists, who have developed a 'bottom-up' or 'Externalist' model which takes 'Grammar' to be a product which is primarily socio-cultural rather than biological.[1] Consequently, each framework operates distinctive methods of analysis and the object of study in typical investigations which rely on these models is also markedly different. Variationists, for example, emphasise the systematic recording and analysis of socially situated language samples with due regard for the so-called

This research was funded by the British Council and the Netherlands Organization for Scientific Research (NWO) *via* the UK-Dutch Joint Scientific Research Programme (Project No. JRP643). We would like to take this opportunity to thank these institutions for their financial support and we are also grateful to Joan Beal, Dave Britain, Carol Fehringer, Frans Hinskens, Dick Hudson, Lesley Milroy, Salikoko Mufwene, Marc van Oostendorp, Ian Roberts and Sali Tagliamonte for their extremely helpful comments on a draft version of this chapter. Any remaining shortcomings are, of course, our own.

[1] The notions 'top-down' and 'bottom-up' are borrowed from language processing models where the former refers to the type of processing which relies on prior knowledge to predict or enhance the perceived event or message. The latter, on the other hand, is used in connection with perceptual processing which extracts information directly from the sensory signal (for example, voice quality). These terms are used metaphorically here to capture the difference between internalist (largely theory-oriented) and externalist (largely data-oriented) models of language as either being a state of mind/brain wholly internal to the individual ('top-down') or a matter of the customs/conventions of (different) speech communities ('bottom-up') (cf. Pinker 1994: 184 *et passim*).

'observer's paradox' and the unreliability of speaker-judgements (cf. Bell 1984; Giles 1984; Labov 1975, 1996; Le Page 1997; and Trudgill 1986). This type of research often focuses on speakers of non-standard dialects who are in contact with others in their community using a standard variety with much greater social prestige.[2] A major task facing analysts operating within this model is to determine whether there is statistical evidence for 'horizontal'/'vertical' convergence or divergence that can be correlated to some degree with social variables. Quantitative analysis in this model is not, however, restricted to ascertaining the significance of the sociocultural correlates of inherent variability, since even the earliest studies engaged with linguistic issues *pur sang* such as ascertaining the probability of occurrence of grammatical constructions in certain linguistic environments (cf. Cedergren and Sankoff 1974; Labov 1969, 1972a, 1994; and Sankoff 1974). By contrast, advocates of the biolinguistic programme contend that such external (performance) evidence is 'irrelevant to linguistics' (Smith 1989: 180) – the goal of which is perceived within this paradigm to be the refinement of our understanding of the underlying rules and principles that constitute an individual's 'knowledge of language' or competence (cf. Chomsky 1976, 1986b; Labov 1972b: 260ff., 1975; Milroy 1984a, 1985, and 1996; and Wilson and Henry 1998). Given this objective, it has been expedient to assert that a suitable investigative tool is native-speaker introspection in an idealised environment. In practice, as we plan to demonstrate in section 2.2, this often means that the resultant analyses reflect the grammaticality judgements of the theorist who may be unaware of the considerable degree of syntactic variation which potentially exists within the same speech community (Milroy and Milroy 1997: 47).

Although there remain certain formal resonances between the generative and variationist paradigms, the methodological differences between the two approaches to grammar created a schism between them which persisted through most of the later twentieth century (cf. Cheshire 1987, 1999; Kroch 1989; Sankoff 1988; Hudson 1985, 1986, 1995, 1997; and Rickford 1988). In this regard, Wilson and Henry (1998: 2) note that 'there have been few real attempts to marry these seemingly divergent positions' and Meechan and Foley (1994: 63), likewise, suggest that theoretical syntacticians and sociolinguists 'rarely, if ever, cross paths'. Nevertheless, researchers have occasionally engaged with

---

[2] Cf. Hinskens (1998b); Milroy (1987: 118); Harris (1984, 1996). In addition, the reader should note that, despite the orientation of 'classic' variationist accounts, there have been relatively few (of the sort outlined here) which handle processes of convergence/divergence as well as might be expected. This is partly due to the prevailing view within this type of research that speech communities are isolated from a perceived standard which obtains outwith its confines, yet is, nevertheless, capable of exerting considerable normative influence. Exceptions to this would include the variationist research that has more recently been developed with reference to contact models by Britain (1997, 2002a); Gerritsen (1999); Hinskens (1996); Kerswill (1994); Schilling-Estes (2000); and Trudgill (1986, 1994) *inter alia.*

the notion that inherent variability that is quantifiable has the potential not only to assess but also to refine theoretical conceptions of linguistic structure.[3] As we observe in sections 2.2–3.5 below, the possibility of utilising convergent/divergent grammatical data for just this purpose has gained momentum since the publication of Chomsky (1981b), which was the first attempt systematically to incorporate cross-linguistic, though not 'inherent', diversity within the paradigm.

2   Literature Review

For present purposes, studies in the literature review which follows are categorised according to their major orientation, ignoring the fact that there is an amount of overlap between approaches by certain authors. The survey is not intended to be an exhaustive one, nor will it be strictly chronological. Instead, we plan to focus on major themes relevant to the original research described in sections 3–3.5 and to the investigation of convergence and divergence in grammar more generally.

2.1   Sociolinguistic approaches to syntactic variation

Although variationist research was initially as focused on matters of morphosyntactic variability as it was on those relating to the lexical and phonological levels, the body of research on the latter outweighs that devoted to morphosyntactic matters.[4] However, as Britain (2002a), Kallen and Kirk (2001), and Schilling-Estes (2000) confirm, researchers in this framework have increasingly begun to refocus on issues relating to syntactic variation and dialect divergence within a dialect contact model as originally articulated in Harris (1984) and (1996). Perhaps the most important signal of this volte-face was the publication in 1991 of a monograph devoted to accounts of grammatical variability edited by Peter Trudgill and Jack Chambers. This collection describes constructions typical of traditional dialects which diverge both vertically and horizontally in that newer, related varieties have innovated from them. As such, they present unusual data for the modelling of linguistic variation and change in the fields of generative linguistics, historical linguistics, and sociolinguistics. The volume also contains analyses from urban communities (Cheshire 1991a; and Eisikovits 1991a, in particular) which augment previous research extending the Labovian

---

[3] Early examples of research with such an orientation can be seen in the collection of papers from a 1987 *CLS* Parasession on variation in linguistic theory edited by Beals *et al.* (1994).

[4] Strictly speaking, we exclude here research on pidgin and creole varieties, such as Winford (1984), in which the relationship between morphosyntax and variability was always more central.

paradigm to processes of linguistic variability at the grammatical rather than the phonological levels.[5]

As noted in section 1, the methodological practices of this framework are distinctive and most investigations begin by specifying a finite set of theoretical assumptions – normally in the form of working hypotheses and often arising from prior knowledge of the speech community in question. A representative sample of speakers is identified and they are recorded under reasonably controlled conditions. Systematic analysis of a substantial quantity of the data which ensues is undertaken and the criteria which govern the description of the speech samples themselves are exacting. In the first place, the identification of tokens must be as specified by the 'Principle of Accountable Reporting', namely, the total number of occurrences and the potential occurrences, i.e. non-occurrences, in the variable environment must be noted (Labov et al. 1968: 70). In addition, the 'Synonymy Principle' presupposes that tokens which have been identified as variants are, indeed, equivocal with regard to referential meaning (i.e. 'alternate ways of saying "the same" thing' Labov (1972b: 118)). The final objective is to contrast speech samples with respect to the frequency of occurrence of each individual variant as a proportion of the number of occasions when it could have occurred without altering referential meaning. The resultant figures can then be used in a sociolinguistic analysis of the data to classify factors (internal and external) in the environment which affect the distribution of variants and with which individual variants can, therefore, be assumed tendentially to co-occur.[6]

There has been a tendency (particularly within those variationist studies conducted in North America such as Sells et al. 1996a,b) to overemphasise the internal constraints on morphosyntactic variation at the expense of external considerations, which is not the case with research within the model on phonological variability. Indeed, one might go so far as to suggest that our knowledge of the degree to which external factors, such as education or ethnicity, are salient to variation at the level of morphosyntax remains considerably less sophisticated as a result.

---

[5] Investigations with this orientation include: Bayley and Pease-Alvarez (1996); Beals et al. (1994); Britain (1997, 1999, 2002a); Cedergren and Sankoff (1974); Cheshire (1982, 1985, 1987, 1998, 1999); Cornips (1994, 1996b, 1998a); Coveney (2000); Cukor-Avila and Bailey (1996); Dines (1980); Eisikovits (1991b); Kikai et al. (1987); King and Nadasdi (1996); Kroch and Small (1978); Labov (1969, 1972a); Lefèbvre (1989); Lemieux (1987); Naro (1981); Policansky (1976, 1982); Romaine (1980a, 1980b, 1982, 1984a); Sankoff (1973, 1974); Sankoff and Vincent (1977); Seppänen (1999); Tagliamonte (1997, 1998); Tagliamonte and Hudson (1999); Tagliamonte and Poplack (1988); Tagliamonte and Smith (1999); and Weiner and Labov (1983).

[6] This is an oversimplification of the method which will suffice for present purposes. Cf. Chambers (1995); Coulmas (1997: Parts I and II); Hudson (1996); Labov (1994); Milroy (1987); and Milroy and Milroy (1997).

As noted above, there has also been a more general reluctance to focus on morphosyntactic aspects of dialectal differences within this paradigm and a number of reasons have been cited as crucial in this regard. Those that have received most attention in the literature are: (i) the quantification of syntactic variation; and (ii) the indeterminacy of synonymy/functional equivalence. Both contribute to Labov's (1991: 277) assertion that 'Syntactic change is an elusive process as compared to sound change', though the latter became less of an issue as the model evolved during the 1990s, as we will demonstrate below.[7] Observing phonological variants in a manner which is accountable to the data is relatively straightforward even when the social dialect corpus is of modest proportions since these are, by their nature, relatively frequently occurring. It is not difficult to meet Labov's (1966: 181) requirement of '10–20 instances' and many researchers have been able to base their analyses on the > 30 tokens per variable per speaker prescription advocated by Guy (1974). The open-ended nature of syntax, by contrast, entails that systematic observations of linguistic and social variability within dialect grammars often produce very small numbers of tokens indeed. Consequently, this level of language is regularly perceived within the paradigm to be less accessible to both speech communities and linguistic analysis for the purpose of creating social indices. In fact, as table 4.1 indicates, there can be a considerable range in the frequency of variants available. Furthermore, the robustness of the data appears to depend as much on the type of variable being investigated as it does on the size of the corpus. Thus, while Corrigan (1997) records a greater number of restrictive relative clause tokens than do Tottie and Rey (1997) or Policansky (1982), the same corpus (n = 52,000 words) contains only 3 tokens of the 'Hot-News' *after* perfect which both Kallen (1991: 63–64), Kallen and Kirk (2001: 73), and Harris (1984: 317) also observe to be relatively infrequent.[8]

Despite the apparent paucity of tokens in some of the research cited in table 4.1, the distributional results which they reveal with respect to age, gender, and grammatical constraints, for example, suggest that the frequency question is not insoluble and that accessibility to robust data sets may not be paramount in certain cases – even when the social and linguistic restrictions operating on

[7] Detailed accounts of (i) are available in: Britain (1999); Cedergren and Sankoff (1974); Cheshire (1998); Hudson (1986, 1996, 1997a, 1997b); Kroch (1994); Labov (1969, 1972a); Naro (1981); Sankoff (1973); Sankoff (1988); Sankoff and Labov (1979); Singh and Ford (1989); and Wilson and Henry (1998). A comprehensive overview of (ii) can be obtained from: Cheshire (1985, 1987, 1999); Coveney (2000); Dines (1980); Fasold (1991); Harris (1984, 1996); Jacobson (1985, 1989); Labov (1978, 1991, 1996); Lavandera (1978); Lefèbvre (1989); Romaine (1980b, 1984b, 1984c); Weiner and Labov (1983); Winford (1996); and Wolfram (1975, 1991).

[8] Examples of these variables from Corrigan (1997) would be: (i) Restrictive relative clauses, namely, 'Subject-Contact/Zero Relative': *The magistrate ø was to try him was an old soldier too;* 'TH-relative': *Matha Locklin **that** lived under the roof with Padgy Bug;* 'WH-relative': *Coulter handed back the bottle of water **which** Smyth placed on the shelf;* and (ii) 'Hot-News Perfect': *One of the farls **was after** breaking.*

Table 4.1 *Tokens of variable X systematically observed in nine sociolinguistic investigations of syntactic variation*[a]

Investigation	Variable construction	N Tokens
Rickford *et al.* (1995: 102)	**AS FAR AS is concerned/ø +NP/ Gerund Complement** *As far as the white servants ø, it isn't clear*	**1,200+**
Corrigan (1997: 337)	**Restrictive Relative Clause** *The magistrate ø was to try him was an old soldier too*	**633**
Tagliamonte and Hudson (1999: 147)	**BE LIKE Quotative** *and they're like, 'Come on, go and get dressed'*	**199**
Tottie and Rey (1997: 226)	**Restrictive Relative Clause** *We killed bears an' panthers an' things like that **what** was eating up the stock*	**164**
Feagin (1979: 128)	**Aux+ Completive DONE +past participle** *I may have **done** lost it*	**161**
Britain (1999: 199)	**AS FAR AS is concerned/ø +NP/ Gerund Complement** *There were divisions **as far as** what roles there might have been*	**156**
Policansky (1982: 43)	**Restrictive Relative Clause** *All the fellers **that** we used to play with lived on the other side of the road*	**122**
Kallen (1991: 66)	**'Hot-News'AFTER Perfect** *It's **after** getting very long*	**114**
Tagliamonte and Smith (1999: 8)	**WERE Past Tense** *She said I **were** going to remain home*	**62**

[a] The reader should note that the studies in this table differ with respect to the size of corpora analysed. Thus, Britain (1999) relies on a 2 million word corpus, whereas in Corrigan (1997) it is a mere 52,000. In some cases (Rickford *et al.* 1995, for example) corpus size is not mentioned at all. In addition, while Tagliamonte and Hudson (1999: 158) expressly comment in their paper that they have observed 199 tokens of *be like* quotatives from a total quotative corpus of 1,277, the studies differ in the degree to which they are explicit about the total number of tokens from which variable X is drawn, and this should be borne in mind when evaluating the extent to which the investigations in table 4.1 are absolutely comparable – at least from a methodological perspective.

the variable are highly complex (cf. Romaine 1980b: 191–192). For instance, although the corpus of Tagliamonte and Smith (1999: 13), by their own admission, is 'severely limited' with regard to the number of *were* tokens that could be isolated, it, nevertheless, reveals a pattern for constructions such as *She **were** young too* for standard *She **was** young too* that conforms to 'that reported for most vernaculars of English, that is, levelling of *was* rather than *were*' (1999: 14), namely, divergence from standard English. Following on from Romaine's (1980b) suggestion (based on findings such as these) that there should be no absolute blueprint with respect to numbers of tokens, Britain (1999) concurs. He suggests that this may well be because: (i) grammatical variables often show sharp rather than gradient patterning; and (ii) 'grammatical variation is generally more socially diagnostic than phonological variation' (1999: 204). Indeed, certain sociolinguistic accounts of syntactic variation, given the low frequency of tokens, have proceeded on the hypothesis that fewer occurrences may be required to uncover statistically significant grammatical patterning within speech communities, though it remains to be seen whether universal principles are involved here that correlate, somehow, with the nature of individual morphosyntactic variables. This approach is particularly successful when investigating 'low-level' morphological variation, since it rests on the assumption that, from a purely external, social perspective, syntax may well be unable to function as subtly as phonological variation can. Hence, the stratification of 'low-level' morphosyntactic variants, even with relatively few tokens, is generally sharp since the middle class and well educated, for instance, will be likely to show near-categorical usage of standard forms (cf. Britain 1999: 200–205; Corrigan 1997; Chambers 1995: 51 and 116; Romaine 1980b; Wolfram 1969: 120–121, 1991: 95).[9]

There are other, 'higher-level' morphosyntactic variables, however, where the frequency problem is compounded by issues relating to pragmatic and semantic conditioning. As we noted earlier, applying the 'Principle of Synonymy' to morphosyntactic data is problematic for reasons that we can only outline in the present context. Central to the issue is deciding precisely how the sociolinguistic variable is to be defined. There was a revision in its interpretation suggested by Labov (1969) which introduced the concept of the 'variable rule', later further refined in Cedergren and Sankoff (1974); and Sankoff and Labov (1979). It

---

[9] We conjecture that it is, indeed, possible to distinguish between types of morphosyntactic variable ('low level' *vs.* 'high level'), though this is an area with respect to convergence and divergence in grammar which is in need of further research. Variables that are termed 'low level' here refer to those that are either purely morphological or purely syntactic, such as the contrast between preterite variants in English dialects (*I **come/came** to York yesterday*) discussed by Cheshire (1994). 'High-level' variables (introduced below) are those which might be classified as operating at the interface of levels of the grammar (between syntax and semantics/pragmatics, say). A potential case in point would be the active/passive contrast discussed at length in Lavandera (1978); and Weiner and Labov (1983).

became an extension of the 'optional rule' construct which was recognised in the generative programme as a means of distinguishing non-'categorical' elements of the grammar. Such rules were neutral in that the choice of one variant over another had no impact on grammaticality and, since syntax was conceived of as autonomous, optional rules were, therefore, assumed to be immune to extra-linguistic factors. The 'variable rule' extended the original by recognising linguistic constraints which favoured/disfavoured the use of particular variants and the degree of variability could be further conditioned by social correlates.[10] Despite the fact that these were originally constructed to accommodate copula usage in African American Vernacular English (AAVE), it remained controversial as to whether one could postulate a syntactic 'variable rule' within the Labovian paradigm. While Sankoff (1973); and Weiner and Labov (1983) contended that it was, Cheshire (1987); Dines (1980); Lavandera (1978); Romaine (1984b,c); Sankoff (1988); and Winford (1996) *inter alia*, argued that there were a number of issues which remained unresolved. The restriction inherent in the definition of a 'variable rule' that it be constrained by 'sameness of meaning' was particularly contentious. Labov (1972b: 118) originally suggested that synonymy should be defined narrowly as 'having the same truth value'. Other scholars argued that this decontextualised view (akin to Chomsky's autonomous theorem) was difficult to apply on the basis that certain morphosyntactic variants normally occur in at least some pragmatic contexts where their propositional content is not synonymous and where they are not functionally equivalent (cf. Jacobson 1989; Lefèbvre 1989; Sankoff 1988; and Winford 1996). Lavandera (1978), for instance, asserts that such a definition of referentiality is too abstract in that the insistence on synonymy entails that in each case the alternating forms refer to the 'same state of affairs' (Weiner and Labov 1983: 82).[11] The dilemma can be illustrated by a brief examination of the 'Hot-News' *after* perfect mentioned earlier and illustrated again in (1) below, which is problematic on account of the fact that it is a 'high-level' variable conditioned by both syntactic and semantic/pragmatic constraints:

(1)   One of the farls [soda bread portion] **was after breaking**[12]
        (Corrigan (1997: 160))

Since the structure often occurs in contexts like this one where recency or completion is being signalled (hence, the term 'Hot-News'), one might postulate that the standard British English construction shown in (2) is a plausible variant:

---

[10] Differences between the traditional generative view of the variable rule and the sociolinguistic version are articulated in Singh and Ford (1989).

[11] Cheshire *et al.* (this volume) address the 'sameness of meaning' problem as well as the fact that it is often very difficult to obtain sufficient numbers of tokens for a given case of syntactic variation (the editors).

[12] In this particular context, the speaker was referring to an event in the recent past, i.e. that a piece of the soda bread had just broken off while it was being cooked on a griddle.

(2)   One of the farls **had just broken**

However, such an alternant would not be unequivocal. In fact, (2) violates the demand of strict synonymy and there is no absolute functional equivalence either since Kallen (1991: 62) has demonstrated that syntactically identical Irish–English perfective constructions to that represented by (1) can also be interpreted pragmatically as the universal perfect in variants such as (3) below:

(3)   All the week **is after being** cold

In 'divergent dialect situations' (Winford 1996: 180) such as this one, it is not at all straightforward to make the necessary assumption that speakers of the dialects in question share a 'panlectal identity' with respect to their grammatical systems and, hence, diverge from one another only superficially (cf. Harris 1996: 32; Hinskens 1998b: 174 and 177; Winford 1984, 1993, and 1996). The number of reported cases of miscommunication between such speakers demonstrates the lack of mutual intelligibility and the degree of deep-seated structural divergence which may actually pertain (cf. Milroy 1984b). This has led to the suggestion that variants such as those exemplified in (1) and (2) above are exponents of underlyingly distinctive grammars (standard vs. dialect) which are clearly divergent.[13]

It has also been argued that other higher level morphosyntactic variants are similarly problematic with respect to synonymy (cf. Cheshire 1987). Meaning in such cases is frequently mutable (non-conventional) and as such is highly contingent on the context of the utterance in spontaneous speech. Consequently, it has been suggested that morphosyntactic variation of this type rarely serves to differentiate social groups because of its dependence on pragmatic and semantic conditioning. Given the distinction, therefore, between 'classic' phonological and morphosyntactic variables which can be adequately handled by traditional variationist techniques, there are strong arguments for either excluding higher level morphosyntactic variables like these from such analyses or for relying on different methods of data collection. Hence, Labov (1975) and Harris (1983) used elicitation techniques in the analyis of internal constraints operating on negative attraction and perfectivity in divergent English dialects. Although it might be argued that this methodology is reminiscent of that favoured within the generative paradigm, there are important differences. In the first place, experimental sociolinguistic research relies on prior knowledge of variability within the speech community gained by observational methods and it is on this basis that hypotheses are formulated and tested. Secondly, sociolinguists who use this approach, unlike their generativist peers, take account of phenomena such as: (i) the observer's paradox;

---

[13] Lesley Milroy (p.c.) proposes that these outcomes are most likely when there is a historical language contact situation and this is corroborated by evidence from similar divergent dialects in Corrigan (1993, 1996, 1997, 2000); and Winford (1993, 1996).

(ii) speakers' attitudes towards stigmatised varieties; (iii) the repetition effect; (iv) the judging of syntactic constructions as ungrammatical simply on the basis of lexical items; and (v) the fact that written forms are unduly influenced by prescriptive educational practices (cf. Cheshire 1985, 1987, 1998, 1999; Cornips 1997, 2000; Coveney 2000; Harris 1983, 1984, 1996; Labov 1975; Milroy 1987; Silva-Corvalán 1994; Winford 1996 *inter alia* (see also the case study in section 3)).

2.2   *Parametric approaches to syntactic variation*

The biolinguistic programme sketched in section 1 conceives of Universal Grammar (UG) as a system of Principles and Parameters (P&P).[14] The latter are integrated within various subsystems of UG (Binding, Case, and Government). Given its 'Internalist' perspective, the P&P model offers no straightforward definition of either language or dialect *per se* since these are attributes of speech communities rather than individuals. Hence, languages are viewed essentially as abstractions and 'variation', in P&P terms, refers primarily to differences between individual grammars rather than between or within languages/dialects. The generic principles of UG would not, solely, accommodate the variation which exists between languages, since they are underspecified. The latter is accounted for by the so-called parameters which permit generative accounts of the extent to which variation is possible and the manner in which it is constrained: (i) between languages; (ii) within the acquisition of the same language; and (iii) between different historical states of the same language (cf. Wilson and Henry 1998: 4–5). Therefore, it would not be unreasonable to infer that a variety which has most parameter settings in common with another will be syntactically closer to it than it will be to others in which the parameter settings are different (cf. Brannigan 1996: 25; and Wilson and Henry 1998: 12). Hence, where a variety 'x' comes to share parameter settings with a variety 'y' as a result of linguistic variation and change, one might conceive of them as converging. By the same token, in cases where 'x' and 'y' share very few settings then this would argue for them being grammatically divergent.[15]

---

[14] For analyses of convergence/divergence in grammar within theoretical models not reviewed in this chapter like Cognitive Grammar (Langacker 1990, 1994; Hudson 1984, 1990, *inter alia*); Head-driven Phrase Structure Grammar (Pollard and Sag 1987, *inter alia*) and Lexical Functional Grammar (Bresnan 1995, *inter alia*), see Börjars *et al.* (1996); Börjars and Chapman (1998); Chapman (1995); and Hudson (1985, 1997a, 1997b).

[15] Intralectal parametric variation at the level of morphosyntax is discussed in: Abraham and Bayer (1993); Belletti (1993); Belletti and Shlonsky (1995); Benincà (1989, 1994, 1996); Bernstein (1991); Brandi and Cordin (1989); Burzio (1986); Christensen and Taraldsen (1989); Elordui (1998); Haegeman (1988, 1990, 1997); Henry (1992, 1994, 1995, 1996, 1997a, 1997b); Holmberg (1986); Jaeggli and Safir (1989); Kayne (1989a, 1989b, 1994); Landa and Franco (1996, 1998); McCloskey (1991, 1992); Muysken (1989); Platzack (1987); Sobin (1987); Suñer

A single abstract grammatical difference or parameter setting can be manifested in a number of constructions which are seemingly unrelated on the surface (like the problematic 'Hot-News' *after* vs. *'Have just'* perfect case outlined in section 2.1).[16] Hence, the classic *pro*-drop parameter is associated not only with the availability of null subjects in those languages which have a positive setting for the parameter ([+*pro*-drop] such as in Irish or Spanish) but also with the occurrence of: (i) post-verbal subjects (4); (ii) apparent violations of *that* trace effects (5); and (iii) a rich verbal morphology (4 and 5), illustrated in the Irish examples given below:

(4) *pro* **Tógaim**   bainne anois
     Ø   take-PR-1SG(post-verbal subject) milk   now
          take   *milk*   *now*
          'I take milk now'

(5) Cé   dúirt   tú   **a**   bposadh   í?
     INTERR say-PAST- you-2SG REL   marry-VN- her-3SG
             2SG   3SG
     who   *said*   *you*   *that* *married* *her*
     'Who did you say married her?'

In the discussion which follows, it will be suggested that it is possible for a single parameter setting, such as [+*pro*-drop] or [+perfective] (see section 3.4.1), to be associated with structural and social variation, irrespective of potential pragmatic incongruities. Indeed, by extension, the same would hold for the full range of syntactic variants attributed to one parameter (cf. Cornips 1994, 1998a). Parametric variation in this regard satisfies one criterion of the notion 'sociolinguistic variable' reviewed in section 2.1 in that the variants attributed to different parameter settings may be considered to be competing forms involved, for example, in processes of language change inducing convergence/divergence between varieties, although it does not share or even imply any sameness of cognitive meaning (cf. Cheshire 1987, 1999; and Winford 1996: 184 *inter alia*).

A distinction should be drawn at this point between the notions 'parametric variation' and what we would like to term 'discrete variation'. The former

and Lizardi (1995); Toribio (1993, 1996, 2000); and Trosterud (1989). The triggering experience of language contact settings has been accounted for using this model by: Corrigan (1993, 1997); De Graff (1997); Guilfoyle (1986); and Lightfoot (1988, 1991, 1999). Parametric variation in historical contexts is described in: Adams (1987); Henry (1997b); van Kemenade (1987, 1993); van Kemenade and Vincent (1997); Kroch and Taylor (1994); Lightfoot (1989, 1991, 1999); Pearce (1995); Pintzuk (1991, 1993); and Roberts (1985, 1993, 1997), *inter alia*.

[16] In the Minimalist Framework of Chomsky (1995), parameters can be reinterpreted as features of functional categories, though this need not concern us here.

refers to that type of syntactic variation outlined immediately above, namely, differences in parameter settings between two languages. Discrete variation, by contrast, describes the object of investigation introduced in section 2.1, i.e. analysing and accounting for the preferential usage by working-class females in community x for English clauses in which subjects [+*pro*-drop] are deleted [-*pro*-drop] in informal contexts (cf. Haegeman 1990). In the latter type of analysis the researcher carefully discriminates all contexts in which the variable can be said to occur or not occur without regard for any associated syntactic phenomena that correlate with this variable cross-linguistically, such as the presence of postverbal subjects, rich verbal morphology, and so on.

However, as we noted in section 1, and as Kallen (this volume) also argues, most research within the generative framework takes account of related structural phenomena using the P&P apparatus but is preoccupied with such internal evidence, leading Trudgill and Chambers (1991: 295) to appeal for 'a more empirically based approach'. In this regard, they refer, for example, to one of the theoretical assumptions of Chomsky (1989) which is derived from the ungrammaticality in standard (American) English of *do*-support in declaratives such as (6) below.

(6)   He **did** burn it
         [Ihalainen (1991: 148) – Wessex English]

The fact that the feature is robust in southwestern British vernaculars and has also been observed elsewhere (cf. Corrigan 1997; and Edwards *et al.* 1984) weakens the universality of Chomsky's position, reinforcing the view advocated in this chapter that formal syntax ignores an important resource for refining and assessing its theoretical models when it overlooks evidence from divergent traditional dialects such as these.[17]

In so far as empirical insights from divergent dialects are considered at all, it is often for the purpose of clinching a theoretical argument. Moreover, analyses – especially in the early research – are restricted to a narrow range of languages, most prominent of which is standard English (cf. Haegeman 1997: 15–16). Hence, Chomsky and Lasnik (1977) invoke an *ad hoc For-to* filter for distinguishing standard American English from divergent North American dialects and British Isles Englishes in which structures such as (7a–t) below are perfectly grammatical:[18]

---

[17] See also: Corrigan (1993, 1997); Docherty *et al.* (1997: 276 and 308); Henry (1992, 1994, 1995, 1996, 1997a, 1997b); Hudson (1995); Milroy (1984a, 1984b, 1986, 1996); Milroy and Milroy (1997: 47); Labov (1975, 1996); and Sobin (1987).

[18] Cf. Carroll (1983); Koster and May (1982); and Lightfoot (1979: 186). Accounts of the same phenomenon are offered in Corrigan (1997, 2003); and Henry (1992, 1995) which demonstrate the recent advances that have been made within P&P in accounting for vertical divergence.

(7) a   Mary wants **for to** leave
          [Carroll (1983: 416) – Ottawa Valley English]
     b   Who did you try **for to** go to the church social with you?
          [Chomsky and Lasnik (1977: 426) – Ozark English]
     c   **For to** tell her like that!
          [Henry (1995: 83) – Belfast English]
     d   The brown mug was sent **for to** use it
          [Corrigan (2003) – South Armagh English]
     e   He's come **for to** collect the rent
          [Miller (1993: 130) – Scots]
     f   The firemen were putting on breathing apparatus **for to** go into
          the house
          [Beal (1993: 200) – Tyneside and Northumbrian English]

Despite recent advances in the use of exemplification from dialects that diverge
from standard English norms within the generative literature (particularly Henry
(1995) *inter alia*),[19] the theory-building orientation of the research continues
to tolerate the analysis of data which is not sociolinguistically accountable in a
variety of ways.[20]

The practice can be illustrated by McCloskey (1992), who has proposed
that selectional restrictions apply to certain predicates in Irish-English which
account for the grammaticality contrasts in utterances like (8a–d), illustrating
'Embedded I(nflection)-to-C(omplementiser) Fronting' ($I°$-to-$C°$) in which the
standard English *if/whether* complementiser is not phonologically expressed
and the subject and auxiliary have been inverted from their usual embedded
question [NP *subject*, $I°$] order.

(8) a   Johnny Matthews **asked** did he ate his supper
    b   *Johnny Matthews **knew** did he ate his supper
    c   Do you **know** why did he eat his supper?
    d   Johnny Matthews **didn't know** did he ate his supper

Since predicates like *ask*, (8a above), *inquire*, and *wonder* might be broadly
described as eliciting information, McCloskey (1992) argues that they could
be construed to function semantically as if they contained the interrogative
operators of matrix questions which we might designate morphosyntactically
as [+Q]. If this is how Irish-English speakers interpret this class of predicates,

---

[19] The fact that Henry's (1995) treatment of Belfast English is a notable exception in this regard,
can be gathered from her comment that 'it is important to check judgements . . . particularly to
ensure that structures said to be ungrammatical have not in fact been so judged simply because
they are non-standard' (1995: 12). See also Milroy (1996).

[20] For a fuller discussion of this theme, see Hale (1994); Klemola (1997); and Labov's distinction
between 'Group A, the "social" group' and 'Group B, the "asocial" group' of linguists in Labov
(1972a: 260ff.).

then it is expected that they would be treated syntactically as [+Q] and, there-fore, be permitted to undergo I°-to-C° fronting just like any other interrogative form, hence the grammaticality of (8a). On the other hand, predicates such as *discover, establish, find out, see*, and *know* (8b) are not interpretable as requests for information and, therefore, must be marked morphosyntactically as [−Q]. Thus, they should be treated by Irish-English speakers in the same way that standard English speakers deal with both classes, namely, as embedded com-plements, the heads of which are filled by lexically selected COMPs blocking the V°-I° complex from fronting to C° which predicts the ungrammaticality of (8b). However, as the acceptability in Irish-English of (8c) and (8d) above suggest, these lexical restrictions are nullified when the [−Q] class appears as a complement to a [+Q] matrix interrogative (8c) and they are also improved when they are embedded under a [+NEG] root verb (8d) (McCloskey 1992b: 34; Corrigan 1997: 134).[21]

The divergence between standard English and Irish-English grammatical norms are crucial to McCloskey's refinement of Chomsky's (1986a: 6) 'Adjunc-tion Prohibition', which is argued to be a universal condition on the categories to which adverbial phrases can be adjoined. To this end, McCloskey (1992: 38) claims that these contrasts are not just specific to Irish-English, but are common to English vernaculars more generally. It is also argued that the range of variation between the acceptance and rejection of embedded inversion with *know*-type predicates is highly constrained cross-dialectally. He proposes, for example, that acceptability among non-standard speakers varies between those who 'adamantly do not' accept inversion in the complement of this subset of verbs to those who will tolerate it but only 'under the right semantic and prag-matic conditions' (when interrogative/negative constructions are involved, for instance, as in (8c/d) cf. McCloskey 1992: 38). However, while these proposals presumably reflect McCloskey's own introspective judgements as a speaker of a particular northern variety of Irish-English,[22] they can easily be countered by empirical evidence from other vernaculars from the same dialect region shown in (9):

(9) a   They used to burn a bit of paper to **see** was there a letter coming
         [Corrigan (1997: 268) – South Armagh English]
    b   The police **found out** had the goods been stolen
         [Henry (1995: 107) – Belfast English]

---

[21] Although McCloskey (1992) does not make this suggestion, the possibility of V2 with the [-Q] class of predicates in this variety of Irish-English may be criterial on the WH- and NEG-criterion, respectively of Rizzi (1991).

[22] The reader is not explicitly informed in the text, though this is not unusual within this framework, as Klemola (1997: 960) observes in connection with the data used by Lightfoot and Hornstein (1994).

In both cases, embedded inversion is grammatical even after the [−Q] subset of verbs which do not permit adverbial adjunction to their CP complements and in the absence of the important contextual factors. In other words, embedded inversion occurs in (9a and b) despite the fact that the verbs in question all belong to the *know* class, which, according to McCloskey (1992: 38), cannot be inverted in this way in positive, non-interrogative environments such as these. This suggests that the lexical restrictions cited by McCloskey (1992) may well not be universally constrained in the manner that he contends them to be, and that Irish-English and standard English diverge from one another in interesting ways that cannot be accounted for simply by recourse to the Adjunction Prohibition. Although the grammaticality judgements exemplified in (8a–d) above may be reliable for some speakers, the counter-examples in (9a and b) add further weight to Labov's (1996) proposals that intuitions – particularly at the grammatical level – may fail to be commensurate with observational data, even in those cases where variants are merely indicators rather than markers or stereotypes (cf. Bard *et al.* 1996; Chambers and Trudgill 1980: 84–85; Labov 1975, 1994: 78, 1996: 102; and Sobin 1987). Indeed, one might go so far as to say that the generalisations emerging from syntactic accounts such as McCloskey (1992) or Lightfoot and Hornstein (1994), which Klemola (1997) has been critical of on similar grounds, are not consistently successful in predicting the patterns of variation which the findings of sociolinguistic accounts of the same communities have revealed. By the same token, the outcomes of sociolinguistic investigations, while occasionally disconfirming the results obtained in purely syntactic accounts, are not used as effectively as they might be to examine, in any principled way, the extent to which their findings with respect to internal constraints, for example, may have a universal dimension. Their outcomes are too often expressed in language-specific terms and there is not enough attention paid to considerations of how dialect or sociolect 'x' is acquired.[23] While it is likely that a degree of the morphosyntactic variability which sociolinguists have found will remain immune to any such universal treatment, it is probable that certain patterns which they demonstrate to be either externally or internally constrained may be predictable from paying closer attention to cross-linguistic data and the evidence available to language acquirers.

In this way, the P&P model which underpins McCloskey (1992) offers a number of advantages to the treatment of convergence and divergence in grammar compared to standard variationist accounts such as those described in section 2.1, particularly when the framework is enhanced by Labov's caveat and

---

[23] While we are not aware of any sociolinguistic accounts of syntactic variability which take this approach, it has begun to emerge in more recent sociophonological accounts such as Foulkes *et al.* (1999); and Docherty *et al.* (2000); and is implicit in Labov (1989).

certain tenets of the latter. This is, principally, because variationist treatments often neglect the implications which their findings may have for current theories of syntax – although they surpass generative treatments in the methodological exactitude that they achieve regarding accountability to the data. Following the P&P assumption that grammar is an integrated, genetically endowed, system, it would not be unreasonable to expect (micro-) variation in one structure containing a CP projection, say, also to be reflected in the usage of similar constructions by a particular community of speakers. For instance, should evidence come to light of a relict English dialect in which the complementiser position in a finite clause can be doubly-filled, say, (*a man **who that** lay dead*),[24] one might reasonably hypothesise that the same may be true of its tenseless clauses, on account of the universal properties attributed to complementisers within the framework. Indeed, in more general terms, it is also likely that variation at one level of the grammar will, necessarily, have implications for other areas of the highly complex mechanism which is the human language faculty (cf. Docherty *et al.* 1997: 275; Hudson 1995: 1514; and Muysken 1995).

However, as Muysken (2000: 48–49) points out, for all its advantages, the P&P approach has yet to fully explain the extent to which languages and, indeed, dialects of the same language can vary so considerably. Moreover, as Corrigan (1997: 136) remarks, there is the additional problem that, although the concept of parameter is a useful device for describing language-particular properties and cross-linguistic differences, we would agree with Muysken (2000: 49) and Platzack (1996: 375) that the parameter concept itself is 'rather fuzzy, and most attempts to find constructions in different languages correlated by a particular value of a single parameter can be severely doubted'. These difficulties were recognised early in the development of the model and can be demonstrated by the fact that Irish, which we described earlier as [+*pro*-drop], lacks some of the well-known properties of such languages (McCloskey and Hale 1984: 487–488). Indeed, McCloskey (p.c.) has suggested that where Irish is concerned, parametric differences appear to be 'a matter of degree rather than reflections of binary on/off settings'.

Further research, such as that outlined in sections 3–3.5, in which the sociolinguistic and biolinguistic paradigms are employed in a 'mutually supportive' manner is, therefore, critical to improving our understanding of processes of

---

[24] This possibility was available, for example, in Old English:

Ure Drihten	arærde		anes ealdormannes dohtor,	**seo ðe**	læg dead
Our Lord	RAISE-PAST	*an*	*alderman's*	*daughter, who that*	*lay dead*

'Our Lord brought to life an alderman's daughter who lay dead'

[*AHP*, VI, 176 in van Kemenade (1987: 224)]. See also Seppänen (1999), who describes the persistence of this doubly filled COMP strategy in Middle and Early Modern English.

convergence and divergence at the grammatical level (cf. Chomsky 1999: 34).[25] This is particularly pertinent in the light of Muysken's (1999b: 72 and 2000: 41–43) suggestion that the opposition between I-language and E-language phenomena is not, necessarily, watertight. He argues, for example, that the cognitive abilities which shape the I-language determine the constraints on forms found in the E-language, and that it is the norms created within E-language which make the I-language coherent. Investigations of this type should have greater explanatory and predictive force with regard to their outcomes than treatments of identical phenomena within the variationist paradigm, yet they rely on similar methodologies (including the quantification of distributions) which makes them accountable to the data in a variety of ways that is not true of conventional biolinguistic treatments relying solely on the introspective method. Indeed, as we hope to demonstrate in section 3, this interdisciplinary approach also indicates the manner in which systematic observation of variable data 'helps us to fix on what the constraints are that the syntactic derivations must respect' (Sells *et al.* 1996a: 624).[26]

3   Parametric Convergence/Divergence and the Extra-linguistic Factors (Real) Time and Geographical Space: A Case Study of Limburg and its Environs

3.1   *Introduction and research question*

This case study of Limburg (the Netherlands) and the neighbouring dialects of Rhineland (Germany) relates the processes of syntactic convergence and divergence to the extra-linguistic factors 'real time' (change between 1885 and 1994) and 'geographical space' (cf. Cornips 1996a). Until 1815, the southern part of Limburg and the area around it in Belgium and Germany formed a political unit with relative linguistic homogeneity within the wider Dutch–German dialect

---

[25] Research with this orientation returns to the arguments of Labov (1969, 1975); and Kroch (1980) which suggested that insights from the variationist paradigm were valuable to the generative-introspective programme and would include: Cameron (1992); Cornips (1994, 1996a, 1997, 1998a, 1998b); Cornips and Hulk (1996, 1999); Corrigan (1993, 1996, 1997, 1998, 2000, and 2003); Sells *et al.* (1996a, 1996b); and Wilson and Henry (1998).

[26] In this way, our approach is somewhat reminiscent of the Optimality Theoretic account of negative inversion in AAVE recently proposed in Sells *et al.* (1996a). Their model takes 'grammar' to be a set of constraints which are ranked and views an 'optimal' derivation therein to be one in which lower- and higher-ranking constraints are equally satisfied. Variation between dialect grammars or, by extension, between different stages of the same language can be accounted for by permitting 'rerankings' to occur. In other words, the strength of certain constraints can weaken relative to others which were once lower ranking so that divergent optimal outputs can be achieved (across time and geographical space, for example).

continuum (cf. Hinskens 1996: 59–63). In 1839, Limburg was incorporated into the kingdom of the Netherlands. However, until 1867 it was in the ambivalent position of being a Dutch province and at the same time a member of the German federation. The linguistic consequence of the separation of Limburg in 1839 from Belgium and Germany was that the dialects which displayed a number of similarities at this juncture came under the influence of divergent languages, namely standard Dutch (SD) and German (SG). It is assumed that the creation of this new Dutch province has potentially significant implications for convergence/divergence phenomena at the grammatical level. In this chapter, however, we will confine our discussion to the following issues: (i) whether 'horizontal' convergences and/or divergences are related to 'vertical' convergences or divergences across a time-span of 100 years; (ii) if this research question can be answered affirmatively, how exactly is this relationship expressed?; (iii) whether internal structural factors interacting with external variables determine the processes of syntactic convergence and divergence and to what extent do they do so? (cf. Auer and Hinskens 1996).

In the case study exploring (i–iii) which follows in sections 3.2–3.5, it is argued that from a diachronic point of view a dialect and/or a standard language x and y are converging if, in the total (abstract) variation space allowed for by the human language capacity, x and y are closer or more alike than in a previous stage of both systems x and y. Consequently, it is claimed that any two varieties are converging with each other if they show a growing clustering of syntactic properties in the variation space. By the same token, if they are divergent then no such clustering will be attested. An important objective of the case study is also to illustrate exactly how the P&P framework can be harnessed to define variation space quite precisely (cf. Arends *et al.* 1995: 12). It will be suggested, for instance, that convergence/divergence at the grammatical level can be reduced to the number of parameter settings which varieties have in common.

3.2   The syntactic variant

As noted above, in this case study of Limburg Dutch (LD), we will explore the idea that variation space can, in fact, be defined by P&P.

Two types of so-called 'middle' construction will be our focus, namely, the adjunct middle and impersonal middle. The basic types are presented in (10a and b) below.[27] It is important to note that the presence of the reflexive marker *zich* is ungrammatical in standard Dutch. In general, it is assumed that

---

[27] The reader should note that orthographic practices in the examples differ between informants and they are copied exactly as the informants gave them in the original questionnaire responses.

middles have one essential property in common with passives, i.e. the logical subject argument is syntactically absent or somehow suppressed, although it is semantically present (cf. Hoekstra and Roberts 1993; Keyser and Roeper 1984).

(10) a   LD   't   zit   **zich**   lekker
              EXPL   (subject)   sit-3SG-PR   REFL   ADV-comfortable
              it   *sits*   *comfortably*
              op   dizze   stool
              P-in   DEM-this   N-chair
              on   *this*   *chair*
     b   LD   Disse   stool   zit
              DEM-this N-chair (grammatical subject)   sit-3SG-PR
              this   *chair*   *sits*
              zich lekker
              REFL   ADV-comfortable
                        comfortably
              'One sits comfortably in this chair'

In the impersonal middle in (10a), for instance, the pronoun *het* 'it' (strong form) or *'t* 'it' (weak form) is always a non-referential or quasi-argument. Further, the impersonal middle requires both the locative PP *op dizze stool* 'in this chair' and the manner adverbial *lekker* 'comfortably'. The adjunct middle in (10b) is the so-called 'personal' variant of the impersonal middle in (10a). The former, however, differs from the latter in that: (i) the locative PP *op dizze stool* 'in this chair' is absent; and (ii) the locative PP complement *disse stool* in (10b) has acquired the status of grammatical subject.

The two types of middle construction in (10a and b) constitute a binary linguistic variable, that is, the reflexive is either present or absent signalling the dialectal and the standard Dutch varieties, respectively (cf. Haeseryn *et al.* 1997: 52, 1420; Hoekstra and Roberts 1993; Cornips 1994, 1997). Similarly, 'plain' and reflexive middles can also be distinguished cross-linguistically, as illustrated for English (E) and French (Fr) in (11a) and (11b) below:

(11) a   E   This   shirt   washes   well
     b   Fr   Cette   chemise   **se**   lave   facilement
              this   *shirt*   REFL   *washes* *easily*
              'This shirt washes well'

However, the situation with respect to this type of variation in Heerlen, a bidialectal community in southeastern Limburg, is that both plain and reflexive middles occur at the levels of the individual and the community in both (regional) standard Dutch and in the local dialect. In particular, a reflexive middle is considered to be a dialect variant in Heerlen by younger as opposed to older speakers ($x^2 = 4,75$, df $= 1$, p $< .05$) and also by speakers with a low as opposed to a high level of education and occupation ($x^2 = 4,75$, df $= 1$, p $< .05$; cf. Cornips 2000).[28]

In this case study we will describe the degree of syntactic convergence/divergence with respect to the presence or absence of the reflexive marker among standard Dutch and standard German and related dialects as well as between the dialects of Limburg and Rhineland. Furthermore, we will assume that the presence of the reflexive marker has been brought about by a chosen value of a parameter setting.

3.3   The database and results

In this study, the data regarding middle constructions in the Limburg and Rhineland dialects were collected by means of written questionnaires, namely, the Willems questionnaire of 1885, the Meertens Instituut questionnaire of 1994, and the Amt für Rheinische Landeskunde (henceforth, Rheinische) questionnaire of 1995. With certain trivial exceptions, the Meertens Instituut questionnaire is similar to that of the Rheinische and both are based on the results of the earlier Willems questionnaire and, as such, can be considered repetitions of it. A written questionnaire has the advantage of systematically gathering dialect data in a large geographical area within a short time-span. Moreover, it is an elicitation technique that enables the researcher to standardise both the collection and the analysis of the material. In this regard it should be noted that the questionnaires upon which this analysis is based include a translation task of two alternatives (Willems questionnaire) and an acceptability judgement task reminiscent of the successful experimental methods described in Labov (1975) and Harris (1983) (Meertens and Rheinische questionnaires). Hence, rather than eliciting direct intuitions by the formula: 'can/do you say X?' or 'do you judge X a grammatical/good sentence?', informants were asked the more indirect: 'do you ever encounter this variant in the local dialect?' and 'which variant do you consider to be the most common in your local dialect?' According to Rickford (1987: 159), such elicited 'intuitions' are in a way similar to those which formal linguists use, but differ from them considerably in at least three respects: (i) they are elicited from a sample of a community members rather than being derived from the linguist's own introspection; (ii) they are combined with and calibrated against the evidence of sociolinguistic interviews and observations in the communities (cf. Cornips 1994); (iii) heterogeneity is assumed by providing several alternatives, and they are designed to reveal competence in bidialectal, heterogeneous varieties rather than in a single, homogeneous

---

[28] However, a distribution of the usage of a reflexive middle in these dimensions cannot be given since only one token of an impersonal middle, e.g. a reflexive one, shows up in 33,5 recorded hours of spontaneous speech (cf. Cornips 1994).

variety. Moreover, the open ended-nature of syntax, illustrated in section 2.1 above, is highly relevant to middle constructions as they are extremely rare in recordings of spontaneous speech (see note 29). In view of this, once various task-effects (as described above in section 2.1) are considered in any resultant analysis, the method is an extremely useful one as demonstrated in Cornips (1996b) for the Willems and Meertens questionnaires described below. In this regard, Rickford (1987: 172) concludes that 'while elicitated intuitions are valuable, and increased use of them seems vital to further progress in the field, their exploitation is not without difficulty. However, the difficulties which they pose – including the problems of vernacular shift and reliability – do not justify our ignoring or neglecting them. . . . more survey sociolinguists should become involved in ongoing efforts to understand intuitive judgements better and use them more fruitfully.' Consequently, analysis of the data provided by these questionnaires makes it possible to conduct a real-time investigation of syntactic change in the LD and Rhineland dialects between the nineteenth and twentieth centuries.

3.3.1 The 1885 Willems questionnaire   In 1885, the Willems questionnaire was distributed throughout the Dutch-speaking regions of Belgium and in the southern part of the Netherlands, including the province of Limburg and the Rhineland area (the total number of localities/villages is 121). In this questionnaire, local dialect respondents were offered a choice of three adjunct middles placed in exactly the same order as in (12a–c) and were asked to 'translate' the SD constructions into their local vernacular. In this regard, the grammatical subject in the adjunct middles below (based on the verbs *slapen* 'to sleep' and *zingen* 'to sing' in (12a) and (12c), respectively) denotes a location whereas the grammatical subject (based on the verb *schrijven* 'to write' in (12b)) denotes an instrument. The construction in (12b) can be defined as an instrumental construction since the corresponding regular transitive contains an instrumental PP headed by *met* 'with': *Ik schrijf met deze inkt* 'I write with this ink'.

(12) a SD Dit bed   slaapt goed
           this bed   sleeps well
           'This bed is comfortable'
     b SD Die inkt   schrijft goed
           this ink   writes   well
           'This ink writes well'
     c SD Die zaal   zingt   licht
           this room/hall   sings   easily
           'This hall has good acoustics [lit. 'sings easily']'

Table 4.2 *Results for the 1885 Willems questionnaire aggregated for the entire research area*

Input: 'Plain' Adjunct Middle (13a)			*Input*: 'Plain' Instrumental (13b)		
Response type:	**n** = 121	%	*Response type*:	**n** = 121	%
• plain adjunct middle *dit bed slaapt goed*	23	19	• plain instrumental *die inkt schrijft goed*	99	82
• reflexive adjunct middle *dit bed slaapt* **zich** *goed*	11	9	• reflexive instrumental *die inkt schrijft* **zich** *goed*	2	2
• plain impersonal middle *in dit bed slaapt het goed*	0	–	• plain impersonal instrumental *met die inkt schrijft het goed*	0	–
• reflexive impersonal middle *in dit bed slaapt het* **zich** *goed*	17	14	• reflexive impersonal instrumental *met die inkt schrijft het* **zich** *goed*	0	–
• corresponding 'active' *men slaapt goed in dit bed*	31	26	• corresponding 'active' *men schrijft goed met die inkt*	3	2
• other type of construction	4	3	• other type of construction	2	2
• 'not a common construction'	17	14	• 'not a common construction'	4	3
• non-response	18	15	• non-response	11	9
total	**121**	**100**	**total**	**121**	**100**

Moreover, Willems also offered the transitive counterparts of (12a) and (12c) as alternatives, namely, *In dat bed slaapt men goed* 'in this bed sleeps one well' and *In dien zaal zingt men gemakkelijk* 'in this hall sings one easily' (see also table 4.2).

Table 4.2 reveals the results regarding the constructions in (12a) (left-hand column) and (12b) (right-hand column) for the 1885 Willems questionnaire from a quantitative perspective.

The quantitative results of this Willems questionnaire reveal a very interesting grammatical and geographical distribution of middles in LD and the neighbouring dialects of Germany in the Rhineland area (RD) (cf. Cornips 1996a). First of all, the adjunct middles in which the grammatical subject denotes a location, as in (12a and c), for instance, is not found in either Limburg or in the Rhineland area. The 23 instances of this plain adjunct middle in table 4.2 are all recorded in the surrounding dialects of Belgium.

Secondly, adjunct middles with the reflexive *zich* (11 tokens in table 4.2) are found exclusively to the north of Limburg and Rhineland area, as illustrated in (13):[29]

---

[29] The reader should note again that orthographic practices in the examples (13a) *dae zâl* and (14a) *die zaol* 'this hall' differ between informants, and they are copied exactly as the informants gave them in the original questionnaire responses.

(13) a   LD north   Dae   zâl   zinkt   **zich**   gôd
                      this   hall   sings REFL   *easily*
      b   RD   Der   saal   sengt   **sich**   legt
                      this   hall   sings REFL   *easily*
                      'This hall has good acoustics'

Thirdly, the reflexive impersonal middle (17 tokens in table 4.2) is also extant across the entire dialect regions of both Limburg and the Rhineland area, though it is important to note that this type of middle (illustrated below) was not present in the questionnaire.

(14) a   LD   In   die   zaol zink et **zech** gemekelek
                in   this   hall sings it REFL   *easily*
      b   RD   En   däne sal   sengt et **sich** god
                in   this   hall sings it REFL   *easily*
                'This hall has good acoustics'

Crucially, despite the fact that the Willems questionnaire offered only adjunct middles in which the grammatical subject denotes a location without a reflexive, an analysis of its response type indicates that this construction (i) is not extant, or (ii) it occurs with a reflexive, or (iii) it is construed as an impersonal middle with a reflexive. These consistent substitutions of the plain adjunct middle presented in the questionnaire provide strong evidence that this construction is not attested for the local dialects of the respondents in the Dutch Limburg and Rhineland areas (Carden 1976: 101).

On the other hand, the adjunct middle in which the grammatical subject denotes an instrument (henceforth, instrumental construction), as in (12b), is found with a reflexive in the Rhineland area (two instances are illustrated in table 4.2) but not a single instance of this type, i.e. with a reflexive, is recorded for the entire province of Limburg. Instead, the instrumental construction occurs as a plain construction (99 tokens in table 4.2) throughout Limburg:

(15) a   RD   Di   Tinte/Enk schriv **sisch** jot
                this   ink   *writes* REFL   *well*
      b   LD   Dieën aenkt   schrif **Ø**   gout
                this   ink   *writes*   *well*
                'This ink writes well'

These distributional differences are highly suggestive of the possibility that the instrumental construction and the adjunct middle are distinctive and, therefore, ought to be analysed separately, and we will return to this disparity below. Note that table 4.2 above reiterates the differences which occur between the

1885		South of Limburg	North of Limburg	Rhineland
impersonal middle	+ **zich**	√	√	√
adjunct middle	+ **zich**	*	√	√
instrumental middle	+ **zich**	*	*	√

Fig. 4.1 Distribution of the instrumental, adjunct, and impersonal middles in 1885.

adjunct middle with/without the reflexive and the instrumental construction with/without the reflexive.

The findings regarding Willems 1885 can be captured as follows. As far as the independent variable area is concerned, figure 4.1 reveals a pattern in which the reflexive instrumental construction implies the existence of the reflexive adjunct middle, whereas this latter implies the existence of the reflexive impersonal middle. In addition, since an impersonal reflexive middle construction is attested in the south of Limburg there is an implication that it will also be present in the north. By contrast, the presence of the adjunct middle in the north of Limburg does not imply its existence in the south. Hence, it is assumed that the syntactic variants, i.e. the constructions with and without the reflexive, as in table 4.2 and figure 4.1 are brought about by different values of a single parameter (cf. sections 2.2 and 3.4.1).

3.3.2 The 1994/1995 databases   In the later Meertens and Rheinische questionnaires, an adjunct middle, an impersonal middle, and the instrumental construction were all offered, as presented in (15) and (16), respectively. Importantly, both questionnaires always administered two variants per type of construction, namely, a variant with and one without the reflexive (i.e. a total of six variants). It is important to note that heterogeneity is assumed by the provision of several alternative choices to informants in the Willems and in the Meertens and Rheinische questionnaires:

Meertens questionnaire in 1994:

(16) a Deze stoel zit   [+ zich]   gemakkelijk
        this   chair sits   *comfortably*
     b Het   zit   [± zich] gemakkelijk op   deze   stoel
        one   sits   *comfortably in   this   chair*
        'One sits comfortably in this chair'
     c Die   inkt   schrijft   [± zich]   goed
        this ink   writes   *well*
        'This ink writes well'

Table 4.3 *Results for the entire province of Limburg from the Meertens Questionnaire*

Input: A = reflexive adjunct middle in (17a);
      B = reflexive impersonal middle in (17b);
      C = reflexive instrumental in (17c).

Response Type:	*A* N = 19		*B* N = 18		*C* N = 24	
	N	%	N	%	N	%
common construction	15	79	18	100	18	75
'not a common construction'	4	21	0	0	6	25

Rheinische questionnaire in 1995:

(17) a Dieser Stuhl sitzt   [± sich]   herrlich
        this   *chair* *sits*   *comfortably*

   b Es   sitzt [± sich] herrlich   auf diesem Stuhl
      it   *sits*   *comfortably* *in*   *this*   *chair*
      'One sits comfortably in this chair'

   c Diese Tinte schreibt [± sich]   gut
      this   *ink*   *writes*   *well*
      'This ink writes well'

For each variant in (16) and (17), the dialect respondents were asked to answer the following two questions: (i) 'do you ever "encounter" the variant in your local dialect?'; and (ii) 'which variant do you consider to be most common in your local dialect?' Their responses are discussed below and we will pay particular attention to the grammatical and geographical distribution of the findings for both the Meertens and Rheinische questionnaires. Table 4.3 displays the quantitative results for responses to the constructions in (16) drawn from the Meertens questionnaire.[30]

The quantified results of the Meertens questionnaire in 1994 reveal interesting syntactic changes through time and space. Specifically, (i) the reflexive adjunct middle in (16a) has become fully grammatical in the southern Limburg dialects; and (ii) the instrumental construction with *zich* as in (16c) has emerged and it too has spread throughout the province of Limburg as exemplified in (18a) and (18b), respectively:

---

[30] As noted above, the Meertens questionnaire was administered throughout the Netherlands and in the Dutch-speaking regions of Belgium. However, the data presented here are the responses for the Dutch province of Limburg only.

	South of Limburg 1885	North of Limburg 1885	Entire province of Limburg 1994	Standard Dutch 1994
reflexive impersonal	√	√	√	*
reflexive adjunct	*	√	√	*
reflexive instrumental	*	*	√	*

Fig. 4.2 Converging dialects in Limburg 1885–1994.

(18) a   LD south   Dèzze stool zit   **zich**   lekker (goöd)
            *this   chair sits   REFL *comfortably*
            'This chair is comfortable'
      b   LD sth./nth. Dieze ink   sjrief   **zich**   plezeerig
            *this   ink   writes   REFL *well*
            'This ink writes well'

This suggests that there has been a convergence of dialects in this region between 1885 and 1994. The findings with respect to the Meertens questionnaire 1994 can be described as follows. Regarding the independent variables 'area' and 'time', figure 4.2 demonstrates a distribution in which the reflexive instrumental construction implies the existence of the reflexive adjunct middle, whereas the latter implies the existence of the reflexive impersonal middle (a pattern which is not dissimilar to that shown in figure 4.1 above).

Moreover, figure 4.2 reveals that speakers in twentieth-century Limburg have more types of reflexive middle in their linguistic repertoire than was the case for speakers in the previous century. In our terms, this suggests that there has been a change over time in the extent to which syntactic properties associated with reflexives cluster in the variation space, the range being greater in 1994 than it was in 1885. It is assumed that these clustering properties, i.e. the presence of a variety of reflexives, are brought about by just one parameter setting, as we will see in section 3.4. Hence, in the later twentieth century, southern Limburg dialects have a parameter setting which is closer to that of northern Limburg varieties of the previous century. Consequently, it would seem reasonable to suggest that convergence has taken place in LD as a whole (cf. Hinskens 1996). Interestingly, figure 4.2 also reveals that this phenomenon does not, necessarily, amount to convergence towards the standard variety since there is robust evidence here for divergence as the reflexive variants remain entirely ungrammatical in standard Dutch and the Limburg dialects have not extirpated their reflexive middles.

The results of our analyses of the Rheinische questionnaire in table 4.4 and figure 4.3 below, indicate a language change in the opposite direction: i.e. the reflexive adjunct and reflexive instrumental middle have (almost) disappeared. In this case, the Rhineland dialects appear to have converged towards the

Table 4.4 *Results for the 1995 Rheinische questionnaire*

Input: A = reflexive adjunct middle in (18a);
B = reflexive impersonal middle in (18b);
C = reflexive instrumental in (18c).

Response type:	*A* N = 19		*B* N = 19		*C* N = 19	
	N	%	N	%	N	%
common construction	2	11	16	84	2	11
'not a common construction'	17	89	3	16	17	89

	Rhineland 1885	Rhineland 1994	Standard German 1994
reflexive impersonal	✓	✓	✓
reflexive adjunct	✓	*	*
reflexive instrumental	✓	*	*

Fig. 4.3 Converging Rhineland dialects and the Standard language, 1885 and 1994.

standard language. Hence, only the reflexive impersonal middle is fully gram-matical in most varieties of RD and in SG (cf. Fagan 1992).

It should be emphasised that the results of both types of questionnaires, the Willems questionnaire and the Meertens and Rheinische questionnaires, are comparable. Although the Willems questionnaire included a translation task there is hardly any reason to assume that a repetition-effect is involved since (i) several alternatives were offered; and (ii) no repetition of the 'plain' middle was found in either Limburg or the Rhineland area. Secondly, the recent questionnaires were designed to reveal competence in heterogeneous varieties since every local dialect speaker nowadays is truly bidialectal. Hence, he/she will also speak the standard language, though this was not, necessarily, the case with regard to the local dialect speakers interviewed at the time of the Willems questionnaire. In sum, the impact of convergence in Limburg has, clearly, led to an increase in the structural distance from the standard language since 1885. By contrast, the use of reflexives by speakers of the Rhineland dialects in 1994/1995 indicates convergence towards the pattern associated with the standard language and divergence from the Limburg dialects.

3.4   Towards an analysis

In the previous section, we observed the degree of syntactic convergence/diver-gence among standard languages and related dialects as well as between the dialects of Limburg and the Rhineland. The presence or absence of the reflexive in the three types of construction may be considered to have been brought about by a chosen value of a parameter setting. Let us first discuss which parameter may be assumed to play a role in middle constructions with and without a reflexive.

3.4.1 Parameter settings manifested in middle constructions   Clearly, not every verb with its internal argument is able to undergo middle formation, as shown in the argument middle constructions in (19):

(19) a   This shirt washes easily
     b   *This book sees easily

This well-known constraint on middle formation is the so-called Affectedness constraint. The common assumption about middle formation is that it is only acceptable if the promoted argument (the logical object) is 'affected' (cf. Jaeggli 1986; Tenny 1987, Hoekstra and Roberts 1993; Fagan 1992, Cornips and Hulk 1999). In that case the 'affected' object is preposable, as in (19a). Apparently, the syntactic property of preposability versus non-preposability of the object appears to correlate with an independent semantic distinction. Although the notion 'affected' object is, to a certain extent, intuitively clear, the precise way to implement this idea has often been left rather vague. In Cornips and Hulk (1999; and Hulk and Cornips 2000), it is argued that the notion affected object or Affectedness is an essential element in the larger question about aspectual properties of verbs and predicates, namely, affectedness is not solely linked to the verb but is crucially linked to the aspectual properties of the predicate as a whole, that is to say, it is related to the event structure of the entire sentence. To illustrate this, consider the following contrast in standard Dutch:

(20) a   SD *Dit   portret   schildert   prettig
                 this portrait   paints   easily
     b   SD Dit   plafond   schildert   prettig
                 this ceiling   paints   easily

The ungrammatical middle in (20a) differs from the grammatical one in (20b) in that the verb *schilderen* 'paint' in the latter combines with a different kind of object, namely *plafond* 'ceiling' instead of *portret* 'portrait'. Apparently, this minimal contrast indicates that only the object in (20b) is an affected object by which middle formation is allowed. This minimal contrast in (20) presents a deeper understanding of the interaction between the aspectual properties of the predicate and the affected object. Interestingly, the corresponding regular transitives of the middles in (20) differ aspectually: the former depicts the event only as telic (bounded, accomplishment), whereas the latter allows both an atelic and telic event reading since it combines with temporal adverbials expressing duration and with temporal adverbials expressing a specific point in time:

(21) a   SD Ik schilder dit portret in een uur/*een uur lang
              I   paint   this portrait in an hour/*for an hour long
     b   SD Ik schilder dit plafond in een uur/een uur lang
              I   paint   this ceiling   in an hour/for an hour long

From the contrast in (21), Cornips and Hulk (1999) assume that (i) middle formation is connected with the whole predicate or the event structure of the entire sentence; and (ii) only predicates which depict the event as atelic and telic may undergo middle formation. Hence, the Affectedness constraint is redefined as an (inner)aspectual property of the predicate. This aspectual property holds for both plain and reflexive languages. Now consider the striking contrasts in acceptability between the standard Dutch plain and the Heerlen Dutch reflexive middles in (22) and (23), respectively. These contrasts reveal that all the transitive verbs selecting unaffected objects in the corresponding regular active constructions can undergo middle formation if the middle combines with the reflexive *zich*:

(22) a   SD *Frans   leert   gemakkelijk
              French   learns   easily
     b   SD *Frans   verwerft gemakkelijk
              French   acquires   easily

(23) a   HD Frans   leert   **zich**   gemakkelijk
              French   learns   REFL   easily
     b   HD Frans   verwerft **zich**   gemakkelijk
              French   acquires   REFL   easily

This is also the case cross-linguistically:

(24) a   Eng *That   tells   easily
     b   Fr   Ça   **se** raconte facilement

Although not explicitly discussed in the literature, the Affectedness constraint also holds for adjunct middles as shown by the following examples:

(25) a   SD *?Dit   park   rent   gemakkelijk
     b   SD Deze   schoenen   rennen   gemakkelijk
              This/these park/shoes run(s)   easily

Intuitively, it is clear that the locational complement of the verb *rennen* (run) in (25a) is not affected by the action expressed by the verb, whereas the locational complement *schoenen* (shoes) is affected by the action of the same verb (cf. Cornips and Hulk 2002). Consider now the corresponding Heerlen Dutch middles with *zich*:

(26) a HD Dit   park   rent   **zich**   gemakkelijk
            this   park   runs   REFL   easily
    b   HD Deze   schoenen rennen   **zich**   gemakkelijk
            these   shoes   walk   REFL   easily

Just as we have seen in the case of argument middles with transitive verbs, (22) to (24), the presence of *zich* allows verbs with unaffected complements to undergo middle formation. The only difference between the grammatical and the ungrammatical examples is the presence and absence of the reflexive marker. Consequently, only the predicates with *zich* as in (23) but not in (22) have the required property to undergo middle formation.[31] This required property is an aspectual one: the reflexive marker does not trigger an event type shift, but it offers a different perspective on the event, in particular, *zich* imparts a sense of achieving an inherent end-point of the event (as will become more clear below) (cf. Cornips and Hulk 1999; Hulk and Cornips 2000). In brief, the aspectual relation between the verb and its (internal) arguments is exactly what is at stake in the Affectedness constraint.

Importantly, it is argued independently by a number of authors that the reflexive marker also plays an aspectual role in other types of constructions (cf. Labelle 1992 for French; and Almagro 1993; Nishida 1994; and Zagona 1994 for Spanish). Compare the following unaccusative constructions with and without a reflexive. The reflexive unaccusative construction in Heerlen Dutch gives rise to an ungrammatical result if it is combined with an adverbial phrase expressing duration, whereas it is fully grammatical if it is linked to an adverbial phrase expressing a specific point in time, as can be seen in (27a) and (27b), respectively:

(27) a HD *dat   het ei   **zich**   3 minuten lang   gekookt heeft
            that   the egg   REFL   for 3 minutes   boiled has
    b   HD dat   het ei   **zich**   in 3 minuten tijd   gekookt heeft
            that   the egg   REFL   in 3 minutes' time   boiled has

Contrary to what is the case in the example in (27b), the unaccusative constructions without a reflexive in both standard Dutch and Heerlen Dutch can

---

[31] Notice that it is important to keep apart the two factors involved in the aspectual 'make-up' of middle constructions. The first is the Affectedness constraint that is a condition which tells us which verbal predicates can undergo middle formation; it doesn't tell us anything about the outcome of such a formation. The notion Affectedness has to do with what has been called Aktionsart: it expresses (inherent) aspectual properties of a verb. *Zich* has a role to play with respect to this type of aspectual impact of the Affectedness constraint. The second aspectual factor involved in middles is the event type of the entire construction after middle formation has taken place. As is well known, in most languages middles denote states. The operation of middle formation somehow abstracts over the kind of event denoted by the verb in its active voice and turns it into a state. *Zich* has no role to play in this operation.

easily be construed with temporal adverbials expressing duration and also with temporal adverbials expressing a specific point in time:

(28)   HD/SD dat het ei   3 minuten lang/ in 3 minuten gekookt heeft
                    that the egg for 3 minutes/   in 3 minutes boiled   has

The aspectual differences between the two constructions with and without a reflexive in (27) and in (28) are very subtle, depending on the way in which the speaker wants to present the situation. According to Labelle (1992) and Cornips and Hulk (1999), when the unaccusative construction occurs without a reflexive, the (aspectual) focus is on the process of transformation of the entity in subject position, whereas when the reflexive is present, the (aspectual) focus is on the end-point or the final state of that entity. So, the occurrence versus absence of *zich* has an influence on the event structure of the whole sentence in representing a certain viewpoint on a (telic) event. The presence of *zich* does not alter the Aktionsart of the verb nor does it modify (sub) parts of events that are characterised by the verb. Rather, it attributes to the state introduced by the event structure of the (unaccusative) verb itself. It is for this reason, that *zich* is considered to be an aspectual marker which supplies more information about the existing aspectual structure. Just as in the case of middles, the reflexive marker has both a syntactic role – triggering a movement analysis, i.e. preposing of the object – and an aspectual one, triggering a different perspective on the event focusing the final state.

Consider now the following alternating transitive predicates denoting consumption in Heerlen Dutch. The reflexive dative 'consumptive' construction in Heerlen Dutch is, in analogy with the reflexive unaccusative construction, ill formed if it is combined with an adverbial phrase expressing duration (cf. (29a)), whereas the construction is fully grammatical if it is linked to an adverbial phrase indicating an end-point of the action expressed by the predicate (cf. (29b)). Note that the alternating constructions without *zich* are again fully acceptable with both types of adverbial phrase:

(29) a   HD   *Zij eet **zich**   5 minuten lang   een boterham
                   she eats. REFL for 5 minutes   a sandwich
     b   HD   Zij eet **zich**   in 5 minuten   een boterham
                   she eats REFL in 5 minutes' time   a sandwich
     c   HD/SD Zij eet   5 minuten lang/   een boterham
                                          binnen 5 minuten
                   she eats   for 5 minutes/in 5   a sandwich
                                          minutes' time

According to Almagro (1993: 136) and Nishida (1994: 442), the presence of the reflexive marker refers to the delimitation of the event or, rather, it highlights the fact that the totality of an object is involved in the situation or that the event is completed.

From the above, it is proposed that the functional category Aspect – that may be presented structurally as [IP [I' [AspP [Asp [VP]]]]] – (cf. Cornips and Hulk 1999; and Hulk and Cornips 2000) functions as a parameter in which the presence of the reflexive is thought to be brought about by the different settings of the parameter (cf. Cornips 1994, 1998a).[32] The syntactic variation can be accounted for by assuming that in Heerlen Dutch the setting [+perfective] is the marked value for the parameter AspP whereas in standard Dutch the AspP projection has a default value. In this way, aspectual differences between standard languages/dialects and cross-linguistically can be viewed in parametric terms. It is very important to note that while this single abstract grammatical difference, i.e. the chosen value of the Aspect parameter, is not visible immediately, it is manifested in a number of very different constructions such as argument middles (see (22), (23), (24)), adjunct middles ((25), (26)), unaccusative constructions ((27), (28)), and 'consumptive' constructions in (29). The holistic view of syntactic variability taken by the P&P model (and also illustrated by McCloskey (1992) in section 2) reflects more clearly the fact that grammars are, in fact, highly integrated systems. Hence, the advantage of the P&P model over a variationist account of this phenomenon is that it is possible to show that seemingly unrelated constructions can belong to the same parameter and that they can be related with respect to structural and social variation which cannot be done by means of the linguistic variable alone (cf. Cornips 1994, 1998a). For this reason, Muysken (1995: 2) argues that the linguistic variable approach forces a perspective on (syntactic) variation in which it always implies isolated, loose elements. Hence, in the Labovian framework, the data revealing optionality within a grammar such as that illustrated above involve three distinct and discrete linguistic variables, namely (i) the middle variants with and without the reflexive; (ii) the unaccusative variants with and without the reflexive; and (iii) the 'consumptive' variants with and without the reflexive.

3.4.2 The notion 'argument structure' as a principle of syntactic organisation   In the present section we hope to demonstrate how this parametric approach accounts for: (i) why variation is possible and why it is constrained with respect to the presence or absence of the reflexive *zich* in the three types of construction, namely adjunct, impersonal, and middle; and (ii) why there is an implicational relationship (from both a chronological and geographical perspective) between the impersonal middle, the adjunct middle, and the instrumental construction with *zich*, revealing why these constructions may or may

---

[32] It is relevant to note that within Generative Grammar there is not a fully elaborated theory of Aspect.

not cluster together in the variation space (cf. Cornips 1996a; figures 4.1 and 4.3). To this end, we will address these issues by considering the hermetic nature of grammar in terms of the notion 'argument structure' as a principle of syntactic organisation.

Consider again the impersonal and adjunct middles in (10) repeated here for convenience as (30):

(30) a   LD 't   zit   **zich**   lekker   op dizze stool
            it   *sits*   REFL   *comfortably*   *in this   chair*
      b   LD Disse stool zit   **zich**   lekker
            this   chair sits   REFL   *comfortably*
            'This chair is comfortable'

We will first assume that: (i) the occurrence of the reflexive *zich* in middles manifests the absorption of the logical subject argument (cf. section 3.2, where absorption should be taken to be neutral regarding the various theoretical instantiations of this phenomenon); and that (ii) the adjunct middle, as in (30b), is derived from an underlying locative PP, (PP_{loc}) such as *op dizze stool* 'in this chair', by means of incorporation of the P_{loc} *op* 'in' into the verb *zit* 'to sit', as illustrated in (20) (cf. Ackema and Schoorlemmer 1994: 174 and 1995):

(31)   LD   **zich** lekker zit [op <u>dizze stool</u>]
         incorporation at the level
         of lexicon=>   **zich** lekker [zit + *op*] <u>dizze stool</u>
         movement in syntax=>   <u>dizze stool</u>*i* **zich** lekker zit t*i*
                                      'One sits comfortably in this chair'

This process of incorporation accounts for the facts that: (i) the preposition in the impersonal middle really 'disappears' in the adjunct middle; and (ii) the DP grammatical subject *dizze stool* 'this chair' is still interpreted as a location as a result of function composition by which the verb expresses the combined semantics of the verb and the PP_{loc} (cf. Ackema and Schoorlemmer 1994 for a more detailed analysis of this process of incorporation). Since *zich* manifests the absorption of the logical subject argument, it is proposed that in the Limburg and Rhineland dialects incorporation takes place at the lexical level and, as a result, the DP *dizze stool* 'this chair' that was embedded in the PP becomes the grammatical subject by means of movement in syntax (cf. Cornips 1996a; Cornips and Hulk 1999). Hence, the analysis of the reflexive adjunct middles involves two operations, namely: (i) incorporation of the PP_{loc} into the verb; and (ii) moving of the embedded DP in PP_{loc} to the subject position.

The notion 'argument structure' imposes constraints on the degree of variation possible in the usage of adjunct middles since not every P_{loc} may incorporate into the verb. Consider, for instance, the following relative clauses in which the relative pronoun *waar* 'where' has been extracted from the PP (so-called R-extraction, cf. Van Ricmsdijk 1978). R-extraction is considered a diagnostic for the adjunct or argument status of locative PPs. According to a barrier theory such as outlined in Chomsky (1986a), the P_{loc} should constitute a barrier for movement, and hence for R-extraction, if it is an adjunct. Since R-extraction is blocked in (32a), whereas it is fully grammatical in (32b), we know that the PP *in het restaurant* in (32a) is an adjunct whereas the PP *in de zaal* in (32b) is an argument.[33] Consequently, deriving an adjunct middle is blocked in the middle counterpart of (32a), i.e. (33a), whereas it is permitted in the middle counterpart of (32b), i.e. (33b). From this distributional evidence, it seems reasonable to conclude that extraction of the prepositional head of the PP_{loc} *in* 'in' or the process of incorporation should also be permitted in these contexts:

(32) a   SD *het restaurant waar$_i$ het prettig [pp in t$_i$] eet
             the restaurant where it   nicely in   eats
             'The restaurant where it eats in nicely'

     b   SD de zaal   waar$_i$ het prettig [pp in t$_i$] zingt
             the hall   where it   nicely in   sings
             'The hall which has good acoustics'

(33) a   SD *Dit   restaurant   eet   prettig
             this   restaurant   eats   nicely
             'This sun sings nicely'

     b   SD Deze zaal   zingt prettig
             this hall   sings nicely
             'This hall has good acoustics'

From the above, it is clear that the formation of the adjunct middle requires one operation more than the formation of the impersonal middle, namely, the process of incorporation of the preposition which can only take place if the PP is an argument. This may explain: (i) the chronological and geographical implicational relationship between both types of middle construction; and

---

[33] Another diagnostic is from Hornstein and Weinberg (cited in Ackema and Schoorlemmer 1994: 85). This test also involves P-stranding, which again allows one to distinguish between argument and adjunct locatives (see the grammaticality contrast between (ib) and (ic)).

(i) a   I slept in my bed in New York
    b   Which bed did you sleep in (in New York)?
    c   ?*Which city did you sleep (in your bed) in?

As the contrast between (ic) and (iia) shows, it depends on the verb whether or not a particular locative PP is an argument:

(ii) a   I lived in New York
     b   Which city did you live in?

(ii) the existence of the impersonal middle in all dialects/standard languages and in both time periods.[34]

The question remains how, exactly, is the instrumental construction linked to the adjunct middle? Let us consider the instrumental construction in more detail:

(34)   SD Deze inkt schrijft goed
             this ink writes well
             'This ink writes well'

It is convincingly argued by Hoekstra and Roberts (1993) that in SD, the verb *schrijven* 'to write' in (34) takes *deze inkt* 'this ink' as a logical subject argument or as an external argument. Their analysis of the instrumental construction differs from that presented above in that the former does not invoke incorporation and assumes that the grammatical subject is an external argument mapped directly onto the subject position. If the grammatical subject in the instrumental construction is, indeed, an external argument, we would expect it to have other properties characteristic of adjunct middles as well. For instance, we would anticipate that a grammatical outcome would result were one to combine it (i) with a different kind of adverb that is ungrammatical in a middle construction (such as *dik* 'thickly' in (35a)); or (ii) with an object such as *de letter 'O'* 'the letter "O"' in (35b). The grammaticality contrasts between (35) and (36) below bear this out:

(35) a   SD Deze inkt schrijft dik
                this ink writes thickly
                'This ink writes thickly'
     b   SD Deze inkt schrijft   de letter 'O' goed
                this ink writes   the letter O   well
                'This ink writes the letter "O" well'

(36) a   SD *Deze zaal zingt dik
                this hall sings thickly
                'This hall has good acoustics'
     b   SD *Deze zaal zingt dit lied goed
                this hall sings this song well

Moreover, we would expect the instrumental construction to be grammatical in languages such as English and standard German, although these varieties do not allow for an adjunct middle. This anticipated outcome is also confirmed as the grammaticality of (37a–b) demonstrates:

---

[34] It is important to note that the formation of the (reflexive) impersonal middle has no such restrictions, i.e. whether the locative PP is an adjunct or an argument.

(37) a E This ink   writes well
     b SG Diese Tinte schreibt gut
           this   ink   writes   well
           'This ink writes well'

Finally, the mandatory absence of *sich* in the SG example (37b), involving an external argument, is accounted for if it is assumed that the reflexive is a morphological marker signalling the absorption of the external argument. Crucially, variation at these specific points in the grammar is possible since the instrumental construction is ambiguous: it may be interpreted both as a regular transitive in which the logical subject argument or the external subject argument is present, as in (35) and (37) or as an adjunct middle in which the logical subject argument is not syntactically overt, as in (36). With respect to the latter interpretation, the verb *schrijven* 'to write' in the instrumental construction extant in the Limburg and Rhineland dialects has been reanalysed as a detransitivised verb which does not project an external argument. Thus, in the instrumental construction, incorporation of the preposition has taken place and the presence of the reflexive is a manifestation of the movement of the embedded DP *die inkt* 'this ink' in PP_{instr} (Cornips 1996a; Cornips and Hulk 1999). This is clear from a comparison of (31) above with (38) immediately below:

(38)   LD **zich** prettig [met deze inkt] schrijft =>
             zich prettig [schrijft + met] deze inkt =>
             deze inkt **zich** prettig schrijft
             'One writes well with this ink'

By contrast, the instrumental construction without the reflexive is interpreted in both the Rhineland and Limburg dialects as a regular transitive construction. Thus, it is assumed that variation with respect to the presence or absence of the reflexive exists at these specific points of the grammar since the instrumental construction is structurally ambiguous. The distributional evidence presented in the previous sections clearly suggests that the formation of the reflexive instrumental implies the presence of an adjunct middle. Hence, the instrumental construction without a reflexive must first be reanalysed as an adjunct middle. This accounts for the geographical and chronological implicational relationship between the adjunct middle and the reflexive instrumental middle. In the dialects of northern Limburg, both middle formation and incorporation were productive processes during the nineteenth century. The 1994 Meertens database, however, reveals that these processes (the reflexive adjunct middle, in particular) have become highly productive and now extend over the entire province of Limburg. In addition, the process of incorporation has produced a new variant, namely, the instrumental construction with the reflexive.

This syntactic change, causing two types of construction to become reflexive, i.e. adjunct and instrumental middles, shows that these constructions cluster together in the variation space which may be explained in terms of parameter theory.

4   General Conclusion

In this chapter we have argued that the variationist approach and the generative programme (since the publication of Chomsky 1981b) are salient frameworks for analysing processes of convergence and divergence between related language varieties at the grammatical level. However, differences in methodology, analyses, and findings with respect to variation have led to the creation of a Janus-like orientation within these two disciplines. Thus, variationists focus on the representativeness of their speakers, controlled recordings of the vernacular, and the collection of a substantial quantity of data in order to achieve descriptive and observational adequacy. By contrast, generativists focus on native-speaker introspection in an idealised environment in their pursuit of explanatory adequacy. Moreover, an integral aim of sociolinguistic accounts is to ascertain the significance of inherent variability for a range of sociocultural correlates with respect to 'community' grammars, whereas the Chomskyan tradition seeks only to delimit the set of possible languages and to discover the universal constraints by which all 'individual' grammars are bound.

In this chapter we hope to have demonstrated that investigations of convergence and divergence at the grammatical level which utilise the interfaces of both frameworks and rely on real time, variable corpora in addition to speaker judgements, have greater observational and explanatory force than that of a single paradigm applied to either type of data in isolation. A good case in point is the empirical evidence provided in section 2.2 which ran counter to McCloskey's claims regarding the distribution of certain predicates in embedded inversion constructions ($I°$-to-$C°$ Fronting) among speakers of divergent Englishes. On the basis of evidence such as this, it was argued that allowing for microvariation within universal constraints so that the resultant analysis remains accountable to the data will eventually bring about important refinements within generative theory.

We have also examined the idea that variation space is defined by parameter theory accounting, at a high level of abstraction, for some of the reasons why certain related varieties cluster together from a syntactic perspective. In this way, processes of convergence/divergence in grammar (or notions such as 'alike'/'different') can be analysed more explicitly than is possible within standard variationist analyses. The case study, for example, demonstrated the manner in which a parametric approach can account for the amount and type of variation, in addition to the restrictions on variability, associated with middle constructions in the Limburg and Rhineland dialects which would not be as transparent within a 'discrete' variationist analysis.

The perspective adopted here is in line with new ways of analysing variation suggested by the findings of other research into the phenomenon of grammatical variability in which theoretical concerns have become much more central. This is partly due to the welcome relaxation of the generative position on the status of social accounts from that of Smith (1989), as can be seen from the quote below:[35]

> Internalist biolinguistic inquiry does not, of course, question the legitimacy of other approaches to language, any more than internalist inquiry into bee communication invalidates the study of how the relevant internal organization of bees enters into their social structure. The investigations do not conflict; they are mutually supportive. In the case of humans, though not other organisms, the issues are subject to controversy, often impassioned, and needless. (Chomsky 1999: 34)

We believe that the analyses and observations made in this chapter suggest interesting avenues for further research. Three issues, in particular, have come to the fore, namely (i) identifying the exact relationship between intuitions and performance data; (ii) exploring the extent to which grammatical theory should attend to introspective judgements about certain types of construction that never surface empirically (cf. Labov 1975, 1996; and Bard *et al.* 1996); and (iii) the hypothesis that morphosyntactic variables can be differentiated into those that are 'low level' and, therefore, accessible to sociolinguistic analysis, and those that are 'high level', where it is less clear that variation serves to differentiate social groups because it is neither purely morphological nor purely syntactic given its dependence on pragmatic/semantic conditioning. Although it has not been possible fully to investigate (i–iii) in the present context, we intend in future research to explore further both introspective and empirical data from divergent Dutch and English dialects. We plan to focus on whether there are cross-linguistic prohibitions operating on the failure of intuitions and to examine empirical observations which are stable across communities of speakers yet run counter to universal constraints postulated within P&P (i.e. question (i)). Similarly, we would like to ascertain the extent to which speakers of divergent Dutch and English varieties share introspective judgements regarding constructions that are grammatically possible intuitively but are not recoverable from observation alone (i.e. question (ii)). We also intend to use cross-linguistic data to explore the hypothesis (following Muysken

---

[35] Such research includes Beals *et al.* (1994); Cornips (1994, 1998a), *inter alia*; Corrigan (1997), *inter alia*; Henry (1992), *inter alia*; Hudson (1995); King and Nadasdi (1996); Klemola (1997); Kroch (1994); Landa and Franco (1996); Muysken (1995), *inter alia*; Pintzuk (1993); Rickford *et al.* (1995); Seppänen (1999); Sells *et al.* (1996a,b); Toribio (1996), *inter alia*; and Wilson and Henry (1998).

1999b) that investigations into the extra-linguistic constraints inducing convergence/divergence at the grammatical level are particularly successful when examining 'low-level' morphosyntactic variation (verbal paradigms, for example), which more clearly pertain to the external domain of language as a social construct than they are when accounting for 'higher level' variables (passivity, for instance), which are associated with areas of the grammar that are more commonly the focus of what Chomsky (1999: 34) terms 'internalist biolinguistic inquiry'.

While we admit that research of this kind is in its infancy, we would argue that the approach that has been taken in this chapter, incorporating as it does a range of variationist and generative criteria, appears to be a fruitful method for interpreting syntactic phenomena associated with processes of convergence and divergence in grammar.

5　Phonology, grammar, and discourse in dialect convergence

Jenny Cheshire, Paul Kerswill, and Ann Williams

1　Introduction

The phenomenon of dialect convergence presents us with an opportunity to examine an issue that is not yet well understood in variation studies: the extent to which linguistic variation in different components of language patterns in similar ways. There have been more studies of phonetic and phonological variation than of any other kind, with the result that we now know a great deal about how sound changes typically spread through a speech community. Studies of morphosyntactic variation have been gently increasing in number, but sociolinguistic analyses of variation in discourse and, especially, in syntax remain relatively scarce. We still do not know, therefore, whether generalisations concerning the spread of sound change apply equally well to other types of language change, nor whether stable linguistic variation in phonology, grammar, and discourse features has a similar sociolinguistic distribution within a community.

The study of dialect convergence might shed light on these questions because the expectation here is, precisely, that there should be considerable commonality in the direction of change and, perhaps, in the rate of change also. If regionally or socially marked phonological features are being levelled within a community, we might expect other regionally or socially marked features to be levelled as well, with perhaps the same speakers or the same social groups driving all types of change. In this chapter we use data from our recent project on levelling in urban dialects in England to explore the question of whether there is isomorphism between patterns of variation and change in phonology, grammar, and discourse. Where grammatical variation is concerned, we will draw a distinction between morphosyntactic variation, where syntax has morphological effects, and syntactic variation, involving changes in word order or in clause structure. Thus, morphosyntactic variation is illustrated by the variable expression of agreement on present tense verbs in some English dialects (*I goes* versus *I go*); and syntactic variation by alternation between a passive construction and its active counterpart (*my phone was stolen* versus *someone stole*

We would like to thank David Adger, Peter Auer, and Frans Hinskens for their many helpful comments and suggestions.

my phone). Our conclusion will be that the fundamental differences between, on the one hand, phonology – and, perhaps, morphosyntax – and, on the other hand, syntax and discourse, result in few parallels other than superficial ones between processes of variation and change in these components of language. We begin, however, with a critical appraisal of what previous writers have seen as the main issues and unresolved problems concerning sociolinguistic variation in components beyond phonology.

2   Literature Review

2.1   *The extent of variation in different components of language*

A fundamental question is whether there is more variation in the phonetics and phonology of languages than in other components of linguistic structure. Hinskens (1998b: 160) states that the proportion of variable phenomena increases the closer one approaches the 'periphery' of the grammar, so that there is less phonological variation than phonetic variation, less morphological variation than phonological variation, and still less variation in syntax. Hudson (1996: 45) suggests one reason why this might be so, albeit as 'a very tentative hypothesis': speakers may use phonological variation to signal the social groups to which they feel they belong, but actively try to suppress variation in syntax because it is the mark of cohesion in society. Romaine (1980c), however, observes that the expansion and elaboration that is part of the standardisation process would be expected to lead to more syntactic variation within a speech community rather than less.

The link between language variation and language change suggests a further reason why there may be more phonetic variation than syntactic variation. Changes in pronunciation can arise spontaneously from the inherent phonetic variability of speech, but endogenous changes at higher levels of structure are rare or non-existent (Kroch 2001). In fact, it has long been assumed that higher-level change is dependent on change at lower levels: for example, phonetic changes can cause phonological weakening at the ends of words, with an accompanying loss of morphological case distinctions. This, in turn, may lead to grammatical reanalysis and a rigid word order to compensate for an increase in ambiguity arising from the loss of case marking. As Kroch says, this presumably accounts for many differences between present-day standard Dutch and standard German, and between classical Latin and its Romance daughter languages. Labov (2001: 12) goes as far as to argue that change in the surface phonetics may be the driving force behind the majority of structural linguistic changes. If higher-level changes stem from phonetic changes, then, there may well be more phonetic changes in progress at any point in time than grammatical changes.

The question of whether there is more variation in some components of the language than others would seem to be an empirical one: indeed, Hinskens also states that because there have been relatively few quantitative studies of dialect features in the realm of syntax (1998b: 159) we do not, in fact, know to what extent the different emphases reflect the actual proportion of variation in and across the dialects in these components of language. There is a similar lack of research into variation in discourse features: Macaulay (2002a: 298) stresses that the study of discourse variation is still at an elementary stage. In our opinion, however, the problem is not only that we lack quantitative sociolinguistic studies of syntax and discourse; we will argue later that variation in syntax and discourse features poses methodological and conceptual problems that prevent us from drawing realistic comparisons with phonological variation.

2.2   Social variation

A further fundamental question is whether sociolinguistic patterns of variation are the same at different levels of structure. In urban English-speaking communities many morphosyntactic variables have been shown to exhibit a sharp pattern of variation, where middle-class speakers show near-total avoidance of the nonstandard variants. In these communities phonological variation typically patterns differently: stratification is not sharp but gradient, with all speakers using all variants but with frequencies that vary in proportion to their position on the social class hierarchy.

It is often assumed that these patterns of gradient phonological variation and sharp grammatical variation tend to hold for all communities (see, for example, Chambers 2002: 350). French, however, shows the reverse pattern: here it is typically phonological variables that are the categorical distinguishers of social class, with gradient stratification exhibited by morphosyntactic variants such as the absence of *ne* in negative clauses (e.g. *je (ne) veux rien*, 'I don't want anything'), and also by some core interrogative structures (Armstrong 1997). Kerswill's (1994a) research into the Norwegian spoken by rural migrants to Bergen reveals a further complication. Here, the sociolinguistic patterns for phonological and morphosyntactic variation resemble those attested in the English-speaking world, but the relevant social factors determining sharp stratification include not only social class but also the rural urban dimension, resulting from the in-migration of people whose rural dialects differ greatly from the urban dialect. For example, in the morpholexis variants could be ascribed unequivocally to either the rural or the urban dialect (for example, the infinitive suffix -*e* is urban whereas -*a* is rural), and there was a clustering of individuals with either relatively high or relatively low usage of urban or rural forms (Kerswill 1994a: 109). Phonological and prosodic features, on the other hand, showed gradient stratification. Patterns of sharp and gradient stratification, then, need to be seen in relation to the social and cultural contexts in which they are found. Interestingly, Kerswill also found that rural speakers acquired features of the urban dialect most readily in the morpholexis, less readily in segmental phonology, and least readily in the prosody. We do not yet know, then, the extent to which sociolinguistic patterns of sharp or gradient variation differ for phonology, grammar, or, indeed, discourse in different languages and dialects, nor how these patterns might relate to processes of convergence and divergence.

2.3   Frequency of occurrence

One well-known reason why the study of syntactic variation has lagged so far behind that of phonological variation is that syntactic alternants recur less frequently in spontaneous speech than phonological features (see Cornips and Corrigan, this volume). Phonological variables show up with high frequencies in sociolinguistic interviews, and can be easily elicited in reading passages and wordlists. Syntactic variables, on the other hand, may occur only in special semantic or pragmatic circumstances, and rarely or unpredictably in interview settings (Rickford *et al.* 1995: 106). This is not an insurmountable problem: researchers have supplemented interview data with material drawn from observation (see, for example, Kallen 1991); from media monitoring and searches of electronic corpora (for example, Rickford *et al.* 1995); or from literature. Elicited introspective judgements are sometimes used, usually mixed with data from other sources (see Sells *et al.* 1996b). However, a data set gathered by such eclectic methods will not normally give equal representation to the different sections of the community; and there may be a random mixing of public and private contexts, and spoken, written, or electronic channels. There are advantages to using a heterogeneous database (see Berrendonner 1993; Cheshire 1995); but an important disadvantage is that we cannot use it to compare the social mechanism of language change in different components of language: for this a more systematically structured data set is needed, so that changes can be accurately charted as they spread from one section of the community to another.

The implications of the relative infrequency of syntactic variants are not confined to methodology: there are important theoretical issues, too. A central tenet of functionalism is that language use can shape grammatical structure, so that sequences of words or morphemes that frequently co-occur may become a single processing unit (see Kemmer and Barlow 2000; Bybee 2003). For example, in spontaneous conversation the English auxiliary *don't* occurs most frequently after a preceding first person singular pronoun and before the verb *know*. As a result, the phrase *I don't know* has come to be produced as a single unit, with phonological reduction to (*I*) *dunno* and with new pragmatic associations: it is still used with its literal meaning in answer to a question, but it is also used to mitigate an assertion or to politely disagree (Bybee 2003; Scheibman 2002). Frequency is a determining factor in grammaticalisation (Hopper and Traugott 1993: 103) and has been argued to be particularly important in syntactic change generally: Lightfoot (1996, 1999), for example, proposes that syntactic change depends on a slow drift in the frequencies with which speakers use various sentence types, so that eventually children are exposed to data that lead them to acquire a different grammar from previous generations. Elements that occur less than 30 per cent of the time, he argues, can be ignored in acquisition. In principle, we can expect this to apply to phonological elements as well. However, as far as rate of change is concerned, the crucial difference is that particular phonological elements occur, on average, much more frequently in the flow of speech than do particular grammatical constructions, and so are likely to change at a faster rate than grammatical, especially syntactic, features.

The relative infrequency of syntactic variants also makes them less available for social assessment, which, in turn, makes them less likely to become associated with a specific social group. If we assume, with Bell (1984), that stylistic variation derives from and echoes social variation, we must conclude that syntactic forms are less likely to function as sociolinguistic markers, in Labov's (1972a) sense. Again, this suggests that syntactic forms are less susceptible to change. Markers are variables to which speakers pay more or less conscious attention (Labov 1972a): in other words, they can be assumed to be salient (Trudgill 1986; Kerswill and Williams 2002a). Salient markers are likely to be involved in processes of dialect convergence and divergence (Trudgill 1986; Auer, Barden, and Grosskopf 1998: 163). Thus, if syntactic forms do not function as markers, they may be less salient, and may not play a role in the processes of speech accommodation that underlie long-term dialect convergence and divergence (though there may, of course, be internal, structural reasons that cause dialects to 'drift' and thereby converge). From this perspective, we would expect morphosyntactic variants to be both more salient and more subject to change than syntactic variants, because they occur more frequently.

There appear to be links, then, between frequency, salience, and processes of convergence and divergence. It has to be said, however, that the relationship between frequency and salience is not yet well understood. Kerswill and Williams (2002a) found that some features that were used infrequently by adolescents in our dialect-levelling project were nevertheless salient for them. Macaulay (1991: 58) points out that the saliency of lack of agreement for the speakers in his study was not because of its frequency: in his Ayrshire data only 7 per cent of third person singular verb forms (past tense forms of BE and most present tense verbs) showed lack of agreement. Hoffman (2002) maintains that low-frequency complex prepositions can be both cognitively salient and involved in change – in this case, in grammaticalisation. Again, then, we see that the impact of the relative infrequency of syntactic forms on their susceptibility to language change is not yet clear.

2.4   Syntactic variation

There are many problems in identifying the linguistic variable for syntax, most notably that of establishing the semantic equivalence of forms that could be considered to be variants. The issues were much discussed during the 1970s and 1980s (see, for example, Lavandera 1978; Cheshire 1987; Levinson 1988; Weiner and Labov 1983; Romaine 1980), and debate has continued since then (see, for example, with reference to French, Blanche-Benveniste 1997; Coveney 1997; Gadet 1997; and for general discussions Coveney 2002; Milroy and Gordon 2003). Cornips and Corrigan (this volume) also discuss several of the issues. Here we will focus on just one issue pointed out by Levinson (1988: 166) with reference to English *ain't*. Levinson asked whether speakers who use *ain't* more frequently than speakers from other social groups do so because for them *ain't* is a marker of group identity, or because *ain't* is a more emphatic form of negation than *isn't*, *aren't*, and the other alternants. If it is because it conveys emphasis, does this reflect an important aspect of the habitual patterns of social interaction of the social group to which the heavy *ain't* users belong? They might, for example, utter emphatic denials more frequently than other social groups in the community because they more often receive accusations. Thus, in order to understand how and why speakers use variation, and the effect that their usage has on language change, it may not be enough simply to analyse the simple alternation of forms: we must also perform qualitative analyses to see how speakers use the forms in social interaction.

The use of passive versus active clauses within a community provides a further illustration of this point. Macaulay's (1991: 98) analysis in Ayrshire found no significant differences between middle-class speakers and working-class speakers in their overall use of passive clauses. Importantly, however, there were social class differences in the use of *get*-passives (for example, *she got run over*), which occurred far more frequently in the interviews with speakers from the lower class. Weiner and Labov (1983: 43) claimed that a shift to the *get*-passive is one of the most active grammatical changes taking place in present-day English. In this context, the social-class differences are an important finding since they suggest a route for the diffusion of this construction through the community. However, Macaulay further reports that the *get*-passive occurred almost exclusively with animate subjects, and that these, in turn, occurred more frequently in the lower-class interviews. *Get*-passives are eventive, aspectually, and this probably contributes to the animacy effect in that events are usually controlled by an actor, and animates are more likely to be able to control such an event. Carter and McCarthy's corpus-based analysis (1999) adds a further dimension that must be taken into account: the *get*-passive highlights the stance of speakers towards the grammatical subject and the event encoded in the verb phrase. Their stance is usually a judgement that the circumstances are adverse, problematic, or otherwise noteworthy. Thus the shift to the *get*-passive could be led by a group-specific discourse preference for using animate subjects,[1] and for expressing the speaker's stance towards these subjects and the event that is mentioned. This is a telling illustration of the way that syntactic variation and syntactic change are intimately and inextricably part of the social construction of discourse. In order to understand fully the ongoing syntactic change, we need to know whether this social distribution reflects a distinctive habitual pattern of social interaction of the lower-class group of speakers. As Carter and McCarthy point out (1999: 55), judgements about adversity, noteworthiness, and the like are socioculturally founded and are emergent in the interaction rather than inherent in the semantics of verb choice or selection of voice or aspect. The type of stance expressed by the speaker can be determined only by examining tokens of the *get*-passive in their discourse context: a qualitative and interpretative dimension to the analysis, then, is essential.

Get-passives are not a unique phenomenon: many syntactic changes appear to have their roots in discourse strategies. Faarlund (1985) explains several changes in terms of 'pragmatic syntax', whereby speakers appear to have found a new form more useful for pragmatic purposes, and this has led to syntactic restructuring. Discourse factors can also play a role in the process of grammaticalisation (see, for example, Epstein (1994, 1995), who takes account of communicative intent, speaker attitude, grounding and thematic continuity in his analysis of the grammaticalisation of the Latin demonstrative *ille* to French *le*). Thus, an essential difference between syntactic variation and phonological variation is that there is a direct link between the syntactic constructions that speakers choose and their construction of discourse in social interaction. Milroy and Gordon (2003: 197) point out that work on higher level variation is often concerned largely with language-internal constraints on variation rather than on the relationship between language variation and the social world. Clearly, however, it is important to explore the social distribution of syntactic alternants if we are to understand processes of syntactic change; and it is necessary, there-fore, as we have said, to look beyond a quantitative analysis of alternating forms to see how speakers use the forms in social interaction. The example of *ain't*, mentioned at the beginning of this section, shows that morphosyntactic variants may raise similar questions. As Cornips and Corrigan point out (this volume),

---

[1] Alternatively (or additionally), *get*-passives might be avoided by middle-class educated speakers because 'got' is prescriptively considered nonstandard: for example, in formal styles *we have some ideas* is preferred to *we've got some ideas*. The expression of stance *in get*-passives would remain an important aspect of their use, however.

more research is needed to determine which grammatical variables (whether morphosyntactic or syntactic) can be considered equivalent in meaning.

2.5   Variation in discourse features

As with the study of syntactic variation, analyses of sociolinguistic variation in the use of pragmatic particles, set marking tags and other discourse features are scarce. We should not conclude, however, that discourse features such as these are never involved in sociolinguistic variation. Variation with social class has sometimes been noted: for example, in Macaulay's Ayrshire study (1991), working-class speakers used more discourse markers overall than middle-class speakers. Dines' (1980) Australian research found that working-class women used set marking tags such as *and that* more than three times as often as middle-class women. Woods (1991) reports that discourse features analysed in the Ottawa survey showed a greater amount of socially stratified variation than phonological variables: the middle-class speakers used a larger number of 'opinion openers' such as *I think, presumably, in my opinion*; whereas the working-class speakers used more markers soliciting or anticipating agreement between speaker and addressee, such as *you know, eh*, or *don't you think*. In New Zealand, Stubbe and Holmes (1995), similarly, found *you know* and *eh* to be more frequent in working-class speech, and *I think* in middle-class speech. In addition, *you know* occurred more frequently in the informal speech styles of both classes, and *I think* was more frequent in the more formal speech styles. Gender differences in the use of discourse markers have also been reported (for example, by Erman 1993; Stubbe and Holmes 1995; and Holmes 1995a; see further below). Nevertheless, Macaulay (2002a) reviews what is currently known about sociolinguistic variation in the use of discourse features, and concludes 'it would take a braver person than I am to assert with confidence that we have much solid information on gender, age or social class differences' (298).

In our view, the analysis of discourse features, like the analysis of syntactic variation, requires a more complex analysis than a simple counting of the number of tokens. Again, we need to consider how speakers use discourse features in interaction. For example, Erman (1993) found that *I mean, you see*, and *you know* were used more frequently by women than men in a sample of speakers from the London-Lund corpus; more importantly, however, there was a gender difference in the functions of these expressions. Women tended to use them between complete propositions, to connect arguments; men, on the other hand, tended to use them as attention-getting devices or to signal repair work. Holmes (1995a) finds a gender difference in the discourse function of both *you know* and *I mean*, with male speakers using them more often to signal referential meaning and female speakers to signal affective meaning. As with syntactic variation, then, important differences in the way that different social groups use discourse features in interaction may be obscured if we simply count numbers of tokens. This is not the case with phonological variation, where the form–meaning relationship is at its most arbitrary, nor, on the whole, with morphosyntactic variation (for an elaboration of this point, see Kerswill in press).

2.6   *The social mechanism of change at higher levels of language*

Finally, we turn to the question of the social mechanism of change at higher levels of linguistic structure. For phonological variation and change it is now possible to generalise from the large number of studies that have been conducted, in order to propose some general principles. Thus Labov (1990: 205), reviewing more than thirty years of research on phonetic and phonological variation, concludes that the clearest and most consistent sociolinguistic patterns concern the linguistic differentiation of women and men. Where there is stable sociolinguistic stratification, men use a higher frequency of nonstandard forms than women do. Gender has an equally important role in the process of sound change: indeed, the linguistic behaviour of female speakers is sometimes taken as a diagnostic of change in progress (for discussion, see Cheshire 2002a).

There are no known general principles of this kind for morphosyntactic changes, and we know still less about the social embedding of changes at other levels of structure, particularly higher level syntax and discourse. The few reports that do exist give a contradictory picture. We argued above that the relative infrequency of syntactic variants makes them unlikely to occur with sufficient frequency to become habitually associated with the speech of particular social groups. This in turn means that there is no reason to suppose that syntactic features will follow similar patterns of change to phonetic and phonological variables. Some studies do suggest a similar social patterning: for example, Rickford *et al.*'s (1995) analysis of topic-restricting *as far as* constructions found women appearing to lead in the loss of the verbal coda. The authors comment, however, that further study is needed of the intersection of gender with social class, which was not included in their study. Ferrara and Bell's (1995) analysis of the grammaticalisation of *like* found sex differentiation at the start of the grammaticalisation process, with a subsequent levelling out of this differentiation as the change proceeds – the reverse, in other words, of the patterns found in sound change, where typically sex differentiation is relatively slight in the early stages of a change, and then increases and interacts with other types of social variation such as social class (Labov 1990). Tagliamonte and Hudson's (1999) analysis of *BE like* leads them to conclude that discourse features may pattern differently from phonological features. As with Rickford *et al.*'s study, however, these studies of *BE like* do not take account of the possible interaction with social class. At present, then, like so many issues concerning variation in syntax and discourse, the question is unresolved.

3   The Milton Keynes, Reading, and Hull Project

We now turn to the results of the research project on dialect levelling and change that we directed between 1995 and 1999, in order to explore some of the unresolved issues mentioned above. The project, funded by the UK Economic and Social Research Council (project number R000236180), analysed the speech of 96 adolescents aged 14–15, in three English towns.[2] The towns contrast on a number of dimensions relevant to the phenomenon of dialect levelling and change. Two of the towns, Milton Keynes and Reading, are in southeast England, approximately the same distance north and west of London, respectively. They differ in that Milton Keynes is Britain's fastest-growing new town, whereas Reading is an older, prosperous, established town. Milton Keynes was founded in 1967 in a district containing some small towns and villages, and since then its population has more than quadrupled from 44,000 to 176,000 in 1991, and 207,000 in 2001. Reading has considerable in-migration, though less than Milton Keynes, but unlike Milton Keynes it also has a stable local population. In contrast, the third town, Hull, is in the northeast, some 200 miles from London. In Hull industries are declining and there is more out-migration than in-migration: unemployment levels are high and the levels of educational achievement in the local schools are low.

In each of the three towns we recorded 32 adolescents aged between 14 and 15; 16 were from a school in a broadly defined 'working-class' area, and 16 were from a school in a contrasting and equally broadly defined 'middle-class' area. There were equal numbers of boys and girls in each school. Thus the 96 adolescent speakers differ by region, gender, and, albeit very broadly, social class. Each speaker was recorded in three settings: in one-to-one 'ethnographic' interviews, mainly with Ann Williams but occasionally with Paul Kerswill; in more spontaneous interactions in pairs with the fieldworker; and in group discussions of 4–6 speakers, guided by the fieldworker. Four working-class elderly speakers (aged 70–80) were also recorded in each town, for comparison. The main focus of the project was on the role of adolescents in dialect levelling. We focused specifically on phonological levelling and diffusion, expecting that syntactic and discourse variants would be unlikely to occur in sufficient quantity for detailed analyses of these types of variables to be carried out. In the event, however, there were enough tokens for us to draw some preliminary conclusions about variation in these components of language, as we will see, and to consider

---

[2] Fuller details of the project are given in Cheshire, Kerswill, and Williams (1999); Williams and Kerswill (1999); and Kerswill and Williams (2002b).

what our analyses can contribute to the questions discussed in the previous section.

3.1   Phonological variation and change in the three towns

We begin by summarising some of the main findings of the analysis of phonological variation and change. Fuller details of this analysis are given in Kerswill and Williams (1999) and Williams and Kerswill (1999); see also Kerswill and Williams (2002a, b). This will serve as a baseline with which to compare variation and change at other levels of structure.

One significant finding concerns the consonant variables that were analysed. Figure 5.1 shows the distribution of T-glottalling and TH-fronting in the three towns. T-glottalling refers to the replacement of [t] by [ʔ] in intervocalic positions within a word, as in [beʔə] for *better*. TH-fronting refers to the variables (th) and (dh). The first has the variants /θ/ and /f/, as in *thin* (which can be pronounced [fɪn] as well as [θɪn]. The (dh) variable represents the equivalent process affecting non-initial /ð/, as in *mother* (which can be pronounced [mʌvə] or [mʌðə]. Figure 5.1 shows that the distribution of each of the incoming, non-standard variants is broadly similar in all three towns: the strongest social factor is social class, with middle-class (MC) teenagers using far fewer of the innovative forms than their working-class (WC) peers. Gender differentiation is, on the whole, slight, and patterning across the three towns is not consistent. All three features are at least a century old in London, and are known to be spreading throughout the southeast (along with a labiodental pronunciation of /r/; see Foulkes and Docherty 2000), albeit at different rates (TH-fronting has been slower to spread than T-glottalling). In Hull, however, all three are recent. The incoming forms have been adopted very rapidly: in Hull there is evidence that TH-fronting has only been common among children since the decade between 1980 and 1990 (Kerswill and Williams 2002a).

A further consonant variable, initial (h) in words such as *head* or *heart*, shows a different social and geographical distribution. All three towns lie in the large central belt in England where initial /h/ is dropped in traditional dialects, and generally in working-class speech. The elderly speakers in the three towns used initial /h/ only 5–12 per cent of the time, as figure 5.2 shows. However, figure 5.2 also shows that working-class teenagers in the two southern towns, especially Milton Keynes, have apparently reinstated the pronunciation of initial /h/, using it up to 83 per cent of the time. In Hull, on the other hand, the young people retain the traditional zero form. Here, then, there is a clear division between the northern town and the southern towns.

This is also true for the vowel variables that were analysed. For these variables there were independent, relatively local, developments which in some cases led to convergence between the two southern towns, though not between the

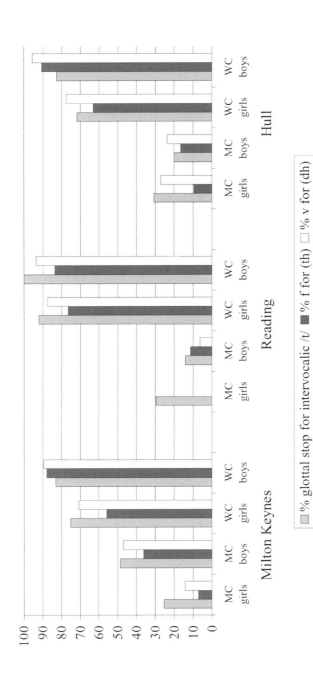

NB: (th) = fronting of /θ/ to [f]

(dh) = fronting of non-initial /ð/ to [v]

Fig. 5.1 Nonstandard variants of three consonantal variables (interview data) (from Cheshire *et al.* 1999).

Table 5.1 *Percentage use of variants (aɪ) (PRICE), Milton Keynes working-class speakers, interview style (from Williams and Kerswill 1999: 156)*

	[aɪ]	[ɑɪ]+	[ɑɪ]	[ɔɪ]	[ʌɪ]+	[ʌɪ]
Elderly age 70–80 (2f, 2m)	0	0	24.4	56.6	15.3	3.4
Girls age 14/15 (n = 8)	25.4	44.6	29.2	0.5	0	0
Boys age 14/15 (n = 8)	1.0	38.0	60.0	0	0	0

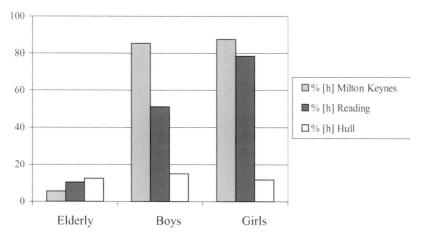

Fig. 5.2 Percentage use of [h] in lexical words, working-class speakers (interview data) (from Cheshire *et al.* 1999).

southern towns and Hull. Table 5.1 gives as an example the distribution of variants of the PRICE[3] vowel in the speech of the working-class teenagers in Milton Keynes. In this new town the young people's families came from outside the area and do not, on the whole, have local ties. As might be expected, there is only a small overlap in the realisations of this vowel by the 16 working-class adolescents and the 4 elderly speakers (these elderly speakers were from Bletchley, one of the small towns that pre-existed Milton Keynes and are now incorporated within the new borough). The dominant variant for boys is a back, diphthongal [ɑɪ], a London-like realisation which is geographically widespread in southeastern urban varieties. This does occur in the speech of the elderly, but for them it is more back and centralised realisations that occur more frequently. The girls have fronter variants, and these are not used at all by the elderly speakers.

[3] These words are used mnemonically following Well's (1982) system.

Table 5.2 *Percentage use of variants (aɪ) (PRICE), Reading working-class speakers, interview style (from Williams and Kerswill 1999: 156)*

	[aɪ]	[ɑɪ]+	[ɑɪ]	[ɔɪ]	[ʌɪ]+	[ʌɪ]
Elderly age 70–80 (2f, 2m)	0	12.4	47.8	21.8	1.7	15.7
Girls' age 14/15 (n = 8)	2.8	21.2	45.1	21.1	4.3	5.1
Boys' age 14/15 (n = 8)	0.6	19.1	63.7	13.7	2.7	0

Table 5.3 *The PRICE vowel with following voiceless and voiced consonants, Hull speakers (from Cheshire et al. 1999)*

	% [aɪ] ~ [aːˈ]	% [aː]
(a) With following voiceless consonant, e.g. *bright*		
WC elderly (n = 4)	100	0
WC girls (n = 8)	100	0
WC boys (n = 8)	100	0
MC girls (n = 8)	100	0
MC boys (n = 8)	100	0
(b) With following voiced consonant, e.g. *bride*		
WC elderly (n = 4)	0	100
WC girls (n = 8)	25.7	74.2
WC boys (n = 8)	17.5	82.5
MC girls (n = 8)	100	0
MC boys (n = 8)	95.0	5.0

Table 5.2 shows that in Reading, where many of the young people are in close contact with older family members from the local area, there *is* continuity in the realisation of this vowel between the elderly speakers and the working-class adolescents. Continuity is not absolute – the young people use the back and centralised variants of the vowel less frequently than the older speakers – but there is overlap in the vowel realisations. As in Milton Keynes, the predominant variant for the working-class boys is the general southeastern form. However, there is no clear pattern of gender differentiation.

In Hull, on the other hand, there is a very different pattern. Table 5.3 shows a complex allophonic patterning, for working-class speakers only, with an [aɪ] diphthong before voiceless consonants (as in *bright* or *pipe*), and an [aː] monophthong before voiced consonants (as in *bride* or *five*). Again, there is no pattern of gender differentiation. It is noteworthy that the allophonic patterning occurs almost exclusively in working-class speech: unusually for English phonological variables, then, the [aː] variant shows sharp stratification. There is evidence in these figures of the incipient loss of this alternation, which is now restricted to the city of Hull and the immediate environs. This loss would represent convergence with other Yorkshire varieties of English.

Williams and Kerswill (1999: 162) see these different social and geographical patterns of variation in terms of the multiple identities of the young speakers participating in the study. In all three towns the young people's linguistic identity was formed, in part, in opposition to the idea of 'being posh' – in other words, to being perceived as snobbish and/or upper class (Kerswill and Williams 1997). Importantly, for the Hull adolescents 'posh' speech was London speech. Although Received Pronunciation (RP) is a social accent, not tied to any region of Britain, there seems no doubt that for young people in the north of England RP is associated negatively both with 'posh' speech and with the south of England, particularly London (see also Cheshire and Edwards 1991). This, then, may account for the Hull adolescents' apparent avoidance of initial [h]. The innovating consonant features, which the same adolescents in Hull have apparently been very happy to adopt, are also southern in origin; but these are associated, we assume, not with RP but with nonstandard southeastern varieties of English (Foulkes and Docherty 1999: 11). They may even have lost any association with London and southeast England: the increase in the number of TV and radio stations and programmes directed at young people has led to a widespread use of informal and nonstandard registers in the broadcast media, many of which emanate from London and the south (Williams and Kerswill 1999: 162). Thus, these features may now be associated with a general youth culture, which is not tied to a particular region. At the same time, the Hull working-class realisation of the PRICE vowel allows young people in that town to retain an allegiance to their local class-based social networks, and their local Hull identity.

In summary, the phonological analysis reveals both convergence and divergence in the three urban centres. There is convergence in the rapid diffusion to all three towns of consonant features presumed to originate in London. However, a regional north–south divide is maintained through the continuing use of H-dropping by Hull adolescents and their divergent realisations of some vowel variables that are converging in the southern towns. Social class is an important factor in all three towns, but gender appears to be a considerably less important factor.

3.2   *Variation and change in morphosyntax*

There is a set of English morphosyntactic variables that have been analysed repeatedly, partly because they occur relatively frequently and partly, perhaps, because they can be analysed as an alternation between a standard English variant and a prescriptively identified nonstandard variant. Six of these well-known variables occurred relatively frequently in the recordings, so for these variables we could analyse patterns of variation across the three towns, and draw some comparisons with the findings of the phonological analysis. All six have nonstandard variants thought to be part of a generalised nonstandard variety of English typical of the urban centres in present-day England (Cheshire, Edwards, and Whittle 1989; Coupland 1988; Hughes and Trudgill 1995). These are:

1. multiple negation e.g. *I like England . . . I'm happy with it . . . we haven't got no diseases . . . no nothing* (Reading; cf. standard English *we haven't got any diseases . . . no anything*)
2. nonstandard *was* e.g. *we just held the brake and we was upside down all the way* (Milton Keynes; cf. standard English *we were upside down*)
3. nonstandard *were* e.g. *we was in the first year and he was in the last year weren't he?* (Reading; cf. standard English *he was in the first year wasn't he?*)
4. third person singular negative *don't* e.g. *my mum don't go to work* (Milton Keynes; cf. standard English *my mum doesn't go to work*)
5. preterite form *come* e.g. *it [my favourite food] used to be steak until the mad cow come about* (Milton Keynes; cf. standard English *came about*)
6. preterite form *done* for full verb DO e.g. *he used to play for Reading football club and he done his knees in so he's had loads of operation*s (Reading; cf. standard English *he did his knees in*)
7. relative pronoun *what* e.g. *have you noticed though there's no lads what want to do it really* (Hull; cf. standard English *no lads who want to do it*)

We have classified these variables as morphosyntactic on the grounds that they involve the morphological expression of a syntactic or semantic relation such as negation, agreement, or tense: in the case of multiple negation, for example, there is alternation between *any-* and *no-*. We calculated a frequency index for each feature following the usual variationist procedure (in other words, calculating the percentage of nonstandard variants relative to the total number of standard and nonstandard variants). Note that we have made no attempt to analyse how speakers use morphosyntactic variants in discourse, following the usual procedure in the analysis of morphosyntactic convergence and divergence (and in analyses of morphosyntactic variation and change generally). Many morphosyntactic variants occur in sufficient numbers for a quantitative analysis; and researchers usually identify variants on a standard – nonstandard dimension, as we have here (though this is not necessarily an appropriate procedure; see

Table 5.4 *Morphosyntactic variables: frequency indices of nonstandard variants and total number of variants in the speech of working-class adolescents in Milton Keynes, Reading, and Hull*

	Frequency index of nonstandard variants (total number of standard and nonstandard forms)		
Variant	Milton Keynes	Reading	Hull
negative concord	33.7 (92)	37.2 (43)	67.0 (68)
nonstandard *was*	20.6 (63)	28.9 (45)	78.3 (69)
nonstandard *were*	66.7 (6)	37.5 (24)	3.1 (224)
nonstandard *don't*	47.2 (36)	63.6 (33)	25.0 (28)
preterite *come*	56.8 (37)	82.4 (17)	72.3 (33)
preterite *done*	85.7 (7)	33.3 (24)	7.7 (13)
relative *what*	3.2 (95)	3.8 (52)	25.5 (51)

Cheshire 1999). Nevertheless analysis of their use in the wider discourse context is potentially important for an understanding of processes of convergence and divergence, for this can help us to understand the micro-interactions where these processes have their roots. For example, Eisikovits (1991: 241) found that nonstandard *don't* was used by male adolescents in her Sydney study to express a tough, anti-establishment identity which came to the fore at different moments in the flow of discourse and which accounted to at least some extent for the variation between *don't* and *doesn't*. Negative concord may well be an emphatic form of negation: if so, the questions we discussed in section 2.4 are also relevant here. Here, however, we will keep to a strictly quantitative analysis and focus simply on the parallels that can be drawn between morphosyntactic and phonological variation. Table 5.4 displays the results of this analysis.

Although the number of tokens is low in a few cases (for example, for preterite *done* in Milton Keynes), the table broadly confirms that several of these common core nonstandard features are robustly used in the three towns.[4] In Hull, nonstandard *were* and preterite *done* are clearly not local dialect features: their low incidence shows that grammatical levelling is not (yet) complete. It is striking, however, that the common core nonstandard features are as frequent overall in the new town of Milton Keynes as in the longer established urban centres of Reading and Hull.

In contrast, table 5.5 gives the frequency indices for two regional features: nonstandard verbal -*s* in Reading; and the zero definite article in Hull. In Reading and the southwest of England generally all present tense verbs can have the -*s*

---

[4] The nonstandard relative pronoun seems a possible exception, but further investigation has to wait for future work.

Table 5.5 *Frequency indices of localised nonstandard variants (total number of standard and nonstandard forms) in the speech of working-class adolescents in Reading and Hull*

	Frequency index of nonstandard forms (total)	
Variant	Reading	Hull
verbal–*s* (lexical verbs)	10.96 (657)	–
zero article	–	9.5 (738)

suffix (e.g. *I wants to be a hairdresser*), unlike standard English where the suffix is confined to third person singular subjects. In Hull there is sometimes no definite article where standard English would require one (e.g. *there was this fellow beating this other fellow up near flats*; cf. standard English *near the flats*). These nonstandard regional variants occur far less frequently than most of the common core nonstandard variants shown in table 5.4.

In both Reading and Hull, then, adolescents seem to be converging on the common core set of widespread urban nonstandard variants, in preference to more localised features. Milton Keynes, as a new town, has no localised features; but here too, as we said, there is convergence among the working-class speakers to the nonstandard rather than the standard English variants.

Thus, there is evidence of convergence across the three towns in the morphosyntax as well as is the phonology. We also note divergence in the morphosyntax, again as with the phonology, in that the speech of working-class adolescents in Hull shows evidence of a continuing north–south regional divide. These young people show continuity with older speakers in the community through their use of certain morphosyntactic forms that do not occur in the southern towns. The forms include past participle forms not heard in the south (for example, *foll* for southern *fell*, as in *I've foll in the river twice*); and [waɪnt] for southern *wound*, as in *you could leave your car unlocked and the window* [waɪnt] *down*). There is a distinctive negative BE paradigm, with [ɪn?] as the third singular present tense form (cf. standard English *isn't*) and [aː?] elsewhere in the present (cf. standard English [ɑːnt]). The adolescents also use several regional lexical forms, such as *twatted*, meaning 'hit' (e.g. *when I'm naughty I get twatted*), *croggy*, 'a ride on the crossbar of a bike' (e.g. *sometimes I give my brother a croggy*), *nowt*, 'nothing', and *owt*, 'anything'. Through their use of lexical and morphosyntactic features, then, the young working-class speakers can display a regional class-based identity, in much the same way as they do with their realisation of the PRICE vowel.

The middle-class adolescents used nonstandard forms once or twice, but never more than sporadically. Social class is an important social dimension here, then, as it was for phonological variation: the effect is sharper, however,

Table 5.6 *Frequency indices (total number of variants) for working-class girls and boys*

	MK girls	MK boys	Rdg girls	Rdg boys	Hull girls	Hull boys
negative concord	20.0 (50)	50.0 (42)	31.6 (24)	41.7 (19)	66.7 (39)	70.0 (29)
nonstandard *was*	15.8 (57)	66.7 (6)	42.3 (26)	10.5 (19)	77.8 (27)	78.6 (42)
nonstandard *were*	*	66.7 (6)	75.0 (8)	18.75 (16)	0.0 (63)	4.35 (161)
nonstandard *don't*	53.6 (28)	25.0 (8)	55.6 (18)	73.3 (15)	6.3 (16)	50.0 (12)
preterite *come*	40.0 (15)	68.2 (22)	*	78.6 (14)	58.3 (12)	80.1 (21)
preterite *done*	*	83.3 (6)	66.7 (6)	25 (6)	*	11.1 (9)
relative *what*	6.4 (47)	0.0 (48)	6.1 (33)	0.0 (19)	32.0 (25)	19.2 (26)
nonstandard *-s*			14.8 (357)	6.3 (300)		
zero definite article					8.3 (337)	10.5 (401)

* Indicates a total number of variants of 4 or lower.

for morphosyntax, which exhibits the usual pattern for English of sharp stratification. The effect of gender is less clear, as table 5.6 shows.

There is no clear pattern of gender variation, perhaps because for many of the gender groups the numbers of tokens are very low: a common obstacle to analyses of variation beyond phonology (see section 2.3). There are statistically significant gender differences only for the use of negative concord in Milton Keynes ($\chi^2 = 9.155$, df = 1, p < 0.001) where, following the conventional pattern, male speakers use a higher proportion of nonstandard forms than female speakers (see Chambers 2003: 116). The differences for negative concord are not significant, however, in Reading and Hull.

Milroy, Milroy, Hartley, and Walshaw (1994) suggest that female speakers may lead in the spread of forms with a supralocal distribution. This may be so for phonological forms, but if it applied equally well to morphosyntactic forms we would expect the regional variants – nonstandard verbal -s and the zero definite article – to occur less often in the girls' speech, since they should be using more of the supralocal standard English forms. In Hull the gender difference is small and not statistically significant; and in Reading it is, in fact, the girls who use a significantly higher proportion of nonstandard verbal -s ($\chi^2 = 12.1057$, df = 1, p < 0.001). Thus, although there is a clear pattern of social-class differentiation, the role of gender in convergence in the morphosyntactic component is unclear – as it was for convergence in the phonological component.

We can observe some parallels, then, between variation and change in the phonological and morphosyntactic components of language in the three towns. In each component there is evidence of convergence: in morphosyntax, convergence lies in the use of forms typical of the generalised nonstandard variety of English among the working-class adolescents, and in a lower frequency of use of the regionally marked forms. There is also evidence of divergence, seen here in the retention of some regionally marked morphosyntactic forms in Hull.

Social class is an important social dimension of variation for both phonology and morphosyntax, but gender appears to be less important.

3.3   Discourse forms

The rapidly innovating consonant features have a parallel in discourse in the rapid grammaticalisation of *like* as a focus marker and a marker of reported speech and thought (as in, respectively, *and we were like rushing home and she was like 'where are you off to?'*). Unlike the consonant features, however, these uses of *like* have been observed not only in Britain but in urban centres throughout the English-speaking world (Tagliamonte and Hudson 1999).[5] The origins are thought to lie in southern Californian 'valley speak' (Dailey-O'Cain 2000), as heard in the early 1980s Frank Zappa song 'Valley Girl'. The rapidity of the spread can be seen for one of the towns by comparing the frequency of occurrence of focus marker *like* in the Reading working-class group with its use by working-class speakers of roughly the same age in an earlier Reading study (Cheshire 1982): in our recent data there are between 6 and 10 tokens of *like* per 1,000 words, whereas in the earlier study the largest group of speakers (the 'Orts Road' group) uttered only 1 token of *like* in 8,948 words.

As with the southeastern consonant features, the rapid dissemination of focus marker *like* has been associated with a general youth culture – though this time, of course, we would have to assume an international dimension to the culture (see Macaulay 2001). The idea that there is an international dimension here is strengthened by the similar contemporary grammaticalisation of forms with an original meaning equivalent to 'like' that are in progress in several other languages, including Hebrew (Maschler 2002), German (Golato 2000), and Swedish (Kotsinas 1994) – though the mechanism by which this cross-linguistic phenomenon could occur is far from understood.

Table 5.7 shows the frequencies per thousand words for adolescents in the three towns. We can observe a parallel with the incoming consonant features in that it is the adolescents in Hull who use focus marker *like* most frequently. In the case of *like*, however, the existence of a clause-final discourse marker *like* in Hull may have played a role in the fast adoption of the focus marker. This is frequent in the speech of the elderly speakers (consider, as an example, *there was only three of us living together like . . . we lost two brothers* from Mrs Roberts), but occurs only rarely in the young people's speech. Individual adolescents varied in the frequency with which they used focus marker *like*, of course, but every speaker in the three towns used this feature, some very often indeed. In Hull there was a clear social-class difference, with the middle-class groups using new *like* more often than the working-class groups, as table 5.7 shows;

---

[5] Glottal realisations of /t/, however, are now found in New Zealand English; see Holmes (1995b).

Table 5.7 *Focus marker* like *in the three towns*

Group	Frequency per 1,000 words	(No. words)
Milton Keynes WC girls	11.05	18,916
Milton Keynes WC boys	14.32	12,703
Milton Keynes MC girls	10.19	24,045
Milton Keynes MC boys	5.96	27,875
Reading WC girls	6.53	15,012
Reading WC boys	9.16	14,274
Reading MC girls	6.0	25,353
Reading MC boys	9.44	15,681
Hull WC girls	10.79	16,214
Hull WC boys	10.41	17,199
Hull MC girls	15.56	23,536
Hull MC boys	14.05	19,287

apart from this, there were no discernible patterns of social class or gender variation. Despite some parallels with the rapidly diffusing consonants, then, the social distribution of this new discourse form differs from the phonological innovations, which were led by the working-class groups.

Another discourse marker that is thought to be rapidly innovating in the urban centres of Britain is *innit* as an invariant tag. This time the origins of the new uses are thought to lie not in the USA but in the speech of British ethnic minorities (Rampton 1995: 127; Andersen 2001: 100). *Innit* is presumably a contraction of *isn't it*, possibly via *ain't* (Andersen 2001: 105–107), but it is now used 'non-paradigmatically' – in other words, not copying *is* and *it* from a preceding main clause. As an example of the non-paradigmatic use, consider Extract 1: here Ann Williams and Dave are discussing the route from Milton Keynes to Chelmsford, where Dave's father's family live. The conventional tag question for Dave's main clause in (f) would presumably be *don't you* (copying the verb *do* in the main clause and an 'understood' subject *you*).

Extract 1

a   AW: so who do you go and see
b   Dave: we mostly go see my Mum's side of the family
c   AW: yeah in Chelmsford
d   Dave: yeah but we sometimes also go down to my Dad's cause it's sort of on the way really
e   AW: on the way out ['cause you come down the M1
→f Dave: [yeah do a little circle really innit
g   AW: and go down whatever it is to Chelmsford
h   Dave: yeah and then come back round on the M25 and back up the M1

In our recordings *innit* occurs far less frequently than the discourse marker *like*: there are only 36 tokens in total. A further difference is that *innit* is used exclusively by working-class speakers. Andersen's analysis of the Corpus of London Teenage Speech (COLT) revealed a similar social distribution for these two discourse forms: in London *like* was used by all social groups (though more frequently by the middle-class speakers); whereas *innit* was used more frequently by working-class speakers. Perhaps, then, convergence in the use of globally innovating features (such as focus marker *like*) is not led by any single social group. This would fit with the idea mentioned earlier that the international media, especially TV and films from the USA, play a role in the dissemination of features that are spreading on a global scale. Global identities are additive, and need not affect existing social or regional identities; and, if the spread of globally diffusing forms does not rely exclusively on face-to-face contact, speakers of all social and regional groups may acquire the forms simultaneously.

The use of *innit* by the two higher social-class groups in COLT as well as the lowest-class group perhaps indicates that *innit* has a longer history in London speech than in the three towns where we conducted our research, and that in London it is now spreading through the different social-class groups: certainly it was reported as used by young people there nearly twenty years ago (Hewitt 1986: 132). Furthermore, in London teenage speech non-paradigmatic uses outnumbered paradigmatic uses (181, or 56 per cent, of the 323 tokens of *innit* in Andersen's sample were used non-paradigmatically)[6] whereas in our data it is paradigmatic uses that are more frequent; 31 of the 36 tokens in our corpus, or 86 per cent, correspond to standard English *isn't it*. Extract 2 below is an example. This suggests to us that the discourse marker *innit* is not yet as 'grammaticalised' in the three towns we have studied as it is in London. A further difference between *innit* and *like*, then, is that *innit* may be spreading by social and regional diffusion.

Extract 2

    Kay: I'm going . . . first thing when I leave school I'm going to go to MacDonalds
        and see if I can get a job there
    R: <LAUGHS> MacDonalds
→ Kay: yeah it's a start though innit then weekly go to college so I've still got a bit of
        money anyway

However, the low frequency of *innit* in our recordings means that we cannot be as certain about its social and regional distribution as we can for the phonological or the morphosyntactic features – nor, indeed, as we can for *like*. A

---

[6] *We might as well go home, innit?* for *we might as well go home, mightn't we?* (though in the spoken standard *shouldn't we* is increasingly preferred to *mightn't we* in examples such as this).

surprisingly high proportion of *innit* tokens in our data – 8 of the 36 tokens – comes from working-class adolescents in Hull: of the remaining 8 tokens, 5 are from Reading and 3 from Milton Keynes. We think it unlikely that these figures accurately reflect the geographical distribution of the form: firstly, because non-paradigmatic *innit* was already used, albeit infrequently, by adolescents recorded in the late 1970s for Cheshire's earlier study in Reading (Cheshire 1982: 61); and secondly, because if geographical diffusion plays a part in the spread of *innit*, it would be strange if the form had reached Hull, the town furthest from London, before Reading and Milton Keynes. Our assumption that the use of *innit* indicates dialect convergence is therefore based largely on a comparison with Andersen's analysis of London teenage speech.

Conventional tag questions such as *don't you*, *aren't you*, and *isn't it* are also relatively rare in adolescent speech in our data. This makes it impossible to comment on whether *innit* is an invariant form that is replacing conventional tag questions in adolescent speech, or on whether its use in Hull indicates convergence in that *innit* is replacing the regionally marked tag form [ɪntɪ?] there. This regional form is used only once in our data (by a middle-class boy). The infrequency of all tags reflects, we assume, the nature of an interview setting. When the adolescents do use tags it is in those sections of the interview where they are talking with a friend as well as the interviewer, and the tags are often directed to their friend: extract 1 contains an infrequent example of *innit* directed to the interviewer. Like syntactic alternants, then, discourse forms may occur rarely or unpredictably in interviews (see section 2.3).

A further problem in the analysis of discourse forms, and a further similarity with syntactic forms, as we will see, lies in their role in social interaction. *Innit* in our data functions as an addressee-oriented positive politeness strategy, indicating that the speaker assumes that the information expressed in the previous clause is shared by the addressee. In extract 1, it is factual information that is assumed to be shared; in extract 2 the speaker assumes that her addressee shares the opinion she has just uttered. On other occasions *innit* functions as a negative politeness marker, softening an utterance where there are conflicting views between the speaker and the addressee. This is illustrated in extract 3, where Charles and his friend, Max, disagree about the ideal age to marry. Charles softens his explicit disagreement in (d) with *innit*, as well as a joke about being a granddad:

Extract 3

a   AW: do you think you'll get married then? what's a good age do you think?
b   Charles: about twenty-five twenty-six
c   Max: I reckon about thirty thirty-five
→d   Charles: too old innit you're going to be a grandad
e   Max: no you've got to live your life first haven't you

Note that the conventional tag *haven't you* in (e) is also used to attenuate disagreement by Max. The pragmatic functions of tags and pragmatic particles are well known to be flexible and to depend on the interactional context. Stubbe and Holmes (1995) point out, further, that discourse markers do not function in isolation. They found that speakers produced complex combinations of pragmatic particles such as *I mean* and *you know*, tag questions, set marking tags (e.g. *or whatever* and *and stuff like that*), and other forms: these clusters of discourse features occurred at key points in interactions to communicate subtle shades of meaning. Often this phenomenon was related to particular discourse or topic types. They conclude that 'the whole is somewhat greater than the sum of its parts' (Stubbe and Holmes 1995: 83). It is difficult to ignore, then, the potential relationship between the working-class adolescents' use of *innit* and their interactional style, as well as the topics they discuss. If there is indeed convergence in the use of *innit* throughout Britain, we can ask whether this represents a convergence simply in the use of a new, invariant tag, or whether it represents a convergence in interactional style. For example, perhaps young working-class speakers prefer a more involved, addressee-oriented interactive style, predisposing them to use new forms that have specific politeness functions. If so, we can ask whether this is an example of age-grading, with the discourse style – and the use of forms such as *innit* – becoming less used as adolescents enter adult life, or whether the discourse style – and *innit* – represents a more permanent aspect of their language use. A further question concerns the apparent diffusion through the social-class hierarchy, as found in Andersen's London study: are we observing diffusion of a more addressee-oriented interactive style, or simply diffusion of a single form that is perhaps replacing *isn't it* and the other paradigmatic tags?

The social and spatial diffusion of the new discourse marker *like* raises similar general questions, but the fact that *like* occurred in such large numbers in our data allowed us at least to chart its regional and social distribution and draw some broad comparisons with phonological features, in the same way that we did for the morphosyntactic features. For a full understanding of its use, however, we would need to consider how speakers use it in interaction.

In summary, we found evidence of convergence in the three towns in the use of discourse markers: most clearly in the widespread use of the new discourse marker *like*; less clearly in the use of *innit*. The social distribution of *like* does not parallel that of the consonant features that are innovating with equal rapidity, since unlike the consonant features there is no clear pattern of differentiation with social class. *Innit*, on the other hand, seems to be confined to working-class speech; here, then, social class remains an important division, as it does for the nonstandard morphosyntactic variants. The relative infrequency of *innit* confronted us with some of the analytical problems discussed in section 2.3. The main point to emerge, however, is that discourse features such as these must be analysed within their interactional context in order fully to understand the nature of any ongoing convergence or divergence. For those discourse features that occur frequently such an analysis would be possible, in principle, using the same recordings as for the analysis of convergence and divergence in phonology (we can do this for a future analysis of *like* in our data, for example). However, a different research design is necessary for features that occur less frequently or less predictably, such as *innit*. None of these issues was raised by our analysis of phonological features, where the link to the construction of discourse is more indirect; and, as we have said, it was possible to ignore the issues in the analysis of morphosyntactic features, although they may well be relevant here. It is not possible to ignore them when analysing syntactic variation, however, as we will see, for here the interactional dimension comes to the fore.

3.4   Analysing syntactic variation

The analysis of syntactic variation in the data set raises similar problems to the analysis of discourse features. We will use clauses with regionally distinctive emphatic pronoun tags briefly to illustrate the problems, and will also consider the question of using a variationist framework for the analysis of syntactic variation.

Emphatic pronouns are illustrated in extract 4.

Extract 4

a	Charlie:	the only time I drink is like at parties or
b	Matt:	yeah . . . not one of the things
		you do every day really is it . . . daft
c	Charlie:	don't like smoking or anything like that . . . no that's disgusting
d	→Matt:	I used to me . . . well I tried it
e	→Charlie:	I haven't even tried it me
f	Matt:	my mam wouldn't say nowt
g	AW:	do your parents smoke?
h	Charlie:	my mam does
i	Matt:	all of them do . . . got my real dad my step dad and my mam
j	→Charlie:	I don't like it me

Clauses with emphatic pronoun tags can be considered, perhaps, as a form of right dislocation. They involve subject copying: thus in (d) the subject *I* of Matt's *I used to me* is copied in the tag to the right of the verb phrase, taking the default form *me*. Although we refer to them as tags, like Macaulay (1991), this is not strictly accurate as they are integrated into the clause, as signalled by the inclusion of the pronoun and the preceding part of the clause within a single tone group. Charlie's *I haven't even tried it me* is a similar construction. We could assume that clauses with tags such as these are alternants to corresponding clauses without tags (here, *I used to* and *I haven't even tried it*). In principle, therefore, a variable could be set up with two different clause structures as the variants.

Emphatic pronoun tags occur in some northern varieties of English, as do 'amplificatory' tags involving subject and operator inversion, such as *she's a lovely girl is Ann* (Quirk *et al.* 1985: 1417). A similar construction where the tag consists of a demonstrative pronoun is widespread in colloquial English generally. As an example consider extract 5, where Kay and Ruth are talking about their favourite TV programmes.

Extract 5

Kay: I like that Tracy and [xxxxxxx]
Ruth: [Birds of a Feather . . . that's funny that
Kay: that's real funny that

Tags such as these are assumed to emphasise either the proposition of the clause (Biber *et al.* 1999: 958) or, in the case of emphatic pronoun tags, the subject of the clause.

As expected, pronoun tags occurred only in the northern town, Hull. Further, they occurred only in the speech of the working-class adolescents in Hull. There seems to be a parallel here, then, with the divergent phonological and morphosyntactic features mentioned earlier, in that by using these tags working-class speakers are maintaining a north–south dialect divide. However, as we mentioned, there are several problems that prevent us from drawing clear parallels.

The first problem concerns methodology: like *innit*, the tags are not very frequent in the data set. There are 30 in total: 16 from 4 of the male speakers, and 14 from 3 of the female speakers; 25 of the 30 tokens came from just 3 of these speakers. It is relevant, of course, that 3 adolescents use the forms relatively frequently, and, as with *innit*, it is necessary to examine the interviews to see why this might be so (for instance, the two boys who were high users of emphatic tags were friends recorded together). For the time being, however, we can simply note that the infrequency of the forms limits the possibilities of a quantitative analysis.

The second problem also concerns methodology, this time the situational context in which speakers use the tags. All the tokens occurred in the parts of the interviews where pairs of friends were recorded with the fieldworker, and where the young people were interacting as much with each other as with the fieldworker. Like *innit*, then, these constructions may never occur within the conventional format of the sociolinguistic interview. The four elderly speakers used no pronoun tags at all, presumably, again, because they were recorded in one-to-one interviews. The result is that we have no way of knowing whether the tags are used less frequently by younger speakers than older speakers, so we cannot draw any conclusions about whether they are declining in use in Hull. As with *innit*, the sociolinguistic interviews that are such a good methodology for investigating convergence in phonology within a socially structured data set do not provide the kind of data that allow us to address the same questions for syntactic convergence; it is not possible, then, systematically to compare convergence and divergence in these different components of language using the same data set.

Third, the choice of analytical framework poses several difficulties. Macaulay (1991) analysed emphatic pronoun tags as the result of syntactic movement, in line with the generativist framework of that time. In extract 6, however, Kay's *Peter André me* can only be considered as the result of movement if we assume an ellipted subject and verb (e.g. *I like*); and if we rely on the notion of ellipsis, we resort to our intuitions about the nature of well-formed utterances. This is a dangerous procedure, since intuitions about language are likely to be influenced by the norms of written standard language, which are not necessarily appropriate for analysing spoken language (for discussion see Cheshire 1999). Unlike generativists, sociolinguists tend to be suspicious of attributing structures in this way to forms that we cannot observe.

Extract 6

a	AW:	right what about a favourite singer then?
→b	Kay:	Peter André me
c	Ruth:	Peter André's alright but
→d	Kay:	he's got a real nice chest him
e	AW:	has he? is it hairy?
f	Kay:	no it's real brown and greasy
g	Ruth:	cos he has baby oil smothered on him

Working within a variationist framework raises a further problem. Rightly or wrongly, when analysing morphosyntactic variation, it is common to set up a variable consisting of a 'standard' and a 'nonstandard' variant. Unlike the morphosyntactic forms we analysed in section 3.2, however, the emphatic pronoun tags do not seem to have attracted the attention of language prescriptivists, and there is no obvious 'standard' equivalent with which they could be said to alternate. We could try, instead, to set up a variable on the basis of the discourse function of the tags; but what exactly is their discourse function? If we accept that they provide emphasis, we might consider setting up a variable consisting of two clause structures, as mentioned earlier (for example, *he's got a real nice chest him* and *he's got a real nice chest*). Emphasis does not affect truth conditions, so the variants are semantically equivalent. But appeals to the concept of emphasis lack theoretical rigour. As Sells *et al.* point out (1996b: 174), we need to specify clearly its status in the grammar, and the extent to which it can affect the form and function of different linguistic phenomena; otherwise the very ubiquity of appeals to this type of affective meaning may reduce its analytic value.

Yet another problem for a variationist analysis is that we surely cannot assume that every clause that is uttered has an equal chance of being expressed emphatically. The tags in our data can, indeed, all be loosely considered 'emphatic', but the emphasis affects the utterances and the ongoing interaction in different ways. For example, in extract 4 the tags mark an explicit contrast between the content of the speaker's clause and the content of the previous turn. Matt and Charlie are discussing smoking with the fieldworker, Ann Williams (AW). Charlie is a keen anti-smoker, and his first utterance about smoking makes it clear that he does not like smoking (*don't like smoking or anything like that . . . no that's disgusting*). Matt, with his *I used to me*, claims, in contrast, to have enjoyed smoking in the past, though he immediately modifies this to state that he has merely tried smoking. Charlie's *I haven't even tried it me* then emphatically contrasts his own experience of smoking with Matt's. His *I don't like it me* in the final clause in extract 4 then contrasts his dislike of smoking with the behaviour of Matt's family, which Matt has described in the previous two turns. The tags in extract 4, then, highlight these contrasts.

In extract 6, on the other hand, the tags are not explicitly contrastive; instead, they emphasise the speaker's stance towards the proposition they express. Perhaps they are implicitly contrastive here: thus Kay's *Peter André me*, given in response to Ann William's enquiry about her favourite singer, might imply that no matter who her friend might prefer, Kay's choice would be Peter André. Ruth's grudging acceptance of this nomination confirms her acceptance of Kay's opinion, and seems to indicate that he is not her own choice. Indeed, perhaps Kay already knew Ruth's opinion. Similarly, the proposition in Kay's *he's got a real nice chest him* expresses her approving stance towards Peter André, and perhaps the tag emphasises this by implicitly contrasting his charms with those of other potential candidates. A further function of the tags in extract 6 is, perhaps, to propose a topic: Ruth elaborates the topic of Peter André in (c), and Ann Williams picks up the topic of his chest in (e).

Speaker stance, in fact, is often explicitly expressed in the part of the clause that precedes the emphatic pronoun. Often there is an adjective and/or an intensifier expressing a positive evaluation, as in Kay's *real nice* in 6(d), or a verb conveying speaker stance, as in Charlie's *I don't like it me* in extract 4. Sometimes, on the other hand, the contrast performed by the tag expresses speaker stance implicitly, as in extract 7. Here Charlie and Matt nominate cider in response to Ann Williams' question about their favourite drink. Since this is an alcoholic drink they are too young to order this for themselves in a bar, and Charlie explains that a friend, Steve, buys his drink for him. Matt then states that he is able to buy his own drink. Using the pronoun tag makes explicit the contrast between what he is able to do and what Charlie is obliged to do. Matt is proud of the fact that he looks older than he is, and so is served without question, and in his next turn, in (k), he drives the point home by telling Ann Williams that he was drinking in the bar on just the previous Saturday.

Extract 7

a	Charlie:	oh I was going to say cider . . . cider cider
b	Matt:	oh cider
c	AW:	any special kind of cider?
d	Charlie:	Pulse Pulse cider yeah
e	Matt:	dry cider I like
f	AW:	are you allowed to buy it?
g	Charlie:	no I get er get . . . I get this kid to go in he's called Steve
→h	Matt:	I can get served though me
i	AW:	is that down here at the =
j	Charlie:	= Battney's Wines yeah
k	Matt:	I was drinking on Saturday as a matter of fact

The tags, then, seem to highlight the stance of speakers towards the proposition that is encoded in the clause, like the *get*-passives mentioned in section 2.4. Clearly, however, where we assume that the stance is implicit, we risk imposing our own interpretation on the utterance. We cannot always establish the function of the tags by inspecting the data. Thus, we are more confident about our interpretation of Matt's tag in extract 7, which seems to be justified by what is said in the subsequent turns, than by our interpretation of Kay's *Peter André me* in extract 6, where we had to make an informed guess at how the emphasis affected the function of the utterance.

In summary, the tags allow speakers to emphasise, or focus on, the subject encoded in the clause. This emphasis can serve several purposes, including marking an explicit contrast, as in extract 1, proposing a topic, as in extract 2, indicating the speaker's stance towards the proposition (or elements of the proposition), and, perhaps, still other purposes that have yet to be determined. These multiple functions do not fit well with the procedures of variationist analysis which, even if the criterion of semantic equivalence is relaxed, insist on equivalence in discourse function.

A sociolinguistic approach will seek to determine how speakers who do not use emphatic pronoun tags perform these discourse functions. Macaulay (1991, 2002b) reports that in his Ayrshire data emphatic pronoun tags were used to express intensity by the lower-class speakers alongside other syntactic constructions such as left dislocation, NP-fronting, and *it*-clefts. The middle-class speakers, on the other hand, conveyed intensity through the use of adverbial intensifiers, such as *extraordinarily* and *awfully*, as in (8) and (9).

(8) I found it extraordinarily boring
(9) oh well Jock it's awfully tasty (Macaulay 1991: 82)

This is an unsuspected finding with potentially important social implications, but it underlines the difficulty of using the linguistic variable for this type of feature (and Macaulay does not attempt to do so). The variable may well be a heuristic construct that does not necessarily map directly onto the units of linguistic structure (see Wolfram 1993; Winford 1996), but to include NP-fronting, say, and *it*-clefts in the same analytic unit as adverbials is surely stretching the concept of the variable beyond all credibility. A consequence is that, once again, we cannot draw a comparison between the use of this feature and the morphosyntactic and phonological features in the data set, since we cannot use the same analytical framework for the analyses.

A sociolinguistic analysis of the emphatic pronoun tags, then, forces us to look beyond a simple alternation of forms and to consider the linguistic strategies that different social groups employ to perform a similar discourse function, with the possibility that groups may converge or diverge on this level, too. If we do not do this, we risk misinterpreting the nature of specific cases of syntactic variation, as García (1985) has argued with reference to some previous research on syntactic variation. We also risk failing to discover important social differences in the construction of discourse. Macaulay's further analyses (see Macaulay 2002b) led him to argue that the greater use of highlighting constructions by working-class speakers in the data he analysed was one aspect of a discourse style that allowed hearers more freedom in interpretation than the style more typical of middle-class speakers. The middle classes' greater use of evaluative adverbs (and adjectives), on the other hand, imposed the speaker's interpretation on the listener.

This fundamental methodological point is further illustrated by the analysis of expletive *there* clauses in our data set (Cheshire 2002a; Cheshire and Williams 2002, Cheshire in press), as in extract 8.

Extract 8

it isn't a school no more . . . it was a swimming baths but it's closed now . . . they've
→   closed it down . . . there was some petitions up to try and open it up but we don't
think anything's happened about that (Mary; Hull)

We became interested in these constructions because previous studies have found them to be an important linguistic environment conditioning the use of *was* rather than *were* – and we assume that the widespread use of nonstandard *was* by all the working-class groups is an example of convergence, as we mentioned earlier. Here, however, we were not interested in whether or not there was agreement between the subject and the verb, but in what patterns of variation existed between expletive constructions and other linguistic forms.

The first step in the analysis, therefore, was to identify the functions of existential clauses in the data set. The most frequent function was their use by speakers to introduce a noun phrase referring to an entity that was new to the discourse, like *petitions* in extract 8. We therefore proceeded to identify the other linguistic forms that speakers used to introduce information that was discourse-new and hearer-new (using Prince's (1992) taxonomy). These forms included syntactic constructions such as fronting and left dislocation, addressee-oriented lexical forms like *sort of*, and performance cues such as hesitations and false starts. We found statistically significant social-class and gender differences in the overall use of these forms, with working-class speakers in all three towns and, especially, female speakers, using a lower number of forms that marked the appearance of new information. In other words, working-class speakers, and female speakers, were more likely to use 'bare' noun phrases to refer to a discourse-new, hearer-new entity, like *smackheads* (people who take drugs) in (g) in extract 9.

Extract 9

a   AW: tell me erm where you live . . . you told me Cranbrook and where do you live
b   Kay: Hillthorp
c   AW: and is that just round here
d   Kay: it's down there
e   AW: just down there and is it this side of Orchard Park
f   Clare: it's across the road over there
g   Kay: it's all the smackheads there
h   AW: who are they then. [where]
i   Clare: [druggies]

The sociolinguistic variation, however, was revealed only when we analysed the full range of forms that speakers used to introduce new entities into their discourse – a range that was far more diverse than we had anticipated, and that took us a long way from the analysis of the existential constructions that had been our starting-point. Like Macaulay, we interpreted our results in terms of discourse style, in this case seeing the greater use of 'elaborated' noun phrases by male speakers as an instance of the well-attested male discourse prefer-ence to focus on the successful communication of referential meaning (Holmes 1995a). This raises the same issues as discourse markers, in terms of whether convergence – or in this case divergence – is better understood as relating to interactional style. Again, then, this points to a deep-seated difference between the study of variation in syntax, and discourse, and the study of phonological and morphosyntactic variation.

4   Conclusions

Our analyses of variation and change in Milton Keynes, Reading, and Hull showed some parallel patterns in phonological and morphosyntactic variation.

We were able to discern similar processes of convergence and divergence in these components of language. Social class was an important factor; gender was less important.

We were also able to see a similar pattern of convergence in the rapid adoption of some specific phonological features and the discourse feature *like*. The social distribution was different, however: although the new phonological and discourse forms were found in the data for all social groups, the adoption of *like* was widespread across all groups. A second discourse feature, *innit*, was used only by working-class speakers, with its social distribution paralleling that of the morphosyntactic forms that were involved in dialect convergence.

We encountered several problems in our analyses of innovative discourse features and syntactic variation. Variation in these components of language seems to us to be of a very different nature from variation in phonology and morphosyntax. Although it is possible, in principle, to analyse syntactic variation in terms of a simple alternation of forms, in our opinion syntax is so central to the construction of discourse that we have to look beyond any superficial alternation to examine what speakers *do* with their grammar – in other words, to focus on social interaction. The point applies equally, we argued, to the analysis of discourse features.

We found no evidence that there is less variation in syntax than in the morphology or the phonology of language (see section 2.1). Our recordings contain, for example, many tokens of the emerging modals *wanna*, *gonna*, and *gotta* (Krug 2000). There is also variation in clause structure, including many passive clauses, clauses with left and right dislocation, fronting, clefting, and existential HAVE and BE constructions. Most of these constructions would not normally be considered as social or regional dialect forms, though Krug (2000) reports both social and regional variation in the distribution of the new modals, and social-class differences have been noted for *get*-passives, as we saw. Syntactic change may well be rare and hard to catch on the fly, as Kroch (2001) tells us; and, indeed, we have not so far found any sign of syntactic convergence in our three cities data. However, this is perhaps because we do not yet know what to look for: the analysis of morphosyntactic, discourse, and syntactic variation brings us face to face with the pervasive ideology of the standard language, which may influence the way in which we conceptualise and analyse syntactic variation (Cheshire and Stein 1997), and may even lead us to overlook its existence.

It seems clear to us that in order to gain a full understanding of how speakers use variation in syntactic and discourse forms, and how and why change occurs in these components of language, quantitative approaches need to be integrated with qualitative approaches. We argued that this is necessary for our understanding of convergence in the diffusion of the new discourse particle *innit*, and for our understanding of what appears to be divergence in the continuing use of emphatic pronoun tags in working-class speech in Hull. We also argued that a more holistic approach to the analysis of syntactic variation may reveal unexpected sociolinguistic patterns in the discourse styles preferred by different social groups, illustrating our argument with a discussion of emphatic pronoun tags and, more briefly, existential *there* constructions.

Finally, although we considered morphosyntactic variation as unproblematic, showing clear parallels with phonological variation, a more holistic qualitative approach might lead to new understandings here, too. Negation, for example, has a range of interactional functions (Cheshire 1998; Ford 2001), some of which may well affect the use of specific morphosyntactic forms, such as *ain't* or those found in multiple negation. It is possible, too, that this type of approach would be revealing for syntactic phenomena that might seem to be neutral in interactional terms. The presence or absence of complementiser *that*, for example, has been associated with speaker stance and speaker point of view (Biber 1988; Cheshire 1995; Dixon 1991). There are many features of this kind whose social and regional distribution has not yet been investigated and that may well turn out to form part of a distinctive discourse style or to have a function in the affective or empathetic aspects of spoken interaction. 'Dialect' can include interactional style, we suggest, as well as specific linguistic features.

There is no reason, then, to expect to find more than a loose isomorphism in patterns of variation and change in phonology, syntax, and discourse. In terms of dialect convergence or divergence, we can talk about structural changes in all linguistic components resulting from contact or isolation of speakers. However, for syntax and discourse, we must additionally take account of differences in the interactional strategies on the part of the social groups involved.

Part 2

Macrosociolinguistic Motivations
of Convergence and Divergence

6   Processes of standardisation in Scandinavia

Inge Lise Pedersen

Viewed from abroad, the three mainland Scandinavian countries of Denmark, Norway, and Sweden are rather similar. They are modern welfare states with ethnically and culturally homogeneous populations that have only recently seen substantial immigration from overseas. Their languages are related and to a great extent mutually intelligible, but as far as language standardisation is concerned there are considerable differences. As we shall see, Danish is one of the most standardised languages in Europe. Swedish standardisation comes close to this, whereas that of Norwegian has taken a very different path.

This chapter will focus on standardisation of spoken language in mainland Scandinavia. It will be based on an analysis of the standardisation process in Denmark, and will attempt to disentangle the interplay between ideological, political, demographic, social, and educational reasons why the standardisation of spoken Danish is as advanced as it is. Besides standardisation, the notions of convergence and divergence (cf. Auer and Hinskens 1996: 1ff.) will be used to refer to internal developments affecting the structure of both dialect and standard varieties.

1   'Standard Language' and 'Standardisation'

The modern tradition of language standardisation studies begins with the Prague School. Characterising the nature of a standard language, they drew attention to the special range of functions in which it was employed, as well as the direct connection with urban culture and civilisation (Joseph 1987: 13). According to this view, we may consider the presence of a standard language to be a major linguistic correlate of an essentially urban culture. With the advent of sociolinguistics in the 1960s, the definition gradually moves away from seeing standardisation as the product of the functional range in which the language is employed, towards standardisation seen as a process.

Weinreich (1954: 396) claimed that it is necessary to distinguish between standardised and non-standardised language. To avoid the ambiguous word 'standard', he proposed that the term standardisation should be used 'to denote a process of more or less conscious, planned, and centralized regulation of language'.

Most definitions of 'standard language' take the form of a description of certain components of language development which have been identified as crucial (overlapping) stages in the move from the presence of exclusively vernacular varieties to the development of a standard. According to Einar Haugen (1966 (1972): 252), the crucial stages are '(1) selection of norm, (2) codification of form, (3) elaboration of function, and (4) acceptance by the community'. This model has been elaborated by Henriksen, who expands the list to eight stages. These are seen by her as an interaction between a number of factors, some of which are linguistic and others social: a social *need* for a common norm; practical *training* in the use of the mother tongue; *propaganda* for the mother tongue; *selection* of the 'best' dialect as a model; *codification* of form in standardised grammars and dictionaries; functional *extension* (of linguistic form); *expansion* of the range of social uses; and *acceptance* of the norm, both officially and on part of the population at large (Henriksen 1979:7*f). Haugen and Henriksen differ only in the degree of specification of the individual stages; they agree that the standard language is by definition the common, or shared, language of a society that is more complex and inclusive than those using only vernaculars.

Milroy and Milroy (1985a: 22–23) stress that, in the case of English, only the written form is so fixed and invariant that it can properly be called a standard language. It is only in the spelling system that (almost) full standardisation has been achieved, as only minute deviations from the norm are tolerated, whereas a good deal of variation is tolerated in speech. Therefore they prefer to speak of standardisation as a historical process, like Haugen, but with greater emphasis on the intolerance of variability, as well as 'to speak more abstractly of standardization as an *ideology*, and a standard language as an idea in the mind rather than a reality'.

2   'Standard Language' as Ideology

Standard languages are founded on the belief that varieties other than the selected one are wrong. This proscription goes hand in hand with codification, operating as a 'standard ideology', and often having a strong influence on speakers' attitudes and on their linguistic behaviour. The presence of such an ideology causes the demarcation of a language characterising a certain geographic area, typically a nation state, making it linguistically distinct from other such states.

The 1980s and 1990s saw an extensive literature on linguistic prescriptivism and standardisation in the UK. A thorough discussion of the emergence of a standard ideology and a spoken standard English norm is presented by Mugglestone (1995). She demonstrates how accent, from the late eighteenth century onwards, came to act as a social symbol, with pronunciation becoming a way of articulating social identity as a part of 'good manners'. This development is related to the reorganisation of society that took place at the same time, the period of the Industrial Revolution, in terms of a change from institutionalised 'rank' to '(social) class' as the conceptual framework for the interpretation of society (Mugglestone 1995; 72, 74).

Bex and Watts (1999) constitutes a widening of the debate, in that spoken standard English is treated at some length, and it also contains some chapters on standard English as seen from outside the UK. Lesley Milroy, in her chapter, suggests that the notion of 'standard English' in the United States is different from that in Britain, because of different ideologies in Britain and the US, related to contrasting national histories and social structures (L. Milroy 1999: 203f.).

James Milroy, in a paper on the ideology of the standard language in Britain, stresses that until the mid-twentieth century the focus on uniformity was less salient than the idea of social prestige and social exclusiveness. 'The variety described as spoken standard English was in reality a supra-regional class dialect that was not used by the vast majority of the population and aspired to only by a few' (Milroy 2000: 20). Another point in Milroy's paper is that the notion of stigma is more explanatory than prestige. Changes in the history of English do not seem to emanate from the highest status groups, and it is by no means clear that the 'standard language' at any given time is a direct product of these groups. On the contrary: features of high-status dialects can be avoided just as low-status dialects are (24). Often people do not want to identify with either the highest-status or the lowest-status usage, and those with the highest social prestige are not necessarily seen as models of language use. Standardisation is a matter of negative identifying and avoidance (i.e. stigmatisation), rather than positive identification, and 'a prestige language is not identical in every respect with an idealised standard language' (25).

In the same volume, Richard Watts traces the ideology of prescription further back than does Mugglestone. He points to the connection with public education and to what he calls the myths of language and ethnicity and language and nationality that form the basis of the ideology (Watts 2000: 30, 34).

3   Studies of Standardisation in Germany

In these and other English-language publications, there is little if any consideration of the contemporary German discussion of standard language and processes
of standardisation. This is true also of most recent Scandinavian discussions –
perhaps more regrettably, since the language histories of at least two of the
Scandinavian countries show greater parallels with, and indeed connections to,
the German situation than to that of Great Britain.

What is common to Germany, Britain, and Scandinavia is that the standard
language becomes a social symbol, as witnessed by the title of Mattheier's

(1991) paper. From the late eighteenth and through the nineteenth centuries language becomes a social symbol in that the written and spoken standard takes over the task of symbolising the new leading social group, the educated members of the bourgeois culture, the *Bildungsbürgertum*.[1] From this social grouping, the standard ideology spreads to other parts of society, and, by the end of the nineteenth century, standard German is no longer a symbol of a particular social group, but has emerged as a national symbol (Mattheier 1991: 41, 43).

Competence in the standard language is an obvious signal of social status, and serves as part of culture and education (*Bildung*) as a line of demarcation between the bourgeoisie proper and petty bourgeoisie and the emerging working class. Due to the difference in timing between Britain and Germany regarding the standardisation of speech and industrialisation (industrialisation is much later in Germany than in Britain), the function of spoken standard German as a class accent is less obvious than is the case with standard English. In other words, it is more obvious that what is signalled in different accents in Germany is differences in status and lifestyle more than purely socioeconomic class differences (though, in practice, these may be hard to tease apart) (Kaschuba 1990: 228). Contributing to this is the ideology of the *Bürgertum* and its role and the ideology of Germany as a cultural nation; both make standard German a national symbol and, later, a tool of rationalisation in industrial society (Mattheier 1991: 49ff.; Polenz 1999: 59).

As pointed out above, standardisation of the spoken language took place at the same time in Britain, Germany, Denmark, and Sweden, but it is not synchronised in the same way with industrialisation. To understand the different courses that standardisation took, and the balance between social and national functions, it is necessary to see how standardisation and modernisation are intertwined.

4   Standardisation: A Summary

In living languages, standardisation is an ongoing process. According to Haugen (cf. above) it consists of a number of elements in a relatively fixed order: selection of a leading variety, codification, elaboration, and acceptance of the

---

[1] The core notions of '*Bildung*' (i.e. education and culture seen as inextricably bound up with each other) and '*Bürgertum*' (the state of being bourgeois, or middle class) merged in a new social grouping united by a critical distance from the privileged aristocracy and absolute monarchy and supporting a modern, secularised, post-corporate, enlightened civil society, i.e. defined by a shared culture. '*Bürgerlich*' means both bourgeois and civil, pointing to a real historical relationship, the interconnection between the rise of the middle classes and of the civil society. It is no mere coincidence that it is difficult to translate the above-mentioned core notions into English (for a thorough discussion, see Kocka 1993: 3ff.), whereas the semantic structure of the Scandinavian languages in this field corresponds better with German, with *Bildung* being translated as *dannelse* (Danish) and *bildning* (Swedish), *Bürgertum* as *borgerskab*. In the following Dan/Norw *dannet* is rendered as *educated*.

norm. As the ideal goals of a standard language, codification may be defined as minimal variation in form; elaboration as maximal variation in function. In other words: a full-fledged standard must be an omnifunctional language, able to fulfil a range of official roles, in addition to being a means of informal communication.

The written language is standardised earlier and to a higher degree than is the spoken language. The standardisation of European written languages started in the early modern period around 1500 with printing (and in some cases the Reformation) as important preconditions, and it was accomplished for orthography, morphology, syntax, and the lexicon during the nineteenth century.

As regards the spoken language, a standard ideology and the selection of 'the best dialect' typically go back to the sixteenth or seventeenth centuries in many countries. A more consistent codification and a simultaneous elaboration of function (not to mention dissemination and acceptance by the public) did not gather momentum until the end of the eighteenth century. This stage is closely connected with the stages of the modernisation process when bourgeois culture and nationalism emerged (Mattheier 1991: 41ff.; Linke 1991: 263; Feldbæk 1994: 139, 144).

5   Linguistic Standardisation in Mainland Scandinavia: An Overview

5.1   *Sketch of the political and linguistic history of mainland Scandinavia*

Linguistic standardisation began after the dissolution of the political union that had united the Nordic countries under the Danish king from 1397 to 1523. From this year to 1905, there were two independent Scandinavian states, Denmark and Sweden. Accordingly, two standard languages, Danish and Swedish, were developed (Haugen 1976: 245–248, 323–332). Norway belonged to the Danish realm until 1814, and was then ceded to Sweden, with internal self-rule, until independence in 1905. Denmark and Sweden, then, both have a long tradition as independent states, while Norway was under Danish hegemony for over 400 years (Haugen 1976: 346–352).

From 1660 to 1814, Denmark was a conglomerate and multilingual state consisting of the kingdoms of Denmark and Norway with the North Atlantic possessions of Iceland, Greenland, and the Faroe Islands, and the duchies of Schleswig and Holstein (Feldbæk 1990: 94–101). Sweden, too, was a multilingual state which, until 1809, included Finland and, for substantial periods, provinces on the south Baltic coast as well as part of Pomerania (Haugen 1976: 346–347).

In the northernmost parts of Norway, Sweden, and Finland, the indigenous population was Sami (Lappish) speaking (Vikør 2002: 9–10). Other parts of the Swedish empire had Swedish, Finnish, Estonian, Latvian, and German as native languages (ignoring the fact that Scania in the south of Sweden was Danish speaking, and some borderlands with Norway were Norwegian speaking). Finland was administered in Swedish, the other Swedish possessions mostly in German.

Danish was the main language in Denmark, and was used in the administration of Norway. The two duchies were German speaking, except for northern Schleswig, where only part of the population of the towns used German (Bjerrum 1973: 51ff). In Norway, Danish was used in church and for primary education. This meant that the Old Norwegian written language disappeared at the end of the medieval period, with the consequence that no modern standard was developed until the middle of the nineteenth century, when two different written standards emerged: a Dano-Norwegian (called *bokmål*, i.e. book language); and a New Norwegian (*nynorsk*) based on selected dialects from the western part of the country (Vikør 2002: 6–7).

Today, then, there are three nation states with three separate languages, but four written standards. Prescription and codification of the *written* languages is quite formal in all three countries, for about fifty years performed by official language boards[2] (in Sweden also the Swedish Academy). In Denmark, this culminated in a 1998 law obliging all public servants to follow regulations (mainly related to orthography) laid down by the language board.

In Denmark and Sweden the *spoken* languages have been standardised, too, although less explicitly. It is a moot point if a spoken standard exists in Norway even today, although it is made likely by the mere existence of a publication subtitled 'A guide to Eastern Norwegian spoken standard language' [Norwegian: 'En veiledning i østnorsk standardtalespråk'] (Vinje 1987; see also Sandøy 1998a: 164). It is clear, however, that a Norwegian spoken standard, to the extent that it exists, is far less functionally elaborated and is used by proportionally far fewer people than is the case for standard Danish and Swedish. It has been estimated that 15–20 per cent of the population use what could be called spoken standard Dano-Norwegian [Norwegian: *bokmålets normaltalemål*] (Vinje 1998: 152).

5.2   Denmark and Sweden: parallel processes of standardisation

The Danish and Swedish written (or rather printed) standards originated in the sixteenth century. They are associated with the Lutheran Reformation of the

---

[2] Danish: *Dansk Sprognævn*; Swedish: *Svenska språknämnden*; Norwegian: *Norsk språknemnd* (since 1972 known as *Norsk språkråd*).

church; linguistically, they are based on dialects in the respective metropolitan areas (Zealand and Mälardalen).

The emerging Danish standard language was morphologically modern, but orthographically more etymological than phonetic (Skautrup 1944–1970 [1947]: 187), while the Swedish orthographical norm from the very beginning (i.e. Gustav Vasa's translation of the Bible 1541) differed from the spoken language (especially regarding inflexional suffixes), in its attempt to establish a link back to the monastic scribal tradition of fifteenth-century Vadstena. At certain points (e.g. the adoption of *ä ö* for *æ ø*, and final unstressed *-a*) the Swedish standard is best described as conditioned by a conscious divergence from the neighbouring language, the formerly hegemonic Danish: the use of *-e* in endings in official documents from the sixteenth century is dependent upon a writing tradition which goes back to the time of the Scandinavian Union and the Swedish–Danish–German civil service language of this time. An abrupt change from *-e* to *-a* in official documents took place in 1612, during the Swedish–Danish War, 1611–1613 (Haugen 1976: 327; Svensson 1981: 132). The change is usually perceived as ideologically conditioned (Teleman 2002: 198).

The translations of the Bible in 1541 and 1550 are considered to be among the first manifestations of deliberate orthographic standardisation in Sweden and Denmark, respectively, although much more variation was tolerated than is usual today. In letters and other handwritten documents, a further one or two hundred years would elapse before a standardised orthography had been established. By the end of the eighteenth century, it is apparent that standardisation was achieved both in Denmark and Sweden. In Sweden, codification of spelling was made explicit in 1801 in a comprehensive manual, followed by a spelling dictionary in 1874, both issued by the Swedish Academy (Vikør 1993: 152; Teleman 2002: 108), while an official Danish orthographic dictionary was published in 1872 (Grundtvig 1872; cf. Jacobsen 1973: 40f.).

Only later did morphology and syntax become subjects of standardisation: conjugation of verbs shows great variability in Danish grammars from the eighteenth century, and word order in subordinate clauses was standardised only during the nineteenth century (Gregersen and Pedersen 2000). In Sweden, standardisation of morphology took place during the seventeenth and eighteenth centuries as well (Teleman 2002: 172f.).

5.3   Standardisation of the spoken language

A spoken standard language proper in these countries is a much later phenomenon, and the standardisation of speech follows a more winding path. It became the received wisdom that the best pronunciation was that which deviated the least from spelling (as for English; cf. Romaine 1998). Both in Denmark and Sweden, the history of the spoken standard language has been described as an approximation to the written language as a result of growing literacy, especially in the nineteenth century (Brøndum-Nielsen 1951: 92f.; Skautrup 1944–70 [1953]: 182; Wessén 1937: 300f.);[3] in the words of the linguist P. K. Thorsen: 'Without exaggeration, it could be claimed that the movement that has created, and is still creating modern common spoken Danish is nothing other than a constant battle between written language and Copenhagen dialect' (Thorsen (1906) 1929: 153, my translation). Most researchers agree on this. Brink and Lund (1975: 241, 768), however, in their thorough description of spoken standard Danish, seem to hold a different opinion. They claim that orthography has exerted only a slight influence on pronunciation, stressing that spoken standard Danish is the result of a natural development; it is not an artifact. This might very well be an apparent disagreement only, partly due to the fact that Brink and Lund are studying the age cohorts from 1840 to 1955, i.e. immediately after many changes had taken place in the (emerging) spoken standard. They do acknowledge that many changes in pronunciation came into spontaneous speech via the language used in recitations and orations throughout the nineteenth century, and this is the means by which orthography was able to influence speech. This is in line with Widmark's (1991) analysis of spoken standard Swedish; according to her, the public spoken language was the mediator between speech and writing in the last part of the nineteenth century.

In what follows, we shall take a closer look at the developments in Denmark, especially during the nineteenth century, and demonstrate that the influence from the public spoken variety is crucial for the standardisation process of spoken Danish, too (cf. Pedersen 1997). In Copenhagen, around 1800, the distinction between public and colloquial language was categorical and based upon general differences, whereas we would find only minor differences between educated colloquial speech and Copenhagen Vernacular. Around the middle of the century, this sociolinguistic structure was changing into two contrasting varieties: a High Copenhagen, with standard language functions; and a stigmatised Low Copenhagen. From now on there are only minor stylistic differences between public and educated colloquial language. Attitudes to dialects outside Copenhagen were not affected by this development; throughout the nineteenth century (rural) dialects were perceived as corrupt (Pedersen in press).

---

[3] In this connection literacy must be specified as writing skills, since reading skills were considerable already in the seventeenth century in both countries. It is evident from parish registers that proficiency in reading is taken for granted at the end of the seventeenth century, since a lack of proficiency is explained or excused (Appel 2001: 363).

6   The Standardisation of Spoken Danish

6.1   Selection of dialect

During the seventeenth century, grammarians engaged in an intense discussion as to which dialect was the 'best' in relation to the written language. The choice was between Zealandic ('like knowledgeable Zealandic men speak, refined and in assembly' (Danish: *sirligen og i Forsamling*, e.g. in council or in court) (Syv 1685: 3)) and the language spoken by individuals born in the capital of Danish parents, or academic people from the university of Copenhagen (Gerner 1690: 30). In both cases, it is emphasised that it is a matter of the public spoken language; it is not a question of the language of the common people, but the language of educated speakers only. In the words of these old grammarians, we glimpse the contours of a tripartite division of spoken Danish varieties.

This three-way split is also found in Høysgaard (1747: 370, 385), and is clearly expressed by most grammarians around 1800. In the introduction to Jacob Baden's grammar, we find this idea expressed thus: 'In all languages cultivated through writing, a threefold pronunciation is found. The common man pronounces the words that he has learnt, not from writings but only from oral tradition, in one way [lit.: "different"]. The pronunciation of the educated man in civil life is different; and that of the public speaker different again' (Baden 1785: 1, my translation). The same categorisation is found in a grammar for German students, where the author distinguishes between four ways of pronouncing Danish: '(1) The formal language, as among preachers and secular orators, and when Danish is taught; (2) decent persons' colloquial language [*die Sprache hübscher Leute im täglichen Umgange*]; (3) ordinary people's pronunciation; and (4) Danish spoken by other Germans' (Tode 1797: 2, quoted from Nielsen 1952: 34).

Time and again throughout the eighteenth and part of the nineteenth century, we are presented with not a bipartite division between dialect and standard but a three-way division; none of these three parts can be labelled a spoken standard language. The standardised written language was matched by two spoken elite varieties, both functionally and socially restricted, and neither qualifying as a spoken standard proper.

6.2   Public vs. educated colloquial speech

We have a description of these two elite varieties from the pen of Jakob Horne-mann Bredsdorff. In 1817, Bredsdorff published what is probably the oldest Danish text in phonetic transcription. It contains a story pronounced as would 'the educated Dane in orations and formal recitations' [Danish: *den cultiverede*

Danske . . . i Taler og det højtidelige Foredrag] and a dialogue in 'colloquial language' [Danish: *Hverdagssproget*]. 'A' speaks a Danish free of all (local) peculiarities (i.e. educated colloquial speech), while 'B' uses Copenhagen vernacular [Danish: *i A's Repliker frit for alle Idiotismer, og i B's efter den sædvanlige kjøbenhavnske Udtale*]. Once more we meet the three-way division; interestingly, the subject of the dialogue is a discussion of the use of the formal orational style. The two speakers do not agree on whether or not one should distinguish between public speech and conversation. A's educated colloquial speech in Bredsdorff's dialogue is characterised by forms like *mæj* (orthographically *mig* 'me'), *gi* (*give* 'give'), *sie* (*sige* 'say'), *jæj, je* (*jeg* 'I'), *sbøre* (*spørge* 'ask'), *føle* (*følge* 'follow'), *øjet* (*øjet* 'the eye'), *inte* (*ikke* 'not'). Bredsdorff's Copenhagen Vernacular is not far from this, though it contains some forms with different vowel qualities, like *maj* (*mig* 'me'), *ge* (*give* 'give'), *jaj* (*jeg* 'I'), *håjeste* (*højeste* 'highest'), *ente* (*ikke* 'not'), all of these characterised by diverging more from writing than do A's corresponding forms.

In contrast to this, Bredsdorff's formal public style is very close to the written language. It is a kind of spelling pronunciation with forms like: *havde* (orthographically *havde* 'had'), *sagde* (*sagde* 'said'), *mig* (*mig* 'me'), *give* (*give* 'give'), *dæt* (*det* 'it'), *sælv* (*selv* 'self'), *sburgte* (*spurgte* 'asked'), *følge* (*følge* 'follow'). In some cases we are presented with different word forms: *eke* (*ikke* 'not', vs. colloquial *inte*), and plural verb forms (vs. colloquial singular forms): *vi skule* (*vi skulle* 'we shall').

A generation later, Israel Levin still distinguished between a spoken literary language, or the type of language characteristic of the public lecture, which was perceived as the main object of grammatical description, and the colloquial language or the idiom in which educated Danes communicated in private conversations [Danish: *Skriftsproget (Bogsproget), eller den Sprogform, der udpræger sig i det offentlige Foredrag . . . fra Talerstolen, prædikestolen, og den tragiske Scenes Bræder, er nærværende Grammatiks Hovedgjenstand; men ogsaa de væsentligste og meest betydende Phænomener af Talesproget (Omgangssproget), eller det idiom, hvori dannede Danske meddele sig hinanden i den private Samtale, angives overalt*]. In his grammar only the most important phenomena from this variety would be described in relation to the written language (Levin 1844: V–VI).

In the nineteenth century, public and educated colloquial language differed on several linguistic levels, as is evident from the above examples, but mostly on the lexical and phonological level. Some phonological differences are lexically conditioned, but the majority of differences are more general.[4] The public forms tend to be closer to the written form.

---

[4] The examples below are taken from a number of texts; for further examples, see also Skautrup (1953).

In educated colloquial speech we find diphthongs like [iw, eːw, øːw, aw, ɒːw] and [ɛj, ʌj], where public spoken language would have a (long) vowel + consonant, e.g. in the words [sgiwʔəð] vs. [sgiʔbət] *skibet* 'the ship', [seːw] vs. [sɛːbə] *sæbe* 'soap', [løːw] vs. [løːbə] *løbe* 'run', [law] vs. [laʔɣ] *lag* 'layer', [sɒːw] vs. [sɔːvə] *sove* 'sleep', [rɒːw] vs. [rɔːbə] *råbe* 'shout', [sdɛjʔ] vs. [sdeʔɣ] *steg* 'roast', [bʌjʔʌ] vs. [bøʔɣʌ] *bøger* 'books'. Another main difference is consonant loss in educated colloquial speech and Copenhagen Vernacular vs. substitution in public language, especially by fricative d in words like *kedel* 'kettle', *hvidkål* 'cabbage', *rødvin* 'red wine', *blødkogt* 'soft-boiled', *Bredgade* 'Broadstreet' (street name).

Besides this, educated colloquial speech was characterised by many assimilations: assimilated /rs/ > /s/, /rv/ > /r/ and /ld/, /lg/, /lv/ > /l/; /nd/ > /n/ and /rd/ > /r/, where public style would prefer unassimilated forms. This applies to a great number of words e.g. *kirsebær* 'cherry', *kurv, arve* 'basket, inherit', *vilde* 'wild', *sælge* 'sell', *kalv, halve* 'calf, half', *gulve* 'floors'; *binde, vinde* 'bind, win'; *myrde, gjorde, jorden* 'murder, did, the earth'.

According to contemporary descriptions, the split between public and colloquial speech was highly salient until the late nineteenth century. As late as 1873, in an article 'Literary language and the dialects', Pauline Worm distinguished between three different kinds of Danish and gave some examples of how they sounded (Worm 1873: 87):

Literary Danish[a]	Cultivated Copenhagen	Ordinary Copenhagen	English
Kan du ikke ryge?	Kan du ikke rye?	Kadunte rye?	Can you not smoke?
De skulle ikke have det	Di skal ikke ha de	Diskante hatte	They shall not have it
Vi vide hvad vi ville	Vi véd va vi vil	Vi vé va vi ve	We know what we will
Pigen har været i vandet	Pien har væred i vanned	Pien ha vætt (våren) i vanned	The girl has been in the water
Hun ligner sin moder;	Hun liner sin mor;	Hun liner hinneses mor;	She looks like her mother;
Hun er mageløs nydelig	Hun er mageløs nydeli	Hun æ maveløs nydelien	She is exceptionally pretty
Jeg kan ikke sluge halve æbler	Jæj kan ikke slue halle æbler	Jækante slue halle ævler	I cannot swallow half apples
Et egetræ i Kjøge og et bøgetræ i Stege	Et æjetræ i Köje å et böjetræ i Stæje	Ed ajetræ i Kåje å ed båjetræ i Staje	An oak in Køge and a beech in Stege

[a] The Danish terms are: *skriftdansk, dannet kjøbenhavnsk*, and *simpelt kjøbenhavnsk*.

In these examples we find both differences in pronunciation (mostly of the type mentioned above), inflectional differences, and enclitics versus non-enclitics.

Worm was the head of a girls' school in a provincial town, and she may have been old fashioned or linguistically conservative, but she demonstrates that in many urban circles formal public language and educated colloquial language (in her terminology literary Danish and educated or cultivated Copenhagen) were still perceived as two different varieties, each of them with a functional area of its own. One was not more correct than the other, but it was important to observe the rules of where and when they could be used.

6.3   Colloquial speech in early bourgeois society

The clear distinction between public and educated colloquial speech corresponds to the sharp differentiation between social spheres. Spoken language both mirrored and maintained the sharp societal distinction between public and private: 'With the differentiation of social spheres (for instance, production, family, politics) . . . individuals became increasingly and continuously tied to forms of specialised activity. This involved a more thorough and reinforced differentiation of roles between those engaged in economic activities and in education, between domestic and non-domestic labour, between production and reproduction, between men and women' (Kocka 1993: 14).

This differentiation between spheres seems to have been more important, linguistically, than were social differences, and the stylistic differences were growing in the first half of the nineteenth century. At the same time, however, bourgeois culture as a style of life, a code of conduct – and a way of speaking – claimed universal social validity for itself, seeing itself as the point of reference for other social groups. This is interconnected with the emerging national identity.

Until this time, and certainly through much of the eighteenth century, the languages of the ruling class in Denmark were to a great extent German and French. For long periods, German had been the preferred language in the royal family, as well as the colloquial language not only of the greater part of the upper classes but also of many ordinary citizens in the major towns, too. Consequently, language choice had not been decisive for an individual to be perceived a good patriot.

Starting in the 1770s, a new Danish national identity entered its formative stages. The members of the royal family who took power at a palace revolution in 1772 identified themselves with a demonstrative Danishness; Danish was introduced as the language of the court, and in 1776 a Law of Indigenous Rights was proclaimed, giving those born in the conglomerate state exclusive rights to hold office. Indigenous rights were defined by place of birth, not by language (Holstein was German speaking), but to the cosmopolitan elite the law was seen as anti-German and as a cultural setback, whereas the Danish bourgeoisie reacted enthusiastically. 'In 1776, the new national identity was entrenched within a numerically small, but dynamic urban section of Danish society which saw itself as the interpreter of the people, the nation' (Feldbæk 1994: 143, my translation).

After another coup d'état in 1784, the ruling circle was again dominated by an aristocratic, German-speaking, and culturally German group, and criticism of the rulers could be construed as anti-Germanness. Here we are presented with a new national discourse in the emerging bourgeoisie, stressing place of birth *and* language (Damsholt 2000: 117), and educated spoken Danish became a social marker of this group. Some German bourgeois families left the country during these years, others consciously shifted to Danish as their colloquial language, since to be German speaking tended to be perceived as pro-German and unpatriotic (Winge 1992: 314).

While the educated Danes of the seventeenth and eighteenth centuries might shift between different languages according to situation, interlocutor, and social domain (cf. Pedersen in press), the new educated bourgeoisie would prefer to speak Danish to all interlocutors competent in this language. Consequently, a new linguistic awareness was emerging, with a stylistic differentiation taking place within spoken Danish; inter-language differences changed into intra-language differences.

We can add to this the demographic development of Copenhagen. The capital had seen rapid growth during the seventeenth century; however, between the beginning of the eighteenth century and the 1840s population growth ceased. Copenhagen was still a medieval type of town, surrounded by ramparts, and because of this stagnation the majority of the inhabitants were born and bred in the capital. Thus, the social conditions were right for the emergence of a close-knit bourgeois community with a focused linguistic norm of colloquial speech.

From the first half of the nineteenth century, we have much contemporary evidence that the same colloquial forms were used by ordinary and higher class people, and no *systematic* class-related differences in pronunciation have been reported in Copenhagen dialect from this time, only insufficient command of foreign words by the common man (cf. Brink and Lund 1975).

6.4   *Public spoken Danish and political and social developments from the mid-eighteenth to the mid-nineteenth centuries*

At the beginning of this period public spoken Danish was used only in a few functional domains. It was heard in courts and in the pulpit, and a Danish theatre was open in 1722–1728, and again from the 1740s. In all other public domains, languages other than Danish were used. There was no public political debate about this, and German remained the language of command in the army (although not in the navy); Latin continued as the language of instruction in grammar schools and at the University of Copenhagen; while Danish was used for elementary teaching, but only in reading. Within the next generation, Danish became used for many more public domains, taking in educational institutions and politics. The first lectures in Danish at the University of Copenhagen were given during the 1770s (from about 1840 all lectures were in Danish); grammar schools changed into mainly Danish-speaking schools around 1800; and compulsory education (in Danish) was introduced in 1814.

By now, many things were changing. Politically, absolutism was on the wane, and an animated public political debate took place, especially within the bourgeoisie in Copenhagen, where the mercantile elite and the intelligentsia formed a political alliance in the National–Liberal party, struggling against absolutism and against the more conservative group of large landowners and loyal urban lower middle classes and their rural counterpart, the freeholders.

From the 1840s all public domains were Danish speaking, and in 1849 a new constitution introduced a democratically elected parliament. Through this development, wider circles were politically mobilised. New groups of people entered the public arena, among them a new 'minor elite' of farmers and primary school teachers (often dialect-speaking farmers' sons). By now, participation in public debate was no longer a privilege of a small bourgeois group in Copenhagen, but had been greatly widened. Many contemporary observers point to the 1850s as a sociolinguistic turning-point (Skautrup 1944–1970 [1953]: 185).

The societal changes of this period may well have had a bearing on the sociolinguistic restructuring and redistribution that was taking place. The public language was the subject of teaching, and in 1814 compulsory education was introduced, and many young people went to evening classes and Folk High Schools. Add to this that through their public activities (in teaching, public meetings, (local) policy, or in one of the numerous co-operative societies and other associations that were formed) broader groups could also learn the public language in natural use, though they did not necessarily have the same opportunity for learning the colloquial language, used among educated individuals in private conversation. To learn this code (and the rules of style shifting) one needed to have access to the bourgeois salons and the opportunity to take part in the social life of the Copenhagen bourgeois families. These circumstances led to some kind of compromise: the borderlines between public and colloquial speech became blurred, and the educated colloquial speech style expanded functionally at the expence of the public style. At the same time this colloquial style was converging on the public style, by adopting certain features from it, especially features that were closer to the written language than were the corresponding features in the older, colloquial variety. This compromise marked the rise of a spoken standard language – and at the same time the beginning of a new dialect split.

6.5   The emergence of a socially stratified spoken standard language

We know from contemporary witnesses that the former local urban dialect in Copenhagen was gradually diverging into two sociolects. A number of variants in the traditional colloquial variety, which was becoming moribund, came to be avoided, primarily those deviating from orthography. These had been perceived as correct when used in private conversation, even among educated citizens, but from now on they were stigmatised. A reallocation took place from stylistic to social markers, the 1840s and 1850s being the decisive years for this development.

The stigmatised forms were primarily diphthongal pronunciations of words like *købe* 'buy', *sæbe* 'soap', *lag* 'layer', *neg* 'sheaf', *bøger* 'books', *låg* 'lid', from this point onwards pronounced with vowel + [b], [ɣ]. Not all diphthongal pronunciations were changed. In highly frequent words, such as the personal pronouns *mig, dig* 'me, you' and the reflexive pronoun *sig*, the diphthongs were maintained, as they were in other frequent words, for instance, *leg* 'play', *steg* 'roast' (but not in the homophone *steg* (pret. of *stige* 'climb')), *løg* 'onion', *røg* 'smoke'. There was also a tendency towards the restitution of assimilated consonants, especially in bisyllabic words, resulting in alternations between singular *gulv, kalv* 'floor, calf' (pronounced with a final /l/) and plural *gulve, kalve* (with /lv/), and in even more unpredictable forms like *jord, mord, færd, på færde* 'earth, murder, expedition', going on with a single /r/, vs. *hjord, hyrde, morder, færdes* 'herd, shepherd, murderer, move', pronounced with /rd/.

The new dialect division was a split between the politically dominant group of professionals and merchants *vis-à-vis* artisans and workers, and it seems to have been the middle classes that were changing their language by stigmatising many features of the former common local dialect, while the lower classes stuck to the traditional dialect features. In place of the stigmatised variants, the middle class adopted phonological features from the public style into the colloquial style.

The dialogue in the musical *Gjenboerne* ('The Neighbours Opposite' 1844, in Hostrup 1889) could be perceived as an example of an early stage of this development, since it indicates a certain divergence between the speech of students and artisans, and between academic people and *petit bourgeois*. Not only the journeymen but also the wife of the rather affluent coppersmith are characterised by using the colloquial features listed above, while the students' pronunciation is unmarked, in so far as their lines have the usual spelling. It is beyond doubt that this lack of marking signals that the students and academic people do observe the current rules of pronunciation, unlike the artisans using an old-fashioned way of speaking that is being stigmatised.

These changes took place during the 1850s when a societal modernisation set in. In 1857 the ramparts round the medieval town were demolished, in 1858 the guild system was abolished and replaced by trade legislation, and a period of growth began. A ring of new suburbs was built, and these suburbs were socially segregated, by contrast with the old town, where different social groups were living closer to each other.

Only now were the foundations laid for the modern spoken standard, built on the Copenhagen dialect. According to Brink and Lund (1975), it is a 'natural development' within the Copenhagen dialect. The majority of changes from this period, however, are restitutions, in some cases hyper-restitutions, e.g. *solgte* 'sold', *valg* 'selection', pronounced with a velar fricative, not originally belonging to the roots of these verbs. These changes are best understood not as local Copenhagen dialect phenomena only but as intimately connected with the social and political societal changes at the national level.

As a reflection of this, we may take a dictionary published (under a pseudonym!) in 1866: *Ordbog over Gadesproget* ('Dictionary of the Urban Lower Class Dialect', literally 'street language'). In the preface, the editor indicates that 'vulgar speech has an overwhelming power, due to the contemporary stronger life of freedom, and due to the popular direction in which society has turned more and more' (my translation). According to the author (Kristiansen 1866: V), these are the reasons for the emergence of slang, especially after 1848. Since this dictionary also includes word forms from the former educated colloquial variety, it tells about the stigmatisation that is going on in these years.

The admission of new members into the middle class from outside the ramparts and outside the close-knit Copenhagen bourgeoisie made the new middle class less locally oriented than the lower classes, who maintained the local dialect features. The sorting out of formerly shared colloquial features led to a reallocation of stylistic features to social dialect features, coinciding with the beginning of the change of the old close-knit Copenhagen speech community into a modern segregated town.

6.6   The rise and fall of the Copenhagen sociolects

During the next generation (from about 1870) the difference increased between educated, or middle-class, speech, and the speech of the working class of the incipient industrialisation, with the working class leading the linguistic change. The new industrial workplaces attracted workers from all over the country, native Copenhageners were a minority in their own city, and the newly built suburbs resembled new towns, where dialect levelling and koineisation outweighed dialect continuity. They were close-knit communities, though their linguistic expression was a series of local workers' dialects differing from the older local dialect in several respects, for example, a split of /a/ into two different qualities depending on the following consonant: fronted [æ] before dentals and back [ɑ] before labials and velars.

In their work on the standard language and the Copenhagen dialects, Brink and Lund (1975) demonstrate that the general differences between 'Low' (L) and 'High' (H) Copenhagen dialects began with speakers born after 1800. Speakers born prior to 1800 might have certain socially correlated words or forms, but no general differences. The social dialects diverge most strongly among speakers from the second half of the nineteenth century. In speakers born after the turn of the century, the general differences diminished.

After about 1900, the Copenhagen sociolects were converging for quite a long time. Features used only by L-speakers would be taken up by H-speakers, and vice versa. The consequence was a convergence of norms, and a tendency that certain features that once were social markers came to function as style markers instead. The result of this development was evident in a sociolinguistic study from the 1980s, where it was concluded that stylistic and gender-related differences were more pronounced than were social class differences (Gregersen and Pedersen 1991).

Twentieth-century developments within the spoken standard, and the relation between the spoken standard and the metropolitan dialects, will not be further commented upon. Instead, we shall take a look at the acceptance of the spoken standard outside the metropolitan area.

6.7   Acceptance of the spoken standard by the population

Spoken standard languages were established in most European countries as part of the modernisation process of the nineteenth century, but the dissemination and acceptance of the standard outside the bourgeois groups of the metropolitan area differs a great deal. In Denmark, all provincial urban dialects have changed into regional standards, presumably during the nineteenth century, judging from contemporary comments and from the fact that the towns in North Schleswig, which was part of Germany in 1864–1920 and therefore less exposed to standard Danish in this period, maintained their traditional dialects at least until the 1940s. The urban dialects in Sweden have been better maintained, and the Norwegian and Fenno-Swedish ones even better (cf. Pedersen 2001).

In a paper on London's role in the standardisation of English (Keene 2000: 98) Keene points to the fact that the force of metropolitan culture has been constantly increasing, and that, within Britain, the rapid growth of London both in size and wealth led to a systematic hierarchy of towns, where the metropolis interacted with these towns more or less intensely, according to their place in the hierarchy. Keene introduces a measure of 'urban potential' that could be used to identify 'those areas of the country where exchange and interaction between individuals is likely to have been most intense' (102). Similar hierarchies of centres might be found in Scandinavia, and their interrelations might well contribute to explaining when or why some provincial towns have either lost or maintained their local dialects (cf. Sandøy 2000: 356; cf. also Chambers and Trudgill 1980: 197).

One of the strongest instruments of the inculcation of the standard has always been the school. In most countries the written standard has been the one and only written language taught in primary schools, and very often it was perceived as 'the language'. Denmark is no exception to this rule; indeed, we find many comments about dialects as corrupted speech, especially from the early nineteenth century. This is doubtless not unconnected with the fact that compulsory education (including writing lessons) had been introduced in 1814, and the 'right' pronunciation has been considered a condition of the correct way of spelling. The school has played a crucial role in the propagation both of the standard language and of standard-language ideology (Kristiansen 1990).

The question arises why the acceptance of the spoken standard language is far more widespread in Denmark than in other European countries (as is widely believed). Is it due to the small size of the country, to (language) ideology, demography, social or political conditions? There can be no doubt that standard language ideology is very strong in Denmark, but we need to consider whether this is the main cause for the extent of standardisation there. It may be that the societal embedding of the standard ideology is crucial. Could the strong ideology be explained by the peculiarities of Danish history?

Three or four such peculiarities are interrelated. One is that the modernisation process took a different course in that the agrarian sector was developed into a market economy prior to industrialisation and was of great importance to the economic upturn (Stilling 1987: 59). The impact of the agrarian reforms around 1790 and the agrarian crisis of 1818–1838, resulting in agrarian capitalism, were the most important political, economic, and social motors of the transformation of Danish society from feudalism to capitalism. During the recession following the Napoleonic wars, urban economic activity was stagnant until the 1840s, especially in Copenhagen (due to the economic consequences of the secession of Norway in 1814). By the mid-nineteenth century, however, the independent farmers' class had been strengthened (cf. for example, Vammen 1990).

Another factor was that the landed aristocracy were politically marginalised. This development can be seen in the context of the policy of the absolute monarchy from 1660 onwards. The Danish absolute monarchy was an anti-aristocratic project, which adhered to a taxation policy that saw the (independent) peasant farmers, and not the landowning nobility, as the central pillar in the agrarian economy. Therefore, modernisation could be accomplished based on an independent class of farmers, who were able to accommodate to the market without being resisted by a nobility with strong political influence (Clemmensen 2002: 458).

A third factor is demography. The increase of population in Denmark was second only to that in England, and by about 1870 a good deal of this increase took place in new rural towns, springing up around the railway stations (in Danish called '*stationsbyer*'). These rural towns were the location for agrarian industries and service companies, and they made up the connecting link between producers and consumers, between country and town (Stilling 1987: 49, 61).

As a fourth factor, it is worth mentioning the particular course of the Danish revivalist movement, compared with many other countries. An important and numerous group developed in a less pietistic direction than many others, inspired by the priest and poet N. F. S. Grundtvig. This movement emphasised that an authentic Christian life implied an active secular life, and that Christianity implied humanity. During the years 1850–1900, they founded a great number of Folk High Schools [Danish: *folkehøjskoler*], spread throughout the countryside, based on this philosophy – but also a product of the profit from the co-operative agrarian capitalism. The Folk High Schools contributed to the creation of a new self-confidence among the peasantry, while at the same time being agents of an urban mentality, at least in some spheres. The result was that the same individualisation process spread simultaneously in the countryside and in the towns, that is, there emerged a more homogeneous mentality among rural and urban people than was the case in many other countries. Almost all leaders of the influential peasant movements in the 1840s and 1850s came from this movement; accordingly, strong class-conscious cultures in opposition to the bourgeoisie did not develop, based either on aristocratic or traditional peasant values (Vammen 1990: 299).

After the war in 1864 and the loss of Schleswig and Holstein, reducing Denmark to a Danish nation state, the National–Liberals, with their ideas about the privileged right to power of the 'educated classes', were repulsed. A protracted constitutional conflict followed, a struggle between left and right over parliamentary government. At the core of the left wing in this constitutional struggle were the freehold farmers. In a wider European context, farmers would more often constitute the rank and file of conservatism.

To sum up: in Denmark, the development of capitalism and industrialisation proceeded in close interaction with the agrarian sector. Class alliances and class compromises, with farmers as the pivot, prevailed (Clemmensen 2002: 464), and Denmark became a bourgeois agricultural country where the formation of a homogeneous mentality, shared by both rural and urban people, had the effect that strong class-conscious cultures did not develop. This should be combined with the fact that the modern market-oriented farmers took an active part both in co-operative societies and in numerous associations, and, accordingly, interacted with many people outside their own village or parish. Their fields of activity were much larger than the local dialect speech communities.

This whole development made the farmers predisposed to standardisation, or, their actual social interaction rather than passive exposure made it less natural for them to maintain the restricted rural dialects. For obvious reasons, a dialect levelling process had set in already before 1900, resulting in regional dialects or accents replacing the former local dialects.

In Sweden, modernisation of the countryside came a little later than in Denmark. The modernisation process as a whole was somewhat different: industrialisation played a greater role, including in the countryside where large industrial firms were founded. However, some parts of agricultural Sweden maintained a traditional way of living throughout the nineteenth century. All this produced a less homogeneous, less consensus-oriented, society. The modern egalitarian orientation of Sweden was a product of the Social Democrats of the early twentieth century.

If this analysis of modernisation in Denmark is correct (and it is the mainstream analysis of Danish historians), the local dialect-speaking communities were much more predisposed, in their mind-set, to be influenced by the standard in schools and via modern mass media, etc., than was the case in many other countries. Add to this the geographical conditions in Denmark (a small country with no natural hindrances to communication) and the fact that most farmers' wives nowadays have a job of their own outside the farm (or indeed are farmers in their own right), with the result that nearly all children go to nurseries from the age of 1, and we find the perfect scenario for complete standardisation, since the standard language or a regional standard is the unmarked speech code of all institutions (cf. Pedersen 2003).

7   A Comparison of the Standardisation Processes in Denmark and Sweden

The sociolinguistic conditions seem to be very much alike in Denmark and Sweden from early modern to modern times. At the same time, the development of the capital cities followed very similar paths. In this section, I examine the extent to which these parallels resulted in similar outcomes for standardisation.

7.1   The demographic development of Copenhagen and Stockholm in the seventeenth to nineteenth centuries

The long-term population growth in Copenhagen and Stockholm is very similar (and similar to the growth of most European metropolises) in that the rapid growth took place in early modern and modern periods, from the seventeenth to the nineteenth centuries. According to the Swedish historian Sven Lilja, the general conclusion from the long-term population development of Stockholm is the city's dependence on, and close links to, the Swedish monarchy as a political entity. Stockholm, as the capital, grew and stagnated in tandem with the growth and stagnation of Sweden's political power (Lilja 1995: 337).

It was not until the early seventeenth century that Stockholm really expanded. In a few decades between 1620 and the 1690s the population of Stockholm increased from round 10,000 to more than 50,000 inhabitants. This was the period when Sweden rose to the status of a European power, and Stockholm became the administrative, political, military, and cultural focus of the early modern Swedish state. After this, there was stagnation until the middle of the nineteenth century, when the next period of expansion began.

In Copenhagen, the growth was already considerable by about 1600, and the following century saw a strong expansion of the capital, due to the organisation of a nationwide administrative apparatus and a standing army as a tool of the new absolutist monarchy (against the Swedish threat!). By about 1690, the number of inhabitants is estimated at 60,000 (Gamrath 1980: 36, 172), but from then on there was a long period of stagnation, until urbanisation following industrialisation gathered speed in the last part of the nineteenth century. Shortly after 1900, the number of inhabitants had reached 500,000 (Lilja 1996: 357).

During the seventeenth century, both Copenhagen and Stockholm were established as capitals proper, with the major political institutions permanently located in the cities. Both rich merchants and the aristocracies were attracted by this, and a general prestige was assigned to the inhabitants and their dialects. The demographic development meant that during the seventeenth century they had few native citizens and many newcomers (many of the newcomers were not native speakers of Danish/Swedish, but native speakers of other languages (mostly German) from within the realms, or else they were foreigners). Linguistically, this would have produced koineisation, with the result that the spoken dialects of the capitals selected for standardisation would already have been levelled and simplified compared to the neighbouring dialects (cf. K. M. Pedersen 1999 on the simplification of gender in the Copenhagen dialect during the sixteenth century).

The eighteenth century was a more stable period; only in around 1850 did another period of rapid growth begin in both cities with many new arrivals, mostly Danes/Swedes from elsewhere in the two countries. The modern industrialised metropolises were born, and new working-class dialects came into being.

7.2   The rise of a spoken standard language in Sweden in comparison with Denmark

The Danish and the Swedish speech communities developed in very much the same way, though at any particular time one or the other might be a little ahead in certain areas. Swedish gained some domains earlier than Danish did: university teaching in Swedish is reported from the 1730s (Teleman 2002: 21); in Danish from the 1780s. The Swedish royal court preferred Swedish and began to use a Swedish court dress during the reign of Gustav III in the second half of the eighteenth century – though at the same time French seems to have figured more prominently in Sweden than in Denmark, especially during the eighteenth century when nobility in Sweden preferred French both in colloquial speech and in written communication (Teleman 2002: 24).

In her inspiring article on literary and spoken Swedish ('*boksvenska och talsvenska*') Gun Widmark examines the standardisation processes of spoken Swedish, which seems to take a course parallel to those of Danish. She goes through the considerable literature on the subject, concluding that for long periods Sweden seems to have been a diglossic society with a sharp line of demarcation between private and public language, comparing this to the contemporary situation in Switzerland (Widmark 1991: 175). Widmark calls particular attention to public spoken language, pointing to the fact that school was perceived as a domain of public language, with many dialect speakers using the public spoken language when reading aloud and saying grace or other prayers. That is to say, many Swedes were bidialectal with public spoken Swedish as one variety in their repertoire and either educated spoken Swedish (i.e. educated Stockholm dialect) or a local dialect as the other (1991: 179).

The establishment of a spoken standard in Sweden was analogous to the similar process in Denmark, as were further developments.

7.3   Linguistic development in Copenhagen and Stockholm in the second half of the nineteenth century

Kotsinas (1988b: 137) describes the linguistic development in Stockholm on the basis of data from speakers born in the 1860s to the present day. The two oldest speakers, born in the 1860s, speak 'quite different varieties', and the same was the case a generation later. Among Stockholmers born round 1900, there is a very marked difference between speakers of 'H' and 'L' varieties. While the L variety seems to have changed very quickly, the H variety seems to be more stable, with continuity between the speakers born forty years apart. There is a marked difference between these two varieties at all linguistic levels, but the two varieties have also some features in common, especially phonological ones. For example, speakers of both varieties use the so-called Stockholm 'e' (instead of 'ä': thus, *mäta* ('to measure') is pronounced as if spelt *meta*, a feature most prominent in the H speakers).

In the speech of informants born in the 1930s, the differences are far less marked. There are still socially conditioned differences, but they are more subtle. A certain convergence between the two varieties has taken place, from both sides.

The Stockholm material gives the impression that Stockholm speech was for a long time divided into two clearly differentiated sociolects, which, in the course of the twentieth century, have converged and have been (at least partly) levelled to one dialect where the social differences are still indicated, but much less obviously. Kotsinas puts forward the hypothesis that periods with social egalitarianism will lead to the convergence of subvarieties within a regional dialect (Kotsinas 1988: 139).

The stages of the standardisation process are analogous in the two capitals, as are the relationships between the metropolitan dialects and the spoken standards. Kotsinas points to socioeconomic and demographic changes in the Stockholm region as an explanation of these linguistic changes, and also draws our attention to the fact that a new dialect split seems to have taken place during the second half of the twentieth century between suburbs with many immigrants and other parts of the metropolitan area. Once more, the parallel between Copenhagen and Stockholm is striking, the difference being that this is happening some years later in Copenhagen (Møller and Quist 2003).

8   The Norwegian Case

Both in Oslo and in Norway as a whole matters were very different. After the dissolution of the Union with Denmark in 1814, the re-establishment of a Norwegian literary language was at the top of the national agenda. The crucial issue was which social group's speech should form the basis of this new Norwegian literary language: the Danicised urban elite or the rural dialect speakers (cf. Mæhlum in press). This choice has not yet been made, or rather both groups have been chosen, one by the advocates of Dano-Norwegian (*bokmål*), the other by the advocates of New Norwegian (*nynorsk*).[5]

Regarding the rise of a spoken standard, there are both resemblances with and differences from the other Scandinavian countries. Among the Norwegian-born, we find the same tripartite division of the speech community as in the other Scandinavian countries. In about 1800 (Kølle 1774, according to Seip 1916: 16), the urban elite groups developed two varieties, a public, official variety (*høitidssproget*) and an educated colloquial language (*den dannede dagligtale*). The official variety could be characterised as a Norwegian-based pronunciation of the Danish literary language, and this was, in fact, in more complete accordance with the written norm than the equivalent Danish variety. Consequently, the Danish spoken by individuals from Oslo was perceived to be one of the 'best' or even the best (Wilse 1790, according to Seip 1916: 13) ways of speaking Danish. In the other variety, the educated colloquial language, the Norwegian base was more prominent, but also this variety was much influenced by Danish written forms. It is assumed that a southeastern variety of Norwegian was perceived as the most prestigious among these 'blended' Danish–Norwegian varieties. The third category of speech was Norwegian dialects, both rural and urban (Seip 1920).

During the second half of the nineteenth century, we find the same functional expansion of the educated colloquial code at the expense of the public official

[5] Before 1929, these two standards were known as *riksmål* and *landsmål*, respectively.

one as in Denmark and Sweden, and the same tendency to adopt features from the official variety. This meant that certain social distinctions were enforced, and the mother tongue of the Norwegian elite diverged from the dialects of the common people, and moved closer to Danish. According to Mæhlum (in press), this may be looked upon as the culmination of a long process in which Danish was perceived as a socioculturally superior code, and Norwegian was devalued. From around 1820 the stage language in Kristiania (now Oslo) was discussed (Løkensgard Hoel 1996: 91ff.), and the result was that Danish actors were hired, and Danish was the only stage language from 1830 to the middle of the century; only from 1863 were Norwegian actors in the majority. This means that during the first half of the nineteenth century, Copenhagen had even confirmed its position as the normative centre for correct spoken language in Norway (Vinje 1984: 222). However, the Norwegian situation differed from that of Denmark in that the social dimension was fused with a national aspect (Jahr 1996: 86). Militant agricultural parties in both countries were fighting what they perceived as urban hegemony, personified as the class of civil servants (Clemmensen 1994: 148), but in Norway this class was Danish or Danicised, i.e. the social opposition was combined with a national one.

This national aspect, combined with the existence of two closely related written standards, an urban Dano-Norwegian and a 'genuine Norwegian' one based on rural dialects, established a different linguistic climate, although in practice the relationship between the two written codes has always been asymmetrical. The very existence of a dialectally based written language has had a symbolic function as an identity marker for the population outside the centres, and has been a means of self-assertion for groups otherwise marginalised in a modern centralised society (Mæhlum in press). It has thus strengthened the position of the dialects, and made this counter-culture more visible than was the case in Denmark and Sweden. This was made easier by the fact that the Norwegian capital was only half the size of Copenhagen and Stockholm, and Norway as a whole was less urbanised than were its neighbours. The result has been that the standardisation process within spoken Norwegian has taken a different course, and the dialects have a more privileged status than is usual in Scandinavia (Vikør 1993: 207).

A resolution of 1878 (Vikør 1993: 206) concerning spoken language in the classroom takes the stance that instruction in primary schools, as far as possible, should take place in the spoken language of the children, i.e. in their dialects. This principle is still valid, although in a somewhat modified version: 'In their oral training, pupils may use the language they speak at home, and the teacher must give due consideration to the speech of the pupils in his vocabulary and manner of expression' (from the Primary School Act of 1969). As a consequence, the Norwegian school has not played the same role in the inculcation and popularisation of the standard norm as have Danish and Swedish schools, and there has never been any codified Norwegian spoken standard variety. Implicitly, this has also had a bearing on the use of dialect in many functional domains where a standard language is the unmarked code in other countries.

It is an open question, though, if this unusual situation in Norway will be maintained in the future, considering societal developments in contemporary Norway. In recent years, there has been a tendency towards 'normalisation', i.e. towards a focused variety based upon a *bokmål*-like norm with a southeast Norwegian pronunciation (Vikør 1994: 204; Mæhlum 2003: 94f.; Akselberg 2003: 157f.; Sandøy 2003: 227).

9   Conclusion

This short account of Scandinavian history has demonstrated that Norway has taken its own course due to its particular political situation. Danish and Swedish, on the other hand, followed very much the same line of development, with Danish being somewhat ahead due to the different course that modernisation took in these two countries. The written languages were standardised at about the same time and to the same degree in both countries, while the selection of the 'best' spoken language also took place in the same way at the same time, in a way that was closely connected to the demographic development of the capitals as a consequence of the societal changes leading to much stronger, centralised states. In both countries, public and educated colloquial styles tended to converge. This simultaneously led to socially divergent varieties, because the lower classes maintained colloquial variants which, from this point on, became stigmatised among middle-class speakers. In this connection, stigma seems to present us with a more plausible explanation than does prestige (cf. the discussion in Milroy 2000).

Stylistic differences were transformed into social ones during the nineteenth century – possibly a little later in Sweden than in Denmark. The emerging sociolects continued to diverge throughout the nineteenth century, whereas they have been converging on each other concurrently with demographic, social, political, and educational changes in the twentieth century.

The discussion in this chapter has allowed us to answer the question why the standardisation of spoken Danish is advanced relative to some neighbouring countries. It has been demonstrated that there is no monocausal explanation, be it standard ideology, prescriptivism, urbanisation, democratisation, or industri-alisation. Both ideology and economic, social, and political contexts have had a bearing on the process. Language ideology is not independent of these societal processes; on the contrary, it is embedded in them.

7   The birth of new dialects

Paul Kerswill and Peter Trudgill

1   New Dialects as Heightened Dialect Convergence: Research Issues

1.1   Introduction

New-dialect formation, as conceptualised by Trudgill and others (e.g. Britain and Trudgill 1999; Trudgill 2004), refers to the emergence of distinctive, new language varieties following the migration of people speaking mutually intelligible dialects to what, to all intents and purposes, is linguistically 'virgin' territory.[1] As such, it is an extreme, and often very rapid, form of dialect convergence. Examples probably abound in world history, but only a few have been described in detail. There seem to be two main scenarios in which new-dialect formation takes place: the settlement of a relatively large territory, either previously uninhabited or in which a previous population is ousted or assimilated; and the formation of a new town in a geographically delimited area in which relatively intense interpersonal communication can take place. Examples of the former are the settlement of New Zealand largely by English speakers in the nineteenth century, and the transport of indentured labourers from the Hindi-speaking areas of the Indian subcontinent to Fiji, Mauritius, Trinidad, and South Africa, also in the nineteenth century. Examples of the latter are the establishment of the Norwegian towns of Høyanger, Odda, and Tyssedal, and the English town of Milton Keynes. In this chapter, we start by outlining the processes and stages found in new-dialect formation. Then we review the sociolinguistic histories of a number of new dialects – or immigrant koines (Siegel 1985: 364; Kerswill 2002a) as they are also known. We follow this with a scrutiny of what is normally considered the crucial stage in the formation of a new dialect: the linguistic strategies of the first native-born speakers, that is, the children of the original speakers.

---

[1] New dialects are also formed by a process of split and subsequent dialect divergence; we are not concerned with this here. A more precise term for Trudgill's concept, but one which is not in common use, might be *koine formation*.

1.2   Processes and stages in new-dialect formation

Because new-dialect formation is never instantaneous, we can expect to isolate chronological stages through which it must pass before reaching completion. At the same time, we can expect these stages to be characterised by a number of processes, both linguistic and social-psychological, which may be found in one or more of the chronological stages. To take an extreme case: we are asking how a disparate collection of migrants, thrown together at random in a new, unpeopled, place, start out as linguistic individualists with no social bonds to each other, and end up forming, within a couple of generations, a cohesive speech community (cf. Patrick 2002). This is both an oversimplification and a caricature, however, because each set of initial circumstances is different, as we have suggested. The type of linguistic input involved, especially in terms of the linguistic differences between speakers, may have an effect on the speed with which an embryonic new dialect 'focuses', or acquires norms and stability (though we will not be discussing the factor of linguistic differences in this article; see Kerswill 2002a). Non-linguistic factors will be crucial, and may override linguistic ones: a new settlement where people are isolated from each other will take much longer to form a 'speech community' than one where there is intensive contact. People may migrate as individuals or in groups. Clear social divisions in the new society will inhibit linguistic uniformity, but will instead promote the appearance of distinct sociolects with focused norms for their use. Thus, we are asking a complex question that has as much to do with forces of social integration and disintegration as with a purely linguistic account of language change. This chapter will attempt to isolate factors that affect the rapidity with which linguistic focusing takes root in new-dialect formation. We turn now to the processes themselves, in a discussion based on our earlier work (Trudgill 1986, 1998; Trudgill *et al.* 2000; Trudgill 2004; Kerswill and Williams 2000).

1.2.1 Mixing   Mixing refers to the coexistence of features with origins in the different input dialects within the new community, usually because speakers have different dialect origins. Trudgill (1986: 129) notes features in modern Newfoundland English which are directly ascribable to its southwest English and Irish origins, respectively; while Siegel (1997: 115) lists grammatical and lexical forms in Fiji Hindi which have origins in different Hindi dialects.

1.2.2 Levelling   Levelling is concerned with the *selection* of forms found in the mix. An early use of the term in the context of new-dialect formation is to be found in Blanc (1968), who describes its operation in the development of Modern Hebrew, which he refers to as a koine. Blanc talks of levelling, first, as

applying to the children of the early migrants whose speech diverged from their parents' non-native, substratum-influenced speech, especially in informal situations. Secondly, he refers to the 'leveling of communal differentiation' (Blanc 1968: 240), referring to the erasure of differences reflecting the speakers' linguistic substrata. Dillard (1972; quoted in Siegel 1985: 364) gives the following definition, which is a useful starting-point:

> Dialect leveling is the process of eliminating prominent stereotypable features of differences between dialects. The process regularly takes place when speakers of different dialects come into contact, such as in migration.

The key word here is 'stereotypable'. Stereotyping of a feature may occur when it is either demographically a minority form in the new community, or when for some reason it has become 'salient', perhaps because it deviates linguistically or because it has become associated with a stigmatised social group (see Trudgill 1986: 11–12; Kerswill and Williams 2002a). An example of this is discussed by Kerswill (1994: 157), who argues that rural migrants in the Norwegian city of Bergen avoid a particular rural dialect vowel because it has attained the status of a stereotype. However, stereotyping is not a necessary condition for the demise of a feature. Trudgill (2004) shows how the purely demographically based proportions of features found in the mix are directly reflected in the features found in the new dialect. The mechanism can be explained in term of Giles and Powesland's (1997/1975) speech accommodation theory:

> When people speak different varieties, as in a new settlement, the dialect differences are likely to be exploited – consciously or passively – as part of accommodation. This can explain the mechanism behind the survival of majority forms in a koine: There will be more 'acts of accommodation' involving the adoption of majority rather than minority variants simply because there are more conversational contexts in which this can take place. (Kerswill 2002a: 680)

– though see Auer and Hinskens (this volume) for a critique of the idea that speech accommodation involving specific features prefigures dialect change involving the introduction of the same features. There are purely linguistic forces at work in addition to levelling, too. In particular, we find the process of SIMPLIFICATION, a notion which refers to 'either an increase in regularity or a decrease in markedness' (Siegel 1985: 358). In practice, this means a decrease in irregularity in morphology and an increase in invariable word forms, as well as the loss of categories such as gender, the loss of case marking, simplified morphophonemics (paradigmatic levelling), and a decrease in the number of phonemes.

   The result of levelling is that, in a given location, there is a reduction in the number of exponents of linguistic units on the phonological level (non-predictable – non-allophonic – variants of phonemes) and on the morpholexical level (distinct, non-predictable forms of lexical items and of exponents of morphological categories). Morphosyntactic and syntactic differences will also be levelled, though on the whole such differences are much fewer in number and crop up very infrequently in conversational speech (see Cornips and Corrigan, this volume; and Cheshire, Kerswill, and Williams, this volume). In general, the new dialect is also characterised by simplification in relation to all or most of its input dialects.

Mixing, levelling, and simplification are the necessary precursors of new-dialect formation. Together, they can be said to constitute *koineisation*.

1.2.3 Interdialect development Interdialect forms can be defined as those which were not actually present in any of the dialects contributing to the mixture but which arise out of interaction between them. Such forms are of three types. They may be (a) forms which are simpler or more regular than any of those present in the original dialect mixture. They may also be (b) intermediate forms (see Kerswill 1994: 161; Trudgill 1986), which are most usually those which are phonetically intermediate between two contributing forms in the mixture. Additionally, morphological or lexical units may combine variants from more than one contributing dialect, giving what are essentially novel coinages. Finally, they may be (c) forms which are the result of hyperadaptation. The best known type of hyperadaptation is 'hypercorrection', in which speakers attempt to use forms from higher status accents, but employ an incorrect analysis and extend changes to items where they are inappropriate.

1.2.4 Reallocation Even after koineisation (mixing, levelling, and simplification), some competing variants left over from the original mixture may survive. Where this happens, reallocation may occur, such that variants originally from different regional dialects may, in the emerging new dialect, become social-class variants, stylistic variants, or, in the case of phonology, allophonic variants (see Britain and Trudgill 1999).

1.2.5 Focusing Focusing is the sociolinguistic process by means of which the new variety acquires norms and stability, and is implicit in the linguistic process of levelling. The term was elaborated by Le Page, who sees focusing as part of an individual's more or less conscious behaviour when interacting with others. Thus,

[w]e engage in activities I call projection and focussing: we project on to the social screen the concepts we have formed, by talking about them, so as to furnish our universe and try to get others to acknowledge the shape of our furniture; we in turn try to bring our concepts into focus with those of others, so that there is feedback from the social screen through language. (Le Page 1980: 15–16)

Among the 'concepts' we form are, we argue, the language varieties which are perceived by the speaker to exist in the community, along with the social groups associated with them and the norms for their use. Our emphasis on 'perception' is important, since these varieties and groups are likely to be simpler and more stereotyped than the detailed and complex picture a linguist or anthropologist might paint. This indeterminacy on the part of speech community members is in line with Le Page's 'hypothesis and four riders' model of linguistic accommodation to groups with which we wish to be associated (Le Page 1980): one of the riders states that we are restricted by 'the extent to which we have sufficient access to [the model groups] and sufficient analytical ability to work out the rules of their behaviour'. It is obvious that, in a stable speech community with clear norms, the 'bringing into focus' of these concepts, including language varieties, is more readily achieved than in a 'diffuse' community, where the social groups are not easily discerned, many language varieties are spoken, and the norms for language use are either not shared or are non-existent.

In the early stages of new-dialect formation, the newly arrived migrants face a maximally diffuse situation. They engage in projection and focusing to make sense of the sociolinguistic melting pot. Over time, certainly over two or more generations, countless attempts lead to greater success in focusing. The outcome is what we call a 'focused' dialect, where there is a measure of uniformity as well as agreement on the social symbolism of the variation that exists. Under Le Page's model, levelling is a direct consequence of speakers' attempts to project and focus. And the model subsumes accommodation theory in that it allows not just for the interpersonal relations that are a prerequisite for accommodation but also for speakers' orientations towards, and beliefs about, social groups and linguistic varieties. In a similar vein, Kerswill (2003) argues that levelling is not only the consequence of face-to-face accommodation but is also dependent on attitudinal and identity-based factors.

We turn now to the stages of new-dialect formation. Trudgill has argued for the following three stages, roughly corresponding to the first three generations of speakers (Trudgill 1998; Trudgill et al. 2000):

Stage	Speakers involved	Linguistic characteristics
I	adult migrants (first generation)	rudimentary levelling
II	first native-born speakers (second generation)	extreme variability and further levelling
III	subsequent generations	focusing, levelling, and reallocation

In Stage I, we find some levelling among the adult migrants, as they avoid what they perceive as 'marked' forms; motivations will be both the maintenance of intelligibility and the avoidance of social stigma. At the same time, people will accommodate to each other linguistically in their conversational interactions – though, as already alluded to, the evidence that this form of 'short-term' accommodation actually involves the adoption of the features that will later end up in the new dialect is far from clear. (See Coupland 1984; Auer and

Hinskens, this volume; Hinskens 1996: ch. 11; and Kerswill 2002a: 680–682 for discussions of this point and the argument that accommodation takes place through 'identity projection' rather than pattern matching.) Stage II (the focus of this chapter) involves the children of the migrants. As we shall see, their speech shows great inter-individual variation. Surprisingly, there is also much greater intra-individual variation than we would normally find in an established community. The nature of the transition to Stage III, during which the new, focused, dialect appears, is at present rather unclear. What we can say is that it must involve further accommodation – both face-to-face and driven by social psychological factors. Because the focusing in Stage III can be achieved by the third-generation speakers, this accommodation must be rather extensive. On the other hand, the focusing may take several generations to occur, and, in some cases, it may never be completed.

1.3   Related contact-induced changes: pidginisation, creolisation, and regional dialect levelling

The processes observed in new-dialect formation are similar to those found in other contact-related changes. New-dialect formation has much in common with both pidginisation and creolisation, in that new language varieties emerge from relatively intense face-to-face contacts between people speaking different varieties. New-dialect formation has more in common, however, with creolisation than with pidginisation, since both lead directly to a new native-speaker generation. As with creolisation, new-dialect formation involves a disturbance in the 'normal' cross-generational transmission of language. Normal transmission is defined by Thomason and Kaufman (1988: 9–10) as taking place when 'a language is passed on from parent generation to child generation and/or via peer group from immediately older to immediately younger'. However, the analogy should not be taken too far, because, in new-dialect formation, there is no need for individuals to abandon their original language varieties, and the process can take many generations. Creolisation, by many definitions, entails language shift by individuals and, for linguistic communication to take place at all, must be rapid – this is essential to Bickerton's (1977) view of creolisation as 'first-language learning with restricted input'. More recent work on creoles suggests, however, that creolisation may take place over more than one generation (Arends 1995). (See also Kerswill 2002a: 695–696.)

As we have seen, new-dialect formation involves levelling. In much of Europe, a related phenomenon of 'regional dialect levelling', or 'dialect supralocalisation' has been reported for local speech generally (Auer and Hinskens 1996; Hinskens 1996, 1998a; Sandøy 1998b; Thelander 1980, 1982; Foulkes and Docherty 1999; Williams and Kerswill 1999; Milroy 2002a; Britain 2002a; Torgersen and Kerswill 2004; Hinskens, Auer, and Kerswill, this volume). By

202 Macrosociolinguistic motivations of convergence and divergence

this is meant that, within a region where mutually intelligible dialects are spoken, there will be a decrease in linguistic differentiation associated with location; the result is the disappearance, or attrition, of local dialects. Differentiation comes to be on a regional, rather than a local, basis. These outcomes, along with simplification, are shared with the levelling found in new-dialect formation, as can be demonstrated in regions where both are taking place at the same time (Kerswill 2002a: 684); in such cases, new dialects are in advance of the levelled regional dialects, anticipating their shape. However, in the discussion of regional dialect levelling, the mechanism that underlies it is rarely examined: we are still at the descriptive stage. It seems to us that the mechanism cannot be the same as that for levelling in new-dialect formation, since the latter relies entirely on the reduction of variants brought about by face-to-face interaction. Across a whole dialect area, this is patently impossible. Instead, we see a continuation of the 'old' process of diffusion (Chambers and Trudgill 1998), with features spreading from large urban centres at a measurable rate, doubtless now accelerated by the increase in mobility and (perhaps) a priming effect caused by the broadcast media (Stuart-Smith 2001). For example, the spread of the use of /f/ for /θ/ in British English varieties can be shown to be geographically gradual, despite being a recent change in much of Britain (Kerswill 2001, 2003).

In what follows, we review a number of cases of new-dialect formation, seeking out factors, linguistic and social, which favour focusing, and those which hinder it.

2 From Melting Pot to Speech Community: Previous Research

Studies of new-dialect formation have been conducted within a number of frameworks. As we shall see shortly, the advantage of this methodological eclecticism is that it allows us to tease out a rather wide range of mainly social factors influencing the progress of new-dialect formation. One tradition is *linguistic* and *descriptive* in orientation, and deals in traditional units of analysis such as the phoneme. It shows a concern for careful linguistic description; origins of features are sought in input dialects and in such processes as levelling. Social explanations are *post hoc* and concentrate on demography. A parallel trend has been much more *interpretive*, dealing with the social symbolism of the varieties from the speakers' point of view. There is a strong emphasis on ethnography, with members' concepts (cf. Le Page) being sought through ethnographic interviews and observation. We deal with each of these two types in turn.

2.1 Linguistic-descriptive studies and the role of demography

Studies of the first kind (the linguistic-descriptive) have given us insights into the processes and stages of new-dialect formation, and are indeed the source of our previous discussion of these. Omdal's brief (1977) study of Høyanger, discussed in Trudgill (1986), demonstrates that Stage II speakers there are still relatively unfocused, focusing being achieved by the third generation (Stage III). Both Siegel's (1987) research on Fiji Hindi and Mesthrie's (1992) investigation of South African Bhojpuri show the importance of demography for the outcomes in the new dialects, by showing how statistics on the origins of the first-generation migrants are reflected in the proportions of morphological and lexical features from different Hindi dialects found in the koines. As we have seen, Trudgill (2004) argues in a similar vein (see also below, section 3.1).

Demographic factors of a different sort are adduced in Britain's (1997a,b) study of the English Fens: that of the opportunities for children to form social relationships *among themselves*. Britain deals with the focusing of two vocalic variables following migrations as long ago as the seventeenth century; interestingly, he finds that one of the features (which is linguistically complex) is only now beginning to resolve the conflicting norms brought about by the migrations. He proposes a partial explanation as follows. In the days before widespread schooling, children living in the sparsely populated Fens had little opportunity to mingle with other children, and so the potential to develop new norms in the mixed dialect situation they found themselves in was severely limited (Britain 1997a: 165). This argument chimes well with Eckert's (2000) contention that, in the developed world, the school is now the chief locale for the socialisation of children, and is therefore the primary setting for language change. We shall have much more to say on the role of children later in this chapter.

Finally, we can observe a third key type of demographic information. This is to do with population stability versus transience. Like Britain's study, Sudbury's (2000, 2001) study of Falkland Islands English is quantitative and makes use of the linguistic variable. She finds that the English spoken there is 'distinguishable from other English varieties' (2001: 64). For example, it has developed distinct allophones of the vowels of /aɪ/ as in PRICE and /aʊ/ as in MOUTH[2] before voiced and voiceless consonants, in the manner of Canadian Raising (Chambers 1979). Yet the allophones are not as distinct as those in Canadian English, and this is perhaps symptomatic of the lack of focusing she finds in Falklands English, despite a settlement history going back to the mid-nineteenth century. Instead, she finds considerable variation within groups defined by sex, age, and residence groups, as well as more-than-expected variation within individual speakers (Sudbury 2001: 64). In explaining this situation, Sudbury's main argument concerns, first, the isolation of communities in the Falklands, leading not only to low rates of inter-community contact but also to a lack of opportunities for children to mix. Second, she points to the transience of the population caused

---

[2] These keywords are used mnemonically following Wells (1982).

by high rates of in- and out-migration, due to the fact that many settlers were contract workers (Sudbury 2000: 374–375). In addition to these demographic factors, there is a continued desire to maintain links with Britain – a factor which contrasts sharply with other southern-hemisphere English-speaking countries. Falklands Islands English is, she argues, still at the transition between Stages II and III (2000: 372). Transience and attitudinal factors will be explored further below.

2.2   Ethnographic studies: dialect as a local identity marker

In this section, we deal with two recent studies of a somewhat different type of new dialect: these are what may be termed DIALECT ISLANDS, by analogy with 'language island' (see Rosenberg, this volume). Dialect islands are the result of the migration of people from a single area to another part of the same language area, while language islands are the consequence of migration to an entirely different language area. The distinction is important because, in dialect islands, we can expect levelling to occur in relation to the surrounding dialects, made possible by mutual intelligibility. At the same time, of course, there will be internal levelling to the extent that there are dialectal differences between the input speakers – as there almost invariably are.

Mæhlum's (1997) study of a dialect island in northern Norway is mainly ethnographic in approach. Over some three decades from 1791, farming families from the east of Norway were encouraged to move to two adjacent regions in the north of the country, Bardu and Målselv, which had not previously been farmed, though Saami reindeer herders were present. Local speech in these regions is to a great extent coloured by the eastern dialects of the settlers, with some speakers even today showing virtually no northern features. The study is especially valuable because of the existence of a previous description published some seventy years after the main settlement (Reitan 1928), which allows us to make some inferences about Stage II, as well to make comparisons with present-day speech. Furthermore, a good deal is known about where the original settlers came from. As Mæhlum points out, Reitan (1928) provides evidence that at least one majority form found in the dialect mix in Bardu had already won out in the speech of Stage II speakers (those of Reitan's informants who were the children of settlers). This is the form of the first person singular pronoun, which took the form /ɛɪ/, this being the variant found in the southeastern district of Tynset, from where Bardu was mainly settled. In the 1920s, there was no evidence of the more general eastern /jeː/ or northern /eː/, which must also have been present to some extent in the mix. However, there was also levelling away from strongly localised and therefore stereotypable Tynset forms, such as /vœtœ/ for 'to know', which was replaced by northern and more general Norwegian /viːtə/.

Despite all this, focusing had clearly not taken place even as late as the 1920s:

> The struggle between southern [i.e. southeastern] and northern dialects has, however,
> not ceased, and the language of the two colonies has therefore not reached any degree of
> uniformity. There is vacillation both with respect to the form and the inflectional mor-
> phology of words, and it is not easy to determine what should be regarded as 'genuine'
> in the dialect. (Reitan 1928, cited in Mæhlum 1997: 19; our translation)

Moreover, individual speakers would show instability in their use of particular forms (Mæhlum 1997: 19). Demography clearly played a part in the slow
koineisation in these two districts: most farms were isolated, and until recently
there were no compact villages or towns in which norms could be developed.
Instead, according to Mæhlum, norms would have been much more local,
perhaps based on an individual valley.

The main thrust of Mæhlum's study, however, lies in its emphasis on finding
reasons for the *maintenance* of a continuum of eastern-derived dialects in the
north of Norway for two hundred years. Historical records reveal that endogamy
was practised right until the Second World War; in the early days, some men
apparently travelled the 1,400 kilometres to their original districts to find wives.
Mæhlum talks of the long-standing 'positive self-image' of the *døl*, or 'valley
person', and the high status that was accorded to *døler* (as pioneers and farmers)
by the authorities. In these communities, members of the out-group (the coastal
residents of north Norwegian descent) were known disparagingly as *skolp*
(a local word referring to coastal people (Mæhlum 1997: 13)). The valley
people's positive self-image continues to this day, as witnessed by Mæhlum's
account of schoolchildren's self-reports, as well as (more recently still) by the
existence of a local information website which *døler* are invited to make use of.

Dyer's (2000, 2002) study of the new town of Corby in the English East
Midlands takes a similarly interpretive approach. Like Mæhlum, she sees the
development and maintenance of a new, distinctive dialect as a reflection of
the maintenance of locally relevant social categories, particularly those concerned with making distinctions between in- and out-groups. The new town
of Corby began in the 1930s with the setting up of an iron and steel works
by a Scottish company. Workers were directly transferred from the depressed
industrial region around Glasgow, with the result that the population rose from
1,500 to 36,000 in thirty years. In 1971, Scottish-born people accounted for
some 30 per cent of the population of the town (Dyer 2002: 101). Dyer shows
that, while most pronunciation features today have an English origin, some
Scottish features have been maintained by the most recent generation of speakers. One such is the monophthongal pronunciation, typically [o], of /əʊ/ as in
GOAT, a clearly Scottish variant that differs strongly from local, southern diphthongs such as [əʊ]. Many young males use this monophthong, while young
females tend to use a fronted variant of the southern diphthong, [əʏ], which

is spreading and is popular among young females in the south of England (Kerswill and Williams 2000: 106; Cheshire, Kerswill, and Williams 1999; Kerswill and Williams 2005). This gender-differentiated pattern holds, regardless of whether a speaker's family is of Scottish origin. Thus, although there has been considerable levelling within the town, with the effect of linking it with its region both linguistically and sociolinguistically, the town's dialect has in certain crucial respects not become part of the regional dialect levelling. Dyer's interpretation of these results, informed by detailed and extensive interviewing, is as follows. She finds that the oldest speakers, most of whom are Scots, perceive both themselves and the younger inhabitants of Corby as speaking a Scottish variety. Outsiders also perceive the accent as Scottish. However, the young people themselves do not see themselves as Scots but as local Corby people, claiming, with some justification, that they all speak the same. Thus, she argues, 'Scots features have been reassigned or reallocated in the new Corby dialect to index local, rather than ethnic identity' (Dyer 2002: 113).

Dyer's findings probably have a consequence for the way we should approach local speech and identity, even in areas which are arguably under strong pressure from the diffusion of London (or, elsewhere, other metropolitan) features, leading to the regionalisation of local speech (that is, levelling leading to distinctiveness at the regional, not local, level). If we find a strong linguistically marked local identity even in a small town in a relatively densely populated region, then this should hold for other places, too, even if the dialect at first hearing is not so distinctive as that of Corby.

However, we should be cautious in the expectation that linguistically marked local identities are powerful everywhere. A related approach to identity factors is to ask whether speakers of new, levelled dialects, such as that in Milton Keynes, can recognise other native speakers. Kerswill and Williams (2002b) find that dialect recognition rates in levelled dialects, including those affected by regional dialect levelling (e.g. Reading), is in fact low, and that this is especially true across generations in cases where the levelling is rapid. Conversely, the study showed high recognition levels for non-levelled urban dialects, such as that of Hull. This suggests that the strength of linguistically signalled identities varies greatly, and that these identities are not necessarily even shared across generations.

The studies we have reviewed (as well as a number of others discussed in Kerswill and Williams 2000 and Kerswill 2002a; cf. also levelling in language islands – Rosenberg, this volume) are remarkably consistent in their findings, suggesting that, at least for new-dialect formation, we really can speak of a finite set of processes and stages. We have also seen how demographic and local identity factors (accessed using both quantitative and qualitative methodologies) appear to account fairly comprehensively for differences in the application of the processes and differences in the rapidity with which the new dialect passes through the stages. We now look in much more detail at the relationships between the stages in terms of the transitions between them. We do this by reporting two of our own studies.

3 The Individual Speaker in the Second Stage of New-Dialect Formation: The New Zealand and Milton Keynes Studies

So far, our picture of new-dialect formation is a rather detailed one, with findings converging in a satisfying manner. However, the studies reviewed are largely silent on Stage II, the highly variable speech of the children of the migrants, which we would argue is central to the whole process. The linguistic choices made collectively by people at this stage are necessarily crucial to the outcome of koineisation, since they provide the input to the next (or a subsequent) generation's focused variety in which the number of available features has been whittled down and final selections made. The studies have, however, given us some insight into the kinds of social factors which favour or inhibit focusing during Stages II and III; these are largely to do with the degree of social interaction which is possible between children (at the micro-level) and across the new community as a whole (on a wider level).

We will be examining in some detail the second stage, particularly the *transitions* into and out of it. That is to say, we are interested in how Stage II speakers differ from those at Stage I, both as a group and in terms of individual parent–child relationships. Secondly, we are interested in the same comparisons between Stage II and Stage III speakers.

Previous studies have looked at the outcomes of new-dialect formation, and have identified the nature of the linguistic changes between the dialect input and the stable new dialect. Necessarily, the second stage has largely been by-passed because access to such speakers was not possible, simply because they are long dead. But two recent projects have been able to examine the second stage in more detail:

1. The Origins of New Zealand English (ONZE) project[3] is unique in that it draws on a substantial historical recorded corpus of second-stage speakers of a known new dialect. The data come from recordings made by the National Broadcasting Corporation of New Zealand in 1946–1948. The recordings were oral history pioneer reminiscences, mostly from people who were the children of the first European settlers in New Zealand. The style of the recordings is relatively informal, often with family members present. Because of

---

[3] Directed by Elizabeth Gordon at the University of Canterbury, Christchurch, and funded by the New Zealand Foundation for Research, Science and Technology, and by the University of Canterbury. Additional funding has also been made available by the British Council and the Marsden Fund.

the subject-matter, fairly extensive incidental information about family history appears on the tapes. About 325 speakers born between 1850 and 1900 were recorded (for more details see Gordon *et al.* 2004). The data presented here are derived from analyses by Peter Trudgill of 84 New Zealand-born speakers representing many regions of New Zealand, and born between 1850 and 1889. This generation of people represents the first native-born speakers of English in New Zealand – though they were elderly by the time they were recorded. From this data, inferences can be made about the way in which this generation's highly mixed speech provided input to the focused variety, as well as ways in which their speech reflects the known demographic origins of the settlers.

2. The Milton Keynes project[4] examines the speech of children and their parents in a koineising new town. It is unique in recording Stage II speakers while they are still children, and in being able to make a direct comparison with the speech of their parents, who are among the original migrants. Milton Keynes, situated some 70 kilometres northwest of London at the boundary between the south Midlands and Home Counties modern dialect areas (Trudgill 1990: 63), was designated a new town in 1967. Between that date and the 1991 Census, the population increased from 44,000 to 176,000, rising further to 207,000 by the 2001 Census. The rationale for the project is the view that children's and adolescents' linguistic choices are the prime sources at least of phonological change (following Eckert 1988; and Aitchison 1981: 180). A socially homogeneous group of 48 children (8 boys and 8 girls from each of three age groups: 4, 8, and 12 years), who had been born in Milton Keynes or who had moved there within the first two years of life, was recorded in 1991. Almost all the children were born to parents who had moved to Milton Keynes as young adults, mainly from elsewhere in the southeast of England, but also northern England and Scotland. This distribution turns out to match rather closely the regional origins of the population as a whole (Kerswill and Williams 2000: 79). One caregiver (in all but two cases the mother) was recorded for each child. The children attended a nursery, a first school, and a middle school, respectively, in two adjacent neighbourhoods which were among the first developments in the new town, with a high proportion of the housing available for rent and with a population showing a relatively high rate of signs of social deprivation (as measured by the proportion of children receiving free school meals). The selection

---

[4] 'A new dialect in a new city: children's and adults' speech in Milton Keynes', directed by Paul Kerswill at the University of Reading, 1990–1994, and funded by the Economic and Social Research Council (ref. R000232376). Ann Williams was the research fellow working on the project. Further data are from the project 'The role of adolescents in dialect levelling', jointly directed by Jenny Cheshire, Paul Kerswill, and Ann Williams, 1995–1999 (ESRC ref. R000236180).

procedures, which involved approaching schools and parents and requesting volunteers, meant that a quasi-random sample was obtained within the broad parameters of age and sex. The children were recorded in same-sex pairs by Ann Williams, with a number of elicitation tasks being conducted in addition to an interview. The variables quantified were phonological.

3.1   Variability in Stage II

3.1.1 New Zealand
The most striking fact about the New Zealand archive is the variability that exists, both between and within individuals. (By contrast, the variability in the Milton Keynes data is much less – for reasons we will return to.) Differences between the speakers, many of whom are siblings or class-mates, are much greater than the expectation would be for an established settlement (village or small town) of similar size. This effect is most likely accentuated by the absence of a stable peer-group variety. In such a situation, adults, especially parents and other caregivers, will have a greater than usual influence on children's speech. We can take the example of Arrowtown, which was settled from about 1860 during a gold rush by people from various parts of the British Isles, other parts of New Zealand, and Australia. Among nine Arrowtown people born between 1863 and 1886, we find the following vowel variants:

FACE:	[e·]	[eᵈ]	[eɪ]	[ɛɪ]	[æɪ]	
PRICE:	[aɪ]	[ɑɪ]	[aᵈ]	[ɑɛ]	[ɑ·ᵉ]	
GOAT:	[o·]	[oᵘ]	[ou]	[ɔu]	[ɵʉ]	[ɐ·ᵘ]
MOUTH:	[ɜʉ]	[ɛʉ]	[ɛu]	[ɛ·ᵘ]	[æʊ]	[æ·ᵊ]
NEAR:	[i·r]	[iəɹ]	[iʲə]	[iə]	[ɪəɹ]	[ɪə]

The fact that most of these can be traced to a British Isles provenance suggests that their users have 'inherited' a British dialect from their parents. This is not the case, however, since none of these speakers uses a variety which is unequivocally localisable to a single area of the British Isles. Instead, we find that speakers appear to have made an idiosyncratic selection of features from the available choice in the dialect mixture. This leads to great inter-individual variability of a kind that is unexpected from people with broadly similar backgrounds. For example, Mr Malcolm Ritchie has the following features:

1. /θ/ and /ð/ are realised as dental stops, [t̪] and [d̪], as in Irish English
2. Syllable-final /l/ may be clear (i.e. non-velarised), as in Irish English
3. He has h-dropping in words like *home*, an English feature absent in Ireland
4. He has a distinction between /ʌ/ and /w/, thus distinguishing *which* and *witch*. This feature is never combined with h-dropping in the British Isles.
5. He distinguishes between [eɪ] reflexes of ME /aː/ as in *gate* and [ɛɪ] reflexes of ME *ai* as in *chain*.

Mr Ritchie's sister-in-law, Mrs H. Ritchie, attended the same school at the same time as he did, yet has some quite different features in her speech. Unlike Mr Ritchie, she has close realisations of /æ/ as [ɛ] and /e/ as [e], while he typically has more open variants. She also lacks the distinction between *gate* and *chain*, found in Mr Ritchie's speech. In Arrowtown as a whole, we find variable rhoticity, variable h-dropping, variable tapping of intervocalic /t/, and variable use of clear (vs. dark) /l/ in syllable-coda positions.

What is happening here is a kind of 'shopping-basket' effect: in situations where there is no stable adult model, children are able to choose from a wider variety of adult models than otherwise. Choice would seem to be highly individual, provided the features are heard sufficiently frequently among the adults to be noticed by the children (what Trudgill 2004 calls the THRESHOLD RIDER). This is not to say that the choices are entirely random. Trudgill argues that though it is impossible to predict which form any individual will select from those available, the proportions of variants present in the accents of the children, *taken as a whole*, derive in a probabilistic manner from, and will therefore reflect – subject to the threshold rider – the proportions of the same variants present in the different varieties spoken by their parents' generation *taken as a whole*.

In the Norwegian Arctic territory of Spitsbergen, which has a highly transient population, Mæhlum (1992) finds children likewise adopting very original combinations of features. Nevertheless, she concludes that there are a number of linguistic tendencies around which the children cluster, by which they signal various kinds of regional and other group allegiances – or a strategy of neutrality. In a similar fashion, ethnographic methods in the Milton Keynes study show children signalling social identities such as these, as we shall see shortly.

The Stage II speakers in the ONZE corpus also show a great deal of intra-individual variation. For example, Mr Riddle, who was born in Palmerston in 1860, shows an astonishing degree of variability:

1. /æ/ as in TRAP can be either [ɛ] or [a] (but not [æ])
2. /iː/ as in FLEECE varies between the short monophthong [i] typical of Scots and a long diphthong [əi] typical of southern England – and individual lexical items can occur with both pronunciations
3. /eɪ/ and /əʊ/ as in FACE and GOAT alternate between Scottish-sounding monophthongal pronunciations with [e] and [o] and very un-Scottish pronunciations with the wide diphthongs [æɪ] and [ɐʊ]
4. similarly, /aɪ/ as in PRICE alternates between a typical Scottish diphthong [ɛɪ] and an open central monophthong [a̠ː], half-way between cardinal 4 and 5 in quality, whose provenance is not entirely clear, but could be Lancashire

The most likely explanation would appear to be that Mr Riddle grew up in a community providing both English English and Scottish English models, and that for some phonological features he acquired both variants. Mr Riddle is by no means the only speaker to display this kind of behaviour. Acoustic analysis, too, shows unusually large envelopes of phonetic space for vowel realisations for a number of informants (Gordon *et al.* 2004).

Care does have to be taken at this point, it is true, since some such variability may be the result of accommodation to the speech of younger New Zealanders during the ONZE informants' long lifetimes. A parallel case is the speech of adult rural migrants in the Norwegian city of Bergen, whose speech shows similar intra-individual variation as part of their long-term accommodation to the city dialect (Kerswill 1994: 148). Nevertheless, the amount of variability in the speech of many individual speakers is very striking indeed and strongly suggests that idiolects formed in dialect mixture situations may be much more variable than idiolects formed in stable speech communities. This kind of variability is paralleled by Stage II speakers in Spitsbergen (Mæhlum 1992) and, if Reitan's (1928) report is correct, in Bardu, too.

3.1.2 *Milton Keynes*   The Milton Keynes children generally show much less variability than the New Zealand informants. This is because the town lies between two regions that have been identified as the most dialectally levelled in the country, and most of the in-migrants also come from these regions (see Kerswill and Williams 2000: 80–81; Edwards 1993: 215–216). However, careful phonetic analysis and quantification can reveal quite detailed patterns. We begin by considering the variable (ou), which refers to the realisation of the offset of the vowel /əʊ/ as in GOAT, which is currently being fronted in the southeast of England. The parents of the children originate from various parts of the British Isles, and would therefore be expected to show a range of pronunciations for this vowel, both from the southeast and elsewhere. In order to see whether any focusing among the children has occurred, we can compare the fronting score for the parent/caregiver recorded for each child (all but one of whom were women) with that of the child. The variable has the following values:

(ou) – 0: [oː], [oʊ]   score: 0   (northern and Scottish realisation)
(ou) – 1: [əʊ], [əʊ̟]   score: 1   (older Buckinghamshire and London)
(ou) – 2: [əɣ]   score: 2   (fronting)
(ou) – 3: [əɪ]   score: 3   (fronting and unrounding)

An index score was calculated for each speaker, on a scale from 0 to 3, in interview style. One of the hypotheses of the Milton Keynes project was that the 4-year-old children would be measurably closer in their speech to their caregiver than are either the 8- or the 12-year-olds. Figure 7.1 shows the correlation of the 4-year-olds' index scores with those of their caregivers. Taking the caregivers' scores first, we note that they cover a very wide range. Four of the 16 have scores close to 0, indicating high-back rounded pronunciations characteristic

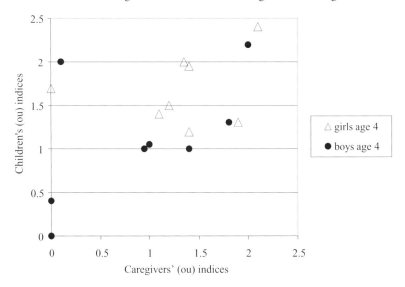

Fig. 7.1 Correlation of 4-year-old children's and caregivers' (ou) indices.

of the north of England and Scotland. The remaining 12 are all from the south of England, and show different degrees of fronting. Like the adults, the children fall into two groups: those using high-back northern variants; and those favouring southern diphthongs. However, all the children are Milton Keynes-born, so we have here a case of some young children acquiring their parents' dialect, while others have either not acquired it or have already accommodated to southeastern speech before the time of the interview. In fact, we have direct evidence of this type of accent mobility in this age group: one of the two boys at bottom left of the figure, the offspring of Scottish parents, was using a mainstream southeastern accent by the time he was recorded for a second time 18 months later.

For these 4-year-olds, the choice between a high-back variant and a central or fronted diphthong is a binary one. Some follow their parents; others turn away from them. However, there is a further, more subtle, pattern in the data. Among the 12 children who have southeastern parents (represented by the large cluster in the centre and top right of the figure), and therefore do not have a gross binary choice to make, there is a strong positive correlation with the degree of fronting of their caregivers, with an r^2 of .3551 (Pearson). This suggests, of course, that these children match their parents' quality for this vowel very closely. The 2 children with non-southern caregivers, at top left, have made the binary choice away from their parents' pronunciation. Interestingly, they have then actually accentuated the difference by going for quite a fronted vowel.

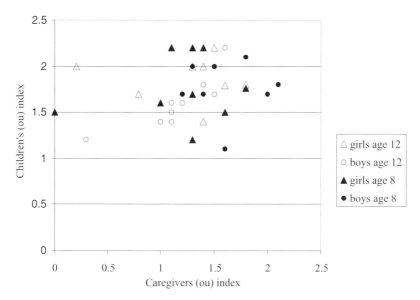

Fig. 7.2 Correlation of (ou) indices for 8- and 12-year-olds and caregivers.

There is a great deal of diversity among the 4-year-olds. Yet we cannot say that these Stage II speakers are following the same track as the ONZE Stage II informants, because they are at a stage in their socialisation where the parental model will still be very strong. However, we can examine the older children to see if the pattern has changed. Figure 7.2 shows the same information for the remainder of the children, divided by age and sex. This time, once the 3 children from northern families have been removed, there is an almost complete absence of correlation ($r^2 = .0532$). By the age of 8, the children are no longer affected at all by their parents' vowel articulations.

Not only is there greater homogeneity but there is also focusing on a different norm even from that of the southeastern caregivers. Figure 7.3 shows the data for all female child subjects along with only those caregivers who are from the southeast (all of whom are female). This is to gain maximum comparability across the age groups. As can be seen, all the children have, on average, a higher fronting score than the caregivers. Of the children, it is the 4-year-olds whose score is closest to that of the adults. This suggests that, as the children grow older, they settle on a new, (in this case) partly external norm. In other words, they change their habitual vowel realisations.

This interpretation was argued for strongly in Kerswill and Williams (2000: 107). A re-examination of the data reveals that, in fact, there is a more complex pattern. The effect illustrated in figure 7.3 is actually rather slight, and is affected

Table 7.1 *Distribution of three variants of (ou) across
sample (%) (children: elicitation tasks; adults: interviews)
(from Kerswill and Williams 2000: 93)*

	[əɪ],[ɐɪ]	[əʏ],[ɐʏ]	[əʊ], [əʊ̈], [ɐʊ], [ɐʊ̈] (also [oʊ] and [o])
4-year-olds	13.5	30.2	55.7
8-year-olds	12.9	53.6	33.3
12-year-olds	3.0	68.6	28.2
Caregivers	3.5	37.3	60.0

Age effect among children: p < .001 (MANOVA)
All children vs. adults: p < .001 (t-test)

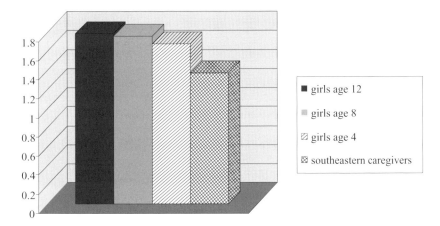

Fig. 7.3 (ou) index scores for all girls and southeastern caregivers.

by the fact that fully front and unrounded vowels get a higher weighting in
the index than their rounded counterparts. The argument in the earlier paper
was based instead on a binary division between front variants ([əɪ], [əʏ], [ɐɪ],
[ɐʏ]) and central or back variants ([əʊ], [əʊ̈], [oʊ], and [o]). This showed a
considerable shift away from the central/back variants of the adults, and a strong
tendency for the older children to lead the way. Data collected from 14-year-
olds in 1996 suggest that children continue to increase their fronting of this
vowel into their teens, albeit slightly (Cheshire *et al.* 1999).

Table 7.1 shows the distribution of three variants on which this argument was
based. Two patterns become apparent, in addition to the clear move away from
central/back variants by the older children. The first is that it is not the most

front and unrounded offsets that are in the ascendancy, but variants with fronted and *rounded* offsets, that is, *not* the most 'shifted' variant (that is, away from the older central/back southeastern diphthong). Second, and this is especially relevant to our argument in this chapter, it is clear that the youngest children exhibit rather greater variation than the older children. Not only do some still use their northern parents' variants but others go for vowels with unrounded offsets, overshooting the use of this variant by the older children. This inter-individual variation is likely to be greater than in established communities because, as in New Zealand, the range of adult models is greater.

However, compared to New Zealand, something quite different is going on here. Focusing seems to have taken place, at least for this vowel, during Stage II. One can suggest a number of reasons for this. First, the linguistic differences involved are less in Milton Keynes than in any of the New Zealand localities studied by ONZE. Second, we are dealing with children who, perhaps, already have a stable (or stabilising) norm to aspire to, not from their parents but from older children and teenagers. We should note that a whole cohort of schoolchildren had already grown up in Milton Keynes in the twenty-four years between designation and the recordings. There may be a contrast between this late twentieth-century new town and many of the earlier cases studied in that there is universal education in quite large schools, with the attendant opportunities for the development of norms. And, finally, it should be remembered that Milton Keynes is not by any means isolated; in this, it differs sharply from all the other settlements we have discussed. (ou)-fronting is, in fact, an external norm, probably (though we can't be sure) being spread from London by diffusion. We have noted it for Reading, where instrumental analysis of the shift has been carried out (Kerswill and Williams to appear). As a new town with (by definition) a mobile population, Milton Keynes is probably extremely receptive to such influences. Added to this is the unstable dialect situation there (relative to other towns), which will favour the adoption and development of new features. In terms of both regional dialect levelling and the adoption of innovations, Milton Keynes may be ahead of neighbouring towns, prefiguring later regional trends in a similar way to the new dialects elsewhere.

Yet there are two ways in which Milton Keynes shows the characteristics of new-dialect formation. The first is that the children indeed show one expected aspect of Stage II speakers, and this is in the amount of inter-individual variability. Children who are socially isolated from other children are likely to rely heavily on their parents as a model for their vernacular as compared to children who are involved in peer groups. In a new town at Stage II, this means that, compared to established towns, there will be a greater presence, among children, of features from dialects elsewhere. In an established town, isolated children will simply sound 'old fashioned', not as if they come from somewhere else. We can again use the (ou) data as an illustration. Kerswill and Williams

(2000: 93–94) argue that individuals who are well integrated into peer groups have high degrees of (ou)-fronting, and that this is part of the mechanism for the establishment of this as a norm. A small number of children in the sample were, however, virtually excluded from participation in peer groups, for a variety of reasons. These children reflected their parents' speech more clearly, and consequently had accent features from elsewhere. The clearest example of this was a 12-year-old, the son of London parents, whose (ou)-fronting score was low, at 1.4, exactly matching that of his mother. He also used London monophthongal variants of MOUTH, typically [æː], which, as we shall see shortly, is not at all characteristic of Milton Keynes children. Like the 'lames' in Labov's (1972b) study of teenage gangs in New York City, this boy was not mentioned as a friend by any of the other children.

For the ONZE data, it is probably unrealistic to infer anything about the quality of the speakers' relationships in early childhood; yet we must assume that the effects noted in Milton Keynes – namely, varying relationships with family and peers mirrored in the degree of use of innovative linguistic features – must have pertained in those communities, too. This means that the 'shopping-basket' model alluded to earlier, whereby the selection of variants by children was seen as a random matter, cannot have been the whole story. Factors such as those just discussed must also have contributed to the inter-individual variation. More generally, they may also help to determine which dialectal 'strategy' a young speaker will home in on, in Mæhlum's (1992) terms.

As alluded to before, there is a second way in which the status of Milton Keynes as a town with a new dialect can be confirmed. A mark of new dialects is the absence of any local, stable model, implying a loss of continuity across generations. The language, with its dialect features, is not transmitted in the 'normal', intergenerational sense identified by Thomason and Kaufman, as we saw in section 1.3. The clearest example of this is the Milton Keynes pronunciation of the vowel /aʊ/ as in MOUTH. Table 7.2 shows the distribution of a number of variants of this vowel, which appears to be converging on a Received Pronunciation-like [aʊ], moving away from local pronunciations such as [ɛɪ] and [ɛʉ]. The child data given here are from recordings of 14-year-olds conducted in 1996.

This table gives an apparent-time snapshot of four generations of the area, with the new town being established between the 'elderly' and 'women's' generations. In Milton Keynes, there appear to be three stages in the development of this vowel: first, a period of stability in which [ɛʉ] and [ɛɪ] predominated (generations 1 and 2), followed at the height of the Milton Keynes settlement in the 1970s by a period of greater heterogeneity in which [æʊ], the form favoured by the majority of the in-migrants (represented here by the women in generation 3), was dominant. A 're-focusing' finally began with the second-generation migrants (today's children, generation 4), who are rejecting [æʊ] and settling

Table 7.2 *Percentage use of variants of /aʊ/ (MOUTH), Milton Keynes working class, interview style (adapted from Kerswill 2002: 697)*

Generation	Stage in new-dialect formation	Speakers	[ɛʊ̯]	[ɛɪ]	[ɛː]	[aːˀ]	[æʊ]	[aʊ]
1	pre-Stage I	*Survey of English Dialects (SED)* informants, 1950–1960s[a]	√					
2	pre-Stage I	Elderly (2f, 2m)	63.2	25.6	9.8	0	1.2	0
3	Stage I	Women age 25–40 (n = 48)	0	0	11.7	17.2	38.6	31.5
4	Stage II	Girls age 14 (n = 8)	0	0	0	5.9	4.7	88.8
		Boys age 14 (n = 8)	0	0	0	12.3	3.8	83.1

[a] Informants recorded in Stewkley, a village 5 km from present-day Milton Keynes (Orton *et al.* 1968)

on [aʊ], probably influenced (in this case) by the fact that this form is spreading in the region. Starting with generation 2, there is a marked discontinuity in the scores between each succeeding generation, shown particularly by the total absence of the older forms in the speech of the women and children. This reflects, we argue, the lack of social continuity in this town, where most children have parents as well as grandparents originating elsewhere. That we really are dealing with koineisation and not just regional dialect levelling by diffusion is demonstrated by data from Reading, a long-established town some 80 kilometres south of Milton Keynes. Here, we see a similar shift towards [aʊ]. In Reading, however, the old form [ɛɪ] is still used by a number of children, thus demonstrating the effect of the demographic continuity there (Kerswill 2002a: 697).

3.2   The transition to Stage III

The relationship between Stage II and Stage III is, on a linguistic level, on the whole very well understood. To summarise, there will be further (probably accelerated) levelling, as the number of variants of a variable reduces from several in Stages I and II to just one, or two or more if reallocation has taken place. Which features survive is largely dependent on demographic factors, as well as on the factor of markedness (Trudgill *et al.* 2000: 311–312). Trudgill (2004) also discusses the contribution to new-dialect formation of DRIFT, a phenomenon first discussed by Sapir (1921): this is the propensity of a language to change in a certain ways. Thus, related languages, such as English and

German, or British English and New Zealand English, may show similar, but independent (that is, not contact-induced) changes.

However, the social mechanism of dialect transmission that is entailed by the rapid focusing that takes place between Stages II and III is less well understood. We offer some thoughts here. Clearly, some general factors come into play, as we have seen. The main one, already discussed, is the degree to which children are able to interact socially with other children. This will be important in determining whether a child will grow up with a mainly parent-based variety, or will start the gradual mutual accommodation process with other children we have witnessed in Milton Keynes. As we have seen, the ONZE informants show both inter-individual and intra-individual variability, and we argue that this in all essential respects reflects their childhood speech as well – at least from the stage in their socialisation when they began to interact outside the home. The Milton Keynes data notwithstanding, we have no evidence of the childhood speech of these or other such individuals. The Milton Keynes children do, however, provide a pointer in that they can be shown to be moving away from parental norms towards new norms as they grow older. But they show none of the variability of the ONZE speakers – with two exceptions: first, non-integrated children's speech will be oriented to varieties in another community (such as London); and second, children with distinctively non-southeastern home accents, such those originating in Scotland, will shift dialect as they begin to interact with other children, and may retain a distinct 'home' variety for use with family members. It may well be the case that many of the New Zealand speakers would, likewise, have had a 'home' and a 'playground' code, and that these would have differed more than they do in a community with cross-generational continuity.

A remarkable fact is the degree of homogeneity in New Zealand English, achieved at least in part, it seems, by 1900 (Woods 2000: 138). Given the degree of variability among the ONZE informants, and the absence of easy communication routes until well after this time, this is very surprising. We argue that a reason for this is that approximately the same mix of forms, in similar demographic proportions, underlay most New Zealand settlements (Trudgill 2004). Since similar mixes formed the input to both Australian and South African English, it is not surprising that rather similar varieties ensued. Yet this alone cannot account for the extreme uniformity of New Zealand English. Trudgill (2004) agrees with Bernard (1969), who argues, in the case of Australia, for geographical mobility and the fact that Australians in different parts of the country kept in touch with one another, mainly though sea travel from one port to another, as accounting for the uniformity. For nineteenth-century New Zealand, Britain (forthcoming) similarly cites high levels of mobility and transience, and suggests that these factors 'led to the emergence of an atomistic society freeing people both from subservience and from the need to conform that tight-knit local communities often engender'. As Britain points out, this was a society with relatively weak social network ties, precisely the sorts of ties that are the breeding ground for rapid supralocal linguistic change. Trudgill also adds diffusion as an explanation: geographical diffusion of linguistic innovations from one place to another would have continued in the normal way during the new-dialect formation period and would have helped, aided by high mobility, to strengthen the reduction of geographical and social differences.

In any case, we can see, even in the ONZE data, very clear changes in speech correlating with the speaker's date of birth. In every case, we see an increase in the use of modern New Zealand English features, and a decrease in features that have died out. An example is so-called *happy*-tensing,[5] the use of a peripheral vowel [i] in some final unstressed syllables (such as that in *happy*), replacing [ɪ]. The feature, which is now universal in New Zealand, is actually absent from the speech of the oldest informants. It then makes an appearance, and subsequently increases. The percentage of speakers who have *happy*-tensing by decade of birth in the ONZE corpus is as follows:

1850–1859   0%
1860–1869   25%
1870–1879   48%
1880–1889   43%

This strongly suggests that *happy*-tensing did not arrive in New Zealand from Britain at all (British varieties, too, have shown an increase in the use of the feature over the same period), but started life independently in New Zealand as an example of drift. It is speakers at the transition between Stage II and III who are gradually adopting it, showing both inter- and intra-individual variation as they do so. Rather than being rapid, we see the process happening over at least forty years. Work on the loss of rhoticity in New Zealand English shows a similar gradualness, and that the process started early in the settlement history (Hay and Sudbury 2002). Hay and Sudbury's results show considerable variability already among the oldest ONZE speakers (born in the 1860s and 1870s), and that the loss of rhoticity was categorical in informants born after about 1910. From the point of view of discovering the geographical spread of a fully focused variety in New Zealand, one result in particular is revealing. This is that, of the two factors 'North Island vs. South Island' and 'year of birth', the former is statistically the stronger predictor. This strongly suggests that focusing was geographically gradual, and (we suggest) that the spread of the loss of rhoticity may, in fact, have been by geographical diffusion; as is well known, rhoticity is a recessive feature that is now restricted to the south of the South Island.

---

[5] This term is taken from Wells (1982).

4   Conclusion

New-dialect formation is in many ways the quintessence of dialect convergence: all the processes described in this chapter can be found in one or more of the other scenarios for dialect contact described in this book. It also has the potential (not always realised) to be a very rapid process, observable using standard techniques from social dialectology. This enables researchers to apply the full range of sociolinguistic techniques, from the quantitative (Labovian) method, through various (ethnographic and quantitative) means of gaining social-psychological information, to examining the contribution of different age groups to dialect convergence in a new community.

Over a longer time perspective and using archive material, it is possible to compare the outcomes of different cases of new-dialect formation, drawing linguistic conclusions that shed light on language change generally. As such, the study of new dialects is a contribution to historical linguistics.

New-dialect formation is related, in particular, to creolisation (cf. Hinskens, Auer, and Kerswill, this volume), in that it implies a lack of generational continuity at the community level. This is an example of dialect divergence, which can also be seen at the family level as the children, through interaction with peers outside the home, begin to form a new dialect. New-dialect formation is the product of linguistic accommodation between speakers, both in the immediate context of conversations and in changes in people's long-term speech habits. We show (Trudgill 2004) that the form of English in New Zealand is highly predictable from knowledge of where in the English-speaking world the immigrants came from, and in what proportions. This does not tell us whether the accommodation was actual (pattern-matching) or more in line with the identity-projection model; in the end, this does not seem to matter for the outcome.

8 Dialect convergence in the German language islands (*Sprachinseln*)

Peter Rosenberg

1 Language Island Research: The Traditional Framework and Some Sociolinguistic Questions

The metaphor of a 'language island'[1] was coined with reference to the 'colonies' of German-speaking settlers in Eastern, Central, and South Eastern Europe, which were mostly founded in the late Middle Ages ('old language islands') and in the eighteenth and nineteenth centuries ('new language islands'), and which for a long time preserved their ethnic, linguistic, cultural, economic, administrative, and sometimes religious distinctness from the surrounding society. Brought in by the state authorities or private colonisers, the settlers cultivated the land, introducing new methods of agriculture, trade, crafts, and mining, stabilising political borders, and increasing the proportion of educated, skilled (and sometimes 'white') population; however, for a long time they did not mingle with the surrounding population.

Since these linguistic communities were founded by settlers speaking different dialects – but lacking the German standard language – they have been subject to dialect convergence from the first days of their existence. The dialects of these language islands are therefore more or less mixed or levelled dialects, as was noted by the Russian dialectologist Victor Schirmunski (1930). For him, the 'language islands' were a 'linguistic laboratory' bringing about the same linguistic processes in short time which over centuries have shaped our contemporary standard languages. Only in the twentieth century did the language islands open to outside linguistic influence from the surrounding language(s).

In this chapter, I will be concerned with convergence in German language islands in Eastern Europe, especially in the former Soviet Union, but also in

---

[1] 'Language islands are internally structured settlements of a linguistic minority on a limited geographical area in the midst of a linguistically different majority' ('Sprachinseln sind räumlich abgrenzbare und intern strukturierte Siedlungsräume einer sprachlichen Minderheit inmitten einer anderssprachigen Mehrheit') (Hutterer 1982: 178, my translation; also cf. Wiesinger 1983: 901). The term 'Sprachinsel' was used for the first time in 1847 to designate a Slavonic community surrounded by a German-speaking population close to Königsberg, East Prussia (now Kaliningrad, Russia; cf. Mattheier 1996: 812).

Poland and Hungary, as well as in Western Europe, and also in Latin America, particularly Brazil, Argentina, Paraguay, Chile, and in the United States.

There is an immense amount of research in this field, which comprises hundreds of historical, philological, ethnological, and folklorist reports and, since the nineteenth century, also dialectological studies. During a first phase, the main interest was in the old language islands close to the German language area, such as in Transylvania, the Zips (Slovakia; Lumtzer 1894; cf. Kuhn 1934), and in the Veneto (northern Italy). Researchers were dialectologists from Germany such as Johann Andreas Schmeller, who included the language-island dialects in the Venetian Alps in his famous Bavarian dictionary (Schmeller 1855). In the late nineteenth century, Gottschee (Slovenia), Temesvar (Banat, Hungary/Romania), and even language islands in Pennsylvania and Australia were included. After the turn of the century several grammars (*Ortsgrammatiken*) were published (e.g. Bohnenberger 1913). In a second phase (after the First World War), the more recent language islands were also subject to dialectological studies by more and more researchers from these communities themselves. Thus, the German-speaking population in Russia attracted the attention of linguists: at first the Germans in the larger cities, then those of the colonies in the Black Sea region, and around St Petersburg (Unwerth 1918; Schirmunski 1928, 1930; Ström/Schirmunski 1926/1927; for the Volga region Dinges 1923, 1925; Dulson 1933, 1941).

Of course, language islands are not a uniquely German phenomenon but exist all over the world.[2]

In German dialectology, language islands were predominantly investigated as relics of the past for the purpose of studies in language change. Most of the linguistic communities examined were rather small with restricted external communication. Since these conservative communities frequently preserved archaic features of German, they were seen as offering access to linguistic elements which had died out in the main German language area.[3] In a way, dialectologists were archivists of linguistic fossils and interpreters of their lives and deaths.[4] The interest in language islands was built on a myth of purity and

[2] Cf. the numerous language islands as a heritage of colonialism, e.g. the enclaves of Portuguese in West Africa, of French in Southern Africa, the complex sociolinguistic situation in South Africa; other language islands are the Finland Swedes in the area around Åbo/Turku, the Yiddish-speaking Jews in Vilnius, Lithuania before the Second World War, the Dutch varieties in northwestern France, the Quechua speakers in Spanish-speaking towns in Peru, the Urdu-speaking communities among the Hindi-speaking majority in Northern India, etc.

[3] The *Sette Communi* in northern Italy are a good example. The Bavarian dialect of these language islands were considered a 'first class linguistic monument' (Hornung 1994: 20, my translation), since it had preserved a number of Old and Middle High German features such as the preterite, the genitive case, and several other characteristics which had vanished in the Bavarian dialects elsewhere four hundred years ago.

[4] This was one of the leading ideas in the Daan and Heikens project, which focused on Dutch dialects in small towns in the American Mid West (cf. Daan 1987).

homogeneity. Language variation and language contact were considered more as a source of data corruption than as a subject of research.

However, in addition to the type of archaic language island there are others which exist under quite different contact settings. What they have in common is (a) a limited geographical area; (b) the fact that they are set off from a linguistically different surrounding community; (c) they are linked internally by a dense communication network (as discussed by Milroy and Margrain 1980; Gumperz 1968) which is to a certain extent more inward- than outward-looking; and (d) a shared attitude of being distinct from the surrounding population.

Language islands are not linguistically and socially homogeneous. They were founded at different times and under different conditions, and they were often inhabited by settlers of different origins, i.e. by speakers of different dialects. After some time social elites emerged: while clergymen and teachers often supported the maintenance of the language island's culture, local authorities were frequently more linked to the world outside.

Language islands also differ in size and settlement structure: they can be remote villages (like those in the Italian Alps, the Brazilian forests, or the Siberian steppe), suburbs in the vicinity of cities (e.g. close to Budapest, Hungary), towns (like Iglau in Moravia, Czech Republic; Bielitz, Silesia/ Poland; cf. Kuhn 1934) or complex structured areas with towns and villages (around Hermannstadt/Sibiu, Transylvania/Romania). 'Introvert' self-contained, mostly religious, language islands like those of the Mennonites in Russia (cf. Rosenberg 1994b), Paraguay (cf. Rosenberg 1998), Mexico and the United States (cf. Kaufmann 1997), or the Hutterites in the USA (cf. Rein 1994: 195ff.) are more resistant to external influence than are 'extrovert' ones in which mobility of the inhabitants, discontinuity of the settlement, and ethnic mixing may induce assimilation (cf. Rosenberg 1994a: 155). 'Expanding' language islands, typically found in Central and South Eastern Europe, have to be distinguished from 'regressive' language islands, i.e. the last remains of a former larger settlement area such as the French-speaking community in Quebec with its partly separatist attitudes (cf. Mattheier 1996; and the language island typology of Kuhn 1934: 324ff.).

Depending on the type and duration of the settlement and the heterogeneity of the linguistic input varieties, language islands display different degrees of levelling: from coexisting local vernaculars (like in Siberia or Kazakhstan) to more or less mixed, levelled, or merged dialects[5] (like those of the Mennonite colonies, Chaco, Paraguay; Volga region, Russia), koines or supraregional varieties (*Hunsrück* variety, South Brazil; Volhynian German, formerly Ukraine) to urban vernaculars with supraregional reach (Hermannstadt, Romania). The Transylvanian can be regarded as an elaborated 'Ausbau' language island (in

---

[5] Cf. Hinskens, Kallen, and Taeldeman (2000: 6ff.).

the terminology of Kloss 1980; also cf. Auburger and Kloss 1979) with a full diasystem.

2   Dialect Convergence in German Language Islands

This section looks in more detail at convergence in the German language islands. The notion of convergence requires some further distinctions: does a dialect variety converge with another variety of the same diasystem (another dialect, a standard language, a 'koine'[6]); or does it converge with an unrelated language? Is the result of dialect levelling or convergence one single new variety or do there still exist several varieties? If there are intralingual or even interlingual convergence phenomena, do they also occur in other German varieties? If so, is this evidence for an internally, maybe typologically motivated, change which all German varieties are subject to? I will focus mainly on dialect–dialect convergence, but since there are links between all the types of convergence mentioned above they will also be taken into account. In the following sections, the three basic problems: convergence as dialect contact (section 2.1); convergence as language contact (section 2.2); and convergence as internal change (section 2.3) will be dealt with in turn.

2.1   *Convergence as dialect contact*

Dialect–dialect convergence has been the classic topic of research on the German language islands in Russia which were founded more than two hundred years ago on the Volga river, in the Black Sea region, in the Caucasus mountains, and later in Siberia and Central Asia. They displayed a unique linguistic setting since the diversity of dialect varieties brought from numerous German regions into these colonies was exceptionally high. In some villages, several dozens of dialects of German coexisted. The German standard existed only among the elites. Convergence during the first hundred years reduced the extreme heterogeneity of the dialects to a still remarkable number of more or less levelled vernaculars. It did not result in the emergence of one common Russian German.

Schirmunski (1930) tried to capture the dynamics of dialect levelling and replacement through his concept of 'primary' vs. 'secondary' dialect features. According to his description, primary features were replaced by those of standard German or of a regional koine, while secondary features were maintained. The criteria for a primary dialect feature for him were, among others, 'articulatory difference', derived by an 'impression of greater or lesser acoustic

---

[6] As a 'koine' I define a higher stratum within the linguistic repertoire of a linguistic community which is the result of levelling of basic language varieties, e.g. a regional colloquial variety used for communication between speakers of different, but closely related, dialects.

similarity', and, more importantly, the 'psycholinguistic difference . . . , which exists between his [the speaker's] way of speaking and the norm of the written language' (Schirmunski 1930: 183, my translation). Obviously, Schirmunski considered the direction of dialect levelling to be given by commonly shared linguistic norms (the written language or some regional koine). However, in the Russian German colonies standard German (and especially the 'written language') was rarely available, as Schirmunski himself admits (cf. Schirmunski 1930: 122), and regional koines were restricted to larger connected settlement areas which hardly existed (cf. Schirmunski 1930: 179).[7] Therefore, this model of dialect levelling is not applicable to those communities where regional linguistic norms did not exist or to colonies which were linguistically extremely heterogeneous, such as in the so-called 'daughter' (secondary) colonies founded by settlers from the old colonies at the turn of the twentieth century (cf. Schirmunski 1930: 176).

Andreas Dulson (1941: 85), who carried out dialectological studies in some extremely heterogeneous Volga German villages, developed another model of dialect–dialect convergence, and argued that Schirmunski's dialect–standard convergence is only one of several possibilities. According to Dulson, dialects of 'compact', close-knit groups of speakers may persist over a long period of time to maintain a demarcation between the groups. 'Compactness' of the group refers to the number of speakers and the distinctiveness of the group, the stability of group norms (in a wide range of linguistic and cultural attributes), attitudes concerning the in- and out-group, and the inclination to accommodate (in the sense of Giles and Coupland 1991). The higher the degree of heterogeneity within the linguistic community, the lower the effect of group norms and the faster the linguistic change. Under extreme linguistic heterogeneity, the direction of convergence is not uniform, but there is what Dulson calls a 'feature-by-feature' struggle. Under these conditions the speakers' perception of dialect differences may focus on subphonemic, non-systematic, differences and even on differences at the level of individual words.[8]

Contrary to the processes of dialect convergence described by Schirmunski and Dulson which are a matter of the past, a second round of convergence is still observable *in vivo* today. It was brought about by the deportation of the German settlers into mixed settlements in Siberia and Central Asia starting in 1938–1941, and the subsequent migrations after the abolition of settlement restrictions in 1956, as well as by the construction of 'central villages' out of small hamlets since the 1970s.

---

[7] Schirmunski (1930: 179) argues that marriage along confessional structures frequently connected distant communities and supported the emergence of 'Catholic' and 'Lutheran' koines.

[8] Dulson (1941) mentions mockeries related to the individual diphthongisation in [broud] Standard German *brot* 'bread' in a Volga German village by the speakers of a neighbouring village, although these speakers themselves systematically use the diphthong [ou] for /o/.

A good example of this recent convergence are the Mennonite settlements in Western Siberia and in the Orenburg region close to the Ural Mountains. Right up to the present day, this religiously and culturally defined group has shown the strongest maintenance of German among the Russian German settlers. The Mennonites have retained their East Low German variety but also have some knowledge of standard German, since it is their language of religion. This is even true for the younger generations, whereas other Russian Germans of this age have shifted to Russian. But even this group is not linguistically homogeneous. There exist at least two major varieties of Mennonite German, which have been brought along from the pre-war settlements in the Ukraine: the oldest Chortica variety; and the more prestigious Molotchna variety.

According to most pre-war studies (Mitzka 1922; Schirmunski 1930; cf. Jedig 1966), upward convergence displaced Chortica features in favour of those of the Molotchna variety. For example, the Chortica rounded front vowel [y:] was replaced by the Molotchna long back vowel [u:], as in [fry:] – [fru:], standard German *Frau* 'woman'. However, in a recent study of dialect convergence among the Mennonites in the Orenburg region, Nyman (1997) describes a more complex type of levelling. He investigated the direction of convergence (on the basis of interview data and so-called 'distinction words') in the twenty-two Mennonite villages of the region. Some features follow the Molotchna pattern, others the Chortica pattern; some did not level at all. For instance, in the [u:] – [y:] variable (as in [u:t] – [y:t], standard German *aus* 'out; out of'), the Chortica feature [y:] has spread to all villages which had been linguistically separated since the colonisation at the turn of the twentieth century.[9] This is hardly compatible with the older findings mentioned above, nor with Schirmunski's assumptions concerning the direction of dialect levelling: Chortica [y:] is more distant from standard German [au] than Molotchna [u:]. Since the Chortica variety is less prestigious than the Molotchna variety, this process looks like downward convergence, but Chortica features may also function as a traditional group symbol because they are perceived as the more authentic, countering the strong assimilatory pressure from Russian.

In the case of the post-schwa [n]-apocope – especially in the infinitive form of the verb (as in [ze:tʲe] – [ze:tʲen] '(to) seek') or in the plural of the weak noun inflection paradigm (as in [tʲoatʲe] – [tʲoatʲen] 'churches') – levelling has occurred towards the Molotchna variety, but only in the surrounding *Unjadarpa* ('lower villages'), which apparently form a subregional geographical unity.

Sometimes *confessional* links cleared the way for convergence. The expression 'to speak Catholic'/'to speak Lutheran' is widespread among Russian Germans, and very often it does not carry a confessional meaning, but rather

[9] The replacement of Molotchna [u:] by Chortica [y:] has taken place in other Mennonite settlements as well (cf. Berend and Jedig 1991: 177).

stands for linguistic varieties. In another of our studies, Dania Asfandiarova (1999) has investigated convergence among 'Catholic' and 'Lutheran' Russian Germans living in the area of Ufa, Bashkortostan. She analysed dialect levelling in a representative study in the Prishib/Alekseevka colony, which consists of four central villages which were amalgamated in the early 1980s from eleven settlements founded around 1900. Each village had its own variety but, after the unification of the settlements, convergence set in. In the vowel system of the speakers, it has led to a complex and sometimes confusing structure. The settlers had come from the Black Sea area and spoke several dialects, the most important ones being Rhine-Franconian (eastern and southern Rhine Palatinate and Hessian), but also Low Alemannic ('Badisch'), Swabian, Bavarian, and others. In the three 'Lutheran' villages Rhine-Franconian features prevail today. The fourth, a 'Catholic' village, is different. But no village is homogeneous. What is striking is that dialect convergence seems to be highly selective: while the front vowel system (unrounded and rounded) and the closed-back vowels are apparently levelled to a very high degree (in the direction of the 'Lutheran' vowel system), this is not the case for (Middle High German) long and short *a* and the diphthongal system. A considerable number of speakers systematically use a backed *a*-vowel (half-open or even closed [o:] for (standard German) /a/ and /a:/ as in [gro:s], std. *Gras* 'grass' or [vo:re], std. *waren* ('[we] were')) which is typical of the 'Catholic' variety (spoken in the Catholic village and by Catholics in the Lutheran villages). These speakers have presumably retained some emblematic elements as markers of their variety which they call *Achterisch* (from the number *acht* 'eight' of their old village at the beginning of colonisation), in contrast to *Sechserisch* (from the number *sechs* 'six'), the variety of the Lutheran majority, even though the varieties have otherwise converged to a great extent. This proves the continuing existence of a 'Catholic' linguistic community which is also supported by certain 'Catholic' cultural traits.

2.2   Convergence as language contact

As far as external influences are concerned, we suggest a comparative method. It seems to be fruitful to compare the linguistic changes in the German language islands in different countries. If we observe different linguistic processes under the dominance of Russian (Slavonic), American English (Germanic), and Brazilian Portuguese (Romance), we will be able to draw some conclusions on contact-induced change. Comparing linguistic processes in language islands in Brazil, Russia, and the United States we will ask to what extent a linguistic change can be related to interlingual convergence in this section.

In Rio Grande do Sul in southern Brazil, the historical conditions under which the German settlements came into being have much in common with those in Russia (cf. Rosenberg 1997, 1998). Brazil has about 1 million speakers of German, who constitute the second-largest German minority group in the world (the territory of the former Soviet Union used to rank first with about 2 million speakers). Settlers lived in small isolated colonies as they did in Russia. Among their dialects the Rhine Franconian and Moselle-Franconian varieties prevailed, but other dialects were present as well, such as Upper German Swabian, Low German Westphalian, Pomeranian, and the Mennonite varieties, and even Volga German. Standard German was taught in school until the political restrictions under the nationalist government (of Getulio Vargas) in the 1940s suspended all educational and political minority rights. As a consequence, redialectalisation took place.

Since dialects were the main means of communication, dialect–dialect convergence set in. In contrast to Russia, a supraregional (so-called *Hunsrück*) variety developed, presumably as a consequence of the numerical dominance of speakers from this area among the first settlers, and due to the more open networks of communication between the settlements. But dialect convergence in Brazil did not mean the complete disappearance of the local vernaculars, which still seem to exist as so-called 'family dialects' ('familetos', i.e. dialects of family settlements). The supraregional *Hunsrück* variety is not homogeneous, but represents a dialect continuum (cf. Altenhofen 1996: 27).[10]

Interestingly, some linguistic features gaining the upper hand in dialect levelling in Brazil and in Russia are similar while others are not, although the input dialect features were to a considerable extent the same. Thus, voicing of consonants in intervocalic position and between vowel and sonorant following stress has spread both in Russia and in Brazil, e.g. [g] for [k]: *drogge* for standard German *trocken* 'dry' (cf. Altenhofen 1996: map 29). On the other hand, nasalisation (as in [tsã:] for standard German *Zahn* 'tooth') is a common feature among the Volga Germans (cf. Wolgadeutscher Sprachatlas 1996, map 143), but not among *Hunsrück* speakers, despite the fact that Brazilian Portuguese has several nasalised vowels. Rhotacism (as in *sore* for standard German *sagten* '(we/they) said'; cf. Altenhofen 1996: map 56) is very common in Brazil, but is found in Russia only among some Upper Hessian speakers. As a rule, it has been replaced by standard forms, perhaps due to the fact that the Volga Germans emigrated at least sixty years earlier than the Brazilian Germans, when rhotacism in Germany was just beginning to spread (cf. Schirmunski 1962: 317ff.; Dulson 1941: 96).

External linguistic influence plays a minor role in these cases. Of course, there are also clear cases of interference; for instance, the loss of the definite

---

[10] It combines for example Rhine-Franconian features with greater, and Moselle-Franconian features with smaller, acceptance (e.g. Rhine-Franconian and standard German *das/was* vs. Moselle-Franconian *dat/wat* 'the (neutr.)'/'what').

article among younger Russian Germans is certainly due to Russian influence (cf. Nöth 1994: 127). Brazilian Germans, on the other hand, velarize lateral /l/, which is probably due to Portuguese interference.

A change which has been much investigated is the reduction of case morphology among German speakers in Russia (Jedig 1966), in Brazil (Altenhofen 1996: 254ff.), Texan Germans (Salmons 1994: 60), Pennsylvania Germans (Louden 1994: 84; Huffines 1994: 50f.), Kansas Volga Germans (Keel 1994: 98), and others. Language contact cannot be excluded in the English/German and Portuguese/German case, and some researchers have argued accordingly (cf. Louden 1994: 90). On the other hand, case reduction is stronger in 'sectarian' Mennonite and Amish groups who consistently use German varieties in everyday conversation than in 'non-sectarian' groups with intensive language contact. In the case of the Russian Germans, a direct Russian influence is rather unlikely anyway (Russian has six cases in the noun, pronoun, and adjective systems). This points to an interpretation of case loss as internally induced language change which will be discussed in the following section.

2.3   Convergence and internal language change

It seems that some changes tend to take place in all 'island' varieties of German, regardless of whether they are in contact with a Slavonic, a Germanic, or a Romance language. But what may influence the direction, the intensity, and the structure of these processes?

Case reduction (as well as the loss of the preterite; cf. Abraham 1999) are part of a long-term development from synthetic to analytic structures in German. Of course, the German linguistic diasystem is still a 'mixed type' (cf. Lang 1996: 12); consequently, some researchers argue that German does not display any uniform typological direction of development. However, there can be little doubt that the development is characterised by the reduction of synthetic elements and the 'externalisation' of syntactic features, i.e. the redistribution of functional category marking to single linguistic elements. Thus, since the Germanic shift to initial stress, the case-marking system in nouns has been reduced (cf. Hutterer 1975: 320). Today, High German noun inflection is, for the most part, restricted to the genitive singular and the plural (Eisenberg 1994: 362); only the strong declension paradigm also marks the dative plural. Dative singular markers are optional. The weak noun paradigm only marks the oblique case singular. Case, number, and gender are generally only marked on the determiner and only on the adjective if no determiner is available (Eisenberg 1994: 367). Grammatical information has moved more and more away from the head of the noun phrase to the left in this originally left-branching language.

The reduction of noun inflection in the German dialects is even more radical than in the standard. This is true for German language island varieties, too. In

Table 8.1 *Case system in Pennsylvania German personal pronouns (Van Ness 1994: 430)*

Person	Nominative	Accusative	Dative
1. Sg.	ix	mix	mir
	'I'	'me'	'me'
2. Sg.	du	dix	dir
	'you'	'you'	'you'
3. Sg. masc.	ar	in	im
	'he'	'him'	'him'
3. Sg. fem.	si	si	ire
	'she'	'her'	'her'
3. Sg. neut.	es	es	im
	'it'	'it'	'it'
1. Pl.	mir/mer	uns	uns
	'we'	'us'	'us'
2. Pl.	dir/ir/der/er/ner/nir	aich	aich
	'you'	'you'	'you'
3. Pl.	si	si	ine
	'they'	'them'	'them'

general, the noun system has two cases (three in some Swabian varieties). The genitive in most functions is substituted by prepositional or dative constructions (plus possessive pronouns following the head). Dative and accusative usually merge into one oblique case (in the south and west sometimes the dative forms, elsewhere the accusative forms). Pronoun inflection exhibits more case distinctions than noun inflection, the masculine more than the feminine and neuter, the singular more than the plural. Since the definite and indefinite determiners are also reduced to a two-case system (especially the masculine and feminine forms), often represented by enclitics, grammatical information is frequently not present at all in the noun, adjective, or determiner. Syntactic functions (e.g. noun–adjective agreement) or semantic information (e.g. direct–indirect object relation) are more and more only a matter of word order and not of morphology.

The German-speaking language islands also share another striking feature which may result from an internal typological drift common to all German varieties or even to all Germanic and other Indo-European languages: while case reduction in the nominal paradigms is extensive, it is not in the pronominal paradigms. Personal pronouns frequently have a three-case system or retain at least the dative, which includes the possibility of marking the direct–indirect object relation (by common case vs. dative).

The full (non-cliticised) forms of the Pennsylvania German personal pronouns (see table 8.1) may serve as an example. The system holds for the

Table 8.2 *Case system in Danish personal pronouns (Haberland 1994: 328)*

Person	Non-oblique	Oblique	Possessive
1. Sg.	jeg	mig	min
	'I'	'me'	'my'
2. Sg.	du	dig	din
	'you'	'you'	'your'
3. Sg. masc.	han	ham	hans
[+ human]		Old Scand. dative: honum	
	'he'	'him'	'his'
3. Sg. fem.	hun	hende [hinne]	hendes
[+ human]		Old Scand. dative: henni	
	'she'	'her'	'her'
3. Sg. neut.	det	det	dets
[+ human]	'it'	'it'	'its'
3. Sg. non neut	den	den	dens
[− human]	'it'	'it'	'its'
1. Pl.	vi	os	vores/vor
	'we'	'us'	'our'
2. Pl.	I	jer	jeres/(eder)
	'you'	'you'	'your'
3. Pl.	de [di]	dem	deres
		Old Scand. dative: þeim	
		(distal demonstrative)	
	'they'	'them'	'their'

linguistically more traditional non-sectarian speakers: they use a three-case system for the 1st and 2nd pers. sg. and the 3rd pers. sg. masc. All other persons have a two-case system (3rd pers. sg. fem. and neut., 3rd pers. pl.: common case vs. dative; 1st and 2nd pers. pl., in some groups, also 3rd pers. masc.: nominative vs. oblique case; cf. Keel 1994: 96, Louden 1994: 84.). Sectarians tend to reduce case marking: they use a two-case system almost exclusively; cf. Huffines 1989: 222f. Other German varieties exhibit a partial shift from dative to accusative, for example Texas German: *spricht er zu mich?* 'Is he talking to me?' (Salmons 1994: 66). But here, too, dative marking is much more extensive on personal pronouns than on determiners (Salmons 1994: 64).

The better retention of case in the pronominal system is not restricted to the varieties of German spoken in the language islands, it also holds for most other Germanic (and some Romance) languages. For instance, the case system of the Danish personal pronouns has a three-term distinction ('non-oblique', oblique, and possessive; table 8.2), whereas the only case distinction in noun inflection is the one between the common case and the genitive. The oblique

Table 8.3 *Case system in Old English personal pronouns (van Kemenade 1994: 121)*

Person	Nominative	Accusative	Dative	Genitive
1. Sg.	ic	me:	me:	mi:n
	'I'	'me'	'me'	'my/of me'
2. Sg.	þu	þe:	þe:	þi:n
	'you'	'you'	'you'	'your/of you'
3. Sg. masc.	he:	hine	him	his
	'he'	'him'	'him'	'his/of him'
3. Sg. fem.	he:o	hi:	hire	hire
	'she'	'her'	'her'	'her/of her'
3. Sg. neut.	hit	hit	him	his
	'it'	'it'	'it'	'its/of it'
1. Pl.	we:	u:s	u:s	u:re
	'we'	'us'	'us'	'our/of us'
2. Pl.	ge:	e:ow	e:ow	e:ower
	'you'	'you'	'you'	'your/of you'
3. Pl.	hi:	hi:	him	hira
	'they'	'them'	'them'	'their/of them'

forms in the 3rd pers. sg. and pl. represent an Old Scandinavian dative. The same is true for the case system in Old English (table 8.3) which used to have a three-term system of personal pronouns in all but the 3rd pers. masc. where a four-term system existed. In Modern English, personal pronouns in the oblique case of the 3rd pers. sg. (masc. and fem.) and pl. refer to Old English dative forms which were lost in Middle English. Nominal inflection only distinguishes between common case and possessive (old genitives). French has lost almost all inflection (cf. Bally 1965: 193), but the system of bound (or enclitic) personal pronouns exhibits a two-term case marking (e.g. *je – me*), and in the 3rd pers. sg. and pl. ('reference' in the terms of Weinrich 1982) even a three-term distinction (*il – le – lui/elle – la – lui; ils/elles – les – leurs*) which is similar to the German dative (table 8.4).[11]

How can case retention (especially of dative) in the pronominal paradigms be explained? We can list seven factors (also cf. Salmons 1994: 64f.).

• The high frequency of pronouns makes them more resistant to change (cf. Salmons 1994: 64; Wängler 1963; Kaeding 1897).

• Pronouns are more likely to have animate referents which demand more morphological distinctions of syntactic roles.

• Pronouns are closed classes.

[11] *lui* goes back to an old Latin dative; cf. Lausberg (1962: 124ff.); Bourciez (1967: 92f., 238ff., 677ff.).

Table 8.4 *Case system in French 'pronoms personnels conjoints'* *(cf. Weinrich 1982: 82)*

	Subject	Object	Partner
Speaker	je	me/m'	me/m'
(Sg.)	'I' ('ich')	'me' ('mich')	'me' ('mir')
Addressee	tu	te/t'	te/t'
(Sg.)	'you' ('du')	'you' ('dich')	'you' ('dir')
Reference (masc.)	il	le/l'	lui
(Sg.)	'he' ('er')	'him' ('ihn')	'him' ('ihm')
Reference (fem.)	elle	la/l'	lui
(Sg.)	'she' ('sie')	'her' ('sie')	'her' ('ihr')
Speaker	nous (on)	nous	nous
(Pl.)	'we' ('wir')	'us' ('uns')	'us' ('uns')
Addressee	vous	vous	vous
(Pl.)	'you' ('ihr, Sie')	'you' ('euch, Sie')	'you' ('euch, Ihnen')
Reference (masc.)	ils	les	leur
(Pl.)	'they' ('sie')	'them' ('sie')	'them' (ihnen)
Reference (fem.)	elles	les	leur
(Pl.)	'they' ('sie')	'them' ('sie')	'them' (ihnen)

- Pronouns function as the head of a noun phrase, and heads normally carry more morphological marking.
- Pronominal paradigms are highly suppletive, and therefore lexicalised. Loss of case marking on nouns seems to be less disruptive than the replacement of entire lexical items.
- The syntactic serialisation of pronouns (in contrast to noun phrases) in the central field of the German sentence shows the order: subject – direct object (accusative) – indirect object (dative). This corresponds with an unmarked order: known before new information, unstressed before stressed (cf. Eisenberg 1994: 383f.).
- Neurolinguistic research gives evidence for a full listing in memory of monomorphemic and polymorphemic irregular words (as well as of less productive morphological paradigms and of semantically less transparent words). This is true precisely for personal pronouns. According to Cholewa (1993), these fully listed items are represented at the deepest lexical level. This might protect them from change.

Thus, we have good reasons to assume that the dynamics and even the structure of case reduction in German language islands is to a great extent an internally motivated, typological change, not directly caused by dialect or interlingual convergence. On the other hand, we may ask what the reasons or conditions for a typological change might be.

3   The Sociolinguistics of Convergence

We have distinguished three processes of change, i.e. convergence of dialects, convergence of languages, and internally motivated linguistic change. However, we have not yet answered the question of why these processes take place at a given moment. Under what conditions do we find convergence, or, when, internally motivated changes? Why are some features at certain times salient in linguistic change while others are not? What are the sociolinguistic conditions under which some features survive, while others are lost? An example will show the complex nature of the problem.

In the past few years, the variety of Low German used by the Russian German Mennonites has undergone remarkable morphological changes, including the reduction of cases mentioned above and a gradual loss of the preterite (cf. Grinjowa 1990). The direction of change is not surprising: it fits the common patterns of change which occur in most German varieties. (The loss of the preterite is typical of Middle and Upper German varieties.) Why has this change occurred so rapidly? On the one hand, the Mennonites have been in contact with other German-speaking groups. Also, the construction of the 'central villages' mentioned above has transformed the formerly homogeneous settlements into more heterogeneous ones. This has caused intensive dialect contact. But, on the other hand, the tight Mennonite networks function as a stronghold of the Low German variety, which can rarely be used for intergroup contact, because only some older non-Mennonite Germans understand it. For intergroup communication, Russian is used.

Our own investigations in a village in the Altai region, West Siberia, a major German settlement area in Russia, prove this point: in intragroup communication about 60 per cent of the Mennonites use (Low) German, in intergroup communication only 20 per cent according to questionnaire data.[12] Additionally, we compiled a sociogramme of a class in the eleventh school year. The students were asked: who are your friends in this class, and which language do you predominantly use for communication with them? The sociogramme displays friendship clusters (multiplex patterns) mainly linking Mennonites among themselves (with differences between boys and girls). Communication is conducted in Russian and German. Russian is used in all clusters, but above all with non-Mennonites. With two exceptions, monolingual German (dialect) is only spoken among Mennonites. Thus, even young Mennonites usually have their own, separate linguistic network. This more or less protects their variety from interference with other German varieties. For this reason, linguistic change due to dialect convergence is not very likely.

---

[12] Cf. Rosenberg (1994b: 294); the study covered about 750 informants, including all school-children and every fifth adult of the village.

The loss of the preterite may also be due to Russian influence, i.e. the Russian perfective verbal aspect. But the Mennonites are the German community with the most separated domains of bilingual language use, and therefore borrowing from Russian occurs less than in other groups.

An explanation needs to refer to the language-internal typological drift typical of the German (or Germanic) languages mentioned above. Its speed depends on the instability of norms. In our case, this stability is reduced by the increased heterogeneity of the mixed Mennonite settlements. Loyalty as an attitudinal matter tends to decline if cultural and linguistic group boundaries become diffuse. This is also true for the Mennonites whose religious and cultural values are weakening, intermarriages are increasing, and mobility is growing.

4   Conclusion

As Eugenio Coseriu states, linguistic (and cultural) norms are in the front line of linguistic change: 'A linguistic change always starts and develops as a "shift" of the norm' (Coseriu 1974: 119; my translation). Since the norm is what is 'normally done' in a language, while the system contains what is possible in a language, the norm will always be the gateway for linguistic change within the limits of the system (and in the same way, the system for typological change). Thus, systematic changes 'are very frequent and widespread in times of weak tradition and cultural decay or in communities with limited linguistic culture' (Coseriu 1974: 117; my translation). Among the Russian German Mennonites, such a decline of linguistic and cultural norms clears the way for language change along the lines of systematic and typologically attested (language internal) patterns.

9   Political borders and dialect divergence/ convergence in Europe

Curt Woolhiser

1   Introduction

Political borders have long been a central concern of geographers, students of international relations, and legal scholars. Since the 1960s, a growing body of sociological and anthropological research has, in addition, provided valuable new insights concerning the sociocultural aspects of border regions. Dialectologists, on the other hand, have given scant attention to the role of modern political borders in the spatial distribution and diffusion of linguistic features, generally viewing such factors as physical geography, earlier migration and settlement patterns, patterns of trade, and the influence of urban centres as linguistically far more significant.[1]

However, with the rise of the modern nation state in the nineteenth century, accompanied in the twentieth century by the emergence of modern communications, improved transportation networks, greater geographical and social mobility of populations, and universal education, political borders have become a far more potent factor in dialect divergence and convergence. In many parts of the developed world, and particularly on the European Continent, dialect areas or dialect continua that are divided by international borders are, in many cases, beginning to show signs of divergence, either as a consequence of cross-border differences in the degree of cross-dialectal levelling or dialect maintenance, or as the result of convergence towards different superposed standard languages.

Obviously, the mere existence of a political border is insufficient to cause dialect divergence, just as the existence of social differentiation does not

Research for this chapter was supported in part by grants from the International Research and Exchanges Board (with funds provided by the National Endowment for the Humanities and the US Information Agency), the Social Science Research Council, the American Council of Learned Societies and the University of Texas at Austin. None of these organisations is responsible for the views expressed.
[1] Where man-made borders were invoked as factors in the diffusion of dialect features, it was more common to refer to early ecclesiastical rather than political divisions, as these presumably played a more significant role in structuring the communication networks of pre-modern, sedentary rural populations.

necessarily entail linguistic divergence within a speech community. What is (socio)linguistically significant about political borders is the extent to which they represent discontinuities in patterns of intra- or interdialectal communication, the ways in which they help to create and maintain linguistic hierarchies and diglossic patterns within a clearly defined geographical area, and how they are reflected in the language attitudes and language ideologies that divide or unite dialect speakers on the two sides of the border. The study of the role of political borders in dialect divergence and convergence thus draws on the concerns and methodologies of such diverse disciplines as dialect geography, social dialectology, the sociology of language, linguistic anthropology, and the social psychology of language. Linguistically relevant insights can also be obtained from studies of the geography, sociology, and anthropology of border regions.

In this chapter, I shall present a conceptual and methodological framework for the investigation of the role of political borders in dialect divergence and convergence. By way of introduction, in section 2 I discuss the key concepts, levels of analysis, and approaches relevant to the study of border effects in social dialectology. In section 3 I proceed with an overview of existing research on the role of political borders in dialect maintenance and change in Europe, a region characterised by an exceptionally rich variety of politically segmented dialect continua. Finally, in section 4, as an illustration of the issues raised in the preceding sections, I present a case study based on an ongoing project investigating structural divergence in the Belarusian dialects of the contemporary Polish–Belarusian border region. The findings of this study support the view that a maximally diversified approach, employing the perspectives and methods of social dialectology, linguistic geography, and the social psychology of language, provides the most satisfactory account of the various mechanisms that promote or hinder dialect divergence and convergence across political borders.

2   The Study of Border Effects in Dialect Maintenance and Change: Conceptual and Methodological Issues

Given the paucity of studies devoted specifically to border effects in dialect divergence and convergence, it is difficult at present to speak of 'border studies' as a distinct area of research in dialectology and sociolinguistics, analogous to what has emerged over the last few decades in such fields as geography, sociology, or anthropology (see, for example, Strassoldo 1973; Rumley and Minghi 1991; Donnan and Wilson 1994; Paasi 1996; Wilson and Donnan 1998). Chambers and Trudgill (1998), for example, have very little to say about political borders other than indicating their importance for the notions of linguistic autonomy and heteronomy, and noting in a very schematic fashion the potential for divergence implied by the imposition of different standard languages within a single dialect continuum (Chambers and Trudgill 1998: 6–7).

Mackey (1988) notes the importance of language–border correspondences in geolinguistic research, but approaches the issue primarily from the standpoint of the sociology of language. Thus, while observing that the geopolitical segmentation of language areas (i.e. the degree of linguistic homogeneity both within and across state boundaries) is of great relevance for the study of ethnolinguistic accommodation and language conflict, Mackey does not indicate what border regions might contribute specifically to the study of language and dialect maintenance and change.

2.1   The linguistic relationship between dialects and standard 'roofs' in border regions

A more explicit, albeit by no means exhaustive, discussion of the problems relating to the linguistic effects of political borders may be found in Kremer and Niebaum (1990b). These authors are primarily concerned with the linguistic relationship between dialects and standard 'roofs' as the basis for a typology of language–border configurations. Using the Continental West Germanic dialect continuum as an illustration, Kremer and Niebaum identify three general types of language–border correspondences with respect to the dialect–standard language dimension:

1. dialect continua divided by national boundaries with different standard languages on the two sides of the border; and
2. dialect continua divided by national boundaries with the same standard language (or national variants thereof) used on the two sides of the border; and
3. dialects within a single state in linguistically heterogeneous areas that share the same standard language.

Kremer and Niebaum note that the outcomes of dialect–standard contact within the borders of a state will depend, at least in part, on the linguistic relationship between the dialects and the standard. Portions of language continua that have a closely related standard 'roof' will be characterised by language change (*Sprachwandel*), i.e. convergence towards the standard, resulting ultimately in the emergence of new regional colloquial varieties (*Umgangsprachen*), replacing earlier diglossic or polyglossic situations. In situations where the linguistic distance between the dialects and a related standard is much greater, for example, in the case of contact between Low German dialects and standard High German, gradual convergence tends to be replaced by more abrupt language shift (*Sprachwechsel*). In their view, exceptional cases such as Swiss German, which does not exhibit any tendency towards convergence with the standard variety, i.e. High German, may be attributed to the exceptionally favourable 'sociocultural' position of the dialects *vis-à-vis* the codified standard language (Kremer and Niebaum 1990a: 16–17).

Auer and Hinskens (1996), in a survey of various aspects of dialect convergence and divergence in contemporary Europe, recognise the potential for political borders (or rather the sociocultural discontinuities they give rise to) to affect the extent and direction of dialect change. They observe that any account of border effects must take into account divergent and convergent change along two axes: the vertical, or dialect–standard axis; and the horizontal, or dialect–dialect axis. In situations where different standard languages dominate on the two sides of a politically divided dialect continuum, Auer and Hinskens argue, vertical convergence towards different standard varieties is likely to be the primary source of horizontal divergence from similar dialects across the border (Auer and Hinskens 1996: 17). However, they note the need for further research to determine the relationship between horizontal divergence and vertical convergence, and the role played by autonomous processes of interdialectal convergence on the two sides of the border.

2.2 *The role of borders in the geographical distribution of language functions*

In discussing border effects on a dialect area or continuum, it is also necessary to distinguish between divergence/convergence in linguistic structure and divergence/convergence in social functions. It remains to be demonstrated whether there is a significant connection between the two, although we might hypothesise that a cross-border mismatch between functions (for example, stable diglossia on one side, and functional overlapping between dialect and standard on the other) is potentially more likely to result in significant structural divergence along a political border than a situation where the dialect functions are identical (and, we should add, the standard 'roof' is essentially the same).

Ideally, in a sociolinguistic study of border effects in dialect divergence/convergence, we should like to be able to map the functions of the dialects and standard languages in different functional domains (education, government, business, religion) and with different interlocutors (family, friends, neighbours, co-workers, visitors from the other side of the border, etc.) in a number of survey sites on the two sides of the border. There are, however, as noted by Auer and Hinskens (1996: 22), certain methodological problems connected with the use of self-report data regarding language use, particularly in situations where the dialect has either very high prestige (in which case informants may over-report use of the dialect) or very low prestige (in which case informants may under-report its use).

2.3   *Political borders and border effects: border regimes and border functions*

In addition to taking into account the linguistic and functional relationship between dialects and their standard 'roofs,' the study of border effects must also be based on a thorough investigation of the geographical structure of border regions. Of particular relevance in this regard are the following:

1. the political status of the border: international vs. internal borders and the border regimes associated with them, i.e. externally (state) enforced restrictions on the cross-border movement of people, information and goods;
2. the degree of cross-border political, economic, and sociocultural integration and interaction. This can be viewed both at the macro-level (in terms of flows of goods and services, the existence of political, economic, and cultural organisations, and institutions in which actors from both sides of the border participate), as well as at the micro-level (frequency of cross-border travel, existence of kinship ties on the other side of the border, density and multiplexity of transborder social networks, exposure to mass media from the other side of the border, etc.). A relatively high degree of transborder political and economic co-operation between states does not, however, necessarily entail a high degree of sociocultural integration of populations on the two sides of the border, as suggested by Lundén (1973) in his study of the individual spatial behaviour of residents of the Swedish–Norwegian border region;[2]
3. the degree of integration of the border region and its population into the national economies and national cultures on the two sides of the border, as reflected in regional infrastructure development, settlement patterns, economic and social structure, patterns of in- and outmigration, etc. Within a border region it is also important to examine differences between urban and rural areas with respect to regional and national integrative processes.

2.4   *The role of borders in the formation and reproduction of language attitudes and ideologies*

While earlier geographical approaches to border regions tended to focus on the relationship between borders and cultural and physical geography, as well as

---

[2] By charting local residents' personal contacts (travel and telephone calls outside their immediate locality) on the basis of diary entries, Lundén demonstrates that inhabitants on the two sides of the Swedish–Norwegian border tend to have more intensive contacts with geographically more distant co-nationals than with the population just across the 'open' border.

border regimes and patterns of cross-border interaction (measured in levels of economic integration, frequency and ease of cross-border movement, etc.), in more recent research (for example, Sahlins 1989; Donnan and Wilson 1994; Paasi 1996; Wilson and Donnan 1998, etc.) there has been a greater emphasis on borders as cultural constructs, as reflected in the attitudes and ideologies that inform and structure the social behaviour of border dwellers. Among the many questions relating to the study of the sociocultural and sociopsychological aspects of political borders, the following are perhaps of greatest importance to the processes of dialect divergence and convergence.

1. Do the residents of the border region identify with the dominant ethnolinguistic group within their country?
2. How strong is local/regional identity on the two sides of the border?
3. Do border residents perceive their counterparts on the other side of the border as members of the same nation or ethnic group?
4. Is there a feeling of cultural superiority or inferiority among border residents *vis-à-vis* the population speaking closely related dialects on the other side of the border?

Borders may thus have an important psychological effect on borderlands populations, in terms of how they view themselves *vis-à-vis* national centres and the populations from whom they are separated by the border. This also applies to the subjective evaluation of different language varieties, both standard and nonstandard, in the verbal repertoire of local communities and of those on the other side of the border.

The language attitudes of border populations may be studied using a variety of experimental techniques developed by social psychologists (for example, matched-guise tests) as well as by qualitative, ethnographic fieldwork methods. Another promising approach for investigating the cultural and sociopsychological correlates of border effects is the study of folk linguistics, or 'perceptual dialectology', as discussed by Preston (1999). By comparing the 'mental maps' of residents of border regions concerning the geographical and social distribution of language varieties and variants on the two sides of the border, it is possible to gain further insights into the ways in which the social discontinuities represented by the border serve to structure local perceptions of linguistic variation within a politically divided dialect continuum.

3   Previous Research on Border Effects in Europe

Europe, the birthplace and first 'testing ground' of the concept of the modern nation state, provides an exceptionally wide variety of examples for the study of the impact of superimposed political borders on pre-existing dialect landscapes. In light of this fact, it is perhaps not surprising that European researchers have so far produced the largest body of research on the impact of political borders in dialect divergence and convergence.[3]

The Germanic languages, and in particular the Continental West Germanic dialect continuum, have unquestionably attracted the greatest amount of attention on the part of dialectologists and sociolinguists working in the field of border impact studies. The first systematic study of this type, Kremer (1979), focuses primarily on lexical aspects of divergence in the central portion of the Netherlands–German border region (Enschede-Gronau) on the basis of a large-scale dialectological survey. The findings from Kremer's survey are systematically compared with mostly pre-Second World War dialect atlas data from the same region, indicating growing cross-border discontinuities in the distribution of the lexical items investigated. The study also maps cross-border differences in the use of the local dialects and standard languages with different interlocutors according to informants' self-report data.

Subsequent studies of this and other sections of the Netherlands–German border, employing both traditional dialectological as well as sociolinguistic methods, have provided further evidence of the divergent restructuring of the dialect landscape (Niebaum 1990) and a growing rift in language attitudes and dialect use (Hinskens 1993a) on the two sides of the border. A recent sociolinguistic study by Gerritsen (1999) of the Limburg dialects, politically divided between the Netherlands, Belgium, and Germany, shows a similar picture with respect to the Netherlands–German border (due largely to dialect attrition on the German side), while the Limburg dialects on the Belgian side of the border, 'roofed' by standard Belgian Dutch, remain essentially the same as on the Netherlands side.

The importance of the function of the standard language(s) for processes of dialect change within national boundaries is highlighted by the case of dialects of Lëtzebuergesch in Luxembourg, formerly considered an integral part of the West Moselle Franconian dialect continuum. Cajot (1990) indicates that, as the result of the spread of certain features of Lëtzebuergesch based on the dialects of Gutland and the city of Luxembourg, the dialects in border regions are becoming less like those of neighbouring parts of Belgium and Germany; i.e. this is an

---

[3] In this connection, it should be noted that the European Science Foundation Network on the Convergence and Divergence of Dialects in a Changing Europe organised the first-ever conference (Gent 1997) dealing specifically with the effects of political borders on dialect divergence and convergence on a pan-European scale. A selection of papers from this conference has been published in the *International Journal of the Sociology of Language* (145 (2000), ed. Jeffrey Kallen, Frans Hinskens, and Johan Taeldeman), and are discussed in this section. This is not to say, however, that border effects in dialectology have not been investigated outside Europe; important work within the variationist paradigm has been done by Boberg (2000), and Zeller (1993) on the Canadian–US border; while Amara (1999) presents a fine-grained study of border effects in Palestinian Arabic as spoken in Barta'a, a village divided between the 'Little Triangle' of Israel and the Israeli-occupied West Bank.

example of horizontal convergence without vertical convergence, contributing to horizontal divergence across state borders. The spread of vernacular linguistic features and the absence of any appreciable influence from standard German are due to the unique sociolinguistic situation in the country: while standard French and standard German (albeit less so) function as the dominant 'H' languages in this largely diglossic society, attitudes towards the local dialects are so favourable as to preclude language shift or vertical dialect convergence.

A similar situation is observed by Scheuringer (1990) in a study of the development of the Middle Bavarian dialect continuum, divided politically between Germany and Austria. Here, the dialects on the Austrian side have retained most of their original structure with minimal influence from standard Austrian German, while the dialects on the German side have diverged from them due to more extensive influence from the regional variety of the standard.

The linguistic effects of the former border between the Federal Republic of Germany (FRG) and the German Democratic Republic (GDR) have also attracted considerable attention among social dialectologists. Schlobinski (1997) notes important differences in the sociolinguistic evolution of the local Berlin vernacular in the FRG and the GDR. While in West Berlin the local vernacular came to be highly stigmatised among the upper and middle classes, in East Berlin it functioned more broadly as an urban colloquial variety, and had even begun spreading to neighbouring regions.

Although the West Romance dialect continuum provides many interesting sociolinguistic parallels to Continental West Germanic, studies focusing on the effects of contemporary political borders on West Romance dialect landscapes are fewer in number and, for the most part, methodologically less innovative. Goebl (2000) presents the results of a macro-level study of dialect similarity within the West Romance dialect continuum employing the dialectometric approach. Focusing on the southeastern French, Franco-provençal, Occitan, and Lombard dialects, Goebl presents evidence that sharp differences between dialects in border regions are characteristic only of the Italian–French border (dialects of Occitan and Franco-provençal) and Swiss–Italian border (Lombard dialects of Italian), while the border effect is minimal in the case of the border between France and Francophone Switzerland. Unfortunately for those not conversant with the dialectometric methodology, Goebl does not discuss which features are employed in measuring linguistic distance between these varieties. In addition, due to the fact that the calculations are based on dialect atlas data and not on the study of ongoing dialect change, they do not provide any indication of the sociolinguistic dynamics involved, i.e. we cannot say for certain whether the modern political borders were established before or after the dialects of the Italian–French or Swiss–Italian border regions began to diverge.

Pohl (1978) discusses some aspects (primarily lexical) of the divergence of Picard and Lorraine dialects along the French–Belgian border. Pohl argues that in the case of the French–Belgian border, linguistic divergence is a consequence of mismatch between what he calls the 'linguistic field' (dialect continuum) linking the Picard and Lorraine dialects on the two sides of the border and the 'communication field' (the communication networks linking groups of speakers with each other, including national media), which in this area is divided into Belgian vs. French zones of influence.

Among the major language families of Europe, the Slavonic languages have probably experienced the greatest number of border shifts (whether in location or political status) over the course of the twentieth century, with far-reaching implications for the evolution of the South Slavonic, West Slavonic, and East Slavonic dialect continua. In light of these circumstances, it is rather surprising that Slavonic dialectologists and sociolinguists have lagged so far behind their colleagues working on Western European languages in the study of border effects. Certainly, during the Communist period, political pressures often prevented such questions from being raised at all (to suppress any manifestations of supposed 'irredentist' tendencies), although the traditional diachronic orientation of Slavonic dialectology was undoubtedly also partly responsible.

The study of divergent language planning in the former Yugoslavia has, for obvious reasons, attracted considerable interest over the last decade. Greenberg (2000) documents the division of 'Serbo-Croatian' into several distinct, although still very similar, standard varieties: Serbian, Croatian, Bosnian, and (potentially) Montenegran. Divergent planning of these varieties is expressed primarily in lexical differences (reflecting both different dialectal sources as well as different attitudes towards lexical borrowing and the sources of such borrowings). It remains to be seen, however, how divergent language planning will be reflected in the dialect landscape of border regions in this area. As Magner (1992) notes in the case of Serbian and Croatian, regional dialects or regional koines are still in a fairly strong position, even in urban areas.

Dialect divergence along the Macedonian–Bulgarian border as a potential by-product of divergent language planning is discussed by Angelov (2000). Herson-Finn (1996) focuses on the impact of the Macedonian–Bulgarian border in the area of perceptual dialectology, observing that Macedonian informants, when presented with samples of written standard Serbian, Macedonian, and Bulgarian, as well as transitional and mixed varieties, typically regarded Serbian and mixed Macedonian–Serbian to be closer to their own language than Bulgarian or transitional Macedonian–Bulgarian varieties (contrary to the majority opinion among linguists).

An interesting case study of the ethnolinguistic impact of political borders in the West Slavonic area can be found in the monograph by Hannan (1996) on the Zaolzie dialect (typologically closest to the Silesian dialects of Polish across the border) in the vicinity of Český Těšín in the Czech Republic. Hannan notes that speakers of the Zaolzie dialect who identify themselves as Czechs lead the way both in the adoption of lexical and syntactic influences from standard Czech and in the shift towards the regional variety of Czech as the predominant form of in-group communication. Those speakers of the Zaolzie dialects who identify themselves as Poles, on the other hand, are more conservative in their linguistic behaviour, and also continue in some cases to use standard Polish alongside Czech in education and other domains (Hannan 1996: 169).

4   Dialect Divergence in the Polish–Belarusian Border Region: A Case Study

As an illustration of the explanatory potential of a multidisciplinary, integrative approach to the study of dialect divergence and convergence along political borders, in this section I shall discuss the preliminary results of an ongoing study of border effects in the Belarusian dialects of the contemporary Polish–Belarusian border region. This region is of particular interest in that it represents a formerly quite homogeneous dialect area that has only relatively recently (that is, after the revision of the Polish–Soviet border in 1945) been divided by a political border. The fact that the political division of the region occurred within the lifetimes of older residents allows us to investigate the process of dialect change, as well as accompanying changes in language attitudes, as responses to major sociopolitical transformations. Another unique feature of this region is that most of the rural population on both sides of the border has only recently, within the last two to three generations, begun to acquire a clearly defined sense of national identity (whether Polish or Belarusian) that transcends traditional local or religious foci of self-identification. Such 'modern' national identities are crucially linked to language – particularly the codified standard 'national language' – which has come to play a central symbolic role in representations of the self as a member of a broader national community. On the Belarusian side of the border, the situation is further complicated by the largely unequal competition between two closely related standard languages, Russian and standard Belarusian, for functional and symbolic dominance as national or state languages.

4 1   Research questions and methodology

In this study I have sought to answer the following questions:
1. To what extent can the process of dialect divergence be observed in apparent time, i.e through comparing the speech of the oldest living residents of the border region with that of the younger generation?
2. How does the degree of linguistic distance between the dialects and the standard 'roof' affect the maintenance or loss of traditional dialect features? What is the relative contribution of Russian and standard Belarusian to the

process of dialect change on the Belarusian side of the border? What is the linguistic effect of continued Polish influence on the Polish side of the border?

3. Is convergence along the horizontal (dialect–dialect) axis observed on either side of the border? If so, to what extent has this horizontal convergence contributed to divergence along the border?

4. To what extent is dialect divergence accompanied by divergence in evaluations of the local dialects and the superposed standard languages on the two sides of the border?

The bulk of the sociolinguistic fieldwork that served as the basis for this case study was carried out from the autumn of 1996 to the spring of 2000. Tape-recorded interviews and sociolinguistic surveys were administered by local fieldworkers under my supervision in twelve Belarusian-speaking villages: six on the Belarusian side; and six on the Polish side. Here I shall focus primarily on the questionnaire data from two villages on the Belarusian side of the border and three villages on the Polish side. On the Belarusian side, the survey sites discussed here include the predominantly Catholic village of Račiču (pop. 500, approximately 90 per cent Catholic), and the large, predominantly Orthodox village of Malaja Berastavica (pop. 1,341). Representing the situation on the Polish side of the border are the neighbouring, confessionally mixed, villages of Dubaśno and Chilmony (with a combined pop. of about 700, 60 per cent Catholic and 40 per cent Orthodox) and the small Orthodox village of Jałowo (pop. 79). In addition, in section 4.4 on language attitudes I shall also discuss findings based on a smaller sample from Reszkowce (pop. 390), an exclusively Catholic village on the Polish side of the border, and the village of Luckaŭljany (pop. 720) on the Belarusian side, where approximately 60 per cent of the inhabitants are Catholics and the remainder Orthodox.

In order to reduce potential observer effects during the interviews, I employed local students from the School of Belarusian Philology at Hrodna University (Belarus) and the Institute for East Slavic Philology at Białystok University (Poland) as fieldworkers. The fieldworkers (all female) were natives of the villages investigated and were themselves speakers of the local Belarusian dialects.[4]

Informants for the study were initially selected by means of a judgement sample of 32 natives of each of the villages investigated, with 4 females and 4 males representing each of the following age cohorts: 10–24 years, 25–39 years, 40–54 years, and 55 years and above. In the presentation of the linguistic

[4] I would like to express my gratitude to the fieldworkers in Poland, Maria Panasewicz-Dubicka (Jałowo), Anna Szczurko (Dubaśno and Chilmony), and Agnieszka Dziełak (Reszkowce); and in Belarus, Iryna Radzivilka (Račiču), Iryna Pir'janovič (Luckaŭljany), and Natallja Vojšal' (Malaja Berastavica), for obtaining the data used for this study. I would also like to express my appreciation to Prof. Michał Kondratiuk (Białystok University) and Vjačaslaŭ Lamaka (Hrodna University) for helping to co-ordinate the fieldwork on the Polish and Belarusian sides of the border.

data I shall focus only on the youngest and oldest groups of informants (10–24 and 55+), inasmuch as the middle two age cohorts do not exhibit any striking deviations from the general trends of maintenance or loss of dialect features reflected in the responses of the other two groups.

The informants for this study were drawn primarily from among my field-workers' social networks in the villages, including family, friends, neighbours, and members of their networks. The informants represent a socially fairly homo-geneous group, i.e. private smallholder farmers and members of their families on the Polish side of the border, and collective farm employees and members of their families on the Belarusian side.[5] Due to incomplete questionnaire data, and in the case of the Polish villages, the tendency of some younger individuals to respond to the interviewer's questions primarily in Polish, a number of the informants originally included in the study had to be eliminated from the sam-ple. As a result, complete data sets were obtained from only 11 informants in the age 10–24 age group on the Polish side of the border, and from 13 informants in the same age group on the Belarusian side. The 55+ age cohort is represented by 16 informants on each side of the border.

Each of the informants for the study participated in a 40-minute tape-recorded interview and responded to two written questionnaires. As the analysis of the interview data is still incomplete, the phonological and morphological data dis-cussed in this section will be based on the questionnaire responses.[6] The first of the written questionnaires provides basic sociological data as well as sociolin-guistic and sociopsychological information regarding the informants' views as to the appropriateness of the use of different language varieties in different social domains, as well as their subjective assessments of the inherent beauty and expressiveness of these different language varieties. The second question-naire, involving oral repetition of sentences read aloud by the fieldworkers as well as sentence completion and morphological transformation tasks, was designed to elicit a variety of local dialectal forms, as well as to gauge the extent of penetration of standard Belarusian, Russian, and Polish features in the dialects. The linguistic questionnaire was particularly important for the study of a number of morphological and syntactic variables for which the number of tokens in the individual interviews may be insufficient for statistical analysis.

4.2   The Polish–Belarusian border: linguistic and sociohistorical context

According to the criteria of dialect geography, the East Slavonic dialects spo-ken in the northeastern portion of the Białystok region near Sokółka and in the

---

[5] Agriculture was collectivised on the Soviet (Belarusian) side of the border in the late 1940s, and collective farms have retained their dominant position in post-Soviet Belarus.

[6] It may be argued, however, that the greater level of formality associated with questionnaire-type tasks is at least partially compensated for by the fact that the fieldworkers are all natives of the villages, and in most cases known by the informants.

western part of the Hrodna region can be classified as part of the southwestern Belarusian dialect, showing features both of the northwestern and western
Belarusian dialect zones and the western dialect group (Avanesaǔ *et al.* 1968;
Glinka *et al.* 1980). For most of its recorded history, the territory where these
dialects are spoken has been part of a single political entity: the ancient Rus'
principalities of Kiev and Volhynia (11th–13th centuries), the Grand Duchy of
Lithuania (late 13th century – 1569), the Polish–Lithuanian Commonwealth
(1569–1795), Prussia (1795–1807), the Russian Empire (1807–1917), and the
interwar Polish Republic (1921–1939). Although united by a common vernacular (Belarusian or transitional Belarusian–Ukrainian dialects further to the
south), the native rural population on both sides of the post-Second World War
Polish–Belarusian border is quite heterogeneous in terms of its ethnonational
affiliations. Historically, the primary focus of supralocal identity was religion,
dividing the local population into divergent communities of faith and cultural
tradition. In more recent times, traditional confessionally based supralocal identities came to be reevaluated in elite, and subsequently in popular, discourse as
national or ethnic identities. Thus, the majority of Roman Catholic speakers of
Belarusian dialects on both sides of the border identify themselves as Poles,
while on the Belarusian side of the border, the vast majority of dialect speakers
of Orthodox heritage claim Belarusian ethnicity. The situation is more complicated in the case of the Orthodox population on the Polish side of the border
(making up a majority in the areas east and southeast of Białystok), who are
divided among those who identify themselves as Belarusians, Poles, or, mainly
among the older generation, simply 'Orthodox'.[7]

Observers have long noted the self-deprecating attitude of many Belarusians
towards their native vernacular varieties. This attitude has its roots, no doubt,
in two important circumstances. First, by the time modern Belarusian linguistic nationalism appeared on the scene in the late nineteenth century, the vast
majority of speakers of East Slavonic dialects that had come to be known in
scholarly discourse as 'Belarusian' were illiterate or semi-literate peasants. The
upper classes of the region, who, as a result of both assimilation of native elites
and immigration, spoke either Polish or Russian as a first language, generally
had a negative view of the Belarusian 'peasant' vernacular. Like speakers of
lower-class vernaculars in other contexts, the Belarusian-speaking peasantry,
while maintaining their dialects as a marker of in-group, local identity, and
solidarity, at times seemed to accept the dominant discourses which portrayed
Polish and/or Russian as more 'refined' and more suitable for use in education, religious life, and other prestigious social domains. Characteristically, the

---

[7] On the complex and dynamic interaction of confessional and ethnonational identities in the region
under the influence of the ideology of the modern nation state, see Tokc' (2000); Straczuk (1999);
Engelking (1999); and Sadowski (1995).

Belarusian-speaking peasantry employed social, rather than ethnolinguistic, terms in defining the language varieties spoken in their communities: to speak Polish was to speak *pa-pansku* ('like a gentleman'), while to speak Belarusian was to speak *pa-mužycku* ('like a peasant'), or *pa-prostu* ('the simple way', 'like plain folk'). It was only gradually, and rather recently, that the ethnonym 'Belarusian' (*belaruski*) began to be applied by the speakers themselves to their vernacular; in some cases, particularly along the contemporary Polish–Belarusian border, to this day villagers distinguish between their local vernacular varieties (*pa-prostu*) and the Belarusian standard language (*pa-belarusku*), despite the relatively minor structural differences between these dialects and the standard.

A second factor that undoubtedly played a significant role in the formation of negative self-perceptions among Belarusian dialect speakers was the ideological legacy of the Tsarist policy of 'Russification' of the western borderlands of the Russian Empire, which began in earnest in the second half of the nineteenth century. Tsarist Russian nationalist ideology, which was often echoed in Russian scholarly opinion, held that Belarusian was simply a dialect of Russian, and was thus destined to merge with the latter.[8] The officially sponsored notion that Belarusian was merely a 'corruption' of Russian, or a haphazard mixture of Russian and Polish, became deeply ingrained in the minds of the educated public in the region, and created further obstacles for the promotion of a standard language based on the Belarusian vernacular. An even more effective means of perpetuating the notion that Belarusian was not a 'proper language', but simply a backward idiom of illiterate peasants, was a Tsarist government ban on Belarusian-language education and 'subversive' Belarusian-language publications (above all those using the Latin rather than Cyrillic alphabet), which remained in force until 1905.

As a result of the journalistic and educational activities of Belarusian intellectuals and social activists in the first two decades of the twentieth century, a Belarusian standard language, based largely on the north central dialects, began to emerge; however, for the reasons noted above, this new standard was slow to gain acceptance by the peasantry. Quite often, the traditional attitudes associated with the peasant vernaculars were simply transferred to the emerging Belarusian standard, which was similarly associated with rural, peasant culture.

The attitudes of the peasantry towards the nascent Belarusian standard language began to change as the cause of linguistic emancipation came to be linked with the cause of social liberation. Following the establishment of the Belarusian Soviet Socialist Republic (BSSR) in 1920, in accordance with the

---

[8] At the same time, as noted by Tokc' (2000: 108), Tsarist Russian administrators and census officials, in their fervor to rid the region of Polish influence, apparently contributed to the spread of the ethnonym 'Belarusian', which had hitherto been virtually unknown to the local East Slavonic-speaking population.

official Soviet policy of 'indigenisation', considerable progress was made in promoting the official use of Belarusian; however, by the end of the 1930s, as a result of Stalin's purges of Belarusian officials and intellectuals, many of the achievements of this period in the language sphere had been reversed. Polish persecution of the Belarusian national movement in the Belarusian-speaking areas of eastern Poland (including both of the regions discussed in this chapter) contributed to pro-Soviet attitudes on the part of the Orthodox peasantry, but effectively limited the exposure of the local population to the newly codified Belarusian standard language.

As a result of the establishment of the contemporary Polish–Belarusian border in the 1940s, the Polish language retained the functional and symbolic dominance which it had enjoyed throughout the region from 1921 to 1939 only on the western side of the border (i.e. the Białystok–Sokółka region). Although concessions in the spheres of education and cultural life were periodically made to the Belarusian minority in the People's Republic of Poland, these concessions affected primarily the predominantly Orthodox areas to the southeast of Białystok, where a distinct Belarusian ethnic identity was relatively stronger. Since the collapse of the Communist system in Poland in 1989, the Polish state has been moderately supportive of Belarusian-language education and media in the Białystok region, part of a broader minority rights policy which was directly linked to Poland's aspirations for membership in the European Union which has meanwhile been realised.

The language situation on the eastern side of the post-Second World War border (i.e. the Hrodna region) is even more complex. Following the annexation of these territories to the Belarusian Soviet Socialist Republic, the Polish language was eliminated from the public sphere as local Polish-speaking elites were repressed or forced into emigration. By the 1950s the Russian language had already become dominant within the republic's Communist party and state apparatus.[9] While primary education, particularly in rural areas, was still conducted mainly in Belarusian, Russian held a dominant position in the sphere of higher education. Thus, by the 1960s, it would appear that for a majority of Belarusians in the BSSR, Russian was the language most closely associated with social mobility, at least outside a relatively limited state-sponsored Belarusian-language 'reservation' in education, scholarship, literature, and the arts. None the less, the fact that officially, at least, Belarusian remained the state language of the BSSR and was recognised in official Soviet discourse as the unique 'national language' of the Belarusians, meant that the dominant position of Russian was not entirely unchallenged. Indeed, the Belarusian side

---

[9] Local Belarusian-speaking personnel who had been active in the Belarusian movement when the region was under Polish rule (1921–1939) were often replaced by Russian-speaking officials from the East, whom Stalin regarded as more loyal.

of the Polish–Belarusian border, far from seeing the imposition of a single standard language as part of a classical nation-building project, became, and continues to be, a battleground for two forms of nationalism with fairly clearly defined linguistic correlates: a Russocentric quasi-Soviet state nationalism; and a 'classical' Belarusian ethnolinguistic nationalism, which since the early 1990s has become increasingly pro-European in orientation. In post-Soviet Belarus under the leadership of President Aljaksandr Lukashenka, it would appear that the former ideological current has gained the upper hand, as policies adopted in the early 1990s to expand the use of Belarusian have been rather dramatically rolled back. Although Belarusian and Russian have had co-official status in the country since 1995, Russian now clearly dominates in most spheres of public life.

According to the 1999 Belarus national census, nearly 63 per cent of the country's 10 million inhabitants (including, apart from the Belarusian majority, Russians, Poles, Jews, and other ethnic groups), concentrated primarily in urban areas, indicated Russian as the language of the home (Itogi 2000); this result has been presented by Lukashenka's administration as justification for its preferential treatment for Russian. None the less, in spite of Lukashenka's policies, according to the same census, the vast majority of ethnic Belarusians in Belarus, almost 86 per cent (i.e. roughly 70 per cent of the country's total population), still consider Belarusian their 'native language' (*rodnaja mova*),[10] although only some 41 per cent claim to speak Belarusian in the home (Itogi 2000).[11] Self-report data of this type are notoriously unreliable; however, they do suggest a considerable discrepancy between the symbolic and communicative functions of the language for many Belarusians. These census data are also somewhat misleading in that respondents were forced to choose between languages as discrete entities, rather than indicating the use of mixed varieties, which, as we shall see below, are an important part of the linguistic landscape in contemporary Belarus.

4.3   Evidence for dialect divergence in the Polish–Belarusian border region

I shall now proceed to an examination of the evidence for dialectal divergence along the northern portion of the contemporary Polish–Belarusian border on the basis of the fieldwork outlined above in section 4.1. As will be seen, the ongoing

[10] This term, which was always included in Soviet-era censuses and was central to official Soviet statements regarding the Soviet Union's 'successful' solution to the nationalities problem, in practice often denoted the language of an individual's ethnic heritage, and not necessarily the language which he or she spoke most fluently.

[11] Interestingly, the ethnic group indicating the highest use of Belarusian in the home (nearly 58 per cent) are self-identified Poles (Itogi 2000).

divergence of the dialects is reflected on all linguistic levels, including not only the lexicon but, more importantly, phonological and morphophonemic rules and inflectional morphology. The overall picture that emerges is one of considerable innovation on the Belarusian side, as compared to a greater conservatism in the Belarusian dialects on the Polish side; in my conclusions in section 5 I shall offer some interpretations of these findings.

4.3.1 Phonology and morphophonemic alternations   In figure 9.1, I present data comparing the retention rates of a traditional regional phonological feature, termed 'incomplete *akanne*', for two age groups, 55+ and 10–24, on the two sides of the Polish (P)–Belarusian (B) border. Incomplete *akanne* involves the maintenance of the distinction between the mid-back vowel /o/ and the low-back vowel /a/ in unstressed word-final position with neutralisation of the opposition (e.g. /o/ > [a]) in pre-tonic and non-final post-tonic position. The following examples illustrate the dialect variants with incomplete *akanne* and their counterparts in standard Belarusian, standard Russian, and standard Polish:

	Hrodna/Sokólka dialect	Standard Belarusian	Polish	Russian
neuter nouns:	[máslo] 'butter'	[másla]	[máswo]	[máslə]
adverbs:	[dórayo] 'expensive'	[dóraɣa]	[drógo]	[dórəgə]
masc. gen. sg. of adjectival declension:	[ɣétaɣo maladóyo] 'that young (one)' (masc. gen. sg.)	[ɣétaɣa-maladó-ɣa]	[tégo mwodégo]	[étəvə məladóvə]

Incomplete *akanne* is characteristic of the entire southwestern Belarusian dialect area, and according to Avanesaŭ *et al.* (1963) and Glinka (1980), was the dominant type of unstressed vocalism in the dialects of the Hrodna–Sokólka type. This contrasts with standard Belarusian as well as Russian, both of which have *akanne (akan'e)* in final position (realised in Russian as [ə], the centralised allophone of /o/ and /a/ in post-tonic position). Standard Polish and most Polish dialects (excepting those that arose on a Belarusian/Lithuanian or Ukrainian substratum) retain unstressed /o/ as [o] in all positions, both pre- and post-tonic.

The questionnaire data summarised in figure 9.1 were taken from the villages of Račičy and Malaja Berastavica on the Belarusian side of the border and Dubaśno/Chilmony and Jałowo on the Polish side. The columns represent group scores for the 55+ and 10–24 age cohorts (consisting of 16 and 11 informants, respectively, on the Polish side; and 16 and 13 on the Belarusian side). To arrive at percentages for each of the groups, I added all of the occurrences of non-reduced word-final /o/ in the responses to the questionnaire and then divided this amount by the total number of tokens of word-final phonemic /o/ in the

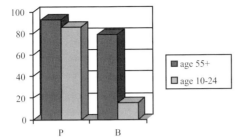

Fig. 9.1 Dubaśno/Chilmony and Jałowo (Poland: first two columns) and Racičy and Malaja Berastavica (Belarus: second two columns): occurrence of incomplete *akanne* ([o] (-stress)/ _#).

responses of the informants in each group.[12] The same approach was taken in the analysis of the other variables in this study.

In figure 9.1 we find that there is marked decline in the retention of unstressed final [o] among the youngest generation in the villages on the Belarusian side of the border. In so far as the phonetic merger of non-high-back vowels in word-final position is as much a feature of standard Russian as of standard Belarusian and the central and northeastern Belarusian dialects, it is difficult to determine the relative contribution of each of these varieties to this innovation. Indeed, it could be argued that the loss of incomplete *akanne* is the result both of convergence on the horizontal axis (i.e. southwestern Belarusian dialects with central and northeastern dialects) and on the vertical axis (standard Russian and standard Belarusian). Significantly, however, the Belarusian Dialectological Atlas (Avanesaŭ *et al.* 1963) indicates on the basis of data collected in the 1950s that there were two locations in the western Hrodna region where incomplete *akanne* already coexisted with full *akanne* – both of them in the immediate vicinity of the regional urban centre, Hrodna. Taking into account the fact that, by the 1950s, Russian was in a dominant position in urban centres such as Hrodna, it seems likely that the co-occurrence of incomplete and full *akanne* in these villages can be attributed primarily to the diffusion of the more innovative

---

[12] Most informants had nine tokens of phonemic /o/ in final position, in the following phrases (dialect variant with non-reduced final vowel is listed first, followed by the standard Belarusian variant): ɣeto moj báć″ko / ɣéta moj báć″ka 'This is my father'; us'ó č'tp'ér náttṷ dóṷ u ɤo / us'ó č″ap'ér nátta dóraɤa 'Everything now is so expensive'; us'ó l'éto byló ɤaračé / us'ó l'eta byló ɤórača 'It was hot all summer'; ɣeto s'ɣ'e žaje maslo / ɣeta s'ɣ'ežaje masla 'This is fresh butter'; Kas'a kaxaje ɣeta ɤo xlopca / Kas'a kaxaje ɣetaha xlopca 'Kasia is in love with that boy'; Pačal'i budavać″ školu ŭ dz̄″ev'anósto dru ɤóm roku / Pačal'i budavać″ školu ŭ dz″ev'anosta dru ɣ'ím ɤodz″e 'They began building the school in '91'. Each of these phrases was read in standard Belarusian (the second variant) by the fieldworker, who then asked the informants to repeat the phrase as they themselves would say it. Since the format of the interview did not foreground the feature of incomplete *akanne*, it is likely that informants were not overly conscious of the difference between their dialect pronunciation and the standard models used for this portion of the questionnaire.

Russian-influenced urban pronunciation to the surrounding rural areas rather than to an older regional pronunciation or diffusion from central Belarusian dialects.

The dialects of the Sokółka and Hrodna regions also show increasing divergence in apparent time with respect to morphophonemic alternations, i.e. the occurrence of alternations of stem-final velars with dental affricates and fricatives in the dative and prepositional cases of Declension II nouns. In contrast to incomplete *akanne*, which is characteristic only of the southwestern Belarusian dialects, velar alternations are a feature also found in standard Belarusian and most of the Belarusian speech territory. Indeed, the presence of stem-final velar alternations, a Proto-Slavonic archaicism, is one of the features distinguishing most traditional dialects of Belarusian from Russian, where the velars in this particular morphological environment simply acquire allophonic palatalisation. The Proto-Slavonic velar alternations are also characteristic of Polish, although it shows distinct reflexes of the palatalised velars /g/ and /x/, as seen in the following examples:

Hrodna/Sokólka dialect	Standard Belarusian	Polish	Russian
[ruká] 'hand'	[ruká]	[rénka]	[ruká]
~ [u ruc:é]/[u ruc:ý] 'in the hand'	~ [u rucé]	~ [v rénce]~	~ [v ruk'é]
[(v)ól'ɣa] 'Olga'	[vól'ɣa]	[ólga]	[ol'gə]
~ [(v)ól'z″i] 'to Olga'	~ [vól'z″e]	~ [óldze],	~ [ól'g'ɪ]
[saladúxa] 'Saladuxa' (surname)	[saladúxa]	[sowodúxa]	[səladúxə]
~ [saladús″i] 'to Saladuxa'	~ [saladús″e]	~ [sowodúše]	~ [səladúx'ɪ]).

Given the presence of velar-dental alternations in standard Belarusian, their gradual attrition in the dialects of the Hrodna region can thus clearly be attributed to influence from Russian. In figure 9.2, we see that on the Belarusian side of the border, the rate of retention of velar-dental alternations declines to around 71 per cent among the age 10–24 cohort, reflecting horizontal divergence *vis-à-vis* the dialects on the Polish side of the border as well as vertical divergence from the closely related Belarusian standard. The loss of velar alternations appears to proceed on a lexical basis, with alternations being lost first in personal names, e.g. *Vol'ɣa Muraška* 'Olga Muraška', *Saladuxa* (surname), and lexical items that have Russian cognates, e.g. *ruká* 'hand', *kn'ɣia* 'book'. However, in certain words related to village life, such as *v'oska* 'village'; *straxá* 'thatched roof', *rečka* 'stream, river', the alternations are more likely to be preserved even by younger speakers.

On the Polish side of the border, the velar alternations were retained in virtually all expected environments by informants of all age cohorts, as illustrated by the data for the villages of Dubaśno/Chilmony and Jałowo in figure 9.2. The conservative influence of Polish, which has analogous, although not entirely identical, velar alternations, together with the absence of any significant Russian influence, appear to account for this fact. The only regular exception

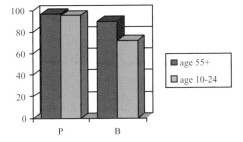

Fig. 9.2 Dubaśno/Chilmony and Jałowo (Poland: first two columns) and Račičy and Malaja Berastavica (Belarus: second two columns). Retention of velar alternations in the prepositional and dative sg. of Decl. II nouns (e.g. *ruká* 'hand' ~ *u ruccý* 'in the hand' vs. Rus. *ruká* ~ *v ruk'é*).

to the expected Belarusian pattern of velar alternations was the sporadic occurrence of the Polish reflex of the second Proto-Slavonic velar palatalisation in dative forms of the personal name *Vol'xa* (that is, [vol'dzy] rather than the expected [vol'z″i]).

4.3.2 Inflectional morphology As in the domains of phonology and morphophonemics, there is also evidence of divergent tendencies in the evolution of the inflectional system, in particular nominal case morphology, in the dialects of the Polish–Belarusian border region. The first variable that I shall discuss is the distribution of the dialectal Declension I stressed masculine nominative plurals in -*é*.[13] Examples of plurals of this type, with the corresponding standard Belarusian, Polish, and Russian forms are shown below:

Hrodna/Sokólka dialect	Standard Belarusian	Polish	Russian
[braté] 'brothers'	[bratý]	[bráća]	[brát'jə]
[syné] 'sons'	[syný]	[sɪnóvje]	[synav'já]
[ɣrybé] 'mushrooms'	[ɣrybý]	[gžíbɪ]	[gr'ibý]
[dubé] 'oaks'	[dubý]	[démbɪ]	[dubý]
[ɣalasé] 'voices'	[ɣalasý]	[gwósɪ]	[gəlasá]
[vawk'é] 'wolves'	[vawk'í]	[v'ílk'i]	[vólk'ɪ]
[b'eraɣ'é] 'shores'	[b'eraɣ'í]	[bžég'i]	[b'ɪr'ɪgá]

As can be seen from the examples, this feature is not found in standard Belarusian (or most Belarusian dialects), Russian, and Polish.[14] According to

---

[13] Belarusian dialectologists generally regard this form as the result of the generalisation of the reflex of the Proto-Slavonic *-j-ŏ* stem accusative plural desinence, *-ě*, to both soft and hard stem types. Many inflectional morphemes in Proto-Slavonic had two variants, a basic form and a fronted variant occurring after the results of jotation and other Proto-Slavonic palatalisations.

[14] Declension I masculine nominative plurals in -*e* do occur in Polish, but with a different distribution, that is, they do not occur under stress (except with non-syllabic stems), and are restricted to stems ending in palatal or historically jotised consonants (e.g. Pol. [nóžé] 'knives', cf. Bel. dial. [nažé], Standard Bel./Russian [nažý]).

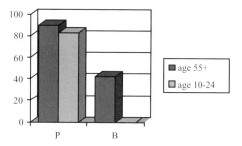

Fig. 9.3 Dubaśno/Chilmony and Jałowo (Poland: first two columns) and Racičy and Malaja Berastavica (Belarus: second two columns). Retention of Decl. I masc. stressed nom. pl. in -é.

the Belarusian Dialectological Atlas (Avanesaŭ *et al*. 1963), this particular feature is characteristic only of the southwestern dialects, where it is encountered in a wedge-shaped zone that widens from west central Belarus to the Polish border. Glinka *et al*. (1980) indicate that stressed Declension I masculine nominative plurals in -*é* predominate in the local Belarusian dialects on the Polish side of the border as well.

As can be seen in figure 9.3, the nominative plural -*é* desinence has virtually died out among younger speakers on the Belarusian side of the border, while its use remains fairly stable in the villages on the Polish side. The percentages here reflect the percentage of plural forms in -*é* out of the total number of end-stressed first declension masculine nouns in the questionnaire (potentially a total of 16 items out of 27 plural forms); respondents were asked to give the plural forms of a series of nouns belonging to different noun classes, with end-stressed Declension I masculine hard and soft stem nouns alternating with stem-stressed Declension I masculine nouns, Declension I neuter, and Declension II (feminine) nouns). While most of the youngest informants in the villages on the Belarusian side of the border showed no instances of these dialectal plural forms, a few did retain the -*é* morpheme in one of the items on the questionnaire: the plural of the noun *syn* 'son', that is, [syné]. Most likely, the retention of this now-exceptional plural form by some younger speakers is due to the relatively high frequency of this given lexeme.

On the Polish side of the border we find that there is a relatively insignificant decline in the use of the stressed -*é* nominative plural from the oldest to the youngest dialect speakers (90 per cent and 83 per cent, respectively). Perhaps more significant is the fact that, overall, the number of end-stressed masculine plural forms has decreased among the younger generation. This innovation can clearly be attributed to Polish influence, both direct, through lexical borrowing, and indirect, via the transfer of Polish-like accentual patterns to native lexemes. One example of direct borrowing is the noun [brek] ('bank, shore', from Polish *brzeg* [bžek]), with the stem-stressed plural form [brég'i], which has supplanted the expected Belarusian form [b'erax], with the plural [b'eraɣ'é] ([b'eraɣ'í] in standard Belarusian). This particular borrowing is now very widespread on the Polish side of the border in the Belarusian-speaking villages in the vicinity of Sokółka.

An example of indirect accentual influence from Polish is the occurrence of fixed initial stress in such lexemes as [l'ésy] 'forests' (cf. traditional dialect [l'asé], Polish [lásɪ]), [dúby] 'oaks' (cf. traditional dialect [dubé], Polish [démbɪ]) and [ɣólasy] 'voices' (cf. traditional dialect [ɣalasé], Polish [gwósɪ]). The last example indicates that the loss of stress alternations does not always involve the transfer of the Polish penultimate stress pattern (i.e. the form *[ɣalósy] is not attested in my data). Still, there is little doubt that the shift from mobile to fixed stress in such cases is primarily a consequence of increasing exposure to Polish accentual models, a conclusion which is supported by the absence of this type of accentual levelling in the speech of the younger generation on the Belarusian side of the border.

Despite an overall decrease in the number of end-stressed masculine nominative plurals in the speech of the younger informants on the Polish side of the border, in those words that retain end stress in the plural (averaging around 11 items out of a potential 16 on the questionnaire), the dialectal -*é* morpheme remains the dominant masculine nominative plural marker.

The loss of the local dialectal plurals in -*é* on the Belarusian side of the border has occurred as the result of two distinct morphological innovations. The first of these is the spread of plurals in -*ý* / -*í*, the exclusive Declension I plural marker in most Belarusian dialects and the standard language, and a variant which also occurs widely in Russian (and, if we disregard differences in stress patterns, in Polish as well). Significantly, in some forms, the loss of the older dialectal variants does not entail the adoption of forms identical to those of standard Russian. In the case of the plurals [bratý] 'brothers' and [syný] 'sons' (for older dialectal [braté], [syné]), the corresponding standard Russian forms [brát'jə] and [synav'já], which have exceptional nominative plural morphology, are not encountered even among the youngest informants. It is evidently the exceptional nature of the standard Russian forms that hinders their adoption, a fact which underscores the koine-like characteristics of the newer village vernaculars.

A second innovation in Declension I plural morphology which has contributed to the decline of plurals in -*é* on the Belarusian side of the border is the spread of plurals in -*á*, a feature that is unquestionably of Russian origin.[15] For the most part, the nouns that regularly have plurals in -*á* in the dialects are those that were recently borrowed from Russian and/or are associated with

---

[15] Indeed, the occurrence of Declension I stressed nominative plurals in -*á* has traditionally been considered one of the morphological diagnostics distinguishing dialects of Russian from those of Belarusian and Ukrainian.

Soviet-era innovations in rural life. Accordingly, among the older informants we find Russian-influenced nominative plurals in -á most frequently with nouns such as [pašpartá]/[paspartá] 'passports' (referring to the internal passports introduced by the Soviets in the late 1940s, cf. standard Russian [pəspartá], Polish [pašpórtɪ]), [traxtará] 'tractors', [damá] 'apartment buildings', and [ɣaradá] 'cities' (which has largely replaced the older local term for city, the polonism [m'esto]). It is only among the younger informants on the Belarusian side of the border that we begin to find plurals in -á even with lexical items native to the dialect, such as [b'erax] ('bank, shore') – [b'eraɣá] (rather than the older dialectal form [b'eraɣ'é] or standard Belarusian [b'eraɣ'í]), [ɣalasá] 'voices', [l'asá] 'forests', etc.

4.4   Sociolinguistic divergence: language attitudes

As Labov (1972a: 121) has argued, a key criterion for determining the boundaries of a speech community is the existence of a shared system of language norms, as reflected both in overt language attitudes and abstract patterns of linguistic variation associated with different contextual styles. In order to determine whether it is still possible to speak of the dialects of the Belarusian–Polish borderlands as constituting a single speech community in this sense, I included in the sociolinguistic survey a series of questions designed to elicit informants' attitudes towards different language varieties in use in their communities, including the local Belarusian dialect (known locally as *pa-prostu* 'the plain/simple way [of talking]', or *pa-svojmu* 'our own way [of speaking]'), standard Belarusian, Russian, Polish, and mixed Russo-Belarusian varieties. The responses to two of these questions – 'Which language do you enjoy speaking most of all?' and 'Which language do you like most of all?' – are summarised in tables 9.1 and 9.2.

In the communities examined, we find that on both sides of the border in everyday communication a sizeable percentage of respondents prefer to use a nonstandard variety, whether dialect (*pa-prostu*) or mixed Belarusian–Russian (on the Belarusian side). At the same time, we find considerable cross-border variation, as well as some variation across communities on the same side of the border, with respect to the overt evaluation of both standard varieties and the local vernacular. The relatively low ratings not only for mixed varieties but also standard Belarusian on the Belarusian side of the border are consistent with what we have observed in section 4.2 with regard to the traditional language attitudes of the Belarusian peasantry. The border effect is reflected primarily in the even lower ratings assigned to standard Belarusian and Russian on the Polish side, and the generally much lower ratings given to Polish on the Belarusian side. In addition, a border effect is seen in evaluations of the traditional local dialects, which are relatively more favourable on the Polish side of the border.

Table 9.1 *Which language do you enjoy speaking most of all?*

	pa-prostu (dialect)	Belarusian	Polish	Russian	Mixed
Poland:					
Jałowo ‡:	66%	0%	34%	0%	0%
n = 29*	(19)	(0)	(10)	(0)	(0)
Dubaśno-Chilmony ✝‡:	48%	0%	52%	0%	0%
n = 31*	(15)	(0)	(16)	(0)	(0)
Reszkowce ✝	37.5%	0%	62.5%	0%	0%
n = 16	(6)	(0)	(10)	(0)	(0)
Belarus:					
Malaja Berastavica ‡✝:	0%	7%	3%	3%	87%
n = 31*	(0)	(2)	(1)	(1)	(27)
Luckaŭljany ✝‡:	6%	13%	0%	40%	40%
n = 30*	(2)	(4)	(0)	(12)	(12)
Račičy ✝:	46.9%	0%	15.6%	37.5%	0%
n = 32	(15)	(0)	(5)	(12)	(0)

✝ = Roman Catholic villages
‡ = Orthodox villages
✝‡ = mixed Roman Catholic/Orthodox villages (Catholic majority)
‡✝ = mixed Orthodox/Catholic villages (Orthodox majority)
* informants who declined to answer the questions are not included in the totals

Table 9.2 *Which language do you like most of all?*

	pa-prostu (dialect)	Belarusian	Polish	Russian	Mixed
Poland:					
Jałowo ‡:	31%	3%	66%	0%	0%
n = 29*	(9)	(1)	(19)	(0)	(0)
Dubaśno-Chilmony ✝‡:	12%	4%	81%	4%	0%
n = 26*	(3)	(1)	(21)	(1)	(0)
Reszkowce ✝:	19%	0%	81%	0%	0%
n = 16	(3)	(0)	(13)	(0)	(0)
Belarus:					
Malaja Berastavica ‡✝:	0%	35%	10%	48%	0%
n = 29*	(0)	(11)	(3)	(15)	(0)
Luckaŭljany ✝‡.	0%	21%	29%	46%	4%
n = 28*	(0)	(6)	(8)	(13)	(1)
Račičy ✝:	0%	3%	63%	34%	0%
n = 32	(0)	(1)	(20)	(11)	(0)

✝ = Roman Catholic villages
‡ = Orthodox villages
✝‡ = mixed Roman Catholic/Orthodox villages
* informants who declined to answer the questions are not included in the totals

The religious make-up of the community also appears to have some impact on language attitudes: this can be seen in the larger number of respondents in Jałowo, an Orthodox village on the Polish side of the border, who indicate *pa-prostu* (Belarusian dialect) as their favourite language, as compared with the mixed Catholic–Orthodox villages of Dubaśno/Chilmony and the Catholic village of Reszkowce in the same region. In the villages studied on the Belarusian side of the border, religious affiliation also has an impact on language attitudes, with the predominantly Orthodox village of Malaja Berastavica showing higher ratings for Belarusian and Russian and much lower ratings for Polish than the exclusively Catholic village of Račičy, where the ratings for Polish approach those on the Polish side of the border.[16]

On the Belarusian side of the border, overt attitudes towards the local dialect are even less favourable, the majority of respondents preferring either Russian, standard Belarusian, or Polish. While the older generations, particularly those born prior to 1940, generally refer to their home language as '*pa-prostu*' ('the plain/simple way of speaking'), '*prostaja mova*' ('simple language'), '*pa-svojmu*' ('our way of speaking'), '*svaja havorka*' ('our own dialect'), the generations born after the 1940s increasingly designate their speech as '*zmešanaja mova/zmešany jazyk*' ('mixed language'), usually implying by this a mixture of Belarusian and Russian. This evaluation, as the linguistic data from the region testify, is a fairly accurate assessment on the part of younger villagers of an ongoing breakdown in the intergenerational transmission of traditional dialect features and their replacement by a combination of Russian and standard Belarusian features.

Thus, the data on language attitudes suggest that the sociolinguistic integration of Belarusian dialect speakers on the two sides of the border into two different regional and national speech communities is well underway. On the Polish side of the border, the majority of Belarusian dialect speakers can be said to be fairly well integrated into a Polish national speech community, at least on the affective level, if not yet entirely on the level of language use. The local Belarusian dialects, still generally referred to in ethnically neutral terms as *pa-prostu*, continue to serve primarily as a marker of local and social (peasant) identity for most respondents. On the Belarusian side of the border, there is evidence for the emergence of a hybrid Russo-Belarusian speech community, with Russian (and, to a lesser degree, standard Belarusian) functioning as the language of formal communication, while mixed Russo-Belarusian forms of speech have largely supplanted the traditional dialects as markers of local solidarity in rural communities.

---

[16] It should be noted, however, that some Catholic villages in the largely Orthodox southern part of the Hrodna region show much higher ratings for Belarusian than for Polish. It thus appears that the majority religious affiliation of a region is a better predictor of language attitudes than religion alone.

5   Conclusions

In comparing the recent evolution of the Belarusian dialects on the two sides of the Polish–Belarusian border, we find a greater number of contact-induced innovations in phonology, morphophonemic alternations, and morphology on the Belarusian side, where standard Russian and, to a lesser extent, standard Belarusian are the dominant official languages, while overall the dialects on the Polish side are more conservative in these linguistic domains. While it is tempting to attribute the greater conservatism in the Belarusian dialects on the Polish side of the border solely to the presence of similar features in Polish (absence of word-final *akanne*, presence of velar alternations, masculine plurals in -*e*), the fact that these are at best only partial similarities, together with the absence of any significant (non-lexical) structural influence from Polish in those areas where there is no formal isomorphism between the local Belarusian dialects and Polish, suggests that we must seek an alternative explanation. A more plausible source for the greater conservatism of the dialects on the Polish side of the border is the greater genetic and typological distance between the dialects and the standard 'roof',[17] which under conditions of language maintenance presents a greater obstacle to the transfer of structurally more integrated features such as inflectional morphemes.[18]

However, the degree of genetic and typological proximity alone do not predetermine the extent of convergence of dialects with a standard variety; social evaluations of the standard (propagated or reinforced through educational

[17] In terms of phonological typology, Belarusian and Russian share the feature of free dynamic stress, in contrast to the penultimate stress characteristic of standard Polish, as well as the phonological merger of the mid vowels /e/ and /o/ in unstressed position with /a/ (in the case of Belarusian) or /i/ and /a/ (in the case of Russian). Polish, a member of the West Slavonic group, also shows a number of early divergent innovations which oppose it to the East Slavonic group (Belarusian, Ukrainian, and Russian). These innovations include: (1) the reflexes of Common Slavonic liquid dipthongs, e.g. Common Slavonic *berg- 'bank, shore', *melko 'milk', and *porg- 'threshold' yield the forms [bžek], [mléko], [pruk] (with metathesis) in Polish, as opposed to the pleophonic reflex in East Slavonic, e.g. Belarusian [b'erax] 'bank, shore', [malakó] 'milk', [paróx] 'threshold', and Russian [b'er'ık], [məlakó], [parók]; (2) reflexes of Common Slavonic *tj, *dj sequences, e.g. Common Slavonic *swětja 'candle' and *sadja 'soot' yield [śf'eca], [sadza] in Polish, as opposed to [s''v'eč-], [saža] in Belarusian and [s'v'ič'á], [sažə] in Russian; (3) reflexes of the Common Slavonic lax high back vowel, or 'jer' in closed syllables: CS *sŭn- 'sleep, dream', *lub- 'forehead' > Polish [sen], [wep] vs. Belarusian/Russian [son], [lop]; (4) reflexes of the Common Slavonic nasal vowels, yielding the Polish nasal diphthongs [čw̃], [õw̃], and their allophones vs. East Slavonic [a], [u], e.g. Polish [p'eńć] 'five', [mõw̃š] 'husband' vs. Belarusian [p'ac''], [muš], Russian [p'at'], [muš]; and other features. There are also more significant differences in inflectional morphology and syntax between Belarusian and Polish than between Belarusian and Russian (Polish having, for example, personal agreement in the past tense of verbs, gender distinctions in the plural of nouns, adjectives and pronouns, and enclitic pronouns, all of which are absent in Belarusian and Russian).

[18] See van Coetsem (2000) for further discussion of the relationship between genetic/structural proximity and the potential for transfer of more structurally integrated features such as inflectional morphology.

policies and national language policies in general) are a crucial factor. The situation on the Belarusian side of the border, where two cognate standard languages, standard Belarusian and Russian, are competing for the linguistic loyalties of vernacular speakers, is an excellent illustration of this point. Although standard Belarusian is structurally the closest 'roof' for the local dialects of the Hrodna–Sokółka type, its influence on the dialects is far less pervasive than that of standard Russian. Here, the difference in the degree of institutional support for the two standard languages, and the resulting popular evaluations of their relative social prestige (as reflected in overt language attitudes), play a decisive role in determining the primary source of standard influence on the local vernacular.

At the same time, we find that there are limits on the extent of Russian influence in the phonology and inflectional morphology of the dialects on the Belarusian side of the border. In the case of nominal inflectional morphology, in those instances where the local dialectal and/or central or standard Belarusian forms are more regular than their standard Russian counterparts (for example, in certain nominative plural forms such as [braté]/[bratý] 'brothers' vs. standard Russian [brat'jə]), Russian influence is limited indeed. Thus, the relationship between the local Belarusian dialects, other varieties of Belarusian (including the central Belarusian standard), and standard Russian shows some features in common with koineisation, where variants that either occur in the majority of the contacting varieties, and/or those features that show the greatest regularity, tend to prevail in the end.

The impact of the contemporary Polish–Belarusian border in these processes is twofold: dialect divergence, i.e. the emergence of a new bundle of isoglosses which largely coincides with the state border, is occurring not only as a result of the relatively weak contacts between the populations on the Polish and Belarusian sides, but also due to the fact that the border delineates the geographical limits of two distinct sociolinguistic hierarchies and their associated linguistic ideologies.[19] The degree to which cross-border horizontal (dialect–dialect) or vertical (dialect–standard) convergence or divergence occur within a politically divided dialect area or continuum is thus determined not only by the linguistic relationship between the roofing varieties and the local vernaculars on the two sides of the border and by the physical obstacles presented by different types of border regimes, but also by the degree of success of national institutions in instilling in local populations a higher level of solidarity with co-nationals than with citizens of the neighbouring state.

---

[19] This is not to say that these dominant sociolinguistic hierarchies and ideologies may not be contested (indeed, in the Belarusian case, the Belarusian standard language has a relatively small, but highly committed, group of advocates on both sides of the border).

10 The influence of urban centres on the spatial diffusion of dialect phenomena

Johan Taeldeman

Urban centres play a prominent part in the spatial diffusion of linguistic phenomena. On dialect maps this is usually reflected by the island-like position of urban dialects (sections 1 and 2). A closer examination of this phenomenon reveals that urban dialects display three types of 'insularity'. Each type will be illustrated by examples from recent sociodialectological literature and from my own investigations in Flanders (section 3). Next we pursue the causes of this urban 'insularity' in greater depth; it appears that besides social factors, social-psychological and structural-linguistic ones (may) also play an important role (section 4). The relevance of the last two kinds of factors leads, finally, to a critique of the use of gravity models in geolinguistics (section 5).

1 Introduction: Patterns of Spatial Diffusion

Social geography has paid a good deal of attention to how innovative phenomena spread across given areas (e.g. Hägerstrand 1967; Brown 1981). Two patterns tend to emerge as the most common modes of diffusion.

a The *contagious diffusion* pattern: innovations spread via social networks, which are bound to have a kind of neighbourhood effect, in the sense that an innovation (including a linguistic innovation) is passed on by means of direct personal contact. The innovation is propagated in waves and step by step.

b The *hierarchical diffusion* pattern: innovations spread by leaps ('parachuting'),[1] according to a hierarchical pattern, beginning in the largest urban centre and spreading to rural areas via smaller and smaller (satellite) towns. This pattern is directly related to Trudgill's gravity model (see Chambers and Trudgill 1980: 196–202), which we discuss in section 4. A schematic representation is given in figure 10.1. However, nearly all studies on the spatial diffusion of social phenomena emphasise that the two patterns usually combine in various mixed forms.

I thank Peter Auer, Frans Hinskens, and Paul Kerwill for their stimulating comments on the first draft of this chapter.
[1] The notion of 'parachuting' was very well known to traditional linguistic geographers (see among others, Weijnen 1977).

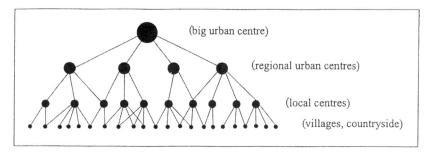

Fig. 10.1 City-hopping: innovations spreading by leaps.

2   The Spatial Diffusion of Linguistic Phenomena

The best-known study of the spatial diffusion of a linguistic phenomenon is probably Trudgill 1974, describing the geographical spread of uvular [ʀ] in Western and Northern Europe. According to Trudgill[2] uvular [ʀ] (with *panlectal* status, i.e. independent of variety and/or register) spread from the French-speaking regions in an insular fashion, namely by hopping from one large urban centre to another. More specifically: *Stuttgart* (→ the whole of the southwest of Germany), *Cologne* (→ the region of the Lower Rhine and the southeast of the Dutch-speaking region, namely Limburg), *Berlin* (→ a large area of northeastern Germany), *Copenhagen* (→ nearly all of Denmark and the southern tip of Sweden with the town of Malmö), and finally the southwestern towns of Norway (*Bergen, Stavanger, Kristiansand*). The initial phase of this process is obviously that of the *hierarchical diffusion* pattern, followed in a second stage by the *contagious diffusion* pattern, in which the urban islands slowly expand and eventually coalesce into homogeneous [ʀ]-areas. The latter stage is clearly illustrated by the two maps that Trudgill takes from Foldvik's undated study on [ʀ] in southwestern Norway. In the case of speakers born around 1900 we are still dealing with small islands around the towns mentioned above, whereas the data for speakers who are two generations younger show that the southwest has already blended into one large [ʀ]-area (see also Torp 2001).

The joint effect of the two diffusion patterns and the dominance of the hierarchical over the contagious pattern has been demonstrated again and again in the geolinguistic literature of the last decade. A well-known case is described in Bailey *et al.* (1993: 368–372) with respect to the unrounding of /ɔ/ to [ɑ] (in words such as *hawk*) in Oklahoma. Among respondents born in or before

---

[2] Although here we reproduce Trudgill's 'classical' interpretation of the distribution pattern, we also refer to the fact that this interpretation has not remained uncriticised. See, for example, Wiese (2001) for an alternative (polygenetic) view on the development of uvular [ʀ] in the German dialects.

1945 the unrounded form was the main variant only in some urban centres, but among respondents born after 1945 it had spread everywhere except for four sparsely populated remote areas.

Another convincing example of the same diffusion pattern can be found in Bücherl (1982). This article deals with the loss of endogenous dialect features in the North Bavarian dialect area. Typical North Bavarian dialect features are gradually replaced by standard High German and Central Bavarian ones. At the time of the investigation this infiltration was still restricted to the North Bavarian towns, but in these towns, the degree of infiltration was proportional to the size (number of inhabitants) of the examined places ('Ortsgröße').

By means of data from the Dutch-speaking part of Belgium, too, the complementarity of both diffusion patterns, but at the same time the dominance of the hierarchical over the contagious pattern, can be convincingly illustrated. Again we turn to the spatial (and social) spread of [ʀ] as against [r], but now focusing on the Flemish and Brabantine dialects. In the 1970s we found that in these dialect areas uvular [ʀ] was still confined to the urban centres. [ʀ] had become general in Brussels (where more than three-quarters of the population speak French anyway) and in Ghent (where there has always been a French-speaking upper class). [ʀ] also scored (fairly) highly in a few other large centres such as Antwerp, Bruges, Mechelen, and Louvain, and even achieved about 10 per cent in small towns such as Lier, Turnhout, and Herentals (see also Goossens 1974). These figures strongly support the validity of the hierarchical diffusion pattern.

Twenty years later Rogier (1994) again subjected the occurrence of [ʀ] to a thorough examination, using as informants 625 youngsters between the ages of 6 and 18 going to school in Ghent. Of that number, 550 lived outside Ghent and they were subdivided, on the basis of where they lived, into three concentric circles around the city:

    zone 1 (closest to Ghent): 254 informants
    zone 2 (middle circle): 173 informants
    zone 3 (most peripheral circle): 124 informants

In the three zones, uvular [ʀ] received scores of 83.9 per cent, 75.7 per cent and 47.6 per cent, respectively. These percentages suggest that the contagious/gradual pattern too can at least partly influence the spatial diffusion of linguistic phenomena.

So all these cases confirm our basic assumptions: (1) the hierarchical diffusion pattern (HP) and the contagious diffusion pattern (CP) interact closely; and (2) in general HP plays a more important role than CP. However, these are not recent findings. They can be traced back, often implicitly, to the many classic studies and handbooks on dialect geography. Bach (1934: 56), for example, makes a distinction between *punktuelle Ziele städtischer Gemeinschaften* (= 'particular targets of urban communities') and the *kontinuierliche Vorrücken*

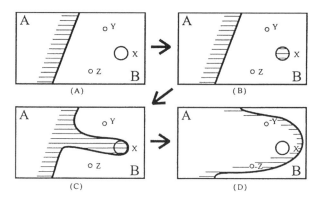

Fig. 10.2 Gradual expansion and urban centres.

(= 'the gradual expansion') in a given region. In particular the many studies from the first half of the twentieth century investigating the spread of features abound with references to the crucial role that *urban centres* have always played in the spatial diffusion of linguistic phenomena and to the hierarchical pattern that was followed. Schematic representations like figure 10.2 were often put forward.

Another case taken from Flemish dialects will make the figure more specific. In 1942 Grootaers wrote on the eastward expansion of *h*-dropping (e.g. *huis* 'house'→ *uis*, *hier* 'here'→ *ier*, *horen* 'to hear'→ *oren*), using dialect data from the period between 1925 and 1940 and presenting the regions with and without initial *h* as in map 10.1.

The map is a visual representation of two noteworthy aspects of diffusion:
1. Initially, i.e. in Middle Dutch, *h*-dropping was a feature of western Flemish, but after it had been taken up by the large towns in Brabant (first Brussels and Antwerp, and later their satellite towns Lier, Mechelen, Leuven, and Tienen) it could expand eastward, towards Limburg.
2. All the (smaller) towns in the west of the *h*-area, namely Turnhout (T), Aarschot (A), Diest (D), Hasselt (H), Zoutleeuw (Z), and Sint-Truiden (ST) have become *h*-less islands as a result of so-called 'parachuting'. Grootaers notes, however, that older people in those urban centres sometimes do pronounce the *h*. In other words, *h*-dropping is clearly an innovation.

The old situation outlined above can now be compared with map 10.2, which I have drawn on the basis of more recent data (of around 1990):[3]

---

[3] For more information on this new collection of dialect data, see Goeman and Taeldeman (1996). The *Fonologische Atlas van de Nederlandse Dialecten*/FAND (Ghent) and the *Morfologische Atlas van de Nederlandse Dialecten*/MAND (Amsterdam), which are now being published, are both based on this new collection.

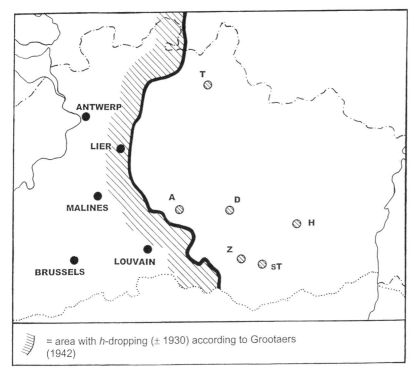

Map 10.1 H-dropping I.

It will be noticed that the area with *h*-dropping has expanded. More particularly, the rural zones between the old *h*-less region and the various *h*-less urban islands of 1942 have now also lost the *h* (the shaded part on the map). This and many other examples show that the prominent role played by urban centres in the spatial diffusion of linguistic innovations is usually revealed on dialect maps by the island-like position of urban dialects, which in itself may, of course, be a temporary state of affairs.

3   Urban Dialects: Three Types of Insularity[4]

3.1   *General*

The above discussion leads to the conclusion that urban dialects – in contrast to rural ones – usually play a pioneering part in the diffusion of linguistic

---

[4] Here we use this term in its literal sense: insular = island-like position.

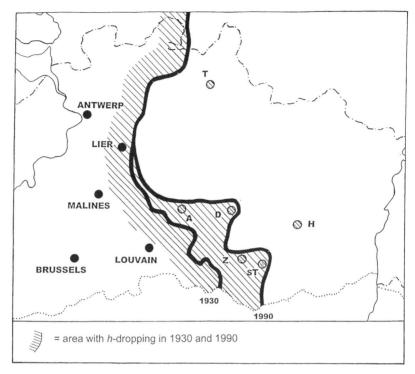

Map 10.2 H-dropping II.

phenomena. However, their susceptibility to change can manifest itself in two different ways.

1. Generating an innovation: urban dialects can themselves *generate* an innovation. For a limited period of time, i.e. before the innovation is adopted by neighbouring smaller centres and by the adjacent rural areas, this innovative action has a *divergent* effect.

2. Adopting an innovation: urban dialects can *adopt* an innovation produced in another (larger) town or in another region enjoying greater social prestige before the surrounding rural areas do. In this case the process has both a *convergent* and a *divergent* effect.

Furthermore, we also find cases (though admittedly much rarer, since this role is principally reserved for the rural dialects) in which urban dialects demonstrate *insular conservatism*, when they resist an exogenous innovation longer than the dialects of the surrounding rural areas do. Such resistance has a *divergent* effect.

By way of summary it may be said that there are three types of urban 'insularity' (See table 10.1).

Table 10.1 *Types of urban insularity*

I	Generating an innovation	Innovative	Divergence
II	Adopting an innovation from somewhere else	Innovative	Convergence + divergence
III	Rejecting an innovation	Conservative	Divergence

3.2   The three types of urban insularity illustrated

The first type of urban 'insularity' mentioned in table 10.1 (consisting of an urban innovation which has not yet been adopted by the adjacent rural areas) has been referred to repeatedly ever since the beginnings of linguistic geography. No doubt seventeenth-century Paris must have displayed this kind of insularity in that uvular [ʀ] was already spreading all over the city but had not yet conquered the rural surroundings.

More recent examples are discussed in – among others – Jahr (1988) and Kerswill (2002a). According to Jahr (1988)[5] during the twentieth century the Oslo dialect has been subject to a marked change in its lateral consonants: in most positions dental *l* was replaced by a retroflex [ɭ]; however, even now the result of this change has remained an exclusive ingredient of Oslo speech.

Kerswill (2002a) focuses on a very special type of (innovative) urban 'insularity', in that new *towns* generate 'new' dialects through a process of *koineisation*. This means that in these new towns as a result of enduring contact between relocated speakers of mutually intelligible varieties of the same language a 'new' koine comes into being through a process of mixing, levelling, and simplification. A well-known example in England is Milton Keynes (see also Kerswill and Williams 2000), which (it is apparent) for some time has taken an island-like position *vis-à-vis* the surrounding countryside. Milton Keynes seems to combine insularity types I and II.

The second type of urban insularity (where an innovation produced in another, larger, town or in another region is adopted before the surrounding rural areas do so) is again well documented in linguistic geography. In fact, it is an inevitable feature of the hierarchical diffusion pattern. For this reason we can refer to the already mentioned instances of this pattern: Trudgill (1974) and Foldvik (n.d.) with respect to uvular [ʀ] in the southwestern towns of Norway (Bergen, Stavanger, and Kristiansand); Bücherl (1982) with respect to the infiltration of standard High German and Central Bavarian features in some North Bavarian towns; and Bailey *et al.* (1993) with respect to the delabialisation of /ɔ/ in some urban islands in Oklahoma. One could add several more examples.

---

[5] I thank Peter Auer for drawing my attention to this case study.

A well-known case is the loss of *h*- in East Anglia (e.g. *(h)ome, (h)appy*; see Trudgill 1983a, 1986), a feature that has been diffused from London within the past two centuries. Until recently *h*-dropping did not occur in the rural areas of East Anglia, whereas in urban centres (such as Norwich) it has become a well-established dialect feature. So, for decades East Anglian urban dialects have taken an island-like position with respect to *h*-lessness.

Another, very similar example of type II insularity is given by Britain (in Radford *et al.* 1999: 82), who convincingly shows that the infiltration of vocalised *l* in the Fens (which lie in East Anglia) has followed an urban hierarchical path, which implies that at least temporarily the dialects of King's Lynn, Wisbech, and Downham Market have taken an island-like position with respect to the adjacent rural areas.

The third type of urban insularity (where urban dialects display insular conservatism, as they resist an exogenous innovation longer than the dialects of the surrounding rural areas) is much less common. In the next section, I shall focus on a Flemish case (with the Ghent dialect in a conservative role) in some depth. Here, I shall restrict myself to discussing briefly three other examples.

The first is found in Goossens (1988), where he describes the drastically changing linguistic situation in northern Germany and more particularly the ongoing replacement of Low German elements/varieties by their High German counterpart(s). In general, it appears that this retreat of Low German started in the cities and that the extent of the retreat correlates with the size of the city or town: the bigger the place, the greater the loss of Low German. Yet, there is one striking exception to this: Hamburg, by far the biggest city in North Germany, displays the greatest resistance to the loss of Low German. In this context Goossens suggests 'urban self-awareness' ('großstädtisches Selbstbewußtsein') as the determining factor: the city and the city dialect as a marker of northern/Low German identity.

Cases like this could also have something to do with the more self-sufficient nature of a big city: working-class people's social networks do not go beyond city boundaries. Bergen in western Norway may be another case in point. It is the oldest city (though no longer the biggest), and for a long time was the most prosperous. Its dialect was, and is, in many ways not part of the general dialect continuum of Norwegian dialects: it displays some eastern features (especially monophthongisation of Old Norwegian diphthongs) and some of its own innovations which have never spread into the hinterland but are still robust, in particular the merger of the masculine and feminine genders into a common gender. See Kerswill (2002c) for a description of the position of the Bergen dialect.

Another case of island-like urban conservatism is signalled by Sandøy (1998). He conducted research into a levelling process in the dialects of central Norway which involves a simplification of noun morphology. According to Sandøy, this simplification process manifested itself 'first in the new centres, which occupy subordinated nodes in the regional hierarchy', whereas the biggest and oldest centre of the region, Trondheim, appeared to resist this innovation in the most persistent way. In this context Trondheim displays another case of 'urban self-awareness'.

3.3   The case of Ghent and the East Flemish dialects

The dialect situation of Dutch-speaking Belgium is characterised by the juxta-position of four areas clearly distinguishable from west to east: West Flemish, East Flemish, Brabantine, and the Limburg area (see map 10.3).

A closer look at the position of the East Flemish dialect group as a whole reveals two groups of characteristics. On the one hand, a number of features really are intermediate stages in the transition from West Flemish to the Brabantine dialect. On the other hand, and this is all the more striking, there are also features which are genuinely and exclusively East Flemish, thus disrupting any continuity from West Flemish to Brabantine. The latter are (not very old) changes, actually innovations, which clearly originated in Ghent (as map 10.4 shows) and which have gradually spread in the last few centuries over the social and economic hinterland of Ghent and its satellite towns Eeklo, Deinze, and Oudenaarde. A few of the long list of typical Ghent and East Flemish innova-tions, which are mainly phonological phenomena, are the following:

1. the neutralisation of the opposition between long and short vowels, the histor-ically short vowels becoming a little longer and the historically long vowels (a little) shorter: e.g. [bo₍ᵥ₎lˀ] = *bol* 'bowl' (< short *o*) vs. [sχo₍ᵥ₎lˀ] = *school* 'school' (< long *oo*);
2. the development of a shwa-inglide after the historically short [ɪ] and [ʏ]: e.g. [vɪˀs] = *vis* 'fish' and [pʏˀt] = *put* 'pit';
3. laxing and voicing of the voiceless stops *p/t/k* ⇒ *b/d/g* in intervocalic position: e.g. [kɑdə] = *kat* 'cat' / [ɑbəl] = *appel* 'apple' / [slægə] = *slak* 'snail';
4. deletion of intervocalic -[ɣ]- (as in *liegen* ⇒ [liːˀn] 'to lie'), -[j]- (as in *bloeien* ⇒ [bluːˀn] 'to bloom') and -[w]- (as in *nieuwe* ⇒ [niːˀ] 'new ones'), in addition to compensatory lengthening of the preceding vowel.

These are illustrated in map 10.4.

The Ghent dialect can be said to have had an innovative role in all these cases and the innovations concerned have already been adopted by the hin-terland as a whole. If the innovations had been generated more recently, the adjacent rural areas would have been slower in adopting the new forms, as the previous section demonstrated with respect to the expansion of the uvular [R] from Ghent. As a matter of fact, there are some innovations in the Ghent dialect which have not yet found their way to the East Flemish countryside at

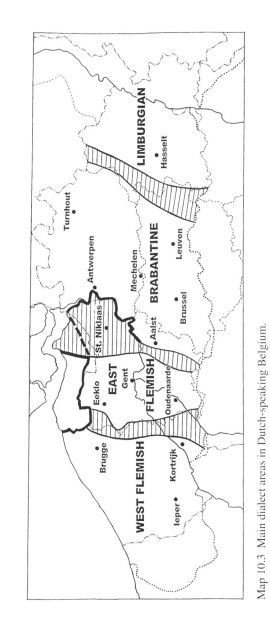

Map 10.3 Main dialect areas in Dutch-speaking Belgium.

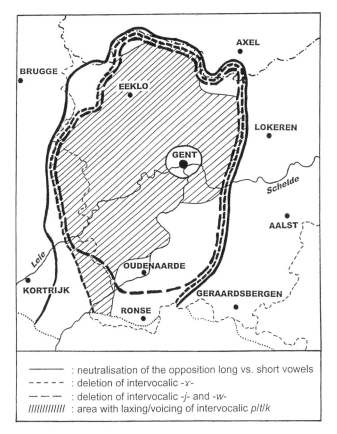

Map 10.4 The East Flemish dialect area.

all, so that the urban dialect continues to be 'insular'. An example of this is the darkening of final -*əl* to [oɫ], as in *sleutel* 'key', *appel* 'apple', *nagel* 'nail', etc.

However, the Ghent dialect is also involved in innovative island formation in a totally different and quite surprising way. Some of the above-mentioned phonological peculiarities of East Flemish undeniably originated in Ghent, as the configuration on the map shows, and have been adopted by the whole of the rural hinterland, *but have since been rejected by the urban dialect*. Two examples:

- the substitution of voiceless *p/t/k* for their intervocalic voiced counterparts *b/d/g* (see (3) above) was neutralised in the Ghent dialect (→ reintroduction of intervocalic *p/t/k*);
- the deletion of -[ɣ]- between a full vowel and ə (see (4) above) was stopped as well in the Ghent dialect (→ reinstatement of intervocalic [ɣ]).

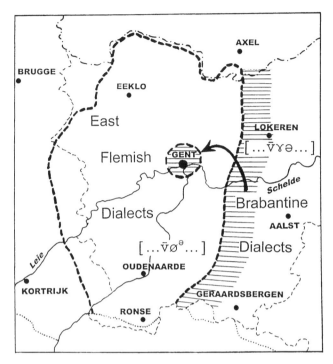

Map 10.5 Re-insertion of intervocalic -[ɣ]- in the Ghent dialect.

One possible explanation is that these East Flemish features, after they had been taken up in the adjacent rural areas, were felt to be too 'peasant-like' by the speakers of the urban dialect. Another, no less plausible, hypothesis is to claim that the Ghent dialect, which is to be considered a spearhead dialect in the East Flemish area, rejected a number of East Flemish peculiarities under pressure from the Brabantine dialect, the dominating dialect of Dutch-speaking Belgium.[6] If the latter theory is correct, the insularity of the Ghent dialect would be an example of type II insularity (table 10.1). In other words, the urban dialect of Ghent in the East Flemish area acts as a bridgehead in adopting a feature of the Brabantine dialect, thus creating a convergent effect in a wider area. The process of island formation by the Ghent dialect is represented visually in map 10.5.

---

[6] This dominance reveals itself in two ways: many elements of the Brabantine dialects have been expanding to adjacent areas (see for example, Taeldeman 1985: 193–196) and at the same time the Brabantine area dominates the standardisation process in Belgian Dutch (see, for example, Geerts 1983).

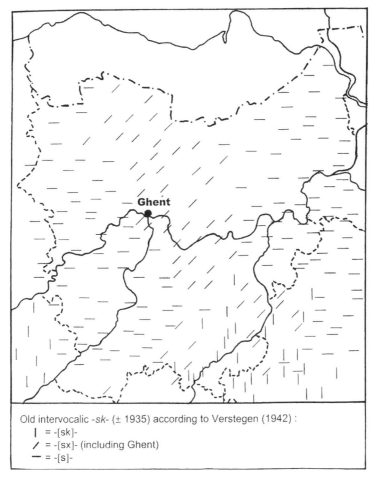

Old intervocalic -*sk*- (± 1935) according to Verstegen (1942) :
 | = -[sk]-
 / = -[sx]- (including Ghent)
— = -[s]-

Map 10.6 Old intervocalic *-sk- (Verstegen 1942).

We can sum this up as follows. The Ghent dialect introduced the deletion of intervocalic -[ɣ]- (type I insularity) a few centuries ago, subsequently passing it on to its East Flemish hinterland. More recently, it also became the first East Flemish dialect to abandon the deletion, thus setting itself apart from its adjacent countryside and conforming to the prestigious dialect of Brabant (type II insularity).

Conservative insularity (type III) is illustrated by a final example of how the rural surroundings adopted an innovation although the Ghent dialect itself did not do so. Map 10.6, taken from Verstegen (1942), presents the way in which the East Flemish dialects handled old intervocalic -sk- in the 1930s.

By that time the majority of East Flemish dialects had already simplified *-sk-* into *-s-*, but a large area, including Ghent, had preserved the intermediate stage of development (with -[sx]-). An example: *vi*[s]*en* vs. *vi*[sχ]*en* = *vissen* 'to fish'.

More recent data (see n. 3) show the -[sx]- area to have disappeared, speakers having adopted -s-, except for Ghent (see also Taeldeman 1985: 231).

4   How Can Urban Insularity be Explained?

When trying to answer this question, we have to distinguish between the *innovative/vanguard* role of urban dialects and the *conservative/rearguard* one.

4.1   The vanguard position of urban dialects (innovative insularity): social factors

Section 3 confirms what dialect geographers have known for nearly a hundred years: on average, urban centres play a more active role in the spatial diffusion of linguistic phenomena than does their rural hinterland. The driving force behind the impact of urban centres is to be found in a number of *social* factors that sociolinguistics has focused on more than classic dialect geography has done.

a An urban population displays a wider and (consequently) more varied social spectrum. More social heterogeneity normally implies more linguistic variation and less linguistic stability.

b The higher degree of migration adds to the above-mentioned social and linguistic diversity and consequently decreases linguistic stability.

c Urban populations are, on average, more mobile, so that city dwellers enjoy more intensive/frequent external contacts and these are quite obviously ideal opportunities for linguistic (ex)change.

d Despite the presence of close-knit networks in some urban neighbourhoods (Milroy 1980), social contact is looser in towns, particularly if compared with the relatively closed nature of rural communities, leading to tighter social control.

All these factors can be perfectly integrated in the *network* model, as it was developed mainly by the Milroys (see Milroy and Milroy 1992, 1993/1998). Social networks are seen as norm-enforcing mechanisms (see Villena, this volume, for a further discussion). The denser the network in which the individual participates, the less he/she will be exposed to external influences and (hence) the more conservatively hc/she will behave. On average social networks are less dense in urban centres than in rural communities. Therefore urban people will (on average) be more open to external contacts and to linguistic features from outside. As a consequence urban dialects will be more liable to language change by generating new forms or by adopting forms from other urban dialects.[7] In addition to this, the external dynamics of an urban centre and its dialect are also related to the centre's *socioeconomic strength*. As shown in greater detail in Taeldeman (1998), the Flemish[8] cities of Antwerp, Ghent, and Bruges are particularly telling examples:

- *Antwerp* (650,000 inhabitants) is the largest city in Flanders. It is also its major commercial and industrial centre. The Antwerp dialect exports its most striking features (e.g. wide diphthongs) to the whole of its hinterland. It is now the most vigorous dialect, not only in the sense that it influences other dialect varieties but also because it has a greater impact on the nonstandard varieties of Belgian Dutch than any other dialect.
- *Ghent* (220,000 inhabitants) is Flanders' second largest city and enjoys a strong industrial and cultural position. Its dialect has remained quite vital within the city's boundaries, but it now exports few of its urban features to the surrounding rural areas. What contemporary expansion there is (e.g. uvular [ʀ]), is very slow in gaining ground.
- *Bruges* (110,000 inhabitants) is now a smaller regional centre, whose major asset is its great attraction for tourists. The town's socioeconomic impact has become (very) limited since all industrial activities have been transferred to a zone around the town and to the port of Zeebrugge. The typical features of the Bruges dialect are disappearing even within the city walls. A kind of general rural West Flemish is superseding the urban dialect.

It is in contexts such as these that a few decades ago Trudgill (1974) and other sociolinguists introduced *gravity models* in order to weigh the socioeconomic strength of cities and towns and, hence, their strength to transmit linguistic elements to other (smaller) centres. Britain (2002b) and also the last section of this chapter contain a critical discussion of this technique.

However, the extent to which an urban centre and its hinterland adapt to each other in the matter of linguistic change (*inter alia*), is not only determined by network factors or by the intensity of contacts of a socioeconomic nature. As I shall argue below, *social-psychological* and *structural-linguistic* factors can also play a major role in this interaction.

4.2   The rearguard position (conservative insularity): social-psychological factors

We often find that urban dialects *do* pass on some of their linguistic features to the adjacent rural area but *do not* transmit others. We have already seen

---

[7] In addition to this Britain (2002: 623–624) also points to the fact that 'interaction between urban centres in modern societies is likely to be greater, and therefore a more frequent and effective conduit for accommodation and transmission of innovations, than between urban and rural. Transportation networks tend to link urban with urbans . . .'.

[8] 'Flemish' and 'Flanders' in this context are used in a broad sense: they refer to the Dutch-speaking part of Belgium.

examples from Ghent: the neutralisation of the opposition between long and short vowels (+ transmission) and the darkening of final -ǝl (−transmission), discussed in section 3.3. above. If no structural-linguistic reasons for this imbalance are apparent, I believe that first of all a *social-psychological* (attitudinal) explanation should be considered. The social-psychological relation between a town and its rural hinterland can vary enormously, ranging between a very positive and a very negative relation. Especially in the case of an antagonistic relationship, a marked urge towards divergence can be the result, in the town as well as in the hinterland. The countryside will not adopt some of the features of the urban dialect and, where it has already done so, the city dwellers will in their turn try to set their dialect apart by introducing new innovations.

The already-mentioned case study by Jahr (1988) clearly illustrates the (possible) impact of attitudinal factors on the outcome of a language change. He convincingly shows that the substitution of dental *l* [l̪] by retroflex *l* [ɭ] in the urban Oslo dialect[9] 'has been stopped at precisely that stage where [the change] was about to cross the borderline between what could be socially accepted as urban "Oslo speech" and what would have to be received by an Oslo speaker as socially unacceptable, rural Østfold speech' (Jahr 1988: 334).

In Flanders it is again Ghent which presents a textbook example. A deep-rooted social-psychological opposition grew between the most industrialised city in Flanders (which used to be called the 'cotton city') and its hinterland (which retained a conservative and agrarian character until the 1960s). I believe it is here that we find the reason why quite a number of features of the urban dialect were *never* adopted by the surrounding East Flemish countryside, so that the Ghent dialect remained an insular dialect as far as all these characteristics are concerned. A few examples:

- open representations of the diphthongs *ij* and *ui*, for which the urban dialect has [aː] as in [baːtǝ] for *bijten* 'to bite' and [ɔˑᵊ] as in [bɔˑᵊtǝ] for *buiten* 'outside', respectively. The rural dialect has [ɛː] and [œː];
- monophthongisation of the general East Flemish diphthongs [iᵊ] and [yᵊ], which become [iː] (as in [iːt] for *heet* 'hot') and [yː] (as in [ʀyːt] for *rood* 'red');
- deletion of final –*n* after ǝ: e.g. urban dialect [baˑtǝ] for *bijten* 'to bite', as against [bɛˑtᵊn] in the rural dialect (see De Wulf-Taeldeman 2002 for a more detailed analysis of final -*n* deletion in the Flemish dialects).

There is, to be sure, no enmity as such between city dwellers and country dwellers, but a marked difference of mentality does separate them, so much so that a native of Ghent does not want to sound like 'a country bumpkin'. Conversely, East Flemish country people will refuse to adopt an accent reminiscent of the Ghent dialect. Nevertheless, the East Flemish countryside has taken up

---

[9] According to Jahr (1988: 330), this sound change 'originated in the non-standard working class variety of Oslo speech, and has made its way into upperclass speech in the last 50 years or so'.

quite a number of features of the urban dialect over the past few centuries, as we have seen in the previous section and in map 10.4. This means that convergence and divergence *vis-à-vis* the Ghent dialect in these rural dialects operate in an eclectic fashion.

The 'tension' between Ghent and its hinterland may also (at least partly) explain two other phenomena already touched upon:

1. the *rejection* by the urban dialect of a number of its *own* innovations as soon as they had been adopted by the adjacent rural areas, and their replacement with sounds closer to the Brabantine dialect and to standard Dutch (see map 10.5);

2. the (not very frequent) *conservative insularity* of type III, as inferred from map 10.6. The fact that the East Flemish countryside adopted an innovation originating somewhere else than in Ghent (e.g. intervocalic -[sx]- → -[s]-), may have triggered a dissociative and divergent reaction of conservation in Ghent.

Yet conservative insularity of urban dialects may (also) be due to social-psychological factors of a different kind. For the most part, we can expect urban centres to function more strongly as spearheads of regional *identity* than rural places. If in a certain region the regional language form x is being challenged (and replaced) by a form y from another more prestigious or economically stronger region/city, the urban centre may (due to its spearhead-function) retain the endogenous form x longer and even reinforce it, so that this form is promoted to a so-called 'primary'[10] dialect feature. The result of this is conservative insularity.

The fact that a dialect feature may become a marker of regional/local identity may – even in rural areas – lead to *polarisation* between dialect areas A and B. Polarisation is preconditioned by a certain awareness of the polarising opposition, in particular, a very positive attitude towards the native dialect feature and a negative one towards the 'foreign' dialect feature. Polarisation[11] may engender processes of extreme divergence among adjacent dialects, such as (cf. Taeldeman 2000):

- abrupt spatial transitions (where isoglosses still have a real status);
- deepened oppositions (with respect to the linguistic/phonological distance between the opposing features); and
- a broadened scope of the opposition: the opposition turns up in as many linguistic forms as possible.

---

[10] In traditional continental dialectology (e.g. Schirmunski 1930) this term was applied to dialect features of which local people are highly conscious and which function as strong linguistic markers of local identity. In more recent sociodialectological work, the terms *'primary/secondary' dialect feature* have been reintroduced in a very fruitful way (see, for example, Hinskens 1986; Auer 1993).

[11] This phenomenon was also mentioned and commented upon by Hock (1991); for a more general account of polarisation we refer to Kallen, Hinskens, and Taeldeman (2000: 6–7).

Table 10.2 *Short vowel height in Flemish and Brabantine*

	Flemish		Brabantine
	West	East	
vis (fish)	[vɛ˛s]	[ʋɪ°s]	[vis]
put (pit)	[pœ˛t]	[pø°t]	[pyt]

Again I illustrate this with a Flemish example. One of the most striking differences between the Flemish and the Brabantine dialects shows up in the vowel system(s): in the Flemish dialects the short vowels (minus *a*) are much lower than in the Brabant area. Examples in table 10.2 illustrate this.

In the rural zone between Ghent and Aalst, the two areas clash in a dramatic way: where the (East) Flemish area 'meets' the Brabantine one (see the shaded zone in map 10.7), the short vowels are lower than anywhere else in East and West Flanders (e.g. [vɛs] = *vis*, [pœt] = *put*) and the transition is very abrupt, even to such an extent that for all words with Old Germanic *ǐ* (e.g. *vis*) and *ǔ* (e.g. *put*) the isogloss separates two small villages (Vlekkem and Ottergem), which are only 2 kilometres apart. In both villages every native is well aware of the local opposition (Vlekkem has mid-low [ɛ]/[œ], whereas Ottergem has high [i]/[ʏ]), and everybody finds his/her pronunciation the only 'proper' one. In other words: the opposition has become so salient, that it turned geographical variants into real markers of local identity (see also Trudgill's 1986 work on 'salience').

4.3   Structural-linguistic factors

Structural-linguistic factors as well can upset the process of accommodation both in the hierarchical and contagious diffusion pattern. A final example from Flemish is illustrated in map 10.8. Map 10.8 shows the geographical spread of the high-front realisations in the region of [y:] from Middle Dutch *ō°* (as, for example, in *brood* 'bread', *lopen* 'to run', etc.). According to various sources (see Taeldeman 1984) this 'spontaneous' fronting emerged in southwestern Brabant (the region of Brussels) and was probably parachuted to Ghent around 1600, from where the [y˛°] permeated into nearly all of East Flanders. Normally one would expect that Aalst and the surrounding countryside, which is situated halfway on the Brussels–Ghent axis, would also have adopted this fronting. Yet, on the map we see that the [y˛°]/[u°]-isogloss makes a clear bend around the region of Aalst (the shaded part on the map), which has a [u˛°]-like sound.

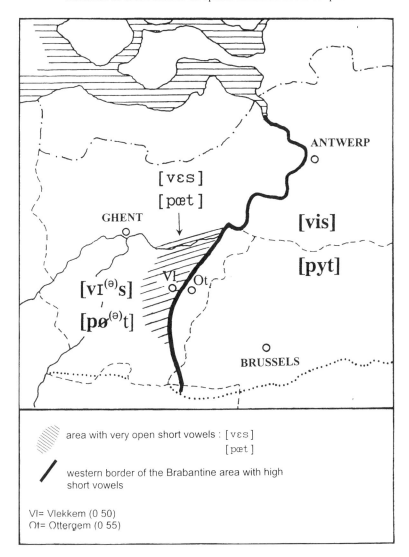

Map 10.7 Polarisation: lowering of short vowels.

Goossens (1962) and Taeldeman (1978) point out that the shaded zone completely overlaps with the Aalst area of unrounding, where all rounded high-front
vowels were (and are) systematically delabialised. This process of unrounding
would also have applied to the front [y.ᵊ] (from the old *ōᵒ), and the result
would have been [y.ᵊ] → [i.ᵊ]. However, the latter would have resulted in a

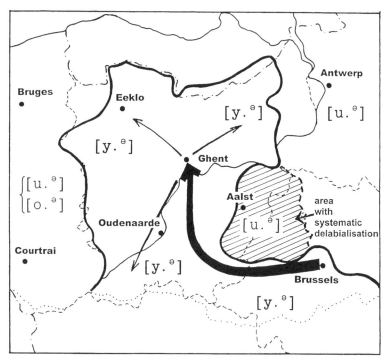

Map 10.8 Historical diffusion pattern of south Brabantine [y.] (<Middle Dutch) to/in East Flanders.

merger with the phoneme [i.ᵊ], which derives from Middle Dutch ē̥ᵊ (as, for example, in [bri.ᵊt] from M.D. *brēəd* 'broad') and which already had many lexical realisations. So this merger would have resulted in the creation of a large number of homophones (e.g. [bri.ᵊt] < *ō̥ᵊ as in *brood* 'bread' and < *ē̥ᵊ as in *breed* 'broad'). Apart from the structural-linguistic argument that the conservation of back [u.ᵊ] blocked the potential homophony, I can see no other reason why the region of Aalst did not adopt the new [y.ᵊ] launched by Brussels and subsequently by Ghent.

5   Concluding Remarks: Why Gravity Models are Bound to Fail

This chapter argues that urban centres play a crucial role in the spatial diffusion of linguistic phenomena. Linguistic maps usually highlight this role by revealing the formation of urban islands, the dialects of which are more often innovative than conservative.

The extent to which an urban centre influences the dialect of its hinterland is naturally determined by measurable factors, namely the town's socioeconomic strength and its corollary, the intensity of human contacts. All this can be measured by means of factors such as:

- the size of the urban centre;
- the nature and the importance of the services that the town can offer (e.g. hospitals, schools, shopping centres, cultural events, recreational amenities, etc.);
- the degree to which the urban centre employs people from the hinterland; and
- the presence or absence of natural barriers (e.g. mountains, forests, and rivers)[12] and political frontiers.

Establishing a mathematical measure of the linguistic impact of urban centre A on a community B in its hinterland is, therefore, theoretically possible, and accordingly *formulas* have been devised for doing so. These *gravity models* have a predictive power and have long been used in social geography. One of Peter Trudgill's many contributions to social dialectology is that he has tried to introduce gravity models in 'geolinguistics' as well (see, among others, Trudgill 1974; Chambers and Trudgill 1980: ch. 11). In Trudgill's gravity model the central idea is that linguistic innovations spread down the urban hierarchy. From the second half of the 1970s we can refer to case studies which (seem to) adduce new evidence (at least partially) for the validity of this idea and of the use of this technique: see, for example, Callary (1975) on [æ]-raising in Illinois; Hinskens (1992: 469–471) with respect to some recent developments in his own Limburg dialect; and Hernández-Campoy (2000) on the penetration of standard Spanish elements into the southeastern Spanish network of cities and towns. Yet, in the last few years, the use of gravity models has become less popular in geolinguistics. This was partly due to the appearance of some studies which contained strong evidence *against* the gravity model (e.g. Horvath and Horvath 2001). At the same time the critical attitude of many geolinguists towards this technique had been fed by a more general insight which, I hope, has been made clear in the last section of this chapter: the spatial diffusion of linguistic phenomena is also influenced, to quite an important extent, by two kinds of factors that are very hard to integrate into formal models: *social-psychological* ones (e.g. the attitudinal relation between the urban centre and its hinterland); and *structural-linguistic* ones. They are liable to promote or to inhibit, or even stop, the expansion of urban innovations.

---

[12] However, German dialect geographers in particular have repeatedly pointed out that rivers, being routes along which trade could develop, can have a *convergent* impact on language change as well. A well-known example is that of the Rhine valley between Mainz and Cologne, which featured as a kind of fan (German: *Fächer*) in adopting quite a large number of innovations originating in the south of the country. It was Koblenz and mainly Cologne which were in the lead in this process (see Frings 1956, among others).

Part 3

Microsociolinguistic Motivations

11 Subjective factors in dialect convergence and divergence

Tore Kristiansen and Jens Normann Jørgensen

1 Objective and Subjective Factors in Language Variation and Change

Since the 1960s new technologies for registering and analysing spoken language have greatly advanced our theoretical and methodological understanding of the many and complex factors involved in language variation and change, including the physiological constitution of our speech organs, the mental capacity of our brains, the structure of linguistic varieties, the linguistic context of particular variables, the social embedding of variation, and the social evaluation of variants and varieties. These factors are commonly divided and grouped in various ways: internal versus external; linguistic versus social versus (socio)psychological; macro versus micro. All of these divisions reflect important aspects of variation and change.

However, if we want to answer the *why* question of variation and change, the fundamental distinction is between necessary and sufficient factors. All the aspects listed above are *necessary* factors in language variation and change, in the sense that they are always involved. But it is our contention that only the sociopsychological, subjective factors can constitute the driving force behind such processes. In that sense, they alone are the *sufficient* factors. Language is a social phenomenon. Without users (in the plural), there is no language. The purpose of language is to contribute to the social construction of reality, including the transmission of collective experience from generation to generation. Languages are not plants with lives of their own, they are tools. Whenever these tools are the objects of tuning or adjustment, it is so because it serves human purposes. In consequence, the driving force behind language variation and change should be sought in terms of motivation rather than causation. If we state, for instance, that the convergence of dialects is *caused* by geographical and social mobility in the population, there may – or may not – be a social-psychological factor involved. But when we think of *motivation* for language change, the subjective factors become the centre of attention, as they should be if we are interested in answering the *why* question. This claim about the role of objective and subjective factors in linguistic change can be studied empirically. Two approaches are possible.

One possibility is to find situations in which the same objective factors hold, and ask whether the same kind of change occurs. One can search for 'natural' changes to be explained in terms of physiological, auditory, or mental factors (or constraints). However, since it always seems possible to find examples of such 'natural' changes not occurring, and of 'non-natural' changes occurring, it must be recognised that 'naturalness does not explain anything' in the sense of being a sufficient factor (Lass 1980). Or one can look at similar social developments in different societies or speech communities and investigate whether language develops in a parallel fashion as well. A comparison of Norway and Denmark, for instance, shows that the languages in the two countries followed very different paths of development in the 1900s – resulting in the loss of the traditional dialects in Denmark, but not in Norway – even though the two countries underwent quite similar processes of urbanisation and show similar patterns of geographical and social mobility. This means that at least these objective factors are not sufficient to explain the different amount of de-dialectalisation in the two countries (Kristiansen 1996).

The second possible approach relates *subjective* factors to linguistic change in order to test their explanatory power. For instance, the presence of a strong Danish *standard* ideology (in the sense of Milroy and Milroy 1985a) as opposed to a strong Norwegian *dialect* ideology constitutes a difference on the subjective level which looks much more like a sufficient explanation of the facts which the objective factors failed to explain (Kristiansen 1996; see also PEDERSEN). In this chapter, we want to follow this second approach, i.e. to raise the issue and study the role of subjective factors in dialect convergence and divergence.

2   Subjective Factors in Sociolinguistic Studies

2.1   *Subjective factors and the macro/micro distinction*

The distinction between a macro and a micro approach is well established in all scientific studies of society. It is easy to argue that some phenomena are best treated at the level of large-scale social structures; others at a level of small-group dynamics and face-to-face interaction. Where do subjective factors influencing language change belong?

It goes without saying that pointing to 'subjective' factors means pointing to the *subject*. Motivation is a psychological concept exactly because it takes a subject to be motivated. Furthermore, to the extent that focusing on the subject entails focusing on the individual, the *micro* aspect of things will obviously be foregrounded.

It is important to notice, however, that there also is a *macro* aspect to subjective factors. This can best be illustrated by referring to another common way of categorising approaches to language change according to whether sociological or social-psychological aspects are considered in addition to the linguistic ones. Sociologically oriented approaches tend to be associated with large-scale social structures and social-psychological oriented approaches with small-scale social structures. But this distinction is not the same as the macro–micro distinction. Very roughly speaking, the sociological perspective gives us the *objective* aspect of social structuring, the social-psychological perspective the *subjective* aspect – in both cases at either a macro or micro level, depending on our focus. Subjective factors such as motivations, representations, feelings, attributions, perceptions, beliefs, values therefore all have a large-scale existence as well as a small-scale existence. They can, and should, be studied at different levels: in individuals; in small social networks; in large social groups; and not the least in the interplay between these different levels. Most reference to subjective factors in sociolinguistics has been in terms of identity and attitudes. These are often used and understood as cover terms for a whole set of social-psychological concepts such as the ones we have listed above. This leads us to a discussion of the place which these two concepts have had in sociolinguistics.

2.2   Attitudes and the study of language change

A common model presents the study of 'language and society' as a continuum, with research focusing on sociological issues at the one extreme and research focusing on linguistic variation and change at the other extreme.[1] The study of 'language attitudes' is commonly treated as not belonging to variationist sociolinguistics, or even as not belonging to sociolinguistics at all. In the first attempts at writing the history of sociolinguistics, for instance, language attitude studies went unmentioned, both when research on language variation and change was the focal point (Koerner 1989), and when the whole continuum of research on language and society was taken into consideration (Shuy 1990).

To the extent that it is conceived of as a sociolinguistic discipline, the study of language attitudes is usually grouped with the kind of sociolinguistics which has a practical interest in social issues, not with the kind of more theoretically and more linguistically oriented sociolinguistics which includes society in order to sharpen our understanding of language. In introductory books and handbooks, language attitudes are therefore usually treated as a 'macro' or 'application' issue: 'attitudes to language have implications in many social spheres and illustrate well the ways in which sociolinguistic research often has

---

[1] Trudgill (1978) discusses this distinction; see also Trudgill (2000).

an applied dimension' (Holmes 1992: 356). A particularly illustrative example of the existing gap between the study of attitudes and the study of language change is Fasold's two-volume *Introduction to Sociolinguistics*. The chapter on language attitudes appears in the volume on the *Sociolinguistics of Society* (Fasold 1984), together with large-scale issues like language maintenance and shift, planning and standardisation – not in the volume on *Sociolinguistics of Language* (Fasold 1990), where the issue of linguistic variation and change is treated. In his introduction to the second book, Fasold is quite explicit: 'I am not able to see very much in common between the issues about the forms and use of language on a small scale that are treated in this book and the large-scale sociopolitical issues that are addressed in the other' (1990: vii). Quite generally, the study of attitudes is considered to be the main subdiscipline of the social psychology of language, a discipline which is concerned not with language change but with the 'contexts and consequences of language' (cf. the title of Giles and Coupland 1991; see also Ryan and Giles 1982; Giles *et al.* 1987, *Journal of Language and Social Psychology* 18:1, 1999).

Trudgill (1978) includes the study of language attitudes under a third category of sociolinguistic research, which is both sociological and linguistic in intent. In his 1986 book, still probably the most comprehensive and profound text on microsociolinguistic factors in dialect convergence and divergence, he seems to assume a 'considerable influence from attitudinal factors' (56). But at the same time these factors are clearly conceived of as facilitating and not driving change: 'the accommodation – may in time become permanent, particularly if attitudinal factors are favourable' (39).

2.3   *Identity and the study of language change*

While it is possible to identify and discuss a particular 'attitudes approach' to the study of language – with theories and methods of its own, and relations to other approaches – it is not in the same way possible to identify an 'identities approach'. Rather, identity has tended to become an omnipresent explanatory concept in most sociolinguistic discourses over the recent years (as it has in the social sciences and in society in general). It may, therefore, be important to notice that the notion of identity has been around in modern sociolinguistics from its very beginnings. In contrast to attitudes, however, identity has become associated more with the micro level of social structure, i.e. with interaction in smaller communities or social groups. The centrality of social identity to ethnographically oriented studies of language is well illustrated by the title of Gumperz's (1982) edited volume *Language and Social Identity*.

In variationist sociolinguistics, too, social identity has featured as the ultimate explanatory concept, in macro- and micro-oriented studies alike, but often more explicitly so in small-scale studies which include some ethnographic methods.

The earliest example of this type of work was William Labov's seminal study on Martha's Vineyard (1963, 1972a). Notice the social psychological orientation implicated by his title 'The social motivation of a sound change'. The study explains the increasingly 'close-mouthed' articulatory style of the native islanders '. . . as a sign of social identity in response to pressure from outside forces' (Labov 1972a: 39, see also 299).

From the subsequent development of variationist sociolinguistics, we shall mention two more studies which, in addition to being prominent examples of the discipline as such, exemplify orientations to social identity as a fundamental explanatory concept.

It is social networks and not social identity which is the pivotal concept in the Belfast study and in later work by James and Lesley Milroy. The social network model operates with a 'close-knit network' as the main norm-enforcement mechanism and 'weak ties' as the main potential for change. The Milroys have repeatedly pointed out that the network model is an account of the social structures which condition language maintenance and change, not of the social psychological processes involved: 'The weak-tie model is not in itself sufficient to provide a full social explanation of linguistic change. What it proposes is a set of conditions that are necessary – but not sufficient – for linguistic change to take place. . . . It is not about psycho-social attitudes to language . . .' (J. Milroy 1992: 204). The sufficient conditions are social psychological processes of identity construction and meaning-making: 'A linguistic change is a social phenomenon, and it comes about for reasons of marking social identity, stylistic difference and so on. If it does not carry these social meanings, then it is not a linguistic change' (J. Milroy 1992: 202). In the same vein, L. Milroy (1987b: 214) says that '. . . it is important to interpret the network measure used in this book as one of social structure. It cannot claim, unfortunately, to reflect consistently an individual's attitude to status or solidarity ideologies . . .'. In accordance with the findings of language attitudes research by social psychologists (e.g. Brown and Gilman 1960; Giles and Ryan 1982), the Milroys propose that an integrated model of sociolinguistic structure must take into account the competing ideologies of solidarity and status (L. Milroy 1987b: 208–209; J. Milroy 1992: 210, 213).

In Penelope Eckert's Belten High study, on the other hand, social identity is no longer an entity which turns up as the explanatory concept *par excellence* at the bottom line of the account. Rather, social identity is the starting point. Eckert (1989a) thoroughly analysed the social categories of 'Jocks' and 'Burnouts', and their hegemonic importance to social identifications among Belten High students. She underlines: 'Thus although the majority of high school students are not members of one category or the other, an important part of most adolescents' social identity is dominated by the opposition between the two categories' (Eckert 1989a: 5). In the subsequent study, *Linguistic Variation as Social Practice*, at Belten High, Eckert points out that '[t]he jock-burnout split . . . is the point of departure, not the end, of an examination of social identity and meaning, and of the analysis of sociolinguistic variation. . . . Based on two years of ethnographic work in and around the school, this study aims to give reality to the identities being associated with linguistic data' (Eckert 2000: 2, 3). Within Eckert's theory of 'variation as social practice', 'giving reality to the identities' means seeing speakers as constituting rather then representing broad social categories, and as constructing as well as responding to the social meaning of variation (Eckert 2000: 3). Meaning-making is central to the theory, and, in Eckert's view, '[t]he co-construction of linguistic change and social meaning will take place in just those interactions in which social identity is at issue . . .' (Eckert 2000: 34).

2.4   The issue of consciousness

A difficult problem in connection with the study of subjective factors is their complex relationship to consciousness. Changes from above and from below are distinguished by 'the level of conscious awareness' in Labov's work (Labov 1966: 338). Also, the distinction between overt and covert norms, values, or prestige refers explicitly to different levels of consciousness (Labov 1972a: 177; Trudgill 1972). These problems have also been treated in terms of salience and awareness (Trudgill 1986; Auer *et al.* 1998; Kerswill and Williams 2002a).

It is often the case that covert values differ from overt values. As a consequence, the values underlying an ongoing change may be difficult to determine: 'The *evaluation* problem is to find the subjective (or latent) correlates of the objective (or manifest) changes which have been observed' (Labov 1972a: 162). In order to find these 'latent correlates', one must have an idea of what to look for. However, the question of what to look for is linked to a serious epistemological dilemma, as has been argued widely within the human sciences in recent years by scholars who advocate a discursive approach (e.g. Potter and Wetherell 1987). Should we conceive of, and look for, social identities as given categories, or as continually negotiated and recreated in communicative practices? How do attitudes, representations, values exist? As frozen sense-making constructs in the brain, ready to be 'tapped' in experiments? Or as communicative practices to be studied primarily in discourse?

Although the answers to these questions are of the greatest importance to the study of subjective factors in general and to the consciousness issue in particular, we have no ambition of answering them here. In fact, the best answer is to reject the 'either – or' option and recognise some kind of conflict and tension – a dialectic relationship – between activity and structure, discourse and cognition. The methodological consequence is to accept the potential value of many and different approaches to the study of subjective factors. It is true that people are often unaware of linguistic phenomena, or at least unable to describe them in anything but *ad hoc* terms (for a discussion, see Preston 1996). To the extent that language users are unaware of their own evaluative reactions to language differences, we refer to, and study, these reactions as *subconscious* attitudes. Speakers may also be unaware of language variation itself, including variation in their own speech. But we find it self-evident that speakers who vary their language use systematically can also be made aware of that variation. And, further, we find it self-evident that linguistic variation which is subject to social evaluation in a speech community, no matter how fine-grained this variation may be, can be brought to the awareness of the speakers. Subconscious attitudes are, therefore, potentially conscious attitudes as long as the speakers can distinguish between the linguistic variants.

3   The Næstved Study

In Denmark, the linguistic features of the traditional dialects have, to a large extent, been replaced by the features of the Copenhagen variety, which has thus become a national standard – a development which began in the 1700s and accelerated tremendously in the 1900s (Kristiansen 1998; Pedersen 2003; Kristensen 2003). Everywhere the new generations talk more like Copenhagen-ers than like the old local-dialect speakers. A study in the town of Næstved, about 90 kilometres to the south of the capital, showed the town's adolescents to use an average of 20 per cent dialect variants in the standard–dialect dimension (Jørgensen and Kristensen 1994, 1995). In fact, the traditional dialect is even less present than this figure seems to indicate; the majority of dialect features are completely gone and cannot be made the object of a quantitative study.

On the other hand, variation within Copenhagen speech is spreading through-out the whole country. This variation has been studied empirically, both in its diachronic (Brink and Lund 1975) and synchronic aspects (Jørgensen 1980; Gregersen and Pedersen 1991a). The general pattern over the last hundred years has been that features of low Copenhagen speech have spread into high Copenhagen speech, and further into other varieties of Danish. Consequently, status-related differences have turned into age-related differences. The older generation's High forms become just old forms, while the older generation's Low forms become the young generation's only and socially unmarked forms. This change is commonly described both in terms of high Copenhagen speech (the traditional standard language of Danish society) versus low Copenhagen speech (the traditional working-class dialect of the capital), and in terms of old standard versus young standard. In Næstved, the adolescents were found to use an average of 80 per cent low or young variants on what we call the 'old – young standard' dimension (Jørgensen and Kristensen 1994, 1995).

POSITIVE <--> NEGATIVE

CONSCIOUS	local		old std	**	young std

SUBCONSCIOUS

competence	young std		old std	***	local
edu. level	young std	***	old std	***	local
sociability	young std	*	local		old std

*** = p < .001 ** = p < .01 * = p < .05

Fig. 11.1 Conscious and subconscious evaluation of the local, old standard, and young standard varieties by Næstved adolescents.

At the same time (late 1980s), considerable amounts of data were gathered in Næstved in order to shed light on the subjective correlates of the observed language-use pattern. Various methods were used, including audio-recorded interviews and group discussions, questionnaires, behavioural reactions to Næstved speech in a naturalistic setting, and a series of experiments including dialect recognition, label ranking, speaker evaluation, and self-evaluation. Studies based on these data reveal a clear discrepancy between overt and covert evaluations in Næstved adolescents.

Overt subjective correlates are the opinions, representations, assessments, and beliefs which subjects display when they are aware of commenting on their speech community, i.e. when language is made a salient feature of data collection (as in questionnaires, interviews, label-ranking experiments). In overt comments the attitudinal disposition of Næstved adolescents is clearly in accordance with the elite discourse of Danish society. The old standard is considered to be the true Danish language from which other varieties are more or less repulsive aberrations – more so in the case of the advancing young standard, less in the case of the dying traditional dialects.

The *covert* subjective correlates were studied in situations where language was not focused on and in which subjects were unaware of displaying attitudes towards language (speaker evaluations in both experimental and natural settings). Here, the Næstved adolescents subconsciously downgraded speakers with even a minimum of local colouring and upgraded speakers with young standard variants (Kristiansen 1991, 1997, 1998). The subconscious upgrading of young standard speakers is general and takes place on the dimensions of both status and solidarity, but is particularly impressive on the dimension of 'dynamism' which cuts across this distinction (Kristiansen 2001).

The patterns of conscious and subconscious attitudes as derived from label ranking and speaker evaluation are shown in figure 11.1. Subconscious evaluations were measured on the dimensions of competence (status) and sociability (solidarity), and these measurements were supplemented by an extra status scale measuring the judged level of education.

It is quite common in Denmark, also among linguists, to talk of the spread of the overtly stigmatised young standard variants in terms of a paradox. Of course, the situation is paradoxical only under the assumption that there should be a positive correlation between linguistic spread and positive evaluation. One solution to the paradox is to deny the relevance of subjective factors to language change. Another solution is to distinguish between surface factors and those at deeper levels of consciousness. This is what was done in the Næstved studies, and it resolved the paradox by discovering a positive correlation between spread and positive evaluation at the subconscious level. However, it seems to us that the postulation of a paradox implies the additional assumption that positive attitudes (motivations) in speakers are a *condition* for the spread of new variants. Indeed, if positive evaluation were a *consequence* which followed from a more or less consciously recognised incorporation of new variants in one's own speech, the existence of (possibly temporary) negative attitudes would be compatible with this spread. So what changes first, attitudes or use?

To throw empirical light on this issue, we have to predict specific developments on the basis of attitudinal patterns and then measure the changes in usage. Speech data have been collected from the Næstved adolescents at later points in time, and we hope to be able to use these data in order to answer the question. In the meantime we suggest that we can find an indirect answer by looking at what happens when our sample of adolescents is broken down according to social-background variables. This is what we shall do in the rest of this section. Attitudinal data gathered in consciousness-oriented and subconsciousness-oriented conditions will be compared with speech data. The attitudes and speech data are from two different samples of adolescents, but since sampling criteria were the same in both cases and significance testing has been applied, the reported patterns are valid for Næstved adolescents in general (with the usually accepted maximum 5 per cent risk of being wrong).

At the end of these comparisons our what-comes-first problem will remain open, since correlation is not explanation. However, if positive evaluation is a consequence and not a condition of spread, we should not be surprised to find, on some or even all background variables, that speakers with the highest frequency of young standard variants are the ones with the more negative attitudes. Such a finding will certainly reduce the attractiveness of the attitudes-come-first hypothesis. Inversely, a good accord between speech patterns and covert attitudinal patterns in the subgroupings would support the attitudes-come-first hypothesis to some extent.

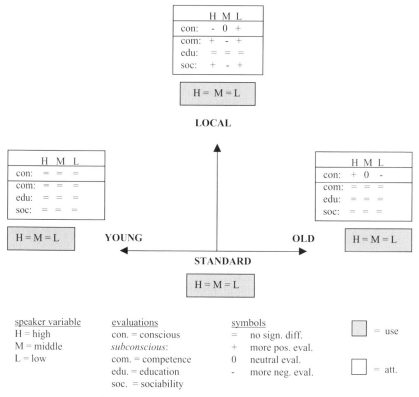

Fig. 11.2 Language use and attitudes across socioeconomic status.

3.1   Use, attitudes, and socioeconomic status

In figure 11.2 we compare language use and linguistic attitudes in Næstved adolescents in three socioeconomic status categories, determined by their parents' occupation. The vertical dimension in the figure represents the local–standard variables. The horizontal dimension represents the old–young standard variables.

There are no significant differences in use across the three socioeconomic status groups, either on the local–standard variables or on the old–young standard variables. Likewise, with respect to attitudes, there are no significant differences with regard to young standard speech, either in conscious or in subconscious evaluation. With regard to old standard and local speech, we find inverse correlations in conscious evaluation. However, we assume the subconscious attitudes to be the more relevant. There is no difference in subconscious evaluation of old standard speech, whereas the middle-status group shows

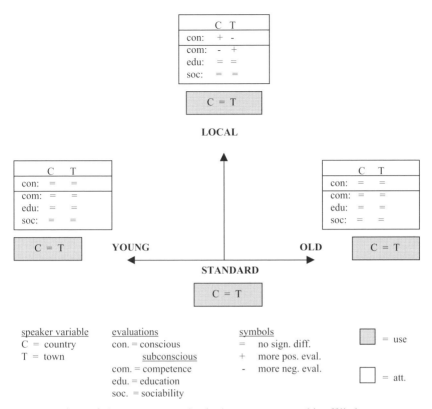

Fig. 11.3 Language use and attitudes across geographic affiliation.

more negative subconscious evaluations of local speech than either the high- and low-status groups. In general, we can say that the good match between patterns of use and attitudes which we found in the adolescents as a whole is confirmed when this relationship is studied across socioeconomic status groups. The attitudes-come-first hypothesis would predict that the further elimination of local variants in Næstved will be spearheaded by adolescents in the middle position of the social status hierarchy.

3.2   Use, attitudes, and geography

In figure 11.3 we compare adolescents from the town of Næstved itself with adolescents from the surrounding countryside who attend some kind of tertiary school in Næstved.

Again, there is no significant difference in language use. There is a differ- ence in the conscious evaluation of local speech, the countryside adolescents

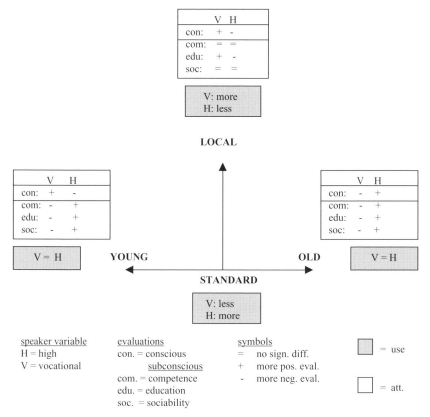

Fig. 11.4 Language use and attitudes across school affiliation.

being the more positive ones. However, in subconscious evaluation (competence dimension) town adolescents turn out to be more positively oriented towards local speech. In sum, we can say that the match between patterns of use and patterns of attitudes is good when these patterns are compared across groups of geographical origin. The difference in attitudes in relation to local speech calls for some attention. It is true that the overall picture shows that even a very light, modern version of the local speech is strongly downgraded by the young informants in general. But the fact that young people from the town itself show a more positive evaluation of local speech in the competence dimension might be taken as an indication that such speech may stand a chance after all.

3.3   Use, attitudes, and school type

With school type as the background variable, we get the results shown in figure 11.4. In the local–standard variables, adolescents who are involved in some kind of vocational training use more local variants than adolescents who attend high school, which is academically oriented, and, of course, the other way round for the standard variants. This corresponds nicely to the attitudinal pattern, with regard to both conscious and subconscious evaluations: the high-school students evaluate local speech more negatively; the vocational students more positively.

In the old–young standard variables, there is no difference in use. When it comes to attitudes, however, high-school students very clearly show a more positive attitude towards both old standard speech and young standard speech. On the basis of this pattern, our prediction is that high-school students will develop into more frequent users of both old standard and young standard variants. This, of course, is only possible where old standard and young standard variants are both opposed to the local variants. Otherwise, the use of more old-standard variants implies the use of fewer young standard variants, and vice versa. In any case, we can predict that the present situation with equal use will change.

3.4   Use, attitudes, and gender

Our last background variable is gender (figure 11.5). Here, the results for usage and those for attitudes for the first time seem to plainly contradict each other: Girls use significantly less young standard variants than boys, although they are more positively oriented towards young standard speech in their subconscious evaluation (both competence and sociability) than the boys. However, we should take into account here that all the voices in the speaker evaluation experiment were male. It is possible that the evaluative pattern would be different if young women's voices were used as stimuli.

If we continue the line of thinking that a change in the social evaluation of speech variants foreshadows a change in language use, we can predict: girls will catch up with, and possibly go beyond, boys in their use of young standard-variants.

4   Conclusion

The dedialectalisation or standardisation which is taking place in Næstved among young people may be seen as a case of convergence towards the Copenhagen-based standard language, and more towards young standard speech than towards old standard speech. Many factors are involved in this process. In this chapter, we have focused on the subjective factors in order to study their role in language variation and change. We now return to the role and place of subjective factors in variationist sociolinguistics.

Social meaning-making and identity-construction are the driving forces underlying maintenance and change in language. With due modifications as to the consciousness issue, we therefore sympathise with Chambers' (2003:

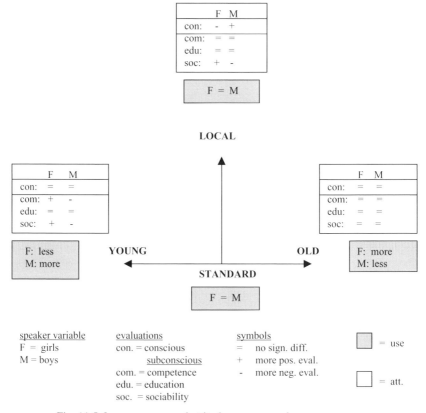

Fig. 11.5 Language use and attitudes across gender.

274) claim that '[t]he underlying cause of sociolinguistic differences, largely beneath consciousness, is the human instinct to establish and maintain social identity', and that the 'common motive' behind difference and unity in language is 'the profound need for people to show they belong somewhere, and to define themselves, sometimes narrowly and sometimes generally'. We also believe that the need for identity-construction is a need to construct a *positive* self-image. One implication is that social identification processes involve evaluative comparisons. A further implication, as argued in the so-called social identity theory developed by Henri Tajfel and his followers (see Hogg and Abrams 1988), may be that people tend to be biased in their representations and evaluations of themselves and others.

Progress in the theory of language change is most likely to result from a better integration of linguistic, sociological, and social-psychological approaches, and also of macro and micro perspectives within these approaches. As Eckert

(2000: 35) states: 'To capture the process of meaning-making, we need to focus on a level of social organization at which individual and group identities are being co-constructed, and in which we can observe the emergence of symbolic processes that tie individuals to groups, and groups to the social contexts in which they gain meaning.' In order to capture such a level of social organisation, Eckert suggests the notion of a community of practice: an aggregate of people who, united by some common enterprise, come to develop and share ways of doing things, ways of talking, beliefs, and values. Eckert points out that an analysis in terms of communities of practice is closely related to network analyses; its potential advantage is that 'it focuses on the day-to-day social membership and mobility of the individual, and on the co-construction of individual and community identity', whereby 'it ties social meaning to the grounded social aggregate at the same time that it ties the grounded aggregate to abstract social structures' (Eckert 2000: 40–41).

By referring to Eckert's work, we do not necessarily wish to embrace the idea that there is one privileged level of social organisation at which social meaning-making is best studied. More important is her strong focus on social meaning-making and the insistence that processes of identity construction cannot be fully captured unless we study them in terms of individuals as members of particular groups in society at large.[2] Neither do we wish to suggest a privileged position for the ethnographic type of methodology associated with Eckert's work, although we do recognise the great potential of this approach. We would rather stress that the complexity of language-mediated identity construction calls for the use of many and different methods. In particular we would like to point to a need for inventiveness in studies of the role of attitudinal factors in linguistic variation and change.

Although most scholars seem to acknowledge the relevance of attitudinal factors for language change, few include separate analyses of attitudes in their projects. This is surprising in view of the fact that the long-standing leading star of this field, William Labov, takes great care to address the 'evaluation problem' both in his theoretical work (e.g. Weinreich, Labov, and Herzog 1968; Labov 1972a) and in his practical work (cf. the way in which he makes language a topic in the sociolinguistic interview and his so-called field experiments, including self-report tests, subjective reactions tests, linguistic insecurity tests, and others; see for example, Labov 1984). Research reports rarely give reasons why little or no effort is put into collecting and analysing attitudinal data. However, the Milroys no doubt express a widely held view when they argue that problems

---

[2] The group-based patterns of use and evaluation among Næstved adolescents reported in this chapter have also been studied in terms of the interrelations between Næstved adolescents, local gatekeepers (graduate school teachers and personnel managers), and the national elite discourse (Kristiansen 2003), and in terms of individual Næstved adolescents' discursive negotiations of their own identities (Kristiansen 2004).

of validity and reliability are too serious for attitudinal data to be of much interest to the study of language change (e.g. L. Milroy 1987a: 141, 1987b: 107). Accordingly, they suggest that 'statistical counts of variants actually used are probably the best way of assessing attitudes' (Milroy and Milroy 1985a: 19). We acknowledge that there can indeed be serious problems of validity and reliability connected with attitudinal data. However, we also believe that there will be little progress unless we deal with these problems instead of avoiding the data. Unless we are to be caught up in circular reasoning, we need to approach the evaluation problem by producing independent evidence to supplement our statistical counts of the variants actually used. If we acknowledge people's striving for a positive social identity as the critical factor underlying variation and change, improving our methods of collecting and analysing attitudinal data becomes a priority.

12 How similar are people who speak alike? An interpretive way of using social networks in social dialectology research

Juan Andrés Villena-Ponsoda

1 Introduction

1.1 Objective

The aim of this chapter is to evaluate the significance of social networks in contemporary language-variation research. A critique of the straightforward *correlational* use of social networks leads to the conclusion that, since they are not able to explain the total amount of variation within the speech community, other factors may be at work, either interacting with the network measures adopted, or intervening between networks and actual language use at a different level of abstraction. To achieve this, I propose a more *interpretive* understanding of the network concept. I will outline a more integrated language-variation theory including subtheories of stratification, social network and the individual speaker. Such a theory implies a revision of methods and techniques with regard to data collection and analysis: the analyst's task should no longer be separated from the participant observer's, since they constitute a unit which guarantees the adequate qualitative interpretation of quantitative results.[1]

1.2 Hypothesis

The major hypothesis proposed in this chapter is that social networks, i.e. the web of ties within which most people's everyday lives are embedded, clearly reflect the main factor underlying language variation at an intermediate level of

The results and data this paper deals with are based on the DGICYT Research Project on UMA Spoken Corpus (UMASC-Project, PB94–1467-CO2-01. 1995–1998). I would like to thank Paul Kerswill and Frans Hinskens for their critical revision and helpful comments. Their comments have very much informed my thoughts on this topic, though I alone am responsible for the manner and content of this chapter. I am indebted to Ann Thacher, Mary Oliver, and Peter Field for their help in revising previous versions of this chapter.

[1] Our theoretical approach has been informed by recent developments in European social dialectology, especially those emerging from the European Science Foundation Network on 'The Convergence and divergence of dialects in a Changing Europe' (1995–1998; see Auer and Hinskens 1996).

social analysis: the speaker's degree of isolation from, or integration with, the speech community. For this reason, intensive research on network properties and qualitative observation of individual behaviour within the speaker's personal network is the best way to capture this decisive factor constraining language variation. Nevertheless, research into very different contexts of language use has shown that such a hypothesis conceals at least two possible interpretations:

1. *strong interpretation*: research on quantitative properties of networks must give an adequate representation of the speaker's position within the community. Hence, a network analysis should serve as a good indicator of language variation. This interpretation is that assumed in the pioneering research by Milroy (1980) and other researchers working around the same time (e.g. Bortoni-Ricardo 1985; Gal 1979).[2]

2. *weak interpretation*: the research results have not always proved to be entirely satisfactory (Labov and Harris 1986; Avila 1994; Gumperz 1997; Marshall 2004; Milroy 2002b). Quantitative correlations between speech and network scores are sometimes weak or non-significant. Therefore, other attributes underlying relationships between speakers have to be sought (interpretive measures). These attributes are related to the quality of contacts (external or internal) and to the speaker's own attitudes (positive or negative) and his or her past or present social life. On this interpretation, the social network would remain as the necessary means of gaining access to this information, which is crucial in accounting for language variation.

Certain properties that derive from the speaker's position in the community (and therefore his or her attitude towards language and language use) are not defined, nor can they be directly obtained from a model which represents links between people as a web of ties (cf. Eckert 2000). Thus, these properties cannot be easily quantified within the frame of network analysis (matrix analysis, density, and so on) nor adequately accounted for with the standardised network measures. We refer to these properties as *interpretive* in the sense that, as analysts, we must have a profound understanding of the speech community in order to use factors such as ruralisation, urbanisation, as well as other interactive factors, as independent variables. If analysts are not familiar with their speakers' lives and attitudes, they cannot go further than merely correlate their network markers with their speech scores. This task cannot be accomplished by an analyst who is not the observer (at least in theory). Interpretation suggests the risk of misunderstanding, but it implies the chance of a more complete knowledge of the social reality.

In network-oriented sociolinguistic studies, the two versions of the hypothesis correspond, respectively, to the application of the concept of social network

---

[2] Milroy and Milroy (1992: 5–9; 1997: 59–61); and Milroy (2002b: 553–568) give an updated report on the most relevant research since their own seminal work in Belfast.

as a methodological procedure and analytical tool (*strong interpretation*), or
to its restricted use as a fieldwork method (*weak interpretation*). In the first
case, social network structure is clearly used as an *independent* variable. In the
second case, however, the discovery of *intervening* and *interacting* variables
would indicate that social networks are, at best, a variable that must be analysed
in conjunction with other variables. At worst, any measured network effect may
simply be a metaphenomenon. Yet, as indicated, they are an important channel
for obtaining relevant information on individual speakers.

To show how this interaction of factors might work, examples from a group
of studies have been selected because they deal with processes of dialect convergence and divergence. The data and results referred to here are mostly from
our own research on the southern varieties of Spanish (Villena 1994, 1996).

The recent focus on dialect convergence and divergence has opened up
new perspectives in language-variation research. Apart from stimulating new
research (Auer and Hinskens 1996), it has revealed (1) that new approaches are
still possible in the study of social variation in language; and (2) that there are
specific historical, social, and geographical circumstances which require new
methods and theoretical approaches.

2   Social Networks and Language Variation

2.1   *The significance of the concept of 'social network' for*
language-variation research

Social network analysis has been successfully used in anthropology, sociology,
and sociolinguistic research for more than forty years. The reason why social
scientists are interested in the observation and description (and often quantification) of individual relations goes beyond the mere collection of case histories.
The basic idea of network analysis is very simple: 'it asks questions about who
is linked to whom, the nature of that linkage, and how the nature of the linkage
affects behaviour' (Boissevain 1987: 169).

Research on social networks arose in the 1920s in the framework of the
American anthropological tradition (Whyte, Wylie, Lewis), and later focused
on the domain of kinship and friendship relations, both as methodological procedure and analytical tool (Fortes, Barnes, Bott, Mitchell). Since the early network
studies were carried out (Barnes 1954; Bott 1957; Mitchell 1969), the level of
refinement in the use of social-network analytical techniques in the field of sociology has been increasing (Knoke and Kuklinski 1982; Wassermann and Faust
1994). Variationist sociolinguistics and social dialectology have been taking
advantage of this for more than twenty years (Dittmar and Schlobinski 1985;
Milroy 2002b). The results of the research in this field clearly showed that the
mesh of ties between social actors and the properties derived from these ties

define the intragroup social order and establish values and individual status in society. This web of links acts as an intermediate configuration between individual subjects and macrosocial and institutional structures, such as class. Thus, prestige or dominance do not directly influence the individual's behaviour, but do so through the constraining effects of networks (Granovetter 1973).

A social network 'may be seen as a boundless web of ties that reaches out through a whole society, linking people to one another, however remotely' (Milroy and Milroy 1992: 5). Nevertheless, for practical reasons, analyses focus on the individual-anchored network of relations (kinship, friends, workmates, and neighbours) a particular actor (*ego*) establishes. Within those personal networks, analysts recognise as the most interesting for their research the *first order zone*, which only includes the directly connected intimate friends and relatives.[3] These people, in turn, are usually connected to one another. From this first order zone, a series of zones (*second, third, n-order zone*) spread, whose actors are not directly linked to *ego*, but only as *friends of a friend*. The *n-order zones* constitute the network's instrumental areas, which allow the core members to communicate with the outer world and receive a flow of external information. The more remote areas of the network are the *extended zone* (Boissevain 1974).

Language-variation researchers accepted quite early on the usefulness of the social network approach, due to the fact that social network typology and dialect maintenance/shift processes have been shown to be interrelated in several ways. Two means of application of social network analysis to the study of language variation have been developed.

1. Firstly, as a tool or strategy in fieldwork methodology (Labov 1972; Labov and Harris 1986) without further use of it as an analytical procedure. Social networks are intermediate social structures which link speakers to one another (i.e. the actual web of ties) and connect them to the macrosocial structures. This is why social networks are supposed to be the best field for observing natural (i.e. not monitored) speech behaviour. It is not accidental at all that this kind of analysis has been practised and developed in Europe and especially in the frame of some critical trends of social and sociolinguistic thought: the need to gain access to 'natural language use' reflects the challenge of finding speech norms different from, or even opposite to, mainstream norms, as a means of understanding the conflict between ideologies in society (Romaine 1982; Milroy 1987; Williams 1992).

2. Secondly, as both a methodological and an analytical tool (Milroy 1980, 1987; Bortoni-Ricardo 1985; Kerswill 1994, etc.). According to Milroy's research in Belfast (L. Milroy 1980), language variation is closely related to the type of social network in which the speakers are embedded. Early

---

[3] The so-called 'personal network' of an individual consists of a subset of the rest of N-1 individuals within the system with whom the actor *i* has direct connection (Knoke and Kuklinski 1982: 51).

observations pointed out that differences in social-network characteristics correlated with the social class and educational level of the speakers. Arguably, this could have been a consequence of the fact that the pioneering studies by the Milroys in Belfast, Bortoni-Ricardo in Brasilia, and even the ethnographically based approaches by Gumperz, all focused on groups of speakers belonging to the same social class. However, it has since become apparent that this homogeneity is due to the social circumstances which affect the individual's life-mode (Milroy and Milroy 1992), where social network and social class seem to be interrelated (J. Milroy 1992: 207–220; Chambers 1995: 66–101).

Statistical analyses (such as matrix analysis, path analysis, multifactorial analysis, and so on) have been built up to account for several kinds of social behaviour (job markets, communication of information in stable and non-stable communities, family and friendship ties, etc.). The research has proved to be successful (Wassermann and Galaskiewicz 1994), especially in ethnographically oriented studies, where, thanks to the use of social-network methodology, researchers have been able to gain access to places where the application of sample survey studies would have been difficult or even impossible. Statistical correlations between linguistic variables and quantitative data taken from direct observation of the speakers' behaviour within their social networks (e.g. points on a scale of 'social integration', 'language attitudes', etc., derived from ethnographic observation by the fieldworker) have been sought with considerable success (Chambers 1995: 68–81; Labov 2001: 325–365; Milroy 2002b). However, more sophisticated analytical techniques from the field of sociology have largely been neglected in dialect-variation research. It is also the case that network analysis, more generally, is underdeveloped in language-variation research, even among the most significant contributions. One of the most surprising things is, for example, the absence of network items in the questionnaires used in survey-based research projects. This failure to seek network data in macrosociolinguistic research projects has led to the erroneous idea that network information is available only through participant observation. This is one of the most urgent tasks to be accomplished in ongoing or future projects (Requena 1996). The Malaga Urban Vernacular project (MUV) has actually been using 'name generators' (cf. Burt 1984; Requena 1996) as a means of collecting social-network data through questionnaire items (Villena and Requena 1996), and the ongoing international Project on Spoken European and American Urban Spanish (PRESEEA) also takes into account this kind of information (Moreno Fernandez 1996).

2.2   Measures of network structure

The concept 'social network' has provided a starting-point for the elaboration of a quantitative measure of community integration permitting statistical

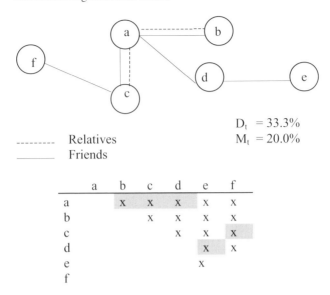

$D_t = 33.3\%$
$M_t = 20.0\%$

- - - - - - - -   Relatives
─────────   Friends

	a	b	c	d	e	f
a		x	x	x	x	x
b			x	x	x	x
c				x	x	x
d					x	x
e						x
f						

Fig. 12.1 Graph of a social network of low density and multiplexity and matrix of relations.

treatment (Milroy and Margrain 1980: 65). A network of interconnected people is considered to be a structure having a series of regularities capable of affecting individual behaviour. To account for these regularities, analysts distinguish between (1) *objective* and (2) *subjective* criteria or measures. Objective measures can be *interactional* (as multiplexity, frequency, and content) or *structural* (as density, centrality, or clustering). Subjective criteria refer to the emotional redefinition of the links within the different network zones, so that five different crowns or zones surrounding *ego* can be detected: (i) personal cell; (ii) intimate zone; (iii) instrumental friends zone; (iv) nominal friends zone; and (v) extended zone (Boissevain 1987: 165–166; Milroy 1980: 46–48).

The most important consequences for language and language-variation theory and practice can be summarised as follows (Milroy 1980: 70–109; Kerswill 1994: 53–57): (1) the morphology and content of these intermediate structures define the degree of the speaker's social integration and how this interacts with social-status pressures to influence his or her speech (*quantitative* or *integrative measures*); (2) the same statement is applicable to the *type of people* with whom an individual has social contacts (*subjective*, *qualitative*, or *interpretive measures*).

2.2.1 Quantitative social network measures   Among the objective or integrative measures, structural criteria, such as *density*, and interactional measures, such as *multiplexity*, are of the greatest importance (see figures 12.1

and 12.2). *Density* is the connectivity, i.e. the number of actual links in relation to the total number of possible links within a group of individuals. A particular social network is said to be highly dense when most of the subjects connected to one individual are in turn connected to one another. Segments of networks which have relatively high density are called *clusters*. Relationships within the cluster are denser than those existing externally (Milroy 1980: 50–51). *Multiplexity* refers to the proportion of multiplex links with reference to the total number of actual links. Within a personal network, people are related through a wide range of capacities. So, multiplex links are ties where more than one type of relation or social role is present in the tie.

Within the network represented in figure 12.1, density D at a time t is equal to the relation between actual links (5) and all possible links (15):

$$D_t = \frac{100a}{k} = \frac{5.100}{15} = 33.3\%$$

When the quantity of ties is high, it is better to compute on the basis of the number of actors:

$$D_t = \frac{200a}{n(n-1)} = \frac{200.5}{6.5} = \frac{1000}{30} = 33.3\%,$$

where a = total number of links and n = total number of actors. Multiplexity M_t of the same network is equal to the relation between the number of multiplex links (2) and the total number of actual ties (5):

$$M_t = \frac{100m}{a} = \frac{2.100}{5} = 20.0\%$$

The network represented in figure 12.1 is one of low density, since only a few of the virtual links between the actors are actual links, as is implied by the shaded cases in the matrix. By contrast, the network shown in figure 12.2 is denser and more multiplex:

$$D_t = \frac{200a}{6.5} = \frac{200.11}{30} = 2200 = 73.3\%$$

Actors linked to a tend to be connected with each other, with the only exception of four virtual links between the two most peripheral subjects (*e/f, d/f, c/e, b/f*). Multiplexity is also higher:

$$M_t = \frac{100a}{k} = \frac{100.5}{11} = 45.5\%$$

Bearing in mind the comparison between both networks, we can expect that union and agreement between actors will be stronger in the second denser and more multiplex network than in the first less dense and uniplex. Consensus of norms and social control will be greater in the latter. The denser and more

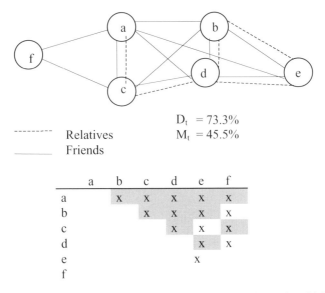

$$D_t = 73.3\%$$
$$M_t = 45.5\%$$

-------- Relatives
_____ Friends

	a	b	c	d	e	f
a		x	x	x	x	x
b			x	x	x	x
c				x	x	x
d					x	x
e					x	
f						

Fig. 12.2 Graph of a social network of high density and multiplexity and matrix of relations.

multiplex a network is (i.e. the closer and stronger the ties between individuals are), and the more multiplex relations it contains (i.e. the more redundant relations there are within the group; for example, *a* connected to *c* as friends and neighbours), so the speakers will be much more closely linked, they will share more things, and will have in common more norms of behaviour. These *integrative* properties are easily quantified (Milroy 1980: 108–176; Milroy and Margrain 1980; Bortoni-Ricardo 1985: 69–97, 150–172; Dittmar and Schlobinski 1985: 163–169), and have been extensively used as analytical tools in language variation research (cf. Milroy and Milroy 1992: 1–9; Milroy and Milroy 1997: 59–61; Dittmar and Schlobinski 1985: 170–185).

Dense and multiplex networks characteristically offer their members close co-operation and local community support. Since Barnes' (1954) and Bott's (1957) work, this particular type of network has been referred to as *close-knit*. Ties are said to be *strong* in the sense that they function as a conservative force resisting pressures for change originating outside the network. Research carried out in the last two decades by Lesley and James Milroy, and lately by others[4] showed that this kind of network structure has the capacity of enforcing local norms and conventions (Milroy 1980: 199; Milroy and Milroy 1992: 5–9). Furthermore, close-knit networks correlate significantly with linguistic

---

[4] Previous work by Blom and Gumperz (1972); and Labov (1972) served as point of departure for Milroy's own research.

variables, in the sense that speakers who belong to close-knit social networks tend to maintain vernacular features and reject standard legitimised usages. Varieties within these networks are then characterised as more regular or *focused* (L. Milroy 1982; Bortoni-Ricardo 1985).

Conversely, less-dense and uniplex networks (*loose-knit networks*) are usually non-territorially based and show a weakening of the strength of ties.[5] Relatively *uniplex*, *weak-tie* networks usually characterise mobile, urban, middle-class speakers, who are open to outside influences, mostly mainstream pressures. As a consequence, the linguistic behaviour associated with these types of speakers tends to be irregular, variable, and *diffuse*. Speakers who do not belong to the core network group or central cluster are said to be peripheral, so that they are less sensitive to network-specific norms of behaviour and to sanctions applied within them. As these speakers are connected to others within the social network through uniplex, non-intense weak ties, and usually have various external contacts (*bridges*), mainstream uses and changes can penetrate the network through them (Granovetter 1973: 1762–1773), since whatever is to be diffused can reach a larger number of people, and traverse a greater distance, when passed through weak rather than strong ties.

Based on Granovetter's (1973) proposals and on their own research, Milroy and Milroy (1992: 9–18) elaborated a cohesive theory about the connection between interpersonal networks and social class. Small-scale structures (such as social networks) and more abstract configurations (such as social class) frequently co-occur in such a way that dense, multiplex kin- and territorially based networks are associated either with working-class speakers or, not surprisingly, with upper-class speakers.[6] The rest of the population would fall between these two extremes (1992: 17). Such speakers are socially and geographically mobile (including second-generation rural migrants) and tend to establish loose-knit networks.

As close-knit networks favour vernacular focusing (at least among lower-class speakers) and loose-knit networks tend to lead to vernacular diffusion (Milroy 1982), the image of a continuum of variation between two poles of focused varieties arises. As mentioned above, strong-tie communities promote convergence in their members' behaviour and tend to avoid or, at least, discourage external contacts. Conversely, weak-tie groups tend to have external contacts with other social groups. The combination of these two features (*low*

---

[5] 'The strength of a tie is a (probably linear) combination of the amount of time, the emotional intensity, the intimacy (mutual confiding), and the reciprocal services which characterize the tie' (Granovetter 1973: 1361).

[6] Upper-class speakers develop loose-knit heterogeneous social networks, which allow them to have non-located weak but useful contacts with many individuals. However, at the same time, they belong either to strong-tie kin and friend networks, as well as elite coalitions (cf. Milroy and Milroy 1992: 18–24).

Table 12.1 *Four types of communities as a function of their network type and degree of isolation (adapted from Trudgill 1996: 3–4)*

Network type	External contact	
	Low	High
Close-knit	A	B
Loose-knit	C	D

or *high* degree of external contacts and the type of network structure: *close-knit* or *loose-knit*) generates four possibilities that cover the total range of variation (table 12.1).

Isolated close-knit communities (A) are likely to maintain vernacular features and to resist changes from outside; as in the case of rural communities (Lippi-Green 1989), or working-class urban areas in industrialised or tourist contexts (Milroy 1980; Villena 1994, 1996). On the other hand, communities with high degrees of external contacts and loose-knit network structures (D) are exposed to dialect contact and favour convergence (levelling and koineisation processes); as, for example, in new-dialect formation processes (Trudgill 1986; Kerswill 1994, 1996). The typology proposed by Trudgill (1996: 5–18) applies to all sorts of processes, both synchronically and diachronically.[7] In Trudgill (1996), examples from the two extreme possibilities (A and D) of this typology are given and commented on. High-external-contact communities with close-knit network structures (B) would correspond to upper-class speakers in urban contexts. In turn, low-external-contact communities with loose-knit networks (C) would be very uncommon, as far as we know.

2.2.2 Interpretive social network measures   So far, regularities regarding the influence of network relationships on a speaker's social, personal, and psychosocial attributes have been focused on. However, factors such as the speaker's gender, age, occupation, education, family background, personality, and so on are factors which obviously influence social networks. Investigating how these factors and other connected variables affect network structure (Boissevain 1987: 167–169) is an interesting way of approaching the interaction between individual and institutional levels, since social networks vary in the characteristics just listed. These interact with the objective (integrative) criteria, intensifying or diminishing the effect of the network structural or interactional features outlined above. Hence, we refer to these factors as *interpretive*,

---

[7] High-contact communities actually develop processes of dialect simplification and admixtures that are similar to those occurring in pidginisation processes (Trudgill 1994).

since they require interpretation by an analyst who is able fully to understand (*Verstehen*) the speech community.

In many cases, these features (more accurately, the *type of people an individual has contacts with*)[8] complement the quantitative information given by density or multiplexity scores. In other cases, however, interpretive data are decisive in interpreting, or even correcting, quantitative network results. Some of these interpretive criteria have been studied as they actually affect dialect or language variation. The main factors are the following:

(1) *biological*: *sex differences* produce sharp distinctions or polarisation between male and female networks (Milroy 1982; Cheshire 1982; Eckert 1989; Villena and Requena 1996).[9] *Ethnicity* splits speech communities and can intensify network closeness, as for instance in black vs. white (Labov and Harris 1986) or in rural, peasant or farming vs. urban (Blom and Gumperz 1972; Gal 1979; Kerswill 1994; Marshall 2004), etc.;

(2) *community*: research into both small rural communities and groups of migrants in industrialised areas has shown a strong correlation between integration into the larger host community and the looseness of network ties (Bortoni-Ricardo 1985).

(3) *Social*: education, occupation, income, as well as other status-dependent variables (media exposure, local loyalty, etc.) can influence network attributes, such as the strength of network ties (Granovetter 1973; Milroy 1980), personal network size (Villena 1996), frequency, centrality, etc.

Nevertheless, the interaction of several of these factors produces unexpected correlations with dialect features, as in the case of farmers' life-styles in Spanish Cantabria (Holmquist 1988).

2.3   Limitations of social network analysis: the speaker's social history

Social networks are the social units that are most closely correlated with linguistic behaviour. As Labov and Harris (1986: 21–22) explain, long and close interaction can produce linguistic convergence. So, speakers of the same social network usually share a common ideology and common experience, which leads to the same directions of style shifting and the same attitudes towards the other dialects. Nevertheless, as pointed out above, certain aspects of the speaker's behaviour remain unexplained. Labov and Harris (1986: 20–22) formulated four 'general principles that have emerged from research in the speech community over the past twenty years'. These principles actually point to the limits of integrative network measures and show the need for different strategies: divergence and diffusion, or convergence and focusing, in dialect-contact situations depend on the social status associated with each variety (prestige), on the

---

[8] Kerswill (1994: 54).   [9] See Coates (1986: 79–95).

speaker's attitude towards these varieties and on the nature of the variable itself. The speaker's attitude eventually comes from his or her own situation within the local speech community and the extent of his or her external contacts.

(1) *Divergence*. Vernacular loyalty towards dialect varieties depends on the degree of cohesion within the community:

> The first [principle] is the fact that linguistic traits are not transmitted across group boundaries simply by exposure to other dialects in the mass media or in schools. This finding appeared in the first study of social stratification in New York City (Labov 1972). The influence of radio and TV may be seen in self-conscious correction of the New York City vernacular in formal styles . . . Our basic linguistic system is not acquired from school, teachers or from radio announcers, but from friends and competitors: those whom we admire, and those we have to be good enough to beat . . . Core groups remain apart and are probably drifting further apart in spite of the fact that members hear standard dialects spoken on radio, TV and at school four to eight hours a day. (Labov and Harris 1986: 20)

(2) *Convergence*. The influence of the dominant varieties over the subordinate varieties is limited and unidirectional. Convergence towards the standard variety affects only speakers definitely open to it and mainly in formal styles. The converse is unusual:

> The second general observation is that the linguistic influence that takes place under these conditions is asymmetrical. Speakers of the dominated dialect acquire unconsciously the rules of the dominant dialect. But the reverse does not happen. (Labov and Harris 1986: 20)

This entails that those speakers who are not core-group members and have external contacts show a profound shift towards the standard uses and tend to diverge from group norms. On the contrary, speakers from the dominant dialect, though accepted within the dominated speech community (here the Black English Vernacular: BEV), do not show a true control of the deep structures of the acquired variety.

(3) *Subordinate dialect*. Contact between varieties produces convergence affecting the surface structures of the language. This statement reflects a situation which has been described at least for the urban context of the USA. A third principle can explain this apparently strange situation:

> This situation is only possible because of a third general fact about language: Abstract linguistic structure has little or no social impact on members of the community. The interface of language and society is narrow, and primarily on the surface: the words and the sounds of the language. Abstract, discontinuous formal elements like the verbal /s/ are not perceived in a systematic way by ordinary listeners and have almost no influence on judgements of ethnic identity. (Labov and Harris 1986: 21)

Verbal /s/ with third person singular subjects in present tense is absent in BEV (*he run* 'he runs'; *John go* 'John goes'). On the other hand, /s/ can appear in other contexts (*he get hurts* 'he gets hurt') or with first or second person (*I says* 'I say', *you runs* 'you run'). The use of this feature is variable and not very frequent in the speech community of north Philadelphia studied by Labov and his associates. The most interesting aspect of this variation is that the use of /s/ tends to specialise for narratives and has become a marker of the narrative past (Labov and Harris 1986: 9–12, 13–20). White people 'who are accepted in the Black community, and are identified as Black by their speech, do not show any important shift towards the BEV grammatical system' (Labov and Harris 1986: 21).

(4) *Degree of integration*. The speakers' position within the personal network of relations where they live strongly constrains their language use and attitudes. However, there is not an exact correlation between both variables, since there are certain regularities beyond network properties, which must explain why very similar people behave so differently. This leads to the fourth principle:

> Members of the same social networks usually share a common ideology and common experience, which leads to the same direction of style shifting and the same attitudes towards other dialects. We have traced small linguistic rules and lexical items that are shared by members of primary networks. But on the whole, social networks have little explanatory value for individual differences in linguistic systems. It is the social history of the speakers that must be taken into account: the kinds of social experience they have had in dealing with members of other groups, the way they have used language in their life. (Labov and Harris 1986: 21)

This does not mean that social networks are useless. On the contrary, only on the basis of the knowledge of the speakers' situation within their personal network would one be able to understand how they define or redefine this position: either by reinforcing the vernacular norms within strong ties networks, or by diverging from them and towards the use of variables associated with other dialects. In both cases, however, *what is decisive is the individual interpretation* of a particular context, whose structure is accessible thanks to the concept of 'social network'. In fact, social-network analysis is a reasonable complement of macrosocial analysis, in the sense that the former can reveal a more integrated vision of the whole system in which the social actors are located (Milroy 1980: 14; Wellman 1998).

2.4   How similar are people who speak alike?

One might think that the nature of the links between people primarily determines speech behaviour. However, as stated in the previous section, any similarity between speakers' use of the variable features of a language is not a matter of the shape of their social networks composed of kin, neighbours, workmates, and friends, but depends fundamentally on their shared *social history* (Labov and Harris 1986: 9). Experiences shared by different speakers, similar types and frequencies of contacts, shared enterprises, etc., are more important than belonging to the same social network or even to the same cluster. Far from convergence affecting only the surface of the language, social networks mirror linguistic structure only when speakers share a common social history (Labov and Harris 1986: 21).

Milroy and Milroy (1992) clearly revealed a network-based theoretical explanation for this issue. The essential similarity of social identities and attitudes among speakers whose idiolects are very close from a structural point of view is a consequence of the type of links (strong or weak) which they establish (contact frequency, duration, and content). Social networks emerge from the conditions associated with the 'life-modes'; i.e. the different subgroups in which the population splits on the basis of the predominant mode of production: self-employed, wage-earners, and professionals (1992: 18–24).

Since social-network structure is likely to conceal other factors which may account for language variation, especially that of less-integrated speakers, research on social networks should address as thoroughly as possible two main issues:

1. the 'integration/isolation' paradox as formulated by Granovetter (1973: 1378): 'weak ties, often denounced as generative of alienation . . . are here seen as indispensable to individuals' opportunities and to their integration into communities; strong ties, breeding local cohesion, lead to overall fragmentation'.[10]
2. the alleged inadequacy of the concept of 'social network' for the explanation of individual language variation (Labov and Harris 1986).

Social network and social class are concepts intended to account for similarities in the speaker's social conduct, which, in turn, can explain similarities in their language use. Sociolinguists have been employing these concepts and their associated techniques for some years. What is needed is the development of more comprehensive models, which integrate class and network (as is the case not only with the above-mentioned intermediate concepts of 'life-mode' or 'social history' but with others like the concept of 'community of practice').[11] As mentioned above, Milroy and Milroy (1992, 1997) have developed a very promising way of doing this. In particular, the weak-ties theory is an interesting way both of exploring Granovetter's paradox about the isolation of strong-tie network speakers and of understanding why social-network analysis has to be supplemented by qualitative individual-centred observation and interpretation.

---

[10] He added: 'Paradoxes are a welcome antidote to theories which explain everything all too neatly' (Granovetter 1973: 1378).
[11] Cf. Eckert (2000); Meyerhoff (2002).

**3   Quantitative Social Network Analysis: Social Networks as
          Independent Variables (Strong Hypothesis)**

A twofold use of the concept of 'social network' arises from the issues discussed
so far: either social network structure is accepted as a good indicator of language
variation; or it is considered only as a way of collecting data or obtaining
social or individual information. In the first case, social networks are used as
independent variables (section 3); in the second case, they are seen as a mere
source of information (section 4).

3.1   Propositions

Convergence and divergence between dialects or towards the standard variety
are dynamic sociolinguistic processes which can be best understood by taking into account the network properties of speakers.[12] Similarity of speakers,
beyond their belonging to the same social class, age, or regional background,
depends on the type of their social networks and the individual's engagement
within them. The outcome of the preceding discussion allows us to formulate
two propositions that are the most important from a quantitative perspective of
network-based sociolinguistic theory.

1. Speakers who are strongly connected to one another (*strong-tie networks*)
   show obvious similarity in their speech use (section 3.2).
   1a. In these circumstances, effective consensus of norms tends to develop,
       so that speech behaviour is expected to show regular and systematic
       patterns. Local loyalty to vernacular varieties is very likely to arise and
       to persist. *Vernacular divergence* from mainstream norms of use seems
       to be usual in a vast majority of cases.
   1b. Speakers who know many others, live at the local community's margins,
       or belong to *weak-tie networks*, are susceptible to mainstream influence
       (*asymmetrical convergence* towards standard-speech norms).
2. Network structure interacts, however, with social and personal variables,
   so that unexpected correlations between network markers and speech variables may occur. More attention paid to these interactions should improve
   correlational network analysis (section 3.3).

These are the main ways in which social network theory can contribute to
dialect contact theory and social dialectology. In what follows, these issues are
commented on and some examples from European Spanish varieties (mainly
southern Spanish) are given, with special emphasis on convergence and divergence processes.

---

[12] Mattheier (1996) gives a thorough exposition of the origin and meaning of the concepts of
convergence and divergence in contemporary social dialectology. See also Auer and Hinskens
(1996).

			Standard Spanish				Andalusian Spanish			
			labial	dental	palatal	velar	labial	dental	palatal	velar
Obstruent	tense		p	t	t͡ʃ	k	p	t		k
	lax		b	d	j	g	b	d		g
	fricative	voiceless	f	θ	ṣ	x	f	θˢ	ʃ	h
		voiced							ʒ	
Sonorant	nasal		m	n	ɲ		m	n	ɲ	
	lateral			l	ʎ			l		
	vibrant	lax		ɾ				ɾ		
		tense		r				r		

Fig. 12.3 Phonemic consonant system of northern/standard Spanish and non-standard Andalusian Spanish.

3.2   Predicting language variation through the use of social networks

The existence of significant correlation between vernacular speech features and social network markers is one of the strongest hypotheses advanced here. The idea is that this correlation may be seen through the analysis of quantitative network data. Research has shown that this hypothesis is correct in predicting inter- and intralinguistic variation. We shall test this hypothesis on data from our correlational study in Malaga.

3.2.1 Standard-dialect convergence and divergence: language variation in Andalusian Spanish   Varieties spoken in Malaga belong to the so-called 'southern Spanish' dialect group. Regional dialects of Spanish can be divided into two main groups, according to phonological and, less significantly, morphological differences: northern and central varieties are phonologically conservative; while southern varieties are innovative compared to medieval Castilian. Standard Spanish is based on the northern dialects, with the result that southern varieties are considered to be less prestigious. Differences between the two sets of varieties are not sharp, so that dialect switching is not observable. Nevertheless, some of them are salient and speakers tend to some extent to have conscious control over them. Some of these differences affect syllable-final consonants and/or vowel quality (cf. Mondéjar 1991).

The differences we refer to here affect the phonemic inventory (figure 12.3). The main differences focus on the subsystems of fricatives and laterals, where standard and northern oppositions between /s/: /θ/ and /l/: /ʎ/ are lacking in the southern phonological inventory. Southern dialects have no alveolar-palatal /ṣ/, but dental /θ/ or /ṣ/, tense palatal /t͡ʃ/ becomes voiceless fricative /ʃ/, and lax palatal /j/ shifts to voiced fricative /ʒ/ (cf. Villena 2001). A chain shift may occur among rural or lower-class urban speakers (/θ^s → h/ /h → Ø/). Standard Spanish and nonstandard southern systems (especially for some of the most advanced varieties) contrast as shown in figure 12.3. Fricative /ş/ is apical in northern varieties and in the national standard. From Alarcos' (1950) analysis onwards, phonologists have been including this phoneme among palatals, since it implies the backing of the front part of the tongue to articulate a fricative relatively close to /ʃ/. When laminal (here /θ/) and apical (here /ş/) sounds contrast at the same closure location, apical sounds are more retracted than laminal (Norval Smith 2000: 259). Retracted articulations are then less natural and more marked than non-retracted. Conservative dialects use these sounds. On the contrary, innovating dialects avoid them and use dental /s̪/ (Villena 2001).

Divergent southern features can be detected among all sorts of speakers, but they are gradually stratified (Villena 1996). Educational and age grading, as well as style variation, show that this vernacular variety is rejected by young educated people, as it is felt to be 'bad Spanish'. Convergence towards the standard Spanish phonemic system (and even through the re-establishment of old or the introduction of previously non-existent phonemic distinctions) is a prestige-motivated challenge. Nevertheless, older and non-educated speakers by and large accept their variety as their own. Loyalty to this vernacular variety (in spite of its very low institutional and macrosocial prestige) may persist within close networks, while convergence towards the standard trends of pronunciation would take place within open networks.

   3.2.2 Data: the MUV project   The MUV project deals with the vernacular varieties spoken in Malaga, a seaside resort city in Andalusia, southern Spain.[13] This city (of around 500,000 inhabitants) and its surrounding area have been the focus of migration for more than thirty years, mainly from its rural hinterland. The total number of speakers included in the first phase of the study was 176 (64 male and 112 female), from lower middle class (LMC) to lower class (LC). Our main objective was to carry out social network research in a variety of neighbourhoods (*barrios*) which had previously been selected (Villena 1994). During the first phase of the project, ten social networks were studied. The fieldwork method was basically ethnographic (participant observer), as data collection was carried out by an insider.

   To illustrate the propositions advanced above, we shall focus on two out of the ten social networks investigated in Malaga. In both of them, the study was intended to analyse phonological variation within the researcher's own social network of kin and friends: (1) Avila's (1994) research into a social

---

[13] Details about the methodological and theoretical foundations of this research project are given in Villena (1996).

network of 31 working-class speakers in a traditional district in Malaga inner city (Capuchinos); (2) Cuevas' (2001) research into a fairly heterogeneous social network (n = 27) within a district in northern Malaga (Nueva Málaga).

3.2.3 Correlation with integrative network markers   Basic general network features such as density or multiplexity are useful when comparing different networks or when contrasting sectors or zones within the same network. As stated above, Milroy (1980: 152–176), Gal (1979: 131–151), Lippi-Green (1989: 218–220, 223–231), and others have used network indexes (such as density and multiplexity) to account for vernacular *focusing*. However, in analysing language variation, the speaker's personal network has been found to be essential. Measures of the speakers' strength of ties and frequency of contacts, as well as their personal network size, have been applied in a thoroughgoing manner.

In the majority of cases, researchers have built scales adapted to their specific objectives. For example, Milroy's 'network-strength scale' or Lippi-Green's complex 17-point 'local-integration' scale were intended to measure the individual's degree of integration into the network structure as well as the intensity of the contacts and the strength of their ties. An adaptation of Milroy's scale was used in Malaga to measure the closeness, intensity, territoriality, and multiplexity of ties (Villena 1994: 32–34). All these measures have been found to be reasonably good indicators of language variation.

As shown in table 12.2, our community-based ethnographic research in Malaga shows that the social-network index scores' prediction of language use is not particularly strong, though it is in many cases significant. The mean probability of using vernacular phonological variables /s → θ/ (as in ['piθo] instead of ['piṣo], *piso* 'flat/apartment'), /x → Ø/ (as in [ro:] instead of ['roxo], *rojo* 'red', /t͡ʃ → ʃ/ (as in ['oʃo] instead of ['ot͡ʃo], *ocho*, 'eight') increases as the network scores increase. This association is particularly significant for /x/-deletion and /t͡ʃ/-lenition. The standard marker /s/: /θ/ (as in ['taθa] *taza*, 'cup' vs. ['tasa] *tasa*, 'tax'), however, tends to behave inversely, so that it is less used as network scores rise. Results displayed in table 12.2 refer to the speaker's number of multiplex ties and his or her score on the 'network-strength scale' (0–9). These network markers measure the speaker's degree of connectedness with the network structure and define the speaker's position within the network: if an actor is connected to the rest of the speakers through strong, close, and multiplex ties, other things being equal, he or she is likely to feel close to the others, and will tend to participate in common activities and share their norms of behaviour.

These results confirm, as expected, that the more one particular speaker is integrated into his or her personal network (density, multiplexity) and the stronger his or her network ties are (network strength), the more frequently he or she uses the variables the local community members feel to be their own.

Table 12.2 *Mean probability for four phonological variables among southern Spanish speakers in six social networks in Malaga. Correlation with two network markers*

Variables	Multiplex ties	K–W	Network strength	K–W
	Number of multiplex ties		Very low (0–2), low (3–4), medium (5), high (>5)	
$\widehat{\text{t}\int} \rightarrow [\int]$	0 = .18 ± .28 1 = .24 ± .32 2–4 = .13 ± .23 >4 = .40 ± .36	$\chi^2 = 13.0392$ Sig. **.0046**	VL = .24 ± .33 L = .28 ± .35 M = .15 ± .20 H = .27 ± .35	$\chi^2 = 2.0624$ Sig. .5595
/s/ → [θ]	0 = .25 ± .29 1 = .32 ± .37 2–4 = .10 ± .17 >4 = .34 ± .31	$\chi^2 = 7.9318$ Sig. **.0474**	VL = .10 ± .13 L = .27 ± .29 M = .31 ± .31 H = .37 ± .37	$\chi^2 = 8.0981$ Sig. **.0440**
/x/ → /ø/	0 = .18 ± .20 1 = .28 ± .22 2–4 = .14 ± .16 >4 = .45 ± .30	$\chi^2 = 20.8360$ Sig. **.0001**	VL = .22 ± .27 L = .30 ± .28 M = .30 ± .27 H = .32 ± .26	$\chi^2 = 3.3700$ Sig. .3380
/s/ : /θ/	0 = .60 ± .35 1 = .55 ± .40 2–4 = .72 ± .27 >4 = .50 ± .38	$\chi^2 = 3.9758$ Sig. .2641	VL = .77 ± .21 L = .58 ± .36 M = .54 ± .36 H = .44 ± .40	$\chi^2 = 9.7458$ Sig. **.0209**

Significant differences in bold type (Kruskal–Wallis non-parametric test). n = 176

Conversely, when speakers are less integrated into the social-network structure and their ties are weaker, they use the vernacular markers less frequently, and tend to converge towards standard models of pronunciation. It seems that the case of /s/: /θ/ is different. However, this contrast is not so clear, as mentioned above, since it is a standard feature whose corresponding southern feature (/s/ = /θ/) fits the pattern described so far. We shall return to this point below (3.2 and 3.3).

3.2.4 Clustering As explained above (2.2.1), *clusters* are the network segments where density is greater than within the rest of the network structure. Within these clusters, the current consensus of norms is expected to be stronger than outside. Therefore, loyalty to vernacular varieties should be high. In Avila's (1994) research, a cluster of middle-aged and elderly speakers was found (mean age = 50.3 ± 15.6 years). Their members (n = 14) had not attained high levels of education (6.0 ± 5.1 years), belonged to a voluntary association called '*Hermandad*' ('Brotherhood'), and spent their free time together. They named one another when asked to name friends. The rest of the network

Table 12.3 *Phonological variation and network density among speakers within a social network in the Capuchinos district of Malaga*

Phonological variables	Probability of use			
	/s/ : /θ/	/t͡ʃ/ → ʃ	/x/ → Ø	/s/ → θ
Brotherhood	.37 ± .33	.29 ± .29	.33 ± .19	.35 ± .36
Rest	.73 ± .26	.17 ± .29	.16 ± 17	.12 ± .24
K–W	$\chi^2 = 7.7922$	$\chi^2 = 2.3113$	$\chi^2 = 5.9733$	$\chi^2 = 2.7174$
	Sig. **.0052**	Sig. .1284	Sig. **.0145**	Sig. .1284
Network scales	NSS		RNSS	
	Mean	N	Mean	N
Brotherhood	3.0 ± .0.0	14	4.5 ± 1.7	8
Rest	1.9 ± .0.9	17	2.5 ± 1.3	14
K–W	$\chi^2 = 14.7680$		$\chi^2 = 7.5303$	
	Sig. **.0001**		Sig. **.0061**	

Significant differences in bold type (Kruskal–Wallis non-parametric test). n = 31

members (n = 17) were younger (24.8 ± 4.5 years), had attained a higher educational level (mean age = 13.2 ± 4.3 years), and were less socially integrated with the local community. With regard to network properties, members of the 'Brotherhood' were found to be more integrated into the social network, as they scored higher than the rest on several network markers. Of particular interest for phonological variation were the 'network-strength scale' scores. Two different scales were applied. The 7-point scale (NSS) affected the total number of speakers (n = 31). The second, more restricted, 5-point scale (RNSS), pointed only to the active worker speakers.[14] As shown in table 12.3, the probability of use of the vernacular variants is higher among speakers within the cluster, the differences being significant for /x/-deletion. With regard to the standard marker /s/: /θ/, its use is lower within the cluster, as expected. Differences of network integration inside and outside the cluster are sharp and significant as the strength of ties measures (NSS and RNSS) clearly show. Correlations between the use of the four phonological variables and the two network scales are weak and not significant for the total number of speakers (n = 31), with the exception of /x/ deletion (R = 0.379, sig. = 0.042). However, separated correlations within each of both clusters show strong and significant association between phonological variables and network scales (especially RNSS) within the *Hermandad*, whereas this association is much weaker and non-significant outside this cluster.

[14] Details about these scales are offered in Villena (1994, 1996).

3.3   Interactions with the structural variables

As reported above, multiplex territory-based networks correlate, as expected, with the use of strong vernacular speech features. Nevertheless, in many cases, correlations between network scores and standard or vernacular speech markers are weak (cf. Kerswill 1994: 102–135). In some other cases, we cannot discount the possibility that such correlations depend on the effect of other underlying variables. In fact, our data, too, have shown that density is not always a reliable predictor of vernacular focusing, as might be expected in line with the data from other research, particularly that of the Milroys (Labov 2001: 326–334; Marshall 2004). The effect of education, age, sex, and ethnicity on network structure can seriously affect the correlations between social network markers and linguistic variables, and produce unexpected results. Therefore, a more detailed consideration of the speech community's specific conditions will, in all probability, refine correlational analyses to a considerable extent.

3.3.1 The effect of the standard   Social networks are often referred to when talking about certain inadequacies of stratification analysis based on social class, education, and so on. The inverse is also true. Differences in vernacular use between clusters are better understood if their members' education and age are carefully considered.

In Cuevas' (2001) research in Nueva Málaga two clusters were identified. Firstly, the cluster of friends (n = 10), in which the participant observer herself was included, was particularly close-knit (D (density) = 75.5 per cent), as its members had frequent and intimate contact, and all of them belonged to a voluntary church organisation. Secondly, the cluster of relatives (n = 7) maintained less-frequent and intense contacts (D = 47.6 per cent). Thirdly, the rest of the speakers (n = 10) within the network did not belong to any well-defined cluster, so we shall treat them as a group on the basis that they, at least, share this characteristic. Variables and network markers, however, did not correlate in the expected direction, as shown in table 12.4.

Let us consider the /s/: /θ/ distinction and the 'Dialectalisation index' (range: 0–1), which is the mean of the vernacular variables examined here. On the one hand, the /s/: /θ/ distinction is much more frequent in the 'friends' cluster, as speakers included are younger and more educated. On the other hand, mean differences of 'Dialectalisation index' between clusters are significant and point to the counter-hypothetical conclusion that the denser a network structure is, the less frequent vernacular focusing will be. Even though the 'friends' cluster is denser than the rest of the groups, its speakers score lower than others in each of the vernacular markers. Furthermore, the speaker's integration into the social network structure is weaker among those individuals (integration = 2.03), though they have contacts with more people than the rest (mean size = 7.5).

Table 12.4 *Mean probabilities of phonological variables in Nueva Málaga.*
Source: Cuevas (2001)

Variables		Probability /s/ : /θ/	Dialect. index	Personal network size	Education	age	Integration index (0–5)
Clusters	N						
Friends	10	.87 ± .12	.14 ± .13	7.5 ± 2.2	18.0 ± 2.9	28.0 ± 1.9	2.03 ± 0.09
Relatives	7	.50 ± .39	.50 ± .39	5.4 ± 1.3	08.9 ± 1.0	48.3 ± 7.6	2.63 ± 0.33
Rest	10	.58 ± .29	.43 ± .29	4.6 ± 1.5	10.9 ± 5.5	47.7 ± 13.5	2.04 ± 0.35
K–W		$\chi^2 = 7.930$	$\chi^2 = 7.909$	$\chi^2 = 7.058$			$\chi^2 = 10.690$
		Sig. **.019**	Sig. **.025**	Sig. **.029**			Sig. **.005**

Significant differences in bold type (Kruskal–Wallis test). n = 27
Spearman's rho coefficient:
standard /s/ : /θ/: Age = −.749 sig. .000. education = .613 sig. .000
dialectalisation: Age = .761 sig. .000. education = −.591 sig. .001

The integration index derives from Bortoni-Ricardo's index, which is adapted for Cuevas' purposes (Bortoni-Ricardo 1985: 162–169; Cuevas 2001: 64–68). The *friends'* density is higher, as their members form a cluster within the total network but are less connected to the rest of the network. With regard to language use, vernacular variants are less used by the 'friends' speakers, since they are more educated and younger than the rest of the network speakers. These young and educated speakers have adapted the prestige norm of pronunciation (/s/ : /θ/) and tend to reject the vernacular norm /s/ = /θ/. Of course, as shown, age and education are highly intercorrelated, with the result that we cannot really treat them as independent variables.[15]

The favoured norms of speech behaviour within close-knit social networks have often been found to be the opposite of the national standard models of use, as discussed above. However, this is far from being a universal principle. Cuevas' analysis clearly revealed that integration into close-knit clusters of kin and friends increases the acceptance of standard variants and norms of use, as these patterns *are* the in-group norms of use (here, as the 'friends' cluster is composed of young educated speakers). The apparently striking statement about the relation between density and vernacular focusing should not be ignored, as social and personal variables within social networks are not as homogeneous as usually believed. This leads to an apparent contradiction, since we do not know if the focusing relates to network variables or to social and personal ones. As is discussed below, networks and personal variables are at different levels of social organisation and interact in often non-predictable ways.

---

[15] The explained variance (R^2) for /s/ : /θ/ = 0.265 and for Dialect, index = 0.208.

Table 12.5 *Spearman correlation between phonological variables and network markers among educated and non-educated speakers within an urban social network in Capuchinos (Malaga)*

Variables	NSS	RNSS	Personal network size
/s/ : /θ/	−.1816	.3028	.6357
	Sig. .615	Sig. .428	Sig. **.048**
/t͡ʃ/ > ʃ	−.0394	−.5320	−.2682
	Sig. .914	Sig. .140	Sig. .168
/s/ > θ	−.0130	−.1284	−.5224
	Sig. .972	Sig. .742	Sig. .121
/x/ > Ø	−.0802	−.0546	−.4852
	Sig. .838	Sig. .898	Sig. .186
Speakers >12 years of education (n = 10)			
NS = 2.25 ± 1.43			
/s/ : /θ/	−.5183	−.8023	.1869
	Sig. **.048**	Sig. **.017**	Sig. .505
/t͡ʃ/ > ʃ	.5348	.8074	−.2989
	Sig. .060	Sig. **.028**	Sig. .321
/s/ > θ	.2823	.6182	−.2773
	Sig. .308	Sig. .102	Sig. 317
/x/ > Ø	.3632	.0426	.0706
	Sig. **.028**	Sig. .880	Sig. .803
Speakers < 8 years of education (n = 15)			
NS = 4.00 ± 1.60			

Significant differences (2-tailed significance) in bold type. n = 25

3.3.2 Education   One of the most interesting findings reported in the context of our community study in Malaga was that scores on network markers are higher among less-educated people (Villena and Requena 1996: 41–46). Network structure is more important for the less-educated speakers, so that they tend more intensely to follow the network consensus of norms and, hence, vernacular linguistic norms. On the contrary, young educated speakers, even though they feel bound to their parents by family ties, are not equally related to the rest of the network links. This is one of the most important factors in explaining why young speakers follow standard norms.[16]

Table 12.5 shows correlation between the four phonological variables studied above and several markers of network strength and size. The objective is to reveal that there are differences between the educational groups with

---

[16] This inequality of network influence on speakers of different sex, age, or educational level has been considered by Milroy and Milroy (1992: 9–16), so that converse patterns have been suggested to exist.

regard to personal network effect on phonological variation. Illiterate speakers or those who had not completed their basic education scored higher than educated speakers in all network markers. The results of Avila's (1994) research into the above-mentioned urban social network of Capuchinos in Malaga inner city confirm this hypothesis. Differences exist and are significant in some cases. Of interest are those referring to the strength of ties. Mean scores of Network Strength Scale (NSS) are sharply different in each group of speakers. The group of less-educated speakers (n = 15) scored 4.00 ± 1.60, while the educated group (n = 10) scored 2.25 ± 1.43 ($\chi^2 = 6.5915$, sig. .0102). The remaining network scores were also divergent, but differences were not significant and showed only tendencies towards statistical significance. Table 12.5 reveals the separate correlation results between network markers and some of the phonological variables studied by Avila (1994) and Villena and Requena (1996). Results for educated speakers (>12 years of education) are much weaker and less significant, or of no significance at all, than those of illiterate speakers (<8 years of education). It is particularly striking how standard uses (/s/ : /θ/) are rejected by less-educated speakers when they are connected by strong ties (NSS, RNSS) to other people and, conversely, how they persist in the use of vernacular markers under the same network conditions. On the other hand, educated speakers behave as expected in that they do not accept vernacular markers of solidarity within the network (correlation is negative in all cases, though weak). In addition, they confirm the tendency observed below towards a positive relation between the number of ties (personal network size) and, let us say, the loyalty to the national standard.

3.3.3 The effect of the speaker's gender   Gender differences affect network composition and size. Male and female personal networks differ in that the former focus on workmates and friends, while the latter are based on relatives. Nevertheless, as differences are considered more carefully, it is obvious that they come from gender structural inequalities. Therefore, when status and labour are the same for both sexes, differences tend to vanish and male and female networks are much more alike (Moore 1990; Requena 1995).

Female speakers often constitute clusters where separate norms of speech behaviour with reference to male norms can be found. Polarised local communities tend then to be established where female variants are closer to the regional or the national standard (Villena and Requena 1996). Gender differences interact with social class, network structure, age and educational group, so that for some linguists, and under certain conditions, gender differences have more impact in the speech community than social structure does (Labov 1990; Milroy 1992). Let us consider again our own community situation.

Southern Spanish speakers alternate between two different models of pronunciation of fricatives /s/ and /θ/ (3.2.1): firstly, the so-called 'standard distinction'

Table 12.6 *Models of pronunciation of fricative /θ/ and /s/ in Spanish regional varieties*

Gloss	Example	Standard D /s̺/ : /θ /	Southern R /θˢ/	
			Sibilant R [s̺]	Nonsibilant R [θ]
house	*casa*	['kas̺a]	['kas̺a]	['kaθa]
hunting	*caza*	['kaθa]		
case	*caso*	['kas̺o]	['kas̺o]	['kaθo]
saucepan	*cazo*	['kaθo]		

(/s/ : /θ/) model (D) and secondly, the 'southern reduction' /θˢ/ model (R). The latter includes the alternative pronunciation of /θˢ/ as a sibilant [s̺] or as a nonsibilant fricative [θ] (i.e. a subphonemic contrast). As a result, speakers switch from one to another phonemic model, and from one to another way of /θˢ/ realisation (table 12.6).

This variation has strong social meaning in southern communities. Within the social network studied by Avila (1994), prototypical male nonsibilant reduction (NsR) and female sibilant reduction (sR) norms were found to be sharply separated, so that gender polarisation of language use was reported (Villena and Requena 1996). This polarisation was detected to increase as the speaker's educational level decreased, and as he or she showed only little media exposure. However, this polarisation tends to diminish as the speaker's educational level rises and his or her personal media exposure increases.

To represent this situation, a bipolar model of variation is proposed (figure 12.4). As shown, illiterate female and male speaker individual scores diverge as they gather, respectively, around mid and high values of sibilant [s̺] (mean $p = .72$) and nonsibilant [θ] (mean $p = .85$) pronunciation of fricative /θˢ/. Educated speakers, in turn, and without regard to their gender, tend to converge and cluster at the lowest values of both axes. This means that, since their scores in sR and NsR are low (mean $p = .10$ and $p = .25$, respectively), their choice is D and their mutual differences small (male $p = .77$, female $p = .64$). All these differences are significant: gender differences affect the subphonemic contrast between sibilant and nonsibilant /θˢ/, and education differences affect /s/ : /θ/ distinction (Villena and Requena 1996).

At the interactional level, network markers seem to confirm the pattern of variation commented on above. As shown in table 12.7 below, non-educated women from Capuchinos have close-knit social networks with fewer ties than do middle-class women. Their ties, however, are stronger and the female speakers are closer to one another. The latter observation can also be applied to men. Moreover, if we look at the educational differences with regard to the speaker's

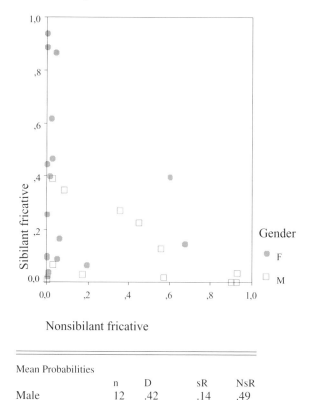

Fig. 12.4 Individual probabilities of sibilant and nonsibilant pronunciation of /θˢ/ among speakers from Capuchinos (Málaga). *Source:* Avila (1994).

Mean Probabilities				
	n	D	sR	NsR
Male	12	.42	.14	.49
Female	18	.50	.48	.11
Sig.		No sig.	.002	.005

role relations (0 vs. 2.50 and 0 vs. 3.00) we observe that they are especially striking. As Bott (1957) and Milroy (1980) showed, segregated gender roles and domestic tasks are very likely to occur within close-knit networks and, conversely, shared gender roles and common activities are usual among loose-knit weak-tie network speakers (cf. Coates 1986: 79–95). Results displayed in table 12.7 confirm this hypothesis with southern Spanish data, and lead to the conclusion that there can be a network-based explanation for gender and class polarisation. This explanation can probably be expressed as follows: a rise in the speaker's educational level leads to a rise in the number of ties and to a lowering in the strength of network ties. The more educated people are, the more people they know. Thus, they have access to other external norms of behaviour. In consequence, educated female speakers do not have to behave as

Table 12.7 *Gender and education differences in social network scores among Malaga speakers in Capuchinos (Málaga). A comparison with fricative pronunciation patterns*

Education						
	Male			Female		
	<8 years	>8 years		<8 years	>8 years	
Personal network size	2.00 ± 0.81	2.87 ± 0.83		2.90 ± 1.45	3.14 ± 1.07	
NSS	2.11 ± 0.92	3.00 ± 0.00		2.54 ± 0.82	2.28 ± 1.11	
RNSS	4.75 ± 2.62	2.62 ± 1.68		3.50 ± 2.38	2.83 ± 0.41	
Relational roles*	0.00	2.50 ± 2.50		0.00	3.00 ± 2.69	
/ṣ/ > θ (NsR)	.83 ± .17	.21 ± .21	**.001**	.15 ± .25	.01 ± .02	**.010**
/θ/ > ṣ (sR)	.01 ± .02	.18 ± .15	**.004**	.42 ± .36	.20 ± .17	**.034**
/ṣ/ : /θ/ (D)	.07 ± .13	.61 ± .29	**.009**	.54 ± .33	.82 ± .14	**.048**

n = 31 (male = 12; female = 18)
* Differences significant p < .002. Significant differences in bold type 'Relational Roles Scale' measures the sharing of roles and tasks within couples

prototypical women, as they do not have to be different from prototypical men. They share household tasks with men as their respective gender roles are no longer segregated. That is why male and female Capuchinos educated speakers are closer, even though women continue to use regional standard sR, as well as the national standard SD, which is the only choice for men.

4 Interpretive Social Network Analysis: Social Networks as Interacting Variables (Weak Hypothesis)

Some of the correlations commented on so far have been found to be weak or nonsignificant, so we must continue to suspect that we are probably dealing with hidden or underlying variables, which should be detected and analysed. Social network data may be used to understand the origin and development of psychosociological factors underlying the speaker's sociolinguistic choices. As shown through significant correlation, quantitative social network analysis is complementary to stratification analysis. What is needed now is the progressive adaptation of network techniques to explain individual variation and motivations. The *natural* way of accessing the speaker's social mode of life and history is his or her personal network.

4.1 Propositions

Inadequacies in speech and network correlation have to be corrected. Network quantitative analysis usually points to broad trends, ignoring details, but we need to fathom the nature of these details, as they are sometimes decisive for a better understanding. The three following propositions are important from an interpretive perspective of network-based sociolinguistic theory.

1. *Interpretive* complements of correlational work are needed if we wish to account for the speaker's entire social motivation in language variation and change. Correlational social network analysis is, then, a means of uncovering personal motivations and attitudes, but cannot on its own achieve this task. The role of the participant observer in fieldwork must be complemented with his or her role in the analysis itself. As far as possible, we should make use of the interpretive capacity of the participant-analyst.

2. The above proposition is based on more general criticism of quantitative network analysis, which constitutes a call to resist a *mechanical* interpretation of social-network theory. Such an interpretation leads to sociolinguistic network-based practice excessively dependent on standardised correlation.

3. The corollary of these statements is the existence within the social network of a *subset of relations* of which the speakers are not primarily conscious and, hence, this subset is beyond the quantitative analyst's scope. These underlying relations become discernible at the 'participant-analyst' stage of work and are a consequence of his or her interpretive role. This capacity springs from the ethnographic methodology adopted by a participant-analyst, who, like the 'modern stranger' has . . . 'his unique character of being both "within" and "without"' (Harman 1988: 3). The 'participant-analyst' combines involvement and detachment to capture relations which are out of the reach of both insiders and outsiders (Harman 1988: 93–160).

Convergence and divergence do not stop, then, with the network structures themselves. Nevertheless, our detailed knowledge of these structures allows us to see beyond them and to focus on individual variation, thus enabling us to carry out more comprehensive descriptions of speech communities. To be specific, what is particularly important at this stage of work is to know how to deal with intranetwork variation.

4.2   Interpretive social network analysis

4.2.1 Passive and active ways of convergence   Research has shown that, in general, people living in the same local community and related to one another through strong network ties, tend to use the same linguistic variants, especially those which are more salient, since they are felt to be signs of cohesion within the group. Hence, one would think that speech communities are formed by strictly split-up homogeneous local communities, where speakers' linguistic behaviour would be highly focused and regular (Milroy 1980: 12–22; Romaine 1982; Kerswill 1994: 22–27, 159–161). However, data from different speech communities reveal that internal social-network speech similarity is not as great as previously thought, and that the speaker's use of variables can converge towards that of models which are far removed from his or her own. Convergence through long-term accommodation is one of the most important mechanisms to explain how and why (Auer *et al.* 1997).[17]

The analyst's target at the 'participant-analyst' stage of work in social-network research is individual language variation. Since people within network clusters of friends or relatives maintain frequent and intense contact, they should speak alike. This is generally true, as seen above, but similarity does not mean *identity*. Even within close-knit core groups of speakers, personal or attitudinal factors and, indeed, individual conditions of social life may produce linguistic differences (cf. Marshall 2004). Such individual variation has been claimed to be the effect of either (1) the speaker's life-history; or (2) his or her position within the network structure (cf. section 2.1):

1. On the one hand, speakers who are connected through weak ties with members of a cluster may not be motivated to accommodate to the core members' varieties. Hence, they may develop external strong ties and converge to different speech norms.
2. On the other hand, practical aspects of individual life (such as job or market conditions) may affect the speaker's performance, as he or she will accommodate to the others' varieties in line with more general psychosocial accommodation.

One way of viewing this is to distinguish between two forms of convergence: (1) an internal or *passive* form of convergence within the peer group (let us say 'passive accommodation', in the sense that the speaker cannot but converge); (2) an *active* form of convergence towards external people (let us say, 'active accommodation', in the sense that the speaker chooses to diverge from his or her own peer group to converge towards the varieties of others). To cope with these types of personal decisions, a network interpretive analyst must start working from the stage where correlational analysis stops. The interpretive analyst must understand the reinterpretation speakers usually make of their own position in ordinary life. This interpretive stage should not be taken as separated from correlational analysis of social and network structures, as we have pointed out above. On the contrary, interpretive analysis is the final complementary stage of the general approach to language and language use. This comprehensive perspective of linguistic analysis allows us to avoid the disadvantages of ethnographic research; i.e. the absence of intersubjectivity.

4.2.2 Intranetwork variation   To give a general idea of what it is meant by this, let us consider once again (cf. section 3.3.1) the social network

---

[17] Cf. Trudgill (1986); and Mattheier (1996) for a thorough overview of this issue. With regard to the 'saliency question' and its influence on speech variation and convergence and divergence of dialects, see Hinskens (1996); and Kerswill and Williams (2002, 2002b).

Table 12.8 *Individual probabilities of two phonological variables among speakers from a network cluster in Nueva Málaga. Source: Cuevas (2001)*

Variables	Gender	/s/ : /θ/	$\widehat{\text{tʃ}} \rightarrow \text{ʃ}$	Network size	Multiplex ties
Speakers					
1	M	**.62**	**.94**	3	1
2	M	.75	.20	4	2
3	M	.78	.06	2	2
4	M	.80	.15	4	3
5	F	.85	.05	4	2
6	M	**.90**	**.65**	4	1
7	F	.97	.00	3	1
8	F	.98	.00	4	1
9	F	.98	.00	4	2
10	F	1.00	.00	2	2
Mean probability		.87 ± .12	.21 ± .33		
Male		.77 ± .10	.40 ± .38		
Female		.96 ± .06	.01 ± .02		

Gender differences significance: /s/ : /θ/ = .008; $\widehat{\text{tʃ}}$/ *Lenition* = .051

from Nueva Málaga (NM) investigated by Cuevas (2001). Two clusters were found: the 'friends' cluster (n = 10) was, according to Cuevas, 75.5 per cent dense. Personal and social variables were homogeneous within the cluster: 'friends' peer group speakers are very similar with regard to age, education, and so on (mean age: M = 28.8 ± 01.8, F = 27.4 ± 01.7; years of education: M = 18.6 ± 02.2, F = 17.4 ± 03.7). The cluster's members maintain frequent and intense contacts, reinforced by their membership of a voluntary church association, as explained above.

In this context of extremely close-knit network ties, which leads to a conspicuous similarity of social status and roles, the expected similarity in linguistic behaviour may be contradicted by the personal motivations of speakers; i.e. the definition of the individual's place within the linguistic market (*marché linguistique*).[18] To investigate that, let us look again at the individual patterns of the /s/ : /θ/ variable and the lenition of /t͡ʃ/ to [ʃ]. Table 12.8 summarises each of the two variables' single probabilities.

As shown, speech behaviour is fairly homogeneous within the cluster. Gender differences are strong and significant. However, network size and multiplexity differences are not significant, nor are media exposure or local loyalty. Lenition of /t͡ʃ/ is relatively high among male speakers (p = .40), but internal variation is also high (s.d. = ±.38). In spite of the strong similarity of social and personal

[18] Cf. Bourdieu (1984).

features, probabilities of lenition $\widehat{/t\int/} \to [\int]$ for speakers 1 and 6 diverge from
the rest of the male individuals (speakers 2, 3, and 4) within the cluster; they
are thus 'outliers'. The range of male probabilities goes from speaker 1 (.94) to
speaker 3 (.06), so that speakers 1 and 6 are responsible for the high male score
of $\widehat{/t\int/}$ lenition (.40 ± .38).

According to Cuevas, closeness and the strength of ties between this cluster's members are based on a shared life-history. They were all born in the
barrio ('neighbourhood'), where they attended school and joined a church voluntary association (*parroquia*). By the time they started university, the group's
contact frequency decreased, as one of the members (speaker 1) attended vocational school to become a skilled labourer, and another (speaker 6) applied to
a different faculty from speakers 2, 3, and 4, who all made the same choice.
Nevertheless, in spite of this slight looseness of ties, all of them maintained
almost daily contact with each other. Furthermore, speakers 1 and 6 are brothers.
Their family moved from another neighbourhood when they were young children. Though they feel very close to their friends, they also maintain some
contact with people from their parents' former neighbourhood. This *barrio* is
a traditional inner-city lower working-class district, called *La Trinidad*. Both
brothers belong to another different voluntary association, a *Cofradía* (church
fraternity), which is strongly associated with *La Trinidad* speakers. Their loyalty to this *Cofradía* is a common issue for discussion within the peer group, as
both brothers are even teased about it by the other cluster members. Therefore,
the use of high percentages of $\widehat{/t\int/}$ lenition by these two speakers is most likely
a consequence of their weak but regular contact with *La Trinidad* speakers at
the *Cofradía* meetings. Vernacular markers, such as $\widehat{/t\int/}$-lenition, among many
other signs of integration into the lower working-class *barrio*, may be seen
as symptoms of long-term accommodation, possibly accounting for something
beyond the network structure. One might say that both brothers, always loyal to
their friends, have slightly accommodated their speech to that of the *Cofradía*.
The standard Spanish distinction /s/ : /θ/ (D) is to them a sign of such a loyalty.
Moreover, the brothers' use of $\widehat{/t\int/} \to [\int]$ would point to a certain redefinition of
these speakers' positions or, indeed, the introduction into the 'friends' cluster
of a covert prestige feature through weak ties. The latter interpretation seems
to be supported by the relatively odd and infrequent co-occurrence of D and
lenited $\widehat{/t\int/}$ pronunciations, since the southern pronunciation of /s/ is dental [s̪],
not alveolar-palatal [s̺] (Villena 2001: 79–104).

5   Conclusion

The degree of the speaker's isolation from, or integration into, the speech
community is the most direct and revealing way of accounting for language
variation. Correlational methods of research have been shown to be useful in

accounting for similarity between speakers, based on their shared class, background, age, gender, etc. However, to penetrate the individual's choices in his or her everyday life, intermediate tools, such as social networks, are needed. Through the study of network structures we can understand why and how speakers are accepted or rejected by a particular group and, hence, know more about individual convergence towards, and divergence from, linguistic uses within the group.

The naturalness of social networks as stable interactive groups, and as a source of norms of behaviour, does not imply that they can necessarily be successfully used for explanatory purposes. Social network structures have been used as independent variables with promising results in some cases, but the impression is that they have been misused, as they have been employed only as correlational tools. However, social networks should be understood as they are. Gumperz (1997: 200) puts it very clearly:

> The social science concept that perhaps comes closest to capturing what is involved here is the notion of network. Although this term has other definitions, I use it here to refer to the kind of sharing that is likely to evolve among individuals who have a common history and have undergone similar communicative experiences within the context of institutional networks of relationships where members cooperate over relatively long periods of time in the achievement of common goals. (Gumperz 1997: 200)

With this in mind, it is possible to consider correlation between speech and network markers only as a means of locating speakers. But it is an important means. Thanks to it, the researcher gains access to the speaker's choices at the individual level and can then perform an interpretive analysis. This is, of course, a rather weak interpretation of the social network's explanatory power, but, in the end, it is the best way to take the investigation beyond a macrosocial correlational analysis. Furthermore, interpretive network analysis constitutes the third step of an integrated sociolinguistic theory with the following range: (1) correlational social-structural analysis (involving age, gender, etc.); (2) correlational social-network analysis; (3) interpretive social-network analysis.

13   The role of interpersonal accommodation in a theory of language change

Peter Auer and Frans Hinskens

1   Introduction

In this chapter, we will discuss the available evidence for Niedzielski and Giles'
claim that 'accommodation theory should be one of the major frameworks to
which researchers in language change should turn' (1996: 338). We will investigate the validity of a model of the implementation of structural language change
which is intricately linked to verbal communication in face-to-face situations,[1]
and which, if only for this reason, is highly appealing. In its prototypical version,
the model stipulates the following (hierarchically ordered) components.

1st component. In face-to-face communication between speakers with more
traditional speech habits and those who use an innovative form, the former
accommodates to the linguistic behaviour of the latter. Accommodation may
consist of either the adoption of the new feature and/or the abandonment of the
older one(s). It is the first case which may, in the long run, lead to the expansion of the innovation in geographical and social space. Thus, interpersonal
accommodation is seen as the root of any structural convergence or advergence
(as it should more correctly be called since in the prototypical case it is unilateral). However, interpersonal accommodation does not always lead to language
change, since it is restricted to the interactional episode at hand, i.e. it does not
always have a lasting effect on the accommodating speaker's linguistic 'habits'.
In order to have such an effect, two further steps are necessary.

2nd component. Short-term accommodation becomes long-term accommodation as soon as it permanently affects the accommodating speakers. This is
the case when they transfer the innovation from direct interaction with the
innovating speakers to situations in which these 'model speakers' fail to
be the addressees. Convergence (advergence), and therefore accommodation

---

[1] More adequate but less widespread than face-to-face communication is the term direct communication. With the advent of long-distance communication by telephone, temporally synchronised
interaction no longer requires face-to-face contact. The notion of direct communication excludes
both unidirectional, mass media communication and communication in which the act of communication is stretched out through the temporal separation of production and reception, as in
prototypical written communication.

of the innovation, now becomes an individual speech 'habit'. The model predicts that a person will be the more likely to take over a given feature into his or her own speech the more often he or she converses with a co-participant who displays the linguistic innovation. But, of course, such speech habits may be idiosyncratic and restricted to individual speakers. For language change in the usual sense of the word, something else is needed.

3rd component. The linguistic innovation may spread into the community at large, eventually leading to language change. Since long-term accommodation presupposes frequent exposure to this feature, spread into the community can be expected to proceed quickly when the innovators (i.e. those who adopt the spreading feature) are part of the same multiplex, dense, networks as the model speakers.

In sum, the model integrates three components into a hierarchy in which higher steps presuppose the lower ones (Auer and Hinskens 1996: 22):

Lowest level (interactional episode): short-term accommodation
   ↓
Middle level (the individual): long-term accommodation
   ↓
Highest level (speech community): language change

This scenario of the origins of language change has a long history which goes back to the beginnings of (social) dialectology, starting with the Neogrammarians (Paul 1870) and with classical dialect geography towards the end of the nineteenth and in the early twentieth centuries (cf. Auer in print). Dialectologists in particular have resorted to explicit or implicit models based on interactional frequency as they have tried to explain bundles of isoglosses at natural or (former) political boundaries by pointing to a lack of communication across these frontiers, or the spread of a feature by means of ease of communication along routes of 'intercourse' (*Verkehr* – in Paul's terminology). Labov (1990: 207), whose arguments are very much in line with the Neogrammarians in this instance (as in many others), calls change-through-accommodation the 'principle of intimate diversification' and describes it as follows: 'Each act of communication between speakers is accompanied by a transfer of linguistic influence that makes their speech patterns more alike.' He believes that this 'automatic and mechanical influence' is responsible for the so-called gravity model according to which innovations spread from larger to smaller communities.

A particularly sophisticated version of the model can be found in Trudgill's book *Dialects in Contact*, where he argues (1986: 39) that

in face-to-face interaction . . . speakers accommodate to each other linguistically by reducing the dissimilarities between their speech patterns and adopting features from each other's speech [= 1st component above]. If a speaker accommodates frequently enough to a particular accent or dialect, I would go on to argue, then the accommodation may in time become permanent, particularly if attitudinal factors are favourable. [= 2nd component above]. . . . People on average come into contact most often with people who live closest to them (40) [= one aspect of the 3rd component].[2]

As the extract makes clear, there is some ambiguity in the model concerning the driving forces behind the first step, or short-term accommodation; while some writers seem to believe in a mechanical process of imitation, or an attempt to optimise information transfer by using maximally overlapping codes, others argue that the accommodated speaker must hold some kind of prestige, and that the accommodating speaker attempts to gain his/her co-participant's social approval by using speech patterns that are familiar to him/her. This ambiguity itself has a long tradition, as it is already present in Bloomfield's account of 'dialect borrowing' in *Language* (1933: 476–477).

The model has undergone a number of revisions and engendered non-orthodox versions; for instance, in social psychological approaches to language variation (Giles *et al.* 1987; Giles, Coupland, and Coupland 1991), a distinction is drawn between objective (actual) and subjective (intended) accommodation (see below). Another revision of the model has been proposed by Bell (1984), who argues that it is not only the addressee that a speaker can accommodate to: speakers may also accommodate to third persons, such as auditors or even overhearers. For Bell, the degree of accommodation decreases the further away the 'audience' is, thus: addressee > auditor > overhearer (160, 163–167, 170–178). Bell's 'responsive' style matching, i.e. the accommodation by an individual speaker to a more or less distant audience, can be the short-term form of what may become 'long-term outgroup initiative style design' (Bell 1984: 187). This is a necessary step in the adoption of a new feature (a process that we will refer to as 'positive accommodation') or the abandonment of an old one ('negative accommodation'). For a critical evaluation, see Kerswill (2002: 680–682).

We will not discuss these non-orthodox versions of the model but, instead, restrict ourselves to the discussion of the original change-by-accommodation model which essentially relies on frequency of (direct) interaction, and on the adaptation of the behaviour of one person to that of another co-present speaker. In this sense, it may be opposed to what could be called an identity projection model[3] according to which the adoption of certain dialect features (or their suppression) is the outcome of the speaker's wish to identify with a certain

---

[2] Also cf.: 'We can assume that face-to-face interaction is necessary before diffusion takes place' (42), and: 'the geographical diffusion of linguistic forms takes place, for the most part, when face-to-face interaction between speakers from different areas happens sufficiently frequently for accommodation to become permanent, and on a sufficiently large scale for considerable numbers of speakers to be involved' (42).

[3] In Anglo-American research, this idea of language change and linguistic variation is often associated with Robert Le Page and his model of verbal 'acts of identity' (cf. Le Page and Tabouret-Keller 1985).

group (i.e. the consequence of projecting a persona of himself or herself); it is irrelevant whether the interlocutor belongs to this group or not. Although it requires the converging speaker to have some (possibly limited, or even mistaken) knowledge of the language of the model group, frequency of contact is not essential, and neither is face-to-face contact. Convergence rather proceeds towards an abstract image of the group.[4]

In the following sections, we will first look at general evidence for interpersonal short-term accommodation (section 2), and then concentrate on the more central issue of whether or not dialect change requires short-term dialect accommodation to proceed in a community (section 3). In section 4, we will briefly deal with evidence from network theory, as the third component of the change-by-accommodation model links the spread of an innovation on the community-level to frequency of interaction.

2   Evidence for Interpersonal Accommodation of Linguistic Features

Accommodation Theory has led to an impressive amount of empirical research. However, many studies cannot directly be linked to language change because the linguistic variables investigated are not those which undergo structural change (such as speaking tempo or the amount of joking), because it is not individual variables but whole varieties which are accommodated (as in code-switching, eventually leading to language shift), or because instead of linguistic variables, it is only the perception and evaluation of these variables by external judges that is investigated. However, there is some evidence for the mechanistic version of the change-by-accommodation model in the literature. Thus, the model receives indirect support from psycholinguistic research on syntactic priming according to which the realisation chosen in prior discourse can influence the choice of one variable form over another. For instance, Levelt and Kelter (1982) tested the matching or non-matching use of the preposition in the responses to Dutch questions such as

> *Aan wie laat Paul zijn viool zien?* (lit. 'To whom lets Paul his violin see?'
>   'Whom does Paul show his violin to?') vs.
> *Wie laat Paul zijn viool zien?* ('Whom lets Paul his violin see?' *idem*).

(In Dutch, both versions are equally acceptable.) They found a high covariation between the syntactic form chosen by the experimenter in the question and the informant's answer. Although the effect was stronger with some prepositions

---

[4] See Bell 2001 for a recent attempt to reconcile the two views, which he calls 'audience design' and 'referee design'.

(*naar*) than with others (*van*), the syntactic form of the question undoubtedly influenced that of the answer.

Corpus-based research on natural discourse supports these and similar results from experimental studies; for instance, in a study on Nigerian Pidgin English, Poplack, and Tagliamonte (1996) found that the best predictor of the use of tense/aspect forms (which are all optional in this variety) was not stylistic, social, or linguistic, but the mere fact of the occurrence of the same form in the preceding sentence.

The reason for this effect seems to be purely cognitive and for the most part unconscious: activated structures tend to be used again for the simple reason of already being available. There are some other studies in which structural repetitions of the words of one speaker by another – verbatim repetitions – were performed consciously. These repetitions usually receive sanctions, because they are perceived as being 'parody', or 'mimicking' by the speaker of the first token. Face-threatening repetitions of this kind have been reported from prosody, particularly intonation. Thus, Couper-Kuhlen shows that pitch register matching on an absolute scale in verbatim repetitions of prior speaker's utterances expresses a critical comment on the utterances (1996). Similarly, Schwitalla (2002) shows that verbatim repetitions (instead of ellipsis) regularly indicate disaffiliation or disagreement. In these cases, it is, of course, highly implausible that the 'accommodating' speaker may (permanently) adapt his or her speech behaviour to that of the speaker whose utterance is repeated.

The studies cited so far deal with local processes of accommodation across sentences or speaking turns. In contrast, the bulk of research on accommodation in social psychology is interested in accommodation over the course of the whole of an interactional episode by the speaker, who is hypothesised to adapt in order to 'gain the receiver's approval' (Giles 1973).

Convincing linguistic evidence for interpersonal accommodation of this type comes from Trudgill's (1986) *ex post hoc* analysis of his own sociolinguistic interviews carried out in Norwich, which shows that he accommodated to the speech of his informants very precisely – at least in some, salient sociolinguistic variables ('markers') such as glottalling/glottalisation of medial and final /t/ (Trudgill 1986: 8; see figure 13.1, below).

Another frequently mentioned piece of evidence for interpersonal accommodation is Coupland's study of a shop assistant in a Cardiff travel agency and her accent convergence towards the customers (Coupland 1984). When her mean values for dialect features, such as h-dropping, tapping of intervocalic /t/, alveolar instead of velar realisation of /ŋ/, and final cluster simplification, are compared with those of her customers (aggregated into occupational classes), the shop assistant's adaptation to the nonstandard speech of her customers becomes evident; cf. table 13.1 for absolute values and correlations.

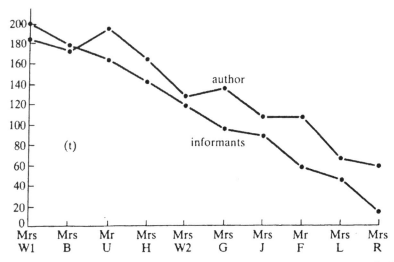

Fig. 13.1 Selected scores for the variable (t) in Trudgill's Norwich study (data reanalysed by the author, 1986: 8).

Table 13.1 *Range of percentual nonstandard usage in 'Sue' and her customers, aggregated into occupational groups (summarised from Coupland 1984)*

	Variation (% of nonstandard forms) in customers	Variation (%) in 'Sue'	Covariation
h-dropping	16.7–88.7	3.7–35.3	.87
/ŋ/ > /n/	0–100	53.8–85.7	.90
t-tapping	0–80	12.0–66.7	.76
cluster reduction	34–77.9	30.1–67.1	.86

Co-variation even increases when adaption is calculated relative to the individual speakers' phonological range.

However, in the interpretation of his results, Coupland rejects the idea of 'direct matching', and advocates an 'interpretive version' of Accommodation Theory which comes rather close to what we have called 'identity projection' above: 'If the participants' pronunciation characteristics converge, it is only as a result of attempts to reduce dissimilarities in social *images*' (1984: 65 [our emphasis]). This is, in fact, the view in many other studies as well: despite the claim by Niedzielski and Giles with which we began this chapter, and despite the contention of sociolinguists such as Labov or Trudgill, most

Table 13.2 *Use of the tag question* eh *by ethnic background and gender (M = Maori, P = Pakeha [Anglo], M = Male, F = Female, I.er = Interviewer, I.ee = Interviewee; data rearranged from Bell (2001: tables 9.2 and 9.3.; arrows: speaker to recipient, e.g. first line: index value 6 for male Maori interviewer speaking to male Maori interviewee, index value 46 for male Maori interviewee speaking to male Maori interviewer)*

Index value	Speaker/recipient constellation	Index value
6	MMI.er ↔ MMI.ee	46
10	MMI.er ↔ MFI.ee	2
0	MMI.er ↔ PMI.ee	0
28	MFI.er ↔ MMI.ee	2
25	MFI.er ↔ MFI.ee	4
35	MFI.er ↔ PFI.ee	0
29	PMI.er ↔ MMI.ee	19
0	PMI.er ↔ PMI.ee	0
14	PMI.er ↔ PFI.ee	0
5	PFI.er ↔ MFI.ee	0
3	PFI.er ↔ PMI.ee	1
9	PFI.er ↔ PFI.ee	0

social-psychological studies on accommodation question the first component of the change-by-accommodation model as stated above. Instead of advergence of one speaker to the observable behaviour of the recipient, they argue that speakers converge to a stereotype of the 'model' receiver, not the actual partner in direct communication.

As an example, consider the use of the discourse particle (tag question) *eh* in New Zealand English, a stereotype particularly of male Maori English. Bell (2001: 152ff.) has investigated this feature and found the *eh*-index values in table 13.2 in interview data.

For some speakers (interviewers and interviewees) there is no evidence of accommodation at all; the female Maori interviewer, the female Anglo interviewer, the female and the male Anglo interviewee and the female Maori interviewee show about the same index value with all partners. Most of them seldom or never use the tag *eh* and they therefore do not provide evidence for, or against, the accommodation hypothesis. The female Maori interviewer, however, shows relatively high index values irrespective of the moderate-to-zero values of her interviewees. This surely contradicts the predictions made by Accommodation Theory. The male Maori interviewer shifts between index values from zero and 10, but not in the predicted way: with the Maori female interviewee, he uses more *eh*-tags (10) than he does with the Maori male interviewee (6), despite the fact that the former hardly uses any but the latter speaker uses the highest amout of particles of all them (index value 46). Also incompatible with the accommodation model is the fact that the Anglo male interviewer, who does not use any *eh* with the Anglo male interviewee, increases their number considerably with the Anglo female interviewee, although both interviewees do not use the tags themselves.

More interesting than these results, which flatly contradict Accommodation Theory, are some others: as already mentioned, the male Maori interviewee uses a high amount of *eh*-tags despite the fact that his recipient, the male Maori interviewer, has very low index values. And the male Anglo interviewer uses the second highest amoung of *eh*-tags when talking to the male Maori interviewee, by far exceeding his co-participant's values. This points to the possibility that the speakers do not actually wish to conform to their co-participants' behaviour, but rather, to some kind of stereotype that they have of the way in which, say, typical Maori men speak (i.e. with many *eh*-tags).

Experimental research done by Giles and colleagues points in the same direction. Giles focused on 'accent mobility' (i.e. regional variation in British phonology) in his earlier work,[5] but in later publications he has replaced the notion of accent convergence/divergence by the more general term 'communicational accommodation', which now includes the accommodation of prosodic features, of 'information density', of 'joking', of gesture and posture, and much more (cf. Giles, Coupland, and Coupland 1991: 7). The link between structural convergence of linguistic features in face-to-face interaction and social psychological accommodation is now stated in very cautious terms (cf. Thakerar, Giles, and Cheshire 1982; Giles, Coupland, and Coupland 1991). One reason for being cautious is that experimental research showed that total convergence on such parameters as pronunciation, speech rate, and message content was not a good strategy to attain the listener's approval, and that phonetic accommodation in particular was often perceived as sounding patronising and was much less efficient in gaining the co-participant's social esteem than, say, accommodation of speech rate or content (Giles and Smith 1979). Other empirical results showed that the 'psychological dimension' (i.e 'individuals' beliefs that they are integrating with and differentiating from one another respectively' thus Thakerar, Giles, and Cheshire 1982: 222) must be strictly separated from the 'linguistic dimension' of convergence in actual speech behaviour. This leads the authors to the conclusion 'that accommodation is often cognitively mediated by our

---

[5] More precisely, he investigated *perceived* accent divergence and convergence, since the 'linguistic' side of his research usually consisted of judgements rather than factual phonological descriptions; cf. Giles (1973); Giles and Powesland (1975).

stereotypes of how socially categorized others will speak' (Giles, Coupland, and Coupland 1991: 16).[6],[7]

All these studies support the identity-projection model rather than the change-by-accommodation model: psychological convergence does not mean imitating the actual speech of one's co-participant, but rather conforming to some stereotyped image of how a person in the social role of the co-participant ought to, or can be expected to, behave.[8] A similar argument is provided by Selting (1983) in an investigation of style shifting in the speech of a then famous German radio presenter (Carmen Thomas in the WDR show *Hallo Ü-Wagen*). Selting demonstrates how the moderator adapts, not so much to the actual style of her callers when she used nonstandard, Ruhr German features, but rather, to a stereotype of colloquial Ruhr German. Similarly Christen (2000) shows how a Swiss German speaker on a TV talk show does not accommodate to the speech of any of his co-participants but orients himself to a general stereotype of 'acceptable' pan-Swiss German.

In sum, there is some evidence that interpersonal accommodation occurs, but is better explained as accommodation towards a stereotypical *persona* or mental representation (model) of a social group than as accommodation to the actually co-present interlocutor.

3   Short-term Accommodation and Language Change

For a theory of language change in general and dialect change in particular, the question of whether interpersonal dialect or accent accommodation exists is of secondary importance. Let us assume for the moment that there are at least some situations and some linguistic parameters in which such accommodation occurs. The crucial point for the convergence-by-accommodation scenario is that *accommodation is the first step to linguistic changes on the community level.* The model predicts that in those communities in which dialect convergence takes place, interpersonal accommodation should be observed as well, and in

---

[6] This shift in perspective was due to the unexpected results of several studies on accommodation in hierarchical situations, where, according to Accommodation Theory, the need to adapt to the speech of the more dominant (high-status) speaker should be particularly strong. In fact, it turned out that speakers *diverged* from each other in these hierarchical situations when compared to their behaviour in the equal-status condition.

[7] Cf. among others Giles and Bourhis (1976); and Beebe (1981). In the latter study, it was shown that Chinese–Thai bilingual children adopted Chinese phonology in an interview with a standard Thai speaker who looked Chinese.

[8] Another often-cited example Giles and colleagues use to illustrate the identity aspect of their model is intersexual attraction 'when two young people are out on a date' (Thakerar, Giles, and Cheshire, 1982: 218); here, masculine and feminine behavioural qualitites (including voice register, accent, dialect use) have to remain distinct, i.e. both partners adopt the norms of an absent group (that of young males or females).

the same linguistic variables that undergo linguistic change. There are several studies we can resort to in order to test this hypothesis.

3.1   Accommodation and change in Rimburg and Luxembourg

In his study of the dialect of Rimburg (southeast Limburg, Netherlands), Hinskens (1992) investigated face-to-face accommodation by speakers of the Rimburg dialect interacting with speakers of two adjoining, increasingly more standard-like, dialects and the regional standard variety. The hypothesis was tested that dialect levelling is foreshadowed in accommodation. It was operationalised in two steps:

(a) dialect use shows gradually differing extents of accommodation depending on both
   • the degree to which dialect features are unique to the speaker's dialect, and
   • the variety spoken by audience members – other things being equal
(b) accommodation and levelling show analogous patterns.

Both accommodation and dialect levelling were studied on the basis of fieldwork data which fit an experimental design. The data make it possible to relate both accommodation and dialect levelling to the parameters (apparent) time, geographical space, linguistic structure, as well as the geographical and structural distance between the varieties in contact.

The databases consisted of spontaneous dialect use in situations of in-group (labelled C1) and out-group contact. Three types of out-group contact were created:

• C2, contact with a speaker of a slightly different dialect variety, spoken a few kilometres west of Rimburg;
• C3, contact with a speaker of a fairly different variety of the dialect, spoken some 15 kilometres west of Rimburg; and
• C4, contact with a speaker of the regional variety of the standard language.

Accommodation was operationalised as the suppression of the usage of those features of the speaker's own dialect that do not occur in the interlocutor's dialect, i.e. as 'non-divergence' or 'negative accommodation'.

Accommodation was traced in the application of the rules for γ'-weakening (a local feature, which only occurs in the Rimburg dialect, i.e. in the C1 condition), n-deletion (which occurs in the dialects spoken in C1 and C2), and t-deletion (a supraregional feature, occurring in the dialects spoken in C1, C2, and C3) to the extent that it is manifested in significantly lower frequencies of use in out-group than in in-group contact situations.

The analyses of *accommodation* were carried out at three levels of specificity. On the first level of specificity, the average overall use of the three dialectal rules in in-group (C1) and out-group contact (aggregated over C2, C3, and C4) were

Table 13.3 *Mean use of the dialectal rules in in-group and out-group contact, the difference between the means and the one-tailed probability of the difference*

	I	O	d	p
ɣ⁻-weakening	31.62	22.26	9.36	.000
n-deletion	45.06	39.31	5.75	.022
t-deletion	80.32	76.52	3.80	.032

analysed. In table 13.3 the means of the overall in-group and the out-group use of the three dialect features are presented; the indexes range from 0 to 100. Remarkably, the out-group means for the use of the three dialect features are systematically lower than the in-group ones. It is particularly interesting that the differences in the use of the dialect features between in-group and out-group contact situations are smaller if the areal spread of the dialect features is wider.

In order to gain an insight into a range of main and interaction effects, multivariate analyses of variance[9] were carried out. On the basis of the outcomes of this statistical approach to the problem, accommodation was studied on a second level of specificity. This concerns the effect of in-group vs. out-group contact on the use of the three dialectal rules, both overall and in certain linguistic conditions. Overall, the in-group vs. out-group effect on ɣ⁻-weakening and t-deletion is highly significant (p = .001) and significant (p = .048), respectively, whereas it is just outside the level of significance for n-deletion (p = .065). These results accord well with those of the univariate analysis shown in table 13.3.

Taking into account the relative number of different linguistic conditions studied, accommodation is more evident as the areal spread of the dialect feature concerned is smaller. So, in this particular respect, accommodation is dialect-geographically gradual; the more a dialect feature is unique for a speaker's dialect, the bigger the relative number of different linguistic conditions in which he will accommodate its use in situations of out-group contact.

Compared to the analyses at the second level of specificity, those on the third level (which were equally based on outcomes of the multivariate analyses of variance mentioned earlier) add systematic differences between the three types of out-group contact situation, C2, C3, and C4. On the assumption that language accommodation is interactionally determined, it must be related not only to a

---

[9] With age group, out-group contact situation, and the interaction between these two as between-subjects factors and IvsO, age x IvsO, out-group contact situation x IvsO and age x out-group contact situation x IvsO as within-subjects factors. The analyses were carried out both on the overall level and in specific linguistic conditions.

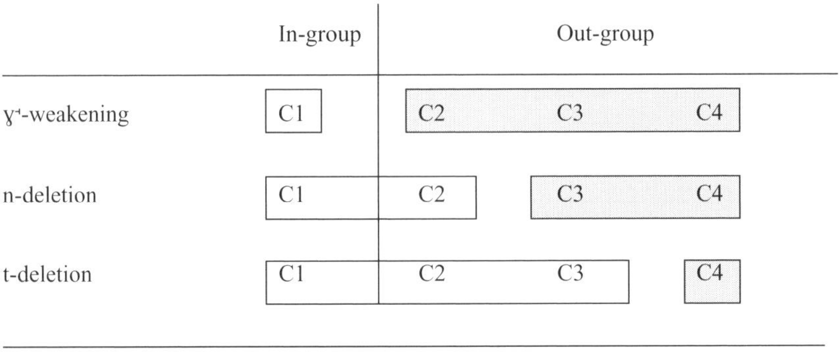

	In-group	Out-group		
ɣ'-weakening	C1	C2	C3	C4
n-deletion	C1	C2	C3	C4
t-deletion	C1	C2	C3	C4

Fig. 13.2 Shaded area: expected accommodation as a function of the distance of the three out-group contact varieties (from Hinskens 1992: section 11.3.2).

speaker's 'normal', everyday language use but also to the language use of his or her interlocutor. In the Rimburg data the first point of reference is the speakers' in-group dialect use (C1); the other one, the variety spoken by the interlocutor, was systematically varied between the three out-group contact situations C2, C3, and C4. Comparing the speakers' out-group dialect use to their in-group speech (C1) shows whether accommodation occurs. Relating accommodation to C2, C3, and C4 makes it possible to establish to what extent accommodation is determined by the language variety spoken by the interlocutors.

In Bell's (1984: 167) audience design, 'a sociolinguistic variable which is differentiated by certain speaker characteristics (e.g. by class, or gender, or age) tends to be differentiated in speech to addressees with those same characteristics'. Following this line of reasoning, one would predict accommodation to increase with the distance between the varieties involved in the out-group contact. This amounts to three predictions (not as such presented here; for details, cf. Hinskens 1992: section 11.3.2). Each of these predictions is a necessary, but not a sufficient, condition. Prediction 1 concerns the probability of the relevant interaction effect. The predictions 2 and 3 concern the direction of the interaction effect, i.e. the 'site' where the break should occur, seen from two different perspectives (cf. figure 13.2). The three predictions are therefore complementary. For a pattern in the data to be considered a case of geographically gradual accommodation in the sense of Bell's hypothesis, all three predictions need to be borne out simultaneously.

The outcomes of the required analyses show that none of the three dialectal rules meets all three predictions. So this part of the research shows (and a superficial inspection of the figures in table 13.4 already suggests this) that there is no evidence in favour of the idea that this kind of accommodation is related to the distance of the variety spoken by the out-group interlocutor, *contra* Bell.

Table 13.4 *Mean use of the three dialect features in the four interactional conditions (from Hinskens 1992: section 11.3.2)*

	In-group C1	Out-group C2	Out-group C3	Out-group C4
ɣ˙-weakening	31.62	22.70	16.30	27.78
n-deletion	45.06	48.95	35.01	33.97
t-deletion	80.32	74.18	80.45	74.94

In short, the claim according to which accommodation in dialect use is gradual is
• supported in so far as the degree to which dialect features are unique to a speaker's dialect allows predictions about the relative number of different linguistic conditions (such as grammatical status, position in the word, degree of stress, etc.; see Hinskens 1992 (section 11.4.2) or 1996 (section 11.3.2)), in which accommodation occurs;
• rejected in so far as the structural distance of the interlocutor's variety is concerned.

So much for part (a) of the operational hypothesis. Moving on to part (b): does this approach produce any evidence for the reflection of *levelling* in *accommodation*? The answer depends partly on how the notion of dialect level- ling is operationalised. If it is operationalised as either the loss of geographically limited dialect features, or the growing use of widely distributed ones, in short as structural homogenisation across dialects, the hypothesis is supported by Hinskens' findings. The effects of the variables age group and in-group vs. out-group contact (second level of specificity) show identical patterns across the three dialect features. Both reach statistical significance in the use of the rules for ɣ˙-weakening and t-deletion, but not in the speakers' application of the n-deletion rule. As for n-deletion, it is most remarkable that the effects of the factors age group (p = .059) and in-group vs. out-group contact (p = .065) on the overall use are both just outside the level of significance.[10] Both accom- modation and levelling seem to hesitate, as it were, in the overall application of the n-deletion rule. And two out of the four linguistic conditions in which this deletion rule is undergoing significant levelling exhibit nearly significant accommodation effects.

In sum, there is sufficient support for the hypothesis that levelling (3rd component) is foreshadowed in accommodation (1st component of the model

---

[10] Note that the p-values in table 13.3 refer to the significance of the *difference* in the mean use of each dialect feature between in-group and out-group contact in a *univariate* analysis, whereas the latter p-value mentioned here refers to the significance of the *effect* of in-group vs. out-group contact in a *multivariate* analysis.

discussed in section 1) if levelling is defined as structural homogenisation across dialects, and operationalised as either the loss of dialect features with a relatively restricted areal spread (ɣ⁻-weakening and n-deletion) or the increasing use of fairly widespread features (t-deletion). If, however, the meaning of the notion dialect levelling is restricted to the loss of dialect features, there is considerably less evidence in favour of the hypothesis, since the use of the t-deletion rule shows accommodation but the opposite of loss.

Another recent investigation in which language change and interpersonal accommodation were studied and which, therefore, can be used to test our hypothesis is Peter Gilles' study of the dialects of Luxembourg (*Letzebuergesch*, Gilles 1999). When compared to the data in the *Luxemburgischer Sprachatlas* (Linguistic Atlas of Luxembourg) which was compiled in 1925–1939, the situation today is characterised by a high amount of levelling between the various dialect areas, usually with the dialect of the capital (Luxembourg city) as the winner.[11] Yet in interdialectal speech (i.e. conversation between speakers from the various dialect areas) Gilles found no accommodation in most of his variables. For instance, the eastern and northern dialects of Luxembourg are today in the process of converging towards the central Luxemburg pronunciations /i/ and /u/ for older /ei/, /ə/, /ig/, etc., and /ou/, /ug/, /aː/, respectively (Gilles 1999: 153). Nevertheless, of the three speakers of the northern and eastern dialects in the sample who in an intradialectal conversation (i.e. with co-participants from the same area) still used a more than negligible number of the older forms at all, two (O1, O2) *increased* the use of the older forms in the interdialect condition, while only one (N1) decreased it (figure 13.3).

All three speakers were investigated in interaction with co-participants who did not, or only rarely, use the diphthongal, non-central forms. It seems that the way in which the three informants adjusted their speech to the interdialectal situation varied on an individual rather than on a systematic basis, and certainly not in accordance with the change-by-accommodation model.

The same picture emerged for the variable (ei), which is also in a process of levelling towards the diphthongal form, typical of the speech of the southern and central areas, i.e. the standard variety (Gilles 1999: 183). Of the four northern and eastern speakers, who still used the areally peripheral monophthongal forms with some frequency in the intradialect condition, three differed only very moderately in the intra- and the interdialectal condition; two of them shifted towards the monophthongal variant, one increased the diphthongal realisation (cf. figure 13.4). Only one informant (N3) accommodated to her co-participant's

---

[11] Gilles shows this to be the case by comparing questionnaire-type wordlists with the LSA data, which were collected in a similar way. In interview data the differences are even more pronounced.

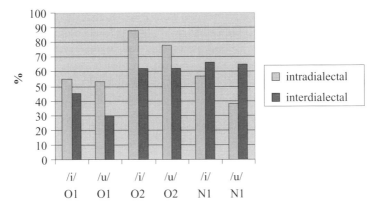

Fig. 13.3 Standard (i.e. non-Luxemburg city) realisations of the variables (i) and (u) in high-scoring dialect speakers from the east (O1 and O2) and the north (N1) (= nonstandard speakers) in intra- and interdialectal condition (from Gilles 1999: 153).

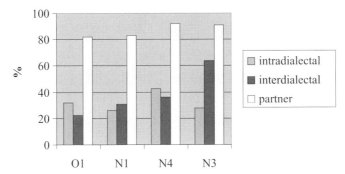

Fig. 13.4 Standard (i.e. Luxemburg city) realisations of the variable (ei) in high-scoring dialect speakers from the east (O1) and the north (N1, N4, N3) in intra- and interdialectal condition, and the scores of their interlocutors (from Gilles 1999: 183).

speech by reducing her northern monophthongs in a way that is unlikely to be due to chance.[12]

Finally, let us look at Gilles' analysis of the variable /aː/ in the inter- and intradialectal condition, the only variable in his study which, at first glance,

[12] In figure 13.4, the scores for the out-group co-participants refer to their speech in the intradialectal condition, since Gilles does not provide the respective figures for the interdialectal condition. The two do not differ in important ways, however (P. Gilles, pers. comm.).

Table 13.5 *Realisation of /aː/ in Luxembourg (shaded areas refer to changes since the 1920s/1930s; from Gilles 1999: 111)*

Variants	North	East	South	Centre (capital)
[aː]	+	+	+	+
[ɔː]	[ɔː~aː]	[ɔː~aː]	[ɔː~aː]	–
[oː]	[oː~ aː]	[aː]	[aː]	–
[ɑː]	[ɑː ~ɑː]	–	–	–

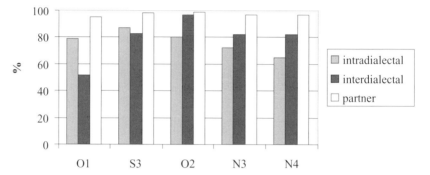

Fig. 13.5 Standard (Luxembourg city) realisation of the variable (aː) in high-scoring vernacular speakers and their partners from the centre area in intra- and interdialectal contexts (from Gilles 1999: 106).

provides evidence for interdialectal interpersonal accommodation. In the variation space /aː (~ æː)~ ɔː/ for the reflexes of OHG /a/ and /ou/, Gilles once again finds massive levelling towards /aː/, the variant of the centre and of Luxembourg city. As shown in table 13.5, older forms different from the Luxembourg city (central) realisation are now in variation with the central form [aː], in the north, the east, and the south. [oː] has disappeared in the east and south entirely. Only the eastern and southern [aː]-forms have resisted levelling towards [aː]. Figure 13.5 illustrates the use of the central form in intradialect and interdialect conversational speech.

All conversational partners in the interdialectal condition used less back/raised, i.e. more standard realisations, than the speakers investigated. In three out of these five cases, accommodation towards the standard forms took place; only in one case was there the opposite effect (O1); one speaker showed no change. This can be interpreted as evidence for face-to-face accommodation. The exceptional case of O1, who used more nonstandard features in interacting with a non-backing/raising partner than with a backing/raising partner, is of some interest, however; whereas all other informants were recorded while speaking to an informant of the central area in the interdialectal condition, speaker O1 talked to another speaker from the east who, on the basis of her highly diverging (but still eastern) dialect, was classified as coming from a different dialect area (Niederdonven vs. Vianden; cf. Gilles 1999: 68). Although this conversational partner of O1 used the standard, non-velarised forms as often as the partners of S3, O2, N3 and N4 did, O1 responded very differently from her, by *increasing* her use of the peripheral forms instead of reducing them. This factual *divergence* is plausibly explained as being a case of 'psychological accommodation' towards the stereotype of the northern and eastern speakers, along the lines of Thakerar *et al.*'s argument mentioned above. It seems that with speakers from the central area the number of non-central forms is suppressed, while in interaction with speakers from the periphery, an increase in the dialectal forms can be observed, independently of the actual speech behaviour of their partners, simply because they are *known* to come from the periphery.

The studies by Hinskens and Gilles therefore do not support the change-by-accommodation model in any straightforward way. Although in both cases (that of the Limburg dialects of Dutch and that of the Luxembourg dialects), an ongoing language change can be observed at the community level, individual speakers do not, or only in a few cases, accommodate to others who do not use the divergent dialect features (Hinskens), or who in their speech already use the spreading feature much more frequently or even exclusively (Gilles).

4   Network Structure

Let us finally turn to the third part of the change-by-accommodation model as outlined above. It seems relatively uncontroversial that long-term accommodation foreshadows change on the community level (cf. Kerswill 2002a); however, the data presented in this article make it less clear whether more *frequent* interaction with persons whose speech displays the new, spreading feature should favour long-term accommodation in the individual and thereby in the community. One way of testing the hypothesis is to build on the insights of network theory, taking the position of the speakers in the network, their types of network contacts, and, in particular, the intensity of these contacts, into account.

The first generation of sociolinguistic studies based on the concept of social networks (Labov 1973; Milroy 1980) focused on the conservative effect of dense and multiplex network structures (i.e. their effectiveness in slowing or preventing change, in particular a shift from more local to more regional or standard way of speaking). There is some evidence, however, that densely structured networks with a tight internal organisation and frequent intensive contacts between members may not only prevent but also favour the diffusion of a change once the change is admitted. This is not as contradictory as it may appear; while densely structured networks will keep an innovation out for a long time, as soon as it has entered the community (at relevant positions in the network) there is a good chance that it will spread fast. For instance, Kerswill and Williams (2000) argue that the emerging local variety of the new town of Milton Keynes is shaped in important ways by older children and adolescents. The adoption of variants which may eventually become features of the Milton Keynes variety, such as fronting of the diphthong /ou/ ([æʏ], [æɪ]) in words like *goat*, seems to crucially depend on the networks of these young speakers. Kerswill and Williams summarise their findings as follows: 'All the high scorers [for fronting of (ou)] . . . are very well integrated into a (mainly school-centred) group of friends; they are sociable and are often cited as friends by other children. By contrast, the low scorers are largely cut off from their peers.' And they conclude, following Labov: 'It is not the socially peripheral . . . groups who innovate, but groups with more resources and more extensive social contacts.' Note, however, that while the peer group had a high linguistic appeal for these young speakers, and a considerable impact on their speech, the language of their mothers, with whom they arguably had just as frequent and intense contacts, was entirely irrelevant to them linguistically. What does seem to be involved are not only matters of frequency or intensity of network contacts, but also issues of identity. Peers have social appeal, mothers do not.

There are other studies which support the idea that strong network contacts favour change. For instance, Siebenhaar (1999) is able to show in his study on language change in Aarau (Switzerland) that those speakers in his sample who had more social contacts with the west (Zurich) used significantly fewer eastern (Berne) phonological variants[13] than did those who had their more important social contacts in the east. Here, lacking network contacts with Berne speakers and having strong contacts with Zurich speakers seem to have shaped the speakers' dialect as well. On the other hand, and following a very different line of thinking in network theory, one which echoes Granovetter's insistence on the importance of 'weak-network' ties for the transmission of information and innovation from one community to another (Granovetter 1973), Milroy and Milroy have claimed that 'outside influence increases in inverse proportion to strength of ties in a group' (Milroy and Milroy 1985b, 1992). According to this view, we need to distinguish between the central areas of a multiplex and dense network and the peripheral areas in which community members may have numerous but superficial network ties with people from diverging social backgrounds. In the central areas, the network impedes innovations from spreading, since people firmly positioned in this zone are too saturated with social contacts to reorient themselves socially and to be willing to accept new forms. But in the peripheral areas, we will find the innovators: those members of the community

---

[13] To be more precise, he found this effect in his factor '2', which he dubs 'phonological', whereas his factor '1' ('morphology') showed no such effect.

who are familiar with many ways of life and, therefore, also with the ongoing innovations.

Barden and Großkopf (1998)[14] address this question in a study on long-term dialect accommodation as a consequence of migration by Saxon (east German) speakers into two different dialect areas in the west and south of Germany during, or shortly after, the collapse of the GDR. Internal migration is a suitable testing ground for the relevance of weak- and strong-network ties for linguistic accommodation, since it is essentially linked to network formation. Migrants are almost always in a situation in which old networks break down and new ones must be constructed. On the other hand, they are confronted with strong local networks. Depending on the way in which they relate to these local networks, three main integration types can be distinguished:

1. Immigrants may join networks with other immigrants from the same background, erecting a dense social structure around them which provides shelter against the new social environment and mutual help to survive socially in relative autonomy. Contacts with local members are restricted to a minimum. Linguistic accommodation is not required and does not take place. Rather, linguistic developments in the group are suppressed, sometimes more than in the society from which the migrant group has originated. This case of segregated but strong networks was never observed in the Saxon migrants but is, of course, well known from overseas migration out of Europe (prototypically in the so-called language islands).

2. Immigrants may join the local networks and become members of a densely structured social aggregate in which the locals are dominant. This applied to 19 out of the 52 informants (integration type 'A'). These Saxons were highly satisfied with their new social environment; contacts with Saxon compatriots no longer played an important role in their new life. According to the third component of the change-by-accommodation model, short- and long-term accommodation of the local speech habits can be expected, since there is frequent interactional contact with local speakers. At the same time, this accommodation will lead to the suppression of the salient features of the Saxon vernacular.

3. Immigrants may not succeed, or not be interested, in establishing strong network ties with any – local or migrant – network; instead, they are engaged in open networks, with unstable, rapidly changing and often superficial contacts. Since this case was quite frequent, three subtypes were distinguished, i.e.

   • migrants who where satisfied with this situation (18 informants, integration type 'B');

   • migrants who were unhappy with this situation, and who attempted to change their situation (although unsuccessfully); in doing so, and in

---

[14] Cf. Barden and Großkopf (1998) as well as for summaries Auer, Barden, and Großkopf (1998); and Großkopf, Barden, and Auer (1996). The figures are taken from Barden and Großkopf (1998).

Table 13.6 *Mean loss of Upper Saxon Vernacular features and adoption of local features*[a]

Integration type	A	B	C	D
loss of Saxon features	38%	27%	−29%	45%
adoption of local features	yes	no	no	yes

[a] For more details, cf. Großkopf, Barden, and Auer (1996); intermediate types AB and BC have been left out of the table here for clarity. They do not alter the argument. The minus value in integration type C indicates an increase of Upper Saxon Vernacular features, i.e. a divergence from the standard-speaking co-participants.

experiencing failure, they developed a strong dislike for the receiving region and for West Germany in general. Their attitudinal and factual orientation was backwards towards Saxony (this applied to a small subgroup of 4 speakers, integration type 'C');

• finally, migrants who were also unhappy with this situation and made an effort to change it (again without much success), but had no orientation towards Saxony; rather, they tried to make their way in the West (a group of 10 informants, integration type 'D').

According to the change-by-accommodation model, informants with weak ties with members of the local community would not be expected to accommodate the local dialect features nor give up their own vernacular; however, they would be ideal carriers of an innovation back into the Saxon context according to Granovetter's and Milroy's theory. The overall results of the longitudinal study which spanned over a period of two years[15] are summarised in table 13.6, above; they refer to the relative loss of Upper Saxon features (average of all 13 phonological variables investigated), i.e. *negative* accommodation (cf. Hinskens' study discussed in section 3.1 above), and to accommodation to the local regiolect (*positive* accommodation).

A look at some phonological variables gives a more concrete picture of the impact of network structure on long-term accommodation (cf. figures 13.6 and 13.7). A typical distribution is the one shown in figure 13.7 for the variables 'lowering of long /eː/' (as in /leːben/ 'to live' → [lɛːbm]), 'unrounding of the high short vowel /y/' (as in /hʏtə/ 'hut' → [huʊtə]), and 'monophthongisation of /au/ (> MHG /ou/)' (only calculated in the word /aux/ 'also' > [ɔːx]). In all these variables, it is integration type D which loses most Upper Saxon Vernacular.[16] The less-frequent pattern, in which type A surpasses type D with

[15] Informants were recorded in three-monthly intervals by speakers of standard German who had neither a local West German nor an East German accent.
[16] Figures include strong and weak Upper Saxon Vernacular realisations.

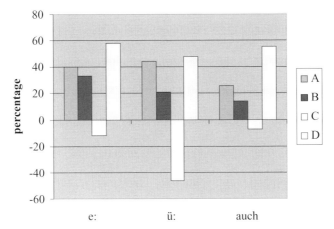

Fig. 13.6 Degree of loss of the Upper Saxon Vernacular features lowering of /eː/, unrounding of /yː/, and monophthongal realisation of /ou/ in the word *auch* according to network types.

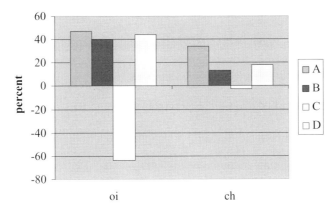

Fig. 13.7 Degree of loss of the Upper Saxon Vernacular features unrounding of /oi/ onset and coronalisation of /x/ according to network types.

respect to the loss of Upper Saxon Vernacular features, is exemplified in figure 13.7 by the variables 'coronalisation of /ch/' (as in /liːgt/ → [liːçt] → [lijt]) and 'unrounding of /oi/' (as in /froind/ 'friend' → [fʀɔ̃int]). As it turns out, integration type D accommodates to the standard variety more than the other integration types in 9 of the 13 variables; integration type A in three variables, integration type B in only one. In types A and D we also find accommodation to the local dialect.

These results clearly show that a fast and successful integration of immigrants into local networks can lead to accommodation, in the sense of taking on local features and losing one's own old regional features. On the other hand, and possibly more surprisingly if one thinks in terms of the change-by-accommodation model, accommodation by the socially integrated speakers of type A is often surpassed by type D speakers, who, with respect to network structure, represent the opposite case: here we find speakers with loose and ephemeral network contacts who are highly dissatisfied with their social life, yet who try to make their way in the West. The amount of linguistic accommodation decreases markedly in those speakers who live in networks similar to those of type D but are quite content with their situation (type B). Finally, there is no accommodation at all, but rather divergence from the local way of speaking (and a return to a more Saxonian Vernacular) in the (few) speakers who show a strong backward orientation to Saxony, again combined with weak network ties and a highly negative perception of one's own situation. It appears that the best predictor of accommodation is not frequency of interaction with speakers of the variety to which they accommodated, but, instead, a strong attitudinal orientation towards the group with whom one wants to associate, or a strong attitudinal dissociation from those from whom one wants to dissociate. This finding supports the identity-projection instead of the accommodation model.

5   Summary and Conclusions

One of the unresolved questions of a theory of language change is how structural change on the level of the speech community relates to the variable use of linguistic features in verbal interaction. In this chapter, we have looked at a relatively simple way of linking the two, which we have called the change-by-accommodation model. It suggests that the driving force of language change is interpersonal accommodation (convergence). After having discussed the results of some studies relevant for testing the validity of this model, we certainly cannot exclude the possibility that participants in interaction accommodate to each other's behaviour, nor can we exclude the possibility that the frequency of exposure to a new, spreading, feature through intensive network contacts with its users can lead to the adoption of this variable. It has been difficult, however, to find evidence for the co-occurrence of interpersonal accommodation and community-level change. Several findings suggest that the driving force behind change in the individual, and also in the community, is not imitation of the language of one's interlocutor but, rather, an attempt to assimilate one's language to the possibly stereotyped characteristics of a group one wants to be part of, or resemble. Only such a view is compatible with the well-known phenomenon of hypercorrection (or, for that matter, hyperdialectalism). The hypercorrecting speaker arguably overshoots the target of the actual speech behaviour of the group he or she wants to resemble; behavioural data are not available to a sufficient degree, or are not perceived with the necessary accuracy, to replicate the target group's speech behaviour, and since the stereotype is different from actual behaviour, the speaker overcompensates. This more abstract, identity-related motivation for the selection of certain forms of speech can go together with interpersonal accommodation if the speaker wants to resemble the group to which his or her co-participants belong, and if his or her stereotype of this group is close to the co-participant's actual behaviour. This, however, is by no means always the case. In the absence of such a fit between behavioural data in face-to-face encounters and stereotyped social personae, the latter seem to override the effect of the former.

References

Abraham, W. (1999). 'Preterite decay as a European phenomenon', *Folia Linguistica* 33 (1): 11–18.

Abraham, W. and Bayer, J. (eds.) (1993). *Dialectsyntax*. Opladen: Westdeutscher verlag.

Abrahamson, W. H. F. (1812). *Versuch einer vollständigen dänischen Sprachlehre für Deutsche.*

Ackema P. and Schoorlemmer, M. (1994). 'The middle constructions and the syntax-semantics interface', *Lingua* 93: 59–90.

(1995). 'Middles and nonmovement', *Linguistic Inquiry* 2: 173–197.

Adams, M. (1987). 'From Old French to the theory of pro drop', *Natural Language and Linguistic Theory* 5: 1–32.

Agard, F. (1971). 'Language and dialect: some tentative postulates', *Linguistics* 65, 5–24.

Aitchison, J. (1981). *Language Change: Progress or Decay?* London: Fontana.

(1991). 2nd edn. *Language Change: Progress or Decay?* Douglas, Isle of Man: Fontana.

Akselberg, G. (2003). 'Talevariasjon i Noreg'. In Mæhlum *et al.* (eds.), *Språkmøte. Innføring i sosiolingvistikk*. Oslo: Cappelen Akademisk Forlag, 144–165.

Alarcos Llorach, E. (1950, 4th edn. 1968). *Fonología española*. Madrid: Gredos.

Alfonzetti, G. (1992). *Il discorso bilingue. Italiano e dialetto a Catania*. Milan: Angeli.

(1996). '"Neutralità" sociolinguistica e "neutralità" strutturale nel discorso italiano-dialetto'. In S. C. Sgroi and S. C. Trovato (eds.), *Letterature e lingue nazionali e regionali*. Rome: Il Calamo, 65–87.

Almagro, A. M. (1993). 'Semantic information in *se*-constructions in Spanish'. *Working Papers in Linguistics: Grammar and the Lexicon* 16: 136–154, University of Trondheim.

Altenhofen, C. V. (1996). *Hunsrückisch in Rio Grande do Sul. Ein Beitrag zur Beschreibung einer deutschbrasilianischen Dialektvarietät im Kontakt mit dem Portugiesischen.* (= *Mainzer Studien zur Sprach- und Volksforschung.* 21). Stuttgart.

Amara, M. H. (1999). *Politics and Sociolinguistic Reflexes: Palestinian Border Villages.* Amsterdam/Philadelphia: John Benjamins.

Andersen, G. (2001). *Pragmatic Markers and Sociolinguistic Variation: A Relevance-theoretic Approach to the Language of Adolescents.* Amsterdam: John Benjamins.

Andersen, H. (1973). 'Abductive and deductive change', *Language* 49 (4): 765–793.

(1988). 'Center and periphery: adoption, diffusion and spread'. In J. Fisiak (ed.), *Historical Dialectology. Regional and Social*. Berlin: Mouton de Gruyter, 39–83.

(1989). 'Understanding linguistic innovations'. In L. Breivik and E. Jahr (eds.), *Language Change. Contributions to the Study of its Causes*. Berlin: Mouton de Gruyter, 5–27.

Angelov, A. (2000). 'A Balkan political border as a factor for language divergence', paper presented at the first international conference on Language Variation in Europe (ICLaVE 1), Barcelona, 29 June–1 July.

Appel, C. (2001). *Læsning og Bogmarked i 1600-tallets Danmark*. Copenhagen: Det Kongelige bibliotek/Museum Tusculanum.

Appel, R. (1999). '"Ik mix gewoon, no span". De straattaal van jongeren in Amsterdam', *Onze Taal* 68 (1): 140–143.

Arašonkava, A. and Mackevič, J. (1968). 'Ab belaruskix dyjalektnyx rysax zaxodnjaha pahranička ['On the Belarusian dialect features of the western border region']. *Slavia Orientalis* 17 (3): 273–280.

Archangeli, D. and Langendoen, D. T. (1997). *Optimality Theory: An Overview*. Oxford: Blackwell.

Arends, J. (ed.) (1995). *The Early Stages of Creolization*. Amsterdam: Benjamins.

Arends, J., Muysken, P., and Smith, N. (eds.) (1995). *Pidgins and Creoles. An Introduction*. Amsterdam/Philadelphia: Benjamins.

Armstrong, N. (1997). *Social and Stylistic Variation in Spoken French*. Amsterdam: John Benjamins.

Arnold, J., Blake, R., Davidson, B., Schwenter, S., and Solomon, J. (eds.) (1996). *Sociolinguistic Variation: Data, Theory and Analysis*. Stanford: CSLI.

Asfandiarova, D. (1999): '>Mir verzehle doch Lutherisch und die Katholisch< – Dialektmischung im Vokalismus in der deutschen Sprachinsel Prišib/Aleksejevka (Baschkortostan, Russische Föderation)'. In G. Brandt (ed.), *Historische Soziolinguistik des Deutschen* IV: *Soziofunktionale Gruppe – Kommunikative Anforderungen – Sprachgebrauch. Internationale Fachtagung, Rostock, 13.-16.09.1998. (= Stuttgarter Arbeiten zur Germanistik*. 372). Stuttgart, 241–262.

Aubin, H., Frings, T., and Müller, J. (1926). *Kulturströmungen und Kultur provinzen in den Rheinlanden. Geschichte, Sprache, Volkshunde*. Bonn (Röhrsheid).

Auburger, L. and Kloss, H. (eds.) (1979). *Deutsche Sprachkontakte in Übersee. Nebst einem Beitrag zur Theorie der Sprachkontaktforschung*. Tübingen.

Auer, P. (1988). 'MHG î and û in the city dialect of Constance'. In Auer and di Luzio, *Variation and Convergence Studies in Social Dialectology*. Berlin: de Gruyter, 44–75.

(1993). Zweidimensionale Modelle fur die Analyse von Standard/Dialekt-Variation und ihre Vorläufer in der deutschen Dialektologie. In W. Viereck (ed.), *Historische Dialektologie und Sprachwandel. Verhandlungen des internationalen Dialektologen-Kongresses Bamberg 1990*: 3–22.

(1997). 'Co-occurrence restrictions between linguistic variables. A case for social dialectology, phonological theory and variation studies'. In F. Hinskens, R. Van Hout, and W. L. Wetzels (eds.), *Variation, Change and Phonological Theory*, Amsterdam/Philadelphia: Benjamins, 69–100.

(1998a). 'Dialect levelling and the standard varieties in Europe'. In P. Auer (ed.), *Dialect Levelling and the Standard Varieties in Europe. Folia Linguistica* 32, 1/2, 1–9.

(1998b). 'Führt Dialektaubbau zur Stärkung oder Schwächung der Standardvarietät? Zwei Fallstudien'. In K. Mattheier and E. Radtke (eds.), *Standardisierung und Destandardisierung europäischer Nationalsprachen.* Frankfurt am Main, etc.: Lang, 129–162.

(1999a). 'Das versteckte Prestige des Türkischen. Zur Verwendung des Türkischen in gemischtetnischen Jugendlichen Gruppen in Hamburg'. In I. Gogolin and B. Nauck (eds.), *Migration, gesellschaftliche Differenzierung und Bildung: Resultate des Forschungsschwerpunktprogramms FABER.* Opladen: Leske and Budrich, 97–112.

(1999b). 'From code-switching via language mixing to fused lects: towards a dynamic typology of bilingual speech', *International Journal of Bilingualism* 3 (4): 309–332.

(in press). 'Phonological Change'. In U. Ammon *et al.* (eds.), *Handbook of Sociolinguistics/Handbuch der Soziolinguistik,* 2nd edn. Berlin: de Gruyter.

(in press). 'Europe's sociolinguistic unity; or, a typology of European dialect/standard constellations'. In N. Delbecque *et al.* (eds.), *Perspectives on Variation.* Berlin, etc.: Mouton de Gruyter.

Auer, P. and Hinskens, F. (1996). 'The convergence and divergence of dialects in Europe. New and not so new developments in an old area,' *Sociolinguistica* 10: 1–30.

Auer, P., Barden, B., and Großkopf, B. (1997). 'Long-term linguistic accommodation and its sociolinguistic interpretation: evidence from the inner German migration after the Wende'. In *Dialect Migration in a Changing Europe.* Frankfurt: Peter Lang.

Auer, P. Barden, B., and Grosskopf, B. (1998). 'Subjective and objective parameters determining "salience" in long-term dialect accommodation', *Journal of Sociolinguistics* 2: 163–187.

Avanesaŭ, R. I., Atraxovič, K. K., and Mackevič, J. F. (1963). *Dyjalektalahičny atlas belaruskaj movy* [Dialectological atlas of the Belarusian language]. Minsk: Vydavectva Akadèmii navuk BSSR.

Avanesaŭ, R. I. *et al.* (1968). *Linhvistyčnaja heahrafija i hrupoŭka belaruskix havorak* [Linguistic geography and the classification of Belarusian dialects]. Minsk: Navuka i tèxnika.

Avila, A. M. (1994). 'Variación reticular e individual de s/z en el Vernáculo Urbano Malagueño: Datos del barrio de Capuchinos'. *Analecta Malacitana* 17 (1994): 343–367.

Bach, A. (1934, 1950). *Deutsche Mundartforschung.* Heidelberg: Carl Winter Verlag.

Baden, J. (1785). *Forelæsninger over det Danske Sprog eller Resonneret Dansk Grammatik.* Copenhagen: P. Horrebow.

Bailey, C.-J. (1973). *Variation and Linguistic Theory.* Arlington, Va: Center for Applied Linguistics.

Bailey, G., Wikle, T., and Tillery, J. (1993). 'Some patterns of linguistic diffusion'. *Language Variation and Change* 5: 359–390.

Bally, C. (1968). *Linguistique générale et linguistique française,* 4th edn. Berne: Francke.

Bakker, P. and Maarten, M. (eds.) (1994). *Mixed Languages. 15 Case Studies in Language Intertwining.* Amsterdam: IFOTT.

Bakker, P. and Marcel, C. (eds.) (1991). *In the Margin of Romani.* Amsterdam (Publikaties van het Instituut voor Algemene Taalwetenschap, Universiteit van Amsterdam, 58).

Bard, E., Robertson, D., and Sorace, A. (1996). 'Magnitude estimation of linguistic acceptability', *Language* 72: 1–31.

Barden, B. and Großkopf, B. (1998). *Sprachliche Akkommodation und soziale Integration: sächsische Übersiedler und Übersiedlerinnen im rhein-/moselfränkischen und alemannischen Sprachraum.* Tübingen: Niemeyer.

Barnes, J. A. (1954). 'Class and committees in a Norwegian island parish', *Human Relations* 7 (1954): 39–58.

Barry, M. V. (1981). 'The southern boundaries of Northern Hiberno-English speech'. In Michael V. Barry (ed.), *Aspects of English Dialects in Ireland: 1*, 52–95. Belfast: The Institute of Irish Studies, The Queen's University of Belfast.

Bauer, L. (1988). 'What is lenition?', *Journal of Linguistics* 24: 381–392.

Bayard, D. (1990). 'Minder, Mork and Mindy? (-t) glottalisation and post-vocalic (-r) in younger New Zealand English speakers'. In A. Bell and J. Holmes (eds.), *New Zealand Ways of Speaking English*. Clevedon: Multilingual Matters, 149–164.

Bayley, R., and Pease-Alvarez, L. (1996). 'Null and expressed pronoun variation in Mexican-descent Children's Spanish', in Arnold *et al.* (eds.): 85–99.

Beal, J. (1993). 'The grammar of Tyneside and Northumbrian English'. In Milroy and Milroy (eds.): 187–213.

Beals, K., Denton, J., Knippen, R., Melnar, L., Suzuki, H., and Zeinfeld, E. (eds.) (1994). *Papers from the 30th Regional Meeting of the Chicago Linguistic Society, Vol. 2: The Parasession on Variation in Linguistic Theory*. Chicago: Chicago Linguistics Society.

Beckman, M. E., De Jong, K., Jun, S.-A., and Lee, S.-H. (1992). 'The interaction of coarticulation and prosody in sound change'. *Language and Speech* 35(1/2): 45–58.

Beebe, L. (1981), 'Social and situational factors affecting communicative strategy of dialect code-switching', *International Journal of the Sociology of Language* 32: 139–149.

Bell, A. (1984). 'Language style as audience design', *Language in Society* 13(2): 145–204.

   (2001). 'Back in style: reworking audience design'. In P. Eckert and John R. Rickford (eds.), *Style and Sociolinguistic Variation*. Cambridge: Cambridge University Press, 139–169.

Belletti, A. (ed.) (1993). *Syntactic Theory and the Dialects of Italy.* Turin: Rosenberg & Sellier.

Belletti, A. and Shlonsky, U. (1995). 'The order of verbal complements: a comparative study', *Natural Language and Linguistic Theory* 13: 489–526.

Bellmann, G. (1998). 'Between base dialect and standard language'. In P. Auer (ed.), 'Dialect levelling and the standard varieties in Europe', *Folia Linguistica*, 32: 1–2, 23–34.

Benincà, P. (1996). 'Agglutination and inflection in northern Italian dialects'. In Parodi *et al.* (eds.), 59–72.

(ed.) (1989). *Dialect Variation and the Theory of Grammar.* Dordrecht: Foris.

(1994). *La Variazione Sintattica.* Bologna: Il Mulino.

(1988). *Piccola storia ragionata della dialettologia Italiana.* Padua: Unipress.

Bennike, V. (n.d.). Three handwritten specimens of the author's own language (Institut for Dansk Dialektsamlings manuskriptsamling).

Bentahila, A. and Davies, Eirlys E. (1998). 'Codeswitching: an unequal partnership'. In R. Jacobson (ed.), *Codeswitching Worldwide.* Berlin and New York: de Gruyter, 25–49.

Berend, N. and Jedig, H. (1991). *Deutsche Mundarten in der Sowjetunion. Geschichte der Forschung und Bibliographie.* Marburg: Elwert.

Bernard, J. R. L. (1969). 'On the uniformity of Australian English', *Orbis* 18: 62–73.

Bernstein, J. (1991). 'DPs in French and Walloon: evidence for parametric variation in nominal head movement', *Probus* 3: 1–26.

Berrendonner, A. (1993). 'Sujets zéro'. In S. Karaloc and T. Muryn (eds.), 'Complétude et incomplétude dans les langues romanes et slaves'. *Actes du VIe Colloque de linguistique romane et slave, Cracovie, sept 29–oct 3*, Cracow: 178–146.

Berruto, G. (1970). *Dialetto e società industriale nella Valle d'Andorno. Note per una sociologia dei sistemi linguistici*, Supplementi al BALI, Torino.

(1989). 'Tra italiano e dialetto'. In G. Holtus, M. Metzeltin, and M. Pfister (eds.), *La dialettologia italiana oggi. Studi offerti a Manlio Cortelazzo*, Tübingen, Narr: 107–122.

(1990). 'Italiano regionale, commutazione di codice e enunciati mistilingui'. In M. Cortelazzo and A. Mioni (eds.), *L'Italiano regionale.* Rome: Bulzoni, 105–130.

(1995). *Fondamenti di sociolinguistica.* Rome, Bari: Laterza.

(1997a). 'Linguistica del contatto e aspetti dell'italianizzazione dei dialetti: appunti di creolistica casalinga'. In G. Holtus, J. Kramer, and W. Schweickard (eds.), *Italica et Romanica. Festschrift für Max Pfister zum 65. Geburtstag*, Tübingen, Niemeyer: 13–29.

(1997b). 'Code-switching and code-mixing'. In M. Maiden and M. Parry (eds.), *The Dialects of Italy.* London, New York: Routledge, 394–400.

Bertz, S. (1975). *Der Dubliner Stadtdialekt.* Doctoral dissertation, Albert-Ludwigs-Universität, Freiburg.

(1987). 'Variation in Dublin English', *Teanga* 7: 35–53.

Bex, T. and Watts, R. J. (eds.) (1999). *Standard English. The Widening Debate.* London/New York: Routledge.

Biber, D. (1988). *Variation across Speech and Writing.* Cambridge: Cambridge University Press.

Biber, D., Johansson, S., Leech, G., Conrad, S., and Finegan, E. (1999). *Longman Grammar of Spoken and Written English.* Harlow: Pearson Education.

Biberauer, T. (to appear). 'How real is embedded V2? Evidence from Afrikaans'. In F. Hinskens, H. den Besten, and J. Koch (eds.), *Afrikaans. Een drieluik.* Leipzig: Leipziger Universitätsverlag.

Bickerton, D. (1975). *Dynamics of a Creole System.* Cambridge: Cambridge University Press.

(1977). 'Pidginization and creolization: language acquisition and language universals'. In A. Valdman (ed.), *Pidgin and Creole Linguistics*, Indiana University Press, 49–69.

Bjerrum, A. (1973). 'On bilingualism in Slesvig'. In A. Bjerrum, *Linguistic Papers*. Copenhagen: Akademisk Forlag, 51–74.

(1990). 'Sprogskiftet i Sydslesvig og dets Årsager', *Danske Folkemål*, 32: 1–34.

Blanc, H. (1968). 'The Israeli koine as an emergent national standard. In J. Fishman, C. Ferguson, and J. Das Gupta (eds.), *Language Problems of Developing Nations*, New York: John Wiley, 237–251.

Blanche-Benveniste, C. (1997). 'La notion de variation syntaxique dans la langue parlée', *Langue Française* 115: 19–29.

Blevins, J. (1995). 'The syllable in phonological theory'. In J. Goldsmith (ed.), *The Handbook of Phonological Theory*. Oxford: Basil Blackwell, 206–244.

Blom, J. P. and Gumperz, J. J. (1972, 2nd edn. 1986). 'Social meaning in linguistic structures: codeswitching in Norway'. In J. J. Gumperz and D. Hymes, *Directions in Sociolinguistics. The Ethnography of Communication*. Oxford and New York: Basil Blackwell, 407–434.

Bloomfield, L. (1933). *Language*. London: Unwin, 9th reprint (1969).

Boberg, C. (2000). 'Geolinguistic diffusion and the U.S.–Canada border, *Language Variation and Change* 12: 1–24.

Boeschoten, H. (1997). 'Convergence and divergence in migrant Turkish'. In K. Mattheier (ed.), *Dialect and Migration in a Changing Europe*. Frankfurt am Main: Lang, 145–154.

Bohnenberger, K. (1913). *Die Mundart der deutschen Walliser im Heimattal und in den Aussenorten*. (= *Beiträge zur Schweizerdeutschen Mundart* 6). Frauenfeld.

Boissevain, J. (1974). *Friends of Friends. Networks, Manipulators and Coalitions*. Oxford: Blackwell.

Boissevain, J. (1987). 'Social network'. In U. Ammon, N. Dittmar, and K. J. Mattheier (eds.), *Sociolinguistics. An International Handbook of Language and Society*, (Vol. 1). Berlin/New York: Walter de Gruyter. 164–169.

Bolognesi, R. (2001). 'L'arcaicità del Sardo fra stereotipi e teoria del mutamento linguistico', MS.

Borer, H. and Wexler, K. (1987). 'The maturation of syntax'. In T. Roeper, and E. Williams (eds.), *Parameter Setting*, Dordrecht: Reidel, 123–172.

Börjars, K. and Chapman, C. (1998). 'Agreement and pro-drop in some dialects of English', *Linguistics* 36: 71–98.

Börjars, K., Vincent, N., and Chapman, C. (1996). 'Paradigms, periphrases and pronominal inflection: a feature-based account'. In G. Booij and J. van Marl (eds.), *Yearbook of Morphology 1996*, Dordrecht: Kluwer, 155–180.

Bortoni-Ricardo, S. M. (1985). *The Urbanization of Rural Dialect Speakers. A Sociolinguistic study in Brazil*. Cambridge: Cambridge University Press.

Bott, E. (1957, 2nd edn. 1971). *Family and Social Network*. London: Tavistock.

Bourciez, É. (1967). *Éléments de linguistique romane*. 5th edn. Révisée par l'auteur et par les soins de Jean Bourciez, Paris.

Bourdieu, P. (1984). 'Capital et marché linguistiques', *Linguistische Berichte* 90: 324.

Boyce-Hendricks, J. (1998). 'Immigration and dialect convergence: on the rise in the use of the reflexive pronoun *zich* in the city dialects of early modern Holland', Paper presented at the ESF Conference. 'The Convergence and Divergence of Dialects in a Changing Europe' September. University of Reading: 17–19.

Bozzini, M. (1994), '*Sulla commutazione di codice italiano/dialetto in Ticino*', unpublished M.A. thesis, University of Zurich.

Brandi, P. and Cordin, P. (1989). 'Two Italian dialects and the null subject parameter'. In Jaeggli and Safir, (eds.): 111–142.

Brannigan, P. (1996). 'Tracing *that-* trace variation'. In J. R. Black and V. Motapanyane (eds.), *Microparametric Syntax and Dialect Variation*. Amsterdam: John Benjamins, 25–40.

Bredsdorff, J. H. 1933 (1817). 'Prøve af en efter Udtalen indrettet dansk Retskrivning'. In J. Glahder (ed.), *J. H. Bredsdorffs Udvalgte Afhandlinger*. Copenhagen: Levin & Munksgaards Forlag.

Bresnan, J. (1995). 'Linear order, syntactic rank and empty categories: on weak crossover'. In M. Dalrymple, R. M. Kaplan, J. T. Maxwell, and A. Zaenen (eds.), *Formal Issues in Lexical-Functional Grammar*, Stanford: CSLI, 241–274.

Brink, L. and Lund, J. (1975). *Dansk Rigsmål 1–2. Lydudviklingen siden 1840 med særlig henblik på sociolekterne i København*. Copenhagen: Gyldendal.

Britain, D. (1997a). '*Was/weren't* levelling in the East Anglian Fens'. *Essex Research Reports in Linguistics*. Colchester: University of Essex.

(1997b). 'Dialect contact, focusing and phonological rule complexity: the koineisation of Fenland English'. In C. Boberg, M. Meyerhoff, and S. Strassel (eds.), *A Selection of Papers from NWAVE 25. University of Pennsylvania Working Papers in Linguistics*, 4 (1): 141–170.

(1997c). 'Dialect contact and phonological reallocation: "Canadian Raising" in the English Fens', *Language in Society* 26: 15–46.

(1999). '*As far as* analysing grammatical variation and change in New Zealand English <*is concerned/ø*>'. In A. Bell and K. Kuiper (eds.), *New Zealand English*. Amsterdam: John Benjamins, 198–220.

(2002a) 'Diffusion, levelling, simplification and reallocation in past tense BE in the English Fens', *Journal of Sociolinguistics* 6(1): 16–43.

(2002b). 'Space and spatial diffusion'. In J. K. Chambers, P. Trudgill, and N. Schilling-Estes (eds.), *The Handbook of Language Variation and Change*. Oxford: Blackwell, 603–637.

(2002c). 'Phoenix from the ashes?: the death, contact, and birth of dialects in England', *Essex Research Reports in Linguistics* 41: 42–73.

(2003). 'Geolinguistics – diffusion of language', in U. Ammon, N. Dittmar, K. Mattheier and P. Trudgill (eds.), *Sociolinguistics/Soziolinguistik. An International Handbook of the Science of Language and Society*. 2nd edn. Vol. I, Berlin: de Gruyter, 34–48.

(forthcoming). 'Where did New Zealand English come from?' In R. Harlow, D. Starks, and A. Bell (eds.), *The Languages of New Zealand*. Wellington: Victoria University Press.

Britain, D. and Trudgill, P. J. (1999). 'Migration, new-dialect formation and sociolinguistic refunctionalisation: *reallocation* as an outcome of dialect contact', *Transactions of the Philological Society*, 97: 245–256.

Brøndum-Nielsen, J. (1951). *Studier og Tydninger*. Copenhagen: Schultz.

Brown, G. (1972). *Phonological Rules and Dialect Variation*. Cambridge: Cambridge University Press.

Brown, L. A. (1981). *Innovation Diffusion*. London: Methuen.

Brown, R. and Gilman, A. (1960). 'The pronouns of power and solidarity'. In T. A. Sebeok (ed.), *Style in Language*. Cambridge, Mass.: MIT Press, 253–276.

Bücherl, R. F. J. (1982). 'Regularitäten bei Dialektveränderung und Dialektvariation. Empirisch untersucht am Vokalismus nord-/ mittelbairischer Übergangsdialekte', *Zeitschrift für Dialektologie und Linguistik* 49: 1–27.

Bullier, A. J. (1981). *Le parler franco-mauricien au Natal: une enclave francophone en Afrique du Sud: éléments d'une phonologie.* Paris.

Burt, R. S. (1984). 'Network items and the General Social Survey', *Social Networks* 6: 293–339.

Burzio, L. (1986). *Italian Syntax: A Government-Binding Approach.* Dordrecht: D. Reidel.

Butskhrikidze, M. and J. van de Weijer (2001). 'On de-affrication in Modern Georgian'. In T. van der Wouden and H. Broekhuis (eds.), *Linguistics in the Netherlands 2001.* Amsterdam Philadelphia: Benjamins, 41–51.

Butters, R. R. (1990). 'Current issues in variation theory'. Paper presented at the *First International Congress of Dialectologists*, 2 August, University of Bamberg.

Bybee, J. (2003). 'Mechanisms of change in grammaticalization: the role of frequency'. In R. Janda and B. Joseph (eds.), *Handbook of Historical Linguistics.* Oxford: Blackwell, 602–623.

Bynon, T. (1983). *Historical Linguistics.* Cambridge: Cambridge University Press.

Byrne, A. (1996). 'An investigation of some extrinsic and intrinsic constraints exerting pressure on phonological variation in Hiberno-English'. Unpublished project report, School of Clinical Speech and Language Studies, Trinity College Dublin.

Cajot, J. (1990). 'Neue Sprachgrenzbildung an der deutschen Staatsgrenze zu Niederländisch-Ostlimburg, Ostbelgien und Luxembourg'. In Kremer and Niebaum (eds.), 125–152.

Callary, R. (1975). 'Phonological change and the development of an urban dialect in Illinois', *Language in Society* 4: 155–170.

Cameron, R. (1992). 'Pronominal and null subject variation in Spanish: constraints, dialects and Functional Compensation. Unpublished Ph.D. diss., University of Pennsylvania.

Carden, Guy (1976). Syntactic and semantic data: replication results. *Language in Society*: S. 99–104.

Carroll, S. (1983). 'Remarks on FOR-TO infinitives', *Linguistic Analysis* 12: 415–451.

Carter, R. and McCarthy, M. (1999). 'The English *get*-passive in spoken discourse: description and implications for an interpersonal grammar', *English Language and Linguistics* 3: 41–58.

Cedergren, H. and Sankoff, D. (1974). 'Variable rules: performance as a statistical reflection of competence', *Language* 50: 333–355.

Chambers, J. K. (1979). 'Canadian English'. In J. K. Chambers (ed.), *The Languages of Canada.* Montreal: Didier.

   (2002). 'Patterns of variation including change'. In J. K. Chambers, P. Trudgill, and N. Schilling-Estes (eds.), *Handbook of Language Variation and Change.* Malden, Mass., and Oxford: Blackwell, 349–372.

   (2003). *Sociolinguistic Theory.* 2nd edn. Oxford: Blackwell.

Chambers, J. K. and Trudgill, P. J. (1980) *Dialectology.* Cambridge: Cambridge University Press.

   (1998). *Dialectology.* 2nd edn. Cambridge: Cambridge University Press.

Chapman, C. (1995a). 'A subject–verb agreement hierarchy: evidence from analogical change in modern English dialects'. In R. M. Hogg and L. van

Bergen (eds.), *Historical Linguistics*, Vol. 2, Amsterdam: John Benjamins, 35–44.

Cheshire, J. (1982). *Variation in an English Dialect: A Sociolinguistic Study.* Cambridge: Cambridge University Press.

  (1985). '*Never* and the problem of where grammars stop', *Polyglot* 6, Fiche 1: Dept of Applied Linguistics, Birkbeck College, London.

  (1987). 'Syntactic variation, the linguistic variable and sociolinguistic theory', *Linguistics* 25: 257–282.

  (1991a). 'Variation in the use of *ain't* in an urban British English dialect', in Trudgill and Chambers (eds.): 54–73.

  (1991b) (ed.), *English Around the World.* Cambridge: Cambridge University Press.

  (1994). 'Standardization and the English irregular verbs'. In D. Stein and I. Tieken-Boon (eds.), *Towards a Standard English.* Amsterdam: Mouton de Gruyter, 115–133.

  (1995). 'That jacksprat: an interactional perspective on English *that*', *Journal of Pragmatics* 25: 369–393.

  (1998). 'Taming the vernacular: some repercussions for the study of syntactic variation and spoken grammar', *Te Reo: Journal of the Linguistics Society of New Zealand* 41: 6–27.

  (1999). 'Spoken standard English', In T. Bex and R. J. Watts (eds.), *Standard English: The Widening Debate.* London: Routledge, 129–148.

  (2002a). 'Sex and gender in variationist research'. In J. K. Chambers, P. Trudgill, and N. Schilling-Estes (eds.), *Handbook of Language Variation and Change.* Malden, Mass., and Oxford: Blackwell, 423–443.

  (2002b). 'Border crossing: syntactic and pragmatic variation'. Plenary lecture, Methods in Dialectology XI, Joensuu, Finland, 6 August 2002.

  (in press). 'Syntactic variation and beyond: gender and social class variation in the use of discourse-new markers', *Journal of Sociolinguistics.*

Cheshire, J. and Edwards, V. (1991). 'Children as sociolinguistic researchers', *Linguistics and Education* 3: 225–250.

Cheshire, J. and Stein, D. (1997). 'Nonstandard and standard syntax'. In J. Cheshire and D. Stein (eds.), *Taming the Vernacular: From Dialect to Written Standard Language.* Harlow: Longman, 1–12.

Cheshire, J. and Williams, A. (2002). 'Information structure in male and female adolescent talk', *Journal of English Linguistics* 30: 217–238.

Cheshire, J., Edwards, V., and Whittle, P. (1989). 'Urban British dialect grammar: the question of dialect levelling', *English Worldwide* 10: 185–225.

Cheshire, J., Kerswill, P., and Williams, A. (1999). 'The role of adolescents in dialect levelling'. Final report submitted to the Economic and Social Research Council (ref. R000236180).

Chirrey, D. (1999). 'Edinburgh: descriptive material'. In P. Foulkes, and G. J. Docherty (eds.), *Urban Voices: Accent Studies in the British Isles.* London: Arnold, 223–229.

Cholewa, Jürgen (1993). 'Störungen der lexikalisch-morphologischen Wortverarbeitung bei Aphasie: Ein Literaturüberblick', In *Neurolinguistik* 7 (2): 105–126.

Chomsky, N. (1976). 'Conditions on rules of grammar', *Linguistic Analysis* 2: 303–351.

  (1981a). *Lectures on Government and Binding.* Dordrecht: Foris.

(1981b). 'Principles and parameters in syntactic theory'. In N. Hornstein and D. Lightfoot (eds.), *Explanation in Linguistics*. London: Longman, 32–75.

(1982). *Some Concepts and Consequences of the Theory of Government and Binding.* Cambridge, Mass.: MIT Press.

(1986a). *Barriers*. Cambridge, Mass.: MIT Press.

(1986b). *Knowledge of Language: Its Nature, Origin and Use*. New York: Praeger.

(1989). 'Some notes on the economy of derivation and representation'. In I. Laka and A. Mahajan (eds.), *MIT Working Papers in Linguistics 10: Functional Heads and Clause Structure,* Cambridge, Mass.: Dept of Linguistics and Philosophy, MIT, 43–74.

(1993). 'A minimalist program for linguistic theory'. In K. Hale and S. J. Keyser (eds.), *The View from Building 20*. Cambridge, Mass.: MIT Press, 1–52.

(1995). *The Minimalist Program*. Cambridge, Mass.: MIT Press.

(1999). 'Derivations by Phase'. Unpublished MS., MIT.

Chomsky, N. and Lasnik, H. (1977). 'Filters and control', *Linguistic Inquiry* 8: 425–504.

Christen, Helen (1998). 'Convergence and divergence in the Swiss German dialects'. In P. Auer (ed.), *Dialect levelling and the standard varieties in Europe. Folia Linguistica*, 32: 1/2, 53–67.

(2000). 'Chamäleons und Fossilien'. In D. Stellmacher (ed.), *Dialektologie zwischen Tradition und Neuansätzen*. Stuttgart: Steiner, 33–47.

Christensen, K. and Taraldsen, K. (1989). 'Expletive chain formation and past participle agreement in Scandinavian dialects'. In Benincà (ed.): 53–84.

Christian, D., Wolfram, W., and Dube, N. (1988). *Variation and Change in Geographically Isolated Communities: Appalachian English and Ozark English*. Publication of the American Dialect Society, 74, Tuscaloosa, Al.: University of Alabama Press.

Clahsen, H. (1991). 'Constraints on parameter setting: a grammatical analysis of some acquisition stages in German child language', *Language Acquisition* 1: 361–391.

Clahsen, H. and Muysken, P. (1986). 'The availability of UG to adult and child learners: the study of acquisition of German word order', *Second Language Research* 2: 92–119.

Clark, T. L. (1972). *Marietta, Ohio: The Continuing Erosion of a Language Island.* Publication of the American Dialect Society, 57. Alabama.

Clarke, S. (1986). 'Sociolinguistic patterning in a New World dialect of Hiberno-English'. In Harris *et al.* (eds.), *Perspectives on the English Language in Ireland*. Dublin: CLCS, Trinity College Dublin, 67–81.

(1991). 'Phonological variation and recent language change in St John's English'. In J. Cheshire, *English Around the World: Sociolinguistic Perspectives.* Cambridge: Cambridge University Press, 108–122.

(1997). 'The role of Irish English in the formation of New World Englishes: the case from Newfoundland'. In J. Kallen (ed.), *Focus on Ireland*. Amsterdam: Benjamins, 207–225.

Clemmensen, N. (1994). 'Bondevenner og bondevenner – to alen af et stykke? En komparativ undersøgelse af de danske og norske bondevenneorganisationer', *Fortid og Nutid* 2: 134–157.

2002. 'Adel under pres. Tysk eller dansk "Sonderweg"', *Historisk Tidsskrift*, 102(2): 451–467.

Clyne, M. (1967). *Transference and Triggering*. The Hague: Nijhoff.

Coates, J. (1986). *Women, Men and Language*. London/New York: Longman.

Coetsem, F. van (2000). *A General and Unified Theory of the Transmission Process in Languge Contact*. Heidelberg: Universitätsverlag C. Winter.

Collins, B. and Mees, I. M. (1996). 'Spreading everywhere? How recent a phenomenon is glottalisation in Received Pronunciation?', *English World-Wide* 17: 175–187.

Cornips, L. (1994). *Syntactische variatie in het Algemeen Nederlands van Heerlen (Syntactic variation in Heerlen Dutch)*. IFOTT 6. Dordrecht: ICG-Printing.

   (1996a). 'The spread of the reflexive adjunct middle in the Limburg dialects: 1885–1994'. In C. Cremer and M. Den Dikken (eds.), *Linguistics in the Netherlands 1996*. Amsterdam: John Benjamins, 45–60.

   (1996b). 'Social stratification, linguistic constraints and inherent variability in Heerlen Dutch: the use of the infinitival complementizers *om/voor*'. In Arnold *et al.* (eds.): 453–468.

   (1997). 'De betrouwbaarheid van de schriftelijke enquête Willems (1885): De adjunct middel in de Limburgse dialecten', *Gramma/TTT* 5 (2): 61–76.

   (1998a). 'Syntactic variation, parameters and their social distribution', *Language Variation and Change* 10 (1): 1–21.

   (1998b). 'Political borders and converging/diverging dialects and dialects/standard languages in Limburg (The Netherlands) and the surrounding area in Rhineland (Germany) between 1885 and 1994', Paper presented at the ESF Conference: *The Convergence and Divergence of Dialects in a Changing Europe*, 17–19 September, University of Reading.

   (2000). 'Variatie in reflexieve middel-constructies in het Heerlense dialect en in de Rijnlandse dialecten'. In H. den Besten, E. Elffers, and J. Luif (eds.), *Samengevoegde Woorden*. Amsterdam: Dept of Dutch Linguistics, University of Amsterdam, 33–45.

   (2000). 'The use of *gaan* + infinitive in narratives of older bilingual children of Moroccan and Turkish descent'. In H. de Hoop and T. van der Wouden (eds.), *Linguistics in the Netherlands 2000*, 57–67.

Cornips, L. and Hulk, A. (1996). 'Ergative reflexives in Heerlen Dutch and French', *Studia Linguistica* 50 (1): 1–21.

   (1999). 'Affected objects in Heerlen Dutch and Romance', *Languages in Contrast* 1(2): 191–210.

   (2002). 'Argumentreductie en aspekt in onpersoonlijke intransitieve constructies', *Nederlandse Taalkunde* 17, 1. 2–19.

Corrigan, K. P. (1993). 'Hiberno-English syntax: nature *vs.* nurture in a creole setting', *Newcastle and Durham Working Papers in Linguistics* 1: 95–131.

   (1996). 'The acquisition and properties of a contact vernacular grammar'. In A. Ahlqvist and V. Čapková (eds.), *Dán do Oide*. Dublin: Linguistics Institute of Ireland, 75–94.

   (1997). 'The Syntax of South Armagh English in its Socio-historical Perspective'. Unpub. Ph.D. diss. University College Dublin.

   (1998). 'Inviting the ugly sisters to the ball'. Paper presented at the ESF Conference: *The Convergence and Divergence of Dialects in a Changing Europe*, 17–19 September, University of Reading.

(2000). 'What are small clauses doing in South Armagh English, Irish and Planter English?' In H. L. C. Tristram (ed.), *Celtic Englishes II*. Heidelberg: Carl Winter Verlag, 75–96.

(2003). '*For-to* infinitives and beyond: interdisciplinary approaches to non-finite complementation in a rural Celtic English'. In H. L. C. Tristram (ed.), *Celtic Englishes III*. Heidelberg: Carl Winter Verlag, 318–338.

Coseriu, E. (1974). *Synchronie, Diachronie und Geschichte. Das Problem des Sprachwandels*. Übers. v. Helga Sohre. Munich.

(1980). '"Historische Sprache" und "Dialekt"'. In J. Göschel, P. Ivic, and K. Kehr (eds.), *Dialekt und Dialektologie*. Wiesbaden: Steiner, 106–122.

(1981). 'Los conceptos de "dialecto", "nivel" y "estilo de lengua" y el sentido proprio de la dialectología', *Lingua española actual* 3 (1): 1–32.

Coulmas, F. (ed.) (1997). *The Handbook of Sociolinguistics*. Oxford: Blackwell.

Couper-Kuhlen, E. (1996). 'The prosody of repetition: on quoting and mimicry'. In E. Couper-Kuhlen and M. Selting (eds.), *Prosody in Conversation*. Cambridge: Cambridge University Press, 366–405.

Coupland, N. (1980). 'Style-shifting in a Cardiff work-setting', *Language in Society* 9: 1–12.

(1984). 'Accommodation at work: some phonological data and their implications', *International Journal of the Sociology of Language* 46: 49–70.

(1988). *Dialect in Use: Sociolinguistic Variation in Cardiff English*. Cardiff: University of Wales Press.

Coveney, A. (1997). 'L'approche variationniste et la description de la grammaire du français', *Langue Française* 115: 88–100.

(2000). 'Vestiges of *nous* and the 1st person plural verb in informal spoken French', *Language Sciences* 22: 447–481.

(2002). 'Supplement: a critical survey of recent research on grammatical variability, negation and interrogation in French', *Variability in Spoken French*. Bristol: Intellect.

Craig, C. (1997). 'Language contact and language degeneration'. In F. Coulmas (ed.), *The Handbook of Sociolinguistics*. Oxford: Blackwell, 257–270.

Crain, S. (1991). 'Language acquisition in the absence of experience', *Behavioral and Brain Sciences* 14: 597–650.

Crowley, T. (1992). *An Introduction to Historical Linguistics*. 2nd edn. Oxford: Oxford University Press.

Cuevas, I. (2001). 'Variación social, reticular e individual de las consonantes obstruyentes palatales y dentales en Nueva Málaga'. Unpublished Ph.D. thesis. Área de Lingüística General. Málaga: Universidad de Málaga.

Cukor-Avila, P. and Bailey, G. (1996). 'The spread of urban AAVE: a case study', in Arnold *et al.* (eds.): 469–485.

Daan, J. (1987). *Ik was te bissie . . . Nederlanders en hun taal in de Verenigde Staten*. Zutphen: Walburg.

Daan, J., Deprez, K., van Hout, R., and Stroop, J. (1985). *Onze veranderende taal*. Utrecht/Antwerp: spectrum.

Dailey-O'Cain, J. (2000). 'The sociolinguistic distribution and attitudes towards focuser *like* and quotative *like*', *Journal of Sociolinguistics* 4: 60–80.

Dal Negro, S. (1998). 'The Swiss/Italian border: The emergence of new verbal mor-phosyntax in a Walser dialect'. Paper presented at the ESF Conference: *The Convergence and Divergence of Dialects in a Changing Europe*, 17–19 September, University of Reading.

Damsholt, T. (2000). *Fædrelandskærlighed og Borgerdyd*. Copenhagen: Museum Tusculanum.

Dauzat, A. (1922). *La géographie linguistique*. Paris: Flammarion.

Davies, P. (1992). 'The non-Bejing dialect component in Modern Standard Chinese'. In K. Bolton and H. Kwok (eds.), *Sociolinguistics Today. International Perspectives*. London/New York: Routledge, 192–206.

De Graff, M. (1997). 'Verb syntax in, and beyond, creolization'. In Haegeman (ed.): 64–94.

De Vink, L. (2004). 'Dialect en dialectverandering in Katwijk aan Zee'. Ph.D. thesis, University of Leiden.

De Wulf, E., Taeldeman, J. (forthcoming). 'Apocope en insertie van –n na sjwa in de zuidelijke Nederlandse dialecten: conditionering en geografie'. To appear in *Taal en Tongval*.

Den Besten, H. Muysken, P., and Smith, N. (1995). 'Theories focusing on the European input'. In Arends, Muysken, L. and Smith (eds.), 87–98.

Denning, K., Inkelas, S., McNair-Knox, F., and Rickford, J. (eds.) (1987). *Variation in Language. NWAV-XV* at Stanford.

Deprez, K. (1981). *Naar een eigen identiteit. Resultaten en evaluatie van tien jaar taalsociologisch en sociolingudstisch onderzoek betreffende de standaardtaal in Vlaanderen*. Ph.D. thesis, University of Leuven.

Déprez, V. and Pierce, A. (1993). 'Negation and functional projections in early grammar', *Linguistic Inquiry* 24: 25–67.

Dewulf, H., Van Keymeulen, J., and Verstraete, F. (1981). 'Westvlaamse expansie en standaardizering: een sociolingudstische benadering', *Taal en tongval* 33, 52–61.

Dillard, J. L. (1972). *Black English: Its History and Usage in the United States*. New York: Random House.

Dines, E. (1980). 'Variation in discourse – and stuff like that', *Language in Society* 9: 13–31.

Dinges, G. (1923). 'Ueber unsere Mundarten'. In *Beiträge zur Heimatkunde des deutschen Wolgagebiets. Mit einer Karte und einer Tabelle*. Pokrowsk a/W: 60–72.
   (1925). 'Zur Erforschung der wolgadeutschen Mundarten. (Ergebnisse und Aufgaben)', *Teuthonista* 1(4): 299–313.

Dittmar, N. and Schlobinski, P. (1985). 'Die Bedeutung von sozialen Netzwerken für die Erforschung von Ortssprachen'. In W. Besch and K. J. Mattheier (eds.), *Ortssprachenforschung. Beiträge zu einem Bonner Kolloquium*. Berlin: Erich Schmidt Verlag, 158–188.

Dixon, R. M. W. (1991). *A New Approach to English Grammar on Semantic Principles*. Oxford: Clarendon Press.

Docherty, G. J. and Foulkes, P. (1999). 'Derby and Newcastle: instrumental phonetics and variationist studies'. In P. Foulkes and G. J. Docherty (eds.), *Urban Voices: Accent Studies in the British Isles*. London: Arnold, 47–71.

Docherty, G., Foulkes, P., Parsons, L., Thompson, J., Tillotson, J., and Watt, D. (2000). 'Phonological variation in child-directed speech'. Paper presented at VIEW 2000, 14–16 September, University of Essex.

Docherty, G. J., Foulkes, P., Milroy, J., Milroy L., and Walshaw, D. (1997). 'Descriptive adequacy in phonology: a variationist perspective', *Journal of Linguistics* 33: 275–310.

Donnan, H. and Wilson, T. (1994). 'An anthropology of frontiers'. In H. Donnan and T. Wilson (eds.), *Border Approaches: Anthropological Perspectives on Frontiers*. Lanham, Maryland: University Press of America, 1–14.

Dressler, W. U. (1986). 'Explanation in natural morphology, illustrated with comparative and agent-noun formation', *Linguistics* 24: 519–548.

Dulson, A. (1933). 'Einige lautliche Eigentümlichkeiten der wolgadeutschen Mundarten'. In *Revolution und Kultur* 5. Engels: 46–54.

(1941). 'Problema skreschtschenija dialektow po materialam jasyka nemzew Powolshja'. In *Iswestija Akademii nauk Sojusa SSR, Otdelenie literatury i jasyka* 3: 82–96.

Dyer, J. A. (2000). 'Language and identity in a Scottish-English community: a phonological and discoursal analysis'. Ph.D. thesis, University of Michigan.

(2002). '"We all speak the same round here." Dialect levelling in a Scottish-English community', *Journal of Sociolinguistics* 6: 99–116.

Eckert, P. (1988). 'Sound change and adolescent social structure', *Language in Society* 17: 183–207.

(1989a). *Jocks and Burnouts: Social Categories and Identity in the High School*. New York: Teachers College Press.

(1989b). 'The whole woman: sex and gender differences in variation', *Language Change and Variation* 1: 245–268.

(2000). *Linguistic Variation as Social Practice*. Oxford: Blackwell.

Edwards, V. (1993). 'The grammar of southern British English.' In J. Milroy and L. Milroy (eds.), *Real English: The Grammar of English Dialects in the British Isles*. London: Longman, 214–238.

Edwards, V., Trudgill, P. J., and Weltens, B. (1984). *The Grammar of English Dialect: A Survey of Research*. London: ESRC.

Eisenberg, P. (1994). *Grundriss der deutschen Grammatik*. 3rd edn. Stuttgart: Metzler.

Eisikovits, E. (1991a). 'Variation in the lexical verb in inner-Sydney English', in Trudgill and Chambers (eds.): 120–144.

(1991b). 'Variation in subject–verb agreement in Inner Sydney English'. In J. Cheshire (ed.), *English around the World: Sociolinguistic Perspectives*. Cambridge: Cambridge University Press, 235–255.

Elordui, A. (1998). 'Changes in the verb–object agreement system of some Basque dialects', paper presented at the conference: *The Convergence and Divergence of Dialects in a Changing Europe*, 17–19 September, Reading.

Engelking, A. (1999). 'The *natsyas* of the Grodno region of Belarus: a field study', *Nations and Nationalism* 5 (2), 175–206.

Epstein, R. (1994). 'The development of the definite article in French'. In W. Pagliuca, (ed.), *Perspectives on Grammaticalisation*. [Current Issues in Linguistic Theory, 109]. Amsterdam: John Benjamins, 63–80.

(1995). 'The later stages in the development of the definite article: evidence from French'. In H. Andersen (ed.), *Historical Linguistics, 1993. Papers from the 11th International Conference on Historical Linguistics 16–20 August, 1993*. [Current Issues in Linguistic Theory, 124]. Amsterdam: Benjamins, 159–175.

Erman, B. (1993). 'Female and male usage of pragmatic expressions in same-sex and mixed-sex interaction', *Language Variation and Change* 4: 217–234.

Ervin, S. and Osgood, C. (1954). 'Second language learning and bilingualism', *Journal of Abnormal and Social Psychology* 49: 139–146.

Faarlund, J. T. (1985). 'Pragmatics in diachronic syntax', *Studies in Language* 9: 363–393.

Fagan, S. (1992). *The Syntax and Semantics of Middle Constructions. A Study with Special Reference to German*. Cambridge: Cambridge University Press.

Farrar, K. and Jones, M. C. (2002). 'Introduction'. In K. Farrar and M. C. Jones (eds.), *Language Change: The Interplay of Internal, External and Extra-Linguistic Factors*. New York: Mouton de Gruyter, 1–16.

Fasold, R. W. (1978). 'Language variation and linguistic competence'. In D. Sankoff (ed.), *Linguistic Variation: Models and Methods*. London: Academic Press, 85–95.

(1984). *The Sociolinguistics of Society*. Oxford: Blackwell.

(1990). *The Sociolinguistics of Language*. Oxford: Blackwell.

(1991). 'The quiet demise of variable rules', *American Speech* 66: 3–21.

Fasold, R. and Schiffrin, D. (eds.) (1989). *Language Change and Variation*. Amsterdam: John Benjamins.

Feagin, C. (1979). *Variation and Change in Alabama English: A Sociolinguistics Study of the White Community*. Washington, DC: Georgetown University Press.

Feldbæk, O. (1990). 'Den lange Fred'. In O. Olsen (ed.), *Gyldendal og Politikens Danmarkshistorie 1700–1800*, Vol. 9. Copenhagen: Gyldendal & Politiken.

(ed.) (1991–92). *Dansk Identitetshistorie*, Vols. 1–4. Copenhagen: C. A. Reitzel.

(1994). 'National identity in eighteenth-century Denmark'. In C. Bjørn, A. Grant, and K. Stringer (eds.), *Nations, Nationalism and Patriotism in the European Past*. Copenhagen: Academic Press, 137–145.

Ferrara, K. and Bell, B. (1995). 'Sociolinguistic variation and discourse function of constructed dialogue introducers: the case of be + like', *American Speech* 70: 265–289.

Filppula, M. (1995). 'The story of language contact in Ireland: how unique, how universal?', *Teanga* 15: 31–48.

Foldvik, A. K. (n.d.). 'The pronunciation of *r* in Norwegian with special reference to the spread of dorsal r'. Unpublished paper.

Foley, J. (1977). *Foundations of Theoretical Phonology*. Cambridge: Cambridge University Press.

Ford, C. E. (2001). 'At the intersection of turn and sequence: negation and what comes next'. In M. Selting and E. Couper-Kuhlen (eds.), *Studies in Interactional Linguistics*. Amsterdam: Benjamins, 51–79.

Foulkes, P. and Docherty, G. (eds.) (1999). *Urban voices. Accent Studies in the British Isles*. London: Arnold.

Foulkes, P., Docherty, G., and Watt, D. J. L. (1999). 'Tracking the emergence of structured variation', *Leeds Working Papers in Linguistics and Phonetics* 7: 1–25.

Foulkes, P. and Docherty, G. (1999). 'Urban voices: overview'. In P. Foulkes and G. Docherty (eds.), *Urban Voices: Accent Studies in the British Isles*. London: Arnold, 1–24.

(2000). 'Another chapter in the story of /r/: "labiodental" variants in British English', *Journal of Sociolinguistics* 4: 30–59.

Franceschini, R. (1998). 'Code-switching and the notion of code in linguistics: proposals for a dual focus model'. In P. Auer (ed.), *Code-Switching in Conversation. Language, interaction and identity*. London/New York: Routledge, 51–72.

Friedemann, M.-A. and Rizzi, L. (eds.) (2000). *The Acquisition of Syntax*. London: Longman.

Frings, Th. (1936). *Die Grundlagen des Meissnischen Deutsch*. Halle (Niemeyer).

Frings, Th. (1956). *Sprache und Geschichte*. Halle: Max Niemeyer Verlag.

Gadet, F. (1997). 'La variation, plus qu'une écume', *Langue Française* 115: 5–18.

Gal, S. (1979). *Language Shift: Social Determinants of Linguistic Change in Bilingual Austria*. New York: Academic Press.

    (1998). 'Cultural bases of language use among German-speakers in Hungary'. In P. Trudgill and J. Cheshire (eds.): *The Sociolinguistics Reader*. Vol. 1: *Multilingualism and Variation*. London: 113–121.

Gamrath, H. (1980). *Københavns Historie*, Vol. 2. Copenhagen: Gyldendal.

García, E. C. (1985). 'Shifting variation', *Lingua* 67: 189–224.

Geeraerts, D., Grondelaers, S., and Speelman, D. (1999). *Convergentie en divergentie in de Nederlandse woordenschat. Een onderzoek naar kleding- en voetbaltermen*. Amsterdam: Publikaties van het Meertensinstituut.

Geerts, G. (1983). 'Brabant als een centrum van standaardtaalontwikkeling in Vlaanderen', *Forum der Letteren* 24: 55–63.

Geerts, G., Haeseryn, W., de Rooy, J., and Van den Toorn, M. (eds.) (1984). *Algemene Nederlandse Spraakkunst*. Groningen: Wolters-Noordhoff.

Gerner, H. 1919 (1690). 'Epitome Philologiæ Danicæ', in H. Bertelsen (ed.), *Danske Grammatikere*, Vol. 3. Copenhagen: Gyldendal, 251–318.

Gerritsen, M. (1999). 'Divergence of dialects in a linguistic laboratory near the Belgian–Dutch–German border: similar dialects under the influence of different standard languages', *Language Variation and Change* 11 (1): 43–66.

Giacalone Ramat, A. (1995). 'Code-switching in the context of dialect/standard language relations'. In L. Milroy and P. Muysken (eds.), *One speaker, Two Languages. Cross-disciplinary Perspectives on Code-switching*. Cambridge: Cambridge University Press, 45–67.

Giegerich, Heinz, J. (1992). *English Phonology*. Cambridge: Cambridge University Press.

Giles, H. (1973). 'Accent mobility: a model and some data. *Anthropological Linguistics* 15, 87–105.

Giles, H. (ed.) (1984). The Dynamics of Speech Accommodation. *International Journal of the Sociology of Language*, 46.

Giles, H. and Bourhis, R. Y. (1976). 'Black speakers with white speech – a real problem?' In G. Nickel (ed.), *Proceedings of the 4th International Congress Applied Linguistics Vol. 1*, Stuttgart: Hochschul-Verlag, 575–84.

Giles, H., Bourhis, R., and Taylor, D. (1977). 'Towards a theory of language in interethnic group relations'. In H. Giles (ed.), *Language, Ethnicity and Intergroup Relations*. London: Academic Press, 307–348.

Giles, H. and Coupland, N. (1991). *Language: Contexts and Consequences*. Milton Keynes: Open University Press.

Giles, H., Coupland, N., and Coupland, J. (1991). 'Accommodation theory. Communication, context, and consequences'. In idem (eds.), *Contexts of Accommodation*. Cambridge: Cambridge University Press, and Paris: Éditions de la maison des sciences de l'homme, 1–68.

Giles, H., Hewstone, M., Ryan, E. B., and Johnson, P. (1987). 'Research on language attitudes'. In U. Ammon, N. Dittmar, and K. J. Mattheier (eds.), *Sociolinguistics*.

An International Handbook of the Science of Language and Society. Berlin/New York: Walter de Gruyter, 585–598.

Giles, H., Mulac, A., Bradac J., and Johnson, P. (1987). 'Speech accommodation theory: the first decade and beyond'. In M. McLaughlin (ed.), *Communication Yearbook*, 10. Beverley Hills: Sage, 13–48.

Giles, H. and Powesland, P. (1997/1975). 'Accommodation theory'. In N. Coupland and A. Jaworski (eds.), *Sociolinguistics: A Reader*. Basingstoke: Macmillan, 232–239. (Reprinted from Giles, H. and Powesland, P. (1975). *Speech Style and Social Evaluation*. London: Academic Press, 154–170.)

Giles, H. and Powesland, P. F. (1975). *Speech Style and Social Evaluation*. London: 154–185.

Giles, H. and Ryan, E. B. (1982). 'Prolegomena for developing a social psychological theory of language attitudes'. In Ryan and Giles (eds.): 208–223.

Giles, H. and Smith, P. M. (1979). 'Accommodation theory: optimal levels of convergence'. In H. Giles and R. St. Clair (eds.), *Language and Social Psychology*. Oxford: Oxford University Press.

Gilles, P. (1998a). 'Virtual convergence and dialect levelling in Luxembourgish'. In P. Auer (ed.), *Dialect Levelling and the Standard Varieties in Europe, Folia Linguistica* 32: 1–2, 69–82.

(1998b). 'Die Emanzipation des Lëtzebuergeschen aus dem Gefüge der deutschen Mundarten', *Zeitschrift für deutsche Philologie*, 117: 20–35.

(1999). *Dialektausgleich im Lëtzebuergeschen: zur phonetisch-phonologischen Fokussierung einer Nationalsprache*. Tübingen: Niemeyer.

Glauser, B. (2000). 'The Scottish/English border in hindsight'. In J. Kallen, F. Hinskens and J. Taeldeman (eds.), 65–78.

Glinka, S., *et al.* (eds.) (1980). *Atlas gwar wschodniosłowiańskich Białostocczyzny* [Atlas of East Slavonic dialects of the Białystok region]. Wrocław: PAN.

Goebl, H. (2000). 'Langues standards et dialectes locaux dans la France du Sud-Est et l'Italie septentrionale sous le coup de l'effet-frontière: une approche dialectométrique', *IJSL* 145: 181–215.

Goeman, A. C. M. and Taeldeman, J. (1996). 'Fonologie en morfologie van de Nederlandse dialecten. Een nieuwe materiaalverzameling en twee nieuwe atlasprojecten', *Taal en Tongval* 48: 38–59.

Golato, A. (2000). 'An innovative German quotative for reporting on embodied action: *Und ich so/und er so* "and I'm like/and he's like"', *Journal of Pragmatics* 32 (1): 29–54.

Goldschmidt, T. (2000). 'Het succes van een blind, passief proces', *NRC Handelsblad*, 15 Dec. 35.

Goossens, J. (1962). 'Die gerundeten Palatalvokale im niederländischen Sprachraum'. *Zeitschrift für deutsche Mundartforschung* XXIX: 312–328.

(1970), 'Niederländische Mundarten vom Deutschen aus gesehen', *Niederdeutsches Wort* Band 10: 61–80.

(1974). 'Historische en moderne taalgeografie'. In A. van Loey and J. Goossens, *Historische Dialectologie*. Amsterdam: K.N.A.W.

(1977). *Deutsche Dialektologie*. Berlin/New York: Sammlung Göschen, 2205.

(1988). 'Zur Lage des Niederdeutschen und ihrer Erforschung', *Michigan Germanic Studies* 12: 1–20.

Gordon, E., Campbell, L., Hay, J., Maclagan, M., Sudbury, A., and Trudgill, P. (2004). *New Zealand English: Its Origins and Evolution*. Cambridge: Cambridge University Press.

Granovetter, M. (1973). 'The strength of weak ties', *American Journal of Sociology* 78: 1360–1380.

Grassi, C. and Pautasso, M. (1989). *Prima roba il parlare . . . Lingue e dialetti dell'emigrazione biellese*. Milan: Electa.

Grčević, M. (2002). 'Some remarks on recent lexical changes in the Croatian language'. In R. Lučić (ed.), *Lexical Norm and National Language. Lexicography and Language Policy in South-Slavic Languages after 1989*. Munich: Sagner, 150–163.

Greenberg, R. (2000). 'Language politics in the Federal Republic of Yugoslavia: the crisis over the future of Serbian', *Slavic Review* 59 (3): 625–640.

Gregersen, F. and Pedersen, I. L. (eds.) (1991a). *The Copenhagen Study in Urban Sociolinguistics*, Vols. 1–2. Copenhagen: C. A. Reitzel.

(1991b). 'Copenhagen as a speech community'. In K. L. Berge and U.-B. Kotsinas (eds.), *Storstadsspråk och storstadskultur i Norden*. Stockholm: Meddelanden från Institutionen för nordiska språk vid Stockholms universitet. MINS 34: 57–69.

(2000). '*A la Recherche du* Word order Not Quite. A methodological progress report'. In S. C. Herring, P. van Reenen, and L. Schøsler (eds.), *Textual Parameters in Older Languages*. Amsterdam/Philadelphia: John Benjamins, 393–431.

Grinjowa, N. M. (1990). 'Interferenzerscheinungen im grammatischen System einer niederdeutschen Mundart in der Sowjetunion infolge intensiver Sprachkontakte'. Unpublished MS.

Grootaers, L. (1942). 'De aangeblazen *h* in het oosten van het land'. In *Verslagen en Mededelingen van de Koninklijke Vlaamse Academie*: 217–225.

Großkopf, B., Barden, B., and Auer, P. (1996). 'Dialektanpassung bei sächsischen "Übersiedlern" – Ergebnisse einer Longitudinalstudie'. In N. Boretzky *et al.* (eds.), *Areale, Kontakte, Dialekte*. Bochum: Brockmeyer, 139–166.

Grundtvig, S. (1872). *Dansk Haandordbog. Med den af Kultusministeriet anbefalede Retskrivning*. Copenhagen.

Guilfoyle, E. (1986). 'Hiberno-English: a parametric approach'. In J. Harris, D. Little, and D. Singleton (eds.), *Perspectives on the English Language in Ireland*. Dublin: CLCS, TCD, 121–132.

Gumperz, J. J. (1968). 'The speech community'. In P. P. Grignioli (ed.), *Language and Social Context*. Harmondsworth: 219–231.

(ed.) (1982). *Language and Social Identity*. Cambridge: Cambridge University Press.

(1997). 'On the interactional bases of speech community membership'. In G. R. Guy, C. Feagin, D. Schiffrin, and J. Baugh (eds.) (1998), *Towards a Social Science of Language. Papers in Honor of William Labov*. Vol. II. Amsterdam/Philadelphia: John Benjamins, 182–203.

Gumperz, J. J. and Wilson, R. (1971). 'Convergence and creolization: a case from the Indo-Aryan/Dravidian border'. In D. H. Hymes (ed.), *Pidginization and Creolization of Languages*. Cambridge: Cambridge University Press, 151–168.

Guy, G. (1974). 'Variation in the group and the individual: the case of final stop deletion', *Pennsylvania Working Papers on Linguistic Change and Variation* 1 (4): 1–75.

(1994). 'The phonology of variation'. In *CLS 30: Papers from the 30th Regional Meeting of the Chicago Linguistic Society. Vol. 2: The Parasession on Variation in Linguistic Theory*. Chicago: Chicago Linguistic Society, 133–149.

Gvozdanović, J. (in press). 'Slavische Sprachen an der zweiten Jahrtausendwende'. In T. Berger (ed.), *Funktionale Studien zur slavistischen Sprachwissenschaft*.

Haag, K. (1929–30). 'Sprachwandel im Lichte der Mundartgrenzen'. *Theutonista* 6 (1): 1–35.

Haas, W. (1978). *Sprachwandel und Sprachgeographie. Untersuchungen zur Struktur der Dialektverschiedenheit am Beispiele der schweitzerdeutschen Vokalsysteme*. Wiesbaden: Steiner.

Haberland, H. (1994). 'Danish'. In E. König and J. van der Auwera (eds.), *The Germanic Languages*. London/New York: 313–348.

Haegeman, L. (1988). 'Register variation in English: some theoretical observations', *Journal of English Linguistics* 20 (2): 230–248.

(1990). 'Understood subjects in English diaries', *Multilingua* 9: 157–199.

(ed.) (1997). *The New Comparative Syntax*. London: Longman.

Haeseryn, W. et al. (1997). *Algemene Nederlandse Spraakkunst*. Second edition. 2 vols. Groningen: Martinus Nijhoff.

Hagen, A. (1982). 'Schuchardts ideeën over dialectvariatie: betekenis en waarderings-geschiedenis'. In P. van de Craen and R. Willemyns (eds.), *Sociolinguistiek en ideologie*. Brussels: 233–261.

Hägerstrand, T. (1967). *Innovation Diffusion as a Spatial Process*. Chicago: University of Chicago Press.

Hale, K. and Keyser, S. (1993). 'On argument structure and the lexical expression of syntactic relations', in K. Hale and S. Keyser (eds.), *The View from Building 20*. Cambridge, Mass.: MIT Press, 53–110.

Hale, M. (1994). 'Review of Lightfoot 1991', *Language* 70: 141–152.

Hannan, K. (1996). *Borders of Language and Identity in Teschen Silesia*. New York: Peter Lang.

Harman, Lesley D. (1988). *The Modern Stranger. On Language and Membership*. Berlin: Mouton de Gruyter.

Harris, J. (1983). 'The Hiberno-English *I've it eaten* construction: what is it and where does it come from?', *Teanga* 3: 30–43.

(1984). 'English in the north of Ireland'. In P. J. Trudgill (ed.), *Language in the British Isles*. Cambridge: Cambridge University Press, 115–134.

(1990). 'Segmental complexity and phonological government', *Phonology* 7: 255–300.

(1994). *English Sound Structure*. Oxford: Blackwell.

(1996). 'Syntactic variation and dialect divergence'. In R. Singh (ed.), *Towards a Critical Sociolinguistics*. Amsterdam: John Benjamins, 31–59.

Harris, J. and Kaye, J. (1990). 'A tale of two cities: London glottaling and New York City tapping', *The Linguistic Review* 7: 251–274.

Harris, J., Little, D. and Singleton, D. (eds.), *Perspectives on the English Language in Ireland*. Dublin: Centre for Language and Communication Studies, Trinity College Dublin: 67–81.

Hartman Keiser, S., Hinskens, F., Migge, B., and Strand, E. (1997). 'The Northern Cities Shift in the Heartland? A study of radio speech in Columbus, Ohio'. In

K. Ainsworth and D. en M. D'Imperio (eds.), *Papers From the Linguistics Laboratory. Ohio State University Working Papers in Linguistics* 50: 41–68.

Haugen, E. (1966/1972). 'Dialect, language, nation'. In *The Ecology of Language. Essays by Einar Haugen.* Selected and introduced by A. S. Dil (1972). Stanford: Stanford University Press, 237–254.

(1976). *The Scandinavian Languages.* London: Faber & Faber.

Hay, J. and Sudbury, A. (2002). 'The fall and rise of /r/: rhoticity and /r/-sandhi in Early New Zealand English. In *Selected Papers from NWAV 30, University of Pennsylvania Working Papers in Linguistics* 8.3: 281–295.

Henriksen, C. C. (1979). 'Indføring'. In [reprint of] H. Bertelsen (ed.), *Danske Grammatikere*, Vols. 1–6. Copenhagen: C. A. Reitzel, Vol. 6: 3*–30*.

Henry, A. (1992). 'Infinitives in a *for-to* dialect', *Natural Language and Linguistic Theory* 10: 279–301.

(1994). 'Singular concord in Belfast English', *Belfast Working Papers in Language and Linguistics* 12: 134–176.

(1995). *Belfast English and Standard English: Dialect Variation and Parameter Setting.* Oxford: Oxford University Press.

(1996). 'Indirect questions in Belfast English and the analysis of embedded verb-second', *Belfast Working Papers in Language and Linguistics* 13: 161–172.

(1997a). 'The syntax of Belfast English'. In J. Kallen (ed.), *Focus on Ireland.* Amsterdam: John Benjamins, 89–108.

(1997b). 'Viewing change in progress: the loss of V2 in Hiberno-English imperatives'. In van Kemenade and Vincent (eds.): 273–296.

Henry, P. L. (1958). 'A linguistic survey of Ireland: preliminary report', *Lochlann* 1: 49–208.

Hernández-Campoy, J. (2000). 'Requisitos teórico-metodológicos para el estudio geolinguístico del dialecto murciano'. In J. M. Jiménez Cano (ed.), *Estudios sociolinguísticos del dialecto murciano.* Murcia: Universidad de Murcia.

Herrgen, J. (1986). *Koronalisierung und Hyperkorrektion; das palatale Allophon des /CH/-Phonems und seine Variation im Westmitteldeutschen.* Wiesbaden: Steiner.

Herson Finn, V. (1996). 'What is "Nash"? Toward a Theory of Ethnolect in the South Slavic Dialect Continuum'. Unpublished Ph.D. diss. Ohio State University.

Hewitt, R. (1986). *White Talk, Black Talk: Inter-racial Friendship and Communication amongst Adolescents.* Cambridge: Cambridge University Press.

Hickey, R. (1999a). 'Developments and change in Dublin English'. In E. H. Jahr (ed.), *Language Change: Advances in Historical Sociolinguistics.* Berlin: Mouton de Gruyter, 209–243.

(1999b). 'Dublin English: current changes and their motivation'. In P. Foulkes and G. J. Docherty (eds.), *Urban Voices: Accent Studies in the British Isles.* London: Arnold, 265–281.

Hinskens, F. (1986). 'Primaire en secundaire dialectkenmerken; een onderzoek naar de bruikbaarheid van een vergeten (?) onderscheid'. In J. Creten, G. Geerts, and K. Jaspaert (eds.), *Werk-in-uitvoering; momentopname van de sociolingudstiek in België en Nederland.* Leuven/Amersfoort: Acco, 135–158.

(1992). 'Dialect levelling in Limburg: structural and sociolinguistics aspects.' Ph.D. thesis, Nijmegen.

(1993a). 'Dialect als lingua franca? Dialectgebruik in het algemeen en bij grensover-schrijdend contact in het Nederrijnland en Twente'. In L. Kremer (ed.), *Diglossi-estudien. Dialekt und Hochsprache im niederländisch-deutschen Grenzland*, Landeskundliches Institut Westmünsterland: Vreden, 209–245.

(1993b). 'Dialectnivellering en regiolectvorming; bevindingen en beschouwingen'. In F. Hinskens, C. Hoppenbrouwers, and J. Taeldeman (eds.), *Dialectverlies en regiolectvorming* (= Taal en tongval 46), 40–61.

(1996). *Dialect Levelling in Limburg: Structural and Sociolinguistic Aspects.* Linguistische Arbeiten, Tübingen: Niemeyer.

(1998a). 'Dialect levelling: a two-dimensional process', *Folia Linguistica* 32: 35–51.

(1998b). 'Variation studies in dialectology and three types of sound change', *Sociolinguistica* 12: 155–193.

(2001). 'Koineisation and creole genesis. Remarks on Jeff Siegel's contribution'. In N. Smith and T. Veenstra (eds.), *Creolisation and Contact.* Amsterdam/Philadelphia: Benjamins, 199–218.

Hinskens, F., Kallen, J. L., and Taeldeman, J. (2000). 'Merging and drifting apart. Convergence and divergence of dialects across political borders'. In J. L. Kallen, F. Hinskens, and J. Taeldeman (eds.), *International Journal of the Sociology of Language 145: Convergence and Divergence of Dialects across European Borders.* Berlin/New York: 1–28.

Hinskens, F. and van Hout, R. (1994). 'Testing theoretical phonological aspects of word-final t-deletion'. In W. Viereck (ed.), *Verhandlungen des Internationalen Dialektologenkongresses Bamberg 1990.* Band 3, 197–310.

Hinskens, F., van Hout, R., and Wetzels, L. (1997). 'Balancing data and theory in the study of phonological variation and change.' In F. Hinskens, R. van Hout, and L. Wetzels (eds.), *Variation, Change and Phonological Theory.* Amsterdam/Philadelphia: Benjamins, 1–33.

Hock, H. (1991). *Principles of Historical Linguistics.* 2nd edn. Berlin: Mouton de Gruyter.

Hock, H. H. and Joseph, B. (1996). *Language History, Language Change and Language Relationship. An Introduction to Historical and Comparative Linguistics.* Berlin/New York: Mouton De Gruyter.

Hoekstra, T. (1992). 'Aspect and theta theory', in I. M. Roca (ed.), *Thematic Structure. Its role in Grammar.* Berlin/New York: Foris, 145–174.

Hoekstra, T. and Roberts, I. (1993). 'Middles in Dutch and English'. In E. Reuland and W. Abraham (eds.), *Knowledge and Language Vol. II, Lexical and Conceptual Structure.* Dordrecht: Kluwer Academic, 185–222.

Hofer, L. (2000). 'Urban dialects in Basel, Switzerland: variation, change and attitudes'. In J. Fontana, L. McNally, M. Turell, and E. Vallduví (eds.), *ICLaVE 1. Proceedings of the first International Conference on Language Variation in Europe.* Barcelona: Universitat Pompeu Fabra, 101–109.

Hoffman, S. (2002). 'Are low-frequency complex prepositions grammaticalised? On the limits of corpus data – and the importance of intuitions'.

Hofmann, E. (1963). 'Sprachsoziologische Untersuchungen über den Einfluß der Stadtsprache auf Mundartsprechende Arbeiter', *Marburger Universitätsbund. Jahrbuch 1963.* Marburg: 201–281.

Hogg, M. A. and Abrams, D. (1988). *Social Identifications. A Social Psychology of Intergroup Relations and Group Processes.* London/New York: Routledge.

Holmberg, A. (1986). *Word Order and Syntactic Features in the Scandinavian Languages and in English.* Unpublished Ph.D. thesis, Stockholm University.

Holmes, J. (1994). 'New Zealand flappers: an analysis of t voicing in New Zealand English', *English World-Wide* 15: 195–224.

Holmes, J. (1992). *An Introduction to Sociolinguistics.* London/New York: Longman.

(1995a). *Women, Men and Politeness.* Harlow: Longman.

(1995b). 'Glottal stops in New Zealand English: an analysis of variants of word-final /t/', *Linguistics* 33: 433–463.

Holmquist, J. C. (1988). *Language Loyalty and Linguistic Variation. A Study in Spanish Cantabria.* Dordrecht/Providence: Foris.

Hoppenbrouwers, C. (1990). *Het regiolect: van dialect tot Algemeen Nederlands.* Muiderberg: Coutinho.

Hopper, P., and Traugott, E. C. (1993). *Grammaticalization.* Cambridge: Cambridge University Press.

Hornung, M. (1994). 'Die sogenannten zimbrischen Mundarten der Sieben und Dreizehn Gemeinden in Oberitalien'. In M. Hornung (ed.), *Die deutschen Sprachinseln in den Südalpen: Mundarten und Volkstum.* Hildesheim, Zürich, New York. (*Studien zur Dialektologie*, 3): 19–43.

Horvath, B. M. (1985). *Variation in Australian English: The Sociolects of Sydney.* Cambridge: Cambridge University Press.

Horvath, B. and Horvath, R. (2001). 'A multilocality study of a sound change in process: the case of /l/ vocalisation in New Zealand and Australian English', *Language Variation and Change* 13 (1): 37–57.

Hostrup, C. (1889). *Komedier*, Vols. 1–3. Copenhagen: Gyldendal.

Høysgaard, J. P. (1920) (1747). 'Accentuered og Raisonnered Grammatica'. In H. Bertelsen (ed.), *Danske Grammatikere*, Vol. 4. Copenhagen: Gyldendal.

Hudson, R. A. (1984). *Word Grammar.* Oxford: Blackwell.

(1985). 'A psychological and socially plausible theory of language structure'. In D. Schiffrin (ed.), *Meaning, Form and Use in Context: Linguistic Applications.* Georgetown: Georgetown University Press, 150–159.

(1986). 'Sociolinguistics and the theory of grammar', *Linguistics* 24: 1053–1078.

(1990). *English Word Grammar.* Oxford: Blackwell.

(1995). 'Syntax and sociolinguistics'. In J. Jacobs, A. von Stechow, W. Sternefeld, and T. Vennemann (eds.), *Syntax: An International Handbook*, Vol. II. Berlin: Walter de Gruyter, 1514–1528.

(1996). *Sociolinguistics.* 2nd edn. Cambridge: Cambridge University Press.

(1997a). 'Inherent variability and linguistic theory', *Cognitive Linguistics* 8: 73–108.

(1997b). 'The rise of auxiliary *DO*: verb-non-raising or category-strengthening', *Transactions of the Philological Society* 95: 41–72.

Huffines, M. (1989). 'Case usage among the Pennsylvania German sectarians and non-sectarians'. In N. Dorian (ed.), *Investigating Obsolescence. Studies in Language Contraction and Death.* Cambridge: Cambridge University Press, 211–226.

(1994). 'Directionality of language influence: the case of Pennsylvania German and English'. In N. Berend and K. J. Mattheier (eds.), *Sprachinselforschung. Eine Gedenkschrift für Hugo Jedig.* Frankfurt am Main: 47–58.

Hughes, G. A. and Trudgill, P. (1995). *English Accents and Dialects*. 3rd edn. London: Arnold.

Hulk, A. and Cornips, L. (2000). 'Reflexives in middles and the syntax-semantics interface'. In H. Bennis and M. Everaert (eds.), *Interface Strategies*. KNAW-series. Amsterdam: Elsevier, 207–222.

Hume, [A.]. (1877–78). 'Remarks on the Irish dialect of the English language', *Transactions of the Historic Society of Lancashire and Cheshire*. 3rd ser., 6: 93–140.

Hunnius, K. (1990). 'Französische Flexionslehre'. In *Lexikon der Romanistischen Linguistik (LRL)*. Hrsgg. v./Edité par Günter Holtus, Michael Metzeltin, Christian Schmitt. Bd./Volume V, 1: *Französisch. Le français*. Tübingen: 59–71.

Hutterer, C. J. (1975). *Die germanischen Sprachen. Ihre Geschichte in Grundzügen*. 2. Aufl. 1987. Budapest.

(1982). 'Sprachinselforschung als Prüfstand für dialektologische Arbeitsprinzipien'. In W. Besch, U. Knoop, W. Putschke, and H. E. Wiegand (eds.), *Dialektologie. Ein Handbuch zur deutschen und allgemeinen Dialektforschung*. Halbbd. 2. Berlin/New York.

Hyams, N. (1986). *Language Acquisition and the Theory of Parameters*. Dordrecht: Reidel.

Hyams, N. and Wexler, K. (1993). 'On the grammatical basis of null subjects in child language', *Linguistic Inquiry* 24: 421–459.

Hyman, L. M. (1975). *Phonology: Theory and Analysis*. London: Holt, Rinehart & Winston.

Hymes, Dell (1971). 'Introduction to section III'. In D. Hymes (ed.), *Pidginisation and Creolisation of Languages*. Cambridge: Cambridge University Press, 65–90.

Ihalainen, O. (1991). 'Periphrastic *do* in affirmative sentences in the dialect of East Somerset', in Trudgill and Chambers (eds.): 148–160.

Itogi (2000). *Itogi perepisi naselenija Respubliki Belarus* [Results of the Population Census of the Republic of Belarus]. Minsk: Gosudarstvennyj komitet statistiki Respubliki Belarus'.

Ivars, A. M. (1998). 'Urban colloquial Swedish in Finland'. In P. Auer (ed.), *Dialect levelling and the standard varieties in Europe. Folia Linguistica*: 32, 1/2, 101–114.

Jacobsen, H. G. (1973). *Sprogrøgt i Danmark i 1930rne og 1940rne*. Copenhagen: Gyldendal.

Jacobson, S. (1985). 'Synonymy and hyponymy in syntactic variation', *Papers from the Third Scandinavian Symposium on Syntactic Variation*, 7–17.

(1989). 'Some approaches to syntactic variation'. In Fasold and Schiffrin (eds.): 381–394.

Jaeggli, O. (1986). 'Passive'. *Linguistic Inquiry* 17: 587–622.

Jaeggli, O. and Safir, K. (eds.) (1989). *The Null Subject Parameter*. Dordrecht: Kluwer.

Jahr, E. H. (1988). 'Social dialect influence in language change: the halting of a sound change in Oslo Norwegian'. In J. Fisiak (ed.), *Historical Dialectology: Regional and Social*. Berlin/New York/Amsterdam, Mouton de Gruyter: 329–335.

(1996). Nynorsk språkforskning – en historisk oversikt, in C. Henriksen *et al.* (eds.), *Studies in the Development of Linguistics in Denmark, Finland, Iceland, Norway and Sweden*. Oslo: Novus, 84–101.

Janich, N. and Greule, A. (eds.) (2002). *Sprachkulturen in Europa*. Tübingen: Narr.

Jaspaert, K. (1986). 'Statuut en structuur van standaardtalig Vlaanderen'. Ph.D. thesis, University of Leuven.

Jaspaert, K. and Kroon S. (1988). 'The relationship between language attitudes and language choice'. In R. van Hout and U. Knops (eds.), *Language Attitudes in the Dutch Language Area*. Dordrecht: Foris, 157–171.

Jedig, H. H. (1966). *Laut- und Formenbestand der niederdeutschen Mundart des Altai-Gebietes*. (*Sitzungsberichte der Sächsischen Akademie der Wissenschaften zu Leipzig. Philologisch-historische Klasse*, 112/5.) Berlin.

Jones, E. and Eyles, J. (1977). *An Introduction to Social Geography*. Oxford: Oxford University Press.

Jørgensen, J. N. (1980). Det flade a vil sejre. *Skrifter om anvendt og matematisk lingvistik* 7. Copenhagen: Institut for anvendt og matematisk lingvistik, 67–124.

Jørgensen, J. N. and Kristensen, K. (1994). *Moderne sjællandsk. En undersøgelse af unge sjællænderes talesprog*. Copenhagen: C. A. Reitzels Forlag.

(1995). 'On boundaries in linguistic continua'. *Language Variation and Change* 7: 153–168.

Joseph, J. E. (1987). *Eloquence and Power. The Rise of Language Standards and Standard Languages*. London: Frances Pinter.

Kachru, B. B. (1983). *The Indianization of English. The English Language in India*. Delhi: Oxford University Press.

Kaeding, F. W. (1897). *Häufigkeitswörterbuch der deutschen Sprache. Festgestellt durch einen Arbeitsausschuss der deutschen Stenographie-Systeme*. In *15 Lieferungen*. Steglitz bei Berlin.

Kahn, D. (1976). *'Syllable-based Generalizations in English Phonology'*. Dissertation, MIT.

Kaisse, E. M. (1993). 'Rule reordering and rule generalization in Lexical Phonology: a reconsideration'. In S. Hargus and E. M. Kaisse (eds.), *Studies in Lexical Phonology*, Phonetics and Phonology, 4. London: Academic Press, 343–363.

Kaisse, E. M. and Shaw, P. A. (1985). 'On the theory of Lexical Phonology', *Phonology Yearbook* 2: 1–30.

Kallen, J. (1991). 'Sociolinguistic variation and methodology: *after* as a Dublin variable'. In J. Cheshire (ed.), *English Around the World: Sociolinguistic Perspectives*. Cambridge: Cambridge University Press, 61–74.

(1994). 'English in Ireland'. In R. Burchfield (ed.), *The Cambridge History of the English Language*, Vol. 5. Cambridge: Cambridge University Press, 148–196.

(ed.) (1997a). *Focus on Ireland*, Varieties of English around the World, G21. Amsterdam: Benjamins.

(1997b) 'Irish English: context and contacts'. In J. Kallen (ed.), *Focus on Ireland*. Amsterdam: Benjamins, 1–33.

(2000). 'Two languages, two borders, one island: some linguistic and political borders in Ireland. *International Journal of the Sociology of Language* 145: 29–63.

Kallen, J. and Kirk, J. (2001). 'Convergence and divergence in the verb phrase in Irish Standard English'. In J. Kirk, and D. ÓBaoill (eds.), *Language Links: The Languages of Scotland and Ulster*. Belfast: Cló Ollscoil na Banríona, 59–79.

Kaschuba, W. (1990). 'German Bürgerlichkeit after 1880. Culture as a symbolic practice. In B. Stråth (ed.), *Language and the Construction of Class Identities*. Gothenburg: Gothenburg University, 223–252.

Katsoyannou, M. and Karyolemou, M. (1998). 'Structural similarities of unrelated dialects: Calabrese and Greco in contact'. Paper presented at the conference on the 'Convergence and Divergence of Dialects in a Changing Europe', Reading, 17–19 September.

Kaufmann, G. (1997). *Varietätendynamik in Sprachkontaktsituationen. Attitüden und Sprachverhalten rußlanddeutscher Mennoniten in Mexiko und den USA.* (*VarioLingua*, 3) Frankfurt am Main.

Kayne, R. (1989a). 'Null subjects and clitic climbing'. In Jaeggli and Safir (eds.): 239–261.

(1989b). 'Facets of Romance past participle agreement'. In Benincà (ed.): 85–104.

(1994). *The Antisymmetry of Syntax.* Cambridge, Mass: MIT Press.

Keel, W. D. (1994). 'Reduction and loss of case marking in the noun phrase in German-American language islands: internal development or external interference?' In N. Berend and K. J. Mattheier (eds.), *Sprachinselforschung. Eine Gedenkschrift für Hugo Jedig.* Frankfurt am Main: 93–104.

Keene, D. (2000). 'Metropolitan values: migration, mobility and cultural norms, London 1100–1700'. In L. Wright (ed.), *The Development of Standard English* 1300–1800. Cambridge: Cambridge University Press: 93–116.

Keller, R. (1994). *Sprachwandel. Von der unsichtbaren Hand in der Sprache.* Tübingen: Francke/UTB.

Kemmer, S. and Barlow, M. (2000). 'Introduction: a usage-base conception of language'. In M. Barlow and S. Kemmer (eds.), *Usage-based Models of Language.* Stanford: CSLI Publications, vii–xxviii.

Kenstowicz, M. (1994). *Phonology in Generative Grammar.* Oxford: Blackwell.

Kerswill, P. E. (1994a). *Dialects Converging: Rural Speech in Urban Norway.* Oxford: Clarendon.

(1994b). 'A new dialect in a new city: children's and adult's speech in Milton Keynes'. Final Report. Project founded by the Economic and Social Research Council (1990–1994 R000232376). Reading.

(1996a), 'Divergence and convergence of sociolinguistic structures in Norway and England'. In P. Auer, F. Hinskens, and K. Mattheier (eds.), *Convergence and Divergence of Dialects in Europe* (*Sociolinguistica* 10), 90–104.

(1996b). 'Children, adults and language change', *Language Variation and Change* 8: 177–202.

(2001). 'Mobility, meritocracy and dialect levelling: the fading (and phasing) out of Received Pronunciation'. In P. Rajame (ed.), *British Studies in the New Millennium: Challenge of the Grassroots.* Proceedings of the 3rd Tartu Conference on British Studies, University of Tartu, Estonia, August 2000. Also at http://www.universalteacher.org.uk/lang/rp.htm.

(2002a). 'Koineization and accommodation'. In J. K. Chambers, P. Trudgill, N. Schilling-Estes (eds.), *The Handbook of Language Variation and Change.* Oxford: Blackwell, 669–702.

(2002b). 'Models of linguistic change and diffusion: new evidence from dialect levelling in British English'. In S. Varlokosta and M. Georgiafentis (eds.), *Reading Working Papers in Linguistics* 6: 187–216.

(2002c). 'A dialect with "great inner strength"? The perception of nativeness in the Bergen speech community'. In D. Long and D. Preston (eds.), *A Handbook of Perceptual Dialectology*, Vol. 2, Amsterdam: Benjamins, 153–173.

(2003). 'Dialect levelling and geographical diffusion in British English'. In D. Britain and J. Cheshire (eds.), *Social Dialectology*. Amsterdam: Benjamins, 223–243.

(2004). 'Social dialectology'. In U. Ammon, N. Dittmar, K. Mattheier and P. Trudgill (eds.), *Sociolinguistics/Soziolinguistik. An International Handbook of the Science of Language and Society*. 2nd edn. Vol. I, Berlin: de Gruyter, 22–33.

(2005). 'Migration and language'. In U. Ammon, K. Mattheier, and P. Trudgill (eds.), *Handbook of Sociolinguistics*, 2nd edn., Vol. 2. Berlin: de Gruyter.

Kerswill, P. E. and Williams, A. (1997). 'Investigating social and linguistic identity in three British schools'. In U-B Kotsinas, A-B Stenström, and A.-M. Malin (eds.), *Ungdomsspråk I Norden. Föredrag från ett forskarsymposium* [Youth Language in the Nordic countries: Papers from a research symposium]. Series: MINS, No. 43. Stockholm: University of Stockholm, Department of Nordic Languages and Literature, 159–176.

(1999). 'Mobility versus social class in dialect levelling: evidence from new and old towns in England', *Cuadernos de Filologia Inglesa* 8: 47–57.

(2000). 'Creating a new town koine: children and language change in Milton Keynes', *Language in Society* 29(1): 65–115.

(2002a). '"Salience" as an explanatory factor in language change: evidence from dialect levelling in urban England'. In M. C. Jones and E. Esch (eds.), *Contact-induced Language Change. An Examination of Internal, External and Non-linguistic Factors*. Berlin: Mouton de Gruyter, 81–110.

(2002b). 'Dialect recognition and speech community focusing in new and old towns in England: the effects of dialect levelling, demography and social networks'. In D. Long and D. Preston (eds.), *A Handbook of Perceptual Dialectology*, Vol. 2. Amsterdam: Benjamins, 175–206.

(2005). 'New towns and koinéisation: linguistic and social correlates', *Linguistics* 43 (5).

Keyser, S. J. and Roeper, T. (1984). 'On the middle and ergative constructions in English', *Linguistic Inquiry* 15: 381–416.

Kikai, A., Schleppegrell, M., and Tagliamonte, S. (1987). 'The influence of syntactic position on relativization strategies'. In Denning *et al.* (eds.): 266–277.

King, R. D. (1969). *Historical Linguistics and Generative Grammar*. Englewood Cliffs, NJ: Prentice-Hall.

King, R. and Nadasdi, T. (1996). 'Sorting out morphosyntactic variation in Acadian French: the importance of the linguistic marketplace'. In Arnold *et al.* (eds.), 113–128.

Kingsmore, R. K. (1995). *Ulster Scots Speech: A Sociolinguistic Study*. Tuscaloosa: University of Alabama Press.

Kiparsky, P. (1968). 'Linguistic universals and linguistic change'. In E. Bach and R. Harms (eds.), *Universals in Linguistic Theory*. New York: Holt, 170–202.

(1972). 'Explanation in phonology'. In S. Peters (ed.), *Goals of Linguistic Theory*. Englewood Cliffs, NJ: Prentice Hall, 189–227.

(1985). 'Some consequences of Lexical Phonology', *Phonology Yearbook* 2: 85–138.

(1992). 'Analogy', in W. Bright (ed.), *International Encyclopedia of Linguistics*. vol. 1. New York: Oxford University Press, 56–61.

(1995). 'The phonological basis of sound change'. In J. Goldsmith (ed.), *The Handbook of Phonological Theory*. Oxford: Blackwell, 640–670.

Kirchner, R. (2000). 'Geminate inalterability and lenition', *Language* 76: 509–545.

Kirchner, R. (2001). *An Effort Based Approach to Consonant Lenition*. London: Routledge.

Klausmann, H. (2000). 'Changes of dialect, code-switching, and new winds of usage: the divergence of dialects along the border between Germany and France in and around the region of the Oberrhein'. In J. Kallen, F. Hinskens, and J. Taeldeman (eds.), 109–130.

Klemola, J. (1997). 'A note on the use of data from non-standard varieties of English in linguistic argumentation'. In R. Hickey and S. Puppel (eds.), *Language History, and Linguistic Modelling: Festschrift für Jacek Fisiak*. Berlin: Mouton de Gruyter. 959–967.

Kloeke, G. (1927). *De Hollandsche expansie in de zestiende en zeventiende eeuw en haar weerspiegeling in de hedendaagsche Nederlandsche dialecten. Proeve eener historisch-dialect-geografische synthese.* 's-Gravenhage: Nijhoff.

Kloss, H. 1967, '"Abstand languages" and "Ausbau languages"', *Anthropological linguistics* 9 (7), 29–41.

(1980). 'Deutsche Sprache außerhalb des geschlossenen deutschen Sprachgebiets'. In H. P. Althaus, H. Henne, and H. E. Wiegand (eds.), *Lexikon der germanistischen Linguistik*. Tübingen: 537–546.

Knoke, D. and Kuklinski, J. H. (1982). *Network Analysis*. Beverly Hills, Calif.: Sage.

Knowles, G. (1973). Scouse: The Urban Dialect of Liverpool. Unpublished Ph.D. thesis, University of Leeds.

Kocka, J. (1993). 'The European pattern and the German case'. In J. Kocka and M. Allen (eds.), *Bourgeois Society in Nineteenth-Century Europe*. Oxford: Berg, 3–39.

Koerner, K. (1989). 'Toward a history of modern sociolinguistics'. *American Speech* 66 (1): 57–70.

König, E. and van der Auwera, J. (eds.) (1994). *The Germanic Languages*. London, New York.

König, W. (2001), *dtv-Atlas Deutsche Sprache*. Munich: Deutscher Taschenbuch Verlag.

Koster, J. and May, R. (1982). 'On the constituency of infinitives', *Language* 58: 116–143.

Kotsinas, U-B. (1988a). 'Immigrant children's Swedish – a new variety?', *Journal of Multilingual and Multicultural Development* 9, (1/2): 129–140.

(1988b). 'Stockholmsspråk i förändring'. In G. Petterson (ed.), *Studier i svensk språkhistoria. Lundastudier i nordisk språkvetenskap*. Lund: Lund University Press, 133–147.

(1994). *Ungdomsspråk*. Uppsala: Hallgren and Fallgren.

Kremer, L. (1979). *Grenzmundarten und Mundartgrenzen*. Köln: Böhlau Verlag.

Kremer, L. and Niebaum, H. (eds.) (1990a). *Grenzdialekte. Studien zur Entwicklung kontinentalwestgermanischer Dialektkontinua* (*Germanistische Linguistik* 101–103).

Kremer, L. and Niebaum, H. (1990b). Zur Einführung: Grenzdialekte als Gradmesser des Sprachwandels. In Kremer and Niebaum (eds.).

Kristensen, K. (2003). 'Standard Danish, Copenhagen Sociolects, and regional varieties in the 1900s'. *International Journal of the Sociology of Language*, 159: 29–44.

Kristensen, K. and Thelander, M. (1984). 'On dialect levelling in Denmark and Sweden', *Folia linguistica* 18: 223–246.

Kristiansen, T. (1990). *Udtalenormering i skolen*. Copenhagen: Gyldendal.

(1991). 'Sproglige normidealer på Næstvedegnen. Kvantitative sprogholdningsstudier'. Ph.D. diss., University of Copenhagen.

(1996). 'Det gode sprogsamfund: det norske eksempel', *Nydanske Studier og almen kommunikationsteori* 21: 9–22.

(1997). 'Language attitudes in a Danish cinema'. In N. Coupland and A. Jaworski (eds.), *Sociolinguistics. A Reader and Coursebook*. London: Macmillan, 291–305.

(1998). 'The role of standard ideology in the disappearance of the traditional Danish dialects'. *Folia Linguistica* 32 (1–2): 115–129.

(2001). 'Two standards: one for the media and one for the school', *Language Awareness* 10(1): 9–24.

(2003). 'The youth and the gatekeepers: reproduction and change in language norm and variation'. In A. Georgakopoulou and J. K. Androutsopoulos (eds.), *Discourse Constructions of Youth Identities*. Amsterdam: Benjamins, 279–302.

(2004). 'Social meaning and norm-ideals for speech in a Danish community'. In A Jaworski, N. Coupland, and D. Galasinski (eds.), *Metalanguage. Social and Ideological Perspectives*. Berlin: Mouton de Gruyter, 167–192.

Kristiansen, V. (1866). *Bidrag til en Ordbog over Gadesproget og saakaldt daglig Tale*. Copenhagen: H. Hagerup.

Kroch, A. S. (1978). 'Toward a theory of social dialect variation', *Language in Society* 7: 17–36.

(1980). 'Resumptive pronouns in English relative clauses'. Paper presented at the *LSA* Annual Meeting, San Antonio.

(1989). 'Reflexes of grammar in patterns of language change', *Language Variation and Change* 1: 199–244.

(1994). 'Morphosyntactic variation'. In Beals *et al.* (eds.): 180–201.

(2001). 'Syntactic change'. In M. Baltin and C. Collins (eds.), *The Handbook of Contemporary Syntactic Theory*. Malden: Blackwell, 699–729.

Kroch, A. S. and Small, C. (1978). 'Grammatical ideology and its effect on speech'. In D. Sankoff (ed.), *Linguistic Variation: Models and Methods*, New York: Academic Press, 45–55.

Kroch, A. S. and Taylor, A. (1994). 'The Loss of OV Word Order in Middle English'. Unpublished MS, University of Pennsylvania.

Krug, M. G. (2000). *Emerging English modals: A Corpus-based Study of Grammaticalization*. Berlin: Mouton de Gruyter.

Kruijsen, J. (1995). 'Geografische patronen in taalcontact. Romaans leengoed in de Limburgse dialecten van Haspengouw'. Unpublished Ph.D. thesis, University of Nijmegen.

Kuhn, W. (1934). *Deutsche Sprachinsel-Forschung. Geschichte, Aufgaben, Verfahren*. Plauen i. Vogtl. (*Ostdeutsche Forschungen*, 2).

Labelle, M. (1992). 'Change of state and valency', *Journal of Linguistics* 28: 375–414.

Labov, W. (1963). 'The social motivation of a sound change', *Word* 19: 273–309.

(1966). *The Social Stratification of English in New York City*. Washington, DC: Center for Applied Linguistics.

(1969). 'Contraction, deletion and inherent variability of the English copula', *Language* 45: 715–762.

(1972a). *Sociolinguistic Patterns*. Philadelphia: University of Pennsylvania Press.

(1972b). *Language in the Inner City: Studies in the Black English Vernacular*. Philadelphia: University of Pennsylvania Press.

(1972c). 'The study of language in its social context'. In W. Labov, *Sociolinguistic Patterns*. Philadelphia: University of Pennsylvania Press, 183–259.

(1972d). 'Negative attraction and negative concord in English grammar', *Language* 48: 773–818.

(1973). 'The social setting of linguistic change'. In T. A. Sebeok (ed.), *Current Trends in Linguistics*, Vol. 11, 195–251.

(1974). 'Language change as a form of communication'. In A. Silverstein (ed.), *Human Communcation*. Hillsdale: Erlbaum, NJ, 221–256.

(1975). *What is a Linguistic Fact?* Lisse: Peter de Ridder Press.

(1978). 'Where does the sociolinguistic variable stop? A reply to B. Lavandera', *Texas Working Papers in Sociolinguistics*, 44. Austin: SW Educational Development Laboratory.

(1981). 'Resolving the Neogrammarian controversy', *Language* 57: 267–308.

(1984). 'Field methods of the project on linguistic change and variation'. In J. Baugh and J. Sherzer (eds.), *Language in Use*. Englewood Cliffs, NJ: Prentice-Hall, 28–53.

(1989). 'The child as linguistic historian', *Language Variation and Change* 1: 85–94.

(1990). 'The intersection of sex and social class in the course of linguistic change'. In *Language Variation and Change* 2, 205–254.

(1991). 'The boundaries of a grammar: inter-dialectal reactions to positive *any more*', in Trudgill and Chambers (eds.): 273–288.

(1994). *Principles of Linguistic Change, Vol. 1: Internal Factors*. Oxford: Blackwell.

(1996). 'When intuitions fail', *Papers from the 32nd Regional Meeting of the Chicago Linguistics Society*, 32: 76–106.

(1997). 'Resyllabification'. In F. Hinskens, R. van Hout, and W. L. Wetzels (eds.), *Variation, Change and Phonological Theory*. Amsterdam: Benjamins, 145–179.

(2001). *Principles of Linguistic Change, Vol. 2: Social Factors*. Blackwell: Oxford.

Labov, W., Cohen, P., Robins, C., and Lewis, J. (1968). *A Study of the Non-standard English of Negro and Puerto-Rican Speakers in New York City*. Co-operative Research Report 3288, Vols. I and II, Philadelphia: US Regional Survey.

Labov, W. and Harris, W. (1986). 'The facto segregation of Black and White vernaculars'. In D. Sankoff (ed.), *Diversity and Diachrony*. Amsterdam/Philadelphia: John Benjamins, 1–24.

Landa, A. and Franco, J. (1996). 'Two issues in null objects in Basque Spanish: morphological decoding and grammatical permeability'. In K. Zagona (ed.), *Grammatical Theory and Romance Languages*, Amsterdam: John Benjamins, 159–168.

Landa, A. and Franco, J. (1998). 'Dialect divergence in Spain and the syntactic stronghold of Basque Spanish'. Paper presented at the ESF conference 'The Convergence and Divergence of Dialects in a Changing Europe', 17–19 September, University of Reading.

Lang, E. (1996). 'Das Deutsche im typologischen Spektrum. Einführung in den Band'. In *Deutsch – typologisch*. Hrsgg. v. Ewald Lang and Gisela Zifonun. (*Institut für deutsche Sprache. Jahrbuch 1995*.) Berlin/New York: 7–15.

Langacker, R. (1990). *Concept, Image and Symbol: The Cognitive Basis of Grammar.* Berlin: Mouton de Gruyter.

(1994). 'Cognitive grammar'. In R. Asher (ed.), *Encyclopaedia of Language and Linguistics.* Oxford: Pergamon Press, 590–593.

Lanthaler, F. (1997). 'Deutsche Varietäten in Südtirol'. In G. Stickel (ed.), *Varietäten des Deutschen. Regional- und Umgangssprachen.* Berlin: De Gruyter, 364–383.

Lass, R. (1980). *On Explaining Language Change.* Cambridge: Cambridge University Press.

Lass, R. and Anderson, J. M. (1975). *Old English Phonology.* Cambridge: Cambridge University Press.

Lausberg, H. (1962). *Romanische Sprachwissenschaft*, Vol. III: *Formenlehre. Zweiter Teil.* Berlin.

Lavandera, B. (1978). 'Where does the sociolinguistic variable stop?', *Language in Society* 7: 171–183.

(1984). *Variación y Significado.* Buenos Aires: Hachette.

Le Page, R. (1997). 'The evolution of a sociolinguistic theory of language'. In F. Coulmas (ed.): 15–32.

(1980). 'Projection, focusing, diffusion, or, steps towards a sociolinguistic theory of language, illustrated from the Sociolinguistic Survey of Multilingual Communities, Stages I: Cayo District, Belize (formerly British Honduras), and II: St Lucia. *York Papers in Linguistics* 9: 9–32.

Le Page, R. B. and Tabouret-Keller, A. (1985). *Acts of Identity: Creole-based Approaches to Language and Ethnicity.* Cambridge: Cambridge University Press.

Leahy, D. J. (1915). 'A Study of English, as Spoken in Cork City'. Unpublished M.A. thesis, University College Cork.

Lefèbvre C. (1989). 'Some problems in defining syntactic variables: the case of *WH*-questions in Montreal French'. In Fasold and Schiffrin (eds.): 351–366.

Lemieux, M. (1987). 'Clitic placement in the history of French'. In Denning *et al.* (eds.): 278–299.

Levelt, W. and Kelter, S. (1982). 'Surface form and memory in question answering', *Cognitive Psychology* 14: 78–106.

Levin, I. (1844). *Dansk Lydlære og Dansk Kjønslære.* Copenhagen: Samfundet til dansk Literaturs Fremme.

Levinson, S. (1988). 'Conceptual problems in the study of regional and cultural style'. In N. Dittmar and P. Schlobinski (eds.), *The Sociolinguistics of Urban Vernaculars.* Berlin: de Gruyter, 161–190.

Lightfoot, D. W. (1979). *Principles of Diachronic Syntax.* Cambridge: Cambridge University Press.

(1988). 'Creoles, triggers and universal grammar'. In C. Duncan-Rose and T. Vennemann (eds.), *Rhetorica, Pragmatica, Syntactica: A Festschrift for R. P. Stockwell.* New York: Routledge, 97–106.

(1989). 'The child's trigger experience: degree-0 learnability', *Behavioral and Brain Sciences* 12(2): 321–334.

(1991). *How to Set Parameters: Arguments from Language Change.* Cambridge, Mass.: MIT Press.

(1996). *Language Acquisition and Language Change.* Oxford: Blackwell.

(1999). *The Development of Language: Acquisition, Change and Evolution.* Oxford: Blackwell.

Lightfoot, D. W. and Hornstein, N. (eds.) (1994). *Verb Movement*. Cambridge: Cambridge University Press.

Lilja, S. (1995). 'Stockholms befolkningsutveckling före 1800', *Historisk Tidskrift* 3: 304–337.

(1996). 'Stockholm under huvudstädernas sekler. Stockholms befolkningsutveckling i jämförande perspektiv', *Historisk Tidskrift* 3: 339–361.

Linke, A. (1991). 'Zum Sprachgebrauch des Bürgertums in 19. Jh'. In R. Wimmer (ed.), *Das 19. Jahrhundert. Sprachgeschichtliche Wurzeln des heutigen Deutsch* (Ids-Jahrbuch 1990). Berlin/New York: de Gruyter, 250–281.

Lippi-Green, R. L. (1989). 'Social network integration and language change in progress in a rural alpine village', *Language in Society* 18: 213–234.

Løkensgard Hoel, O. (1996). *Nasjonalisme i norsk målstrid 1848–1865*. KULT skriftserie nr. 51. Oslo: Norges forskningsråd.

Louden, M. L. (1994). 'Syntactic change in multilingual language islands'. In N. Berend and K. J. Mattheier, Klaus, J. (eds.), *Sprachinselforschung. Eine Gedenkschrift für Hugo Jedig*. Frankfurt am Main: 73–91.

Lumtzer, V. (1894). *Die Leibitzer Mundart*. Halle/J. (= H. Paul and W. Braune (eds.) *Beiträge zur Geschichte der deutschen Sprache und Literatur*, 18).

Lund, J. (1996). 'Guldalderens lyd. Om diktion og hverdagssprog'. In Scaverius, B. (ed.), *Guldalderens verden*. Copenhagen: Gyldendal: 177–183.

Lundén, T. (1973). 'Interaction across an "open" international boundary: Norway–Sweden'. In Strassoldo, R. (ed.) (1973). *Contini e regiono*. Trieste: Edizioni LINT. 147–161.

Macaulay, R. K. S. (1991). *Locating Dialect in Discourse: The Language of Honest Men and Bonnie Lasses in Ayr*. New York: Oxford University Press.

(2001). 'You're like "why not?" The quotative expressions of Glasgow adolescents', *Journal of Sociolinguistics* 5(1): 3–21.

(2002a). 'Discourse variation'. In J. K. Chambers, P. Trudgill, and N. Schilling-Estes (eds.), *Handbook of Language Variation and Change*. Malden, Mass., and Oxford: Blackwell, 283–305.

(2002b). 'Extremely interesting, very interesting, or only quite interesting? Adverbs and social class', *Journal of Sociolinguistics* 6: 398–417.

Mackey, W. F. (1988). 'Geolinguistics: its scope and principles'. In C. H. Williams (ed.), *Language in Geographic Context*. Clevedon: Multilingual Matters, 20–45.

MacMahon, M. K. C. (1998). 'Phonology'. In S. Romaine (ed.), *The Cambridge History of the English Language*, Vol. 4. Cambridge: Cambridge University Press, 373–535.

Mæhlum, B. (1992). 'Dialect socialization in Longyearbyen, Svalbard (Spitsbergen): a fruitful chaos'. In E. H. Jahr (ed.), *Language Contact and Language Change*. Berlin: Mouton de Gruyter, 117–130.

(1996). 'Code-switching in Hemnesberget – myth or reality?', *Journal of Pragmatics* 25: 749–761.

(1997). *Dølamål: dialektene i Bardu og Målselv*. Målselv: Målselv Mållag.

(2003). 'Normer'. In Mæhlum *et al.* (eds.): *Språkmøte. Innføring i sosiolingvistikk*. Oslo: Cappelen Akademisk Forlag, 86–102.

(in press). 'Sociolinguistic structures chronologically III: Norwegian'. In *The Nordic Languages. An International Handbook of the History of the North Germanic Language*. Vol. 2. Berlin: de Gruyter.

Magner, T. (1992). 'Urban vernaculars and the standard language in Yugoslavia'. In R. Bugarski and C. Hawkesworth (eds.), *Language Planning in Yugoslavia*. Columbus, Oh.: Slavica Publishers, 189–199.

Mak, G. (1998). *Hoe God verdween uit Jorwerd. Een Nederlands dorp in de twintigste eeuw*. Amsterdam/Antwerp: Atlas.

Marcato, G., Ursini, F., and Politi, A. (1974). *Dialetto e italiano. Status socioeconomico e percezione sociale del fenomeno linguistico*. Pisa: Pacini.

Marshall, J. (2004). *Language Change and Sociolinguistics. Rethinking Social Networks*. Basingstoke: Palgrave Macmillan.

Maschler, Y. (2002). 'On the grammaticalization of *ke'ilu* "like", lit. "as if", in Hebrew talk-in-interaction', *Language in Society* 31: 243–276.

Matras, Y. (2001). 'Identifying and explaining convergent processes', talk delivered at the 23rd Annual Meeting of the German Linguistics Society (DGfS), Leipzig, 28 February–1 March.

Mattheier, K. (1980). *Pragmatik und Soziologie der Dialekte; Einführung in die kommunikative Dialektologie des Deutschen*. Heidelberg.

(1991). 'Standardsprache als Sozialsymbol'. In R. Wimmer (Hrg.) *Das 19. Jahrhundert. Sprachgeschichtliche Wurzeln des heutigen Deutsch*. Berlin/New York: IdS Jahrbuch 1990: 41–72.

(1996). 'Varietätenkonvergenz. Überlegungen zu einem Baustein einer Theorie der Sprachvariation'. In P. Auer, F. Hinskens, and K. Mattheier (eds.), *Convergence and Divergence of Dialects in Europe* (*Sociolinguistica* 10), 31–52.

(1997). 'Methoden der Sprachinselforschung'. In H. Goebl, P. H. Nelde, Z. Stary, and W. Wölck (eds.), (1996/97). *Kontaktlinguistik/Contact linguistics/Linguistique de contact. Ein internationales Handbuch zeitgenössischer Forschung. An international handbook of contemporary research. Manuel international des recherches contemporaines*. Halbbd. 1. Berlin/New York: 812–819.

Mazur, J. (1996). 'Konvergenz und Divergenz in den polnischen Sprachvarietäten'. In P. Auer, F. Hinskens, and K. Mattheier (eds.), *Convergence and Divergence of Dialects in Europe* (*Sociolinguistica* 10), 53–74.

McCafferty, K. (1998). 'Shared accents, divided speech community? Change in Northern Ireland English', *Language Variation and Change*, 10(2): 97–121.

McCloskey, J. (1991). 'Clause structure, ellipsis and proper government in Irish', *Lingua* 85: 259–302.

(1992). 'Adjunction, selection and embedded verb second', *Working Paper LRC-92-07*. Linguistics Research Center, University of California at Santa Cruz.

McCloskey, J. and Hale, K. (1984). 'On the syntax of person-number inflection in Modern Irish', *Natural Language and Linguistic Theory*: 1, 487–533.

McConvell, P. (1988). 'Mix-im-up: aboriginal codeswitching, old and new', in M. Heller (ed.), *Codeswitching. Anthropological and Sociolinguistic Perspectives*. Berlin: Mouton de Gruyter, 97–149.

McMahon, A. M. S. (1995). *Understanding Language Change*. Cambridge: Cambridge University Press.

Meechan, M. and Foley, M. (1994). 'On resolving disagreement: linguistic theory and variation – *There's bridges*', *Language Variation and Change* 6: 63–85.

Mees, I. (1987). 'Glottal stop as a prestigious feature in Cardiff English', *English World-Wide* 8: 25–39.

Mesthrie, R. (1992). *Language in Indenture: A Sociolinguistic History of Bhojpuri-Hindi in South Africa*. London: Routledge.

Meyerhoff, M. (2002). 'Communities of practice'. In J. K. Chambers, P. Trudgill, and N. Schilling-Estes (eds.), *The Handbook of Language Variation and Change*. Oxford: Blackwell, 526–548.

Mhac an Fhailigh, É. (1968). *The Irish of Erris, Co. Mayo*. Dublin: Dublin Institute for Advanced Studies.

Miller, J. (1993). 'The grammar of Scottish English', in Milroy and Milroy (eds.): 99–138.

Miller, J. and Brown, K. (1982). 'Aspects of Scottish English syntax', *English World-Wide* 3: 3–17.

Milroy, J. (1992). *Linguistic Variation and Change*. Oxford: Blackwell.

(2000). 'Historical description and the ideology of the standard language'. In L. Wright (ed.), *The Development of Standard English 1300–1800*. Cambridge: Cambridge University Press: 11–28.

Milroy, J. and Milroy, L. (1985a). *Authority in Language. Investigating Language Prescription and Standardization*. London: Routledge.

(1985b). 'Linguistic change, social network and speaker innovation', *Journal of Linguistics* 21: 339–384.

(1993/1998). 'Mechanisms of change in urban dialects: the role of class, social network and gender', *International Journal of Applied Linguistics* 3: 57–78. Reprinted in P. Trudgill and J. Cheshire (eds.), *The Sociolinguistic Reader* I (1998): 179–195.

(1997). 'Varieties and variation'. In F. Coulmas (ed.), *The Handbook of Sociolinguistics*. Oxford: Blackwell, 47–64.

Milroy, J., Milroy, L., and Hartley, S. (1994). 'Local and supra-local change in British English: the case of glottalisation', *English World-Wide* 15: 1–33.

Milroy, J., Milroy, L., Hartley, S., and Walshaw, D. (1994). 'Glottal stops and Tyneside glottalization: competing patterns of variation and change in British English', *Language Variation and Change* 6: 327–358.

Milroy, L. (1980). *Language and Social Networks*. Oxford: Blackwell.

(1982). 'Social network and linguistic focusing'. In S. Romaine (ed.) (1982), *Sociolinguistic Variation in Speech Communities*. London: Edward Arnold, 141–153.

(1984a). 'What a performance! Some problems with the competence-performance distinction'. In R. Hawkins and J. Harris (eds.), *Sheffield Working Papers in Linguistics*. Sheffield: University of Sheffield, 40–55 (also published in 1985 with the same title in *Australian Journal of Linguistics* 51: 1–17).

(1984b). 'Comprehension and context: successful communication and communicative breakdown', in P. J. Trudgill (ed.), *Applied Sociolinguistics*. London: Academic Press, 7–31.

(1986). 'Questions and answers; an analysis of the discourse structure of interviews'. In Harris, J., Little, D. and Singleton, D. (eds.), *Perspectives on the English Language in Ireland*. Dublin: Centre for Language and Communication Studies, Trinity College, Dublin, 49–63.

(1987a). *Observing and Analysing Natural Language*. Oxford: Blackwell.

(1987b). *Language and Social Networks*. 2nd edn. Oxford: Blackwell.

(1992). 'New perspectives in the analysis of sex differentiation in language'. In K. Bolton and H. Kwok (eds.), *Sociolinguistics Today. International Perspectives.* London/New York: Routledge, 163–179.

(1996). 'Review of Henry (1995)', *Language in Society* 25: 471–475.

(1999). 'Standard English and language ideology in Britain and the United States'. In Bex and Watts: 173–206.

(2002a). 'Introduction: mobility, contact and language charge – working with contemporary speech communities?' *Journal of Sociolinguistics*, 6(1): 3–15.

(2002b). 'Social networks'. In J. K. Chambers, P. Trudgill, and N. Schilling-Estes (eds.), *The Handbook of Language Variation and Change.* Oxford: Blackwell: 550–572.

Milroy, L. and Gordon, M. (2003). *Sociolinguistics. Method and Interpretation.* Oxford: Blackwell.

Milroy, L. and Margrain, S. (1980). 'Vernacular language loyalty and social network'. In *Language in Society* 9: 43–70.

Milroy, L. and Milroy, J. (1992). 'Social network and social class: towards an integrated sociolinguistic model', *Language in Society* 21(1): 1–26.

(eds.) (1993). *Real English: The Grammar of English Dialects in the British Isles.* London: Longman.

Minervini, L. (1998). 'Dialect convergence in the formation of Judeo-Spanish (16th cent.)'. Paper presented at the conference on The Convergence and Divergence of Dialects in a Changing Europe, Reading, 17–19 September.

Mitchell, J. C. (ed.) (1969). *Social Network in Urban Situations.* Manchester: Manchester University Press.

Mitzka, W. (1922). 'Dialektgeographie der Danziger Nehrung'. In *Zeitschrift für deutsche Mundarten.*

Møller, J. and Quist, P. (2003). 'Research on youth and language in Denmark', *International Journal of the Sociology of Language* 159: 57–72.

Mondéjar, J. (1991). 'Andaluz'. In *Lexikon der Romanistischen Linguistik* VI. Tübingen: Max Niemeyer, 430–446.

Montoya Abad, B. (1995). 'L'observació del canvi fonologic en el català balear', in M. T. Turrell Julià (ed.), *La sociolingüítica de la variació.* Barcelona (PPU), 165–219.

Moore, G. (1990). 'Structural determinants of men's and women's personal networks', *American Sociological Review* 55: 726–735.

Moreno Fernández, F. (1996). 'Metodología del "Proyecto para el estudio sociolingüístico del español de España y de América' (PRESEEA), *Lingüística* 8: 257–287.

Moretti, M. (1988). *La differenziazione interna di un continuum dialettale. Indagine a Cevio (TI).* Zurich: Zentralstelle der Studentenschaft.

Mugglestone, L. (1995). *'Talking Proper'. The Rise of Accent as Social Symbol.* Oxford: Oxford University Press.

Mühlhäusler, P. (1997). *Pidgin and Creole Linguistics.* Expanded and revised edition. London: University of Westminster Press.

Mummendey, A. (1999). 'Gesellschaftlicher Umbruch und soziale Identität. Sozialpsychologische Perspektiven'. Talk delivered to the SFB 417, Universität Leipzig, 24 November 1999.

Münstermann, H. and van Hout, R. (1986). 'Taalattitudes contra geschiktheid en gebruik'. In J. Creten, G. Geerts, and K. Jaspaert (eds.), *Werk-in-uitvoering; momentopname van de sociolinguïstiek in België en Nederland*. Leuven/ Amersfoort: Acco, 235–248.

Muysken, P. (1981). 'Halfway between Spanish and Quechua: the case for relexification'. In A. Highfield and A. Valsman (eds.), *Historicity and Variation in Creole Studies*. Ann Arbor: Karoma, 52–78.

(1989). 'The morphology/syntax interface in Quechua dialectology'. In Benincà (ed.): 41–52.

(1995). 'Ottersum revisited: style shifting and code-switching'. Paper presented at the Dutch *Tweede Sociolinguïstische Conferentie*, 18–19 May, 1995, Lunteren, The Netherlands.

(1999a). 'Three processes of borrowing: borrowability revisited'. In G. Extra and L. Verhoeven (eds.), *Bilingualism and Migration*. Berlin/New York: Mouton de Gruyter, 229–246.

(1999b). *Talen. De Toren van Babel*. Amsterdam: Amsterdam University Press.

(2000). 'Radical modularity and the possibility of sociolinguistics'. Paper presented at the *Sociolinguistics Symposium 2000*, 27–29 April, University of the West of England, Bristol.

Muysken, P. and Smith, N. (1995). 'The study of pidgin and creole languages'. In J. Arends, P. Muysken, and N. Smith (eds.), *Pidgins and Creoles. An Introduction*. Amsterdam: John Benjamins, 3–14.

Muysken, P. and Veenstra, T. (1995). 'Universalist approaches'. In J. Arends, P. Muysken, and N. Smith (eds.), *Pidgins and Creoles. An Introduction*. Amsterdam: John Benjamins, 121–134.

Myers-Scotton, C. (1993). *Duelling Languages. Grammatical Structure in Codeswitching*. Oxford: Clarendon Press.

(1997). '"Matrix language recognition" and "morpheme sorting" as possible structural strategies in pidgin/creole formation'. In A. K. Spears and D. Winford (eds.), *The Structure and Status of Pidgins and Creoles*. Amsterdam/Philadelphia: Benjamins, 151–174.

(1999). 'Compromise structural strategies in codeswitching'. In G. Extra and L. Verhoeven (eds.), *Bilingualism and Migration*. Berlin/New York: de Gruyter, 211–227.

Naro, A. (1981). 'The social and structural dimensions of a syntactic change', *Language* 57: 63–98.

Nelde, P. (2001). 'Die neue Mehrsprachigkeit – Perspektiven einer europäischen Sprachpolitik'. Inaugural address upon the accession to the 'Leibnizprofessur' at the University of Leipzig.

Nespor, M. and Vogel, I. (1986). *Prosodic Phonology*. Dordrecht/Riverton: Foris.

Nesse, A. (1998). 'Determining linguistic contacts in the past: the case of Low German and Bergen Norwegian'. Paper presented at the conference on The Convergence and Divergence of Dialects in a Changing Europe, Reading, 17–19 September.

Newbrook, M. (1999). 'West Wirral: norms, self-reports and usage'. In P. Foulkes and G. J. Docherty (eds.), *Urban Voices: Accent Studies in the British Isles*. London: Arnold, 90–106.

Newton, B. (1972). *The Generative Interpretation of Dialect*. Cambridge: Cambridge University Press.

Niebaum, H. (1990). 'Staatsgrenze als Bruchstelle? Die Grenzdialekte zwischen Dollart und Vechtegebiet'. In Kremer and Niebaum (eds.): 49–83.

Niedzielski, N. and Giles, H. (1996). 'Linguistic accommodation'. In H. Goebl *et al.* (eds.), *Kontaktlinguistik – Ein internationales Handbuch zeitgenössischer Forschung*, Vol. 1(1), 332–342.

Nielsen, N. Å. (1952). 'Abrahamsons og Todes oplysninger om rigsmålsudtalen omkring 1800'. In *Sprog og Kultur*, Vol. 19: 33–57.

Nishida, C. (1994). 'The Spanish reflexive clitic se as an aspectual class marker', *Linguistics* 32: 425–458.

Nortier, J. (2001). *Murks en straattaal. Vriendschap en taalgebruik onder jongeren.* Amsterdam: Prometheus.

Nöth, D. (1994). 'Spuren der verlernten Muttersprache? Beobachtungen zum Artikelgebrauch beim Sprachwiedererwerb von Rußlanddeutschen'. Unpublished MS. Berlin.

Nyman, L. (1997). 'Einige Beobachtungen zu Varietäten und Varietätenausgleich im Niederdeutsch der Orenburger Rußland-Mennoniten'. In *Historische Soziolinguistik des Deutschen* III. *Sprachgebrauch und sprachliche Leistung in sozialen Schichten und soziofunktionalen Gruppen. Internationale Fachtagung Rostock/Kühlungsborn 15.–18.9.1996.* Hrsgg. v. Gisela Brandt. Stuttgart: 261–276.

Ó Baoill, D. P. (1990). 'Language contact in Ireland: the Irish phonological substratum in Irish-English'. In G. A. Edmondson *et al.* (eds.), *Development and Diversity: Language Variation across Time and Space.* Dallas: Summer Institute of Linguistics and University of Texas at Arlington, 147–172.

(1997). 'The emerging Irish phonological substratum in Irish English'. In J. Kallen (ed.), *Focus on Ireland.* Amsterdam: Benjamins, 73–87.

Ó Cuív, B. (1944). *The Irish of West Muskerry, Co. Cork.* Dublin: Dublin Institute for Advanced Studies.

Ó Curnáin, B. (1998). 'Polygenesis of a third plural pronoun in West Galway Irish'. Paper presented at the ESF Conference: The Convergence and Divergence of Dialects in a Changing Europe, 17–19 September, University of Reading.

Odlin, T. (1989). *Language Transfer: Cross-Linguistic Influence in Language Learning.* Cambridge: Cambridge University Press.

Omdal, H. (1977). 'Høyangermålet – en ny dialekt', *Språklig Samling* 18: 7–9.

(1994). 'From the valley to the city: language modification and language attitudes'. In B. Nordberg (ed.), *The Sociolinguistics of Urbanization. The Case of the Nordic Countries.* Berlin: de Gruyter, 116–148.

Orton, H., Dieth, F., and Wakelyn, M. (1968). *The Survey of English Dialects, Vol. 4 (the Southern Counties).* Leeds: E. J. Arnold.

Paardekooper, P. (2001). 'Hoe zacht is saft?' *Onze taal* 6: 153.

Paasi, A. (1996). *Territories, Boundaries and Consciousness: The Changing Geographies of the Finnish–Russian Border.* New York: Wiley.

Pandeli, H., Eska, J. F., Ball, M. J., and Rahilly, J. (1997). 'Problems of phonetic transcription: the case of the Hiberno-English slit-t', *Journal of the International Phonetic Association* 27: 65–75.

Paolillo, J. C. (1997). 'Sinhala diglossia: discrete or continuous variation?', *Language in Society* 26(2): 269–296.

Pardy, A. (1987). 'To examine the distribution of the sociolinguistic variable (t) across different contexts'. Unpublished project report, School of Clinical Speech and Language Studies, Trinity College Dublin.

Parodi, C., Quicoli, C., Saltarelli, M., and Zubizareta, M. L. (eds.) (1996). *Aspects of Romance Linguistics*. Washington, DC: Georgetown University Press.

Patrick, P. (2002). 'The speech community'. In J. K. Chambers, P. Trudgill, and N. Schilling-Estes (eds.), *Handbook of Language Variation and Change*. Oxford: Blackwell.

Paul, H. (1870/5th edn. 1920). *Prinzipien der Sprachgeschichte*. 5e Auflage. Halle: Niemeyer.

Pautasso, M. '"Competenza sbilanciata" e parlato narrativo: passaggi di codice e enunciati mistilingui in emigrati biellesi di ritorno'. In G. Berruto and A. A. Sobrero (eds.), *Studi di sociolinguistica e dialettologia italiana offerti a Corrado Grassi*, Galatina, Congedo: 123–150.

Pearce, E. (1995). 'Diachronic change and negation in French'. In L. Haegeman (ed.), *Rivista di Linguistica* (thematic issue) *The Syntax of Sentential Negation*, 301–328.

Pedersen, I. L. (1996). 'Regionalism and linguistic change'. In P. Auer, F. Hinskens, and K. Mattheier (eds.), *Convergence and Divergence of Dialects in Europe (Sociolinguistica* 10), 75–89.

— (1997). 'Sprogarter og sprogforandring i 1800-tallet'. In P. Widell and M. Kunøe (eds.), *6. Møde om Udforskningen af Dansk Sprog til minde om Peter Skautrup 1896–1996*. Århus: Institut for Nordisk Sprog og Litteratur, 237–245.

— (1998). 'Stylistic convergence and social divergence: on the emergence of socially stratified spoken standards in the Nordic countries'. Paper presented at the conference on The Convergence and Divergence of Dialects in a Changing Europe, Reading, 17–19 September.

— (2000). 'Urban and rural dialects of Slesvig: political boundaries in the millenial retreat of Danish in Slesvig'. In J. Kallen, F. Hinskens, and J. Taeldeman (eds.), *Dialect Convergence and Divergence Across European Borders = International Journal of the Sociology of Language* 145: 131–151.

— (2001). 'Bymålenes stilling i Danmark'. In M. Saari (ed.), *Våra språk i tid och rum*. Helsingfors: Institutionen för nordiska språk och litteratur, 169–180.

— (2003). 'Traditional dialects of Danish and the de-dialectalization 1900–2000', *International Journal of the Sociology of Language* 159: 9–28.

— (in press). 'Sociolinguistic structures chronologically I: Danish'. In *The Nordic Languages. An International Handbook of the History of the North Germanic Languages*. Vol. 2. Berlin: de Gruyter.

Pedersen, K. M. (1999). 'Genusforenklingen i københavnsk', *Danske Folkemål* 41: 79–106.

Pellegrini, G. B. (1972). 'La classificazione delle lingue romanze e i dialetti italiani'. In G. B. Pellegrini (ed.), *Saggi sul ladino dolomitico e sul friulano*, Adriatica: Bari, 239–268.

Peterson, J. (1996). 'Sociolinguistic interviewer style variation: hyperconvergence in the other informant'. In M. Meyerhoff (ed.), *(N)WAVES and MEANS: A Selection of Papers from NWAVE 24 = University of Pennsylvania Working Papers in Linguistics* 3(1): 159–170.

Pierce, A. (1992). *Language Acquisition and Syntactic Theory.* Dordrecht: Kluwer.

Pinker, S. (1994). *The Language Instinct: How the Mind Creates Language.* New York: Harper-Collins.

Pintzuk, S. (1991). 'Phrase Structures in Competition: Variation and Change in Old English Word Order'. Unpublished Ph.D. diss., University of Pennsylvania.

— (1993). 'Verb seconding in Old English: verb movement to INFL', *The Linguistic Review* 10: 5–35.

Pizzolotto, G. (1991). *Bilinguismo ed emigrazione in Svizzera. Italiano e commutazione di codice in un gruppo di giovani.* Bern: Lang.

Platzack, C. (1987). 'The Scandinavian languages and the null subject parameter', *Natural Language and Linguistic Theory* 5: 377–401.

Poeppel, D. and Wexler, K. (1993). 'The full competence hypothesis of clause structure in early German', *Language* 69: 1–33.

Pohl, J. (1978). 'Communication field and linguistic field: the influence of the border (France and Belgium) on the French Language', *International Journal of the Sociology of Language* 15: 85–90.

Polenz, P. von (1999). *Deutsche Sprachgeschichte vom Spätmittelalter bis zur Gegenwart. Bd. 3. 19. und 20. Jahrhundert.* Berlin/New York: de Gruyter.

Policansky, L. (1976). 'Syntactic variation in Belfast English', *Belfast Working Papers in Language and Linguistics* 5: 217–231.

— (1982). 'Grammatical variation in Belfast English', *Belfast Working Papers in Language and Linguistics* 6: 37–66.

Pollard, C. and Sag, I. (1987). *Information-based Syntax and Semantics.* Stanford: CSLI.

Pop, S. (1950). *La dialectologie. Aperçu historique et méthodes d'enquêtes linguistiques. Première partie: dialectologie Romane.* Louvain: 'Chez l'auteur'.

Poplack, S. (1980). '"Sometimes I'll start a sentence in English *y termino en español*": toward a typology of code-switching', *Linguistics* 18: 581–618.

Poplack, S. and Tagliamonte, S. (1996). 'Nothing in context: variation, grammaticization and past time marking in Nigeria Pidgin English'. In P. Baker (ed.), *Changing Meanings, Changing Functions.* London: University of Westminster Press, 71–94.

Potter, J. and Wetherell, M. (1987). *Discourse and Social Psychology: Beyond Attitudes and Behaviour.* London: Sage.

Preston, D. (1996). 'Whaddayaknow?: the modes of folk linguistic awareness', *Language Awareness* 5(1): 40–74.

— (ed.) (1999). *Handbook of Perceptual Dialectology.* Vol. 1. Amsterdam/Philadelphia: John Benjamins.

Prince, E. (1992). 'The ZPG letter: subjects, definiteness and information status'. In William C. Mann and Sandra A. Thompson (eds.), *Discourse Description: Diverse Linguistic Analyses of a Fundraising Text.* Amsterdam: John Benjamins, 295–325.

Pulleyblank, D. (1997). 'Optimality Theory and features'. In D. Archangeli and D. T. Langendoen (eds.), *Optimality Theory: An Overview.* Oxford: Blackwell, 59–101.

Quirk, R., Greenbaum, S., Leech, G., and Srantrik, J. (1995). *A Grammer of Contemporary English.* Harlow: Longman.

Radford, A. (1990). *Syntactic Theory and the Acquisition of English Syntax*. Oxford: Blackwell.

Radford, A., Atkinson, M., Britain, D., Clahsen, H., and Spencer, A. (1999). *Linguistics: An Introduction*. Cambridge: Cambridge University Press.

Ramge, H. (1982). *Dialektwandel im mittleren Saarland*. Saarbrücken: Veröffentlichungen des Instituts für Landeskunde im Saarland – Band 30.

Rampton, B. (1995). *Crossing: Language and Ethnicity among Adolescents*. Harlow: Longman.

Rein, K. (1994). 'Die Geschichte rußlanddeutscher Täufergruppen in Amerika und ihre Bedeutung für die Sprachinsel- und Sprachkontaktforschung'. In N. Berend and K. J. Mattheier (eds.), *Sprachinselforschung: eine Gedenkschrift für Hugo Jedig*. Frankfurt am Main: 193–203.

Reitan, J. (1928). 'Oplysninger om målet i Bardo og Målselven', *Maal og Minne 1928*: 1–35.

Requena, F. (1995). 'Determinantes estructurales de las redes sociales en los hombres y las mujeres'. Papers 45 (1995): 33–41.

(1996). *Redes sociales y cuestionarios*. Madrid: CIS.

Rickford, J. (1987). The haves and have nots: sociolinguistic surveys and the assessment of speaker competence. *Language in Society*: 16(2): 149–177.

(1988). 'Connections between sociolinguistics and pidgin-creole studies', *International Journal of the Sociology of Language* 71: 51–57.

Rickford, J., Mendoza-Denton, N., Wasow, T., and Espinoza, J. (1995). 'Syntactic variation and change in progress: loss of the verbal coda in topic-restricting *as far as* constructions', *Language* 71: 102–131.

Riehl, C. (2001). 'Das Deutsche im Sprachkontakt: individuelle und universelle Entwicklungstendenzen'. Paper presented at the 23rd Jahrestagung of the Deutsche Gesellschaft für Sprachwissenschaft. Leipzig, March.

Rizzi, L. (1991). 'Residual verb second and the *wh*-criterion', *Technical Reports in Formal and Computational Linguistics*, 2, University of Geneva.

Roberts, I. G. (1985). 'Agreement parameters and the development of English modal auxiliaries', *Natural Language and Linguistic Theory* 3: 21–57.

(1993). *Verbs and Diachronic Syntax: A Comparative History of English and French*. Dordrecht: Kluwer Academic.

(1997). 'Directionality and word order change in the history of English'. In van Kemenade and Vincent (eds.): 397–426.

Robertson, R. (1993). *Globalization. Social Theory and Global Culture*. Repr. London: Sage.

Roeper, T. and Weissenborn, J. (1990). 'How to make parameters work: comments on Valian'. In L. Frazier and J. de Villiers (eds.), *Language Processing and Language Acquisition*. Dordrecht: Kluwer, 147–162.

Rogier, D. (1994). 'De verspreiding van een sociaal hooggewaardeerd taalkenmerk: de huig-R rond Gent', *Taal en Tongval, themanummer 7: R- zes visies op een kameleon*: 45–53.

Romaine, S. (1980a). 'The relative clause marker in Scots English: diffusion, complexity and style as dimensions of syntactic change', *Language in Society* 9: 221–247.

(1980b). 'A critical overview of the methodology of urban British sociolinguistics', *English World Wide* 1(2): 163–198.

(1980c). 'On the problem of syntactic variation: a reply to Beatriz Lavandera and William Labov'. *Working Papers in Sociolinguistics* 82. Austin, Texas: South-West Educational Development Laboratory.

(1981). 'Syntactic complexity, relativization and stylistic levels in Middle Scots', *Folia Linguistica Historica* 2: 56–77.

(1982a). *Socio-historical Linguistics: Its Status and Methodology.* Cambridge: Cambridge University Press.

(1982b). 'What is a speech community?' In S. Romaine (ed.), *Sociolinguistic Variation in Speech Communities.* London: Edward Arnold, 13–24.

(1984a). 'Relative clauses in child language, pidgins and creoles', *Australian Journal of Linguistics* 4: 257–281.

(1984b). 'The status of sociological models and categories in explaining linguistic variation', *Linguistische Berichte* 90: 25–80.

(1984c). 'On the problem of syntactic variation and pragmatic meaning in sociolinguistic theory', *Folia Linguistica* 18: 409–437.

(1989a). 'Pidgins, creoles, immigrant and dying languages'. In N. Dorian (ed.), *Investigating Obsolescence.* Cambridge: Cambridge University Press, 369–384.

(1989b). *Bilingualism.* Oxford: Blackwell.

(1998). 'Introduction'. In S. Romaine (ed.), *The Cambridge History of the English Language, vol. IV 1776–1997.* Cambridge: Cambridge University Press.

Rosenberg, P. (1994a). 'Varietätenkontakt und Varietätenausgleich bei den Rußlanddeutschen: Orientierungen für eine moderne Sprachinselforschung'. In N. Berend and K. J. Mattheier (eds.), *Sprachinselforschung: eine Gedenkschrift für Hugo Jedig.* Frankfurt am Main: 123–164.

(1994b). 'Sprachgebrauchsstrukturen und Heterogenität der Kommunikationsgemeinschaft bei den Deutschen in der GUS – eine empirische Studie'. In P.-P. König and H. Wiegers (eds.), *Satz – Text – Diskurs. Akten des 27. Linguistischen Kolloquiums, Münster 1992.* Bd. 2. Tübingen: 287–298.

(1997). 'Die Sprache der Deutschen in Rußland'. In G. Stricker (ed.), *Deutsche Geschichte im Osten Europas. Rußland.* Berlin: Siealer, 585–608.

(1998). 'Deutsche Minderheiten in Lateinamerika'. In *Particulae particularum. Festschrift zum 60. Geburtstag von Harald Weydt.* Herausgegeben von Theo Harden und Elke Hentschel. Tübingen: 261–291.

Rosewarne, D. (1984). 'Estuary English', *Times Educational Supplement* 42, 19 October.

Røyneland, U. (2000). 'Is age-grading always a potential problem in apparent time studies?' In J. Fontana, L. McNally, M. Turell, and E. Vallduví (eds.), *ICLaVE 1. Proceedings of the First International Conference on Language Variation in Europe.* Barcelona, Universitat Pompeu Fabra, 187–196.

Rumlcy, D. and Minghi, J. (eds.) (1991). *The Geography of Border Landscapes.* London: Routledge.

Russell, P. (1995). *An Introduction to the Celtic Languages.* London: Longman.

Russo, M. and Roberts, J. (1999). 'Linguistic change in endangered dialects: the case of alternation between *avoir* and *être* in Vermont French', *Language Variation and Change* 11(1): 19–41.

Ryan, E. B. and Giles, H. (eds.) (1982). *Attitudes Towards Language. Social and Applied Contexts.* London: Edward Arnold.

Ryckeboer, H. (2000). 'The role of political borders in the millenial retreat of Dutch (Flemish) in the north of France'. In J. Kallen, F. Hinskens, and J. Taeldeman (eds.), 79–108.

Sadowski, A. (1995). *Pogranicze polsko-białoruskie: tożsamość mieszkańców* [The identity of the inhabitants of the Polish–Belarusian border region]. Białystok: Transhumana.

Sahlins, P. (1989). *Boundaries: The Making of France and Spain in the Pyrenees.* Berkeley: University of California Press.

Salmons, J. (1994). 'Naturalness and morphological change in Texas German'. In N. Berend and K. J. Mattheier (eds.), *Sprachinselforschung. Eine Gedenkschrift für Hugo Jedig.* Frankfurt am Main: 59–72.

Samuels, M. (1972). *Linguistic Evolution – with Special Reference to English.* Cambridge: Cambridge University Press.

Sándor, K. (1998). 'Political changes as an accelerating factor in syntactic change in varieties of Hungarian'. Paper presented at the ESF conference The Convergence and Divergence of Dialects in a Changing Europe, 17–19 September, University of Reading.

Sandøy, H. (1998a). 'Talenorm i NRK'. In R. Vatvedt Fjeld and B. Wangensteen (eds.), *Normer og Regler. Festskrift til Dag Gundersen 15. januar 1998.* Oslo: Nordisk forening for leksikografi: 158–170.

  (1998b). 'The diffusion of a new morphology in Norwegian dialects'. In P. Auer (ed.), *Dialect Levelling and the Standard Varieties in Europe* (= *Folia Linguistica* 32(12): 83–100).

  (2000). 'Utviklingslinjer i moderne norske dialektar', *Folkmålsstudier* 39: 345–384.

  (2003a). 'Språkendring, kontakt og spreiing'. In Mæhlum *et al.* (eds.), *Språkmøte. Innføring i sosiolingvistikk.* Oslo: Cappelen Akademisk Forlag, 196–247.

  (2003b). 'Types of society and language change in the Nordic countries'. In B.-L. Gunnarson *et al.* (eds.), *Language Variation in Europe.* Uppsala: Uppsala University, Dept. of Scandinavian Languages, 53–76.

Sankoff, D. (1988). 'Sociolinguistics and syntactic variation'. In F. Newmeyer (ed.), *Linguistics: The Cambridge Survey, IV.* Cambridge: Cambridge University Press, 140–161.

Sankoff, D. and Labov, W. (1979). 'On the uses of variable rules', *Language in Society* 8: 189–223.

Sankoff, G. (1973). 'Above and beyond phonology in variable rules'. In C.-J. Bailey and R. W. Shuy (eds.), *New Ways of Analysing Variation in English.* Washington DC: Center for Applied Linguistics, 44–61.

  (1974). 'A quantitative paradigm for the study of communicative competence'. In R. Bauman and J. Sherzer (eds.), *Explorations in the Ethnography of Speaking.* Cambridge: Cambridge University Press, 18–49.

Sankoff, G. and Vincent, D. (1977). 'L'emploi productif du *ne* dans le Français parlé à Montréal', *Le Français Moderne* 45: 243–256.

Sapir, E. (1921). *Language. An Introduction to the Study of Speech.* San Diego: Harcourt Brace Jovanovich.

Saporta, S. (1965). 'Ordered rules, dialect differences, and historical processes', *Language* 41: 218–224.

Sarhimaa, A. (2000). 'The divisive frontier: the impact of the Russian–Finnish border on Karelian'. In J. Kallen, F. Hinskens, and J. Taeldeman (eds.), *Dialect Convergence and Divergence across European borders* (*International Journal of the Sociology of Language* 145: 153–180).

Sasse, H.-J. (1985). 'Sprachkontakt und Sprachwandel: Die Gräzisierung der albanischen Mundarten Griechenlands'. *Papiere zur Linguistik* 32: 37–95.

Saville-Troike, Muriel (1982). *The Ethnography of Communication. An Introduction.* Oxford: Blackwell.

Scheibman, J. (2002). *Point of View and Grammar: Structural Patterns of Subjectivity in American English Conversation.* Amsterdam: John Benjamins.

Scherre, M. M. P. (2001). 'Phrase-level parallelism effect on noun phrase number agreement', *Language Variation and Change* 13(1): 91–107.

Scheuringer, H. (1990). 'Bayerisches Bairisch und österreichisches Bairisch. Die deutsch-österreichische Staatsgrenze als "Sprachgrenze"?' In Kremer and Niebaum (eds.): 361–381.

Schilling-Estes, N. (2000). 'On the nature of insular and post-insular dialects: innovation, variation and differentiation'. Paper presented at Sociolinguistics Symposium 2000, 27–29 April, University of the West of England. [To appear in a Special Issue of the *Journal of Sociolinguistics*, edited by Lesley Milroy.]

Schilling-Estes, N. and Wolfram, W. (1994). 'Convergent explanation and alternative regularization patterns: *were/weren't* levelling in a vernacular English variety', *Language Variation and Change* 6: 273–302.

Schirmunski, V. M. (1928). *Die deutschen Kolonien in der Ukraine. Geschichte, Mundarten, Volkslied, Volkskunde.* Charkow.

(1930). 'Sprachgeschichte und Siedelungsmundarten', *Germanisch-Romanische Monatschrift* XVIII, 113–122 (Teil I), 171–188 (Teil II).

(1962). *Deutsche Mundartkunde. Vergleichende Laut- und Formenlehre der deutschen Mundarten.* Berlin.

Schlobinski, P. (1997). *The Sociolinguistics of Berlin Urban Vernacular.* Berlin: Mouton de Gruyter.

Schmeller, J. A. (1984). *Cimbrisches Wörterbuch, das ist deutsches Idioticon der VII und XIII communi in den venetianischen Alpen.* Edited and introduced by J. Bergmann. Vienna: Bracemüller. Re-edited as *Über die Sogenannten Cimbern der VII. und XIII. Communen auf den Venedischen Alpen und ihre Sprache.* Landshut: Curatorium Cimbricum Bavarense, 1985.

Schmidt, J. (1872). *Die Verwandtschaftsverhältnisse der indogermanischen Sprachen.* Weimar: Böhlau.

Schmieger, R. (1998). 'The situation of the Macedonian language in Greece: sociolinguistic analysis', *International Journal of the Sociology of Language* 131: 125–155.

Schuchardt, H. (1870). *Über die Klassifikation der romanischen Mundarten. Leipziger Probevorlesung.* Graz, 1900.

(1885). *Über die Lautgesetze, gegen die Junggrammatiker.* Berlin: Oppenheim.

Schwitalla, J. (2002). 'Kohäsion statt Kohärenz. Bedeutungsverschiebungen nach dem Sprecherwechsel – vornehmlich in Streitgesprächen'. In A. Deppermann and T. Spranz-Fogasy (eds.), *Be-deuten: Wie Bedeutung im Gespräch entsteht.* Tübingen: Stauffenburg, 106–118.

Sebba, M. (1997). *Contact Languages: Pidgins and Creoles.* London: Macmillan.

Seip, D. A. (1916). *Grundlaget for det norske Riksmaal*. Kristiania: Olaf Nordlis Forlag. (1920). 'Til Riksmålets Forhistorie'. *Maal og Minne* 1920: 129–142.

Selkirk, E. O. (1982). 'The syllable'. In H. van der Hulst and N. Smith (eds.), *The Structure of Phonological Representations*, Vol. 2. Dordrecht: Foris, 337–383.

(1984). *Phonology and Syntax: The Relation Between Sound and Structure*. Cambridge, Mass.: MIT Press.

Sells, P., Rickford, J. R., and Wasow, T. (1996a). 'An optimality theoretic approach to variation in negative inversion in AAVE', *Natural Language and Linguistic Theory* 14: 591–627.

(1996b). 'Variation in negative inversion in AAVE: an optimality theoretic approach'. In J. Arnold, R. Blake, B. Davidson, S. Schwenter, and J. Solomon (eds.), *Sociolinguistic Variation: Data, Theory, and Analysis*. Stanford: CSLI, 161–176.

Selting, M. (1983). 'Institutionelle Kommunikation: Stilwechsel als Mittel strategischer Interaktion', *Linguistische Berichte* 86: 29–48.

Seppänen, A. (1999). 'Dialectal variation in English relativization', *Lingua* 109: 15–34.

Shuy, R. (1990). 'A brief history of American sociolinguistics', *Historiographia Linguistica* 17(1/2): 183–209.

Siebenhaar, B. (1999). *Sprachvariation, Sprachwandel und Einstellung. Der Dialekt der Stadt Aarau in der Labilitätszone zwischen Zürcher und Berner Mundartraum*. Stuttgart: Steiner.

Siegel, J. (1985). 'Koines and koineization', *Language in Society* 14(3): 357–378.

(1987). *Language Contact in a Plantation Environment*. A Sociolinguistic History of Fiji. Cambridge: Cambridge University Press.

(1992). 'Language change and culture change among Fiji Indians'. In T. Dutton (ed.), *Culture Change, Language Change. Case Studies from Melanesia* (= *Pacific Linguistics* C120: 91–113).

(1993). 'Dialect contact and koineization'. In J. Siegel (ed.), *Koines and koineization* (= *International Journal of the Sociology of Language* 99: 105–121).

(1997). 'Mixing, leveling, and pidgin/creole development'. In A. K. Spears and D. Winford (eds.), *The Structure and Status of Pidgins and Creoles*. Amsterdam/Philadelphia: John Benjamins, 111–149.

(2001). 'Koine formation and creole genesis'. In N. Smith and T. Veenstra (eds.), *Creolisation and Contact*. Amsterdam/Philadelphia: Benjamins, 175–197.

Sihler, A. L. (2000). *Language History: An Introduction*. Amsterdam: Benjamins.

Silva-Corvalán, C. (1994). *Language Contact and Change: Spanish in Los Angeles*. Oxford: Clarendon Press.

Singh, R. (1981). 'On some "redundant compounds" in modern Hindi', *Recherches linguistiques à Montreal/Montreal working papers in linguistics*: 17, 169–175.

(1995). 'Rethinking the relationship between phonology and loan phonology', *Folia Linguistica* 29: 395–405.

Singh, R. and Ford, A. (1989). 'A closer look at so-called variable rule processes'. In Fasold and Schiffrin (eds.): 367–379.

Skautrup, P. (1944–1970). *Det danske sprogs historie*, Vols. 1–5. Copenhagen: Gyldendal.

Smith, Neil (1989). *The Twitter Machine: Reflections on Language*. Oxford: Blackwell.

Smith, Norval (2000). 'Dependency Theory meets OT: a proposal for a new approach to segmental structure'. In J. Dekkers, F. van der Leeuw, and J. van der Weijer (eds.), *Optimality Theory. Phonology, Syntax, and Acquisition*. Oxford/New York: Oxford University Press, 234–276.

(1979). 'The nonacquisition of a phonological rule: a case of Frisian influence?' In M. Gerritsen (ed.), *Taalverandering in Nederlandse dialekten. Honderd jaar dialektvragenlijsten 1879–1979*. Muiderberg: Coutinho, 244–249.

Smits, C. (1996). *Disintegration of Inflection. The Case of Iowa Dutch*. The Hague: Holland Academic Graphics.

Snyder, W. (2001). 'On the nature of syntactic variation. Evidence from complex predicates and complex word-formation', *Language* 77(2): 324–342.

Sobin, N. (1987). 'The variable status of COMP-trace phenomena', *Natural Language and Linguistic Theory* 5: 33–60.

Sobrero, A. A. (1996). 'Italianization and variations in the repertoire: the Koinai', *Sociolinguistica* 10: 105–111.

'Sprachwandels'. In Kremer and Niebaum (eds.): 7–21.

Stilling, N. P. (1987). *De nye Byer. Stationsbyernes befolkningsforhold og funktion 1840–1940*. Viborg: Selskabetfor Stationsbyforskning.

Straczuk, J. (1999). *Język a tożsamość człowieka w warunkach społecznej wielojęzyczności* [Language and identity in the context of societal multilingualism]. Warsaw: Wydawnictwo Uniwersytetu Warszawskiego.

Strassoldo, R. (ed.) (1973). *Confini e regioni*. Trieste: Edizioni LINT.

Strassoldo, R. and Gubert, R. (1973). 'The boundary. An overview of its current theoretical status'. In Strassoldo (ed.): 29–57.

Stråth, B. (ed.) (1990). *Language and the Construction of Class Identities*. Gothenburg: Gothenburg University.

Ström, A. and Schirmunski, V. M. (1926/1927). 'Deutsche Mundarten an der Newa'. In *Teuthonista* 3(1–2): 39–62.

Stroop, J. (1998). *Poldernederlands. Waardoor het ABN verdwijnt*. Amsterdam: Bert Bakker.

Stuart-Smith, J. (1999). 'Glasgow: accent and voice quality'. In P. Foulkes and G. J. Docherty (eds.), *Urban Voices: Accent Studies in the British Isles*. London: Arnold, 203–222.

(2001). 'Should variationists worry about the influence of TV on speech?' Plenary lecture given at the 3rd UK Language Variation Conference, Department of Language and Linguistic Science, University of York, 19–22 July.

Stubbe, M. and Holmes, J. (1995). '"You know", "eh" and other "exasperating expressions": An analysis of social and stylistic variation in the use of pragmatic devices in a sample of New Zealand English', *Language and Communication* 15: 63–88.

Sudbury, A. (2000). 'Dialect contact and koinéisation in the Falkland Islands: development of a southern hemisphere English?' Ph.D. thesis, University of Essex.

(2001). 'Falkland Islands English: a southern hemisphere variety?', *English World Wide* 22: 55–80.

Sundgren, E. (2000). 'A Swedish case study of language change in real time: the impact of integration in the local community on linguistic behaviour'. Paper presented at the Ist International Conference on Language Variation in Europe (ICLaVE 1), Barcelona, 29 June–1 July.

Suñer, M. and Lizardi, C. (1995). 'Dialectal variation in an argumental/non-argumental asymmetry in Spanish', in J. Amastae, G. Goodall, M. Montalbetti, and M. Phinney (eds.), *Contemporary Research in Romance Linguistics*. Amsterdam: John Benjamins, 187–203.

Svensson, L. (1981). *Ett fall av språkvård under 1600-talet*. Lundastudier i nordisk språkvetenskap. Lund: Walter Ekstrand.

Swigart, L. (1992). 'Two codes or one? The insiders' view and the description of codeswitching in Dakar'. In C. M. Eastman (ed.), *Codeswitching*, Multilingual Matters, Clevedon: 83–102.

Syv, P. (1919) (1685). 'Den danske Sprog-Kunst'. In Henrik Bertelsen (ed.), *Danske Grammatikere*, Vol. 3. Copenhagen: Gyldendal: 147–250.

Taeldeman, J. (1978). *De vokaalstruktuur van de Oostvlaamse dialecten*. Amsterdam: K.N.A.W.

    (1984). 'Joas Lambrechts "Nederlandsche Spellijnghe" (1550) als spiegel van het (Laat-) Middelgentse vokaalsysteem'. In W. J. J. Pijnenburg, K. Roelandts, and V. F. Vanacker (eds.), *Feestbundel Maurits Gysseling*. Leuven: 325–334.

    (1985). *De klankstruktuur van het Gentse dialect*. Ghent: Recueil Faculteit Letteren en Wijsbegeerte.

    (1993). 'Dialectresistentie en dialectverlies op fonologisch gebied'. In F. Hinskens, C. Hoppenbrouwers, and J. Taeldeman (eds.), *Dialectverlies en regiolectvorming* (*Taal en tongval* 46, 102–119).

    (1998). 'Levelling phenomena in the Flemish dialects: some observations on their teleology'. In P. Auer (ed.), *Dialect Levelling and the Standard Varieties in Europe*, *Folia Linguistica* 32, 11–22.

    (1999). 'Het Gents. Een eiland in het Oost-Vlaamse dialectgebied'. In J. Kruijsen and N. van der Sijs (eds.), *Honderd jaar stadstaal*. Amsterdam/Antwerp: Uitg. Contact, 273–287.

    (2000). 'Polarisering', *Taal en tongval* 52, 227–244.

Tagliamonte, S. (1997). 'Obsolescence in the English perfect? Evidence from Samaná English', *American Speech* 72(1): 33–68.

    (1998). '*Was/were* variation across the generations: view from the city of York', *Language Variation and Change*, 10(2): 153–191.

Tagliamonte, S. and Hudson, R. (1999). '*Be like et al.* beyond America: The quotative system in British and Canadian youth', *Journal of Sociolinguistics* 3(2): 147–172.

Tagliamonte, S. and Poplack, S. (1988). 'How Black English PAST got to the present: evidence from Samaná', *Language in Society* 17(4): 513–533.

Tagliamonte, S. and Smith, J. (1999). 'Analogical levelling in Samaná English', *Journal of English Linguistics* 27(1): 8–26.

Teleman, U. (2002). *Ära, rikedom & reda. Svensk språkvård och språkpolitik under äldre nyare tid*. Stockholm: Norstedts ordbok.

Tenny, C. L. (1987). *Grammaticalizing Aspect and Affectedness*. Cambridge: Cambridge University Press.

Thakerar, J. N., Giles, H., and Cheshire, J. (1982). 'Psychological and linguistic parameters of speech accommodation theory'. In C. Fraser and K. R. Scherer (eds.),

Advances in the Social Psychology of Language. Cambridge: Cambridge University Press, 205–255.

Thelander, M. (1980). 'De-dialectalisation in Sweden'. FUMS Rapport No. 86. Uppsala: Uppsala University.

(1982). 'A qualitative approach to the quantitative data of speech variation'. In S. Romaine (ed.), *Sociolinguistic Variation in Speech Communities.* London: Edward Arnold, 65–83.

Thomas, A. R. (1972). 'A note on dialect borrowing', *Studia Celtica* 7: 163–167.

Thomason, S. G. and Kaufmann, T. (1988). *Language Contact, Creolization, and Genetic Linguistics.* Berkeley: University of California Press.

Thorsen, P. K. (1929) (1906). 'Hvor gammelt er det nye i det danske sprog?' In *Afhandlinger og Breve*, Vol. 2. Copenhagen: Schønbergske 84–86.

Thurneysen, R. (1946). *A Grammar of Old Irish.* Dublin: Dublin Institute for Advanced Studies.

Tibiletti Bruno, M. G. (1974). 'Integrazione linguistica degli anziani in un paese del Varesotto'. In *Dal dialetto alla lingua*. Pisa: Pacini, 195–227.

Tode, J. C. (1797). Neue Dänische Grammatik für Deutsche. Copenhagen.

Tokc', S. (2000). 'Etničnyja pracesy na terytoryi belaruska-pol'skaha pamežža ŭ XIX – na pačatku XX stahoddzja [Ethnic processes on the territory of the Belarusian-Polish border region in the nineteenth and early twentieth centuries]. In E. Smułkowa and A. Engelking (eds.), *Język a tożsamość na pograniczu kultur* [Language and identity in cultural borderlands]. Białystok: Katedra Kultury Białoruskiej Uniwersytetu w Białymstoku, 101–114.

Tollfree, L. (1999). 'South East London English: discrete versus continuous modelling of consonantal reduction'. In P. Foulkes and G. J. Docherty (eds.), *Urban Voices: Accent Studies in the British Isles.* London: Arnold, 163–184.

(2001). 'Variation and change in Australian consonants: reduction of /t/'. In D. Blair and P. Collins (eds.), *English in Australia*. Amsterdam: Benjamins, 45–67.

Tönnies, F. (1887). *Gemeinschaft und Gesellschaft.* Leipzig: Fues.

Torgersen, E. N. and Kerswill, P. E. (2004). 'Internal and external motivation in phonetic change: dialect levelling outcomes for an English vowel shift', *Journal of Sociolinguistics* 8(1): 24–53.

Toribio, A. J. (1993). 'Parametric Variation in the Licensing of Nominals'. Unpublished Ph.D. thesis, Cornell University, Ithaca, NY.

(1996). 'Dialectal variation and the licensing of null referential and expletive pronouns', in Parodi *et al.* (eds.): 409–432.

(2000). 'Intralingual variation', Paper presented at Sociolinguistics Symposium 2000, 27–29 April, University of the West of England, Bristol.

Torp, A. (2001). 'Retroflex consonants and dorsal /r/: mutually excluding innovations? On the diffusion of dorsal /r/ in Scandinavian'. In H. Van de Velde and R. van Hout (eds.), *R-atics*. Etudes et Travaux (Bruxelles), No. 4: 75–90.

Tottie, G. and Rey, M. (1997). 'Relativization strategies in Earlier African American Vernacular English', *Language Variation and Change* 9: 219–247.

Trask, R. L. (1996). *Historical Linguistics.* London: Arnold.

Trautmann, M. (1880). 'Besprechung einiger schulbücher nebst bemerkungen über die rlaute', *Anglia* 3, 201–222.

Trosterud, T. (1989). 'The null subject parameter and the new mainland Scandinavian word order: a possible counter example from a Norwegian dialect'. In J. Niemi (ed.), *Papers from the 11th Scandinavian Conference of Linguistics* 1: 87–100.

Trudgill, P. J. (1972). 'Sex, covert prestige and linguistic change in the urban British English of Norwich', *Language in Society* 1: 179–195.

(1974a). *The Social Differentiation of English in Norwich*. Cambridge: Cambridge University Press.

(1974b). 'Linguistic change and diffusion: description and explanation in sociolinguistic geography', *Language in Society* 3: 215–246.

(1978). 'Introduction: sociolinguistics and sociolinguistics'. In P. Trudgill (ed.), *Sociolinguistic Patterns in British English*. London: Edward Arnold, 1–18.

(1983a). 'Linguistic change and diffusion. Description and explanation in geolinguistics'. In P. Trudgill (ed.), *On Dialect*. Oxford: Blackwell, 52–87.

(1983b). *On Dialect*. Oxford: Blackwell.

(1986). *Dialects in Contact*. Oxford: Blackwell.

(1988). 'On the role of dialect contact and interdialect in linguistic change'. In J. Fisiak (ed.), *Historical Dialectology. Regional and Social*. Berlin/New York/Amsterdam: Mouton de Gruyter, 547–563.

(1990). *The Dialects of England*. Oxford: Blackwell.

(1992). 'Dialect contact, dialectology and sociolinguistics'. In K. Bolton and H. Kwok (eds.), *Sociolinguistics Today. International Perspectives*. London/New York: Routledge, 71–79.

(1994). 'Language contact and dialect contact in linguistic change'. In K. Ulla-Britt and J. Helgander (eds.), *Dialektkontakt, Språkkontakt och Språkförändring i Norden. Föredrag Från ett Forskarsymposium*. Stockholm: Institutionen För Nordiska Språk, Stockholms Universitet, 13–22.

(1996). 'Dialect typology: isolation, social network and phonological structure'. In G. R. Guy *et al.*, *Towards a Social Science of Language*, Vol. 1. Amsterdam/Philadelphia: John Benjamins, 3–22.

(1998). 'The chaos before the order: New Zealand English and the second stage of new-dialect formation'. In E. H. Jahr (ed.), *Advances in Historical Sociolinguistics*. Berlin: Mouton de Gruyter, 1–11.

(1999). 'Norwich: endogenous and exogenous linguistic change'. In P. Foulkes and G. J. Docherty (eds.), *Urban Voices: Accent Studies in the British Isles*. London: Arnold, 124–140.

(2000). 'Sociolinguistics and sociolinguistics once again'. *Sociolinguistica* 14: 55–59.

(2002a). 'The sociolinguistics of modern RP'. In P. Trudgill, *Sociolinguistic Variation and Change*. Edinburgh: Edinburgh University Press, 171–180.

(2002b). 'Linguistic and social typology'. In J. K. Chambers, P. Trudgill, and N. Schilling-Estes (eds.), *The Handbook of Language Variation and Change*. Oxford: Blackwell. 707–728.

(2004). *New-Dialect Formation: The Inevitability of Colonial Englishes*. Edinburgh: Edinburgh University Press.

Trudgill, P. J. and Chambers J. K. (eds.) (1991). *Dialects of English: Studies in Grammatical Variation*. London: Longman.

Trudgill, P. J., Gordon, E., Lewis, G., and Maclagan, M. (2000). 'Determinism in new-dialect formation and the genesis of New Zealand English', *Journal of Linguistics* 36: 299–318.

Turner, B. (1996). *The Blackwell Companion to Social Theory*. Oxford: Blackwell.

Valian, V. (1991). 'Syntactic subjects in the early speech of American and Italian children', *Cognition* 40: 21–81.

Vammen, H. (1990). 'Bourgeois mentality in Denmark 1730–1900'. In B. Stråth (ed.), *Language and the Construction of Class Identities*. Gothenburg: Gothenburg University, 283–310.

Van Bree, C. (1990). *Historische Taalkunde*. Leuven/Amsterdam: Acco.

(1994). 'The development of so-called Town Frisian'. In P. Bakker and M. Mous (eds.), *Mixed Languages. 15 Case studies in language intertwining*. Amsterdam: IFOTT, 69–82.

(1997). *Een oud onderwerp opnieuw bekeken: het Ingweoons*. Farewell address, Leiden University: Leiden University Press.

Van Coetsem, F. (1988). *Loan Phonology and the Two Transfer Types in Language Contact*. Dordrecht/Providence: Foris.

(2000). *A General and Unified Theory of the Transmission Process in Language Contact*. Heidelberg: Winter.

Van de Velde, H. (1996). 'Variatie en verandering in het gesproken Standaard-Nederlands (1935–1993)'. Unpublished Ph.D. thesis, University of Nijmegen.

Van der Horst, J. and Marschall, F. (1992). *Korte geschiedenis van de Nederlandse taal*. Amsterdam: Nijgh & Van Ditmar.

Van Kemenade, A. (1987). 'Syntactic Case and Morphological Case in the History of English'. Unpublished Ph.D. diss., Rijksuniversiteit, Utrecht.

(1993). 'Parametric change and the history of English impersonals'. Paper presented at the *LAGB*, 14 September, Bangor, UCNW.

(1994). 'Old and Middle English'. In E. König and J. van der Auwera (eds.), *The Germanic Languages*. London/New York: 110–141.

Van Kemenade, A. and Vincent, N. (eds.) (1997). *Parameters of Morphosyntactic Change*. Cambridge: Cambridge University Press.

Van Marle, J. (1997). 'Dialect versus standard language: nature versus culture'. In J. Cheshire and D. Stein (eds.), *Taming the Vernacular. From Dialect to Written Standard Language*. London/New York: Longman, 13–34.

Van Ness, S. (1994). 'Pennsylvania German'. In E. König and J. van der Auwera (eds.), *The Germanic Languages*. London/New York: 420–438.

Van Oostendorp, M. (1997). 'Style levels in conflict resolution'. In F. Hinskens, R. van Hout, and L. Wetzels (eds.), *Variation, Change and Phonological Theory* Amsterdam/Philadelphia: Benjamins, 207–229.

Van Riemsdijk, H. C. (1978). *A Case Study in Syntactic Markedness*. Dordrecht: Foris.

Vandekerckhove, R. (1998). 'Code-switching between dialect and standard language as a graduator of dialect loss and dialect vitality. A case study in West Flanders'. *Zeitschrift für Dialektologie und Linguistik* 65: 280–292.

Verstegen, V. (1942). 'De Westgermaanse *sk* in de Zuidnederlandse dialecten'. In *Handelingen Koninklijke Commissie voor Toponymie en Dialectologie* 16: 31–42 + 2 maps.

Vikør, L. S. (1993). *The Nordic Languages*. Oslo: Novus.

(1994). *Språkplanlegging. Prinsipp og praksis*. Oslo: Novus.

(2001). *The Nordic languages. Their Status and Interrelations*. Oslo: Novus.

(2002). 'The Nordic language area and the languages in the north of Europe'. In *The Nordic Languages. An International Handbook of the History of the North Germanic Languages*, Vol. 1. Berlin/New York: de Gruyter: 1–12.

Villena, J. A. (1994). *La ciudad lingüística. Fundamentos críticos de la sociolingüística urbana*. Granada: Universidad.

(1996). 'Convergence and divergence in a standard dialect continuum: networks and individuals in Malaga'. In Auer and Hinskens (eds.) (1996): 112–137.

(2001). *La continuidad del cambio lingüístico. Tendencias conservadoras e innovadoras en la fonología del español*. Granada: Universidad.

Villena, J. A. and Requena, F. (1996). 'Género, educación y uso lingüístico: la variación social y reticular de s y z en la ciudad de Málaga'. *Lingüística* 8: 548.

Vinje, F. E. (1984). '"Damer sier kjød". Dannet dagligtale dengang og nå'. In B. Fossestøl *et al.* (eds.), *Festskrift til Einar Lundeby, 3 Oktober 1984*. Oslo: Novus, 211–236.

(1987). *Rent ut sagt – En veiledning i østnorsk standardtalespråk*. Oslo: Novus.

(1998). 'Talemålsnormering i NRK'. In Vatvedt Fjeld and B. Wangensteen (eds.), *Normer og Regler. Festskrift til Dag Gundersen 15. januar 1998*. Oslo: Nordisk forening for leksikografi, 143–157.

von Unwerth, W. (1918). *Proben deutschrussischer Mundarten aus den Wolgakolonien und dem Gouvernement Cherson*. (*Abhandlungen der Preußischen Akademie der Wissenschaften. Philologisch-historische Klasse*. 11). Berlin.

Voortman, B. (1994). *Regionale variatie in het taalgebruik van notabelen. Een sociolinguïstisch onderzoek in Middelburg, Roermond en Zutphen*. Ph.D. thesis University of Amsterdam: IFOTT.

Wang, W. S.-Y. (ed.) (1977). *The Lexicon in Phonological Change*. The Hague: Mouton.

Wängler, H. H. (1963). *Rangwoerterbuch hochdeutscher Umgangssprache*. Marburg.

Wassermann, S. and Galaskiewicz, J. (eds.) (1994). *Advances in Social Network Analysis. Research in the Social and Behavioural Sciences*. London & Thousand Oaks: Sage.

Wassermann, S. and Faust, K. (1994). *Social Network Analysis: Methods and Applications*. New York: Cambridge University Press.

Watt, D. and Milroy, L. (1999). 'Patterns of variation and change in three Newcastle vowels: is this dialect levelling?' In P. Foulkes and G. J. Docherty (eds.), *Urban Voices: Accent Studies in the British Isles*. London: Arnold, 25–46.

Watts, R. J. (2000). 'Mythical strands in the ideology of prescriptivism'. In L. Wright (ed.), *The Development of Standard English 1300–1800. Theories, Descriptions, Conflicts*. Cambridge: Cambridge University Press, 29–48.

Weijnen, A. (1977). *The Value of the Map Configuration*. Special issue of Mededelingen van de Nijmeegse Centrale voor Dialect- en Naamkunde.

Weiner, E. J. and Labov, W. (1983). 'Constraints on the agentless passive', *Journal of Linguistics* 19: 29–58.

Weinreich, U. (1953). *Languages in Contact*. The Hague: Mouton.

(1954). 'Is a structural dialectology possible?', *Word* 10(2/3): 388–400.

Weinreich, U., Labov, W., and Herzog, M. (1968). 'Empirical foundations for a theory of language change'. In W. Lehmann and Y. Malkiel (eds.), *Directions for Historical Linguistics; a Symposium*. Austin: University of Texas Press, 95–188.

Weinrich, H. (1985). *Textgrammatik der französischen Sprache*, 1. Aufl. 1982. Stuttgart: Nachdruck.

Weissenborn, J., Goodluck, H., and Roeper, T. (eds.) (1992). *Theoretical Issues in Language Acquisition*. Hillsdale, NJ: Erlbaum.

Wellman, B. (1998). 'Structural analysis: from metaphor to substance'. In B. Wellman and S. D. Berkowitz (eds.), *Social Structures: A Network Approach*. Cambridge: Cambridge University Press.

Wells, J. C. (1982). *Accents of English*, 3 vols. Cambridge: Cambridge University Press.

Wessén, I. (1937). 'Vårt riksspråk. Några huvudpunkter av dess historiska utveckling'. In *Modermålslärarnas förenings årsskrift*.

White, L. (1989). *Universal Grammar and Second Language Acquisition*. Amsterdam: John Benjamins.

Widmark, G. (1991). 'Boksvenska och talsvenska. Om språkarter i nysvenskt talspråk', *Språk och Stil* Ny följdl: 157–197.

Wiese, R. (2001). 'The unity and variation of (German) /r/'. In H. Van de Velde and R. van Hout (eds.), *R-atics*. Etudes et Travaux (Brussels), No. 4: 11–26.

Wiesinger, P. (1983). 'Deutsche Dialektgebiete außerhalb des deutschen Sprachgebiets: Mittel-, Südost- und Osteuropa'. In W. Besch, U. Knoop, W. Putschke, and H. E. Wiegand (eds.), *Dialektologie. Ein Handbuch zur deutschen und allgemeinen Dialektforschung*. Halbbd. 2. Berlin/New York: 900–929.

Williams, A. and Kerswill, P. (1999). 'Dialect levelling: change and continuity in Milton Keynes, Reading and Hull'. In P. Foulkes and G. Docherty (eds.), *Urban Voices: Accent Studies in the British Isles*. London: Arnold, 141–162.

Williams, G. (1992). *Sociolinguistics. A Sociological Critique*. London/New York: Routledge.

Wilson, J. and Henry, A. (1998). 'Parameter setting within a socially realistic linguistics', *Language in Society* 27: 1–21.

Wilson, T. M. and Donnan, H. (eds.) (1998). *Border Identities: Nation and State at International Frontiers*. Cambridge: Cambridge University Press.

Winford, D. (1984). 'The linguistic variable and syntactic variation in creole continua', *Lingua* 62, 267–288.

   (1993). 'Variation in the use of perfect *have* in Trinidadian English: a problem of categorial and semantic mismatch', *Language Variation and Change* 5: 141–187

   (1996). 'The problem of syntactic variation'. In J. Arnold, R. Blake, B. Davidson, S. Schwenter, and J. Solomon (eds.), *Sociolinguistic Variation: Data, Theory, and Analysis*. Stanford: CSLI Publications, 177–192.

Winge, V. (1992). *Dänische Deutsche – deutsche Dänen. Geschichte der deutschen Sprache in Dänemark 1300–1800 mit einem Ausblick auf das 19. Jahrhundert*. Heidelberg: Carl Winter Universitätsverlag.

Wolfram, W. (1969). *A Sociolinguistic Description of Detroit Negro Speech*. Washington, DC: Center for Applied Linguistics.

(1975). 'Variable constraints and rule relations', in R. Fasold and R. Shuy (eds.), *Analysing Variation in Language*. Washington DC: Center for Applied Linguistics, 70–88.

(1991). 'The linguistic variable: fact and fantasy', *American Speech* 66(1): 22–32.

(1993). 'Identifying and interpreting variables'. In D. R. Preston (ed.), *American Dialect Research*. Amsterdam: John Benjamins, 193–222.

Wolfram, W. and Hazen, K. (1996). 'Isolation within isolation: the invisible Outer Banks dialect'. In M. Meyerhoff (ed.), *(N) WAVES and MEANS: A Selection of Papers from NWAVE 24 = University of Pennsylvania Working Papers in Linguistics* 3(1): 141–157.

Wolgadeutscher Sprachatlas (WDSA) (1996). Aufgrund der von Georg Dinges 1925–1929 gesammelten Materialien. Bearb. und hrsg. von Nina Berend. Unter Mitarb. von Rudolf Post. Tübingen/Basle.

Wollersheim, H.-W. (1998). 'Identifikation'. In H.-W. Wollersheim, S. Tzschaschel, and M. Middell (eds.), *Region und Identifikation*. Leipzig: Leipziger Universitätsverlag, 47–55.

Woods, H. B. (1991). 'Social differentiation in Ottawa English'. In J. Cheshire (ed.), *English Around the World: Sociolinguistic Perspectives*. Cambridge: Cambridge University Press, 134–149.

Woods, N. J. (2000). 'Archaism and innovation in New Zealand English', *English World Wide* 21: 109–150.

Worm, P. (1873). 'Skriftsproget og Folkemaalene'. *Nordisk Maanedsskrift*. Odense: Den Miloske Boghandel, 81–115.

Wrede, F. (1919). 'Zur Entwicklungsgeschichte der deutschen Mundartforschung', *Zeitschrift für deutsche Mundarten*: 3–18.

Zagona, K. (1994). 'Compositionality of aspect: evidence from Spanish aspectual *se*'. *Communication LSRL* 24. Los Angeles.

Zeller, C. (1993). 'Linguistic symmetries, asymmetries and border effects within a Canadian/American sample'. In Clarke, Sandra (ed.), *Focus on Canada*. Amsterdam/Philadelphia: John Benjamins, 179–199.

Zipf, G. (1946). 'The P_1P_2/D hypothesis: on the intercity movement of persons', *American Sociological Review* 11(6): 677–686.

Index